falstaff
ULTIMATE WINE GUIDE

AUSTRIA/NEIGHBORING COUNTRIES
2023/24

Austria's Best Producers and Wines
Recommended wineries from neighboring countries
reviewed and rated

IMPRINT

falstaff
ULTIMATE WINE GUIDE

Copyright © 2023
by Falstaff Publications Ltd.
(Falstaff Verlags GmbH)

All rights reserved including the right of reproduction in whole or in part in any form.

Peter Moser is hereby identified as author of this work in accordance with Section 77 of the Copyright, Designs and Patents Act 1988

Editor in chief: Peter Moser
Managing editor: Petra Kirchmayer
Editor: Claudia Schindlmaisser
Tasting assistant: Konstantin Schindlmaisser
Translation: Artemis Burger
Art director: Marcus Wiesner
Art Dir. Marketing & Sales: Thomas Kepplinger
Producer: Michael Lenhart
Technical support: Robert Pleniger

Supported by:
Georg Morawitz-Holeschofsky
Noah Neururer

First published in 2002 by
Falstaff Publications Ltd. Schottenring 2-6,
A - 1010 Vienna, Austria

Printed by
ppm Fulda GmbH & Co. KG

Frankfurter Straße 8
36043 Fulda
www.ppm-fulda.de

Peter Moser
Born in 1961 in Krems, descendant of the famous Austrian wine dynasty. Since 1997 he has been Editor-in-Chief of the Falstaff magazine, responsible for the wine department. He has travelled the world's wine regions since the mid-1980s, but his expertise lies in the field of Austrian wine. The Falstaff Weinguide is an annual compilation of Moser's scores and wine descriptions of Austria's leading wineries.
(E-Mail: peter.moser@falstaff.com)

Falstaff Publications Ltd.
Publisher:
Angelika and Wolfgang M. Rosam
Managing director:
Elisabeth Kamper, Wolfgang M. Rosam, Ronald Tomandl

The publishing house, established in 1980 in Vienna by Hans Dibold and Dr. Helmut Romé, publishes ten issues per year of the wine and gourmet magazine Falstaff in German language, the Falstaff Weinguides presenting Österreich/Nachbarländer, Deutschland, Italien, Schweiz, the Falstaff Rotweinguide Österreich (E-Mail: wein@falstaff.com), the Falstaff Restaurantguide, Beizenguide, Barguide (E-Mail: guides@falstaff.com) and numerous other guides. (www.falstaff.com)

DEAR READERS, DEAR FRIENDS OF AUSTRIAN WINE

We are delighted to present the 26th edition of this guide, in which you will find more great wines across all local varietals and categories than ever before. Thanks to a whole series of excellent vintages since 2015, with the exception of the frost-ridden year of 2016 (and what little there was is not to be dismissed), wine enthusiasts have been blessed by Mother Nature and the work of our winemakers.

Although the war in Ukraine and persistent inflation have left their mark on the economy, the end of the Corona pandemic has hastened the revival of the wine industry. Trade fairs and presentations have resumed in their usual format and are well received, and Austrian wines are once again in demand on the international stage, as recently witnessed at the new Falstaff Wine & Gourmet Festival in Baden-Baden, Germany.

Let's take a brief look back at 2022, which was a very positive year for the country's winegrowers. Not only was the quality of the wine very promising in all regions, but the harvest of 2.53 million hectolitres was above the average of 2.38 million hectolitres. Last year, 67.7 million litres of Austrian wine were exported, bringing in 231.3 million euros. According to the Austrian Wine Marketing Association, the most significant increase in value abroad was for wine and sparkling wine. In 2020, Austrian wines were particularly in demand in Canada, the USA and Northern Europe. The downer in 2022 was the United Kingdom (-38.0% value). There it was clearly noticeable that trade had become more difficult and costly as a result of Brexit. In Asia, the volatile Chinese market showed a

Peter Moser
Editor-in-Chief

slight downward trend (-15.8% value) after a healthy increase in 2021 (+77.9% value). After several years of stagnation, positive signals came from Japan, which recorded a significant increase (+61.3%). There was also strong growth in South Korea (+26.4% in value terms), which is beginning to establish itself as a promising future market for Austrian wines.

The development of domestic vineyards is encouraging: 20% of the 44,728 hectares are cultivated by winegrowers certified as „Sustainable Austria", and with 22% of the area certified as organic and/or biodynamic, Austria has already achieved a leading international position. This important development towards organic viticulture is reflected in the top wineries; never before has the proportion of organic wines been as high as in this edition of the Falstaff Wine Guide.

Twenty years after the Weinviertel received its first DAC in 2003, the Thermenregion is now the latest region to protect its regionally-typical wines under the DAC sys-

EDITORIAL

The Wachau, one of the oldest wine and cultural landscapes of Europe

tem. The focus is on the autochthonous white wine varieties Rotgipfler and Zierfandler, as well as Chardonnay, Weißburgunder, St. Laurent and Pinot Noir. DAC wines are divided into three levels of origin: Gebietsweine (regional wines), Ortsweine (local or village wines) and Riedenweine (single vineyard wines). Bottling will begin with the 2023 vintage, and by next year's Wine Guide, the DAC range will be comprehensive for all Austrian wine regions.

The positive development of the domestic sparkling wine sector continues this year: Never before have so many sparkling wines been submitted to the Falstaff Wine Guide. This is a positive sign that marketing efforts are beginning to bear fruit. The sparkling wine pyramid and the introduction of the new term Sekt Austria are resonating with consumers. In the alternative segment, Pet Nats is very popular and appeals to a younger target group in the sparkling wine segment. The greatest challenge for the future of viticulture will be global climate change, and it will be necessary to respond to this phenomenon with foresight.

Exciting and varied times lie ahead for both winemakers and consumers, and we look forward to continuing to guide them with our expert analytical commentary and advice on the best wines.

I would like to take this opportunity to express my special thanks to all the contributors to this 26th edition, and to all the wineries that have entrusted us with their wines during this special period. It is their skill and admirable work that makes this guide possible. And so that our winemakers can continue to produce the best possible wines in the future for their customers, they must receive a worthy price for their excellent products. So let's continue to enjoy our wines at a fair price.

PETER MOSER
Falstaff Ultimate Wine Guide Austria

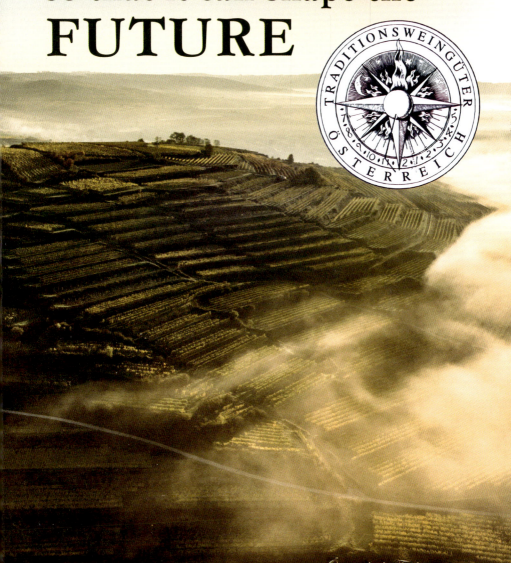

CONTENT

AUSTRIA'S BEST WINES REVIEWED AND RATED

5	Editorial	32	Austrian wine regulations
10	Overview	34	The Falstaff Wine Guide – its practical side
12	The 2022 vintage	37	Importer's country codes
14	The 2021 vintage	38	Organizations in Austria
18	Austria's grape varieties	412	Index

WINEGROWING IN AUSTRIA & NEIGHBORING COUNTRIES
Short Descriptions, Maps of the Regions and the Wineries in Detail

40	Wien/Vienna	254	Burgenland
		258	Eisenberg DAC
56	Niederösterreich/Lower Austria	266	Leithaberg DAC
60	Carnuntum DAC	280	Mittelburgenland DAC
76	Kamptal DAC	294	Neusiedlersee DAC
108	Kremstal DAC		
142	Thermenregion	324	Steiermark/Styria
152	Traisental DAC	328	Südsteiermark DAC
164	Wachau DAC	376	Vulkanland Steiermark DAC
202	Wagram DAC	388	WeststeierMark DAC
228	Weinviertel DAC		
		396	Viticulture in Neighboring Countries

Wachau. Guaranteed origin since 823 AD.

ik-wachau.at

In guaranteeing the origin of our wines, we in the Wachau region have always been a step ahead, most recently with the new **Wachau DAC designation.** And our wines are still labelled according to the established styles of Steinfeder®, Federspiel® and Smaragd®. True Wachau quality, guaranteed.

Riedeweine or single-vineyard wines, either Grüner Veltliners or Rieslings, provide the unique Wachau experience. At the pinnacle of the Wachau's origin classification, these wines mirror the finest grade of Wachau terroir: the Riede. No noticeable oaking or any other enrichment is permitted.

Ortsweine are wines produced from grapes grown around a single town or village. Only traditional Wachau grape varieties are pressed, and no noticeable oaking is allowed.

Gebietsweine – wines originating from grapes grown throughout the region – reflect the Wachau's rich diversity. Explore the abundant variety and choice of wine styles the Wachau has to offer. Discover for yourself the many surprises this region holds in store.

The Wachau label stands for 100% hand-harvested grapes.

The designation "Wachau" originally dates back to 823 AD.

OVERVIEW

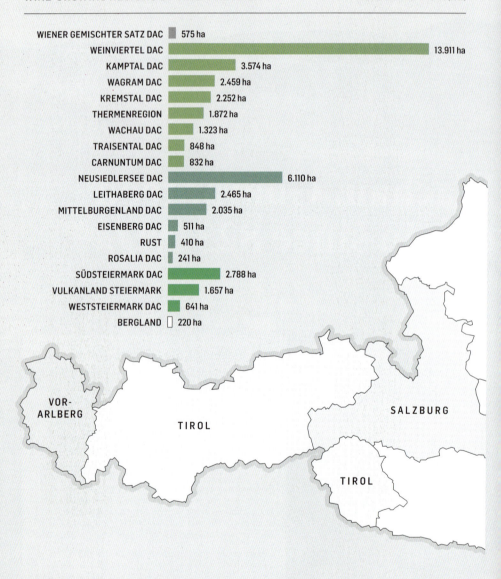

WINE-GROWING REGIONS BY VINEYARD AREA SOURCE: BMLRT nach INVEKOS (2022)

- WIENER GEMISCHTER SATZ DAC — 575 ha
- WEINVIERTEL DAC — 13.911 ha
- KAMPTAL DAC — 3.574 ha
- WAGRAM DAC — 2.459 ha
- KREMSTAL DAC — 2.252 ha
- THERMENREGION — 1.872 ha
- WACHAU DAC — 1.323 ha
- TRAISENTAL DAC — 848 ha
- CARNUNTUM DAC — 832 ha
- NEUSIEDLERSEE DAC — 6.110 ha
- LEITHABERG DAC — 2.465 ha
- MITTELBURGENLAND DAC — 2.035 ha
- EISENBERG DAC — 511 ha
- RUST — 410 ha
- ROSALIA DAC — 241 ha
- SÜDSTEIERMARK DAC — 2.788 ha
- VULKANLAND STEIERMARK — 1.657 ha
- WESTSTEIERMARK DAC — 641 ha
- BERGLAND — 220 ha

The vineyard areas of the federal states of Oberösterreich/Upper Austria, Kärnten/Carinthia, Salzburg, Tirol/Tyrol and Vorarlberg are combined in the wine-growing area »Bergland«.

WINE REGIONS IN AUSTRIA

Parndorfer Platte at Lake Neusiedl

VINTAGE 2022: A VERY GOOD VINTAGE IN ALL RESPECTS

At the end of the harvest, there was a very positive resonance from all regions. Both white and red wines were of above average quality in good quantities. Although the acidity of many whites is slightly below that of the great 2021 vintage, the wines still show good balance and freshness.

The 2022 vintage was a challenge for Austrian winemakers due to the unusual weather conditions. At first it seemed to be a year of severe drought, were it not for sporadic rainfall - not always at the most opportune times. However, with much dedication and meticulous work, the winemakers were ultimately able to produce ripe, balanced white wines with fine fruit. The reds are outstanding, with power, structure and velvety tannins. Depending on the grape variety, microclimate and soil composition, the 2022 vintage was slightly more varied than the 2021 vintage. Overall, however, the wines show great maturity, fine fruit and harmonious acidity. At 2.5 million hectolitres, the 2022 harvest is slightly above the long-term average.

THE WINE WEATHER IN 2022
First, let's review the year's climatic conditions: After an extremely mild winter with

very little rainfall, vegetation development was initially very similar to that of 2021. The vines did not bud until the end of April, which was relatively late. However, the danger of the dreaded late frosts was averted. On the other hand, after a long period of drought, the vines flowered quite early in warm weather, although, in most areas, this was accompanied or influenced by rainfall at this vulnerable time. Winegrowers in these regions have had their hands full with the threat of fungal infection, particularly peronospora (downy mildew). In addition, there was a natural thinning out of the crop due to the regional occurrence of coulure.

The summer months were then characterised by numerous hot days and, above all, extreme drought, the likes of which had hardly ever been experienced before. Naturally, young plants and vines on poor soils that survive without irrigation suffered most from these conditions. Fortunately, there were no severe hailstorms or widespread heavy rainfall.

However, the tide turned before the main harvest, which began around 20 August. There was rain, quite heavy in some areas, followed by two more spells of rain before the main harvest - usually a rather unfavourable date for rain, but this time it was welcomed in most wine-growing areas. While the must weight had been relatively modest before, the timely rains triggered a real ripening surge. At the beginning of September, gradations were suddenly recorded, as in the excellent 2019 vintage. The acidity was lower than in the previous two years, but on a par with the 2017 and 2012 vintages, which were also excellent. All the conditions were in place for another remarkable vintage. However, the unexpected rainfall required rapid action in the vineyards to prevent the risk of rot and botrytis. One consequence of these weather conditions was the almost simultaneous ripening of most grape varieties, which also required rapid action.

As a result, in many wine regions the harvest was completed in record time by the end of September. Of course, this was only the case for some regions and varieties. Riesling, for example, was given the extra ripening time it needed in its growing areas north of the Danube, but at the expense of volume. Finally, even in the sweet wine strongholds along Lake Neusiedl, beautiful botrytis was able to develop, allowing for top quality Prädikat wines. There were also a few frosty nights before Christmas, allowing the harvest of the coveted ice wines.

VARIETAL WHITES, GOOD ACIDITY

In general, mature white wines with fine fruit aromas and slightly lower acidity than the previous two years are to be expected. Powerful single vineyard or reserve wines were also easily achieved. Distinct varietal expression can be seen in the leading variety, Grüner Veltliner, as well as in the surprisingly racy Rieslings and the Pinot varieties, which benefited from the prevailing conditions. The acidity is slightly lower, without affecting the balance of the wines. The aromatic varieties such as Sauvignon Blanc, Muskateller and Traminer are also very promising.

The same goes for regional varieties such as Roter Veltliner from Wagram and Rotgipfler and Zierfandler from the Thermenregion. In addition, a few very cold nights in December made it possible to harvest the rare Eiswein. The Viennese vineyards of Nussberg, Grinzing, Neustift, Bisamberg and Mauer also achieved optimum sugar ripeness with lower acidity levels. After an unusually dry spell, the long-awaited showers arrived, aiding the ripening process and bringing the harvest forward from last year to early October. The result is round and balanced Wiener Gemischter Satz wines, as well as well-balanced, fruit driven Rieslings that can be enjoyed a little earlier than in previous years.

DENSE, STRUCTURED RED

In Conditions were very dry, especially in the wine producing areas along Lake Neusiedl. There was no late frost or hail damage and the grapes were very healthy with excellent ripeness and adequate acidity. The conditions for a great red wine vintage were ideal, especially as the ratio of pulp to skins of the very small berries was also optimal.

HARMONY IN STYRIA

A very good vintage was recorded in all three Styrian wine-growing regions, which will probably be compared to the excellent, albeit somewhat different, 2021. Precipitation was average for Styrian conditions. The rain just before the main harvest was also considered essential for the further development of the grapes, even if it meant a little more sorting. The harvest period was quite short, with most of the harvest completed in September - earlier than ever before. Another key factor was that most of the varieties reached optimum ripeness almost simultaneously. Sauvignon Blanc, which has become the leading variety in Styria, was particularly good, but Gelber Muskateller, Morillon (Chardonnay), Pinot Blanc and Welschriesling also pleased even the most discerning palates. The high must weights allowed the white wines to develop their full potential of succulence and power potential, but above all their elegance and structure. This time the balance of all the components has been achieved right from the start, so that even the young wines are very juicy, round and harmonious. The Traminers in the Vulkanland region have also benefited from good conditions, while in western Styria, at the foot of the Koralpe, the Schilcher wines have developed a distinct texture and succinct red berry fruit.

VINTAGE 2021: A DREAM VINTAGE IN WHITE AND RED

Rarely has a vintage produced such a dreamlike result across all winegrowing regions. In particular, a magnificent autumn ensured optimal grape quality and ripe acidity, resulting in balanced, elegant white wines with intense fruit and a vibrant structure, as well as powerful, complex red wines.

With a harvest of around 2.4 million hectolitres, the 2021 vintage is in line with the long-term average. This is a cause for celebration, as the 2021 vintage was less positive in comparison with the rest of Europe: some German wine-growing regions suffered drastic crop losses; the major wine-growing countries of Italy, France and Spain also suffered losses, some of them severe, largely due to late frosts.

THE WINE WEATHER IN 2021

Let's take a quick look back at the year's weather: After a rather dry winter, spring took a long time to arrive. April was cool and much too dry, and May brought little sun but plenty of rain, although the amount

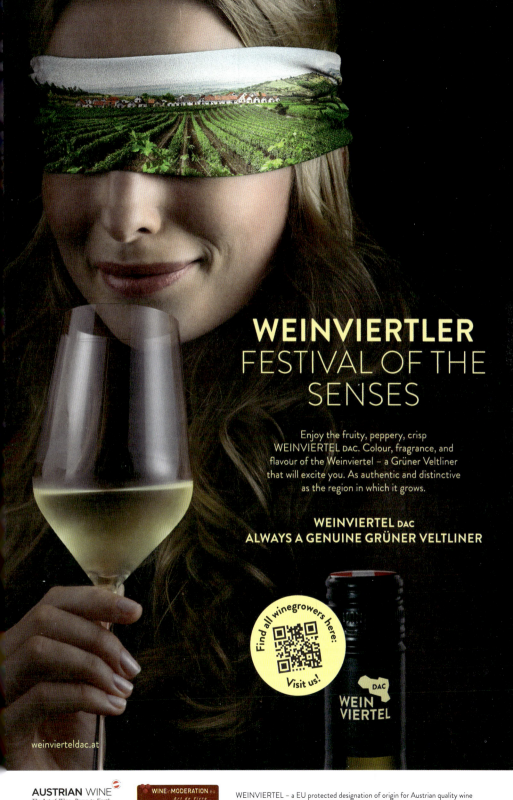

varied from region to region. Vine budding and flowering were delayed, and unlike the wine-growing countries to the south and west of the main Alpine ridge, Austria was spared late frosts this time. June finally brought sunshine and warmth. The vines did not blossom until the end of the month, when a hot spell set in, causing some coulure and loose clusters. The heat also increased the risk of storms: Already on 24 June, a huge thunderstorm cell with heavy hail unleashed itself in the northern Weinviertel, causing severe damage to around 1,000 hectares of vineyards, some of which were completely destroyed. A tornado even touched down in the neighbouring Czech Republic.

At the end of July, a hailstorm hit the wine villages of Rührsdorf and Rossatz in the Wachau, and there was also some damage to the Dürnstein and Loibner vineyards, as well as vineyards near Göttweig and in the Traisental. The red wine heartland of Mittelburgenland was also severely damaged by hail, while some vineyards on the Nussberg in Vienna, in the Styrian Vulkanland and in southern Styria were somewhat less affected. Overall, however, this year's harvest suffered only minor losses due to the storms. Otherwise, July was a beautiful summer month as usual, but was replaced by a rather dull, rainy and cool August.

On 1 September, however, the break the winegrowers had been waiting for arrived: a six-week period of sunny weather with only two days of rain. By mid-September, however, the nights had become quite cool, with a marked difference between day and night temperatures. This resulted in great aromatic development in the whites and vibrancy in the reds. At the end of October, a warm spell gave the Rieslings north of the Danube a welcome final push towards optimal ripeness. Oidium, peronospora and unwanted botrytis never stood a chance in these conditions, and in some areas, experienced winemakers and winegrowers said they had never seen such beautiful, perfectly healthy grapes at harvest time. Harvest was stress-free and spot-on.

WHITE WINES WITH FRUIT AND OPTIMUM ACIDITY

From the Wachau to Carnuntum, from the Weinviertel to southern Styria, there is pure delight in the wonderfully harmonious white wines whose components have been concentrated by the long growing season. This has resulted in wines with optimal sugar levels, rich extract, distinct freshness, exceptional aromatic diversity and a racy acidity structure. This is particularly beneficial for the main variety, Grüner Veltliner. In the 2021 vintage, the Grüner Veltliner has a fine savouriness as well as deep stone-fruit succulence and creamy suppleness. The Rieslings are also very promising, with full body and elegance thanks to a great acidity structure. Equally compelling are the ripe, powerful Sauvignon Blancs and Chardonnays, as well as the highly aromatic Muskateller. White wine enthusiasts will find their money's worth in all regions and categories. Rarely has a vintage offered such superb and exciting wines.

RED WINES WITH STRUCTURE AND POTENTIAL

Carnuntum produced excellent red wines from all varieties and at all stages of maturity. The late harvest and long growing season may have been particularly beneficial for the sensitive Pinot Noir and St Laurent. As with the white single vineyard and reserve wines, they are expected to have great structure and maturity potential. In Burgenland, red wines benefited from optimal autumn conditions, especially the two leading varieties, Zweigelt and Blaufränkisch. The long vegetation period and late harvest, as well as the analytical data, point to a 2019 red wine style, with a high degree of maturity, elegant structure and razor-sharp fruit. Some even see the most promising red wines of all time maturing in their barrels, which could rival the powerful and pronounced fruit wines of the exceptional 2011 and 2017 vintages. Among the French varietals, Cabernet in its Sauvignon and Franc variants could be particularly exciting this time around.

THE EXHILARATING ASCENDANCY OF VIENNESE WINE IS NO ACCIDENT.

Behind it stands the renowned winegrower group WienWein, and their vision: to lead Vienna's wine to a position among the world's finest. The picturesque vineyards and their panorama of the Danube metropolis are inextricably woven into the heart & soul of the city. They present themselves full of pride to the beholder, and provide the WienWein winegrowers with ideal conditions for vinifying wines of great character.

WWW.WIENWEIN.AT

The Leopoldsberg, Vienna's most famous hill, towering over the Danube and the Nussberg vineyards

AUSTRIA'S GRAPE VARIETIES

The small wine country of Austria has a very diversified assortment of grape varieties, with more than thirty different grape varieties currently permitted for the production of quality wines.

Due to the very long and eventful history of Austrian viticulture, the present list of grapes is a colourful mixture of old indigenous varieties, fairly recent cross-breedings, and classic international varieties, which make up only a small part of the totaal. This latter group includes mostly whites like Chardonnay and Sauvignon Blanc, but black Bordeaux varieties like Cabernet Sauvignon, Cabernet Franc and Merlot are included and have been permitted for Austrian quality wines since 1986. In 2001, the Syrah was added to this list. Only scant basic information is provided here about these worldwide-known varieties. Our focus shall be the typical Austrian specialties that are often little known over the country's borders. Scientific ampelographic classification began in Austria around 200 years ago during the era of the Habsburg Monarchy. Vineyards were typically planted with a mixture of several different varieties during the Austro-Hungarian Empire. Hundreds of varieties thrived and were often difficult to distinguish from one another. Further complicating categorization, were multiple names for the very same variety, which differed from district to district and even from village to village. It was not until the second half of the 19th century that a vague comprehension about the enormous variety that had developed during the Habsburg Monarchy solidified. At the end of the 19th century, major vineyard epidemics spread. Oidium and peronospora followed by phylloxera decimated vineyards in all of Europe. After the propagation of European vines on disease and phylloxera resistant American rootstocks was discovered, planting of vineyards with a single selected variety was initiated. Until World War II, vineyards were cultivated in bush or gobelet styles and it was not until the 1950s that wire-frame trellis systems caught on. The so-called Lenz Moser cultivation, conceived and propagated by a well-known Austrian winery owner and viticulture engineer revolutionized the country's viticulture and made mechanical cultivation possible for the first time. Grüner Veltliner in particular adapted well to this specific form of planting and the variety became Austria's predominant grape. Today young vines are preferably established in a cordon training system with high leaf canopies and high density of vines. It is no longer the potential quantity that is the priority, but physiologically ripe and aromatic grapes of high quality. Subsidization from the European Union has further supported the concentrated efforts on improvements in Austrian vineyards. Consumer demand is clearly moving towards red wine consumption and new plantings in suitable vineyards and microclimates reflect this. Some less fashionable or less interesting white varieties are being replaced with red wine varieties. It is easily imaginable that the number of grape varieties, which are really used for the production of high-quality wine in Austria, will decrease. Already today, wines from some of the varieties stated on the list are rarely found on the market. The Federal College and Research Centre for Viticulture and Pomology Klosterneuburg near Vienna is the country's leader in research and cultivation innovation. This is where Professor Fritz Zweigelt worked in the early 1920s and cultivated the Blauer Zweigelt variety by crossing St. Laurent and Blaufränkisch, resulting in Austria's most successful and popular black grape. Leading scientists like Dr. Ferdinand Regner are currently researching the genetic origin of indigenous Austrian varieties and their clones by means of DNA-sequencing. Dr. Ferdinand Regner succeeded in documenting the significant role of Traminer, whose genes can be found in numerous Austrian varieties. The Austrian wine landscape offers broad varietal diversity, which is multiplied by quite differing soils and microclimates. In the end, it is the responsibility of every single vintner to select varieties most suited for each vineyard site.

WHITE WINE VARIETIES

GRÜNER VELTLINER
Synonyms: Weissgipfler, Grüner, Manhardsrebe, Grüner Muskateller

Grüner Veltliner is the main grape variety in Austria, grown predominantly in the wine-growing areas Weinviertel, Kamptal, Kremstal, Traisental, Wagram, and Wachau. Grüner Veltliner is not botanically related to other Veltliner varieties like Brauner Veltliner, Roter Veltliner or Frühroter Veltliner. Traminer has long been known as one of the parents of Grüner Veltliner, but the other parent remained unknown until recently. An

Grüner Veltliner

old, unrecognizable variety was discovered in Burgenland and through DNA-sequencing was determined to be the second parent. This grape was named after is discovery location, St. Georgen, because its identity did not correspond to any other known variety. Nearly one third of the Austrian vineyard area is planted with Grüner Veltliner; in Niederösterreich it comprises half of the vineyards. The preference for this variety is due in part to its compatibility with the Lenz Moser vine trellising and training system. After World War II there was a search for productive varieties requiring little care. Grüner Veltliner fulfilled both these needs and moreover thrives in several different soil types. When cultivation is geared towards high yields, the resulting wine from Grüner Veltliner is light and racy, but still spicy and appetizing for everyday consumption. The typical peppery-spicy aroma and flavour of the variety is often referred to as "Pfefferl". When cultivation concentrates on quality rather than quantity, Grüner Veltliner amplifies its terroir with corresponding changes in taste and character. Meagre, poor primary rock soil, as is found in the Wachau, Krems, or Kamptal, bring wine dominated by firm mineral character and pleasant vegetal spiciness. When Grüner Veltliner is planted on fertile loess terraces in the Wagram or in the Weinviertel, the wine displays a supple, juicy fruitiness reminiscent of an exotic fruit cocktail. Yield restrictions bring intense, expressive wines of impressive depth and complexity. Another important quality of Grüner Veltliner is its longevity. Riesling is considered internationally to be particularly capable of ageing, yet tastings of mature wines prove Grüner Veltliner to be at least as long-lived. I have tasted and drunk Grüner Veltliners on several occasions that were 50 years old or more with considerable enjoyment. In recent years experiments were performed in fermenting and maturing Grüner Veltliner in small oak barrels. These experiments have proved quite legitimate and have occasionally resulted in very interesting wines indeed. These concentrated wines are often very potent, sometimes with as much as 14.5 % alcohol. The first maturation results show, however, that after some years in the bottle, the character of Grüner Veltliner variety is obscured by the influence of new oak and prolonged contact with the fine lees. Nevertheless, these new Veltliner types have their fans. Falstaff magazine stages an annual competition called the "Grüner Veltliner Grand Prix", which addresses the classic medium-bodied style of Grüner Veltliner. The wines involved are fermented dry with a maximum of four grams of residual sugar, have no more than 13% alcohol, and display crisp acidity. They provide refreshing drinking pleasure and are suited as ideal accompaniment to many foods. As the white wine variety that is most associated with Austria, this unique grape offers vintners a broad spectrum of styles, from light wines all the way up to noble sweet Trockenbeerenauslese. Grüner Veltliner is increasingly popular internationally and has become more easily available in recent years.

BOUVIER

This rare variety has a striking fragrance, putting it among the aromatic varieties. It was first cultivated from a Burgundy seedling around 1900 in Radkersburg, Steiermark, by the estate owner Clotar Bouvier. The best Bouviers in Austria can be found among the sweet wine predicates Beerenauslese, Trockenbeerenauslese, and Eiswein. Though it is a white wine, it has rather low acidity. Because it has little character, its popularity in the vineyard is decreasing.

Bouvier

WHITE WINE VARIETIES

CHARDONNAY
Synonym: Morillon

When Chardonnay became fashionable in Austria 20 years ago, much was labelled Chardonnay that actually wasn't. Many a Pinot Blanc attempted to profit from word creations like Pinot Chardonnay. Styrian Morillon is identical to Chardonnay. The term Feinburgunder was once often used in the Wachau for the variety, but since 1999, this synonym is no longer permitted. Chardonnay is vinified both in steel tanks and in new oak in Austria. Terms like "classic" and "tradition" can be misleading to international consumers since they denote the fresh and fruity style without oak influence. A clue can be found in the specified alcohol content on labels since only the more potent wines, with over 13%, are matured in new oak barrels. Chardonnay occupies very small but widespread cultivation areas all over Austria, (around 3 % of Austria's vineyard area). Despite this, the variety is of increasing importance, particularly in the upper quality segment. Chardonnay is found in every Austrian wine-growing area.

Frühroter Veltliner

FRÜHROTER VELTLINER
Synonym: Malvasier

This natural cross of Roter Veltliner x Sylvaner is not demanding in terms of its location and can even cope with meagre lime-rich soils. It is resistant against both winter and late frosts, and even against humidity. On the other hand, it ripens too early. The resulting wine has no particular bouquet, tends to be of high alcohol content, and is mild in acidity. The Frühroter Veltliner is by no means a trendy variety and makes up only 0.9 % of the Austrian vineyards.

FURMINT

This rare variety originates from the Tokaj region in north-eastern Hungary. It is the main component of the Hungarian Tokaji wine and has nothing to do with the Tokay d'Alsace. In Austria it is encountered almost exclusively in Burgenland, particularly in the region around Rust where it is experiencing a small renaissance. The Furmint is demanding of its location and requires warm, well-drained soils. It is sensitive to oidium, but has good resistance to botrytis. The wine is yellow-green when fermented dry and golden yellow in colour when sweet. It is intense in bouquet, often reminiscent of chamomile and quince, usually high in alcohol, and possesses racy acidity. Because it can achieve high degrees of extract and alcohol, it is very well suited to vinification of sweet predicated wines.

GELBER MUSKATELLER
Synonym: Muscat Blanc á petits grains

Muscat is usually fermented dry in Austria and comprises a fragrant, light aperitif wine with refreshing acidity. Muscat has been documented in the Wachau since 1400. This variety also has a long tradition in Steiermark and Burgenland, yet the vineyard area remains very small since it is extremely susceptible to rot. It is very demanding of its location, sensitive to frost and fungal attacks, matures late, but is suitable for almost any soil, except lime. In addition to racy, fragrant, light, dry wines, fascinating sweet wines are also made from this variety in Austria. The best sweet examples can age for decades.

GEWÜRZTRAMINER
Synonyms: Roter Traminer, Gelber Traminer, Traminer

In Austria, Traminer finds its most significant dissemination in Burgenland, the Thermenregion, and Steiermark. It is very demanding of its location and soil, has a low tolerance for lime, and is sensitive to frost. The wine

AUSTRIA'S GRAPE VARIETIES

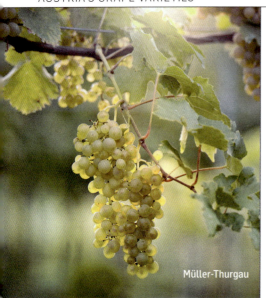
Müller-Thurgau

typically displays an intense medium yellow to golden-yellow colour, occasionally with a slightly reddish shimmer. The fragrance is intense and reminiscent of rose petals and marshmallow. Gewürztraminer achieves its best quality in the upper predicated sweet wine categories and is quite capable of extended ageing. Despite being considered a noble, aristocratic wine, it is not currently the trend among consumers. Fortunately there is a committed community of fans, and its continued existence in Austria is secured.

GRAUER BURGUNDER
Synonyms: Ruländer, Pinot Gris
This noble variety stems from Burgundy and was brought into Austria and Hungary in the 14th century by Cistercian monks. Its highest density can be found in northern Burgenland, where the Cistercians were once very diligent viticulturists. Pinot Gris requires deep soils that are rich in nutrients and a good well-drained location with regular access to a good supply of water. Fruit maturity is reached relatively soon, however the vintage is usually not until the beginning of October. A wine with an intensive golden-yellow colour that sometimes has a mild reddish shimmer and a delicious varietal bouquet with a touch of honey. It is typically full bodied and can reach high levels of alcohol. It currently makes up less than 0.5 % of Austrian vineyards.

GRÜNER SYLVANER
It is proven that this old indigenous vine variety is a cross of Traminer x Österreichisch Weiss. It is also common in Germany, where it was mentioned for the first time in 1665 in a monastery inscription. The acreage has been decreasing in Austria, and today Grüner Sylvaner is found nearly only in Niederösterreich. This variety needs fertile soils with good nutrients and water supply, as well as good hillside locations. It is sensitive to winter frost and botrytis. The wine is greenish-yellow, mild and subtly fruity. In short, it is rather neutral.

MÜLLER-THURGAU
Synonym: Rivaner
Cultivated in 1882 by Dr. Hermann Müller from Thurgau in Switzerland at the University of Geisenheim in Germany, it is a cross of Riesling x Madeleine Royal. For years it was believed to be a cross of Riesling x Sylvaner which is the base for its synonym Rivaner. This new variety was introduced in Franken in 1913, and by the 1950s it was distributed throughout the world. Fritz Salomon of the Undhof Winery in Kremstal introduced this variety in Austria in 1926. Once the second-most important grape variety in Austria, its popularity has declined rapidly over the past two decades. It is cultivated predominantly in Lower Austria and Burgenland where it occupies 4.6% of the area under vine. Although not very demanding, it does favour cooler sites and deep loam and loess soils that are rich in nutrients and have a good water supply. Müller-Thurgau is sensitive to winter frost and prone to disease. The wines are usually soft and mild, with a discreet bouquet slightly reminiscent of Muscat. Apart from the sweet predicated wines made, Müller-Thurgau is preferably drunk young.

MUSKAT OTTONEL
This aromatic variety stems from a crossing of Chasselas x Muscat d'Eisenstadt first breen in the Loire at the end of the 19th century. The main centre of Austrian plantings is in northern Burgenland, and it totals 0,8% of the Austrian area under vine. It requires deep, fertile soil with good water supply and loves a sunny site protected from the wind. The ripening is early but with unrelia-

© WSNA

ble yields. The wine exhibits a greenish-yellow colour and an intense spicy bouquet reminiscent of nutmeg. It is mild, usually low in alcohol and extract and most suited for the production of remarkable sweet predicated wines.

NEUBURGER

This typical Austrian variety is an old cross of Roter Veltliner x Sylvaner which apparently stems from the Spitzer Graben community in the Wachau. Today it is found in Burgenland and Lower Austria, with only a few plantings in Styria and Vienna. Neuburger is not demanding of its location. It is even thrives on heavy, lime-rich soils, but brings its best results in primary rock. It is prone to variable fruit set if the weather is poor during flowering. The Neuburger results in restrained, classy wines that are sometimes somewhat neutral in fragrance, but aristocratic in expression. Interesting Neuburger wines can be discovered in Burgenland, Thermenregion, and especially in the upper Wachau region.

RIESLING
Synonym: Weisser Riesling

The existence of this variety is documented in Rüsselsheim in Germany as early as 1435. The Wachau also lays claim to being the origin of this variety, according to a document that mentions a vineyard by the name of Ritzling. Despite the theory being based solely on hypothesis, it is nevertheless an ingenious idea. Riesling is encountered in Austria predominantly in the Wachau, Kremstal, Kamptal, Traisental and Wagram wine-growing areas where it is the source of outstanding wines. It places high demands both on location and soil. The most fragrant and raciest wines stem from schist and primary rock. Riesling is therefore also found in other areas of Austria where primary rock or schist is found, such as Röschitz in the Weinviertel, Donnerskirchen, or Jois in Burgenland. The variety matures very late with the harvest usually at the end of October or beginning of November. It tests the patience of the vintner nearly each and every year. Its aristocratic bouquet exhibits peach, apricot, and citrus. Riesling is very racy and well structured. It develops continuously, gaining in complexity making

it very suitable for ageing. This holds particularly true for the late harvested Spätlese and Auslese categories, or for the Smaragd wines of the Wachau.

ROTGIPFLER

The rare Rotgipfler is a natural cross of Savagnin x Roter Veltliner, most probably from Austria's Thermenregion, and is therefore a half-sibling of Frühroter Veltliner, Neuburger and Zierfandler.. Its oldest documentation is from Styria in 1840. Together with Zierfandler, it established the reputation of the famous wines from Gumpoldskirchen. This variety exists almost exclusively in Austria, particularly in its Thermenregion origin. It favours fertile medium-weight lime soils and warm hillside locations. It is sensitive to winter frosts, prone to botrytis, and matures late. The wine is golden-yellow and possesses a pronounced bouquet. It is refreshing and spicy, and for the most part, full-bodied, and rich in extract and alcohol. It is vinified dry, off-dry and sweet and is often paired with Zierfandler in a blend.

ROTER VELTLINER

The origin of this very old variety has not yet been clearly established. It is likely from Niederösterreich (Lower Austria), where it is grown today in small quantities in the Kremstal and Wagram areas. The Roter Velt-

Neuburger

AUSTRIA'S GRAPE VARIETIES

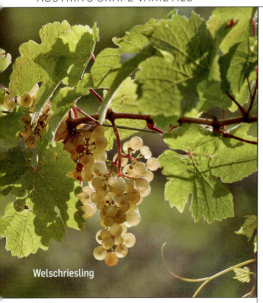
Welschriesling

liner places moderate demands on soil, but high demands on location, requiring warm, southern hillside aspects. It is sensitive to frost and yields are unreliable. Roter Veltliner matures late. The wine is greenish-yellow, fruity and fragrant, with a subtle spicy aroma, and often exhibits racy acidity.

SAUVIGNON BLANC

In its present form, this variety probably comes from the south of France where it has been documented since the first half of the 18th century. It originates from a Traminer crossing, but seems to have developed from a preliminary stage. It is most common in Styria, but due to its general popularity is now planted in all regions. The name "Muskat-Sylvaner" was permitted until 1999. The variety places high demands on location and thrives on fertile, not overly dry soils. High humidity is important. It brings moderate, irregular yields and is sensitive to winter frost. The wine exhibits a greenish yellow colour and its grassy spiciness reminiscent of fresh bell peppers evolves into aromas of asparagus, elderflower and cassis at high stages of maturity. Sauvignon Blanc is an elegant, refreshing wine with racy structure and inimitable, stimulating character. The variety is suitable for medium-term ageing. More potent wines are sometimes vinified in new oak.

SCHEUREBE
Synonym: Sämling 88

This variety is a cross of Riesling and an unknown variety, but not Silvaner as was once suspected. In terms of quality, this is perhaps the most successful of all the German crossings and was developed by Dr. Scheu in 1916. The variety is valued in Burgenland for noble sweet wines and in Styria for light, dry, crisp wines. Despite its quality, the variety is currently declining. It makes little demand on soil, but high demand on location. The Scheurebe matures late and provides moderate yields. Scheurebe wines are usually golden-yellow, have a subtle, aromatic bouquet, and exhibit elegant acidity and body.

WEISSBURGUNDER
Synonym: Pinot Blanc, Klevner

Burgundy is considered to be the home of this highly acclaimed variety as it was documented there in the 14th century. Pinot is quite prone to mutation and its different colour variations, – Pinot Blanc, Pinot Gris, and Pinot Noir – all have a very similar genetic fingerprint. Weissburgunder is mainly planted throughout Austria's wine regions and makes up 4.3 % of the vineyard area. This noble variety is demanding of location and soil, requiring plenty of nutrients and sufficient moisture. It is sensitive to late frost, and yields reliably and consistently. When allowed to gain full maturity, Weissburgunder develops into a white wine rich in substance with a subtle, almond flavour and racy acidity. The variety, internationally known as Pinot Blanc, usually develops very well in the bottle. Due to its discreet character, it is also suitable for blends with other varieties and for fermentation and/or maturation in new, small oak barrels.

WELSCHRIESLING

The different interpretations of its origin point towards Italy and France. Welschriesling makes up 7.8% of Austrian vineyards and is the country's second most important white grape variety behind Grüner Veltliner (29.4 %). The variety is planted predominantly in Burgenland and Niederösterreich, but it is also very popular in Steiermark. The vine requires deep, warm soils, rich in nutrients and places high demands on its location.

The Rubin CARNUNTUM Wineries

30 Years — WINE REGION CARNUNTUM

The figurehead of an entire region.

www.carnuntum.com

AUSTRIA'S GRAPE VARIETIES

Zierfandler

cious sweetness finds perfect balance in its inherent acidity. A Welschriesling Trockenbeerenauslese can bring tremendous drinking pleasure even after two decades of bottle maturation.

ZIERFANDLER
Synonym: Spätrot

DNA parentage analysis at the Federal College and Research Centre for Viticulture and Pomology Klosterneuburg has suggested that Zierfandler could be a natural cross between Roter Veltliner and a relative of Savagnin that took place near Gumpoldskirchen in the Thermenregion of Niederösterreich (Lower Austria). Gumpoldskirchen continues to be one of the few places in the world where the variety is found. Together with another rare autochthon variety Rotgipler, Zierfandler is the foundation on which the fame of the historic wine village Gumpoldskirchen is based. It is a fickle and demanding variety that ripens late and irregularly, providing no more than moderate yields. The wine has a golden yellow colour, a distinct fruity bouquet, full body, and racy acidity. It is spicy and rich in extract and alcohol content, and is often produced with residual sweetness, blended with Rotgipfler variety and marketed as Spätrot-Rotgipfler.

Because it is sensitive to dryness, it favours south-facing slopes protected from the wind. It provides generous, reliable yields. When fermented dry, Welschriesling brings fresh, fruity wines with subtle spice, best enjoyed in their youth. The variety is perhaps at its best as a noble sweet predicated wine for its lus-

RED WINE VARIETIES

BLAUFRÄNKISCH
Synonyms: Limberger, Lemberger

Although Blaufränkisch is not Austria's number one black grape in terms of planted area – with 3,225 hectares it ranks second – it is the most important variety to many Austrian red wine specialists. Its exact origin has not yet been determined, but for many centuries it has certainly been at home in Austrian vineyards. The root of the word, "fränkisch", was associated with the German Franks just as the stem "Wälsch" was connected with Italian, as is exemplified by Welschriesling. One assumes, however, that the term Blaufränkisch was meant to hint at the positive properties of the wine – "Frankish" in the sense of good,

fine. By contrast, the name "Heunisch" meaning "Hunnish" was still used last century to denote a weak, less valuable wine. Both in the Viennese dialect and in English, the term "frank" also has the connotation of "honest". But enough on etymology: Blaufränkisch thrives in deep soils and even does quite well in lime soils. It ripens relatively late and is harvested after advantageously long hang times. While not particularly susceptible to mildew diseases, it is prone to botrytis-related stem necrosis. Typically, it displays pronounced dark berry aromas reminiscent of boysenberry, sometimes intertwined with mineral notes derived from its terroir. Appetizing acidity and firm tannin structure are its trademarks. The grape calls for at least two years of ageing before it becomes approachable. Wines from good vintages exhibit surprising ageing capacity. The best Blaufränkisch wines are vinified according to international models in new French oak bar-

RED WINE VARIETIES

rels and are often blended with small quantities of Cabernet Sauvignon or Merlot. Blaufränkisch thrives best on the west and south sides of Lake Neusiedl in Burgenland an also finds suitable locations in Carnuntum in Niederösterreich (Lower Austria). The best sites in Südburgenland are located in the Eisenberg DAC. Mittelburgenland is also referred to as "Blaufränkischland", and this is the predominant variety in prime vineyards in Neckenmarkt, Horitschon, and Deutschkreutz. Farther north on the west side of Lake Neusiedl in the Neusiedlersee-Hügelland wine-growing area and the Leithaberg DAC, Blaufränksich brings exquisite results from marine limestone and mica-schist soils slopes. It is here that the vintner Ernst Triebaumer crafted Austria's first hallmark wine in 1986 from the single vineyard Marienthal. This legendary wine, although almost completely exhausted, rings a bell for every Austrian wine buff.

ZWEIGELT
Synonyms: Blauer Zweigelt, Rotburger

The variety with the intense cherry fruit aromas and flavours is an Austrian crossing and by far the most widely planted red vine variety in the country and the second most prolific variety after Grüner Veltliner. It grows in all Austrian wine-growing regions on 6,476 ha, covering 14.1% of the total area under vine. This successful grape goes back to Professor Fritz Zweigelt (1888–1964), who developed this cross of Blaufränkisch and St. Laurent at the ederal College and Research Centre for Viticulture and Pomology Klosterneuburg in 1922. Although the name Zweigelt may appear justified in honour of the originator, it has turned out to be a real tongue twister for non-German speaking people. The oenologist himself in a more self-effacing manner chose the designation Rotburger – to the credit of the place where it all came about. He was referring to "red from Klosterneuburg". The name "Blaue Zweigeltrebe" was officially introduced in 1975 upon intervention of another one of Austria's winegrowing pioneers – Lenz Moser, founder of the widely used high culture training system. The reasons why the Zweigelt grape is so popular among vintners are manifold: it is frost-resistant, ripens early, sets no special demands on location or soil, and has proved to be relatively disease resistant. Consumers appreciate Zweigelt for its vibrant fruitiness that bursts with fresh amarelle cherry flavour. Some of the very best Zweigelts come from the Neusiedlersee DAC on the east side of Lake Neusiedl in Burgenland and from Carnuntum to the north in Niederösterreich, but the variety finds well suited locations throughout Austria's wine regions. Weather easy-drinking approachable examples or more complex oak-matured growths, Zweigelt is the indisputable crowd-pleaser among Austria's black grape varieties. Quite frequently, the best lots of Zweigelt are added to a winemaker's master blend.

ROESLER

This new variety was developed by Dr. Gertraud Mayer at the Federal Viticulture Research Centre Klosterneuburg and the vine nursery Langenzersdorf. The crossing of Zweigelt x Sevye-Villard 18-402 x Blaufränkisch is named after the former director of Austria's oldest viticultural college and research centre, Leonard Roesler. The variety brings not only interesting aromas, deep colour, and abundant extract, it is also advantageous for vintners in cooler regions. The variety is quite frost resistant and can withstand temperatures of up to $-25°$ C ($-13°$ F) and is also resistant to both mildew varieties.

Blaufränkisch

AUSTRIA'S GRAPE VARIETIES

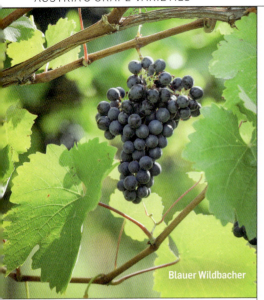
Blauer Wildbacher

BLAUER BURGUNDER
Synonyms: Blauer Spätburgunder, Pinot Noir

Blauburgunder, otherwise known as Pinot Noir, stems from Burgundy and ranks among the great classic international red wine varieties. In Austria it was first mentioned in 1394, when it was planted by Cistercian monks who had brought it directly from France to Gumpoldskirchen where the Freigut Thallern monks still own the Heiligenkreuz Abbey. Blauburgunder is regarded as the prima donna among the classic grape varieties. It sets high demands on location, requiring warm and fertile soils. Bunches are rather small and compact with berries that are round, thin-skinned, and juicy. It takes a highly skilled winemaker to bring the best out of Pinot Noir: the subtle finesse on the nose, its complex and fruity flavours, the silky texture and a longevity exceeding that of most other varieties. The increasing skill of Austrian vintners has inspired them to plant more Blauburgunder (Pinot Noir) and the variety now makes up 903 hectares of the country's vineyards. The best producers are rewarded with expressive reds; the lesser engaged vintners only too frequently obtain thin, stingy wines which lack ripeness. Top varietal representatives are found in the Thermenregion, Vienna, and on both sides of Lake Neusiedl in Burgenland.

ST. LAURENT
Synonyms: Saint Laurent, Sankt Laurent, Lorenzitraube

August 10th is the feast of Saint Laurentius and the day on which this variety usually turns colour. Its history of origin was repeatedly associated with the Bordeaux village of the same name, but it was actually discovered by a certain Mister Bronner from Wieloch in Alsace, who designated it "Schwarzer" and reported Burgundy as its original home. There are, in fact, some similarities with Pinot Noir both in the vineyard and in terms of aromas and flavours, which seem to indicate a certain relationship between the two varieties. St. Laurent grows well on light soils. Unlike Pinot Noir it is characterized by early bud-break. It is thicker skinned than Pinot Noir and produces more robust, dark, velvety reds. Yields must be limited rigorously to promote concentration and ageing capacity. Its amarelle cherry aromas and flavours, which are sometimes offset by a delicate tartness, have gained it many fans. It profits tremendously from bottle ageing. Experience has also proved St. Laurent to be a good blending partner.

BLAUBURGER

Blauburger is an Austrian crossbreed between Blauer Portugieser and Blaufränkisch and dates back to 1923. The final syllable "burger" points to the Federal College and Research Centre for Viticulture and Pomology Klosterneuburg. Its intention at that time was to surpass Zweigelt, but this eventually failed. Since the Blauburger is deeply coloured, it was soon degraded to a colouring wine in blends. In terms of aromas and flavours it resembles a milder version of Blaufränkisch. Today, some excellent oak-matured wines are made from this grape, which fell into unfortunate disrepute, but is truly worthy of note.

BLAUER WILDBACHER
Synonym: Schilcher

Schilcher is the special name of a rosé made from Blauer Wildbacher grapes. This designation is only allowed in Steiermark. Blauer Wildbacher is an old Austrian variety that is said to go back to the Celts. Manuscripts from the 16th century show the first record of the name. Genuine Schilcher comes exclusively from Weststeiermark where vines thrive up to 600 meters above sea level. Despite this, commercial success in the eighties inspired a wave of new plantings throughout Steiermark (Styria). Blauer Wildbacher is also used for the production of fragrant and refreshing bottle-fermented sparkling wine as well as deeply coloured red wine. The variety is not very demanding in terms of soil, requiring only warm and aerated sites due to its proneness to rot. The grapes ripen late and bring only moderate, often inconsistent yields. The colour spectrum of the wine ranges from onion skin shades to ruby-pink. Its red berry and herbal flavour is backed up by a tart acidity and a refreshing character.

CABERNET SAUVIGNON

The world's most famous grape variety also found its way to Austria from Bordeaux. The wine-growing pioneer Robert Schlumberger planted both Cabernet and Merlot on his estate in Bad Vöslau in the 19th century. Although Schlumberger's Privatkeller was a great "liquid" success for decades, his venture eventually fell into oblivion. The first vintner to reinstate this noble grape was Anton Kollwentz from Burgenland. In Mailberg in Niederösterreich (Lower Austria), Lenz Moser carried out tests that showed promising results on the Schlossweingut Malteser Ritterorden estate in Weinviertel, on much less suitable terroir than in Neusiedlersee-Hügelland. Progressive Austrian winegrowers really had to fight for Cabernet Sauvignon. They planted experimental vineyards and their efforts were constantly supported by Falstaff Magazine. After triumphantly showing their expected positive results, the bureaucratic hurdles were also finally cleared and Cabernet Sauvignon was officially authorized as a permitted quality grape variety on June 11, 1986. Contrary to many a false prophecy, it has not spread like a flood, drowning all indigenous grapes below it. Cabernet Sauvignon thrives almost everywhere, is disease and pest resistant and can withstand dryness – even low temperatures do not bother it. A miracle grape? Not at all! If you tackle this grape as a winegrower rather than a jungle-ranger, enough work still awaits. Although yields are low, additional crop restriction and rigorous green harvests are necessary to bring in ripe fruit at the end of the growing season. As the vines growing older, Cabernet Sauvignon displays its exceptional potential to an ever-increasing extent. Connoisseurs love its pronounced cassis nose, its succulence and inherent harmony. Cabernet Sauvignon turned out to be a perfect blending partner for indigenous Austrian varieties, wherein only small amounts are employed for structure and texture. Unfortunately, if weather conditions prevent the fruit from ripening fully, heavy losses will be suffered. In problematic years, many producers refrain from making varietal Cabernets altogether. In good vintages, this grape produces wines with impressive structure, pronounced aromas and flavours, and a firm tannic backbone.

MERLOT

This grape was mentioned for the first time in the Bordeaux region in the 18th century. It was permitted as a quality variety in Austria first in 1986. At present, Merlot plantings remain on a rather limited scale. The grape is mainly employed as a blending partner. Merlot is not very demanding on soil and site. It prefers dry soils and warm, medium-quality sites as well a mild climate,

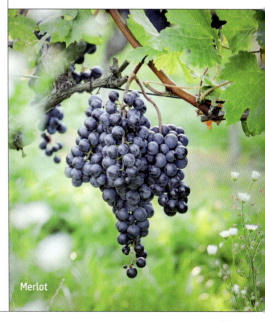
Merlot

AUSTRIA'S GRAPE VARIETIES

Syrah

being sensitive to winter frost. The wine has a ruby-red colour, slightly grassy-spicy aromas and a supple mouthfeel. It is rarely bottled as a single-varietal wine in Austria.

CABERNET FRANC

This grape comes from France, having been documented there for the first time in 1635. It was not permitted in Austria as a quality variety until 1986. Plantings in Austria are limited and very selective. Cabernet Franc is not very demanding on soil, yet it thrives best on fertile loam, while requiring sites with excellent sun exposure. It is highly frost-resistant. The wine has a garnet colour and is very dark. It tastes similar to Cabernet Sauvignon, but has less acidity and less abundant tannins.

SYRAH
Synonym: Shiraz

This top-variety from the Rhône Valley first had to go to Australia to become famous before Austrians began showing some interest in it. Until 2001, wines made from this black grape were marketed without indication of the vintage, because plantings were initially permitted for experimental purposes only. Consequently, resulting products could not be sold as vintage designated "Qualitätswein". In the meantime, Syrah was officially accepted into the catalogue of Burgenland's quality varieties. The origin of Syrah is laden with mystery and hypothesis. It was ascribed to the Persian city of Shiraz and to Egypt, Cyprus, and Greece alike. In 2001, the less prosaic truth was established. After years of DNA research work carried out by Professor Carole Meredith from the University of California at Davis and the leading French ampelographer Jean-Michel Boursiquot from L'École Nationale Supérieure Agronomique in Montpellier, the parents of Syrah could finally be determined. The prominent grape is a spontaneous cross between two lesser known French grapes. One of them is Mondeuse Blanche, which is related to the Savoie-based and better known Mondeuse Noire. The other one is called Dureza and is sporadically encountered in the northern Ardèche region between the upper courses of the Rhône and Loire Rivers.

RED CUVÉE

The category in which different vine varieties are combined in a harmonious blend enjoys great popularity among Austrian red wine vintners. While in previous years blends had the negative connotation of a mixed concoction of leftover wine batches, today's blends frequently represent the high-end wines of a winery. They are often the flagship of their respective producer, who has the chance to express his personal style preference. Like the Super Tuscan models, they often bear symbolic names that have become just as familiar to wine enthusiasts as the names of single vineyards in the case of Austria's white wines. These often-fanciful designations are borrowed from the most diverse worlds of concepts. From dogs to the universe, from mythology to song titles – anything goes; it's actually a matter of taste and marketing savvy. Austrian red-wine blends are usually aged in new French oak barrels. Many of them include a portion of Cabernet Sauvignon, Merlot, or more recently, Syrah, which marries especially well with indigenous grapes such as Blaufränkisch and Zweigelt. As a rule, such wines require sufficient maturation before its components homogenize. The category "Cuvée" to some extent also guards against annual fluctuations, offering more flexibility to the vintner than a single-varietal wine.

© WSNA

AUSTRIAN WINE REGULATIONS

Austrian wine law is incorporated in the hierarchical structure of EU wine legislation. As with the other EU member countries, the national wine laws of Austria form a "bridge" between the general rules of the EU wine market organization and the specific circumstances within the country. Wines are put into two general categories: wines of origin (Landwein, Qualitätswein / land wine, quality wine) and wines without a specific origin (Wein aus Österreich /Wine from Austria).

For Qualitätswein (quality wine), grapes must come from one of the official Austrian wine-growing area. For Landwein (land wine), the origin of the wine is a larger wine-growing region. Wine labels must contain the following information; origin, variety, vintage, quality designation, alcohol content by volume, reference to its residual sugars (i.e. dry, etc), as well as the official state control number and name of the producer or bottler. The Austrian wine law defines a maximum yield of 9,000 kg of grapes or 6,750 litres of wine per hectare for wines of origin (Landwein and Qualitätswein). If the yield is larger, then the total volume must be declassified as a wine without origin and may only be sold if there is no declaration of origin, variety or vintage on the wine label.

LANDWEIN – LAND WINE

In Austrian wine law, the traditional term "Landwein" replaces the EU wine law term "wine with protected geographical indication". Landwein comes from one of the three Austrian wine regions: Weinland (encompassing the federal states Niederösterreich/ Lower Austria, Burgenland, and Wien/Vienna), Bergland (encompassing the federal states Oberösterreich/Upper Austria, Salzburg, Kärnten/Corinthia, Tirol/Tyrol), or Steirerland (encompassing the federal state Steiermark/Styria).

QUALITÄTSWEIN – QUALITY WINE

In Austrian wine law, the traditional term "Qualitätswein" replaces the EU wine law term "wine with protected designation of origin". Quality wine must be produced from any single variety or blend of the 35 permitted grape varieties for Austrian Qualitätswein, and must come from the 25 wine-growing areas. Wine-growing areas include each of the 9 federal states and 16 specific wine-growing areas. Austrian Qualitätswein (quality wine) is given a unique state control number (for each wine submitted). This confirms that the wine submitted has undergone a chemical and sensorial analysis in a federal bureau of oenology. In Austria, bottled Qualitätswein (quality wines) can be easily recognised by the red-white-red (to symbolise the national flag) seal, imprinted with the winery registration number, on either the capsule or screwcap closure.

DAC – QUALITY WINE WITH REGIONAL CHARACTER

DAC wines are Qualitätsweine (quality wines) from demarcated wine-growing areas that display regional typicity and place of origin. The names of the DAC wine-growing areas are defined by EU legislation as Protected Designation of Origin (PDO). Since the year 1999, Austria has been working on specifications for the classification of wine according to demarcated origins with typical corresponding style along the lines of Romanic wine laws (as in France, Italy, Spain). This means that specific wine-growing areas will become better known on the market for a specific style typical for the region. This does not mean that the diversity of varieties and wine styles will be neglected; wines that are produced from other grape varieties and styles will be marketed under the name of the generic area (federal state). Thus, the consumer shall be able to associate a specific wine type/style with the name of a demarcated region. Branding wines with demarcated origins is preferable to branding with grape varieties; grape varieties can be planted anywhere, but specific places of origin are irreplaceable. The development of DAC regulations is the responsibility of Regional Wine Committees made up of representatives from wineries, wine trade, cooperatives and sparkling wine producers according to their significance in the wine-growing area. The coordination and technical control of this wine-growing political development is regulated by the joint composition National Wine Board, in which member experts of the Ministry of Agriculture and the Austrian Wine Marketing Board have an advisory role. Typical wines of demarcated origin proposed by the National Committee are legally established by the Agriculture Minister by regulation. The wine label contains the term "Districtus Austria Controllatus" (abbreviated to DAC), and is placed next to the name of the demarcated origin.

A dual strategy continues to ensure the preservation of diversity: Austria has managed to square the circle by employing the benefits of both the Romanic system of classification according to origin and the Germanic system according to Prädikat (predicate).

PRÄDIKATSWEIN – QUALITY WINES WITH PREDICATE

In Austria, Qualitätsweine of a special ripeness and harvest method can be categorized in predicates. Prädikatsweine (predicated wines) carry their wine-growing area of origin on the label. There are currently no DACs for Prädikatsweine, but it is imaginable that one could be created in the future. The system for Prädikatswein – i.e. to distinguish wines with a higher, natural residual sugar level and different harvest and maturation techniques – is a Germanic wine tradition. The declaration of a Prädikatswein based on the quality of the grapes harvested must be confirmed in the presence of a federal wine inspector. Chaptalization of the grape must is prohibited and the residual sugar may only come from the premature arrest of the fermenting must (but not by the addition of grape must to the wine).

OVERVIEW OF QUALITY LEVELS

Wine without origin: minimum of 10,7° KMW (see conversion table). No specific region of origin is permitted, only the description of "Österreich" or "Österreichischer Wein" or similar.

Landwein (land wine): minimum 14° KMW. A more specific region of origin declaration than the wine-growing region or larger sites is not permitted on the label.

Qualitätswein /quality wine/DAC: minimum 15° KMW. Grapes may only come from the list of classified Austrian varieties and only from one wine-growing area.

Kabinettwein: minimum 17° KMW. Regarded as a Qualitätswein, but must not be chaptalized. Maximum alcohol content total is 13%.

Prädikatswein: Spätlese, Auslese, Beerenauslese, Eiswein, Stohwein/Schilfwein, Ausbruch, Trockenbeerenauslese Must not be chaptalized. A Spätlese cannot be sold before March 1 following the harvest, other Prädikatswein not before May 1.

Spätlese: minimum 19° KMW. Grapes must be fully ripe.

Auslese: minimum 21° KMW. All faulty or unripe grapes must be excluded.

Beerenauslese (BA): minimum 25° KMW. Produced from overripe grapes or grapes with noble rot.

Ausbruch: minimum 27° KMW. Exclusively from overripe grapes, naturally shrivelled and affected by noble rot.

Trockenbeerenauslese (TBA): minimum 30° KMW. Produced from overripe grapes, naturally shrivelled and affected by noble rot.

Eiswein: minimum 25° KMW. Grapes must be frozen when harvested and pressed (contents are concentrated; water remains in the pressed grape skins).

Strohwein /Schilfwein: minimum 25° KMW. Produced from overripe grapes which are stored and airdried on straw or reeds for at least three months (similar to Vin Santo).

THE FALSTAFF WINE GUIDE – ITS PRACTICAL SIDE

WINERY CLASSIFICATIONS AND WINE SCORES

Each wine in this book is scored according to the international 100-point scale. Cask samples are signified by scores in parentheses and are predicted scores based on the assessed potential of the yet unfinished wine. The wines are tasted and assessed with knowledge of their origins and based on knowledge and past experience with the development of each individual winery's terroir and style. This has proved to be particularly valuable when assessing cask samples and very young wines, resulting in more accurate predictions than in blind tastings. A classification of each winery is also included in this guide and is not based solely on the assessment of the current wines. This attempt at winery classifications is quite a subjective undertaking, yet it does follow specified criteria that follow in the next paragraphs.

Since the beginning of the Austrian wine branch's era of tremendous quality improvement, which began at the end of the 1980s, Peter Moser has regularly tasted wines from leading producers, aspiring newcomers, and wineries which would like to be one of the two. Wines from more than 400 producers are tasted each year, which currently mean more than 50,000 individual tasting notes throughout the year. The English guide includes only a fraction of these. Continuous tastings of these wines allow a dependable overview. Apart from personal preferences, it is only natural that through regular contact friendly relationships develop, but despite this there are still objective elements that allow a fair classification. The ability of a producer to optimally express unique terroir is naturally a primary focus. Vineyards, clone selection, and just how consistently outstanding quality, even in difficult vintages, is produced are also considered. To summarize, it is talent, terroir, consistency, and sometimes originality that are desired. These are criteria not just in Austria, but in every wine-producing country. To what extent a producer has been able to achieve these goals over the past 10 years is reflected in a 5-star classification. In the past years this has been a 3-star classification, but the country's constant quality development has proved this to be too imprecise. This classification occurs in steps, or stages, beginning from a producer's acceptance into this guide,

CLASSIFICATIONS

which is simultaneously a recommendation. Five stars are awarded to only an elite few and they are the country's very best producers with wines of best international standards. The five stars now allow the author the possibility to differentiate more precisely.

TASTING NOTES
EXTRA TROCKEN (EXTRA DRY):
Up to 4 g/l residual sugar.

TROCKEN (DRY):
Up to 9 g/l residual sugar, if the total acidity is less than the residual sugar by a maximum of 2 g/l. For example, a wine with 8 g/l residual sugar must have at least 6 g/l acidity in order to be "trocken".

HALBTROCKEN (OFF-DRY):
Up to 12 g/l residual sugar.

LIEBLICH (SEMI-SWEET):
Up to 45 g/l residual sugar.

SÜSS (SWEET):
Over 45 g/l residual sugar.

ORGANIC
 Wines made organically or biodynamically.

CERTIFIED SUSTAINABLE AUSTRIA
 The "Sustainable Austria" certification programme regulates the use of the term "sustainability" in Austrian winemaking.

RATING
The rating of the wines follows the internationally accepted system of 100 points which allows a very differentiated and exactly accentuated rating. In addition to this, the 100-point system provides the possibility of an international comparison, since a large number of publications, especially in English-speaking countries, relies on this system.

Falstaff Rating Scale
100	not to be surpassed
95–99	absolute world class
90–94	excellent wine, among the best of its vintage
85–89	good to very good
(–)	barrel sample rating

PRICE CATEGORIES

€	up to	€ 5,–
€€	up to	€ 10,–
€€€	up to	€ 15,–
€€€€	up to	€ 20,–
€€€€€	up to	€ 40,–
€€€€€€	more than	€ 40,–

THE 5-STAR CLASSIFICATIONS

5 stars: A winery that always produces extraordinary quality which can be sourced only from the country's best terroir. This producer is among the best in the world and enjoys international recognition and demand.

4 stars: A producer of wines with consistent outstanding quality and class. A winery with significant international recognition.

3 stars: A producer of very high qualities that are consistently among the best of their category in Austria.

2 stars: A winery of national recognition that regularly produces wines with typical varietal and regional character of very good quality.

1 star: A winery with more than regional significance that regularly produces wines with typical varietal and regional character of good quality.

Without a star: A recommendable winery of regional significance that produces wines of dependable quality.

ABBREVIATIONS USED
The full page coverage of vintners provides you with a wealth of information. In order to save space, we have used abbreviations that are explained further on. The best-rated wine of every producer was described in addition to those wines that are of interest due to their style. The older ratings were taken from the relevant edition of the German-language Falstaff Wein Guide.

CLASSIFICATIONS

White Wine Varieties
BO Bouvier
CH Chardonnay/Feinburgunder/Morillon
FU Furmint
FV Frühroter Veltliner/Malvasier
GM Gelber Muskateller, Muscat Lunel
GO Goldburger
GS Grüner Sylvaner
GV Grüner Veltliner
MO Muskat-Ottonel
MT Müller-Thurgau/Riesling-Sylvaner now: Rivaner
NB Neuburger
PG Pinot Gris/Grauburgunder/ Ruländer
RG Rotgipfler
RR Riesling/Rheinriesling
RV Roter Veltliner
SÄ Sämling 88/Scheurebe
SB Sauvignon Blanc, Muskat-Sylvaner
SE Semillon
TR Gelber -/ Roter -/Gewürz- Traminer
WB Weissburgunder/Pinot Blanc
WR Welschriesling
ZF Zierfandler

Red Wine Varieties
BB Blauburger
BF Blaufränkisch
BP Blauer Portugieser
BW Blauer Wildbacher/Schilcher
CF Cabernet Franc
CS Cabernet Sauvignon
ME Merlot
PN Pinot Noir/Blauer Burgunder/Spätburgunder
RO Roesler
SG Sangiovese
SL St. Laurent
SY Syrah
TN Tannat
ZW Blauer Zweigelt

Sweet Wine Categories
AB Ausbruch
EW Eiswein
BA Beerenauslese
TBA Trockenbeerenauslese
STW Strohwein/Schilfwein (vin de paille)

SYMBOLS
🅂 Sparkling Wine
🅑 organic
🆅 vegan
🅕 low fructose
🅢 low sulphur
🅗 low histamine
🅘 natural wine
🅞 orange wine
* DAC
** DAC Reserve
*** DAC Rosé

IMPORTERS' COUNTRY CODES

Below you will find the country abbreviations we use in our publications. As the guide is published annually, it is therefore not entirely possible to keep up to date with distribution partners. This is due to the fact that there are too many distributors worldwide who stock Austrian wine. Therefore we only list the respective export countries on the winery pages in this guide. On the websites of the wineries you can usually find all the distribution partners in detail.

AUS	Australia		NZ	New Zealand
BDS	Barbados		NO	Norway
BE	Belgium		PE	Peru
BY	Belarus		RP	Philippines
BER	Bermuda		PL	Poland
BG	Bulgaria		PT	Portugal
BR	Brazil		RO	Romania
CDN	Canada		RUS	Russia
CL	Chile		SRB	Serbia
RC	China		SGP	Singapore
HR	Croatia		SK	Slovakia
CY	Cyprus		SLO	Slovenia
CZ	Czech Republic		ZA	South Africa
DE	Germany		ES	Spain
DK	Denmark		CL	Sri Lanka
EST	Estonia		SE	Sweden
FIN	Finland		CH	Switzerland
FR	France		RC	Taiwan
GB	Great Britain		TH	Thailand
GR	Greece		TR	Turkey
HK	Hongkong		UA	Ukraine
HU	Hungary		UAE	United Arab Emirates
IS	Iceland		USA	United States of America
RI	Indonesia			
IRL	Ireland			
IL	Israel			
IT	Italy			
JP	Japan			
ROK	Korea			
LV	Latvia			
LT	Lithuania			
LU	Luxembourg			
MAL	Malaysia			
MT	Malta			
MV	Maldives			
NL	Netherlands			

ORGANIZATIONS IN AUSTRIA

Bundesministerium für Land- und Forstwirtschaft, Umwelt und Wasserwirtschaft
(Federal Ministry for Agriculture, Forestry, Environment and Water Management)
Stubenring 1, 1010 Wien/Vienna
Tel.: +43/(0)1/711 00
Fax: +43/(0)1/513 16 79-9900
www.lebensministerium.at

ÖWM Österreichische Weinmarketing GmbH
AWMB – Austrian Wine Marketing Board, Ltd.
Prinz-Eugen-Strasse 34, 1040 Wien/Vienna
Tel.: +43/(0)1/503 92 67-0
Fax: +43/(0)1/503 92 67-70
info@austrianwine.com
www.austrianwine.com

Weinakademie Österreich GmbH
(Austrian Wine Academy)
Dr. Josef Schuller, MW
Hauptstrasse 31, 7071 Rust
Tel.: +43/(0)2685/68 53
Fax: +43/(0)2685/64 51
www.weinakademie.at
info@weinakademie.at

Wirtschaftskammer Österreich
(Austrian Economic Chamber)
Wiedner Hauptstrasse 63, 1045 Wien/Vienna
Tel.: +43/(0)5 90 900
Fax: +43/(0)5 90 900-250
www.wko.at

Weinbauverband Niederösterreich
(Lower Austrian Wine Growers' Association)
Managing Director: DI Konrad Hackl
Sigleithenstrasse 50, 3500 Krems
Tel.: +43/(0)5 0259 48200
Fax: +43/(0)5 0259 95 48200
office@wbv.lk-noe.at

Landesweinbauverband Burgenland
(Burgenland Provincial Wine Growers' Association)
Managing Director: Ing. Verena Klöckl
Esterhazystrasse 15, 7001 Eisenstadt
Tel.: +43/(0)2682/702-652
Fax: +43/(0)2682/702-691
wbv-bgld@lk-bgld.at

Weinbauverband Steiermark
(Styrian Provincial Wine Growers' Association)
Managing Director:
Ing. Werner Luttenberger
Hamerlinggasse 3, 8011 Graz
Tel.: +43/(0)3168/0 50-1333
Fax: +43/(0)3168/0 50-1510
wein@lk-stmk.at

Landesweinbauverband Wien
(Vienna Provincial Wine Growers' Association)
President: DI Herbert Schilling
Gumpendorfer Strasse 15,
1060 Wien/Vienna
Tel.: +43/(0)1/587 95 28
Fax: +43/(0)1/587 95 28-21
office@lk-wien.at

Österreichischer Weinbauverband
(Federal Wine Growers' Association)
Schauflergasse 6, 1014 Wien/Vienna
Tel.: +43/(0)1/534 41-8553
Fax: +43/(0)1/534 41-8549
President: NR Johannes Schmuckenschlager
www.lk-oe.at

THE PREMIUM PLATFORM FOR WINE, FOOD & TRAVEL

FINE WINE, GOOD FOOD, MEMORABLE JOURNEYS:

These are the themes that Falstaff covers at the highest level – with stunning visuals and dynamic content, optimised for desktop & smartphone, written from international perspectives by passionate writers with an exceptional nose for the best things in life.

For the best things in life:
falstaff.com

Subscribe to our weekly newsletter
falstaff.com/newsletter

WIEN/VIENNA

WIENER GEMISCHTER SATZ

DAC

View from the Bisamberg over Vienna

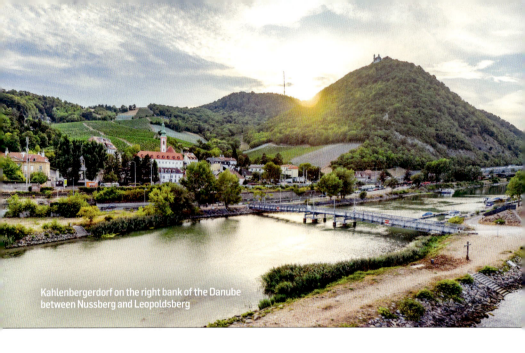

Kahlenbergerdorf on the right bank of the Danube between Nussberg and Leopoldsberg

A NEW WINE CULTURE – A LONG HEURIGER TRADITION

Winegrowing in the city? That usually means an exhibition vineyard as a tourist attraction. That's not the case in Vienna. The 575 vineyard hectares are the source of high quality wines and make a significant economic contribution while preserving the city's green belt. The wines range from the traditional field blend (Gemischter Satz), elegant Rieslings and powerful Weissburgunders to outstanding reds.

Up to the Late Middle Ages, vines were grown within the ramparts of Vienna, right up to the city centre. Today's vineyards are situated mainly on the outskirts of Vienna. Vintners from Strebersdorf, Stammersdorf and Jedlersdorf cultivate Burgundian varieties and red wines on Bisamberg north of the Danube River. In Heiligenstadt, Nussdorf, Grinzing, Sievering and Neustift am Walde, all districts of northwest Vienna, the varieties Riesling, Chardonnay and Weissburgunder (Pinot Blanc) prevail due to limestone-rich soils. In the southern parts of Vienna, namely Mauer, Rodaun and Oberlaa, cambisol soils favour powerful white wines and opulent red wine blends. A new discovery is the prime vineyard Nussberg, which seems to magically attract ambitious new vintners crossing over from other professions. The leading producers of the capital city have united their marketing efforts in the vintner association "WienWein". There is hardly a vintner that does not produce the traditional Gemischter Satz (field blend) that is sourced from a vineyard planted with diverse grape varieties that are harvested and fermented together. What was once an insurance policy for irregular harvest conditions is now a highly sought-after Viennese specialty. The Slow Food Foundation recognized the Wiener Gemischter Satz as a "Presidia" product in 2008, making it the first Austrian product

WIEN/VIENNA — WIENER GEMISCHTER SATZ DAC

that was awarded this seal of approval. Wiener Gemischter Satz became a DAC protected designation of origin in 2013. For this wine, all grapes must stem from a vineyard in Vienna that is planted with at least three different quality grape varieties that are harvested and vinified together. The predominant variety may not exceed 50 % and the third largest share must make up at least 10 %. Vienna's Heurigens (wine taverns) are, without a doubt, legendary. Regardless of whether they offer their generous warm and cold buffets all year round, or are one of the small, seasonal Heurigens hidden in the cellar alleys, they are popular with people from all walks of life, locals and tourists. Another pleasant aspect of Viennese viticulture is the fact that modern cellars and technological equipment are seamlessly integrated into the traditions of old, established family wine estates.

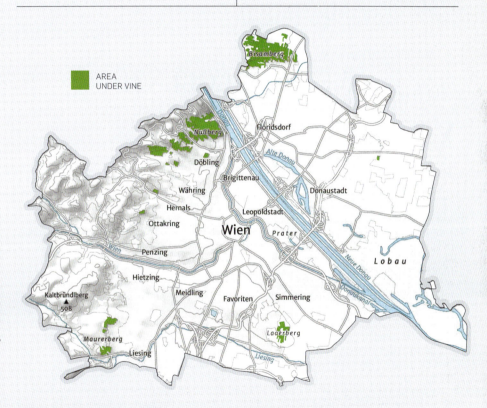

WINE-GROWING AREA VIENNA

Austria total:	44.728 ha		Wine-growing area Vienna:	575 ha	(1 %)
White wine total:	460 ha	(80 %)	**Red wine total:**	115 ha	(20 %)
Gemischter Satz:	224 ha	(40 %)	Zweigelt:	33 ha	(5,7 %)
Grüner Veltliner:	135 ha	(23,4 %)	Pinot Noir:	19 ha	(3,3 %)
Riesling:	65 ha	(11,3 %)	Cabernet Sauvignon:	7 ha	(1,2 %)
Chardonnay:	40 ha	(7 %)	Blauburger:	6 ha	(1 %)
Weißburgunder:	37 ha	(6,4 %)	Sankt Laurent:	5 ha	(0,9 %)

SELECTED WINERIES

★★★★★
Weingut Wieninger, Wien

★★★★
Weingut Mayer am Pfarrplatz, Wien
Weingut Rotes Haus, Wien

★★★
Weingut Cobenzl, Wien
Weingut Hajszan Neumann, Wien
Schlumberger Wein- und Sektkellerei, Wien

★
Landhaus Mayer, Wien

★★★

WEINGUT COBENZL

Vienna is unique: the city is home to the only wine-growing region in the world that lies entirely within the boundaries of a major city and, thanks to its unique wine and Heurigen tradition, helps to shape the particular atmosphere of the city.

The Vienna Cobenzl Winery is one of Vienna's most important wineries and has been owned by the City of Vienna for over 110 years. Here, under the management of Thomas Podsednik, outstanding quality wines are produced from around 60 hectares of vineyards in Grinzing, on the Nussberg and on the Bisamberg. The unique microclimate with Pannonian influence and the proximity to the Danube are the ideal conditions for fine-fruited, mineral wines. The vineyards with resounding names such as Ried Pfeffer, Ried Seidenhaus and Ried Bellevue ("Beautiful View") have always been among the best in the city.

In accordance with the size and the variety of sites and grape varieties, a wide range of quality wines is offered: The "Classic" wines are, deliberately, somewhat lighter, with pronounced fruit and designed to be uncomplicated food wines. The single vineyard wines and the "ÖTW Erste Lage" wines fascinate with their complexity, finesse and the character achieved by the terroir typical of their provenance.

The Vienna City Winery was one of the first domestic wineries to achieve the prestigious "Sustainable Austria" award. The particular sustainability measures here range from grape production and work in the vineyard to environmentally-friendly electricity generated from solar power.

Since August 2020, the winery Wien Cobenzl is in the process of organic conversion. Thus, wines that will be vinified from 2023 onwards will be certified organic. The holistic nature of the winery is also evident in the fine details: such as owning their own bee colonies, which diligently create honey for the delicious "Wiener Bio-Honig vom Cobenzl".

92 ☉ **Gemischter Satz Sekt Austria Reserve Wien g.U. Brut 2018**
CH/TR/GV/GM/MO/RR/WB
13 Vol.-%, cork, bottle fermentation, €€€€€

92 ☉ **Gemischter Satz Sekt Austria Reserve Wien g.U Brut 2017**
CH/TR/GV/MO/GM/WB/RR

90 ☉ **Sekt Austria Rosé Brut Wien g.U. 2021**
12,5 Vol.-%, cork, bottle fermentation, €€€

93 * **Ried Steinberg 1ÖTW 2021**
13,5 Vol.-%, cork, steel tank/bottle maturation,
€€€€€ V

93 * **Ried Steinberg 1ÖTW 2020**
Light greenish yellow, silver reflections. Fine nuances of yellow tropical fruit, hints of apple and mango, delicate blossom honey, fresh orange zest, mineral in the background. Full-bodied, balanced, white fruit, fresh acidity, salty finish, lime on the back palate. It has good development potential.

93 * **Ried Steinberg 1ÖTW Grinzing 2019**

WIENER GEMISCHTER SATZ DAC

WEINGUT COBENZL
1190 Wien
Am Cobenzl 96
T: +43 (1) 3205805
office@weingutcobenzl.at
www.weingutcobenzl.at

Winemaker: Ing. Georg Königsbauer
Contact: Ing. Thomas Podsednik, Akad. Dipl.-Önol.
Production: 400,000 bottles
1 % sparkling, 80 % white, 4 % rosé, 15 % red, 60 hectares
Certified: Sustainable Austria
Fairs: Foodex Japan, ProWein Düsseldorf, VieVinum, DAC-Presentations
Distribution partners: JP

Team Weingut Cobenzl in the vineyard Ried Reisenberg

92 * Ried Reisenberg 2022
13,5 Vol.-%, screwcap, amphore, €€€ V
92 * Ried Reisenberg 2021
91 * Ried Reisenberg Grinzing 2020

(92) * Nussberg 2022
13,5 Vol.-%, screwcap, steel tank, €€€
92 * Nussberg 2021

89 Wiener Gemischter Satz DAC 2022
12,5 Vol.-%, screwcap, steel tank, €€
90 Wiener Gemischter Satz DAC 2021
88 Wiener Gemischter Satz DAC 2019

93 Riesling Ried Preussen-Nussberg 1ÖTW 2021
13,5 Vol.-%, DIAM, large wooden barrel/bottle maturation, €€€€€ V
93 Riesling Ried Preussen-Nussberg 1ÖTW 2020
93 Riesling Ried Preussen-Nussberg 1ÖTW 2019

90 Riesling Nussberg 2021
13 Vol.-%, screwcap, steel tank, €€€
92 Riesling Nussberg 2020
91 Riesling Nussberg 2018

93 Weißburgunder Ried Seidenhaus 1ÖTW 2021
13,5 Vol.-%, DIAM, barrique/bottle maturation, €€€€€ V
94 Weißburgunder Ried Seidenhaus 1ÖTW Grinzing 2020
Light golden yellow, silver reflections. Pear fruit underpinned with fine savouriness and a hint of caramel, candied orange, some blossom honey. Juicy, silky texture, elegant, fine nuances of white stone fruit, delicate acidity, lemony mineral, good length, a grown-up food wine with sure ageing potential.

93 Weißburgunder Ried Seidenhaus 1ÖTW Grinzing 2019
91 Weißburgunder Ried Reisenberg Grinzing 2020
90 Weißburgunder Ried Reisenberg Grinzing 2018
89 Weißburgunder Ried Reisenberg Grinzing 2017

90 Weißburgunder Grinzing 2021
13,5 Vol.-%, screwcap, steel tank, €€
89 Weißburgunder Grinzing 2020
88 Weißburgunder Grinzing 2017

91 Grüner Veltliner Ried Pfeffer 2021
92 Grüner Veltliner Ried Pfeffer 2020
90 Grüner Veltliner Ried Pfeffer 2019

(89) Grüner Veltliner Grinzing 2022
13,5 Vol.-%, screwcap, steel tank, €€ V
90 Grüner Veltliner Grinzing 2021
89 Grüner Veltliner Grinzing 2020

88 Grüner Veltliner Bisamberg 2020
89 Grüner Veltliner Bisamberg 2019
89 Grüner Veltliner Bisamberg 2017

* Wiener Gemischter Satz DAC

WIEN/VIENNA

92	Atrium 2018 ZW/CS/ME/PN
92	Bisamberg-Wien Ried Jungenberg 2018 ZW/ME/CS
92	Ried Jungenberg Bisamberg Wien 2016 ME/ZW/CS
91	Ried Jungenberg Bisamberg-Wien Cuvée 2015 CS/ME/ZW

| 92 | Pinot Noir Ried Bellevue Sievering 2018 |
13,5 Vol.-%, cork, barrique, €€€€
91	Pinot Noir Ried Bellevue-Sievering Reserve 2017
90	Zweigelt Ried Hofbreiten-Bisamberg 2017
91	Zweigelt Ried Hofbreiten Bisamberg 2016

WEINGUT HAJSZAN NEUMANN
ORGANIC

The Hajszan Neumann winery is located in Grinzing at the foothill of Nussberg, probably the most traditional wine region in Vienna. With a lot of passion, prestigious wines are produced here according to biodynamic principles. Fritz Wieninger, the pioneer of the highest quality wines in Vienna, took over the winery in 2014 and focuses on Wiener Gemischter Satz as well as Riesling and Grüner Veltliner. The vineyards, the majority of which belong to star architect Heinz Neumann, are located in the best Viennese sites, with the Nussberg site playing a central role. The mineral shell limestone and limestone weathered soils give the wine a lot of depth and expression. The secret behind the wine quality is biodynamic viticulture: the winery has been working according to these principles since 2006. The focus is on the vineyard ecosystem with all its facets, and the vines enjoy a lot of manual work. In the wine cellar, too, work is done gently and in a reduced manner. You can taste all of this in Hajszan Neumann's lively wines: each has a characteristic soul that develops from the natural aroma of the grape and the terroir. Fritz Wieninger goes one step further with his "Natural" line. These wines fermented on the skins are characterized by complete restraint in the cellar and are vinified without any intervention and bottled unfiltered. Since March 2016, the German top chef Juan Amador has

Gelber Muskateller

WEINGUT HAJSZAN NEUMANN
1190 Wien
Grinzinger Straße 86
T: +43 (1) 2901012
weingut@hajszanneumann.com
www.hajszanneumann.com

Winemaker: Luis Teixeira
Contact: Fritz Wieninger
Production: 66,667 bottles
80 % white, 20 % red, 20 hectares
Fairs: ProWein Düsseldorf, VieVinum
Distribution partners: BE, DK, DE, JP, RUK, LT, NO, PL, SE, CH, ES, USA

WIENER GEMISCHTER SATZ DAC

been running the "Amador Restaurant" on the wine estate, which has three Michelin stars!

93 Pet Nat 2022 NB/MT/RR
11,5 Vol.-%, crown cap, bottle fermentation, €€€€ Ⓑ

92 Pet Nat 2021

(94) * Ried Weisleiten 2022
13 Vol.-%, screwcap, steel tank, €€€€ Ⓑ

93 * Ried Weisleiten 2021

93 * Ried Weisleiten 2020

(92) * Nussberg 2022
13 Vol.-%, screwcap, steel tank, €€€ Ⓑ

92 * Nussberg 2021

92 * Nussberg 2020

(93) Gemischter Satz Natural Wine 2022
13 Vol.-%, DIAM, amphore, €€€€ Ⓑ Ⓞ

92 Gemischter Satz Natural Wine 2021

92 Gemischter Satz Natural Wine 2020

94 Riesling Ried Steinberg 1ÖTW 2021
12,5 Vol.-%, DIAM, steel tank, €€€€ Ⓑ

93 Riesling Ried Steinberg 1ÖTW 2020

94 Riesling Ried Steinberg 1ÖTW 2019

93 Riesling Nussberg 2022
13,5 Vol.-%, screwcap, steel tank, €€€€ Ⓑ

92 Riesling Nussberg 2021

92 Riesling Nussberg 2020

93 Grüner Veltliner Ried Steinberg 1ÖTW 2021
14 Vol.-%, DIAM, steel tank, €€€ Ⓑ

93 Grüner Veltliner Ried Steinberg 1ÖTW 2020

93 Grüner Veltliner Ried Haarlocke 2019

93 Grüner Veltliner Ried Haarlocke 2018

93 Grüner Veltliner Ried Haarlocke 2017

92 Grüner Veltliner Nussberg 2022
12,5 Vol.-%, screwcap, steel tank, €€€ Ⓑ

91 Grüner Veltliner Nussberg 2021

92 Grüner Veltliner Nussberg 2020

92 Grüner Veltliner Natural Wine 2022
12 Vol.-%, DIAM, amphore, €€€€ Ⓑ Ⓞ

91 Grüner Veltliner Natural Wine 2021

91 Grüner Veltliner Natural Wine 2020

(94) Traminer Natural Wine 2022
13 Vol.-%, DIAM, amphore, €€€€ Ⓑ Ⓞ

Bellevuehöhe, Sievering

93 Traminer Natural Wine 2021
Pale golden yellow, silver reflections. Fine nuances of marshmallow paste, a touch of rose oil, spicy nuances, attractive bouquet. Taut, tightly meshed, fine white tropical fruit, fresh and clinging, some marshmallow on the finish, salty aftertaste, very good varietal typicity.

93 Traminer Natural Wine 2020

95 Weißburgunder Ried Gollin 1ÖTW 2021
13,5 Vol.-%, screwcap, large wooden barrel, €€€€€ Ⓑ

94 Weißburgunder Ried Gollin Nussberg 1ÖTW 2020
Light greenish yellow, silver reflections. Delicate blossom honey, a touch of caramel, nuances of yellow tropical fruit, inviting bouquet. Juicy, round and elegant, well-integrated acid structure, fine fruit, well-balanced and already drinking well, it has sure ageing potential.

93 Weißburgunder Ried Gollin 1ÖTW 2020

93 Muskateller Natural Wine 2022
12,5 Vol.-%, DIAM, amphore, €€€€ Ⓑ Ⓞ

92 Muskateller Natural Wine 2021

91 Muskateller Natural Wine 2020

93 Zweigelt Natural Wine 2021
13 Vol.-%, DIAM, cement, €€€€ Ⓑ Ⓞ

92 Zweigelt Natural Wine 2020

92 Zweigelt Natural Wine 2019

WIEN/VIENNA

Nussberg and Leopoldsberg

LANDHAUS MAYER
1190 Wien
Eroicagasse 4
T: +43 (1) 3360197
office@landhausmayer.at
www.landhausmayer.at

Winemaker: Gerhard J. Lobner and Dr. Dragos Pavelescu
Contact: Gerhard J. Lobner
Production: 90 % white, 10 % red
Fairs: ProWein Düsseldorf, VieVinum, Vinexpo Bordeaux
Distribution partners: BE, DE, FIN, UK, JP, HR, NL, PL, CH, ES, CZ, USA

LANDHAUS MAYER

Landhaus Mayer has entered into a special cooperation with Niederösterreich winegrowers who have been passionately cultivating top sites for generations. Together with the vine growers, production manager Gerhard J. Lobner decides which steps to take in the vineyards. From pruning to foliage work to the optimal harvest time, the vines are followed. "It is indescribable what certain ageing potential you can draw on in these areas," Lobner is enthusiastic. Many of these top vineyards are in extreme danger of being abandoned due to structural change. Landhaus Mayer wants to counteract this development by working out promising perspectives together with local vintners.

90 Riesling 2022
12,5 Vol.-%, screwcap, steel tank, €€
90 Riesling 2021
Light yellow-green with silver reflections. Fine herbal notes, white stone fruit, and a touch of lime underlaid with blossom honey. Juicy, fresh and lively, with citrus touches on the finish and a salty aftertaste, the wine lingers and makes for uncomplicated drinking pleasure.
90 Riesling 2020

89 Sauvignon Blanc 2021
89 Sauvignon Blanc 2018

89 Gelber Muskateller 2022
12,5 Vol.-%, screwcap, steel tank, €€
90 Gelber Muskateller 2021
90 Gelber Muskateller 2020

89 Grüner Veltliner 2022
12,5 Vol.-%, screwcap, steel tank, €€
89 Grüner Veltliner 2021
90 Grüner Veltliner 2020

89 Rosé 2022
12 Vol.-%, screwcap, steel tank, €€
88 Rosé 2021
88 Rosé 2020

91 Zweigelt 2020

WIENER GEMISCHTER SATZ DAC

WEINGUT MAYER AM PFARRPLATZ

This traditional winery has been creating Vienna's finest wines in Döbling and Grinzing since 1683. The charming villa on Pfarrplatz is synonymous with wine quality and Viennese Heurigen culture. Ludwig van Beethoven stayed here in 1817. During his time in Heiligenstadt, he worked on his greatest composition, the 9th Symphony. The estate's wines come from the best vineyards in Vienna: Nussberg and Alsegger sites. Their elegant fruit aromas, balance and minerality are characteristic of Vienna's best vineyard sites. The traditional Viennese Gemischter Satz is the classic of the diverse range: it is made from Grüner Veltliner, Riesling, Rotgipfler and Zierfandler, which are harvested and vinified together. The Riesling brings out the fine nuances of the Nussberg and Alsegger sites. Grüner Veltliner, Sauvignon Blanc and Gelber Muskateller round off the white wine range. Weingut Mayer am Pfarrplatz also offers an elegant Blauer Burgunder red wine.

92 ✪ Riesling Sekt Brut Wien g.U. Grosse Reserve 2017
12 Vol.-%, cork, bottle fermentation, €€€€
93 ✪ Riesling Sekt Brut Wien g.U. Grosse Reserve 2016

94 * Ried Langteufel-Nussberg 1ÖTW 2021
14 Vol.-%, screwcap, steel tank, €€€€€
95 * Ried Langteufel Nussberg 1ÖTW 2020
Light greenish yellow, silver reflections. White pome fruit underlaid with subtle spice aromas, delicate chamomile, somewhat restrained scent of peach. Good complexity, taut, lively acidity, delicately spicy, pear, nutty finish, multi-faceted food wine, good ageing potential.
95 * Ried Langteufel Nussberg 1ÖTW 2019

93 * Ried Preussen-Nussberg 1ÖTW 2021
14 Vol.-%, screwcap, steel tank, €€€€€
94 * Ried Preussen-Nussberg 1ÖTW 2020
93 * Ried Preussen Nussberg 1ÖTW 2019

93 * Nussberg 2022
13 Vol.-%, screwcap, steel tank, €€€€
93 * Nussberg 2021
92 * Nussberg 2020

91 Wiener Gemischter Satz DAC 2022
12,5 Vol.-%, screwcap, steel tank, €€€
91 Wiener Gemischter Satz DAC 2021
90 Wiener Gemischter Satz DAC 2020

(95) Riesling Nussberg Weißer Marmor 2022
13 Vol.-%, cork, steel tank, €€€€€€
96 Riesling Nussberg Weißer Marmor 2021
Pale greenish yellow, silver glints. Gentle blossom honey notes, a touch of yellow stone fruit, a hint of passion fruit and papaya, underlaid with kumquats. Juicy, taut, sweet extract redolent of vineyard peach, dark minerality, tightly woven acidity structure, remains persistent. A complex food companion with potential.
95 Riesling Nussberg Weißer Marmor 2020

94 Riesling Ried Preussen-Nussberg 1ÖTW 2021
13,5 Vol.-%, screwcap, steel tank, €€€€€
94 Riesling Ried Preussen-Nussberg 1ÖTW 2020
94 Riesling Ried Preussen-Nussberg 1ÖTW 2019

93 Riesling Nussberg 2022
13,5 Vol.-%, screwcap, steel tank, €€€€
93 Riesling Nussberg 2021
93 Riesling Nussberg 2020

WEINGUT MAYER AM PFARRPLATZ
1190 Wien
Pfarrplatz 2
T: +43 (1) 3360197
weingut@pfarrplatz.at
www.pfarrplatz.at

Winemaker: Dr. Dragos Pavelescu
Contact: Gerhard J. Lobner and Paul Kiefer
Production: 90 % white, 8 % red, 2 % sweet, 61 hectares
Certified: Sustainable Austria
Fairs: Austrian Tasting London, VieVinum, DAC-Presentations
Distribution partners: BE, DE, FIN, UK, JP, HR, NL, PL, RUS, CH, SK, SLO, CZ, USA

*Wiener Gemischter Satz DAC

WIEN/VIENNA

93 Riesling Hernals Ried Alsegg 2022
13,5 Vol.-%, screwcap, steel tank, €€€
92 Riesling Ried Alsegg Hernals 2021
91 Riesling Ried Alsegg Hernals 2020

91 Sauvignon Blanc 2022
13,5 Vol.-%, screwcap, steel tank, €€€
91 Sauvignon Blanc 2021
92 Sauvignon Blanc 2020

92 Sauvignon Blanc Hernals 2022
13,5 Vol.-%, screwcap, steel tank, €€€€
92 Sauvignon Blanc Hernals 2021
92 Sauvignon Blanc Hernals 2020

92 Gelber Muskateller 2022
12,5 Vol.-%, screwcap, steel tank, €€€
91 Gelber Muskateller 2020
91 Gelber Muskateller 2019

93 Grüner Veltliner Grinzing Ried Schenkenberg 1ÖTW 2021
14 Vol.-%, screwcap, steel tank, €€€€

92 Grüner Veltliner Ried Schenkenberg Grinzing 2017
91 Grüner Veltliner Schenkenberg 2015

92 Grüner Veltliner Grinzing 2022
14 Vol.-%, screwcap, steel tank, €€€
90 Grüner Veltliner Grinzing 2020
91 Grüner Veltliner Grinzing 2019

90 Grüner Veltliner 2022
13 Vol.-%, screwcap, steel tank, €€
90 Grüner Veltliner 2021
88 Grüner Veltliner 2019

(93) Pinot Noir Nussberg 2020
13,5 Vol.-%, cork, large wooden barrel, €€€€
91 Pinot Noir Nussberg 2019
90 Pinot Noir Nussberg 2018

94 Sauvignon Blanc Nussberg TBA 2018

WEINGUT ROTES HAUS

Since 2001, Weingut Rotes Haus has been cultivating around nine hectares of vineyards in Vienna's most famous vineyard location, the Nussberg. In the heart of this unique vineyard lies the picturesque Rotes Haus am Nussberg. Under the motto "quality instead of quantity", Nussberg wines represent the exceptional character of this prestigious Viennese vineyard. The unique terroir and microclimate are the basis for the elegance and Burgundian style of the wines.

White grape varieties dominate the vineyards of the Rotes Haus. Chardonnay, Pinot Gris, Pinot Blanc, Neuburger and Traminer grow in harmony in one vineyard and form the basis of the Wiener Gemischter Satz DAC. Chardonnay and Grüner Veltliner varietals complete the range.

95 * Ried Langteufel-Nussberg 1ÖTW 2021
13,5 Vol.-%, cork, large wooden barrel, €€€€€
95 * Ried Langteufel-Nussberg 1ÖTW 2020
Medium golden yellow, green reflections. Ripe tropical fruit underlaid with fine wood spice, soft notes of pineapple, some candied orange zest, a hint of pear, some papaya.

Juicy, complex, light on its feet, lemony touch, salty finish, white stone fruit on the aftertaste, long lasting, multi-faceted acidity, definite ageing potential.
95 * Ried Langteufel Nussberg 1ÖTW 2019

94 * Ried Preussen-Nussberg 1ÖTW 2021
13,5 Vol.-%, cork, large wooden barrel, €€€€€
95 * Ried Preussen-Nussberg 1ÖTW 2020
Medium greenish yellow, silver reflections. Inviting scent of pineapple and pear, blossom honey underlaid with a hint of lime, multi-faceted bouquet. Complex, rich, balanced acidity, delicately nutty, ripe apple fruit on the finish, long-lasting echo, spicy aftertaste, good food wine with ageing potential.
94 * Ried Preussen Nussberg 1ÖTW 2019

93 * Nussberg 2022
13 Vol.-%, screwcap, steel tank, €€€€
93 * Nussberg 2021
92 * Nussberg 2020

90 Wiener Gemischter Satz DAC 2022
12,5 Vol.-%, screwcap, steel tank, €€€
92 Wiener Gemischter Satz DAC 2021
91 Wiener Gemischter Satz DAC 2020

WIENER GEMISCHTER SATZ DAC

WEINGUT ROTES HAUS
1190 Wien
Pfarrplatz 2
T: +43 (1) 3360197
office@ptarrplatz.at
www.rotes-haus.at

Winemaker: Dr. Dragos Pavelescu
Contact: Gerhard J. Lobner and Paul Kiefer
Production: 95 % white, 5 % red, 9 hectares
Certified: Sustainable Austria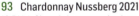
Fairs: Austrian Tasting London, ProWein Düsseldorf, VieVinum, Vinexpo Bordeaux, DAC-Presentations
Distribution partners: BE, DE, EST, FIN, UK, JP, HR, LV, LT, NL, PL, CH, SLO, ES, CZ, HU, USA

Nussberg

93	Chardonnay Nussberg 2021	
13,5 Vol.-%, cork, large wooden barrel, €€€€€		
93	Chardonnay Nussberg 2020	
93	Chardonnay Nussberg 2019	

92	Grüner Veltliner Nussberg 2022	
14,5 Vol.-%, screwcap, steel tank, €€€		
92	Grüner Veltliner Nussberg 2021	
92	Grüner Veltliner Nussberg 2020	

★★★

SCHLUMBERGER WEIN- UND SEKTKELLEREI

ORGANIC

For over 180 years, the Schlumberger brand has been synonymous with qualitative excellence within Austria. Founded in 1842 by Robert Alwin Schlumberger, the company boasts an exciting and eventful history - from its beginnings as a small family business to its rise as the largest domestic sparkling wine producer.

In the production of sparkling wine, according to the Méthode Traditionelle, great importance is attached to the processing of exclusively Austrian grapes and the maximum usage of the domestic supply chain. The Austrian three-tier quality pyramid for Sekt Austria was developed to raise consumer awareness of the diversity of the products, regional production, and the high-quality standards of Austrian sparkling wine. The quality level of sparkling wine can be recognized at first glance by the label on the bottle and the red-white-red banderole. The quality pyramid serves primarily as an orientation aid when buying and distinguishes Austrian sparkling wines in three different quality levels: Sekt Austria, Sekt Austria Reserve, and Sekt Austria Grosse Reserve.

93 Schlumberger Chardonnay Brut Sekt Austria Reserve 2017
12 Vol.-%, cork, bottle fermentation, €€€€€

WIEN/VIENNA

Schlumberger Sparkling Wine Cellar

SCHLUMBERGER WEIN- UND SEKTKELLEREI
1190 Wien
Heiligenstädter Straße 41-43
T: +43 (1) 3682258
services@schlumberger.at
www.schlumberger.at

Winemaker/Contact:
Aurore Jeudy
Production: 10+250 hectares
Fairs: ProWein Düsseldorf, VieVinum
Distribution partners: AUS, BY, BE, BR, RC, DK, DE, EST, FIN, FR, GR, UK, HK, IRL, IS, IL, JP, ROK, MT, NL, NO, PL, PT, RO, SE, CH, SRB, SGP, SK, SLO, ES, TH, TR, UA, USA, PT

---

93 ● Schlumberger Chardonnay Brut Österreichischer Sekt g. U. Niederösterreich Reserve 2016

93 ● Schlumberger Chardonnay Sekt g. U. Brut Reserve 2015

94 ● Schlumberger Chardonnay Sekt Austria Große Reserve brut Niederösterreich g.U. Poysdorf 2015
Medium golden yellow, silver reflections, fine mousse. Yellow tropical fruit underlay with a touch of caramel, delicate mango, peach and candied orange zest, some biscuit. Complex, substantial, fine nuances of pastry, a touch of nougat, mineral and persistent, lemony finish, a juicy food wine with definite further ageing potential.

94 ● Schlumberger Große Reserve 2015 CH

93 ● Schlumberger Prestige Cuvée Sekt g.U. Reserve Wien brut 2015

92 ● Schlumberger Prestige Cuvée Brut Reserve Sekt g.U. 2012

93 ● Schlumberger Cuvee 1842 Brut Sekt Austria Reserve 2015 CH/PN
12 Vol.-%, cork, bottle fermentation, €€€€€

92 ● Schlumberger Cuvée 1842 Sekt Austria Reserve brut Niederösterreich g.U. 2015
Medium golden yellow, silver reflections, fine, persistent mousse. Ripe fruit notes of quince underlaid with blossom honey, a hint of tangerine, subtle hints of cherries, attractive bouquet. Taut, fine pear fruit, a touch of caramel, some nougat on the finish, a reliable food wine.

92 ● Schlumberger Blanc de Noirs Brut Reserve Sekt g.U. 2012

92 ● Schlumberger Grüner Veltliner Sekt g.U. brut Klassik 2017 GV

92 ● Schlumberger Grüner Veltliner Sekt g.U. Klassik brut 2016

93 ● Schlumberger Grüner Veltliner brut 2015

92 ● Schlumberger Grüner Veltliner Brut Bio Sekt Austria 2021
12 Vol.-%, cork, bottle fermentation, €€€ Ⓑ

92 ● Schlumberger Grüner Veltliner Bio Sekt Austria Brut 2020

92 ● Schlumberger Grüner Veltliner BIO Brut Niederösterreich g.U. Klassik 2019

92 ● Schlumberger Sparkling Brut Sekt Austria 2019 WR/WB/CH

92 ● Schlumberger Sparkling Brut Sekt Austria 2019 WR/WB/CH
12 Vol.-%, cork, bottle fermentation, €€€ Ⓕ

93 ● Schlumberger Sparkling Brut Sekt Austria 2018 WR/WB/CH

92 ● Schlumberger Sparkling Brut Österreichischer Sekt g. U. Niederösterreich Klassik 2017 WR/WB/CH

92 ● Schlumberger Pinot Blanc Brut Nature Reserve Sekt g.U. 2015

93 ● Schlumberger Pinot Noir Brut Sekt Austria Reserve 2017
12 Vol.-%, cork, bottle fermentation, €€€€€

© Philipp Lipiarski

| 91 | ❂ Schlumberger Rosé Brut Sekt Austria 2021 ZW/PN/SL | 91 | ❂ Schlumberger Rosé Brut Klassik 2019 ZW/PN/SL |

12 Vol.-%, cork, bottle fermentation, €€€

| 91 | ❂ Schlumberger Sekt Austria Rosé brut Burgenland g.U. 2020 ZW/PN/SL |

WEINGUT WIENINGER

ORGANIC

The Wieninger name is synonymous with a commitment to excellence. And Fritz Wieninger has been doing just that for many years. Here, a traditional wine tavern has developed into a top-quality winery. For some years now, Wieninger has been processing grapes from both sides of the Danube. With the famous and best sites on Vienna's Nussberg, the dynamic winemaker has excellent grape material at his disposal, and he knows how to turn this into an extensive range of top wines.

Wieninger is famous in Austria for his barrique-aged Grand Select Chardonnays and Pinot Noirs, and his cassis-savoury Bordeaux blend (Cabernet/Merlot), Danubis Grand Select, is also worthy of note. A particular speciality is the traditional "Wiener Gemischter Satz". For this authentic terroir wine, the vines of different varieties are mixed in the vineyard and contribute their respective characteristics. Since the 2013 vintage, it has also been awarded DAC status.

This export-oriented winery is the only Viennese winery to have found recognition in Austria's top gastronomic scene. Wieninger has long been the undisputed number one in quality wine in the metropolis, exporting 40 per cent of its production to 31 countries on three continents. Its share of the Viennese gastronomy scene has also risen sharply in recent years. To make Vienna's top wine even more popular, the winemaker has joined forces with the Christ, Edlmoser, Cobenzl, Mayer am Pfarrplatz and Fuhrgassl-Huber wineries to form the "WienWein" group. With the 2017

WEINGUT WIENINGER
1210 Wien
Stammersdorfer Straße 31
T: +43 (I) 2901012
weingut@wieninger.at
www.wieninger.at

Winemaker: Luis Teixeira
Contact: Fritz Wieninger
Production: 300,000 bottles
67 % white, 2 % rosé, 30 % red, 1 % sweet, 55 hectares
Fairs: ProWein Düsseldorf, VieVinum, Summa Margreid
Distribution partners: BE, RC, DE, FIN, UK, JP, CDN, ROK, LU, NZ, NL, NO, PL, RUS, SE, CH, SGP, SK, ES, TH, CZ, UA, USA

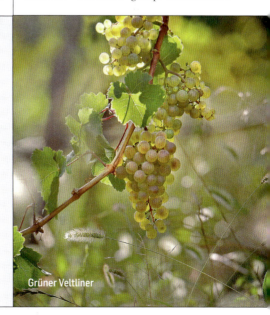

Grüner Veltliner

* Wiener Gemischter Satz DAC

WIEN/VIENNA

In den Falkenbergen, Stammersdorf

vintage, twelve Viennese vineyards were classified as "Erste Lagen" for the first time by the association "Traditionsweingüter Österreich", four of which are cultivated by the Wieninger winery.

94 ❂ **Blanc de Noirs Brut Nature Große Reserve 2017**
11,5 Vol.-%, cork, bottle fermentation, €€€€€ ⓑ

93 ❂ **Cuvée Katharina Rosé Brut nature NV Wien Reserve PN/ZW**
Deg. 05/2022, 12 Vol.-%, cork, bottle fermentation, €€€€ ⓑ
91 ❂ **Cuvée Katharina Rosé Sekt g.U. PN/ZW**
92 ❂ **Cuvée Katharina Rosé Zero Dosage Österreichischer Sekt g.U. Wien Klassik NV PN/ZW**

(95) * **Ried Rosengartel 1ÖTW 2021**
14 Vol.-%, glass, large wooden barrel, €€€€ ⓑ
94 * **Ried Rosengartel 1ÖTW 2020**
Light golden yellow, silver reflections. White pear fruit, a touch of blossom honey, yellow tropical fruit, inviting bouquet. Juicy, finely spicy and complex, good acidity, finesse, mineral, persistent, already developed, certain very good ageing potential, a versatile food wine.
95 * **Ried Rosengartel 1ÖTW 2019**

94 * **Ried Ulm Nussberg 1ÖTW 2021**
13,5 Vol.-%, DIAM, large wooden barrel, €€€€ ⓑ
95 * **Ried Ulm Nussberg 1ÖTW 2020**

94 * **Ried Ulm Nussberg 1ÖTW 2019**

(93) * **Bisamberg 2022**
13 Vol.-%, DIAM, steel tank, €€€€ ⓑ
93 * **Bisamberg 2021**
93 * **Bisamberg 2020**

94 * **Ried Falkenberg 1ÖTW Jeunes Restaurateurs 2021**
13,5 Vol.-%, DIAM, steel tank, €€€€€ ⓑ
93 * **Ried Falkenberg 1ÖTW Jeunes Restaurateurs 2020**
93 * **Ried Falkenberg 1ÖTW Jeunes Restaurateurs 2019**

(92) Wiener Gemischter Satz DAC 2022
12,5 Vol.-%, screwcap, steel tank, €€€ ⓑ
92 Wiener Gemischter Satz DAC 2021
92 Wiener Gemischter Satz DAC 2020

97 Chardonnay Grand Select 2020
14 Vol.-%, DIAM, barrique/steel tank, €€€€€€ ⓑ
97 Chardonnay Grand Select 2019
Medium greenish yellow, silver glints. Remarkable wood savouriness, yellow stone fruit nuances, a hint of white nougat, and candied orange zest. Complex. Succulent peach, expressive fruit, filigree acidity, silky-creamy style, soft nutty notions on the finish. Well-balanced and long, definite ageing potential. A Viennese Grand Cru.
96 Chardonnay Grand Select 2018

93 Chardonnay Select 2020
13 Vol.-%, DIAM, barrique, €€€€ ⓑ
93 Chardonnay Select 2019
93 Chardonnay Select 2018

(92) Chardonnay Wien 2022
13,5 Vol.-%, screwcap, steel tank, €€€ ⓑ
91 Chardonnay Wien 2021
91 Wiener Chardonnay 2020

95 Riesling Ried Rosengartel 1ÖTW 2021
13 Vol.-%, DIAM, steel tank, €€€€ ⓑ
95 Riesling Ried Rosengartel Nussberg 1ÖTW 2020
95 Riesling Ried Rosengartel 1ÖTW 2019

95 Riesling Ried Preussen 1ÖTW 2021
13,5 Vol.-%, DIAM, steel tank, €€€€ ⓑ
94 Riesling Ried Preussen Nussberg 1ÖTW 2020
94 Riesling Ried Preussen 1ÖTW 2019

WIENER GEMISCHTER SATZ DAC

(93) Riesling Nussberg 2022
13,5 Vol.-%, glass, steel tank, €€€€ Ⓑ
93 Riesling Nussberg 2020
93 Riesling Nussberg 2019

(92) Riesling Wien 2022
14 Vol.-%, screwcap, steel tank, €€€ Ⓑ
92 Riesling Wien 2021
91 Wiener Riesling 2020

94 Grüner Veltliner Ried Preussen Nussberg 1ÖTW 2020
14 Vol.-%, DIAM, large wooden barrel, €€€€ Ⓑ
94 Grüner Veltliner Ried Preussen 1ÖTW 2019
94 Grüner Veltliner Ried Preussen 1ÖTW 2018

(94) Grüner Veltliner Ried Kaasgraben 2021
14 Vol.-%, glass, large wooden barrel, €€€€ Ⓑ
93 Grüner Veltliner Ried Kaasgraben Sievering 2020
94 Grüner Veltliner Ried Kaasgraben 2020

(93) Grüner Veltliner Nussberg 2022
13 Vol.-%, glass, steel tank, €€€ Ⓑ
93 Grüner Veltliner Nussberg 2021
92 Grüner Veltliner Nussberg 2020

(94) Grüner Veltliner Ried Herrnholz 2022
13,5 Vol.-%, glass, steel tank, €€€ Ⓑ
93 Grüner Veltliner Ried Herrnholz 2021
92 Grüner Veltliner Ried Herrnholz 2020

93 Grüner Veltliner Bisamberg 2022
12,5 Vol.-%, screwcap, steel tank, €€€ Ⓑ
92 Grüner Veltliner Bisamberg 2021

(92) Grüner Veltliner Wien 2022
12,5 Vol.-%, screwcap, steel tank, €€€ Ⓑ
91 Grüner Veltliner Wien 2021
90 Wiener Grüner Veltliner 2020

(93) Sauvignon Blanc SoMa 2022
13 Vol.-%, DIAM, 500-l-barrel, €€€€ Ⓑ

(91) Muskateller Wien 2022
12,5 Vol.-%, screwcap, steel tank, €€€ Ⓑ
91 Muskateller Wien 2021
90 Wiener Muskateller 2020

(93) Blaufränkisch KaSoMa 2022
13 Vol.-%, DIAM, barrique, €€€€ Ⓑ

94 Merlot Grand Select 2019
13,5 Vol.-%, DIAM, barrique, €€€€ Ⓑ
95 Merlot Grand Select 2018
94 Merlot Grand Select 2017

97 Pinot Noir Tribute 2019

94 Pinot Noir Grand Select 2020
13 Vol.-%, DIAM, barrique/steel tank, €€€€€ Ⓑ
95 Pinot Noir Grand Select 2019
Medium crimson garnet, purple reflections, wide water rim. Inviting aroma of fresh red berries, some herbal tobacco savouriness, a hint of figs, candied orange zest, multi-faceted aromatics. Complex, taut, balanced tannic structure, ripe heart cherry fruit on the finish, mineral aftertaste, complex food companion with a long sweet finish.
95 Pinot Noir Grand Select 2018

92 Pinot Noir Select 2020
14 Vol.-%, DIAM, barrique, €€€€ Ⓑ
92 Pinot Noir Select 2019

93 Pinot Noir Cuvée Ritz Carlton 2018
93 Pinot Noir Cuvée Ritz Carlton 2017

(95) Danubis Grand Select 2019 CS/ME/ZW
13,5 Vol.-%, DIAM, barrique, €€€€€ Ⓑ
94 Danubis Grand Select 2018 CS/ME/ZW
94 Danubis Grand Select 2017 CS/ME/ZW

(92) Wiener Symphonie 2020 ZW/CS/ME
13 Vol.-%, DIAM, used barriques, €€€€ Ⓑ
92 Wiener Trilogie 2019 ZW/CS/ME
92 Wiener Trilogie 2018 ZW/CS/ME

(93) St. Laurent Grand Select 2020
12,5 Vol.-%, DIAM, barrique, €€€€ Ⓑ
94 St. Laurent Grand Select 2019
93 St. Laurent Grand Select 2018

93 Grinzing Beerenauslese 2020 RR/NB

94 Muskateller Auslese 2020

The Wachau, here near Rossatz, is one of the best known wine-growing regions of Austria

NIEDER-ÖSTERREICH/ LOWER AUSTRIA

AUSTRIA'S LARGEST WINE-GROWING REGION

The Urbanuskapelle in Traiskirchen, Thermenregion

DIVERSITY HAS A NAME

Lower Austria is the largest wine-growing region for quality wine in Austria. It unites a rich potential of wine history and wine styles of domestic wine rarities, but also international grape varieties. The eight specific wine-growing regions located in Lower Austria – Wachau, Kremstal, Kamptal, Traisental, Wagram, Weinviertel, Thermenregion and Carnuntum – can be roughly divided into three climatic areas: the Weinviertel in the north, the Danube region to the west and the Pannonian region to the south and east of Vienna.

The great Weinviertel made positive headlines in 2003 when it decided to market only its showpiece wine, the peppery Grüner Veltliner, under the name Weinviertel. Since then, the designation "Weinviertel DAC" on the label guarantees peppery, spicy, fresh Grüner Veltliner. The diverse range of varieties of fresh white wines, fruity red wines and even sweet wine specialities from the Weinviertel can be found under the "Niederösterreich" (Lower Austria) specified wine growing region.

Along the Danube from Melk to Klosterneuburg and its tributaries Krems, Traisen and Kamp, one discovers quaint wine villages, strung together like a string of pearls. Here, besides Grüner Veltliner, Riesling has also positioned itself as a flagship variety. These two grape varieties find their typical expression in the Kremstal DAC, Kamptal DAC, Traisental DAC, Wachau DAC and recently, in addition to Roter Veltliner, also in the Wagram DAC. In the eastern part of the neighbouring Krems Valley, the steep primary rock slopes of the Wachau merge into loess terraces, which also shape the wine character of wines from Wagram. South of Krems, in Traisental, conglomerate soils with numerous limestone islands dominate. In Kamptal, predominantly pri-

NIEDERÖSTERREICH/LOWER AUSTRIA

mary rock soils give the wines their unmistakable character. Specialities such as Roter Veltliner, Pinot Blanc, Chardonnay, but also elegant red wines from these parts of Lower Austria complete the picture. Some of Austria's most outstanding red wines grow in the Pannonian region of Lower Austria to the south and east of Vienna, with Zweigelt and Blaufränkisch setting the tone in Carnuntum and Sankt Laurent and Blaufränkish in the Thermenregion. And everywhere you will find specialities such as Zierfandler and Rotgipfler around Gumpoldskirchen, but also noble sweet rarities and modern red cuvées. Lower Austria, depicts diversity from the vast land of great wines.

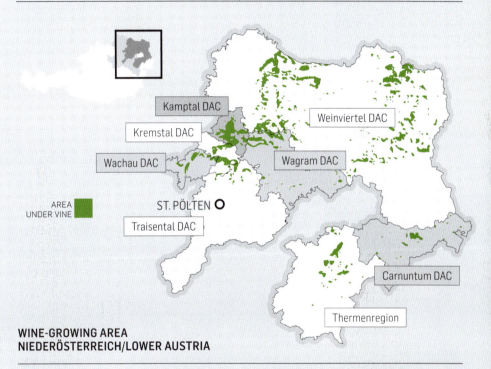

WINE-GROWING AREA
NIEDERÖSTERREICH/LOWER AUSTRIA

Austria total	44.728 ha	**White wine total**	**20.859 ha (77 %)**
Wine-growing area		Grüner Veltliner	13.284 ha (49 %)
Lower Austria	27.074 ha (60,5 %)	Riesling	1.804 ha (6,7 %)
		Welschriesling	1.112 ha (4,1 %)
SPECIFIC WINE-GROWING AREAS		Müller-Thurgau	874 ha (3,2 %)
Carnuntum DAC	832 ha	Weißburgunder	695 ha (2,6 %)
Kamptal DAC	3.574 ha		
Kremstal DAC	2.252 ha	**Red wine total**	**6.227 ha (23 %)**
Thermenregion	2.872 ha	Zweigelt	3.478 ha (12,8 %)
Traisental DAC	848 ha	Blauer Portugieser	479 ha (1,8 %)
Wachau DAC	1.323 ha	Blauburger	371 ha (1,4 %)
Wagram DAC	2.459 ha	St. Laurent	291 ha (1,1 %)
Weinviertel DAC	13.911 ha	Pinot Noir	290 ha (1,1 %)

The Braunsberg near Hainburg

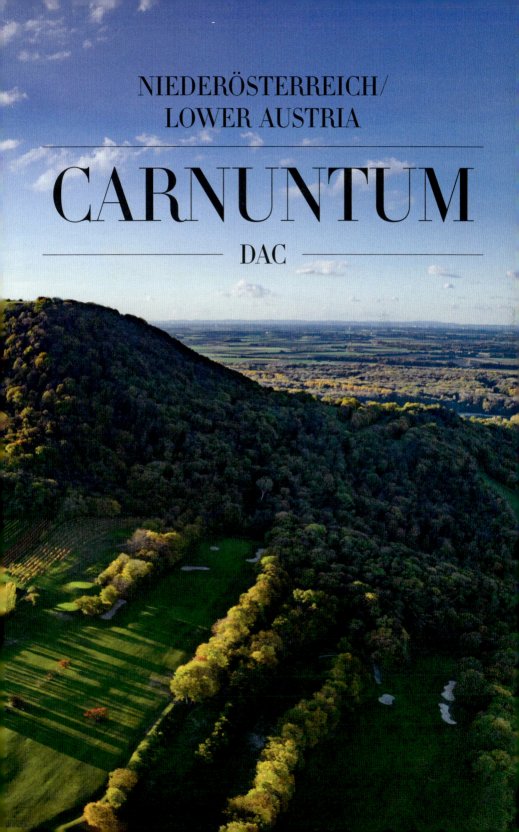

CARNUNTUM DAC

NIEDERÖSTERREICH/
LOWER AUSTRIA

The terraced southern slope of the Spitzerberg is primarily planted with Blaufränkisch

HISTORICAL SITES, ELEGANT RED WINES

Archaeologists excavate evidence of Roman culture from the soils of historical Carnuntum. Equally remarkable are the treasures of the 832 vineyard hectares, in particular the typical regional red wines. A league of successful vintners decorates its "Rubin Carnuntum" labels with the ancient Roman "Heidentor", a fitting symbol of regional identity that is now further enhanced with the Carnuntum DAC protected designation of origin.

The wine-growing area of Carnuntum extends east of Wien (Vienna) to the borders of Slovakia. The vineyards spread south of the Danube River over a landscape of rolling hills including the Leitha, Arbesthaler, and Hainburger Mountains. Stony, heavy soils with clay, loess, sand and gravel offer excellent conditions for red wine varieties. The leading grape is Blauer Zweigelt, which is bottled here in its easy-drinking version under the "Rubin Carnuntum" label. Accompanying Zweigelt are St Laurent and Pinot Noir as well as the international varieties Cabernet Sauvignon, Merlot and Syrah. Blaufränkisch is currently experiencing a renaissance, particularly in the community of Prellenkirchen where it finds ideal conditions on the slopes of Spitzerberg. The hot summers and cold winters of the Pannonian climate are tempered by the Danube River and Lake Neusiedl and allow black grape varieties to ripen fully.

A generation of younger winemakers know how to exploit this natural potential and have led this wine-growing area to success within a short period of time with harmonious red wines that unite fruit and elegance. The wines are modern in style yet remain unique expressions of their provenance. Despite the importance of black grape varieties, white wines with power and structure are also

NIEDERÖSTERREICH/LOWER AUSTRIA CARNUNTUM DAC

produced: Grüner Veltliner and increasingly Sauvignon Blanc and Pinot varieties. The new Carnuntum DAC protected designation of origin divides wines into three quality levels: "Gebietswein" (regional wines), "Ortswein" (village wines) and "Riedenwein" (single-vineyard wines). The red Carnuntum DAC wines are made from Zweigelt, Blaufränkisch or from blends dominated by these varieties. The white Carnuntum DAC wines are made from Chardonnay, Weissburgunder (Pinot Blanc) and/or Grüner Veltliner.

The close proximity of the beautifully renovated baroque castles in Marchfeld, the Archaeology Park Carnuntum, the Donau-Auen National Park and Slovakia's capital Bratislava provide numerous opportunities for vintners to introduce visitors to the local wines. The wine villages Göttlesbrunn, Höflein and Prellenkirchen are well known for their winery taverns and have always been attractive excursion destinations for the Viennese. A more recent fine-dining culture is attracting an increasing number of discerning gourmet travellers. The Carnuntum wines dominate the region's wine lists precisely because they accompany the evolving local cuisine so well.

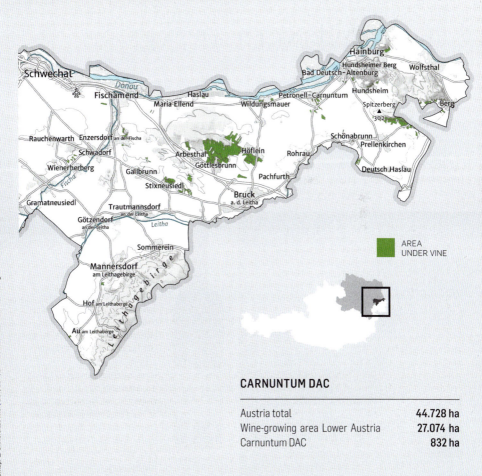

CARNUNTUM DAC

Austria total	44.728 ha
Wine-growing area Lower Austria	27.074 ha
Carnuntum DAC	832 ha

NIEDERÖSTERREICH/LOWER AUSTRIA

SELECTED WINERIES

★★★★★

Weingut Philipp Grassl, Göttlesbrunn
Weingut Gerhard Markowitsch, Göttlesbrunn

★★★★

Weingut Artner, Höflein
Weingut Walter Glatzer, Göttlesbrunn

★★★★

Weingut Franz und Christine Netzl, Göttlesbrunn
Bioweingut Robert Payr, Höflein

★★

Weingut Gerhard Pimpel, Göttlesbrunn

★★★★

WEINGUT ARTNER

ORGANIC

The history of Weingut Artner estate dates back to the 1650s. Their ancestors had already recognised the region's potential for viticulture. Since the 1980s, the family has increasingly focused on producing wines of character and distinction on what was once a mixed farming estate. Höflein is located in the Carnuntum wine region, which stretches east of Vienna and south of the Danube to the Slovakian border. The area is characterised by rich loess and limestone soils. The Pannonian climate and the cooling influence of the Danube provide ideal conditions for growing grapes. Since the winery became a member of Traditionsweingüter Österreich in 2018, the issue of or-

WEINGUT ARTNER
2465 Höflein
Dorfstraße 93
T: +43 (2162) 63142
weingut@artner.co.at
www.artner.co.at

Winemaker: Peter Artner
Contact: Hannes and Christoph Artner
Production: 40 % white, 60 % red, 40 hectares
Fairs: Austrian Tasting London, ÖGW Zürich, ProWein Düsseldorf, London Wine Fair, VieVinum, DAC-Presentations, Hong Kong International Wine & Spirits Fair
Distribution partners: BE, RC, DE, UK, HK, LU, NL, PL, PT, SE, CH, USA

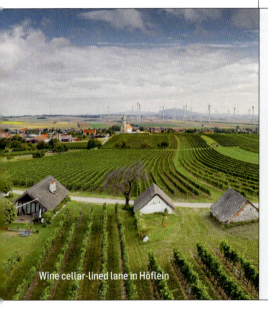

Wine cellar-lined lane in Höflein

© Weingut Glatzer

CARNUNTUM DAC

igin has become even more important in the work undertaken in the vineyards. The members of the association see it as their duty to express the characteristics of their region's soil, climate, grape varieties and respective wineries.

The Artner family is made up of three generations: Hannes Artner, who took over the business from his father and was the creative force behind the company's early focus on quality; his son Peter, who is cellar master and brings all his knowledge and passion to the wines; and Hannes' brother Christoph, who is responsible for international sales and administration. They work in harmony as a team on all fronts - and at the end of the day, they all share the belief that they should always maintain their own high standards of quality. They now cultivate 40 hectares of vineyards and have been certified as an organic winery since the 2021 vintage.

Syrah

94 Chardonnay * massive a. [weiß] 2021
14 Vol.-%, cork, €€€€€

93 Chardonnay * massive a. [weiß] 2020
Medium greenish yellow, silver reflections. Delicate herbs and vanilla, fine yellow tropical fruit, delicate pineapple and mango, some caramel and blossom honey. Juicy, white pear fruit, finely structured, elegant and balanced, fresh acidity, lemony touch on the finish, good ageing potential.

93 Chardonnay * massive a. [weiß] 2019

(93) Grüner Veltliner * Ried Kirchberg 2022
13,5 Vol.-%, screwcap, €€€ Ⓑ

91 Grüner Veltliner * Ried Kirchberg 2021
91 Grüner Veltliner * Ried Kirchberg 2020

91 * Höflein Weiss 2022 GV/CH
13 Vol.-%, screwcap, steel tank, €€€ Ⓑ
90 * Höflein Weiss 2021 GV/CH

**(93) Blaufränkisch *
Ried Kirchweingarten 1ÖTW 2021**
14 Vol.-%, cork, €€€€€ Ⓑ
**93 Blaufränkisch *
Ried Kirchweingarten 1ÖTW 2020**
**94 Blaufränkisch *
Ried Kirchweingarten 1ÖTW 2019**

93 * Ried Aubühl 1ÖTW 2019 BF/ZW
93 * Ried Aubühl 1ÖTW 2018 BF/ZW
94 Ried Aubühl 1ÖTW Höflein 2017 BF/ZW

(92) * Amarok 2021 ZW/BF/SY/ME
14 Vol.-%, cork, €€€€€ Ⓑ
92 * Amarok 2020 ZW/BF/SY/ME
93 * Amarok 2019 ZW/BF/SY/ME

90 * Höflein Rot 2021 ZW/BF/ME
13,5 Vol.-%, cork, €€€ Ⓑ
91 * Höflein Cuvée Barrique 2020 ZW/BF
91 * Höflein Cuvée Barrique 2019 ZW/BF

(94) Zweigelt * Ried Steinäcker 1ÖTW 2021
14 Vol.-%, cork, €€€€€ Ⓑ
94 Zweigelt * Ried Steinäcker 1ÖTW 2020
Deep dark ruby, purple glints, faintly lighter at the rim. Softly scented with liquorice and cassis underlaid with sweet cherries, and subtle savoury wood notes redolent of cedar. An alluring bouquet. Succulent, fresh blackberries, vibrant structure, fine tannins, saline-mineral finish. Good ageing potential.
93 Zweigelt * Ried Steinäcker 1ÖTW 2019

91 Zweigelt * Rubin Carnuntum 2021
92 Zweigelt Rubin * 2020

(95) massive a. [rot] 2020 SY/ZW/BF
14,5 Vol.-%, cork, €€€€€€
96 massive a. [rot] 2019 SY/ZW/BF
98 massive a. [rot] 2018 SY/ZW/BF

(93) Syrah And ever 2021
14 Vol.-%, cork
92 Syrah and ever 2020
93 Syrah and ever 2019

* Carnuntum DAC

NIEDERÖSTERREICH/LOWER AUSTRIA

WEINGUT WALTER GLATZER
★★★★
ORGANIC

The Glatzer family infuses their passion for their craft into every bottle of wine. On a total of 50 hectares of vineyard, red and white grapes flourish; their character is determined by nature and the climate. The 2018 vintage was the first to be released with organic certification. The white wines have a fruity-mineral character with a vintage specificity. All the red wines, which account for around 65 per cent of the vineyards, are fermented on the skins in steel tanks or wooden fermentation vats and then aged for up to 15 months in barriques and large wooden casks.

A new addition to the range is a Göttlesbrunn local wine made from Blaufränkisch and a white wine cuvée called »Göttlesbrunn Weiß«. The »Gotinsprun« cuvée, vinified by Walter Glatzer since 1992, is considered a trendsetter for local wines in Carnuntum. The St. Laurent Altenberg was renamed St. Laurent Alte Reben in accordance with the new DAC rules. Since 2019, the Glatzer winery has been a member of the »Traditionsweingüter Österreich«. The 1ÖTW site wines are the Zweigelt Ried Haidacker, the Cuvée Ried Rosenberg and the Blaufränkisch Ried Bärnreiser.

Meanwhile, daughter Hanna is already making her third vintage of »Hannas Bunte Weine«. In this project, Traminer, Welschriesling, Cabernet and Pinot are free to express themselves.

(92) Chardonnay * Ried Kräften 2021
13 Vol.-%, cork, partial barrique, €€€ B H V

92 Chardonnay * Göttlesbrunn Ried Kräften 2020
92 Chardonnay * Ried Kräften Göttlesbrunn 2019

91 * Göttlesbrunn Weiß 2020 WB/CH/GV/SB
92 * Göttlesbrunn weiss 2019 CH/GV/WB/SB
91 Göttlesbrunn weiss 2018 CH/WB/GV/SB

93 Traminer Hanna Glatzer Bunte Weine 2021
12,5 Vol.-%, DIAM, small wooden barrel, €€€€ B O

95 * Gotinsprun 2019 BF/ZW/ME/SY
95 * Gotinsprun 2018 BF/ME/ZW/SY

94 * Ried Rosenberg 1ÖTW 2020 BF/ZW/ME
94 * Göttlesbrunn Ried Rosenberg 1ÖTW 2019 BF/ME/ZW
94 * Ried Rosenberg 1ÖTW Göttlesbrunn 2018 BF/ME/ZW

The Glatzer family

WEINGUT WALTER GLATZER
2464 Göttlesbrunn
Rosenbergstraße 5
T: +43 (2162) 8486
info@weingutglatzer.at
www.weingutglatzer.at

Winemaker/Contact:
Walter Glatzer
Production: 250,000 bottles
30 % white, 5 % rosé, 65 % red, 38+10 hectares
Fairs: ProWein Düsseldorf, VieVinum, DAC-Presentations
Distribution partners: BE, DK, DE, UK, NL, PL, SE, CH, CZ, USA

© Weingut Glatzer

CARNUNTUM DAC

(94) Blaufränkisch * Ried Bärnreiser 1ÖTW 2021
14 Vol.-%, cork, 500-l-barrel, €€€€ ⓑ ⓘ ⓗ

92 Blaufränkisch * Ried Bärnreiser 1ÖTW 2020
Dark ruby, purple reflections, subtle ochre brightening on the rim. Ripe cherries, a touch of plums, fine nuances of nougat, candied orange zest. Juicy, balanced, hints of cloves and red cherries, fine tannins, mineral and lasting, nougat also in the finish.

94 Blaufränkisch * Ried Bärnreiser 1ÖTW 2019

(93) Zweigelt * Ried Haidacker 1ÖTW 2021
13,5 Vol.-%, cork, 500-l-barrel, €€€€ ⓑ ⓘ ⓗ

93 Zweigelt * Ried Haidacker 1ÖTW 2020
Dark ruby, deep core, purple reflections, subtle brightening on the rim. Fine cherry fruit, floral touch, in the background some red wild berries, a hint of orange zest, hints of liquorice. Juicy, fine cherry fruit also on the palate, discreet fruitiness, freshly structured, round tannins, a touch of caramel in the finish, a versatile wine for the table.

93 Zweigelt * Ried Haidacker 1ÖTW 2019

(93) Sankt Laurent Alte Reben 2021
12,5 Vol.-%, cork, used barriques, €€€€ ⓑ ⓕ

93 St. Laurent Alte Reben 2020

93 St. Laurent Alte Reben 2019

91 Pinot Noir Hanna Glatzer Bunte Weine 2021
12,5 Vol.-%, DIAM, large wooden barrel, €€€€ ⓑ ⓘ

92 Pinot Noir Hanna Bunte Weine 2020

★★★★★

WEINGUT PHILIPP GRASSL
ORGANIC

The Grassl winery is relatively small with an area of 27 hectares, but it is nevertheless well-situated and manageable. The Grassls conscientiously pursue their clearly outlined strategy. Their concept: focus on red wines, clear assortment, purist outward expression, functional cellar, labels without frills, no fashion fad wines. What counts is quality. Grassl produces "in harmony with nature" wines in the best sense of the term, but at an international level of quality: the local varieties Zweigelt, Blaufränkisch and St. Laurent are the most important, and at least 50 percent of them are also included in all cuvées. Cabernet, Merlot and Syrah are merely intended to better bring out the existing strengths of the Zweigelt. Instead of 3,500 vines as in the past, there are now 5,000 to 6,500 vines per hectare in the vineyards. In the cellar, they work meticulously without intervention and treat the grapes as gently as possible in order to get their exceptional quality into the bottle. White wines and classic red wines are fermented and matured in stainless steel tanks or in large wooden barrels. The premium red wines are fermented in wooden fermentation vats - partly with the natural yeasts from the vineyard - and with manually submerged cap management. The premium red wines, the cuvées "Bärnreiser" and "Neuberg", as well as St. Laurent are matured in French barriques. A large part of the barrels are renewed annually to impart the dark fruit aromas with the structure of the wood. The wood note is not overemphasised, but accompanies and refines the maturation until bottling. 80 percent of the production are red wines, half of which are made up of the main variety Zweigelt. Pinot Noir and St. Laurent, which are traditional highlights of the winery, account for 25 per-

WEINGUT PHILIPP GRASSL
2464 Göttlesbrunn
Am Graben 4–6
T: +43 (2162) 8483
office@weingut-grassl.com
www.grassl.wine

Winemaker/Contact:
Philipp Grassl
Production: 150,000 bottles
25 % white, 75 % red,
30+10 hectares
Certified: Sustainable Austria ⓢ
Fairs: ProWein Düsseldorf,
VieVinum, MondoVino
Distribution partners: BE, DK, DE, LU, NL, PL, RUS, CH, SK, CZ, CY

NIEDERÖSTERREICH/LOWER AUSTRIA

Vineyards near Göttlesbrunn

cent. The remaining 25 percent are distributed among Blaufränkisch, Merlot and other international grape varieties. Philipp Grassl was named "Falstaff Winemaker of the Year" in 2018, and he is also always among the winners at the Falstaff Red Wine Awards.

93 Chardonnay * Höflein Ried Rothenberg 2021
13,5 Vol.-%, cork, tonneaux barrel, €€€€

93 Chardonnay * Göttlesbrunn Ried Rothenberg 2020
Medium golden yellow, silver reflections. Fine yellow tropical fruit, some caramel, white peach and lime zest, inviting bouquet. Juicy, white apple, light on its feet, freshly structured, delicate fruit on the finish, salty aftertaste, a fine and already accessible food wine.

93 Chardonnay * Ried Rothenberg Göttlesbrunn 2019

(91) Chardonnay * Höflein 2022
13,5 Vol.-%, cork, large wooden barrel, €€€€ ⓑ

92 Welschriesling Alte Reben Weiss 2021
13,5 Vol.-%, cork, amphore, €€€

92 Welschriesling Alte Reben Weiss 2020

93 Welschriesling Alte Reben weiss 2019

96 Grassl Reserve 2020 ME/BF/ZW
14,5 Vol.-%, cork, tonneaux barrel/used barriques, €€€€€

97 Reserve 2019 ME/BF/ZW
Deep ruby, purple glints, faintly broader ochre hue at the rim. Delicately scented notes of candied orange zest and fresh figs, red berry nuances, dark cherries, and a hint of nougat. A multidimensional bouquet. Juicy, elegant and sweet, silky tannins, lush sweetheart cherries, pleasantly refreshing, mineral reverberations. Already accessible and offers promising ageing potential.

99 Reserve 2018 ME/BF/ZW

(94) * Höflein Ried Bärnreiser 1ÖTW 2021 ZW/ME/BF
14 Vol.-%, cork, barrique/500-l-barrel, €€€€€

95 * Höflein Ried Bärnreiser 1ÖTW 2020 ZW/ME/BF
Deep ruby, purple glints, faintly lighter ochre hue at the rim. Tobacco nuances, subtle toasty scents, black cherries, blackberries, and a hint of nougat. Rich, refined fruit expression, elegant and well-balanced, ripe tannins, superseded by a soft caramel finish and mineral reverberations. Excellent length, a bold supper accompaniment with ageing potential.

95 * Ried Bärnreiser 1 ÖTW 2019 ZW/BF/ME/CS

(92) * Göttlesbrunn Ried Neuberg 2021 ZW/BF/ME
14 Vol.-%, cork, barrique/500-l-barrel, €€€€

91 * Göttlesbrunn Ried Neuberg 2020 ZW/BF/ME

92 * Ried Neuberg Göttlesbrunn 2019 ZW/BF/ME

(92) Zweigelt * Göttlesbrunn Ried Schüttenberg 1ÖTW 2021
13,5 Vol.-%, cork, 500-l-barrel, €€€€

93 Zweigelt * Göttlesbrunn Ried Schüttenberg 1ÖTW 2020

93 Zweigelt * Ried Schüttenberg Göttlesbrunn 1ÖTW 2018

91 Zweigelt * Rubin Carnuntum 2021

91 Zweigelt Rubin * 2020

91 Zweigelt * Rubin Carnuntum 2019

91 Blaufränkisch * Prellenkirchen 2019

93 Blaufränkisch * Prellenkirchen 2018

93 Pinot Noir Reserve 2019

(92) Sankt Laurent Alte Reben 2021
12,5 Vol.-%, cork, 500-l-barrel/small wooden barrel, €€€€

92 St. Laurent Alte Reben 2020

92 Sankt Laurent Alte Reben 2019

WEINGUT GERHARD MARKOWITSCH

In a very short time, the Markowitsch winery has become one of Austria's elite wineries. This has been achieved through a relentless pursuit of quality, which was rewarded in 1999 with the title of ‚Winemaker of the Year' by Falstaff magazine. The reds are dominated by Zweigelt, Blaufränkisch and Pinot Noir, and the whites by Grüner Veltliner, Chardonnay and Pinot Blanc. To meet the international demand for top quality wines, an additional 40 hectares of grapes from contracted growers are processed according to strictly controlled guidelines. In 2001, the Markowitsch family built one of the most modern wineries in Austria to meet the challenges of modern viticulture. Gerhard Markowitsch's goal is to make the terroir of Carnuntum palpable in his wines. For him, this means increasing the use of indigenous grape varieties such as Zweigelt but also using international varieties to create a clear profile in the global wine market. Gerhard Markowitsch won the prestigious Erste Bank Reserve Trophy at the Falstaff Red Wine Awards in 2007 with the 2004 vintage of M1 and came second overall in 2012 with the 2010 Rosenberg. In the autumn of 2015, Gerhard Markowitsch again won the Erste Bank Reserve Trophy with the 2012 vintage M1, and in November 2017, he became the second Falstaff winner with the Cuvée Rosenberg. Finally, in 2019, he brought the coveted Falstaff Red Wine Award to Lower Austria with the 2017 Cuvée Ried Rosenberg, and in the autumn of 2020, he again took second place. An unparalleled consistency!

97 Chardonnay * Ried Schüttenberg Filetstück 2021
13,5 Vol.-%, cork, barrique, €€€€€€ Ⓥ
96 Chardonnay * Ried Schüttenberg Filetstück 2019

93 Chardonnay * Ried Schüttenberg 2021
13,5 Vol.-%, cork, barrique, €€€€ Ⓥ
93 Chardonnay * Ried Schüttenberg 2020
Light greenish yellow, silver reflections. Delicate tangerine zest, vanilla, some mint and lime zest, very attractive aroma. Medium body, white apple, fine acidity, elegant, mineral, delicate melon, stylistically close to Chablis, a great food wine.
94 Chardonnay * Ried Schüttenberg 2019

90 Chardonnay * 2019
91 Chardonnay 2018

93 Weißburgunder * Prellenkirchen 2021
13,5 Vol.-%, screwcap, large wooden barrel/cement, €€€€ Ⓥ
93 Weißburgunder * Prellenkirchen 2020
93 Weißburgunder * Prellenkirchen 2019

92 * Göttlesbrunn Weiss 2021 CH/WB
13 Vol.-%, screwcap, large wooden barrel, €€€€ Ⓥ
92 * Göttlesbrunn Weiss 2020 CH/WB
91 * Göttlesbrunn Weiss 2019 CH/WB

(95) * Ried Rosenberg 1ÖTW 2021 ZW/ME/BF
14 Vol.-%, cork, barrique, €€€€€ Ⓥ
94 * Ried Rosenberg 1ÖTW 2020 ZW/ME/BF
Dark ruby, purple reflections, faint ochre brightening on the rim. A still somewhat restrained bouquet with black forest berries, soft floral notes, some leather and tobacco and dark cherries. Good complexity, taut texture, underpinned with fine fruit, well-integrated tannins, salty-mineral finish, still very restrained overall.

WEINGUT GERHARD MARKOWITSCH
2464 Göttlesbrunn
Pfarrgasse 6
T: +43 (2162) 8222
weingut@markowitsch.at
www.markowitsch.at

Winemaker: Gerhard Markowitsch
Contact: Christine and Gerhard Markowitsch
Production: 30 % white, 70 % red, 79 hectares
Certified: Sustainable Austria Ⓞ
Fairs: ProWein Düsseldorf, VieVinum, MondoVino
Distribution partners: BE, RC, DK, DE, JP, CDN, NL, SE, CH, SGP, CZ, USA, PT

NIEDERÖSTERREICH/LOWER AUSTRIA

95 * Ried Rosenberg 1ÖTW 2019 ZW/ME/BF

97 M1 2020 ME/BF
14,5 Vol.-%, cork, barrique, €€€€€
97 M1 2019 ME/BF
Deep ruby, purple glints, slightly fainter ochre hue at the rim. A scented array of black-coloured berries, a hint of sea buckthorn, nuances of cassis and blackberries, hardwood, and soft notions of nougat. Multifaceted bouquet. Complex, sweetheart cherries, a sophisticated arc of acidity, ripe, supporting tannins, and smooth, supple chocolate superseded by mineral reverberations. Exhibits excellent length and has promising potential for development.
96 M1 2018 ME/BF

92 * Redmont 2018 ZW/BF/ME
91 Redmont 2017 ZW/BF/ME
91 Redmont 2016 ZW/BF/ME

(93) Zweigelt * Ried Kirchweingarten 1ÖTW 2021
13,5 Vol.-%, cork, 500-l-barrel, €€€€ Ⓥ
93 Blauer Zweigelt *
    Ried Kirchweingarten 1ÖTW 2020
93 Zweigelt * Ried Kirchweingarten 1ÖTW 2019

(93) Pinot Noir Reserve 2021
13 Vol.-%, cork, 500-l-barrel, €€€€ Ⓥ
93 Pinot Noir Reserve 2020
94 Pinot Noir Reserve 2019

★★★★

WEINGUT
FRANZ UND CHRISTINE NETZL
ORGANIC

Christina Netzl and her parents Franz and Christine Netzl are a well-coordinated team. Together they vinify wines that are full of character, finesse and, above all, depth from the family-run vineyards around Göttlesbrunn, in the heart of the Carnuntum wine-growing region. The family winery was established around 1860 and developed from a mixed agricultural business. Constant striving for the highest quality in the vineyards, as well as in the cellar, has been the hallmark of the last few generations and allowed the winery to grow to its current 30 hectares of vineyards. The personal goal of the winegrowing family as a member of the "Österreichische Traditionsweingüter" (Austrian Traditional Wine Estates) is to bring out the uniqueness and typicity of the individual grape varieties with a focus on their provenance. Above all, the characteristics of the individual vineyards are increasingly coming to the fore. The basis for this is, of course, the vines and therefore the cultivation of the vineyards according to organic guidelines. Together they spend hours tinkering in the vineyard and cellar. While Franz contributes his experience, knowledge and tradition, Christina provides new ideas and innovations - in short, they complement each other perfectly, and it is precisely this combination that forms the unmistakable basis of Netzl wines.

Zweigelt is, and remains, the absolute king among the varieties, because it suits the climatic conditions of Carnuntum and its soils. As the basis of almost all wines, Zweigelt fascinates above all with its incredible versatility, because everything from classically fruity to a savoury, refined glass of wine can be made from this grape. For example, as a single-vineyard Zweigelt from the Ried Haidacker 1ÖTW and as the most important part of the top cuvée Anna-Christina from the Ried Bärnreiser 1ÖTW, it forms wines at the top of the range.

"This is exactly the direction we will continue to take, as the old Zweigelt vineyards produce the highest quality every year and thus great ageing potential for the future - indigenous, archetypal and simply ingenious!"

92 Weißburgunder * Ried Altenberg 2022
13,5 Vol.-%, cork, 500-l-barrel/amphore, €€€€ Ⓑ Ⓥ
92 Weißburgunder * Ried Altenberg 2021
92 Weißburgunder * Ried Altenberg 2020

91 Grüner Veltliner * Ried Rothenberg 2022
13,5 Vol.-%, cork, 500-l-barrel, €€€€ Ⓑ Ⓥ
92 Grüner Veltliner * Ried Rothenberg 2021
92 Grüner Veltliner * Ried Rothenberg 2020

CARNUNTUM DAC

WEINGUT FRANZ UND CHRISTINE NETZL
2464 Göttlesbrunn
Rosenbergstraße 17
T: +43 (2162) 8236
weingut@netzl.com
www.netzl.com

Winemaker: Christina Artner-Netzl & Franz Netzl
Contact: Christina Artner-Netzl
Production: 200,000 bottles
35 % white, 65 % red, 30 hectares
Fairs: ProWein Düsseldorf, VieVinum
Distribution partners: AUS, BE, RC, DK, DE, EST, FIN, UK, IRL, CDN, LU, NL, NO, PL, RUS, SE, CH, SK, CZ, USA

The Netzl family

90 Chardonnay * 2020
91 Chardonnay * 2019
89 Chardonnay 2018

92 Chardonnay Wilde Liebe 2021
12 Vol.-%, DIAM, amphore, €€€€ ❷ ❶

(89) * Göttlesbrunn weiß 2022 CH/GV
13 Vol.-%, screwcap, amphore, €€€ ❷ ❼
89 Göttlesbrunn weiß * 2020 CH/GV/SB

(95) * Ried Bärnreiser 1ÖTW Anna-Christina 2021 ZW/BF/ME/CS
14 Vol.-%, cork, barrique, €€€€ ❷
94 * Ried Bärnreiser 1ÖTW Anna-Christina 2020 ZW/ME/BF/CS
Deep dark ruby garnet, purple reflections, soft brightening on the rim. Herbal spice, wild blackberries, a touch of sweet dark cherries, subtle hints of cloves and nougat. Powerful, juicy, sweet cherries, vivid, well-integrated tannins, subtly chocolatey finish, shows length, has ageing potential.
96 * Ried Bärnreiser 1ÖTW Anna-Christina 2019 ZW/ME/CS

(93) * Göttlesbrunn Edles Tal 2021 ZW/ME/SY
14 Vol.-%, cork, used barriques, €€€€ ❷
91 * Göttlesbrunn Edles Tal 2020 ZW/BF/SY
91 * Göttlesbrunn Edles Tal 2019 ZW/ME/SY

96 Netzl Privat 2020 ZW/ME
14,5 Vol.-%, cork, barrique, €€€€€ ❼

96 Netzl Privat 2019 ZW/ME
Deep dark ruby, opaque core, purple glints, faintly lighter at the rim. Intense berry fruit, subtle hints of plush wood, a touch of cardamom and vanilla, with gentle candied violets and liquorice undertones. Juicy, opulent, and sweet, ripe berry fruit, sweetheart cherries, robust, ripe tannins, with a nougat finish. Mineral and persistent, chocolatey aftertaste, excellent length, and calibre.
96 Netzl Privat 2018 ME/CS/ZW

(93) Zweigelt * Ried Haidacker 1ÖTW 2021
13,5 Vol.-%, cork, 500-l-barrel, €€€€ ❷ ❼
92 Zweigelt * Ried Haidacker 1ÖTW 2020
93 Zweigelt Ried Haidacker 1ÖTW 2019

(91) Zweigelt * Rubin Carnuntum 2022
13,5 Vol.-%, DIAM, used barriques, €€€ ❷ ❼
90 Zweigelt * Rubin Carnuntum 2021
90 Zweigelt * Rubin Carnuntum 2020

92 Syrah 2020
93 Syrah 2019
93 Syrah 2018

94 Merlot 2020
94 Merlot 2019
94 Merlot 2018

91 Cabernet Sauvignon 2020
92 Cabernet Sauvignon 2019
92 Cabernet Sauvignon 2018

* Carnuntum DAC

NIEDERÖSTERREICH/LOWER AUSTRIA

BIOWEINGUT ROBERT PAYR
ORGANIC

The Payr Winery is located in Höflein in the Carnuntum winegrowing region southeast of Vienna between the Danube and Lake Neusiedl. It is run by the fifth generation of the family, Robert Payr, and is dedicated to the artisanal production of authentic and regionally typical wines. Today, twelve hectares of vineyards are cultivated around Höflein and Prellenkirchen. Since 2018, the winery has been a member of the "Traditionsweingüter Österreich". There is evidence that vine growing in the family goes back to the 18th century. An old wine cellar dating back to 1772, which is still owned by the family today, bears witness to this.

Robert Payr combines traditional craftsmanship with contemporary commitment and develops wines whose taste is based on the experience and passion of now five powerful winemaking personalities. Today, he is carefully developing the heritage of his ancestors and is always breaking new ground. In addition to the reduction of yields in the vineyards and the conversion to organic viticulture, he focuses above all on the sites. He has bought new vineyards, completely reoriented existing ones and given some soils a rest.

In an intensive examination of the vine, the soil and the climate, the experienced winemaker relies on the finesse of nature and carefully works out the unique taste structure of the individualistic sites, wine for wine.

Restful and restless - in a positive sense - is how Robert Payr could be described. The winery has been officially certified as "Sustainable Austria" since 2015 and has been in conversion to organic since January 2017. The grapes from their own vineyards are harvested by hand, selected and processed from the fruit to the seeds to the stalk. Robert Payr's wines are powerful characters that tell their own story. They are structured and savoury and are internationally appreciated due to their density and long storage ageing potential.

(93) Grüner Veltliner * Höflein Ried Rothenberg 2022
13,5 Vol.-%, screwcap, steel tank, €€€€ Ⓑ

93 Grüner Veltliner * Höflein Ried Rothenberg 2021

93 Grüner Veltliner * Ried Rothenberg Höflein 2020

Robert Payr

BIOWEINGUT ROBERT PAYR
2465 Höflein
Dorfstraße 18
T: +43 (2162) 62356
robert@weingut-payr.at
www.weingut-payr.at

Winemaker/Contact:
Robert Payr
Production: 1 % sparkling, 26 % white, 3 % rosé, 71 % red, 1 % sweet, 12 hectares
Certified: Sustainable Austria Ⓒ
Fairs: VieVinum
Distribution partners: CL

CARNUNTUM DAC

Blauer Zweigelt

89   Grüner Veltliner * Löss 2022
12,5 Vol.-%, screwcap, steel tank, €€ Ⓑ
90   Grüner Veltliner * Löss 2021
90   Grüner Veltliner * Löss 2020

(93) Chardonnay * Höflein Ried Kirchberg 2022
13,5 Vol.-%, screwcap, steel tank, €€€€ Ⓑ
93   Chardonnay * Höflein Ried Kirchberg 2021
92   Chardonnay * Ried Kirchberg Höflein 2020

91   Chardonnay * Lehm 2022
12,5 Vol.-%, screwcap, steel tank, €€ Ⓑ
91   Chardonnay * Lehm 2021
90   Chardonnay * Lehm 2020

92   Sauvignon Blanc Selection 2022
13,5 Vol.-%, screwcap, steel tank, €€€ Ⓑ
92   Sauvignon Blanc Selection 2021
91   Sauvignon Blanc 2020

(95) Blaufränkisch * Prellenkirchen
     Ried Spitzerberg 1ÖTW 2021
13,5 Vol.-%, cork, used barriques, €€€€€€ Ⓑ
94   Blaufränkisch * Prellenkirchen
     Ried Spitzerberg 1ÖTW 2020
Strong ruby, purple reflections, faint ochre brightening on the rim. Floral nuances of violets and hibiscus, with ripe red cherries, a hint of cranberries and a mineral touch in the background. Juicy, elegant, ripe cherries, fresh acidity, tight-meshed and salty, persistent, definite ageing potential.
94   Blaufränkisch * Ried Spitzerberg 1ÖTW
     Prellenkirchen 2019

(94) * Höflein Ried Bühl 2021 ZW/BF/ME
13,5 Vol.-%, cork, barrique, €€€€ Ⓑ
93   * Ried Bühl 2020 ZW/BF/ME
93   * Ried Bühl Höflein 2019 ZW/BF/ME

(93) * Höflein Granat 2021 ZW/CS
13,5 Vol.-%, cork, barrique, €€€€ Ⓑ
92   * Höflein Granat 2020 ZW/CS
92   * Höflein Granat 2019 ZW/CS

93   * Höflein Ried Bühl 1ÖTW 2020 BF/ZW
93   * Ried Bühl Höflein 2019 ZW/BF/ME
93   * Ried Bühl Höflein 2018 ZW/BF/ME

(92) * Höflein Matthäus 2021 ZW/BF/ME
13,5 Vol.-%, screwcap, barrique, €€€€
92   * Höflein Matthäus 2020 ZW/BF/ME
92   * Höflein Matthäus 2019 ZW/BF/ME

(91) * Cuvée Carnuntum Prestige 2021
     ZW/BF/ME/CS
13,5 Vol.-%, screwcap, partial barrique, €€€€ Ⓑ

(89) * Cuvée Carnuntum Selection 2022 ZW/BF
13 Vol.-%, screwcap, partial barrique, €€ Ⓑ
90   * Cuvée Carnuntum Selection 2021 ZW/BF
89   * Cuvée Carnuntum Selection 2020 ZW/BF

(94) Blauer Zweigelt * Höflein
     Ried Steinäcker 1ÖTW 2021
13,5 Vol.-%, cork, barrique, €€€€€ Ⓑ
93   Blauer Zweigelt * Höflein
     Ried Steinäcker 1ÖTW 2020
Dark ruby, opaque core, purple reflections, delicate bright rim. Dark cherry, fine blackberry confit, gentle savouriness, some liquorice and candied orange zest. Juicy, tight, dark fruit of the forest, vivid, well-integrated tannins, mineral finish, hint of nougat, it will benefit from bottle age.
93   Zweigelt * Ried Steinäcker 1ÖTW
     Höflein 2019

(90) Blauer Zweigelt * Rubin Carnuntum 2022
13,5 Vol.-%, DIAM, used barriques, €€€ Ⓑ
91   Blauer Zweigelt * Rubin Carnuntum 2021
90   Zweigelt * Rubin Carnuntum 2020

WEINGUT GERHARD PIMPEL

★ ★

For Gerhard Pimpel, being a winemaker entails appreciating, observing and cherishing nature, along with a sense for the vines and grapes. He has an intuition for a natural product, from the grape's growth cycle to the final product, the wine. Pimpel creates dense yet elegant wines with harmony and finesse. One gets the impression here that he knows every single vine personally. With the Rosenberg, Schüttenberg and Bärnreiser sites, Gerhard Pimpel's vineyards are among the best in the entire winegrowing region.

Gerhard Pimpel is a calm winemaker who pursues his path - focused and committed, accompanying the work of nature. "You have to pay attention to the interaction between the soil, the variety and the rootstock," he says. Drawing on this experience, he is able to produce autochthonous, terroir-based wines. With "Optime", Latin for "the best", soil, climate, grapes, and wood blend optimally - hence: Ergo bibamus Optime.

The Carnuntum winegrowing region of Lower Austria stretches to the east of Vienna and south of the Danube. Rich loess and barren limestone soils, as well as the continental Pannonian microclimate with the cool influences of the Danube, offer ideal conditions for appealing red wines that combine fruit and elegance. The wines are modern in style but unique and true to their origins.

92 Chardonnay * Göttlesbrunn Ried Rosenberg 2021
13,5 Vol.-%, cork, barrique, €€€€

92 Chardonnay * Göttlesbrunn Ried Rosenberg 2020

90 Pinot Noir Rosé 2021

93 * Göttlesbrunn Ried Rosenberg 1ÖTW 2020 ZW/ME
14,5 Vol.-%, cork, barrique, €€€€

93 * Göttlesbrunn Ried Rosenberg 1ÖTW 2019 ZW/ME
Dark ruby, purple reflections, broad faint ochre brightening on rim. Tobacco, fine plum confit, a touch of wood spice, delicate hints of candied orange zest, dark berry fruit. Juicy, complex, fine blackberry touch, ripe tannins, nougat on the finish, long lasting, versatile food wine with further ageing potential.

93 * Ried Rosenberg 1ÖTW 2017

Gerhard Pimpel

WEINGUT GERHARD PIMPEL
2464 Göttlesbrunn
Kirchenstraße 19
T: +43 (664) 4636650
weingut@gerhardpimpel.at
www.gerhardpimpel.at

Winemaker/Contact:
Gerhard Pimpel
Production: 30 % white, 70 % red, 13 hectares
Fairs: VieVinum

© www.ludwig-rusch.com

CARNUNTUM DAC

92 Zweigelt * Selektion Göttlesbrunn 2019
91 Zweigelt * Selektion Göttlesbrunn 2017

91 Zweigelt * Rubin Carnuntum 2020
14 Vol.-%, cork, used barriques, €€
90 Zweigelt Rubin Carnuntum 2018

93 Zweigelt * Höflein
   Ried Bärnreiser 1ÖTW 2020
14,5 Vol.-%, cork, barrique, €€€€

92 Zweigelt * Höflein
   Ried Bärnreiser 1ÖTW 2019
92 Zweigelt * Höflein
   Ried Bärnreiser 1ÖTW 2018

93 Merlot Optime 2020
14,5 Vol.-%, cork, barrique, €€€€€
93 Merlot Optime 2019
14,5 Vol.-%, cork, barrique, €€€€
93 Merlot Optime 2018

SPACE FOR YOUR
WINE NOTES

* Carnuntum DAC

The Kalvarienberg between Stiefern and Schönberg am Kamp

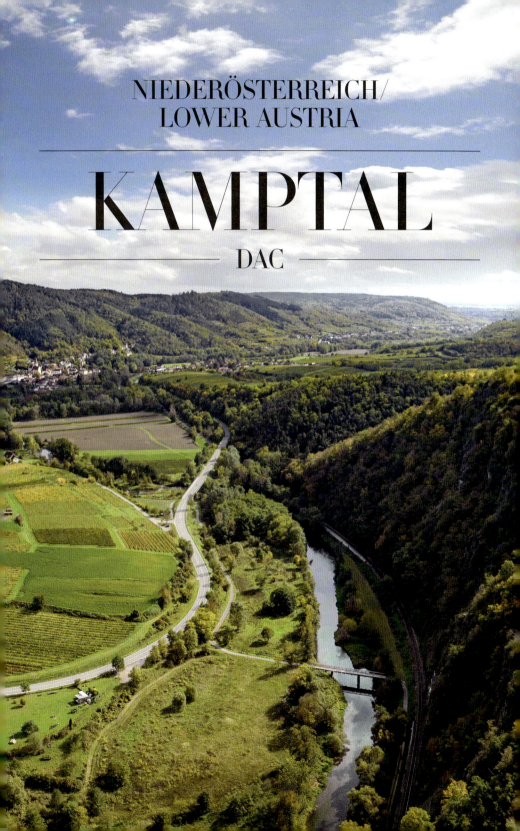

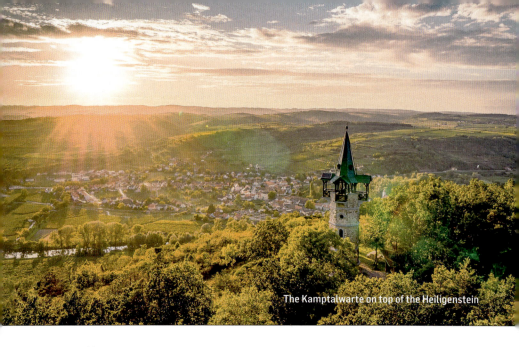
The Kamptalwarte on top of the Heiligenstein

GRÜNER VELTLINER KAMPTAL DAC AND RIESLING KAMPTAL DAC FROM ANCIENT SOILS

The Kamp River lends its name to this region and Langenlois has the greatest vineyard area of any city in Austria. With 3,574 hectares, Kamptal is also one of the country's larger wine-growing areas.

Culture and tourism play a very important role in Kamptal, which is further enhanced with winery taverns and wine shops. In Heiligenstein, Kamptal has one of the most striking vineyards in Austria with unique soil: desert sandstone with volcanic components dating back to the Permian period 270 million years ago. Powerful, age-worthy Rieslings grow on its steep, terraced south-facing slope. Toward the Danube River soils alter; loess and loam terraces provide excellent conditions for numerous other wine styles.

Next to Grüner Veltliner, Burgundian varieties and Blauer Zweigelt thrive excellently. The interplay of a hot Pannonian climate and cool influences from the Waldviertel (Forest Quarter) to the north are noticeable. The two main varieties, Grüner Veltliner and Riesling have defined the Kamptal DAC since 2008. The initial, two-tier classification system is currently experiencing a change. Origin plays a greater role in the new hierarchy of 2017, which applies to all producers. The regional Kamptal DAC wines build the base of the pyramid. Ortswein (village wines) are the next level and carry the additional name of the community in which they are grown. The single-vineyard wines comprise the peak of the pyramid. These are easy to recognize because the word "Ried" precedes the name of the vineyard and in many cases also the name of the wine village. The term "reserve" is also allowed for single-vineyard wines, but

© Robert Herbst

NIEDERÖSTERREICH/LOWER AUSTRIA **KAMPTAL DAC**

there will be fewer on the market than previously. Wines labelled with "reserve" may first be released in September. Many vintners don't label their wines in this way, but still choose to release their wines at a later date. A highly recommendable tourist attraction is the Loisium, a futuristic wine theme park with mystical underground wine adventures, a wine shop and seminar hotel. The ensemble represents the symbiosis of tradition and innovation. Ursinhaus is another recommendable address for the discovery of Kamptal wines. Langenlois and the communities of Gobelsburg, Kammern, Zöbing and many other villages are exemplary for Austrian wine culture.

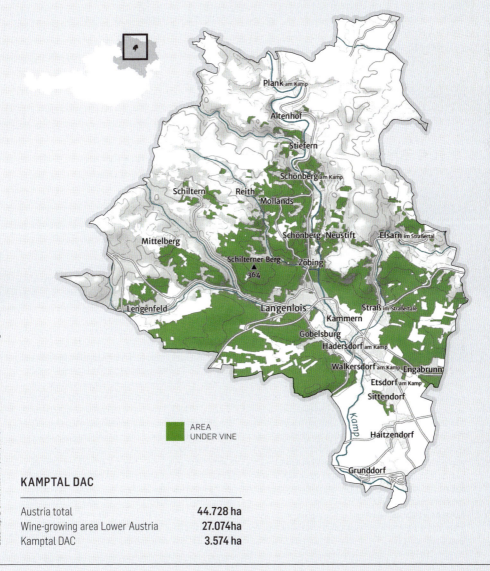

KAMPTAL DAC

Austria total	44.728 ha
Wine-growing area Lower Austria	27.074 ha
Kamptal DAC	3.574 ha

NIEDERÖSTERREICH/LOWER AUSTRIA

SELECTED WINERIES

Weingut Bründlmayer, Langenlois
Weingut Schloss Gobelsburg, Gobelsburg
Weingut Hirsch, Kammern

Weingut Jurtschitsch, Langenlois
Weingut Fred Loimer, Langenlois
Weingut Steininger, Langenlois
Weingut Topf, Straß im Straßertale

Weingut Leindl, Zöbing
Weingut Rudolf Rabl, Langenlois

Weingut Weixelbaum, Straß im Straßertale

Weingut Gerhard Deim, Schönberg am Kamp
Weingut Christoph Edelbauer, Langenlois
Laurenz V., Wien/Zöbing
Weingut Christian Nastl, Langenlois
Winzerhof Sax, Langenlois
Weingut Peter Schweiger, Zöbing

—
Weingut Schmid, Langenlois

WEINGUT BRÜNDLMAYER

ORGANIC

There is much to admire about the Bründlmayer estate: the people, the high quality of the wines produced here in Langenlois, and finally the friendly and unassuming nature of the man who has been responsible for the success of this flagship estate since 1980. Almost every wine - from the lightest Grüner Veltliner to the red and sparkling wines - has the potential to be the best of the vintage in its category.

The vineyards are mostly terraced and have been organically farmed since 2015. About a third of the vineyards are trained in the so-called "Lyra" system. The geologically oldest and most interesting vineyard is the Zöbinger Heiligenstein, the soil of which dates back to the Permian period, 270 million years ago. This desert sandstone with volcanic deposits creates the conditions for the production of outstanding wines. The finest Riesling and Cabernet Franc grapes ripen high up in a self-contained nature reserve.

Grüner Veltliner is the winery's main grape variety, ranging from pleasant, light quality Kabinetts to complex, long-lasting Spätlese wines.

Riesling grapes grow on the barren, rocky soils of the Steinmassl and Heiligenstein sites, and the resulting wines can reach almost legendary ages. Chardonnay and Burgundy varieties (Pinot Noir, Pinot Gris and Pinot Blanc) are also considered specialities of the house. Even though the red wines shine with finesse rather than power, it is still a challenge for Willi Bründlmayer to cultivate beautiful, digestible red wines with a striking personality in this climatic border region. The "Bründlmayer Brut" is in a class of its own. After traditional fermentation, it is left on the lees for about three years, then riddled by hand and disgorged in the cellar. Since 1947, the most valuable vintages have been kept in the wine archive. Intensive internal tastings are held to learn about the sites, the character of the vintage and the style of development.

With an export share of 30 per cent, the family business is also very successful internationally. The American Wine & Spirits Magazine has named Bründlmayer 'Winery of the Year' five times in a row, and the British Financial Times calls it 'a beacon of Austrian viticulture'.

KAMPTAL DAC

WEINGUT BRÜNDLMAYER
3550 Langenlois, Zwettler Straße 23
T: +43 (2734) 21720
weingut@bruendlmayer.at
www.bruendlmayer.at
Winemaker: Christopher Forst
Contact: Willi Bründlmayer, Andreas Wickhoff, Thomas Klinger
Production: 600,000 bottles
15 % sparkling, 59 % white, 10 % rosé, 15 % red, 1 % sweet, 90 hectares
Certified: Sustainable Austria
Fairs: Austrian Tasting London, Foodex Japan, Millésime Bio, ProWein Düsseldorf, VieVinum, Vinexpo Bordeaux, MondoVino, véritable St. Martin, Summa Margreid
Distribution partners: AUS, BDS, BY, BE, BR, BG, RC, DK, DE, EST, FIN, FR, GR, UK, HK, IRL, IS, IT, JP, CDN, ROK, HR, LV, LT, LU, NZ, NL, NO, PL, RUS, SE, CH, SRB, SGP, SK, SLO, ES, TH, CZ, TR, UA, PT

Langenlois

All the current wines can also be tasted by the glass at the Heurigenhof Bründlmayer, a Renaissance building dating back to the 16th century.

96 Bründlmayer Brut Nature Blanc de Blancs Langenlois Große Reserve 2017
Medium golden yellow, silver glints, fine mousse. Pleasant apple fruit, delicate hints of guava, a touch of herbs, mango notes, mineral touch, and white tropical fruit. A multidimensional bouquet. Juicy, tight-knit, citrus and brioche, delicate hints of Williams pear, persistent. A complex food accompaniment with promising ageing potential. (Deg. January 2022)

96 Bründlmayer Blanc de Blancs Langenlois Große Reserve Extra Brut 2014

94 Sekt Austria Reserve Niederösterreich g.U. Blanc de Noirs Extra Brut 2016
12 Vol.-%, cork, steel tank, small wooden barrel/large wooden barrel/bottle fermentation, €€€€€

95 Bründlmayer Blanc de Noirs Extra Brut Langenlois Grosse Reserve 2015

94 Sekt Austria Reserve Niederösterreich g.U. Blanc de Blancs Extra Brut Reserve
Deg. 09/2022, 12 Vol.-%, cork, steel tank/large wooden barrel/used barriques/bottle fermentation, €€€€€

94 Bründlmayer Blanc de Blancs Extra Brut Reserve Niederösterreich g.U. NV

93 Sekt Austria Reserve Niederösterreich g.U. Brut CH/PN/PG/WB/GV
Deg. 11/2022, 12 Vol.-%, cork, steel tank/large wooden barrel/used barriques/bottle fermentation, €€€€€

93 Sekt Austria Reserve Niederösterreich g.U. Brut Rosé PN/SL/ZW
Deg. Dezember 2022, 11,5 Vol.-%, cork, bottle fermentation/steel tank, €€€€€

92 Bründlmayer Brut Rosé Reserve Niederösterreich g.U. NV PN/SL/ZW

99 Riesling * Ried Heiligenstein 1ÖTW Alte Reben 2021
13 Vol.-%, cork, steel tank/wooden barrel, €€€€€€

97 Riesling * Zöbing Ried Heiligenstein 1ÖTW Alte Reben 2020
Medium yellow-green, silver glints. Peach and pineapple fruit underlaid with candied limes, delicately mineral, with traces of white tropical fruit and hints of flint. A multifaceted bouquet. Juicy, complex, tightly woven, vibrant acid structure, softly spicy, white stone fruit, prolonged persistence with ripples of expressive fruit nuances. A concise food accompaniment with a lot of potential for development.

97 Riesling * Ried Zöbinger Heiligenstein 1ÖTW Alte Reben 2019

95 Riesling * Ried Zöbinger Heiligenstein 1ÖTW Lyra 2019

95 Riesling ** Ried Zöbinger Heiligenstein 1ÖTW Lyra 2018

* Kamptal DAC   ** Kamptal DAC Reserve

NIEDERÖSTERREICH/LOWER AUSTRIA

95 Riesling ** Zöbinger Heiligenstein Lyra
    1ÖTW 2017

(94) Riesling * Ried Heiligenstein 1ÖTW 2022
13 Vol.-%, cork, steel tank, €€€€ B
95 Riesling * Zöbing Ried Heiligenstein 2021
95 Riesling * Zöbing Ried Heiligenstein
    1ÖTW 2020

(94) Riesling * Ried Steinmassl 1ÖTW 2022
12,5 Vol.-%, cork, steel tank, €€€€ B
94 Riesling * Langenlois Ried Steinmassl
    1ÖTW 2021
94 Riesling * Langenlois Ried Steinmassl
    1ÖTW 2020

92 Riesling * Terrassen 2022
12,5 Vol.-%, screwcap, steel tank, €€€ B V
92 Riesling * Terrassen 2021
92 Riesling * Terrassen 2020

98 Grüner Veltliner * Ried Lamm 1ÖTW 2021
13 Vol.-%, cork, barrique, €€€€€€ B V
96 Grüner Veltliner * Kammern Ried Lamm
    1ÖTW 2020
Medium golden yellow, silver glints. Subtle toasty aromas are underpinned by ripe honeydew melon and pineapple, a hint of herbs, white nougat, and candied orange peel. Juicy, complex, tightly woven, multifaceted acidity structure, nutty touch, followed by a yellow apple finish, and persistence. Assured ageing potential.

97 Grüner Veltliner * Ried Kammerner Lamm
    1ÖTW 2019

97 Grüner Veltliner * Ried Spiegel Langenlois
    1ÖTW Vincent 2021
13,5 Vol.-%, cork, barrique/large wooden barrel,
€€€€€€ B
95 Grüner Veltliner * Langenlois Ried Spiegel
    1ÖTW Vincent 2019
94 Grüner Veltliner ** Langenloiser
    Ried Spiegel 1ÖTW 2018

95 Grüner Veltliner * Ried Käferberg
    1ÖTW 2021
13 Vol.-%, cork, steel tank/large wooden barrel,
€€€€€€ B V
94 Grüner Veltliner * Langenlois
    Ried Käferberg 1ÖTW 2020
95 Grüner Veltliner * Ried Langenloiser
    Käferberg 1ÖTW 2019

(94) Grüner Veltliner * Langenlois
    Alte Reben 2022
13 Vol.-%, cork, large wooden barrel, €€€€€ B

95 Grüner Veltliner * Langenloiser
    Alte Reben 2021
94 Grüner Veltliner * Langenloiser
    Alte Reben 2020

(93) Grüner Veltliner *
    Ried Loiserberg 1ÖTW 2022
12,5 Vol.-%, cork, steel tank/large wooden barrel,
€€€€ B V
93 Grüner Veltliner * Langenlois
    Ried Loiserberg 1ÖTW 2021
93 Grüner Veltliner * Ried Loiserberg 1ÖTW
    Langenlois 2020
93 Grüner Veltliner * Ried Rosenhügel 2021

92 Grüner Veltliner * Ried Berg Vogelsang 2022
12,5 Vol.-%, screwcap, steel tank, €€€€ B V
92 Grüner Veltliner * Ried Berg Vogelsang 2021
92 Grüner Veltliner * Ried Berg Vogelsang 2020

91 Grüner Veltliner * Terrassen 2022
12,5 Vol.-%, screwcap, steel tank, €€€ B V
91 Grüner Veltliner * Terrassen 2021
91 Grüner Veltliner * Terrassen 2020

89 Grüner Veltliner L + T 2022
11 Vol.-%, screwcap, steel tank, €€€ B V
90 Grüner Veltliner L + T (leicht & trocken) 2021
89 Grüner Veltliner L + T (leicht & trocken) 2020

95 Chardonnay Reserve Ried Steinberg 2021
13 Vol.-%, cork, barrique, €€€€€ B V
95 Chardonnay Ried Steinberg Reserve 2020
95 Chardonnay Reserve 2019

93 Grau- und Weißburgunder Ried Spiegel
    2019 PG/WB
93 Ried Spiegel Grau- und Weißburgunder
    2018 PG/WB

93 Gelber Muskateller Langenlois
    Ried Rosenhügel 2021
92 Gelber Muskateller Ried Rosenhügel 2019

92 Merlot Vincents Rosé 2022
12,5 Vol.-%, screwcap, steel tank, €€€€ B

93 Cabernet Franc Reserve 2018
13 Vol.-%, cork, barrique, €€€€€ B

93 Pinot Noir Reserve Ried Käferberg 2019
93 Pinot Noir Reserve 2017
92 Pinot Noir Reserve 2016

92 Pinot Noir 2018
93 Pinot Noir 2017

KAMPTAL DAC

91 Pinot Noir 2016	97 Gelber Muskateller Ried Rosenhügel TBA 2018
92 Zweigelt Reserve 2018	
93 Zweigelt Reserve Ried Hasel Langenlois 2017	95 Gelber Muskateller Eiswein Ried Langenloiser Rosenhügel 2016
92 Zweigelt Reserve 2016	
90 Zweigelt 2019	96 Riesling Eiswein Ried Langenloiser Steinmassl 2016
91 Zweigelt 2018	
92 Cabernet Franc & Merlot Willi & Vincent 2015 ME/CF	94 Grüner Veltliner Langenloiser Alte Reben Auslese 2018

WEINGUT GERHARD DEIM

Schönberg am Kamp, located in a basin at the northernmost part of the Kamptal, is characterized by a microclimate with hot days and particularly cool nights. Weingut Gerhard Deim focuses on the region's strengths: Grüner Veltliner and Riesling. The winery's foundation is laid through intergenerational teamwork, the combination of time-honoured methods, and the spirit of youthful innovation. Old and young are united by the pursuit of uncompromisingly high quality, and this begins with the tending and nurturing of each individual vine, both in the case of estate and reserve wines and of local and regional wines.

Schönberger local wines are characterized by freshness, elegance, and palatability. They reflect the most diverse soil formations and the microclimate characterized by the unique location of the village within the basin. In the Irbling vineyard, Riesling grows on the foothills of the Waldviertel gneiss-slate plateau, and Grüner Veltliner at Kalvarienberg thrives on weathered soil of silicate rock with a thin layer of alluvial loess loam. In the Bernthal vineyard, the vines grow on metre-thick loess-loam terraces. Some Ried wines are aged in 500-litre barrels until the

WEINGUT GERHARD DEIM
3562 Schönberg am Kamp
Kalvarienberg 8
T: +43 (2733) 8763
wein@deim.at
www.gerharddeim.at

Contact: Gerhard Deim
Production: 10 % sparkling, 80 % white, 10 % red, 20 hectares
Certified: Sustainable Austria
Fairs: Austrian Tasting London, VieVinum, Vinobile Feldkirch
Distribution partners: DE, NL, PL, SE, CZ

Gerhard Deim jr. and sen.

* Kamptal DAC   ** Kamptal DAC Reserve

NIEDERÖSTERREICH/LOWER AUSTRIA

Ried Kalvarienberg

next harvest - an ideal size that simultaneously guarantees a balance between natural oxygen permeation and not too much wood influence. The many small terraces and plots in the vineyards can be vinified separately year after year due to the barrel size and thus optimally accompanied in their development until bottling.

93 Riesling * Ried Irbling 2021
13 Vol.-%, cork, steel tank, €€€

93 Riesling * Schönberg Ried Irbling 2021
Bright pale green yellow. Passionfruit and ripe peach, underlaid with blossom honey, delicate tangerine zest, a hint of guava. Good complexity, lemon-salty nuances, fresh acidity, mineral, white peach on the finish, long lasting, a complex food companion.

93 Riesling * Schönberg Ried Irbling 2020

92 Riesling * Schönberg 2022
12,5 Vol.-%, screwcap, steel tank, €€€
91 Riesling * Schönberg 2021
92 Riesling * Schönberg 2020

93 Grüner Veltliner * Ried Kalvarienberg 2021
14 Vol.-%, cork, 500-l-barrel, €€€€
93 Grüner Veltliner * Ried Kalvarienberg 2020
93 Grüner Veltliner * Ried Schönberger Kalvarienberg 2019

92 Grüner Veltliner * Ried Bernthal 2021
14 Vol.-%, cork, 500-l-barrel/large wooden barrel, €€€€
92 Grüner Veltliner * Schönberg Ried Bernthal 2020
93 Grüner Veltliner * Ried Schönberger Bernthal 2019

92 Grüner Veltliner * Schönberg 2022
13 Vol.-%, screwcap, large wooden barrel, €€€
92 Grüner Veltliner * Schönberg 2021
92 Grüner Veltliner * Schönberg 2020

91 Grüner Veltliner * 2022
12,5 Vol.-%, screwcap, steel tank, €€
90 Grüner Veltliner * 2021
90 Grüner Veltliner * 2020

WEINGUT CHRISTOPH EDELBAUER
ORGANIC

For winemaker Christoph Edelbauer in Langenlois, everything is in harmony with nature and the Kamptal region: Winery, work and wine. He knows what he wants, loves the challenge and follows his path straightforwardly and consistently. Christoph Edelbauer pressed his first vintage in 2003, and today the winemaker cultivates twelve hectares of vineyards and processes the grapes at his architecturally-sophisticated winery in the middle of the Langenlois vines, which was completed in 2013. "Sustainable thinking and mathods are deeply rooted in me. That is why it is important to me that our winery maintains a manageable size. Only in this way can I dedicate myself with conviction to the entire process of vinification," explains Edelbauer, who consistently pays attention to the conscious use of resources. He cultivates his vineyards organically, he had his new building constructed according to energy efficient principles, and the air conditioning in his

KAMPTAL DAC

WEINGUT CHRISTOPH EDELBAUER
3550 Langenlois
Im Neuberg, Kremser Straße 86
T: +43 (676) 7734811
info@weingut-edelbauer.at
www.weingut-edelbauer.at

Winemaker/Contact:
Christoph Edelbauer
Production: 10 % sparkling, 50 % white, 38 % red, 2 % sweet, 12 hectares
Fairs: Millésime Bio, ProWein Düsseldorf, VieVinum
Distribution partners: BE, DK, DE, IT, CDN, CZ, NL, CH, SK, USA

Grüner Veltliner

cellar is provided by environmentally-friendly ground air collectors.
The design of Edelbauer's equipment is also reduced and all the more memorable: Direct screen printing on the bottles replaces the labels, the cartons are printed in a minimalist manner, and business cards and stationery are produced on natural paper - an overall concept for sustainability right down the line.
Christoph Edelbauer's wines are captivating in their simplicity; they are unfussy, relaxed and exciting at the same time - this applies to the entire range, with Grüner Veltliner, Riesling and Pinot Noir being his flagships. As a winemaker, he is consistent. In his work he relies on sustainability; the essence is and remains the Kamptal: Christoph Edelbauer is preparing to show what the new Kamptal is all about.

92 🌱 Pet Nat Rosé 2022 ZW/SL
12,5 Vol.-%, cork, bottle fermentation, €€€€€ 🅑
91 🌱 Pet Nat Rosé 2021 ZW/SL
90 🌱 Zweigelt zero dosage Pet Nat Rosé 2019

93 Grüner Veltliner * Ried Neuburg 2018
Bright yellow green, gold reflections. Delicate blossom honey, yellow apple, mineral, faint pineapple, tight bouquet. Juicy, complex, well-integrated acid structure, spicy, yellow stone fruit, somewhat restrained, peppery touch, versatile, with certain ageing potential.
92 Grüner Veltliner ** Ried Neuburg 2017

93 Grüner Veltliner * Ried Thal 2020
13,5 Vol.-%, cork, steel tank, €€€€€ 🅑
93 Grüner Veltliner Kamptal Langenlois DAC Ried Thal 2019

92 Grüner Veltliner * Langenlois 2022
12,5 Vol.-%, screwcap, steel tank, €€€ 🅑
92 Grüner Veltliner * Langenlois 2021
91 Grüner Veltliner * Langenlois 2020

(92) Riesling * Langenlois 2022
12,5 Vol.-%, screwcap, steel tank, €€€ 🅑
92 Riesling * Langenlois 2021
91 Riesling * Langenlois 2020

92 Chardonnay 2022
12,5 Vol.-%, screwcap, steel tank, €€€ 🅑
89 Chardonnay 2021
89 Chardonnay 2019

90 Abartig Einfach! 2020 GM/TR
91 Abartig Einfach! 2019 GM/TR

92 Pinot Noir Ried Spiegel 2017
13 Vol.-%, cork, 500-l-barrel, €€€€€ 🅑

94 Sauvignon Blanc TBA 2017

* Kamptal DAC   ** Kamptal DAC Reserve

NIEDERÖSTERREICH/LOWER AUSTRIA

★★★★★
WEINGUT SCHLOSS GOBELSBURG

Schloss Gobelsburg is the oldest winery in the Danube Kamptal region, with a documented winegrowing history dating back to the 12th century. In 2021, Schloss Gobelsburg celebrated its 850th vintage. The Cistercian monks of Zwettl Abbey were given their first vineyards in 1171 and have had a lasting influence on Austrian viticulture over the past 850 years. Over the centuries, the monks have cultivated vineyards in some of the best locations in Austria. Today, the winery focuses on the typical wines of provenance of the Danube appellations in the three categories of Regional, Local and Riedenwein, including internationally renowned names such as Ried Heiligenstein and Ried Lamm. Sustainable viticulture has always been close to everyone's heart. From pruning to foliage work, the vineyards are tended with care and expertise. In autumn, when the leaves are already golden in October and November, the grapes are harvested by hand in small crates and carefully transported to the cellar for further sorting. Simplicity and rigour are the Cistercian way of life and the way to excellent wines. The much-needed time factor has become a rare commodity these days. The Gobelsburg wines, however, have the luxury of developing in peace and quiet in the cool cellars.

In addition to the typical appellation wines, the cellars at Schloss Gobelsburg also produce other speciality wines. The winery is a renowned producer of quality Austrian sparkling wines and cool climate red wines based on Pinot Noir, St. Laurent & Zweigelt. Gobelsburg also produces a small but fine selection of sweet wines. The winery produces Prädikat wines at all levels and ice wines. The winery is also known for its commitment to traditional and heritage winemaking, which is reflected in its "Tradition" wine range.

95 ❃ Schloss Gobelsburg Vintage 2010
GV/RR/PN

95 ❃ Sekt Austria Grosse Reserve
Niederösterreich g.U. Langenlois Extra Brut Vintage 2012 GV/PN/RR
12 Vol.-%, cork, bottle fermentation, €€€€€ V

93 ❃ Sekt Austria Reserve Niederösterreich g.U. Brut GV/PN/RR
12 Vol.-%, cork, bottle fermentation, €€€€ V

92 ❃ Sekt Austria Reserve brut Niederösterreich g.U. NV GV/PN/RR

93 ❃ Sekt Austria Reserve Niederösterreich g.U. Blanc de Blancs Brut CH/WR/GV
12 Vol.-%, cork, bottle fermentation, €€€€ V

93 ❃ Sekt Austria Reserve brut Niederösterreich g.U. Blanc de Blancs NV GV/WR/CH

93 ❃ Sekt Austria Reserve Niederösterreich g.U. Brut Rosé ZW/PN/SL
11,5 Vol.-%, cork, bottle fermentation, €€€€ V

93 ❃ Sekt Austria Reserve Rosé brut Niederösterreich g.U. SL/ZW/PN

98 Riesling * Ried Heiligenstein 2021
13,5 Vol.-%, cork, large wooden barrel, €€€€€ V

95 Riesling * Ried Heiligenstein 1ÖTW 2020
Medium yellow-green, silver reflections. Delicate herbal notes, a bit of orange zest, touch of peach, subtle notes of greengage, with some chamomile underneath. Good complexity, well-integrated acidity, citrus-mineral finish, plus some apricot, long-lasting, fresh with finesse, secure ageing potential.

95 Riesling * Zöbing Ried Heiligenstein 1ÖTW 2019

95 Riesling * Ried Gaisberg 1ÖTW 2021
13,5 Vol.-%, cork, large wooden barrel, €€€€ V

94 Riesling * Ried Gaisberg 1ÖTW 2020
94 Riesling * Ried Gaisberg 1ÖTW 2020

93 Riesling * Zöbing 2022
13 Vol.-%, cork, large wooden barrel, €€€ V
92 Riesling * Zöbing 2021
92 Riesling * Zöbing 2020

94 Riesling Tradition 2018
94 Riesling Tradition 2017
93 Riesling Tradition 2016

97 Grüner Veltliner * Ried Lamm 1ÖTW 2021
13,5 Vol.-%, cork, large wooden barrel, €€€€€ V
95 Grüner Veltliner * Ried Lamm 1ÖTW 2020

© Schloss Gobelsburg

KAMPTAL DAC

WEINGUT SCHLOSS GOBELSBURG
3550 Gobelsburg
Schloss Straße 16
T: +43 (2734) 2422
schloss@gobelsburg.at
www.gobelsburg.at
Winemaker/Contact:
Michael Moosbrugger
Production: 10 % sparkling, 70 % white, 20 % red, 85 hectares
Certified: Sustainable Austria
Fairs: Austrian Tasting London, Foodex Japan, ProWein Düsseldorf, VieVinum, Vinexpo Shanghai
Distribution partners: AUS, BY, BE, RC, DK, DE, EST, FIN, FR, GR, UK, HK, IRL, IL, IT, JP, CDN, ROK, HR, LV, LT, LU, MV, NZ, NL, NO, RP, PL, PT, RUS, SE, CH, SGP, SK, ES, TH, CZ, TR, HU, USA, CY, UAE, PT

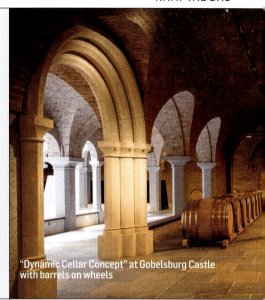

"Dynamic Cellar Concept" at Gobelsburg Castle with barrels on wheels

94 Grüner Veltliner * Ried Lamm 1ÖTW 2019

96 Grüner Veltliner * Ried Grub 1ÖTW 2021
13,5 Vol.-%, cork, large wooden barrel, €€€€€ ⓥ
96 Grüner Veltliner * Ried Grub 1ÖTW 2020
Bright golden yellow, silver glints. Delicate herbal notes, nuances of yellow fruit, hints of mango, a touch of lemon balm, and fig chutney. Juicy, good complexity, dark minerality, Golden Delicious apples, soft savoury wood nuances, fruit forward, and prolonged persistence. A lovely accompaniment to food with ageing potential.
94 Grüner Veltliner * Ried Grub 1ÖTW 2019

96 Grüner Veltliner * Ried Renner 1ÖTW 2021
13,5 Vol.-%, cork, large wooden barrel, €€€€€ ⓥ
94 Grüner Veltliner * Ried Renner 1ÖTW 2020
93 Grüner Veltliner * Ried Renner 1ÖTW 2019

(93) Grüner Veltliner * Ried Spiegel 2022
13,5 Vol.-%, cork, large wooden barrel, €€€€€ ⓥ
93 Grüner Veltliner ** Ried Spiegel 2021
92 Grüner Veltliner * Ried Spiegel 2018

(93) Grüner Veltliner * Ried Steinsetz 2022
13,5 Vol.-%, cork, large wooden barrel, €€€€ ⓥ
92 Grüner Veltliner * Ried Steinsetz 2021
92 Grüner Veltliner * Ried Steinsetz 2020

92 Grüner Veltliner * Langenlois 2022
13 Vol.-%, cork, large wooden barrel, €€€ ⓥ
92 Grüner Veltliner * Langenlois 2021
92 Grüner Veltliner * Langenlois 2020

93 Grüner Veltliner Tradition 2018
94 Grüner Veltliner Tradition 2017
93 Grüner Veltliner Tradition 2016

96 Tradition Heritage 10 years Edition 851 GV/RR
13 Vol.-%, cork, large wooden barrel, €€€€€ ⓥ
95 Tradition Heritage 10 years Edition 850 GV/RR

94 Tradition Heritage 3 years Edition 851 GV/RR
Medium golden yellow, silver reflections. Fine tobacco spice, a bit of mango, a touch of pear, candied orange zest, nutty nuances, blossom honey hints. Juicy, taut, multi-faceted acid structure, mineral salty, peach touch, powerful, lingers, versatile food wine with certain ageing potential.

93 Tradition Heritage 50 years RR/GV/GS/MO/WR

93 Pinot Noir Reserve 2019
92 Pinot Noir Reserve 2018
94 Pinot Noir Reserve 2017

92 St. Laurent Reserve 2019
92 St. Laurent Reserve 2017

92 Zweigelt Reserve 2019
91 Zweigelt Reserve 2018

* Kamptal DAC   ** Kamptal DAC Reserve

NIEDERÖSTERREICH/LOWER AUSTRIA

97 Grüner Veltliner TBA 2017
94 Grüner Veltliner Eiswein 2018
94 Grüner Veltliner Beerenauslese 2017
93 Grüner Veltliner Auslese 2017

97 Riesling Trockenbeerenauslese 2015
95 Riesling Beerenauslese 2017
94 Riesling Auslese 2017

★★★★★

WEINGUT HIRSCH

ORGANIC

In a 500 year old farmstead in the picturesque village of Kammern in Kamptal, the Hirsch family devotes all their passion to winemaking. The philosophy is: "the soil creates the wine," even more than the grape variety. The site determines the character of the wines. Hirsch wines are, therefore, always wines of origin. The renowned winemaker Johannes Hirsch focuses all his attention on the varieties Grüner Veltliner and Riesling. The unique sites, which Johannes Hirsch has farmed biodynamically for many years, are right on the doorstep of the charming winery. These include the well-known Riesling sites Zöbinger Heiligenstein-Rotfels and Zöbinger Gaisberg and the magnificent Veltliner sites Kammerner Lamm, Kammerner Grub and Kammerner Renner. Every year, these sites produce distinctive wines, full of power, taut minerality, finesse and suppleness, impressively and unmistakably reflecting the characteristics of the soil.

100 Riesling * Zöbing Ried Heiligenstein-Rotfels 1ÖTW 2021
13 Vol.-%, screwcap, steel tank/large wooden barrel, €€€€€ ⓑ

97 Riesling * Zöbing Ried Heiligenstein 1ÖTW 2021
13 Vol.-%, screwcap, steel tank/large wooden barrel, €€€€ ⓑ

96 Riesling * Zöbing Ried Heiligenstein 1ÖTW 2020
Bright medium greenish yellow. Fragrantly fine blossom honey, a little hint of meadow herbs, fresh orange zest, underlaid with a delicate mint note, a hint of papaya, and a mineral touch. Juicy, multifaceted, well-integrated acidity structure, with hints of peach on the finish and saffron nuanced reverberations marked by a reserved finish, remains persistent. A versatile style with good ageing potential.

97 Riesling * Ried Zöbinger Heiligenstein 1ÖTW 2019

96 Riesling * Zöbing Ried Gaisberg 1ÖTW 2021
13 Vol.-%, screwcap, steel tank/large wooden barrel, €€€€ ⓑ

95 Riesling * Zöbing Ried Gaisberg 1ÖTW 2020
Medium golden yellow, silver reflections. Delicate peach and herbs, a hint of passion fruit, fresh bouquet, kumquat and passion fruit hints. Juicy, tight-knit, racy acidity, mineral, pineapple hints, spicy finish, multi-layered finish, certain ageing potential.

95 Riesling * Ried Gaisberg 1ÖTW Zöbing 2019

93 Riesling * Zöbing 2022
12,5 Vol.-%, screwcap, steel tank, €€€€ ⓑ

92 Riesling * Zöbing 2021

Riesling

KAMPTAL DAC

WEINGUT HIRSCH
3493 Kammern
Hauptstraße 76
T: +43 (2735) 2460
info@weingut-hirsch.at
www.weingut-hirsch.at

Winemaker/Contact:
Johannes Hirsch
Production: 100 % white,
30 hectares
Fairs: ProWein Düsseldorf,
VieVinum
Distribution partners: AUS, BE, DK, DE, FR, UK, IT, JP, CDN, LV, LT, NZ, NL, NO, SE, CH, SK, TH, CZ, USA, CY

View towards Heiligenstein

90 Riesling * Zöbing 2020

96 Grüner Veltliner * Kammern Ried Renner 1ÖTW 2021
13 Vol.-%, screwcap, steel tank/large wooden barrel, €€€€€ ⓑ

93 Grüner Veltliner * Kammern Ried Renner 1ÖTW 2020

94 Grüner Veltliner * Ried Renner 1ÖTW Kammern 2019

95 Grüner Veltliner * Kammern Ried Lamm 1ÖTW 2021
13 Vol.-%, screwcap, steel tank/large wooden barrel, €€€€€ ⓑ

97 Grüner Veltliner * Kammern Ried Lamm 1ÖTW 2020
Medium greenish yellow. Delicately scented tobacco whiffs, slightly smoky, white stone fruit, a hint of quince, and meadow herbs. Compact bouquet. Good complexity, multilayered, expressive papaya nuances, orange touch, multifaceted acidity, marked by saline-minerality. Compellingly persistent, excellent potential.

99 Grüner Veltliner * Ried Lamm 1ÖTW Kammern 2019

95 Grüner Veltliner * Kammern Ried Gaisberg 1ÖTW 2021
13 Vol.-%, screwcap, steel tank/large wooden barrel, €€€€€ ⓑ

95 Grüner Veltliner * Kammern Ried Gaisberg 1ÖTW 2020

94 Grüner Veltliner * Ried Gaisberg 1ÖTW Kammern 2019

95 Grüner Veltliner * Kammern Ried Grub 1ÖTW 2021
13 Vol.-%, screwcap, steel tank/large wooden barrel, €€€€€ ⓑ

94 Grüner Veltliner * Kammern Ried Grub 1ÖTW 2020

96 Grüner Veltliner * Ried Grub 1ÖTW Kammern 2019

92 Grüner Veltliner * Kammern 2022
12,5 Vol.-%, screwcap, steel tank, €€€€ ⓑ

92 Grüner Veltliner * Kammern 2021

91 Grüner Veltliner * Kammern 2020

90 Grüner Veltliner * Hirschvergnügen 2022
11,5 Vol.-%, screwcap, steel tank, €€€ ⓑ

91 Grüner Veltliner * Hirschvergnügen 2021

91 Grüner Veltliner * Hirschvergnügen 2020

92 Riesling Hirschin 2018

92 Riesling Hirschin 2017

92 Riesling Hirschin 2015

* Kamptal DAC   ** Kamptal DAC Reserve

NIEDERÖSTERREICH/LOWER AUSTRIA

★★★★

WEINGUT JURTSCHITSCH
ORGANIC

The Jurtschitsch family's traditional winery, with its 16th century vineyard and 700-year-old natural underground cellar, is one of the most charming wineries in Austria. Alwin and Stefanie Jurtschitsch cultivate their vines and wines with great passion and sensitivity. Out of conviction and affinity with nature, they decided in 2006 to attain organic certification for the winery. The conversion of their vineyards was accompanied by a fundamentally new approach to winemaking. The single-vineyard wines are fermented in large wooden barrels with wild yeasts from the vineyard.

The old cellar vaults, which were revitalised in 2016, provide optimal conditions for the wines from the best sites in the Kamptal: Zöbinger Heiligenstein, Loiserberg, Dechant, Schenkenbichl, Käferberg, Lamm and Tanzer. Few other Austrian wineries are able to offer such consistent quality across the entire range. Over the years, milestones have also been set for the region's red and sweet wines. Its uncompromising commitment to quality has been rewarded with numerous national and international awards. The "GrüVe®" is a bestseller in restaurants and specialist shops. This youthful, elegantly light Grüner Veltliner, with its label by Christian Ludwig Attersee, has outlasted many wine fads and fashionable wines at home and abroad.

Those who miss one or the other site wine in this year's ratings will have to be patient. Stefanie and Alwin Jurtschitsch have decided to release their best wines fashionably late.

94 ❂ Grüner Veltliner Brut Nature Sekt Austria Grosse Reserve g.U. Niederösterreich 2018
94 ❂ Grüner Veltliner Sekt Austria Große Reserve brut nature Niederösterreich g.U. Langenlois 2017
93 ❂ Jurtschitsch Grüner Veltliner Brut Nature Sekt g.U. Langenlois Große Reserve 2016

92 ❂ Brut Rosé Klassik ZW/SL/PN

95 Grüner Veltliner * Ried Lamm 1ÖTW 2021
13 Vol.-%, cork, large wooden barrel, €€€€ Ⓑ
96 Grüner Veltliner * Ried Lamm 1ÖTW 2020
Medium yellow-green with silver reflections. Delicately savoury tobacco underlies notes of pineapple and mango, and fine blossom honey with orange zest in the background. Elegant and full-bodied on the palate, there is pronounced fine fruit, ripe yellow apple, rich finesse to the acidity and delicate blossom honey on the finish. This has very good length and ageing potential.
96 Grüner Veltliner * Ried Lamm 1ÖTW 2019

94 Grüner Veltliner * Ried Käferberg 1ÖTW 2021
13 Vol.-%, cork, large wooden barrel, €€€€ Ⓑ
95 Grüner Veltliner * Ried Käferberg 1ÖTW 2020
95 Grüner Veltliner * Ried Käferberg 1ÖTW 2019

94 Grüner Veltliner * Ried Schenkenbichl 1ÖTW 2021
13 Vol.-%, cork, large wooden barrel, €€€€ Ⓑ
94 Grüner Veltliner * Ried Schenkenbichl 1ÖTW 2020
94 Grüner Veltliner * Ried Schenkenbichl 1ÖTW 2019

93 Grüner Veltliner * Ried Dechant 1ÖTW 2021
13 Vol.-%, cork, large wooden barrel, €€€€ Ⓑ
94 Grüner Veltliner * Ried Dechant 1ÖTW 2020
93 Grüner Veltliner * Ried Dechant 1ÖTW 2019

93 Grüner Veltliner * Langenlois 2022
12,5 Vol.-%, screwcap, large wooden barrel, €€€ Ⓑ
92 Grüner Veltliner * Langenlois 2020
92 Grüner Veltliner * Langenlois 2019

92 Grüner Veltliner * Ried Loiserberg 1ÖTW 2021
92 Grüner Veltliner * Ried Loiserberg 1ÖTW 2020
93 Grüner Veltliner * Ried Loiserberg 1ÖTW 2019

© www.pov.at

KAMPTAL DAC

WEINGUT JURTSCHITSCH
3550 Langenlois
Rudolfstraße 39
T: +43 (2734) 2116
weingut@jurtschitsch.com
www.jurtschitsch.com

Winemaker: Stefanie Jurtschitsch
Contact: Alwin Jurtschitsch
Production: 74 % white, 25 % red, 1 % sweet, 60 hectares
Certified: Sustainable Austria
Fairs: Millésime Bio, ProWein Düsseldorf, VieVinum
Distribution partners: DK

Stefanie and Alwin Jurtschitsch

92 Grüner Veltliner * Löss 2022
12,5 Vol.-%, screwcap, steel tank, €€€ B
91 Grüner Veltliner * Löss 2021
91 Grüner Veltliner * Löss 2020

92 Grüner Veltliner * Urgestein 2022
12,5 Vol.-%, screwcap, steel tank, €€€ B
91 Grüner Veltliner * Stein 2021
90 Grüner Veltliner * Stein 2020

91 Grüner Veltliner Belle Naturelle 2020
92 Grüner Veltliner Belle Naturelle 2019
91 Grüner Veltliner Belle Naturelle 2018

95 Riesling * Ried Heiligenstein 1ÖTW
     Alte Reben 2021
13 Vol.-%, cork, large wooden barrel, €€€€€ B
96 Riesling * Ried Heiligenstein 1ÖTW
     Alte Reben 2020
Medium lemon-green with silver reflections. Attractive ripe yellow fruit nuances of pineapple and peach, with a whisper of apricot in the background, and a mineral touch. Tight and close-knit, with delicate blossom honey, white apple, and lemony nuances on the finish, it is lively and long lasting. It should be allowed to mature for some years yet.
97 Riesling * Ried Heiligenstein 1ÖTW
     Alte Reben 2019

94 Riesling * Ried Heiligenstein 1ÖTW 2021
94 Riesling * Ried Heiligenstein 1ÖTW 2020
95 Riesling * Ried Heiligenstein 1ÖTW 2019

93 Riesling * Ried Loiserberg 1ÖTW 2021
93 Riesling * Ried Loiserberg 1ÖTW 2020
94 Riesling * Ried Loiserberg 1ÖTW 2019

92 Riesling * Langenlois 2022
12,5 Vol.-%, screwcap, large wooden barrel, €€€€ B
92 Riesling * Langenlois 2020
92 Riesling * Langenlois 2019

92 Riesling Platin 2022
12 Vol.-%, screwcap, steel tank, €€€ B

92 Zweigelt Tanzer Reserve 2017
91 Zweigelt Ried Tanzer Reserve 2016

98 Grüner Veltliner Ried Spiegel TBA 2017

95 Grüner Veltliner Ried Spiegel
     Beerenauslese 2019

95 Grüner Veltliner Eiswein 2017

92 Grüner Veltliner Ried Spiegel Auslese 2018

97 Riesling Ried Loiserberg TBA 2018

97 Riesling Ried Heiligenstein
     Beerenauslese 2018

93 Riesling Ried Loiserberg Spätlese 2019

* Kamptal DAC   ** Kamptal DAC Reserve

NIEDERÖSTERREICH/LOWER AUSTRIA

LAURENZ V.

In the wine industry, everyone has their own story. Ours is that we have contributed to making Grüner Veltliner internationally renowned" - this is how LAURENZ V associates himself with the Austrian flagship grape variety. The declared goal is to establish Grüner Veltliner internationally, among the best white wines in the world.

LAURENZ V. only produces Grüner Veltliner - fruity, elegant, complex and with an animating drinking flow. In addition to the very approachable wine style, interesting names also provide a contemporary "twist": The "Charming" Grüner Veltliner is the flagship wine of LAURENZ V. (Kamptal Reserve), the "Friendly" Grüner Veltliner - the classic from Kamptal (Kamptal DAC). With "Singing" and "Forbidden Grüner" is a range of wines which are produced for everyday drinking. In the best years, "L5", a selection from the Ried Zöbinger Gaisberg, is produced from hand-picked grapes and aged for 24 months in French oak. The winery produces the full stylistic range of Grüner Veltliner, taking into account the whole variety of tastes provided by the grape variety. Today, LAURENZ V. exports to more than 40 countries on all five continents, markets about 80 hectares of Grüner Veltliner and stands for elegant, well-balanced and complex wines that are meant to live up to the winery's motto: "Strictly Grüner & Sheer Drinking Pleasure".

**92 Grüner Veltliner ** Charming
by Laurenz V. 2021**
Medium greenish yellow in colour with silver reflections. Aromas of ripe tropical fruit, some herbs, a hint of guava, delicate lemon balm and apple. The medium-bodied palate is balanced, with fine acidity, minerality, and a touch of mango on the delicately spicy finish. A good food wine.

**92 Grüner Veltliner ** Charming
by Laurenz V. 2020**

**92 Grüner Veltliner * Charming
by Laurenz V. 2019**

92 Grüner Veltliner * Zöbing Ried Grub 2021
13 Vol.-%, screwcap, steel tank, €€€€€

92 Grüner Veltliner L5 by Laurenz V. 2020
13 Vol.-%, screwcap, barrique, €€€€€

**(91) Grüner Veltliner * Langenlois Friendly
by Laurenz V. 2022**
12,5 Vol.-%, screwcap, steel tank, €€€

**91 Grüner Veltliner * Langenlois Friendly
by Laurenz V. 2021**

**91 Grüner Veltliner * Friendly
by Laurenz V. 2020**

**90 Grüner Veltliner * Singing
by Laurenz V. 2022**
12 Vol.-%, screwcap, steel tank, €€

**90 Grüner Veltliner * Singing
by Laurenz V. 2021**

**90 Grüner Veltliner * Singing
by Laurenz V. 2020**

**90 Grüner Veltliner Forbidden
by Laurenz V. 2022**
11 Vol.-%, screwcap, steel tank, €€ Ⓥ

**90 Grüner Veltliner Forbidden
by Laurenz V. 2021**

**89 Grüner Veltliner Forbidden
by Laurenz V. 2020**

LAURENZ V.
1070 Wien/Zöbing, Mariahilfer Straße 32
T: +43 (1) 5224791, info@laurenzfive.com
www.laurenzfive.com
Winemaker: Peter Schweiger
Contact: Dieter Hübler
Production: 100 % white
Certified: Sustainable Austria
Fairs: Austrian Tasting London, Merano WineFestival, ProWein Düsseldorf, London Wine Fair, The Shanghai International Wine & Spirits Expo, VieVinum, Vinexpo Bordeaux, Vinexpo Hongkong, Vinexpo Shanghai, ProWine China, ProWine Asia, MondoVino, Hong Kong International Wine & Spirits Fair
Distribution partners: AUS, BE, BG, RC, DK, DE, EST, FIN, UK, HK, JP, CDN, LV, LT, LU, MAL, MT, NL, NO, RP, SE, CH, SGP, SK, TH, CZ, TR, UA, HU, USA

WEINGUT LEINDL

Weingut Leindl in Zöbing in the Kamptal is a young, dynamic business. During his 20 years of work as an oenologist in research, teaching and consulting, Georg Leindl's desire to vinify his own wines grew, which he put into practice by founding the winery in 2013.

The main focus is on Grüner Veltliner and Riesling and in particularly good vintages, a wine from the Viognier grape variety is also made. The vineyards are located in the Kamptal and the wines are accordingly characterised by the terroir of the vineyards. The soils give the wines their minerality and freshness.

(95) Riesling * Zöbing Ried Heiligenstein 1ÖTW 2022
13 Vol.-%, cork, large wooden barrel, €€€€€

94 Riesling * Zöbing Ried Heiligenstein 1ÖTW 2021
Light greenish yellow. Fine notes of passion fruit, a bit of white peach, delicate orange zest, fresh bouquet, floral touch. Juicy, taut, well-integrated acid structure, mineral, light tropical fruit on the finish, lemony aftertaste, powerful food companion.

94 Riesling * Zöbing Ried Heiligenstein 1ÖTW 2020

(94) Riesling * Zöbing Ried Kogelberg 1ÖTW 2022
13 Vol.-%, cork, large wooden barrel, €€€€

94 Riesling * Zöbing Ried Kogelberg 1ÖTW 2021

94 Riesling * Zöbinger Ried Kogelberg 1ÖTW 2020

92 Riesling * Stieferner Ried Irbling 2020
92 Riesling * Ried Irbling 2019
92 Riesling * Ried Stiefener Irbling 2018

(94) Grüner Veltliner * Langenlois Ried Seeberg 1ÖTW 2022
13 Vol.-%, cork, large wooden barrel, €€€€€

93 Grüner Veltliner * Langenlois Ried Seeberg 1ÖTW 2021
Bright yellow green, silver reflections. Inviting bouquet of passion fruit, hints of tropical fruit, citrus zest, meadow herb touch. Juicy, elegant, fine acid structure, good spice, yellow apple fruit, powerful finish, versatile.

92 Grüner Veltliner * Ried Seeberg 1ÖTW 2020

93 Grüner Veltliner * Langenlois Ried Eichelberg 2022
13 Vol.-%, screwcap, large wooden barrel, €€€€

93 Grüner Veltliner * Langenlois Ried Eichelberg 2021

92 Grüner Veltliner * Ried Eichelberg 2020

91 Grüner Veltliner * Langenlois 2022
12,5 Vol.-%, screwcap, steel tank, €€

90 Grüner Veltliner * Langenlois 2021

91 Grüner Veltliner * Langenlois 2020

94 Viognier 2021
15 Vol.-%, cork, barrique, €€€€€

93 Viognier 2019

93 Viognier 2018

WEINGUT LEINDL
3561 Zöbing
Am Wechselberg 12
T: +43 (676) 5082313
info@weingutleindl.at
www.weingutleindl.at

Winemaker/Contact:
Georg Leindl
Production: 8 hectares
Fairs: ProWein Düsseldorf, VieVinum, Vinobile Montfort
Distribution partners: DK, CZ, USA

* Kamptal DAC   ** Kamptal DAC Reserve

NIEDERÖSTERREICH/LOWER AUSTRIA

★★★★
WEINGUT FRED LOIMER
ORGANIC

Authentic wines are always characterised by their origin - and they convey a message. Fred Loimer's wines express origin, the power of nature, and the respectful handling of the soil, plants, animals, and people. His strategic concept is based on the idea of running the winery as a "closed operating organism" that generates as many elements of the agricultural production cycle as possible, independently.

The result is pure origin: unique wines, shaped by their place of origin, dominated by nature's biological rhythms, created with patience, precision, and minimal intervention, unique, sometimes controversial - but always authentic.

95 ⊕ Loimer Langenlois Große Reserve Blanc de Blancs Brut Nature 2014 CH/WB/PG
12 Vol.-%, DIAM, bottle fermentation, €€€€€€ Ⓑ

95 ⊕ Langenlois Große Reserve Blanc de Blancs Brut Nature 2016 CH/WB/PG

95 ⊕ Gumpoldskirchen Große Reserve Blanc de Noirs brut nature 2016

94 ⊕ Loimer Langenlois Blanc de Blancs Sekt g.U. extra brut Große Reserve 2017 CH/WB/PG
12 Vol.-%, DIAM, bottle fermentation, €€€€€€ Ⓑ

94 ⊕ Loimer Langenlois Blanc de Blancs Sekt g.U. extra brut Große Reserve 2014 CH/WB/PG

93 ⊕ Loimer Extra Brut Reserve ZW/PN/CH/SL
12 Vol.-%, DIAM, bottle fermentation, €€€€€ Ⓑ

92 ⊕ Extra Brut Reserve ZW/PN/CH/SL

93 ⊕ Loimer Brut Rosé Reserve ZW/PN/SL
12 Vol.-%, DIAM, bottle fermentation, €€€€€ Ⓑ

92 ⊕ Brut Rosé Reserve ZW/PN/SL

(95) Riesling * Zöbing Ried Heiligenstein 1ÖTW 2021
13,5 Vol.-%, cork, large wooden barrel, €€€€€€ Ⓑ

96 Riesling * Zöbing Ried Heiligenstein 1ÖTW 2020
Bright golden yellow, silver glints. Subtle tobacco-herbal notes, an appealing bouquet of yellow peach, and subtle hints of candied calamansi with resonating guava nuances. Complex, mineral, mango notes with citrus nuances on the finish,

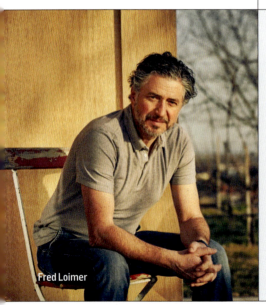
Fred Loimer

WEINGUT FRED LOIMER
3550 Langenlois
Haindorfer Vögelweg 23
T: +43 (2734) 2239
weingut@loimer.at
www.loimer.at

Winemaker/Contact:
Fred Loimer
Production: 15 % sparkling, 80 % white, 5 % red, 80 hectares
Certified: Sustainable Austria Ⓐ
Fairs: Millésime Bio, ProWein Düsseldorf, VieVinum
Distribution partners: AUS, BY, BE, RC, DK, DE, EST, FIN, FR, GR, UK, HK, IL, IT, JP, CDN, ROK, HR, LV, LT, LU, NL, NO, PE, RP, PL, PT, RO, RUS, SE, CH, SGP, SK, ES, TH, CZ, TR, UA, HU, USA, UAE, PT

KAMPTAL DAC

and prolonged persistence. A lovely multilayered accompaniment to food, with secure potential for development.

95 Riesling * Ried Heiligenstein 1ÖTW Zöbing 2019

(95) Riesling * Langenlois Ried Steinmassl 1ÖTW 2021
12,5 Vol.-%, cork, steel tank, €€€€€ Ⓑ Ⓥ

95 Riesling * Langenlois Ried Steinmassl 1ÖTW 2020

94 Riesling * Langenlois Ried Steinmassl 1ÖTW 2019

(94) Riesling * Ried Loiserberg 1ÖTW 2021
12,5 Vol.-%, screwcap, steel tank, €€€€ Ⓑ

93 Riesling * Ried Loiserberg 1ÖTW 2020
93 Riesling * Ried Loiserberg 1ÖTW 2019

91 Riesling * Langenlois 2022
12,5 Vol.-%, screwcap, steel tank, €€€ Ⓑ Ⓥ

91 Riesling * Langenlois 2021
92 Riesling * Langenlois 2020

(95) Grüner Veltliner * Langenlois Ried Käferberg 1ÖTW 2021
13,5 Vol.-%, cork, wooden barrel, €€€€€ Ⓑ

95 Grüner Veltliner * Langenlois Ried Käferberg 1ÖTW 2020
Medium yellow-green, silver glints. Subtle smoky savouriness, a hint of guava, dark minerality, luscious apples, and orange nuances. Juicy, good complexity, elegant, multifaceted acidity structure, white stone fruit, and persistent. A versatile food companion with potential.

94 Grüner Veltliner * Langenlois Ried Käferberg 1ÖTW 2019

93 Grüner Veltliner * Ried Loiserberg 1ÖTW 2021
13 Vol.-%, screwcap, steel tank, €€€€€ Ⓑ Ⓥ

93 Grüner Veltliner * Langenlois Ried Loiserberg 1ÖTW 2020

93 Grüner Veltliner * Ried Loiserberg 1ÖTW Langenlois 2019

92 Grüner Veltliner * Langenlois 2022
12,5 Vol.-%, screwcap, steel tank, €€€€ Ⓑ Ⓥ

91 Grüner Veltliner * Langenlois 2021
92 Grüner Veltliner * Langenlois 2020

94 Pinot Noir Dechant Langenlois 2021
12 Vol.-%, cork, oak barrel, €€€€€€ Ⓑ

93 Pinot Noir Langenlois Dechant 2020
95 Pinot Noir Dechant Langenlois 2019

(95) Pinot Noir Anning Gumpoldskirchen 2021
12 Vol.-%, cork, oak barrel, €€€€€€ Ⓑ

93 Pinot Noir Gumpoldskirchen Anning 2020
94 Pinot Noir Gumpoldskrichen Anning 2019

WEINGUT CHRISTIAN NASTL

Anyone who comes across the mighty, 150-year-old wooden press at the Nastl Heurigen immediately realises that viticulture has a long tradition in this family business - with the emphasis on the word "family". Today, Christian Nastl, together with his parents Renate and Günter Nastl and his siblings Alexander and Petra, are entrusted with the family estate. The family's winemaking history continues unabated.

In the unique microclimate of the Kamptal, the distinctive Nastl wines mature. Whether "VelKam" (VELtliner from the KAMptal), as the light, fruity regional representatives are called, or the local/village wines of Veltliner and Riesling, or the extraordinary Veltliner from the single vineyards of Kittmannsberg, Käferberg and Steinmassl: there is a suitable companion for every occasion.

"Enjoyment at every level" is the motto of the wine-growing family. This is taken quite literally in the three-storey wine cellar: Level one is accessed through the traditional cellar entrance in the Kühsteingraben cellar lane. It includes a hall with stainless steel tanks and connecting corridors to the 300-year-old wooden barrel cellar and Vinotheque.

The gently working press is on the second floor, after which the grapes are transferred to the third floor.

All operations are carried out by gravity flow. From here, you have a breathtaking view over the best vineyards of Langenlois, such as Loiserberg, Steinhaus, Steinmassl or Käferberg.

* Kamptal DAC   ** Kamptal DAC Reserve

NIEDERÖSTERREICH/LOWER AUSTRIA

Zweigelt

WEINGUT CHRISTIAN NASTL
3550 Langenlois
Gartenzeile 17
T: +43 (2734) 2903
office@nastl.at
www.nastl.at

Winemaker/Contact:
Christian Nastl
Production: 1 % sparkling, 85 % white, 3 % rosé, 10 % red, 1 % sweet, 12+3 hectares
Certified: Sustainable Austria
Fairs: Austrian Tasting London, ProWein Düsseldorf, VieVinum, DAC-Presentations
Distribution partners: DK, DE, UK, CDN, NL, NO, RUS, SE, CZ, USA

The Grüner Veltliner, Riesling, and Zweigelt varietals are in a designated area called ‚Reservebereich' and belong to the category known in-house as "Gigant", meaning giant. These are wines of particular expression and pronounced volume. Produced only in years when the conditions for grape ripening are perfect, they are characterised by a rich structure, acidity, sweetness and a long finish. These ‚giants' are a valuable investment with long-term ageing potential. With each year of ageing, they reveal new flavour components.

91 ❂ Riesling Sekt Brut
12,5 Vol.-%, cork, bottle fermentation, €€€€
91 ❂ Riesling Sekt brut 2019

93 Grüner Veltliner * Ried Liss Gigant 2020
13 Vol.-%, screwcap, large wooden barrel, €€€€€
92 Grüner Veltliner ** Ried Liss Gigant 2019
92 Grüner Veltliner * Ried Liss Gigant 2019

93 Grüner Veltliner * Ried Steinmassl 2021
13,5 Vol.-%, screwcap, steel tank, €€€
90 Grüner Veltliner * Ried Steinmassl 2020
91 Grüner Veltliner * Ried Steinmassl 2019

(92) Grüner Veltliner * Ried Käferberg 2022
13,5 Vol.-%, screwcap, large wooden barrel, €€€

92 Grüner Veltliner * Ried Kittmannsberg 2021
92 Grüner Veltliner * Ried Kittmannsberg 2020

91 Grüner Veltliner * Ried Kittmannsberg 2018

90 Grüner Veltliner * Langenlois 2022
12,5 Vol.-%, screwcap, steel tank, €€
89 Grüner Veltliner * Langenlois 2021
89 Grüner Veltliner * Langenlois 2019

93 Riesling * Ried Steinmassl Gigant 2021
Pale yellow-green, silver reflections. Fine herbal citrus notes, a hint of peach, a touch of lemon balm, floral touch, underlaid with blossom honey. Juicy, elegant, tightly meshed, dark mineral, white stone fruit, remains well lasting, a versatile food companion.

93 Riesling * Ried Steinmassl Gigant 2020
92 Riesling ** Ried Steinmassl Gigant 2017

91 Zweigelt Reserve Gigant 2020
13,5 Vol.-%, screwcap, used barriques, €€€€€
90 Zweigelt Reserve Ried Ladner Gigant 2017

WEINGUT RUDOLF RABL

Rudi Rabl prides himself on the traditional history of his family winery, which dates back to 1750. Originally run as a mixed farm, the family business has now developed into a winery covering 80 hectares and cultivating vineyards in the best Kamptaler Rieden (sites). With Johanna and Tobias, the next generation is already training to be winemakers and oenologists. The love for nature and the grapes, the ecological vineyard work with herbal plants as well as the knowledge of professional processing ensure excellent quality of the different wine varieties. In the cellar, modernity is combined with traditional values. Ecology is an important factor, which is why the winery has been "Sustainable Austria" certified since 2015.

One of the most important awards in recent years was undoubtedly the title of "White Wine Maker of the Year 2019" at the IWSC in London, a title that Rudi Rabl was also able to achieve in 2021. Other successes include the two Decanter Trophies "Winner Grüner Veltliner Dechant Alte Reben" and "Winner Riesling Ried Steinhaus Rote Erde", as well as the 2017 regional victories in the Riesling and Sauvignon Blanc categories. The winery is also continuously represented with its wines in the "SALON Österreich Wein". And ultimately, the winery was awarded "Winery of the Year - Langenlois Champion" in the Kamptal.

94 Riesling ** Ried Schenkenbichl Alte Reben 2021
13 Vol.-%, screwcap, steel tank, €€€€

93 Riesling ** Ried Schenkenbichl Alte Reben 2020

92 Riesling ** Ried Schenkenbichl Alte Reben 2019

93 Riesling ** Ried Steinhaus Rote Erde 2021
13 Vol.-%, screwcap, steel tank, €€€€

94 Riesling ** Ried Steinhaus Rote Erde 2020
Medium greenish yellow, silver reflections. Fine mango notes, deliacte papaya, a bit of honey blossom, clementine zest, pineapple notes. Juicy, good complexity, mineral-salty, sweet tropical fruit, apricots on the finish, citrus in the aftertaste, complex food companion, certain ageing potential.

93 Riesling ** Ried Steinhaus Rote Erde 2019

WEINGUT RUDOLF RABL
3550 Langenlois
Weraingraben 10
T: +43 (2734) 2303
office@weingut-rabl.at
www.weingut-rabl.at

Winemaker/Contact:
Rudolf Rabl
Production: 68 % white, 30 % red, 2 % sweet, 80 hectares
Certified: Sustainable Austria
Fairs: ProWein Düsseldorf, VieVinum
Distribution partners: AUS, BY, BE, BG, RC, DK, DE, EST, FIN, FR, UK, IRL, IT, CDN, LV, LT, LU, NL, NO, RP, PT, RUS, SE, CH, SGP, SK, TH, CZ, HU, USA

Ried Spiegel

*Kamptal DAC   **Kamptal DAC Reserve

NIEDERÖSTERREICH/LOWER AUSTRIA

Grüner Veltliner

91 Riesling * Steinberg 2022
13 Vol.-%, screwcap, steel tank, €€€
92 Riesling * Steinberg 2021
92 Riesling * Steinberg 2020

91 Riesling * Langenlois 2022
12,5 Vol.-%, screwcap, steel tank, €€
91 Riesling * Langenlois 2021
91 Riesling * Langenlois 2020

89 Riesling * Terrassen 2022
12 Vol.-%, screwcap, steel tank, €€
90 Riesling * Terrassen 2021
89 Riesling * Terrassen 2020

94 Grüner Veltliner ** Ried Käferberg Alte Reben 2021
14 Vol.-%, screwcap, wooden barrel, €€€€
92 Grüner Veltliner ** Ried Käferberg Alte Reben 2020
93 Grüner Veltliner ** Ried Käferberg Alte Reben 2019

93 Grüner Veltliner ** Ried Loiserberg Alte Reben 2021
14 Vol.-%, screwcap, wooden barrel, €€€€
93 Grüner Veltliner ** Ried Loiserberg Alte Reben 2020
Bright golden yellow, silver reflections. Some gunpowder and ripe passion fruit, a touch of quince, floral touch, mineral, pear notes. Juicy, elegant, good complexity, salty, powerful, a bit of papaya, substantial finish, savoury aftertaste, versatile.

93 Grüner Veltliner ** Ried Loiserberg Alte Reben 2019

93 Grüner Veltliner ** Ried Dechant Alte Reben 2021
14,5 Vol.-%, screwcap, wooden barrel, €€€€
93 Grüner Veltliner ** Ried Dechant Alte Reben 2020
93 Grüner Veltliner ** Ried Dechant Alte Reben 2019

92 Grüner Veltliner * Ried Spiegel 2021
32 Grüner Veltliner * Ried Spiegel 2020
92 Grüner Veltliner * Ried Spiegel 2019

92 Grüner Veltliner * Ried Kittmansberg 2022
13,5 Vol.-%, screwcap, steel tank, €€€
92 Grüner Veltliner * Ried Kittmansberg 2021
91 Grüner Veltliner * Ried Kittmansberg 2020

91 Grüner Veltliner * Ried Panzaun 2022
13,5 Vol.-%, screwcap, steel tank, €€€
91 Grüner Veltliner * Ried Panzaun 2021
90 Grüner Veltliner * Ried Panzaun 2020

90 Grüner Veltliner * Vinum Optimum 2022
13 Vol.-%, screwcap, steel tank, €€
91 Grüner Veltliner * Vinum Optimum 2021
90 Grüner Veltliner * Vinum Optimum 2020

90 Grüner Veltliner * Langenlois 2022
12,5 Vol.-%, screwcap, steel tank, €€
90 Grüner Veltliner * Langenlois 2021
90 Grüner Veltliner * Langenlois 2020

89 Grüner Veltliner * Terrassen 2022
12,5 Vol.-%, screwcap, steel tank, €€
89 Grüner Veltliner * Terrassen 2021
89 Grüner Veltliner * Terrassen 2020

KAMPTAL DAC

WINZERHOF SAX
3550 Langenlois
Walterstraße 16
T: +43 (2734) 2349
office@winzersax.at
www.winzersax.at

Winemaker: Rudolf Sax
Contact: Michael Sax
Production: 240,000 bottles
5 % sparkling, 75 % white, 5 % rosé, 10 % red, 5 % sweet, 30 hectares
Fairs: ProWein Düsseldorf, VieVinum
Distribution partners: DK, DE, UK, IL, JP, NL, RUS, CH, SK, CZ, USA

Michael & Rudolf Sax

★★

WINZERHOF SAX

The Sax family has been an integral part in Austrian winemaking history since 1660. Under the term "vinification", the twin brothers Sax understand the passion to press varietal, vintage and regionally typical wines that reflect the climate and soil of Kamptal. A high degree of sunshine hours and cool nights ensure wines of high quality and fruit intensity. The estates best vineyards are Steinhaus, Steinmassl, Schenkenbichl, Spiegel and Panzaun, which are also among the most renowned vineyards of Kamptal. The aim is to take yield-regulating measures as early as the pruning stage, which are adapted to the different varieties. The main focus is traditionally on Grüner Veltliner and Riesling. Due to the different taste ideals, customers are now offered five varieties of Grüner Veltliner: From the light Grüner Veltliner "Luftikus" to the Grüner Veltliner "Panzaun", the Sax twins offer the right taste for every palate. With their own line, the youngest generation of vintners have already won many a prize in international competitions. The aim of the twins is to press wines from the ripest grapes of the Pinot line, which has caused an internationally sensation due to their charm. These wines are very balanced and elegant, above all due to their adequate maturation in small wooden barrels, which offer gentle nutty and wonderfully creamy aromas.

93 Riesling ** Ried Käferberg 2021
13,5 Vol.-%, screwcap, steel tank, €€€

91 Riesling ** Ried Käferberg 2020
Medium yellow-green, silver reflections. Floral touch, a touch of mango and pineapple, soft notes of vanilla, meadow herbs sound. Juicy, elegant, tropical fruit, spicy, slightly creamy texture, lemony finish, individual.

92 Riesling ** Ried Käferberg 2019

93 Riesling ** Ried Loiserberg 2021
13,5 Vol.-%, screwcap, steel tank, €€€

91 Riesling ** Ried Loiserberg 2020

91 Riesling ** Ried Loiserberg 2019

91 Riesling ** Ried Steinmassl 2020

92 Riesling ** Ried Steinmassl 2019

92 Grüner Veltliner Un.konventionell 2021
12,5 Vol.-%, cork, steel tank, €€€€€ ◯

92 Grüner Veltliner ** Ried Thal 2021
13,5 Vol.-%, screwcap, 500-l-barrel, €€€€

* Kamptal DAC   ** Kamptal DAC Reserve

NIEDERÖSTERREICH/LOWER AUSTRIA

91 Grüner Veltliner ** Ried Panzaun 2021
13,5 Vol.-%, screwcap, steel tank, €€€
90 Grüner Veltliner ** Ried Paznaun 2018

90 Grüner Veltliner * Zwillingslauser 2021
90 Grüner Veltliner * Zwillingslauser 2020

WEINGUT SCHMID

Weingut Schmid is located in Gobelsburg in the Kamptal winegrowing region. Fertile, lime-rich loess and gravel soils that date back to the Tertiary Period characterise the wines here in a distinctive way. Precise manual work with the use of modern, as well as traditional methods of vinification, guarantee the high quality of the estate's wines. The certifications "Sustainable Austria" and "VEGAN" document the responsible use of resources. In addition, wine connoisseur tours are offered. A hike through the vineyards in Gobelsburg ends with a snack and convivial get-together at the winery - in keeping with the motto: "Von der Traube bis zum Wein in der Flasche", which literally translates as the process from grape to the wine in the bottle. The southern Kamptal with its mild climate offers the best conditions for high-quality wines. The family's oldest vines thrive on the fertile, lime-rich loess soils of the Spiegel vineyard and on the gravelly soils of the Haid vineyard, guaranteeing exceptional DAC wines.

89 Grüner Veltliner ** Alte Reben 2020

92 Chardonnay Barrique Saxess XIII 2021
13,5 Vol.-%, cork, barrique, €€€€

90 🍷 Pinot Noir Rosé Vintage extra brut 2020
13 Vol.-%, DIAM, bottle fermentation/bottle maturation, €€€€ V

92 Riesling ** Ried Haid 2021
13 Vol.-%, screwcap, steel tank, €€€€ V

90 Riesling * Langenlois Ried Loiser Berg 2020

89 Riesling * Gobelsburg 2022
12 Vol.-%, screwcap, steel tank, €€ V
89 Riesling * Gobelsburg 2019
89 Riesling * Gobelsburg 2018

91 Grüner Veltliner ** Ried Haid 2021
91 Grüner Veltliner ** Gobelsburg Ried Haid 2019
Bright golden-yellow, green reflections. Delicate floral honey scent, ripe tropical fruit, a hint of orange zest and apricot. Juicy fruit, powerful, mango notes, salty, a touch of honey on the finish; already easy to drink, a likeable food companion.

90 Grüner Veltliner ** Ried Haid 2017

90 Grüner Veltliner * Ried Spiegel 2021
14,5 Vol.-%, screwcap, steel tank, €€€ V
90 Grüner Veltliner * Ried Spiegel 2019
88 Grüner Veltliner * Ried Spiegel 2018

90 Grüner Veltliner * Gobelsburg Ried Kirchgraben 2021

88 Grüner Veltliner * Gobelsburg 2022
12 Vol.-%, screwcap, steel tank, €€ V
90 Grüner Veltliner * Gobelsburg 2021
89 Grüner Veltliner * Gobelsburg 2019

WEINGUT SCHMID
3550 Langenlois
Schloß Straße 56
T: +43 (2734) 2188
trink@schmidwein.at
www.schmidwein.at

Winemaker: Ing. Andreas Schmid
Contact: Ing. Andreas and Alexandra Schmid
Production: 10 % sparkling, 73 % white, 1 % rosé, 15 % red, 1 % sweet, 20 hectares
Certified: Sustainable Austria

KAMPTAL DAC

88	Grüner Veltliner * 2021
89	Gelber Muskateller art of essentials 2021
89	Pinot Noir Tradition 2021

14,5 Vol.-%, DIAM, 500-l-barrel, €€€€

WEINGUT PETER SCHWEIGER

Weingut Schweiger is situated in the village of Zöbing, in the heart of the Kamptal region. Peter Schweiger and his son Peter attach particular importance to environmentally friendly and sustainable viticulture. Both generations are particularly devoted to respecting the terrain and nature. In order to vinify great wines, two things are crucial for them: the special appreciation of nature and the prudent treatment of the vines. This awareness pervades their entire existence as winemakers and can ultimately be tasted in their excellent wines.

The grapes, which are exclusively hand-picked and selected, come from the main vineyard sites of the Kamptal: Zöbinger Heiligenstein, Kogelberg, Gaisberg, and Lamm. The labels of the wines convey the philosophy of the winery to the outside world: the compass embodies the connection with the region, and the clock stands for the intention to give the wines enough time to mature. And thus, the first wines of the past year come onto the market in April ("IV") at the earliest.

The much-loved Grüner Veltliner is vinified into eight different wines: from light and fruity to full-bodied and mineral to bold and savoury, aged in barriques. Peter Schweiger junior, born in 1996, who has been working actively since 2013, not only in terms of craftsmanship but also with new ideas, creates particularly sophisticated wines with his own "96" line, which he vinifies exclusively by himself.

| 94 | Grüner Veltliner ** Ried Lamm 1ÖTW 2021 |

14,5 Vol.-%, screwcap, steel tank, €€€€€

| 93 | Grüner Veltliner ** Ried Kammerner Lamm 2019 |

| 92 | Grüner Veltliner ** Ried Gaisberg 1ÖTW 2021 |

13,5 Vol.-%, screwcap, steel tank, €€€€

| 92 | Grüner Veltliner ** Ried Gaisberg 1ÖTW 2020 |

Medium yellow green in colour with silver reflections. On the nose, aromas of yellow stone fruits are underpinned by a dark minerality, with a touch of clementine, meadow herbs and hint of greengage. The palate is juicy and powerful with fine acidity and a touch of apple on the minerally finish. A good food wine that will benefit from bottle ageing.

| 91 | Grüner Veltliner ** Ried Gaisberg 2018 |
| 91 | Grüner Veltliner ** Ried Heiligenstein 1ÖTW 2021 |

13,5 Vol.-%, screwcap, steel tank, €€€€

92	Grüner Veltliner ** Ried Heiligenstein 1ÖTW 2020
92	Grüner Veltliner ** Ried Heiligenstein 2019
91	Grüner Veltliner * Ried Kogelberg 2022

12 Vol.-%, screwcap, steel tank, €€

| 91 | Grüner Veltliner * Ried Kogelberg 2021 |
| 90 | Grüner Veltliner * Ried Kogelberg 2020 |

WEINGUT PETER SCHWEIGER
3561 Zöbing
Im Grübl 25
T: +43 (664) 2104748
office@schweiger-wein.at
www.schweiger-wein.at

Winemaker: Peter Schweiger jr.
Contact: Peter Schweiger
Production: 1 % sparkling, 95 % white, 1 % rosé, 3 % red, 18 hectares
Certified: Sustainable Austria
Fairs: VieVinum
Distribution partners: AUS, BE, BG, DK, DE, FIN, FR, UK, HK, IRL, JP, CDN, MAL, MV, NL, NO, SE, CZ, USA

* Kamptal DAC   ** Kamptal DAC Reserve

NIEDERÖSTERREICH/LOWER AUSTRIA

89 Grüner Veltliner * Zöbing 2021
89 Grüner Veltliner * Zöbing 2020
90 Grüner Veltliner * Zöbing 2019

92 Riesling * Ried Kogelberg 2022
12,5 Vol.-%, screwcap, steel tank, €€€€
92 Riesling ** Ried Kogelberg 2021

92 Riesling ** Ried Kogelberg 2020

92 Riesling ** Ried Heiligenstein 1ÖTW 2021
13,5 Vol.-%, screwcap, steel tank, €€€€
91 Riesling ** Ried Heiligenstein 1ÖTW 2020
92 Riesling ** Ried Heiligenstein 2019

WEINGUT STEININGER

The Steininger family has found its own Austrian sparkling wine philosophy with the vintage-pure sparkling grape varieties of the Kamptal. The secret of the success of the classic line is based on two factors: the excellent quality of the base wines, which are distinct, fruity, and fragrant, and the subsequent gentle second fermentation in the bottle. These two factors work together to bring out the varietal character and the base wine's flavour. The single vineyard wines, Riesling Ried Heiligenstein, Pinot Blanc Ried Panzaun, and Grüner Veltliner Ried Steinhaus, highlight the variety and terroir.

The Steininger family also focuses on premium quality still wines. The focus is on Grüner Veltliner and Riesling. Each individual vine expresses its terroir and gives the wine its character; fruit and varietal distinctions. Channelling the grapes' aromas from the vineyards into the wine is their main priority and reflects the cool Kamptal climate. The winery's most important vineyard sites are Ried Loisium, Ried Lamm, Ried Kittmannsberg, Ried Kogelberg, Ried Steinhaus, and Ried Seeberg.

95 ❂ Grüner Veltliner Sekt Austria Große Reserve brut Niederösterreich g.U. Langenlois Ried Steinhaus 2017
13 Vol.-%, cork, large wooden barrel/bottle fermentation, €€€€€ Ⓥ
93 ❂ Grüner Veltliner Sekt Langenlois g.U. brut Große Reserve Steinhaus 2016
Pale golden yellow, silver glints, fine mousse. Floral white apple, and a hint of candied lime. Good complexity, fresh stone fruit, finely fruit forward, silky texture, pleasant acidity, and persistent followed by soft nutty nuanced reverberations. A versatile style of wine.
94 ❂ Grüner Veltliner Sekt g.U. brut Große Reserve 2015

94 ❂ Riesling Sekt Austria Große Reserve Niederösterreich g.U. Zöbing Ried Heiligenstein 2018
13 Vol.-%, cork, large wooden barrel/bottle fermentation, €€€€€ Ⓥ
94 ❂ Riesling Sekt Langenlois g.U. Große Reserve Heiligenstein 2017

93 ❂ Riesling Elementar Sekt NV
13 Vol.-%, cork, bottle fermentation, €€€€€ Ⓥ
93 ❂ Riesling Elementar Sekt NV

92 ❂ Riesling Sekt Austria Reserve brut Niederösterreich g.U. 2020
13 Vol.-%, cork, bottle fermentation, €€€€€ Ⓥ
93 ❂ Riesling Sekt Austria Reserve brut Niederösterreich g.U. 2019
92 ❂ Riesling Sekt g.U. brut Reserve 2018

94 ❂ Weißburgunder Sekt Austria Große Reserve g.U. Niederösterreich Ried Panzaun 2017
13 Vol.-%, cork, large wooden barrel/bottle fermentation, €€€€€ Ⓥ
94 ❂ Weißburgunder Sekt Langenlois g.U. Grosse Reserve Ried Panzaun 2016

93 ❂ Weißburgunder Elementar Sekt NV
13 Vol.-%, cork, bottle fermentation, €€€€€ Ⓥ

92 ❂ Weissburgunder Brut Österreichischer Sekt g. U. Niederösterreich Reserve 2017

93 ❂ Sauvignon Blanc Brut Österreichischer Sekt g. U. Niederösterreich Reserve 2017

93 ❂ Chardonnay Sekt Austria Reserve brut Niederösterreich g.U. 2020
13 Vol.-%, cork, bottle fermentation, €€€€€ Ⓥ

KAMPTAL DAC

WEINGUT STEININGER

3550 Langenlois
Walterstraße
T: +43 (2734) 2372
office@weingut-steininger.at
www.weingut-steininger.at

Winemaker: Peter Steininger
Contact: Eva Steininger
Production: 30 % sparkling, 50 % white, 10 % rosé, 9 % red, 1 % sweet, 70 hectares
Certified: Sustainable Austria ⊙
Fairs: ProWein Düsseldorf, VieVinum
Distribution partners: BE, DK, DE, FIN, IRL, JP, CDN, LU, NL, NO, PL, SE, CZ, USA

The Steininger family

---

93 ⊙ Chardonnay Sekt Austria Reserve brut Niederösterreich g.U. 2019
93 ⊙ Chardonnay Sekt g.U. Brut Reserve 2018

93 ⊙ Burgunder Sekt brut g.U. Reserve 2015

92 ⊙ Muskateller Sekt 2021
13 Vol.-%, cork, bottle fermentation, €€€€€ Ⓥ
93 ⊙ Muskateller Sekt 2020
92 ⊙ Muskateller Sekt 2019

93 ⊙ Cabernet Sauvignon Rosé Sekt 2021
13 Vol.-%, cork, bottle fermentation, €€€€€ Ⓥ
92 ⊙ Cabernet Sauvignon Rosé Sekt 2020
92 ⊙ Cabernet Sauvignon Rosé Sekt 2019

94 Riesling ** Zöbing Ried Kogelberg 1ÖTW 2020
95 Riesling ** Zöbing Ried Kogelberg 1ÖTW 2019
93 Riesling ** Ried Kogelberg 1ÖTW 2018

(93) Riesling ** Langenlois Ried Steinhaus 1ÖTW 2022
13 Vol.-%, screwcap, steel tank, €€€€ Ⓥ
92 Riesling ** Ried Steinhaus 1ÖTW 2021
93 Riesling ** Langenlois Ried Steinhaus 1ÖTW 2020

(93) Riesling ** Langenlois Ried Seeberg 1ÖTW 2022
13 Vol.-%, screwcap, steel tank, €€€€ Ⓥ

93 Riesling ** Ried Seeberg 1ÖTW 2021
94 Riesling ** Langenlois Ried Seeberg 1ÖTW 2020

(94) Grüner Veltliner ** Ried Kittmannsberg 1ÖTW 2022
13,5 Vol.-%, screwcap, steel tank, €€€€ Ⓥ
93 Grüner Veltliner ** Ried Kittmannsberg 1ÖTW 2021
92 Grüner Veltliner ** Langenlois Ried Kittmannsberg 1ÖTW 2020

(93) Grüner Veltliner ** Zöbing Ried Kogelberg 1ÖTW 2022
13,5 Vol.-%, screwcap, large wooden barrel, €€€€€ Ⓥ
93 Grüner Veltliner ** Ried Kogelberg 1ÖTW Terrassen 2021
93 Grüner Veltliner ** Zöbing Ried Kogelberg 1ÖTW 2020

(93) Grüner Veltliner ** Grand Grü 2022
13,5 Vol.-%, screwcap, wooden barrel, €€€€ Ⓥ
92 Grüner Veltliner ** Grand Grü 2021
92 Grüner Veltliner ** Grand Grü 2020

(92) Grüner Veltliner ** Kammern Ried Lamm 1ÖTW 2022
13,5 Vol.-%, screwcap, wooden barrel, €€€€€ Ⓥ
94 Grüner Veltliner ** Ried Lamm 1ÖTW 2021
Medium yellow-green, silver reflections. Discreet honeydew melon, candied orange zest, some bourbon vanilla, a hint of apricot and fine spice in the background. Juicy, good com-

---

* Kamptal DAC   ** Kamptal DAC Reserve

plexity, multi-faceted, mineral, velvety texture, passion fruit on the finish, good food wine with certain ageing potential.

93 Grüner Veltliner ** Kammern Ried Lamm 1ÖTW 2020

92 Grüner Veltliner * Ried Loisium 2022
13 Vol.-%, screwcap, steel tank, €€€

90 Grüner Veltliner ** Ried Loisium 2021
90 Grüner Veltliner ** Ried Loisium 2020

90 Grüner Veltliner * 2022
12,5 Vol.-%, screwcap, steel tank, €€

90 Grüner Veltliner * 2021
89 Grüner Veltliner * 2020

91 Weißburgunder 2022
13,5 Vol.-%, screwcap, large wooden barrel, €€

91 Weißburgunder 2021
91 Weißburgunder 2020

WEINGUT TOPF

At the foot of the Gaisberg mountain in the southern Kamptal, lies the picturesque village of Straß im Straßertale, home to the Topf family's traditional winery. Here, where knowledge and passion have been passed down consistently over five generations since 1885, wines with a unique signature are created. Preserving tradition, passing on the skilled craft, and taking great care in the vineyards are part of the daily routine. Together with his sons, Hans Topf vinifies single-vineyard and sparkling wines and brings them to market with optimum maturity. The brothers Hans-Peter and Maximilian work in harmony with nature and complement their father's portfolio with their own single-vineyard wines, which additionally bear their initials "M" and "HP" respectively.

The great potential and pride of the winegrowing family is based on the Erste Lage single vineyard sites, Offenberg, Gaisberg, Wechselberg Spiegel, and Heiligenstein. Conglomerates of mica schist, paragneiss, and arkoses as well as the influence of different microclimates are responsible for the uniqueness and distinctiveness of these sites. As a member of the Traditionsweingüter Österreich (Association of Austrian Traditional Wine Estates), the Topf family focuses on the experience of the single vineyard site wines under the motto "Herkunft im Glas kostbar machen", loosely translated as "treasure provenance within the glass."

94 ❂ Grosse Reserve Sekt g.U. brut 2016 GV/PN/CH/WB
Bright golden yellow, green reflections, persistent fine mousse. Inviting bouquet of orange zest and ripe stone fruit, a bit of apricot, a hint of caramel and figs, meadow herbs in the background. Juicy, elegant, multi-faceted acidity, salty-minerality, finely spicy, mango touch on the finish, very good persistency, taut food wine.

95 ❂ Grosse Reserve Sekt g.U. brut 2014 GV/PN/CH/WB

92 ❂ Blanc de Blancs Sekt g.U. brut Reserve NV GS/GV/WB/CH

92 ❂ Topf Sekt g.U. Reserve Niederösterreich Rosé brut NV

95 Grüner Veltliner * Ried Renner 1ÖTW 2021
12,5 Vol.-%, screwcap, steel tank, €€€€

95 Grüner Veltliner * Ried Offenberg 2021
13,5 Vol.-%, screwcap, steel tank, €€€€

93 Grüner Veltliner * Ried Offenberg 1ÖTW 2020

93 Grüner Veltliner ** Strass Ried Offenberg 1ÖTW 2019

93 Grüner Veltliner * Ried Gaisberg 1ÖTW 2021
13 Vol.-%, screwcap, steel tank, €€€€

93 Grüner Veltliner * Ried Gaisberg 1ÖTW 2020

94 Grüner Veltliner * Strass Ried Gaisberg 1ÖTW 2019

93 Grüner Veltliner * Ried Rosengartl 1ÖTW 2020
12,5 Vol.-%, screwcap, wooden barrel, €€€€

94 Grüner Veltliner Ried Rosengartl »M« 2019

92 Grüner Veltliner Ried Rosengartl M 2017

KAMPTAL DAC

WEINGUT TOPF
3491 Straß im Straßertale
Talstraße 162
T: +43 (2735) 2491
office@weingut-topf.at
www.weingut-topf.at
Winemaker: Maximilian & Hans-Peter Topf
Contact: The Topf family
Production: 306,667 bottles
10 % sparkling, 70 % white, 20 % red, 50 hectares
Certified: Sustainable Austria
Fairs: Alles für den Gast Salzburg, Austrian Tasting London, ProWein Düsseldorf, VieVinum, Vinitaly, Wein & Genuss Festival Sylt, DAC-Presentations
Distribution partners: BE, DK, DE, EST, FIN, UK, HK, IT, JP, NL, NO, PL, RUS, SE, CH, PT

Maximilian, Hans Peter and Hans Topf

---

92 Grüner Veltliner * Ried Wechselberg 1ÖTW 2022
13 Vol.-%, screwcap, steel tank, €€€
91 Grüner Veltliner * Ried Wechselberg 2021
91 Grüner Veltliner * Ried Wechselberg 2020

91 Grüner Veltliner * Strass im Strassertal 2022
12,5 Vol.-%, screwcap, steel tank, €€
90 Grüner Veltliner * Strass im Strassertal 2021
91 Grüner Veltliner * Ried Strass im Strassertaler Wechselberg 2020

95 Riesling * Ried Heiligenstein 1ÖTW 2021
12,5 Vol.-%, screwcap, steel tank, €€€€€
93 Riesling * Ried Heiligenstein 1ÖTW 2020
92 Riesling * Ried Zöbinger Heiligenstein 1ÖTW 2019

94 Riesling * Ried Heiligenstein-Steinwand 1ÖTW 2021
12,5 Vol.-%, screwcap, steel tank, €€€€€
94 Riesling * Ried Heiligenstein-Steinwand 1ÖTW 2020
Medium greenish yellow, gold reflections. A bit of honey blossom and papaya, passion fruit, deliacte meadow herbs, plus guava, a hint of lemon zest. Good complexity, juicy, well-integrated acid structure, white vineyard peach on the finish, mineral aftertaste, complex food companion with certain ageing potential.

94 Riesling * Ried Zöbinger Heiligenstein 1ÖTW »M« 2021

93 Riesling * Ried Heiligenstein "M" 1ÖTW 2019

93 Riesling * Ried Wechselberg Spiegel 1ÖTW 2021
13,5 Vol.-%, screwcap, steel tank, €€€€€
93 Riesling * Ried Wechselberg Spiegel 1ÖTW 2020
93 Riesling * Ried Wechselberg Spiegel 1ÖTW 2019

93 Riesling * Ried Wechselberg 1ÖTW 2022
13 Vol.-%, screwcap, steel tank, €€€€
92 Riesling * Ried Wechselberg 2021
92 Riesling * Ried Wechselberg 2020

92 Riesling * Strass im Strassertal 2022
13 Vol.-%, screwcap, steel tank, €€€
91 Riesling * Strass im Strassertal 2021
91 Riesling * Strass im Strassertal 2020

93 Chardonnay Ried Hasel 2020
13,5 Vol.-%, screwcap, large wooden barrel, €€€€€
93 Chardonnay Ried Hasel 2019
92 Chardonnay Ried Hasel 2018

93 Sauvignon Blanc Ried Hasel 2017
92 Sauvignon Blanc Ried Hasel 2016

92 Pinot Noir Ried Stangl "HP" 2017
93 Pinot Noir Ried Stangl HP 2016

---

* Kamptal DAC   ** Kamptal DAC Reserve

NIEDERÖSTERREICH/LOWER AUSTRIA

WEINGUT WEIXELBAUM
ORGANIC

Living in harmony with nature and taking a comprehensive and holistic approach are the principles by which we live and love wine and by which we have run our family winery in Strass for three generations. Throughout the year, these values guide the family in the vineyard, in the cellar and in our lives. The passion with which we approach our work is expressed in Heinz Weixelbaum's explicit goal: to produce wines that he himself enjoys drinking and sharing this pleasure with others. True values do not mean stagnation but rather a cautious approach to the future. The past provides support, grounding, and valuable treasures for the Vinothèque. They are now looking to the future with their children, Theresa and Pauli, who already participate in the "family meeting" in the vineyard to decide which grape varieties to plant.

On 30 hectares of vineyards in the wine-growing region of Kamptal, the passionate winemaking family tends and nurtures 140,000 vines. The focus is on white wine, with a small but fine range of red wines. The winery's success is based on holistic ecological principles and the preservation of traditional values: hospitality, humour, and genuine passion flow through the winery. When the wine reflects these values, that's when the family rejoices. "Then our profession becomes as much an elixir of life as a good glass of wine".

95 Riesling ** Ried Heiligenstein 1ÖTW 2021
13,5 Vol.-%, screwcap, large wooden barrel, €€€€€

94 Riesling ** Strass Ried Gaisberg 1ÖTW 2021
13,5 Vol.-%, screwcap, large wooden barrel, €€€€€

93 Riesling ** Ried Gaisberg 1ÖTW 2020

93 Riesling ** Strass Ried Gaisberg Wahre Werte 1ÖTW 2019

92 Riesling ** Ried Renner 2019

95 Riesling Anno Dazumal 2017
Bright yellow, gold reflections. Inviting bouquet of apricots and linden blossom honey, a bit of candied orange zest, floral touch, fine spicy touch. Good complexity, multi-layered, mineral, subtle notes of ripe vine peach, fruit, powerful, but still tight-knit, spicy aftertaste, has good ageing potential.

94 Riesling Anno Dazumal 2016

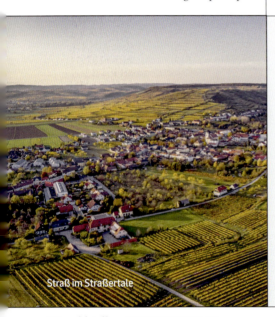

Straß im Straßertale

WEINGUT WEIXELBAUM
3491 Straß im Straßertale
Weinbergweg 196
T: +43 (2735) 2269
weixelbaum@invinoweix.at
invinoweix.at

Winemaker: Heinz Weixelbaum
Contact: Heinz and Gabi Weixelbaum
Production: 90 % white, 4 % rosé, 5 % red, 1 % sweet, 30 hectares
Fairs: ProWein Düsseldorf
Distribution partners: DK, DE, UK, IRL, NL, PL, RO, CH, CZ, USA

KAMPTAL DAC

94 Grüner Veltliner ** Strass Ried Gaisberg 1ÖTW 2021
13,5 Vol.-%, screwcap, large wooden barrel, €€€€ V
92 Grüner Veltliner ** Ried Gaisberg 1ÖTW 2020
93 Grüner Veltliner ** Ried Gaisberg 1ÖTW Wahre Werte 2019

90 Grüner Veltliner * Ried Stangl 2021
90 Grüner Veltliner * Ried Stangl 2020
90 Grüner Veltliner * Ried Stangl 2019

92 Grüner Veltliner * Alte Reben 2022
12,5 Vol.-%, screwcap, steel tank, €€€ B V

94 Grüner Veltliner Anno Dazumal 2017
93 Grüner Veltliner Anno Dazumal 2015

94 Sauvignon Blanc Anno Dazumal 2017
Bright greenish yellow, silver reflections. Tight-knit bouquet of white pome fruit and gooseberries, soft herbal notes, a hint of blossom honey and some pineapple. Good complexity, juicy, velvety texture, mineral, baby banana, ripe tropical fruit on the finish, tobacco spice echo, complex food wine with certain ageing potential.
94 Sauvignon Blanc Anno Dazumal 2016

92 Sauvignon Blanc Wahre Werte 2021
92 Sauvignon Blanc Wahre Werte 2020
90 Sauvignon Blanc Ried Wechselberg-Himmel Wahre Werte 2018

93 Chardonnay Wahre Werte 2020
13 Vol.-%, screwcap, large wooden barrel, €€€€

92 Roter Veltliner Wahre Werte Reserve 2020
93 Roter Veltliner Wahre Werte 2017

92 Weißburgunder Wahre Werte 2022
13 Vol.-%, screwcap, large wooden barrel, €€€ B V
91 Weißburgunder Wahre Werte 2021
91 Weißburgunder Wahre Werte 2019

Chardonnay

* Kamptal DAC   ** Kamptal DAC Reserve

Krustetten south-east of the Göttweiger Berg

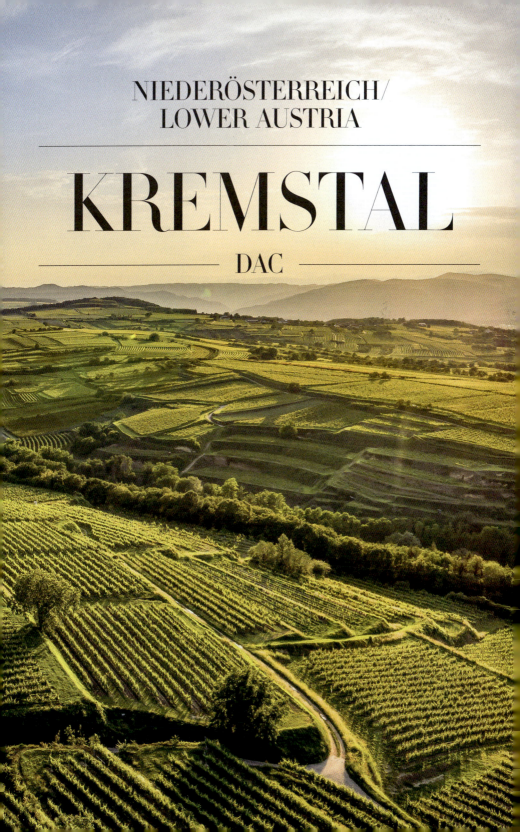

Göttweig Abbey

HIGH CULTURE OF WINE

If vineyards could speak, there would be endless hours of exciting discussion in Kremstal. The 2,252 vineyard hectares are distributed in three distinct zones: the picturesque twin cities Krems and Stein, the eastern lying areas, and the small wine villages south of the Danube River near the Göttweig Abbey. The uniting elements for the region are Grüner Veltliner and Riesling under the "Kremstal DAC" designation of origin – and art and culture.

In the old wine-culture city of Krems and its twin city, Stein, the intimate link to wine is more than evident. This is a place that has superbly fulfilled its role as an ambassador of Austrian wine culture throughout the ages. Many of the estates in Krems have existed for centuries. This tradition continues to thrive due to the many young and successful vintners, an innovative wine co-operative and an outstanding wine school. Like its neighbour Wachau, metamorphic rock prevails in the vineyards in and around the city.

Representative is the renowned Steiner Pfaffenberg, which produces elegant, mineralic wines. Microclimates such as Senftenberg and its surrounding wine villages along the river Krems are home to truly unique wines. The vineyards to the east, in stark contrast, yield much richer, rounder, full-bodied wines. The massive loess terraces in the wine villages of Rohrendorf (home of the internationally famed viticultural pioneer Prof. Dr. Lenz Moser) and Gedersdorf add a very special appeal to the landscape.

The magnificent Benedictine Göttweig Monastery (founded in 1083) is perched on a mountaintop on the southern side of the Danube River and appears to stand guard over the wine villages of Furth-Palt, Krustetten, Hollenburg, Oberfucha and Tiefenfucha at its feet. As with the neigh-

NIEDERÖSTERREICH/LOWER AUSTRIA **KREMSTAL DAC**

bouring Wachau and Kamptal wine-growing areas, the Kremstal lies in the centre of climatic tension. Cool air from the adjacent Waldviertel (Forest Quarter) meets the dry warm influences of the Pannonian Basin to the east. The Danube Valley benefits from the temperature-regulating effect of the river's large flowing surface.

Juicy white wines of great finesse, particularly Grüner Veltliner and Riesling, and to a lesser extent concentrated, expressive red wines distinguish this wine-growing area. The vintners are very conscious of the provenance of their wines and welcome the opportunity to realize the diversity of unique individual vineyards. The three-tier DAC hierarchy is similar to that of Kamptal with the only difference being the point at which the wines may be released onto the market.

KREMSTAL DAC

Austria altogether	**44.728 ha**
Wine-growing area Lower Austria	**27.074 ha**
Kremstal DAC	**2.252 ha**

AREA UNDER VINE

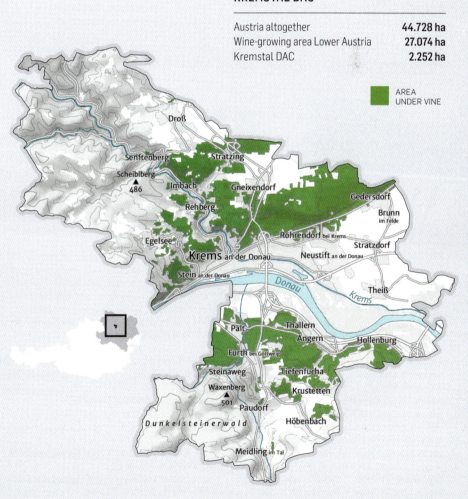

NIEDERÖSTERREICH/LOWER AUSTRIA

SELECTED WINERIES

Weingut Mantlerhof, Brunn im Felde/ Gedersdorf
Wein-Gut Nigl, Senftenberg
Weingut Familie Proidl, Senftenberg
Weingut Salomon Undhof, Stein an der Donau

Weingut Buchegger, Droß
Weingut & Hotel Malat, Palt
Weingut Josef Schmid, Stratzing
Weingut Stadt Krems, Krems

Weingut Aigner, Krems

Weingut Philipp Bründlmayer, Grunddorf
Winzerhof Familie Dockner, Höbenbach
Weingut Meinhard Forstreiter, Krems-Hollenburg
Weingut Müller, Krustetten
Weingut Stift Göttweig, Furth bei Göttweig

Weingut Felsner, Grunddorf
Weinkellerei Lenz Moser, Rohrendorf
Wandraschek Weinmanufaktur, Krems

Weingut David Harm, Krustetten

WEINGUT AIGNER

Wolfgang Aigner was born into the world of wine-making. The son of a winemaker, he took over the family winery in Krems at the age of 21. From the very beginning, Aigner worked consistently to exploit the potential of the excellent sites. After all, it is in the terroir of the Sandgrube and Weinzierlberg sites, that the strength of the winery lies, which today produces some of the most interesting white wines in the Krems region on around 16 hectares.

Most of the vines were planted by Aigner's grandfather 40 years ago. The focus is on the Grüner Veltliner and Riesling varieties. The wines have an unmistakable style: they are full-bodied but not overbearing, feel fresh, and have a distinctive savouriness as well as a bold bouquet. Aigner vinifies his wines for long-term storage. The reserves are still invigoratingly fresh after 20 years, displaying clear fruit and multilayered tertiary aromas.

94 Grüner Veltliner ** Ried Frechau Elitär 2019
95 Grüner Veltliner ** Frechau Elitär 2017

93 Grüner Veltliner ** Ried Obere Sandgrube Privat 2021
14 Vol.-%, screwcap, large wooden barrel, €€€€
93 Grüner Veltliner ** Ried Obere Sandgrube Privat 2019
Medium yellow-green, silver glints. Pleasant herbal notes, a hint of passion fruit, ripe apple, as well as delicate hints of blossom honey. Savoury bouquet. Juicy, elegant, powerful, balanced acidity, delicately creamy, followed by candied orange zest marked by a dark finish. A lovely food companion.
94 Grüner Veltliner ** Ried Obere Sandgrube Privat 2018
92 Grüner Veltliner ** Ried Obere Sandgrube 2020
93 Grüner Veltliner ** Obere Sandgrube 2016
92 Grüner Veltliner * Krems 1773 Tradition 2022
12,5 Vol.-%, screwcap, large wooden barrel, €€€
90 Grüner Veltliner * Krems Sandgrube 2022
12,5 Vol.-%, screwcap, €€
91 Grüner Veltliner * Krems Sandgrube 2020
91 Grüner Veltliner * Kremser Sandgrube 2019

KREMSTAL DAC

WEINGUT AIGNER
3500 Krems
Weinzierl 53
T: +43 (2732) 84558
info@aigner-wein.at
www.aigner-wein.at

Winemaker/Contact:
Wolfgang Aigner
Production: 97 % white, 3 % red, 16 hectares
Fairs: VieVinum
Distribution partners: UK, NL, CZ

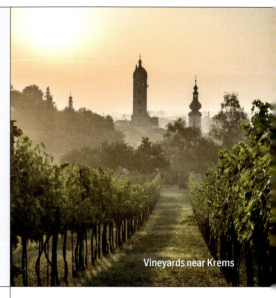

Vineyards near Krems

90 Grüner Veltliner * Weinzurl 2022
12 Vol.-%, screwcap, €€
90 Grüner Veltliner * Weinzurl 2021
90 Grüner Veltliner * Weinzurl 2020

92 Riesling * Ried Weinzierlberg 2021
13,5 Vol.-%, screwcap, €€€€
91 Riesling * Ried Weinzierlberg 2020
Medium yellow-green, silver glints. Candied orange zest on the nose, followed by yellow peach and ripe pineapple, as well as a hint of blossom honey. Juicy, distinctly fruit-forward, vibrant arc of acidity, persistent, with a zesty citrus finish. Will benefit from bottle ageing.
92 Riesling * Ried Weinzierlberg 2019

92 Riesling ** Ried Frechau 2019

92 Riesling Ried Kremsleithen 2021
13,5 Vol.-%, screwcap, steel tank, €€€€

90 Muskateller 2022
12 Vol.-%, screwcap, steel tank, €€
90 Muskateller 2021
90 Muskateller 2020

91 Sauvignon Blanc 2021
90 Sauvignon Blanc 2020
91 Sauvignon Blanc 2019

91 Chardonnay 2022
13 Vol.-%, screwcap, steel tank, €€
89 Chardonnay 2020
91 Chardonnay 2019

WEINGUT PHILIPP BRÜNDLMAYER

Passionately dedicated to the craftmanship of producing wine is still the best prerequisite for quality. This is especially true for Philipp Bründlmayer, who has inherited this trait. Consequently, his wines are true bliss: authentic, varietal, and of unmistakable origin.
In Grunddorf, the farthest part of Kamptal, the wines are aged in stainless steel tanks and large wooden barrels. However, they originate from the mighty loess terraces of Gedersdorf and Rohrendorf and thus bear the Kremstal designation of origin. A truly breathtaking landscape, ideal for viticulture. Here you will find the climatic conditions needed to develop the aromas and character of the wines.
In addition to knowledge, craftsmanship, and climate, soil quality is a decisive factor in creating great wines. In Kremstal, loess and conglom-

* Kremstal DAC   ** Kremstal DAC Reserve

NIEDERÖSTERREICH/LOWER AUSTRIA

Philipp Bründlmayer

WEINGUT PHILIPP BRÜNDLMAYER

3485 Grunddorf
Ortsring 44
T: +43 (2735) 5112
office@jpbm.at
www.philipp-bruendlmayer.at

Winemaker/Contact:
Philipp Bründlmayer
Production: 90 % white, 8 % rosé, 2 % red, 25 hectares
Certified: Sustainable Austria
Fairs: ProWein Düsseldorf, VieVinum
Distribution partners: AUS, BE, DK, DE, FIN, UK, PL, CH, CZ, USA

erate form the ideal terroir for the distinctive dry wines for which Austria is so highly regarded. Philipp and Josef Bründlmayer are winemakers with a strong sense of tradition and a hands-on approach to winemaking. The vineyards that the estate cultivates could not be better suited to this philosophy: they are unruly, impassable, and require manual cultivation. But they are also - if left to their own devices and approached properly - an ideal habitat for the varieties for which this region is so well known and loved.

At Philipp Bründlmayer, the wines are allowed to reveal their origins without any disguise. On 25 hectares, the winemaker cultivates over 100 vineyards in a wide range of microclimates. He bottles wines that are not only representative of their varietal typicity but also bear his unmistakable signature. With no more than one gram of residual sugar, all wines are particularly dry and thus ambassadors of their region - the very essence of Kremstal.

(94) Grüner Veltliner * Gedersdorf Ried Wieland 2022
13,5 Vol.-%, screwcap, 500-l-barrel, €€€€€

94 Grüner Veltliner * Gedersdorf Ried Wieland 2021
Medium yellow-green, silver reflections. Delicate anise and cumin, yellow tropical fruit, nuances of mango, fresh yellow apple. Spicy, full-bodied, fine yellow tropical fruit, salty minerality, discreet acidity, compact and long lasting, definite ageing potential.

(93) Grüner Veltliner * Gedersdorf Ried Vordernberg 2022
13,5 Vol.-%, screwcap, 500-l-barrel, €€€€€

93 Grüner Veltliner * Gedersdorf Ried Vordernberg 2021

92 Grüner Veltliner * Ried Vordernberg Gedersdorf 2020

93 Grüner Veltliner ** Selection Widnau 2018

93 Grüner Veltliner * Credo 2020

(92) Grüner Veltliner * Gedersdorf Ried Moosburgerin 2022
13,5 Vol.-%, screwcap, 500-l-barrel, €€€€€

93 Grüner Veltliner * Gedersdorf Ried Moosburgerin 2021

92 Grüner Veltliner * Ried Moosburgerin Gedersdorf 2020

91 Grüner Veltliner * Kaiserstiege 2022
92 Grüner Veltliner * Kaiserstiege 2021
92 Grüner Veltliner * Kaiserstiege 2020

90 Grüner Veltliner * Jakobsweg 2022
91 Grüner Veltliner * Jakobsweg 2021
91 Grüner Veltliner * Jakobsweg 2020

95 Grüner Veltliner Reserve 2017
13,5 Vol.-%, cork, €€€€€

(94) Riesling * Gedersdorf Ried Altmandl 2022
13 Vol.-%, screwcap, 500-l-barrel, €€€€€

© Atelier Schulte

KREMSTAL DAC

(93) Riesling * Gedersdorf Ried Steingraben 2022
13 Vol.-%, screwcap, 500-l-barrel, €€€€€
94 Riesling * Gedersdorf Ried Steingraben 2021
Light yellow-green, silver reflections. White tropical fruit background with LIME, delicate hints of pineapple and passion fruit, floral touch, multi-faceted bouquet. Juicy, tightly meshed, fresh vineyard peach, lively lemon, salty touch on the finish, crisp dry style, a racy food wine with certain ageing potential.
91 Riesling * Ried Steingraben Gedersdorf 2020

(92) Riesling * Gedersdorf Ried Moosburgerin 2022
13 Vol.-%, screwcap, 500-l-barrel, €€€€€
93 Riesling * Gedersdorf Ried Moosburgerin 2021
93 Riesling * Ried Moosburgerin Gedersdorf 2020

91 Riesling * Kaiserstiege 2022
92 Riesling * Kaiserstiege 2021
92 Riesling * Kaiserstiege 2020

90 Riesling * Jakobsweg 2022
91 Riesling * Jakobsweg 2021
91 Riesling * Jakobsweg 2020

92 Weißburgunder Reserve 2021
90 Weißburgunder Reserve 2020
91 Weißburgunder Konglomerat 2019

(91) Neuburger Reserve 2022
13 Vol.-%, screwcap, 500-l-barrel, €€€€€
92 Neuburger Reserve 2021
91 Neuburger Ried Vordernberg 2020

WEINGUT BUCHEGGER

At Vorspannhof Dross, winemaker Silke Mayr focuses on achieving the very highest quality at Weingut Buchegger. In the very east of the Kremstal winegrowing region, in Gedersdorf, the Buchegger wines flourish. The unique interaction of soil and climate produces wines of exceptional finesse and diversity, with elegance and minerality. At the traditional Buchegger winery, terroir and origin are of utmost importance, and the preservation of the humus-rich soil is of importance at all times. Only the best sites make the best grapes, and only good judgment produces the best wine. Silke Mayr and her dedicated team with cellar master Michael Nastl invest an extra portion of work where it is required and makes sense: "And we let nature take its course where necessary." The excellent know-how in all areas characterises Buchegger wines.

94 ❂ Chardonnay Sekt Austria Große Reserve extra brut Niederösterreich g.U. Gedersdorf 2017
12 Vol.-%, cork, bottle fermentation, small wooden barrel, €€€€€
94 ❂ Chardonnay Sekt g.U. Extra Brut Große Reserve 2016

(95) Grüner Veltliner ** Gedersdorf Leopold 2022
13,5 Vol.-%, screwcap, wooden barrel/steel tank, €€€€
92 Grüner Veltliner ** Leopold 2021

93 Grüner Veltliner ** Leopold 2020

(95) Grüner Veltliner ** Ried Moosburgerin 1ÖTW 2021
13 Vol.-%, screwcap, steel tank, €€€€€
93 Grüner Veltliner ** Ried Moosburgerin 1ÖTW 2020
94 Grüner Veltliner ** Ried Moosburgerin 1ÖTW 2019

WEINGUT BUCHEGGER
3552 Droß
Droß 300
T: +43 (2719) 30056
buchegger@vorspannhof.at
www.buchegger.at

Winemaker: Michael Nastl
Contact: Silke Mayr
Production: 90 % white, 10 % red, 11 hectares
Distribution partners: BG, DK, DE, EST, JP, LT, NL, CH, CZ, USA

* Kremstal DAC   ** Kremstal DAC Reserve

NIEDERÖSTERREICH/LOWER AUSTRIA

(94) Grüner Veltliner ** Ried Vordernberg 1ÖTW 2021
13 Vol.-%, screwcap, large wooden barrel, €€€€€

94 Grüner Veltliner ** Ried Vordernberg 1ÖTW 2020

94 Grüner Veltliner ** Ried Vordernberg 1ÖTW 2019

93 Grüner Veltliner * Ried Pfarrweingarten 2022
13 Vol.-%, screwcap, steel tank, €€€€

93 Grüner Veltliner * Pfarrweingarten 2021
Pale yellow, green hints, silver reflections. Aromas of fresh tropical fruit, pineapple and mango, a touch of orange blossom and nuances of herbal savouriness. Complex and round on the palate, fine fruit expression, fresh structure, minerality and a long, salty finish. Definite ageing potential.

93 Grüner Veltliner * Gedersdorf Ried Pfarrweingarten 2021

91 Grüner Veltliner Kamptal DAC Ried Geppling 2022
12,5 Vol.-%, screwcap, steel tank, €€€

91 Grüner Veltliner Kamptal DAC Ried Geppling 2021

92 Grüner Veltliner Kamptal DAC Ried Geppling 2020

95 Riesling ** Ried Moosburgerin 1ÖTW 2021
Light green-yellow, silver reflections. Fine aromas of white tropical fruit, a hint of lime zest, mineral touch, inviting, still somewhat shy bouquet. Juicy, elegant, fine fruity expression, racy acidity, precise and radiating with great freshness, white peach on the aftertaste, delicate, animating style, certain ageing potential.

94 Riesling ** Ried Moosburgerin 1ÖTW 2020

95 Riesling ** Ried Moosburgerin 1ÖTW 2019

(94) Riesling ** Ried Vordernberg 1ÖTW 2021
13 Vol.-%, screwcap, steel tank, €€€€

93 Riesling ** Ried Vordernberg 1ÖTW 2020

93 Riesling ** Ried Vordernberg 1ÖTW 2019

(94) Riesling * Ried Tiefenthal 2022
13,5 Vol.-%, screwcap, steel tank, €€€

94 Riesling * Ried Tiefenthal 2021

92 Roter Veltliner Ried Tiefenthal 2022
13 Vol.-%, screwcap, used barriques, €€€€

92 Roter Veltliner Ried Tiefenthal 2021

92 Roter Veltliner Ried Tiefenthal 2020

WINZERHOF FAMILIE DOCKNER

The Dockner family from Höbenbach in southern Kremstal are very pleased with their latest vintage. In recent years, they have enjoyed numerous successes. In the meantime, wines from a good 80 hectares of their own land and 70 hectares of contracted land are farmed. Grüner Veltliner is the estates main variety, but the Docknors also produce outstanding Riesling wines. The wines from these two varieties are divided into regional wines, local wines, and single-vineyard site wines. The fact that father Sepp, who is responsible for vineyards and marketing, and his son Josef, cellar master of the house, can also offer excellent red wines is not entirely new - and that in a region where reds are not necessarily among the mainstream wines. Especially with the Cuveé "Sacra", the two have been able to show repeatedly that top red wines are also possible in the Kremstal.

An additional project is the production of their own traditional method of sparkling wine. For this purpose, several old cellars in the Kellergasse at Frauengrund in Krems were restored and converted into the new sparkling wine facility, which was opened in 2014. Sparkling wines from all three quality levels of the Austrian sparkling wine pyramid are offered: Classic, Reserve and Great Reserve. In 2017, the new JOE-Keller was opened in Höbenbach, a new production facility that is one of the most modern cellars in Austria. Guided tours for 20 or more people are available by appointment.

92 ❂ Josef Dockner Blanc de Blancs Sekt Austria g.U. Grosse Reserve Brut Krems Ried Frauengrund CH/WB/PG
13 Vol.-%, cork, large wooden barrel, bottle fermentation, €€€€€

© chris rogl

KREMSTAL DAC

WINZERHOF FAMILIE DOCKNER
3508 Höbenbach
Ortsstraße 30
T: +43 (2736) 7262
winzerhof@dockner.at
www.dockner.at/

Winemaker: Josef Dockner jr.
Contact: Josef Dockner sen.
Production: 70 % white, 29 % red, 1 % sweet, 90+90 hectares
Certified: Sustainable Austria
Fairs: ProWein Düsseldorf, VieVinum
Distribution partners: BE, DK, DE, IT, NL, NO, PL, SK, CZ

Sepp and Josef Dockner

92 ⓘ Josef Dockner Brut Große Reserve "Blanc de Blancs" - Ried Kremser Frauengrund 2015 CH/WB/PG
92 ⓘ Josef Dockner Blanc de Blancs Große Reserve Frauengrund 2014

90 ⓘ Josef Dockner Reserve 2015

90 ⓘ Josef Dockner Sekt g.U. Klassik Brut CH/WB
12 Vol.-%, cork, bottle fermentation, steel tank, €€€
92 ⓘ Josef Dockner Sekt g.U. brut Klassik 2017 CH/WB
90 ⓘ Josef Dockner Brut Klassik CH/WB

91 ⓘ Josef Dockner Sekt Austria g.U. Reserve Brut Rosé Reserve PN/ZW
12,5 Vol.-%, cork, bottle fermentation, steel tank, €€€€

93 Riesling * Ried Rosengarten 2021
13 Vol.-%, screwcap, steel tank, €€€
93 Riesling * Tiefenfucha Ried Rosengarten 2020
93 Riesling * Tiefenfucha Ried Rosengarten 2019

93 Riesling * Ried Gottschelle 1ÖTW 2021
13 Vol.-%, screwcap, steel tank, €€€€
92 Riesling * Furth Ried Gottschelle 2020
91 Riesling * Furth Ried Gottschelle 2019

91 Riesling * Ried Steinleithen 2022
12,5 Vol.-%, screwcap, steel tank, €€€

93 Riesling ** Tiefenfucha Ried Leiten 2020
Medium green yellow, silver reflections. Delicate apricot notes, a hint of papaya, underlaid with tobacco herbal savouriness, ripe fig. Juicy, elegant, silky texture, mineral, mango notes on the finish, savoury aftertaste, long lasting, a good food companion.
94 Riesling ** Tiefenfucha Ried Leiten 2019
94 Riesling ** Tiefenfucha Ried Leithen Privatfüllung Sepp 2018

90 Riesling * Höbenbach 2022
12 Vol.-%, screwcap, steel tank, €€

91 Riesling * Krems 2021
91 Riesling * Krems 2020
90 Riesling * Krems 2019

94 Grüner Veltliner * Ried Steinbühel 1ÖTW 2021
13 Vol.-%, screwcap, large wooden barrel, €€€€
93 Grüner Veltliner ** Palt Ried Steinbühel 2020
Bright yellow, hints of green and silver reflections. Fresh herbal savoury aromas, yellow tropical fruit, a touch of red apple and a hint of candied tangerine. On the palate, good complexity, juicy and creamy with pronounced fruit and honeydew melon on the finish. A versatile wine.

94 Grüner Veltliner ** Tiefenfucha Ried Leiten 2020
94 Grüner Veltliner ** Tiefenfucha Ried Leiten 2019
93 Grüner Veltliner ** Tiefenfucha Ried Leiten Privatfüllung Gudrun 2018

* Kremstal DAC   ** Kremstal DAC Reserve

NIEDERÖSTERREICH/LOWER AUSTRIA

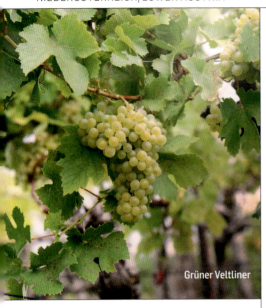
Grüner Veltliner

93 Grüner Veltliner * Ried Lusthausberg 2021
13 Vol.-%, screwcap, large wooden barrel, €€€
92 Grüner Veltliner * Hollenburg
Ried Lusthausberg 2020
92 Grüner Veltliner * Hollenburg
Ried Lusthausberg 2019

93 Grüner Veltliner * Ried Gottschelle
1ÖTW 2021
13 Vol.-%, screwcap, large wooden barrel, €€€€
91 Grüner Veltliner * Furth
Ried Gottschelle 2020
91 Grüner Veltliner * Furth
Ried Gottschelle 2019

92 Grüner Veltliner * Furth
Ried Oberfeld 2021
91 Grüner Veltliner * Furth
Ried Oberfeld 2020
90 Grüner Veltliner * Furth
Ried Oberfeld 2019

92 Grüner Veltliner * Ried Frauengrund 2022
12,5 Vol.-%, screwcap, steel tank, €€
92 Grüner Veltliner * Krems
Ried Frauengrund 2021
90 Grüner Veltliner * Krems
Ried Frauengrund 2020

90 Grüner Veltliner * Ried Himmelreich 2022
12,5 Vol.-%, screwcap, steel tank, €€

91 Grüner Veltliner * Höbenbach
Ried Himmelreich 2021
90 Grüner Veltliner * Höbenbach
Ried Himmelreich 2020

90 Grüner Veltliner * Krems 2022
12 Vol.-%, screwcap, steel tank, €€
91 Grüner Veltliner * Krems 2021
89 Grüner Veltliner * Krems 2020

91 Grüner Veltliner Wachau DAC
Alte Reben 2022
13 Vol.-%, screwcap, steel tank, €€
92 Grüner Veltliner Wachau DAC Reserve
Alte Reben 2021
92 Grüner Veltliner Wachau DAC Reserve
Alte Reben 2020

91 Grüner Veltliner Reserve JOE 2021
90 Grüner Veltliner Reserve JOE 2019
90 Grüner Veltliner Reserve JOE 2018

93 Sacra Grande Reserve 2017 CS/ME/ZW
93 Sacra Grande Reserve 2015 CS/ME

91 Sacra 2020 CS/ME/ZW
13,5 Vol.-%, cork, barrique, €€€€
92 Sacra 2019 CS/ME/ZW
91 Sacra 2018 CS/ME/ZW

90 Sankt Laurent Reserve 2018

90 Pinot Noir Reserve - Wachau 2017

90 Zweigelt Reserve Joe 2019
89 Zweigelt Reserve Joe 2018

91 Cabernet SauvignonReserve 2019

95 Gelber Muskateller Strohwein 2018

93 Grüner Veltliner Ried Leithen Tiefenfucha
Auslese 2017

93 Riesling Eiswein Ried Rosengarten 2017

92 Grauburgunder Beerenauslese 2018

KREMSTAL DAC

WEINGUT FELSNER

With the support of his family, Manfred Felsner cultivates 16 hectares of prime vineyard sites in Gedersdorf and Rohrendorf. His focus can be described as having three pillars: Typicality, varietal character and terroir. Since the, then, young winemaker took over the winery in 1990, he has placed special emphasis on expressing the fruit type of the Krems Valley and at the same time bringing out the character of the respective varieties. The foundation comes from a selection of old vines, which are used for grafting when new vines are planted. Manfred Felsner is an uncompromising advocate of terroir as well as near-natural viticulture. The greatest goal of the Veltliner specialist is to bring out the many different varieties of this quintessentially Austrian variety. Grüner Veltliner thrives excellently on his exposed terraced vineyards with glacial loess or lime-rich conglomerate soils.

The mild Pannonian influence from the east and the cool winds from the Waldviertel give the wines their spiciness and finesse. From the fragrant Grüner Veltliner Ried Moosburgerin to the full-bodied Grüner Veltliner Ried Vordernberg and the mineral Grüner Veltliner Ried Gebling to the complex Grüner Veltliner Alte Reben, each wine has its own personality.

(91) Grüner Veltliner ** Ried Schnabel 2022
13 Vol.-%, screwcap, steel tank, €€€€
92 Grüner Veltliner ** Ried Schnabel Alte Reben 2021
Medium yellow green colour with silver reflections. Fine meadow herbs, yellow apples, a hint of spices, a bit of orange peel. Juicy, elegant, multi-faceted acidity, powerful, orchard fruit notes on the finish, fruity and sweet aftertaste, a good food wine.
92 Grüner Veltliner ** Ried Schnabel Alte Reben 2020
90 Grüner Veltliner * Gedersdorf Ried Moosburgerin 2022
12,5 Vol.-%, screwcap, steel tank, €€
89 Grüner Veltliner * Gedersdorf Ried Moosburgerin 2021

89 Grüner Veltliner * Ried Moosburgerin 2020

(92) Riesling * Ried Gebling 2022
12,5 Vol.-%, screwcap, steel tank, €€€
91 Riesling * Rohrendorf Ried Gebling 2021
92 Riesling * Ried Gebling 2020

92 Riesling * Gedersdorf Weisser Stein 2020

91 Neuburger Ried Reisenthal 2021
13 Vol.-%, screwcap, steel tank, €€€
90 Neuburger Ried Reisenthal 2020
91 Neuburger Ried Reisenthal 2019

89 Gelber Muskateller 2022
12 Vol.-%, screwcap, steel tank, €€
88 Muskateller 2021
89 Gelber Muskateller Gedersdorfer Lössterrassen 2019

88 Rosé 2022
12 Vol.-%, screwcap, steel tank, €€
89 Rosé 2020 ZW/SL
88 Rosé Hesperia 2019 ZW/SL

WEINGUT FELSNER
3485 Grunddorf
Ortsring 61
T: +43 (2735) 5122
office@weingut-felsner.at
www.weingut-felsner.at

Winemaker/Contact:
Manfred Felsner
Production: 68 % white, 30 % red, 2 % sweet, 16 hectares
Fairs: ProWein Düsseldorf

* Kremstal DAC   ** Kremstal DAC Reserve

NIEDERÖSTERREICH/LOWER AUSTRIA

Wetterkreuzkirche

WEINGUT MEINHARD FORSTREITER
3506 Krems-Hollenburg
Hollenburger Kirchengasse 7
T: +43 (2739) 2296
weingut@forstreiter.at
www.forstreiter.at

Winemaker: Meinhard and Daniel Forstreiter
Contact: Meinhard Forstreiter
Production: 80 % white, 19 % red, 1 % sweet, 54 hectares
Certified: Sustainable Austria
Fairs: ProWein Düsseldorf, VieVinum
Distribution partners: BE, DE, CDN, NL, PL, SE, CH, USA

★ ★ ★

WEINGUT MEINHARD FORSTREITER

Like hardly any other winery in the Kremstal region of Lower Austria, the Forstreiter winery succeeds in combining tradition and innovation. With Tabor, for example, the winery owns the oldest vineyard in Austria with Grüner Veltliner vines, and its winery has continually expanded for decades and is now one of the most modern wine production facilities in the region. Located in Hollenburg, the south-easternmost district of the white wine capital Krems, the organic vineyard has been family-owned since 1868 and, although it has grown from 28 to 54 hectares over the past decades, is still run as a family business in harmony with nature by the current winemaker Meinhard Forstreiter. The main variety is Grüner Veltliner, but Riesling, Sauvignon Blanc, Gelber Muskateller as well as red wines from Zweigelt and St. Laurent are also vinified and successfully exported to 17 different countries. "We are proud to carry the ‚Sustainably Produced Wine from Austria' certificate since 2019 and are pleased to be able to make an ecological, economic and social contribution." The wines are appreciated by both the private and the gastronomy sector, and great importance is attached to personal customer service here.

93 ❂ Chardonnay Forstreiter Brut 2017

94 Grüner Veltliner ** Krems Ried Hollenburger Kreuzberg Das Weiße Mammut 2020
13,5 Vol.-%, cork, barrique, €€€€ Ⓥ

95 Grüner Veltliner ** Ried Kreuzberg Das weiße Mammut 2019
Pale greenish yellow, silver glints. Luscious tropical fruit, delicate melon, a hint of herbal savouriness, salted caramel, a touch of tobacco, and candied orange zest. Juicy, good complexity, finely savoury, hints of quince, and dark minerality. A multifaceted food accompaniment with good ageing potential.

93 Grüner Veltliner ** Ried Kreuzberg Hollenburg Das weiße Mammut 2019

94 Grüner Veltliner * Ried Schiefer 2021
13,5 Vol.-%, screwcap, steel tank, €€€€ Ⓥ

92 Grüner Veltliner * Ried Schiefer 2020

92 Grüner Veltliner * Ried Schiefer 2019

93 Grüner Veltliner * Ried Kogl 2022
12,5 Vol.-%, screwcap, steel tank, €€ Ⓥ

92 Grüner Veltliner * Krems Ried Kogl 2021

92 Grüner Veltliner * Ried Kremser Kogl 2020

93 Grüner Veltliner ** Ried Tabor 2020

KREMSTAL DAC

| 93 | Grüner Veltliner ** Ried Tabor 2019 |
| 93 | Grüner Veltliner ** Tabor 2018 |

92 Grüner Veltliner * Krems Alte Reben 2021
14 Vol.-%, screwcap, steel tank, €€€ V

92 Grüner Veltliner * Alte Reben 2019
91 Grüner Veltliner * Alte Reben 2017

92 Grüner Veltliner * Little Mammut 2020

91 Grüner Veltliner * Krems Kalk & Stein 2022
12,5 Vol.-%, screwcap, steel tank, €€

91 Grüner Veltliner * Kalk & Stein 2021

94 Grüner Veltliner Maische 2021
13,5 Vol.-%, screwcap, 500-l-barrel, €€€€ V

93 Grüner Veltliner Maische 2020
Medium yellow, green hints and silver reflections. Ripe herbal notes, a hint of white peach, candied lime zest and a mineral touch. Juicy on the palate with good complexity, powerful with subtle nutty flavours and tropical fruit with a savoury note on the finish. A multi-faceted food companion.

90 Grüner Veltliner Wagram Ried Rosengarten 2021
91 Grüner Veltliner Ried Rosengarten 2020
90 Grüner Veltliner Ried Wagramer Rosengarten 2019

93 Riesling * Ried Schiefer 2021
13,5 Vol.-%, screwcap, steel tank, €€€€ V

92 Riesling ** Ried Schiefer 2020
92 Riesling ** Ried Schiefer 2019

91 Riesling * Krems Schotter 2022
13 Vol.-%, screwcap, steel tank, €€ V

92 Riesling * Schotter 2021
91 Riesling * Schotter 2020

90 Gelber Muskateller 2022
12,5 Vol.-%, screwcap, steel tank, €€

91 Gelber Muskateller 2021

89 Weißburgunder 2021

88 Sauvignon Blanc 2022
12,5 Vol.-%, screwcap, steel tank, €€

88 Sauvignon Blanc 2021

92 Das Mammut Reserve 2015 ZW/RÖ/SL

93 Grüner Veltliner Strohwein 2021
8 Vol.-%, screwcap, steel tank, €€€€ V

94 Grüner Veltliner TBA 2021
13,5 Vol.-%, screwcap, steel tank, €€€€ V

★
WEINGUT DAVID HARM
ORGANIC

Weingut David Harm is a haven for connoisseurs. "Life is about good wine and good food!" is a straightforward way for Katharina and David Harm to describe their motivation for their work at the family winery. The winery, idyllically situated, elevated above the Danube, south of the city of Krems in the small village of Krustetten, is a delightful place for gourmets and wine lovers alike, an area for hiking, biking and, of course, a haunt for fine wine. The most famous varieties of the region are Grüner Veltliner and Riesling. These grow in the Krems Valley on a wide variety of soils. At the Harm winery, too, the vines are rooted in loess, gravel, primary rock, or conglomerate. The Hollenburger Kreuzberg site is particularly charming. The rare conglomerate rock found there, which is gorgeously pink due to iron deposition, gives the Riesling Kreuzberg its unique scent and taste. "Capturing scents and tastes from all over the world is our passion, each site is allowed to epitomize itself in the wine and is given leisurely time to do so," David Harm tells us. "We rely on hand harvesting, organic and vegan vinification, spontaneous fermentation, wood and long aging." This diversity is also found in the vineyard, where an abundance of herbs, fruit trees, and insects, such as the vine hawk moth, which also adorns the logo, can be found.

93 Riesling * Hollenburg Ried Kreuzberg 2022
13 Vol.-%, screwcap, steel tank, €€€€ B V

93 Riesling * Hollenburg Ried Kreuzberg 2021
Bright yellow green, silver reflections. Attractive tropical fruit, nuances of lychee and peach, lime zest and blossom

---

* Kremstal DAC   ** Kremstal DAC Reserve

NIEDERÖSTERREICH/LOWER AUSTRIA

David Harm

WEINGUT DAVID HARM
3508 Krustetten
Am Brunnen 14
T: +43 (2739) 2520
office@weinschwaermer.at
www.weinschwaermer.at

Winemaker/Contact:
David Harm
Production: 80,000 bottles
85 % white, 15 % rosé, 10 hectares
Fairs: VieVinum
Distribution partners: DE, RO, CH, CZ

honey. Complex, juicy, ripe white fruit, fresh acidity, fine fruit expression in the finish, shows length and certain ageing potential.

93 Riesling * Ried Hollenburger Kreuzberg 2020

92 Riesling * Kalk & Löss 2022
13 Vol.-%, screwcap, steel tank, €€€ Ⓑ Ⓥ

94 Weißburgunder Ried Gottschelle 2021
13 Vol.-%, screwcap, used barriques, €€€€ Ⓑ Ⓥ

93 Grüner Veltliner Wachau DAC Ried Zaum 2022
13 Vol.-%, screwcap, 500-l-barrel/steel tank, €€€€ Ⓑ

92 Grüner Veltliner Wachau DAC Ried Silberbichl 2022
13 Vol.-%, screwcap, steel tank, €€€ Ⓑ Ⓥ

93 Grüner Veltliner Hollenburg Ried Schiefer 2021
13 Vol.-%, screwcap, steel tank, €€€€ Ⓑ Ⓥ

WEINGUT & HOTEL MALAT

Weingut Malat is one of those special wineries that produce a top-quality range of products in all categories: white, red, sparkling, and sweet - and exclusively from grapes grown in their own vineyards. Since 2008, Michael Malat has been running the family business founded in 1722 in Furth bei Göttweig and producing his own style of wine here. "I want to make wines that people enjoy drinking, not just tasting, and my personal signature should be clearly evident: elegance, finesse, and easy to drink!"

Michael Malat pursues a style of wine that was already embraced by his father Gerald, the winegrowing pioneer of the Krems Valley, who propelled the winery to the forefront with his visionary work. "The diversity of our assortment reflects, on the one hand, the long tradition, but on the other hand also the potential of our wine-growing region," Michael Malat is pleased about the great opportunities he encounters as a winemaker in the Kremstal. He deliberately refrains from irrigating the vines, which is common in many places: "It would change the character of the vineyards. Only when the vines are forced to root deeply in order to access water and min-

© @ Atelier Schulte

KREMSTAL DAC

erals does the character of the vineyard express itself authentically in the wine." Spontaneous fermentation for all site wines and the complete renunciation of grapes with botrytis also ensure a precise, recognisable profile for all wines. These wines are clear and transparent, varietally typical and animating, opulently finesse, multilayered and authentic, but never overpowering.

The Malats know how to master the entire range perfectly, from light white wines to complex red wines. Since 1976, Austria's first sparkling wines, Malat Brut and Malat Brut Rosé have been produced according to the traditional method. Traditional noble sweet wines complete their product range - these are also always among the best in the country. At the Malat winery, perfection has always been the guiding principle for many generations.

WEINGUT & HOTEL MALAT
3511 Palt
Hafnerstraße 12
T: +43 (2732) 82934
weingut@malat.at
www.malat.at

Winemaker/Contact:
Michael Malat
Production: 10 % sparkling, 74 % white, 5 % rosé, 10 % red, 1 % sweet, 45 hectares
Certified: Sustainable Austria
Fairs: ProWein Düsseldorf, VieVinum
Distribution partners: BE, RC, DK, DE, FIN, UK, IRL, IT, JP, CDN, LU, NL, NO, PL, RUS, SE, CH, SGP, TH, CZ, HU, USA, PT

96 ❶ Sekt Austria Große Reserve Niederösterreich g.U. Furth Blanc de Blancs Brut Nature 2016
12,5 Vol.-%, cork, bottle fermentation, €€€€€ Ⓑ

95 ❶ Chardonnay Sekt Austria Große Reserve brut nature Niederösterreich g.U.Furth 2014
Pale golden yellow, fine, persistent mousse. Soft yellow tropical fruit, nuances of peach and pineapple, a hint of lime and French biscuit, and white flowers. Juicy, fine fruit expression, pleasant nutty nuances, saline touch on the finish, with finesse and persistence followed by lime-nuanced reverberations. Ethereal, delicate, and well-developed with the potential to age further.

93 ❶ Sekt Austria Reserve Niederösterreich g.U. Brut Nature 2017 CH/PN
12 Vol.-%, cork, bottle fermentation, €€€€ Ⓑ

92 ❶ Malat Brut Nature Österreichischer Sekt g. U. Niederösterreich Reserve 2015 CH/PN

92 ❶ Malat Brut Reserve Sekt g.U. 2014

93 ❶ Sekt Austria Reserve Niederösterreich g.U. Brut Rosé 2018
12 Vol.-%, cork, bottle fermentation, €€€€ Ⓑ

93 ❶ Pinot Noir Sekt Austria Reserve Rosé brut nature Niederösterreich g.U. 2017

93 ❶ Malat Brut Rosé Reserve 2016

(95) Riesling * Ried Pfaffenberg 1ÖTW 2021
13 Vol.-%, cork, large wooden barrel, €€€€ Ⓑ

93 Riesling * Ried Pfaffenberg 1ÖTW 2020
13 Vol.-%, cork, large wooden barrel, €€€€ Ⓑ

(94) Riesling * Ried Steinbühel 1ÖTW 2021
13 Vol.-%, cork, large wooden barrel, €€€€ Ⓑ

94 Riesling * Ried Steinbühel 1ÖTW 2020
13 Vol.-%, cork, large wooden barrel, €€€€ Ⓑ

95 Riesling * Ried Steinbühel 1ÖTW 2019

94 Riesling Große Reserve (1,5l Magnum) 2016
95 Riesling * Große Reserve 2015
Bright golden yellow, silver reflections. Ripe yellow tropical fruit with a touch of herbal spice, nuances of mango and peach, some saffron and candied orange zest, a touch of honey. Complex, juicy, fine nuances of apple and pineapple, well-integrated acidity, ripe fruit on the finish, subtle sweetness on the aftertaste, apricot on the palate, fully developed, a robust food wine.

(94) Grüner Veltliner * Ried Gottschelle 1ÖTW 2021
13 Vol.-%, cork, wooden barrel, €€€€ Ⓑ

93 Grüner Veltliner * Ried Gottschelle 1ÖTW 2020
13 Vol.-%, cork, wooden barrel, €€€€ Ⓑ

94 Grüner Veltliner * Ried Gottschelle 1ÖTW 2019

(93) Grüner Veltliner * Ried Leukuschberg 2021
13 Vol.-%, cork, used barriques, €€€€ Ⓑ

93 Grüner Veltliner * Ried Leukuschberg 2019

92 Grüner Veltliner * Ried Höhlgraben 2022
12,5 Vol.-%, screwcap, large wooden barrel, €€€ Ⓑ

92 Grüner Veltliner * Ried Höhlgraben 2021

92 Grüner Veltliner * Ried Höhlgraben 2019

* Kremstal DAC   ** Kremstal DAC Reserve

NIEDERÖSTERREICH/LOWER AUSTRIA

91 Grüner Veltliner * Crazy Creatures 2022	92 Pinot Gris Ried Zistel 2019
91 Grüner Veltliner * Crazy Creatures 2021	92 Pinot Gris Ried Zistel 2017
91 Grüner Veltliner * Crazy Creatures 2019	
	91 Gelber Muskateller Raw 2020
(93) Chardonnay Ried Hochrain 2021	90 Gelber Muskateller RAW 2019
13 Vol.-%, cork, barrique, €€€€€ Ⓑ	
93 Chardonnay Ried Hochrain 2020	90 Cabernet Sauvignon Furth Rosé 2022
13,5 Vol.-%, cork, barrique, €€€€ Ⓑ	90 Cabernet Sauvignon Furth Rosé 2020
93 Chardonnay Ried Hochrain 2019	
	93 Pinot Noir Ried Satzen 2019
90 Chardonnay Furth 2021	13 Vol.-%, cork, barrique, €€€€ Ⓑ
92 Pinot Blanc Ried Am Zaum 2022	90 Pinot Noir Furth 2019
12,5 Vol.-%, screwcap, large wooden barrel, €€€€ Ⓑ	
91 Pinot Blanc Ried Am Zaum 2021	94 Weißburgunder Beerenauslese
91 Pinot Blanc Ried Am Zaum 2020	Leopold 2016
92 Gewürztraminer RAW 2021	94 Grüner Veltliner TBA 2018

WEINGUT MANTLERHOF

ORGANIC

On approaching Weingut Mantlerhof, in the centre of Brunn im Felde, a twinkle from the picturesque pond catches the eye. To the pond's west is an impressive courtyard with an early classicist façade. The Mantlerhof dates back to Admont Abbey, which owned the stately farmstead until the mid-16th century. It was acquired by the Mantler family 200 years ago. One aspect is immediately apparent at first glance: solidity and consistency; even the label reflects this. Margid and Sepp Mantler and their three children not only cultivate the vines but also farm arable land. Since 2003, both branches of the business have been gradually converted to organic farming and are now certified.

The Mantlers cultivate the classic white wines of the region on the impressive loess terraces, the light yellow walls of which reflect far to the south. The Grüner Veltliner and Riesling are vinified in the Kremstal DAC style on a variety of sites. A particular speciality of the Mantlerhof is the cultivation of Roter Veltliner, with very impressive results. To a lesser extent, but with the same passion, Chardonnay, Gelber Muskateller and Neuburger are also cultivated. The latter was planted because an ancestor of Margid Mantler-Ferstl, who was born in the Wachau, was one of the pioneers of this variety.

The best sites from which the estate's wines are bottled are Spiegel (Grüner Veltliner), Wieland (Riesling), Steingraben (Riesling) and Moosburgerin (Grüner Veltliner). All are classified as Erste Lagen according to the 2010 classification of the Traditionsweingüter Österreich.

With its high lime content, the glacial loess shapes the fundamental character of these wines, even the light ones: juicy, full-bodied, and long-lasting. The wines of the Mantlerhof are very distinct in their varietal characteristics and have earned a reputation for long ageing potential. Although the majority of the wines are dry, there is a wide range of noble sweet wines with great depth. The collection of old and rare bottles from their own winery dates back to 1947. Their main marketing focus is on specialist retailers and the gastronomy sector, with exports accounting for 45% of sales.

100 Riesling * Gedersdorf Ried Wieland 1ÖTW 2021
13 Vol.-%, cork, steel tank/bottle maturation, €€€€€
Ⓑ Ⓥ

KREMSTAL DAC

94 Riesling * Gedersdorf Ried Wieland 1ÖTW 2020
Light greenish yellow, silver reflections. Fine yellow tropical fruit, light blossom, almost red berry nuances, fresh orange zest, mineral background. Juicy, white peach fruit, fresh, fine savoury touch, salty-lemon in the aftertaste, lively style, limes, certain ageing potential.

94 Riesling * Ried Wieland 1ÖTW 2019

96 Riesling * Gedersdorf Ried Steingraben 1ÖTW 2021
12,5 Vol.-%, cork, steel tank/bottle maturation, €€€€€ Ⓑ Ⓥ

93 Riesling * Gedersdorf Ried Steingraben 1ÖTW 2020

94 Riesling * Ried Steingraben 1ÖTW 2019

90 Riesling * Ried Zehetnerin 2019
91 Riesling * Ried Zehetnerin 2018
90 Riesling * Ried Zehetnerin 2017

96 Grüner Veltliner * Gedersdorf Ried Spiegel 1ÖTW 2021
13,5 Vol.-%, cork, steel tank/bottle maturation, €€€€€ Ⓑ Ⓥ

95 Grüner Veltliner * Gedersdorf Ried Spiegel 1ÖTW 2020
Medium yellow-green, silver glints. Subtle herbal savoury nuances, a little honeydew melon, delicate hints of apple, mango, tangerine zest, and a dash of minerality. Firm, white apple fruit, tightly woven and vibrant structure, citrus-minerality, exhibiting excellent length. A silky-smooth food accompaniment with good ageing potential. Already accessible.

93 Grüner Veltliner * Ried Spiegel 1ÖTW 2019

94 Grüner Veltliner ** Gedersdorf Ried Moosburgerin 1ÖTW 2021
13 Vol.-%, cork, steel tank/bottle maturation, €€€€€ Ⓑ Ⓥ

93 Grüner Veltliner * Gedersdorf Ried Moosburgerin 1ÖTW 2020

93 Grüner Veltliner * Ried Moosburgerin 1ÖTW 2019

93 Grüner Veltliner * Gedersdorf Lössterrassen 2022
12,5 Vol.-%, screwcap, steel tank, €€€ Ⓑ Ⓥ

91 Grüner Veltliner * Lössterrassen 2019

94 Roter Veltliner Gedersdorf Ried Ungut 2020
Medium yellow-green, silver reflections. Delicate nuances of yellow fruit, hints of figs and nougat, with fresh mango and some blossom honey underneath. Lean but sturdy on the palate, a hint of linden blossom, fine acidity, mineral-citrus notes on the finish, very good length, fresh and persistent, shows what this rare variety has to offer.

WEINGUT MANTLERHOF
3494 Brunn im Felde/ Gedersdorf
Hauptstraße 50
T: +43 (2735) 8248
weingut@mantlerhof.com
www.mantlerhof.com

Winemaker: Josef Mantler
Contact: Margid Mantler
Production: 98 % white, 2 % sweet, 15 hectares
Fairs: Austrian Tasting London, Millésime Bio, ProWein Düsseldorf, VieVinum
Distribution partners: DK, DE, EST, FIN, UK, HK, IT, JP, MT, NL, NO, RUS, CH, CZ, USA

95 Roter Veltliner Ried Ungut 2019

94 Roter Veltliner Gedersdorf Ried Reisenthal 2022
13,5 Vol.-%, cork, steel tank, €€€€€ Ⓑ Ⓥ

93 Roter Veltliner Ried Reisenthal 2021
92 Roter Veltliner Ried Reisenthal 2020

93 Roter Veltliner Gedersdorf Ried Reisenthal Selection 2021
13,5 Vol.-%, cork, steel tank, €€€€€ Ⓑ Ⓥ

94 Roter Veltliner Ried Reisenthal Selection 2019

92 Neuburger Hommage 2022
12,5 Vol.-%, screwcap, steel tank, €€€€ Ⓑ Ⓥ

93 Neuburger Hommage 2021
92 Neuburger Hommage 2020

91 Chardonnay Gedersdorf 2019

93 Grüner Veltliner Beerenauslese 2017

95 Riesling Beerenauslese 2017

* Kremstal DAC   ** Kremstal DAC Reserve

WEINKELLEREI LENZ MOSER

Internationally, the wines of Lenz Moser are an integral part of the Austrian wine scene. The winery, based in Rohrendorf near Krems, is not only the market leader in Austrian quality wine but has also always been an innovator. Among other things, the screw cap was introduced here in 1984, and since 2008 you can find it on almost all of Lenz Moser's wines.

"Small is beautiful". This also applies to the Lenz Moser winery, as a large number of winegrowers, who collectively look after around 2,700 hectares of vineyards, deliver their grapes to the winery in small batches in the autumn. To ensure that only healthy, perfectly ripened grapes are delivered, the team led by Head Oenologist Michael Rethaller maintains close contact with the winegrowers and advises them throughout the year.

In addition to the excellent quality of all the wine lines and the certainty that they have been created with the greatest attention to detail, consumers also appreciate the highly reasonable price range. Lenz Moser wines have also received the recognition they deserve from renowned wine experts at home and abroad.

90 Grüner Veltliner * Rohrendorf Lenz Moser 2022
12,5 Vol.-%, screwcap, steel tank, €€

90 Grüner Veltliner * Rohrendorf 2021
Medium yellow-green, silver reflections. Fresh orange zest, hints of yellow apple and mango, subtle tobacco. Medium body, white stone fruit, freshly structured, salty minerality, lingers, a versatile food wine.

91 Grüner Veltliner * Rohrendorf 2020

90 Grüner Veltliner Lenz Moser Prestige 2022
12,5 Vol.-%, screwcap, steel tank, €€

90 Grüner Veltliner Lenz Moser Prestige 2021
90 Grüner Veltliner Lenz Moser Prestige 2020

89 Grüner Veltliner Lenz Moser Selection 2022
12 Vol.-%, screwcap, steel tank, €€

89 Grüner Veltliner Lenz Moser Selection 2021
89 Grüner Veltliner Lenz Moser Selection 2020

89 Pinot Gris Lenz Moser Prestige 2021
90 Pinot Gris Lenz Moser Prestige 2020
89 Pinot Gris Prestige 2018

89 Riesling Lenz Moser Prestige 2022
12,5 Vol.-%, screwcap, steel tank, €€

88 Riesling Prestige 2019
89 Riesling Prestige 2018

92 Lenz Moser Noah 2017 ZW/CS/ME

90 Blaufränkisch Barrique Lenz Moser Prestige 2020
13,5 Vol.-%, screwcap, barrique, €€

90 Blaufränkisch Barrique Lenz Moser Prestige 2019
89 Blaufränkisch Barrique Prestige 2017

90 Blauer Zweigelt Reserve Lenz Moser Prestige 2020

89 Blauer Zweigelt Lenz Moser Prestige Reserve 2019

89 Blauer Zweigelt Prestige Reserve 2018

94 Lenz Moser Carpe Diem Mariage 2015 CS/ME

Grüner Veltliner

KREMSTAL DAC

WEINKELLEREI LENZ MOSER
3495 Rohrendorf
Lenz-Moser-Straße 1
T: +43 (2732) 85541
marketing@lenzmoser.at
www.lenzmoser.at

Winemaker: Michael Rethaller
Contact: Christoph Bierbaum
Production: 55 % white, 44 % red, 1 % sweet
Fairs: Anuga, ProWein Düsseldorf, VieVinum, Vinexpo
Distribution partners: DK, DE, EST, FIN, UK, JP, CDN, NL, NO, PL, RUS, SE, SK, CZ, USA

View over Krems

94 Trockenbeerenauslese Lenz Moser Prestige 2018 BO/WR
8,5 Vol.-%, cork, steel tank, €€€€
93 TBA Prestige 2017 CH/WB/WR/GV/SÄ

91 Beerenauslese Prestige 2018 WB/SÄ/CH/WR/BO/SB/MO
92 Beerenauslese Prestige 2017 WR/CH/WB

SCHLOSSWEINGUT MALTESER RITTERORDEN WEINVIERTEL

90 🛈 Malteser Ritterorden Sekt brut 2017

90 Grüner Veltliner * 2022
12,5 Vol.-%, screwcap, steel tank, €€
89 Grüner Veltliner * 2021
90 Grüner Veltliner * 2020

92 Grüner Veltliner Reserve 2019
14 Vol.-%, screwcap, steel tank, €€€€
92 Grüner Veltliner Reserve 2018
92 Grüner Veltliner Reserve Magnum 2015

91 Grüner Veltliner Ried Hundschupfen 2022
13 Vol.-%, screwcap, steel tank, €€
90 Grüner Veltliner Ried Hundschupfen 2021
91 Grüner Veltliner Ried Hundschupfen 2020

88 Chardonnay 2020
88 Chardonnay 2019

89 Chardonnay 2018

91 Kommende Mailberg 2019 CS/ME
14 Vol.-%, cork, barrique, €€€
91 Kommende Mailberg 2018 CS/ME
91 Kommende Mailberg 2017 CS/ME

91 Merlot 2020
14 Vol.-%, cork, barrique, €€€
90 Merlot 2019
91 Merlot 2018

89 Blauer Zweigelt 2020
13 Vol.-%, screwcap, large wooden barrel, €€
88 Blauer Zweigelt 2019
88 Blauer Zweigelt 2018

KLOSTERKELLER SIEGENDORF LEITHABERG

90 Weißburgunder 2020
90 Weißburgunder 2018
89 Weißburgunder 2017

89 O'Dora 2019 CF/CS
91 O'Dora 2018 CF/CS
90 O'Dora 2017 CF/CS

89 Cabernet Sauvignon 2017

88 Siegendorf Rot 2017 CS/ME

* Kremstal DAC ** Kremstal DAC Reserve

NIEDERÖSTERREICH/LOWER AUSTRIA

The Müller family

WEINGUT MÜLLER
3508 Krustetten
Hollenburger Straße 12
T: +43 (2739) 2691
info@weingutmueller.at
www.weingutmueller.at

Winemaker: Leopold Müller
Contact: Leopold and Stefan Müller
Production: 1 % sparkling, 80 % white, 1 % rosé, 17 % red, 1 % sweet
Certified: Sustainable Austria
Fairs: ProWein Düsseldorf, VieVinum, Vinexpo
Distribution partners: BE, DK, DE, FIN, FR, UK, IRL, IT, CDN, LU, NL, NO, PL, RUS, SE, CH

★ ★ ★

WEINGUT MÜLLER

Nestled in the picturesque wine village of Krustetten in the southern Krems Valley is the Müller family winery. It was first mentioned in a document in 1270 as Lesehof (wine press house) in the Göttweig Abbey archives and has been run by the Müllers as a family business since 1936. Viticulture on the Göttweiger Berg has a long tradition, which has been appreciated and cultivated by the Müller family for three and four generations. Grandfather Leopold started viticulture with just 0.7 hectares of vineyards, but since then the Müllers have expanded the area to 120 hectares. Stefan tends the vineyards with love and passion, while Leopold is in charge of everything from grape picking to bottling. Their philosophy is to work in harmony with nature and to make targeted use of the diverse conditions around the Göttweiger Berg to bring out the best in each vineyard. Leopold and Stefan Müller agree: "Our landscape gives us an immense variety of soils - from deep loess to weathered conglomerate to barren primary rock soils - and unique climatic conditions for high-quality grapes and wines full of character! We feel obligated to keep our landscape viable for generations to come, and try to run our winery in the most sustainable way possible."
Through their determination, the strict criteria of the "Sustainable Austria" certification could be achieved. The wines can be tasted in the wine cellar at the winery or at the ‚Top Heurigen', which is open four times a year, and are also available from many retailers.

92 ❶ Riesling Sekt g.U. Große Reserve 2015

91 ❶ Müller Grüner Veltliner Brut Österreichischer Sekt g. U. Ried Göttweiger Berg Grosse Reserve NV

91 ❶ Grüner Veltliner Sekt g.U. Große Reserve 2015

95 Grüner Veltliner ** Ried Eichbühel 2021
13,5 Vol. %, cork, wooden barrel, €€€€

92 Grüner Veltliner ** Ried Eichbühel 2020
Medium green yellow colour with silver reflections. Delicate orange zest, a touch of pineapple and mango, fine blossom honey. Complex, juicy, delicate nuances of quince,

KREMSTAL DAC

silky texture, ripe yellow apples, subtle honey on the finish, already approachable.
- 93 Grüner Veltliner ** Ried Eichbühel 2018

- 92 Grüner Veltliner * Ried Gottschelle 2021
- 92 Grüner Veltliner ** Ried Further Gottschelle 2020
- 92 Grüner Veltliner * Ried Further Gottschelle 2019

- 91 Grüner Veltliner * Ried Kremser Kogl 2022

12,5 Vol.-%, screwcap, steel tank, €€
- 90 Grüner Veltliner * Ried Kremser Kogl 2021
- 92 Grüner Veltliner * Ried Kremser Kogl 2020

- 92 Grüner Veltliner * Ried Neuberg 2022

13 Vol.-%, screwcap, steel tank, €€
- 92 Grüner Veltliner * Ried Neuberg 2021
- 92 Grüner Veltliner * Ried Neuberg 2020

- 91 Grüner Veltliner * Ried Frauengrund 2022

12,5 Vol.-%, screwcap, steel tank, €€
- 91 Grüner Veltliner * Ried Frauengrund 2021
- 91 Grüner Veltliner * Ried Kremser Frauengrund 2020

- 90 Grüner Veltliner * Göttweiger Berg 2022
- 89 Grüner Veltliner * Göttweiger Berg 2021
- 90 Grüner Veltliner * Göttweiger Berg 2020

- 93 Riesling ** Hollenburg Ried Goldberg 2021

13 Vol.-%, cork, wooden barrel, €€€€
- 91 Riesling ** Ried Goldberg 2020

Light golden yellow, silver reflections. Nuances of blossom honey, fresh apricot, some mango, ripe fruit bouquet, a touch of caramel. Juicy, substantial, elegant, fruity, silky texture, well matured, some nougat on the finish, shows length, mild style.
- 93 Riesling ** Hollenburg Ried Goldberg 2019

- 92 Riesling * Ried Leiten 2021
- 92 Riesling * Ried Leiten 2020

- 91 Riesling * Ried Silberbichl 2022

12,5 Vol.-%, screwcap, steel tank, €€€
- 91 Riesling * Furth Ried Silberbichl 2021
- 91 Riesling * Ried Further Silberbichl 2020

- 90 Riesling * Göttweiger Berg 2022
- 88 Riesling * Göttweiger Berg 2021
- 90 Riesling * Göttweiger Berg 2020

Neuburger

- 90 Chardonnay Ried Fuchaberg Reserve 2022

13,5 Vol.-%, screwcap, large wooden barrel, €€€
- 91 Chardonnay Ried Fuchaberg Reserve 2020
- 90 Chardonnay Reserve Ried Fuchaberg 2019

- 89 Sauvignon Blanc Göttweiger Berg 2021
- 89 Sauvignon Blanc Göttweiger Berg 2020

- 90 Gelber Muskateller Göttweiger Berg 2022

12 Vol.-%, screwcap, steel tank, €€

- 91 Neuburger Ried Kremser Kogl Reserve 2021

13 Vol.-%, cork, wooden barrel, €€€€€

- 92 Diana 2019 ZW/CS/ME

13,5 Vol.-%, cork, barrique, €€€€€
- 91 Diana 2018 ZW/CS/ME
- 92 Diana 2017 ZW/CS/ME

- 89 Zweigelt Reserve 2020

13,5 Vol.-%, screwcap, barrique, €€€
- 89 Zweigelt Reserve 2019
- 90 Zweigelt Reserve 2018

- 93 Grüner Veltliner Eiswein 2021

- 96 Neuburger TBA Therese 2017

- 94 Riesling Ried Leiten Beerenauslese 2017

* Kremstal DAC   ** Kremstal DAC Reserve

NIEDERÖSTERREICH/LOWER AUSTRIA

★★★★★
WEIN-GUT NIGL

Weingut Nigl is located on the outskirts of Senftenberg, near the foothills of the Burgberg. Today, the winery has 30 hectares of vineyards spread over the best sites of the Kremstal. The most important are Pellingen, planted with Riesling and Grüner Veltliner, and Hochäcker, planted with Riesling. The vineyards are located near Senftenberg, Rehberg, and the Kremser Rieden.

The best wines in the Nigl range are called "Privat". The two "Privat" selections come from old vineyards in the Pellingen area of Senftenberg. The yields of the 40-year-old vines are very low on the barren primary rock soils, but the quality is all the higher: year after year, two great wines are produced here, with great concentration and minerality. Stuart Pigott says of Martin Nigl's wines: "From the simplest wine to these ultimate pinnacles, Nigl's whites are crystal clear and extremely precise in aroma and flavour. Here, almost indecent charm and great elegance are combined; simply brilliant! We can only agree with this statement." The Nigl family also runs a restaurant and a small hotel in Senftenberg, making for a comfortable stay in the Kremstal.

90 ❂ Brût de Brût Sekt g.U. Klassik NV

(97) Riesling * Ried Hochäcker 1ÖTW 2022
13 Vol.-%, screwcap, wooden barrel, €€€€€€
97 Riesling * Ried Hochäcker 1ÖTW Privat 2021
Pale yellow-green, silver glints. Pleasant meadow herbs, subtle vineyard peach, delicate hints of blossom honey, candied orange peel. A multidimensional mineral-nuanced bouquet. Complex, elegant, filigree acidity structure, intensely redolent of white stone fruit, and passion fruit on the finish, with mineral reverberations. A complex food accompaniment with potential.
98 Riesling * Ried Hochäcker 1ÖTW Privat 2020

(94) Riesling * Rehberg Ried Goldberg 1ÖTW 2022
13 Vol.-%, cork, wooden barrel, €€€€€
95 Riesling * Rehberg Ried Goldberg 1ÖTW 2021
Light yellow-green, silver reflections. Fine stone fruit nuances, fresh white vine peach, a touch of lime zest. Complex, powerful, juicy white tropical fruit, underpinned with a racy acidity, mineral-lemon finish, solid fruit expression, shows length, good ageing potential.
94 Riesling * Ried Goldberg 2020

92 Riesling * Piri 2022
13 Vol.-%, screwcap, steel tank, €€€€
92 Riesling * Piri 2021
93 Riesling * Piri 2020

(96) Grüner Veltliner * Ried Kirchenberg 1ÖTW Herzstück 2022
13 Vol.-%, cork, wooden barrel, €€€€€€
95 Grüner Veltliner * Ried Kirchenberg 1ÖTW Herzstück 2021
Pale yellow-green, silver glints. Zesty orange underlaid with subtle yellow tropical fruit, delicate tobacco nuances, and hints of mango and blossom honey. Powerful, dense, subtle fruit expression, lush yellow apple, silky-mineral texture, sweet and persistent. An opulent style, with a dash of caramel on the finish, exhibiting length. Will profit from further bottle ageing.

WEIN-GUT NIGL
3541 Senftenberg
Kirchenberg 1
T: +43 (2719) 2609
info@weingutnigl.at
www.weingutnigl.at

Winemaker/Contact:
Martin Nigl
Production: 90 % white, 9 % red, 1 % sweet, 30 hectares
Fairs: ProWein Düsseldorf, VieVinum
Distribution partners: BE, RC, DK, DE, GR, HK, IT, JP, CDN, HR, LT, NL, NO, PL, RUS, CH, SK, SLO, ES, ZA, CZ, HU, USA

KREMSTAL DAC

95 Grüner Veltliner * Ried Kirchenberg Herzstück 2020	90 Grüner Veltliner Niederösterreich 2021
	89 Grüner Veltliner 2020
(95) Grüner Veltliner * Ried Pellingen 1ÖTW Privat 2022	92 Chardonnay Toas 2018
13 Vol.-%, screwcap, steel tank, €€€€	91 Sauvignon Blanc 2022
94 Grüner Veltliner * Ried Pellingen 1ÖTW Privat 2021	13 Vol.-%, screwcap, steel tank, €€€
	91 Sauvignon Blanc 2021
95 Grüner Veltliner * Ried Pellingen 1ÖTW Privat 2020	90 Sauvignon Blanc 2020
	89 Gelber Muskateller 2022
93 Grüner Veltliner * Ried Zwetl 2022	11,5 Vol.-%, screwcap, steel tank, €€€
13 Vol.-%, screwcap, steel tank, €€€€	91 Gelber Muskateller 2021
93 Grüner Veltliner * Ried Zwetl 2021	90 Gelber Muskateller 2020
93 Grüner Veltliner * Ried Zwetl 2020	
	91 Pinot Noir 2019
93 Grüner Veltliner * Alte Reben 2022	13,5 Vol.-%, cork, wooden barrel, €€€€€
13 Vol.-%, screwcap, steel tank/large wooden barrel, €€€€	90 Pinot Noir 2018
	92 Pinot Noir 2017
92 Grüner Veltliner * Alte Reben 2020	
93 Grüner Veltliner * Alte Reben 2019	94 Gelber Muskateller Eiswein 2019
	93 Grüner Veltliner Eiswein 2018
92 Grüner Veltliner * Piri 2022	92 Grüner Veltliner Eiswein 2017
12,5 Vol.-%, screwcap, steel tank, €€€	
91 Grüner Veltliner * Piri 2021	94 Riesling TBA 2018
92 Grüner Veltliner * Piri 2020	

WEINGUT FAMILIE PROIDL

The Proidl family winery operates between tradition and modernity. The family's ancestors emigrated from the Bremen area in 1650 and have been cultivating vines in Senftenberg, north of Krems and at the gateway to the Kremstal, since 1738. It combines the Wachau wine region with the typical Waldviertel landscape of deeply incised river valleys separated by forests and rugged rocky terrain. The Proidl family's long history of winemaking has given them a great deal of expertise in dealing with the diverse vineyard sites. They are meticulous observers of nature and passionate winegrowers. The Proidls see themselves as craftsmen and mountain winegrowers with a past, a present and a promising future.

Minimalism reigns in the cellar. Patrick Proidl is convinced that the highly mineralised soils of Senftenberg and the close-to-nature cultivation of the vineyards mean that there is little need for intervention in the cellar. The most important tasks are patience, tasting and observation. Instead of tinkering with barrels and tanks, the Proidl family gives the wines the time they need to mature. Wines from the Proidl estate do not mature for two to three weeks but for three to twelve months. This results in wines that can be stored without an expiry date - that's the Proidl's unique definition of sustainability.

(96) Riesling ** Ried Ehrenfels 1ÖTW 2022
13 Vol.-%, screwcap, large wooden barrel
96 Riesling ** Ried Ehrenfels 1ÖTW 2021
Medium greenish yellow, silver glints. Delicate floral nuances underlaid with fresh vineyard peach fruit, a hint of lime, and a mineral touch. Inviting bouquet. Complex, tightly woven, white apple, racy-citrus texture, saline reverberations, finely chiselled, and long lasting. Good future potential.

* Kremstal DAC   ** Kremstal DAC Reserve

NIEDERÖSTERREICH/LOWER AUSTRIA

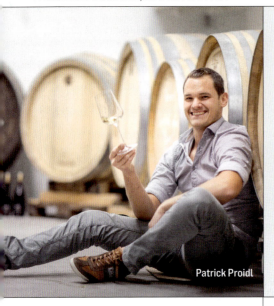

Patrick Proidl

WEINGUT FAMILIE PROIDL
3541 Senftenberg
Oberer Markt 5
T: +43 (2719) 2458
weingut@proidl.com
www.proidl.com

Winemaker/Contact:
Patrick and Franz Proidl
Production: 90 % white, 5 % red, 5 % sweet, 25 hectares
Certified: Sustainable Austria
Fairs: VieVinum
Distribution partners: BE, DE, NL, NO, PL, CH, CZ, USA

---

95   Riesling ** Ried Ehrenfels 1ÖTW 2020

(96) Riesling ** Ried Pfeningberg 1ÖTW 2022
13 Vol.-%, screwcap, large wooden barrel, €€€€€
94   Riesling ** Ried Pfeningberg 1ÖTW 2021
95   Riesling ** Ried Pfeningberg 1ÖTW 2019

(95) Riesling ** Ried Hochäcker 1ÖTW 2022
13 Vol.-%, screwcap, large wooden barrel, €€€€€
94   Riesling ** Ried Hochäcker 1ÖTW 2021
95   Riesling ** Ried Hochäcker 1ÖTW 2019

95   Riesling ** Senftenberg Katzengold 2021
14 Vol.-%, screwcap, wooden barrel, €€€€
93   Riesling * Senftenberg Alte Reben 2020

92   Riesling * Senftenberg Steilheit 2022
92   Riesling * Senftenberg Steilheit 2021
92   Riesling * Senftenberg Steilheit 2020

97   Riesling Senftenberg Generation X 2021
13,5 Vol.-%, screwcap, wooden barrel, €€€€€
94   Riesling Senftenberg Generation X 2020
Medium greenish yellow, silver reflections. Delicate orange zest, plus kumquats and yellow peach fruit, underlaid with pineapple, multi-faceted bouquet. Juicy, elegant, nuances of yellow fruit, fine acidity, mineral, already very balanced, delicately salty on the finish, versatile.
94   Riesling Senftenberg Generation X 2019

95   Riesling »Proidl spricht Deutsch« 2019

(95) Grüner Veltliner ** Ried Ehrenfels 1ÖTW 2022
13,5 Vol.-%, screwcap, large wooden barrel, €€€€€
96   Grüner Veltliner ** Ried Ehrenfels 1ÖTW 2021
95   Grüner Veltliner ** Ried Ehrenfels 1ÖTW 2020
Medium greenish yellow, silver glints. Delicately scented with pineapple and mango, nuances of candied orange zest, and mineral notes. Attractively delicate floral bouquet. Complex, full-bodied, subtle white tropical fruit, richly refined acidity structure, persistent with definite ageing potential. An elegant food accompaniment.

93   Grüner Veltliner * Senftenberg Grande Reserve Holzhammer51 2019
94   Grüner Veltliner Grande Reserve Holzhammer50 2018

(93) Grüner Veltliner ** Ried Pellingen 1ÖTW 2022
13,5 Vol.-%, screwcap, large wooden barrel, €€€€€
93   Grüner Veltliner ** Ried Pellingen 1ÖTW 2021
94   Grüner Veltliner ** Ried Pellingen 1ÖTW 2020

92   Grüner Veltliner * Ried Hausberg 2022
93   Grüner Veltliner * Ried Hausberg 2021
92   Grüner Veltliner * Ried Hausberg Senftenberg 2020

© Edwin Dullinger

KREMSTAL DAC

91 Grüner Veltliner * Senftenberg Rameln 2022	94 Gelber Traminer 2021 15 Vol.-%, screwcap, wooden barrel, €€€€€
92 Grüner Veltliner * Senftenberg Rameln 2021	93 Traminer 2017
92 Grüner Veltliner * Senftenberg Rameln 2020	93 Chardonnay Generation X 2021 13,5 Vol.-%, screwcap, wooden barrel, €€€€€
90 Grüner Veltliner * Senftenberg Freiheit 2022	92 Chardonnay Senftenberg Generation X 2019
92 Grüner Veltliner * Senftenberg Freiheit 2021	
92 Grüner Veltliner * Senftenberg Freiheit 2020	95 Riesling Proidl spricht Deutsch 2021 9,5 Vol.-%, screwcap, steel tank, €€€€€
97 Grüner Veltliner Generation X 2021 15 Vol.-%, screwcap, wooden barrel, €€€€€€	93 Traminer TBA 2017
94 Grüner Veltliner Generation X 2020	
94 Grüner Veltliner Generation X 2019	

★★★★★

WEINGUT SALOMON UNDHOF

Salomon Undhof is a notable icon of Austrian viticultural history and is one of Austria's oldest privately owned wineries. White wines have been produced here for 230 years from some of the best Grand Cru sites along the Danube, including such famous vineyards as ‚Ried Steiner Kögl', ‚Ried Pfaffenberg', ‚Ried Wachtberg' and ‚Ried Lindberg'.

The winery's notability was established in the early 1930s with one of Austria's first wine-bottling plants. Today, through Bertold Salomon, the estate is best known for its excellent dry Riesling and Grüner Veltliner - the long-lived, elegant wines for which it is renowned. More than half of the 25 hectares of vineyards are planted with Riesling, the rest with Grüner Veltliner, and a small part with Gelber Traminer. Salomon Undhof's original parish terraces are located in the westernmost part of the Kremstal, where the soils are predominantly primary rock. The

WEINGUT SALOMON UNDHOF
3500 Stein an der Donau
Undstraße 10
T: +43 (2732) 83226
office@salomonwines.com
www.salomonwein.at
Winemaker: Bert Michael Salomon
Contact: Fanny Marie and Bert Michael Salomon, Dr. Bertold and Mag. Gertrud Salomon
Production: 100 % white, 25 hectares
Certified: Sustainable Austria
Fairs: VieVinum
Distribution partners: AUS, BE, BG, RC, DK, DE, EST, FIN, UK, HK, IL, IT, JP, CDN, ROK, LV, LT, LU, NZ, NL, PL, RUS, SE, CH, SGP, SK, SLO, TH, CZ, USA

Bert Michael, Fanny Marie, Gertrud and Bertold Salomon

* Kremstal DAC   ** Kremstal DAC Reserve

NIEDERÖSTERREICH/LOWER AUSTRIA

wine-growing region of Kremstal and the World Heritage Site of Wachau converge in Stein an der Donau to form this unique viticultural area. The old wine town of Stein takes its name from the predominance of primary rock soils on the stone terraces. Controlled integrated vineyard management and the renunciation of herbicides keep these vineyards in a healthy balance. The ninth generation of siblings, Bert and Fanny Marie, have now taken over. After 25 years of two harvests each (in Austria and Australia), parents Bertold and Gertrud are handing over the reins to the next generation and are primarily focused on the premium red wines of their Australian "Salomon Estate" in Finniss River and on their joint venture "Salomon & Andrew" in New Zealand.

92 ⊕ Pet Nat »Wolke für Zwei« 2022
13 Vol.-%, crown cap, bottle fermentation, €€€€€
93 ⊕ Pet Nat »Wolke für Zwei« 2021
92 ⊕ Wolke für Zwei Pétillant Naturel 2020

92 ⊕ Zweigelt Rosé Sekt g.U. Brut Nature 2020
12,5 Vol.-%, cork, bottle fermentation, €€€€€
91 ⊕ Rosé Sekt g.U. brut nature 2019
91 ⊕ Rosé Sekt g.U. brut nature 2018

(97) Riesling * Ried Steiner Kögl 1ÖTW
Alte Reben 2022
13,5 Vol.-%, cork, steel tank, €€€€€€
97 Riesling ** Ried Steiner Kögl 1ÖTW
Alte Reben 2021
Pale greenish yellow, silver glints. Inviting fragrance of ripe tropical fruit, touches of pineapple, delicate blossom honey, mineral tones, clementine zest, and savoury nuances. Good complexity, taut, vibrant acidity structure, apricot on the finish, mineral reverberations, prolonged persistence. Assured ageing potential.
96 Riesling ** Ried Steiner Kögl 1ÖTW
Alte Reben 2020

(95) Riesling * Ried Pfaffenberg 1ÖTW
Alte Reben 2022
13 Vol.-%, cork, steel tank, €€€€€€
96 Riesling * Ried Pfaffenberg 1ÖTW
Alte Reben 2021
Medium greenish yellow, silver glints. Fragrant herbal savoury scents, a hint of aniseed, a touch of white stone fruit, delicate honeydew melon, and candied orange peel. Juicy, good complexity, taut, dark bristling minerality, expressive fruit redolent of apricot, citrus reverberations followed by a bold finale. Good ageing potential.
95 Riesling * Ried Pfaffenberg 1ÖTW
Alte Reben 2020

(93) Riesling * Ried Steiner Kögl 1ÖTW 2022
13 Vol.-%, screwcap, steel tank, €€€€€
94 Riesling * Ried Kögl 1ÖTW 2021
93 Riesling * Ried Kögl 1ÖTW 2020

92 Riesling * Stein a. d. Donau 2022
12,5 Vol.-%, screwcap, steel tank, €€€
93 Riesling * Stein a. d. Donau 2021
92 Riesling * Stein a. d. Donau 2020

(96) Grüner Veltliner * Ried Lindberg 1ÖTW
Alte Reben 2022
14 Vol.-%, cork, steel tank, €€€€€€
97 Grüner Veltliner * Ried Lindberg 1ÖTW
Alte Reben 2021
Bright pale greenish yellow, silver glints. Meadow herbs underlaid with blossom honey, delicate passion fruit, a hint of peach, and tobacco savouriness. Multidimensional bouquet. Complex, succulent, lush apple, well-integrated, lively acidity structure, finely savoury, prolonged sweet persistence superseded by pineapple reverberations with mineral undertones. Good ageing potential.
95 Grüner Veltliner * Ried Lindberg 1ÖTW
Alte Reben 2020

(95) Grüner Veltliner * Ried Goldberg
Alte Reben 2022
13,5 Vol.-%, cork, steel tank, €€€€€
95 Grüner Veltliner * Ried Goldberg
Alte Reben 2021
94 Grüner Veltliner * Ried Goldberg
Alte Reben 2020

(93) Grüner Veltliner * Ried Wachtberg 1ÖTW 2022
13,5 Vol.-%, screwcap, steel tank, €€€€
94 Grüner Veltliner * Ried Wachtberg 1ÖTW 2021
93 Grüner Veltliner * Ried Wachtberg 1ÖTW 2020

92 Grüner Veltliner * Wieden 2022
12,5 Vol.-%, screwcap, steel tank, €€€
92 Grüner Veltliner * Krems a. d. Donau
Wieden 2021
92 Grüner Veltliner * Krems a. d. Donau
Wieden 2020

92 Grüner Veltliner ** Kremser Tor Alte Reben 2021
92 Grüner Veltliner ** Kremser Tor Alte Reben 2019
92 Grüner Veltliner ** Kremser Tor Alte Reben 2018

93 Gelber Traminer Wildrosen 2021
14,5 Vol.-%, screwcap, steel tank, €€€€
91 Gelber Traminer Lumiere 2020
91 Gelber Traminer 2020

WEINGUT JOSEF SCHMID

The Schmid winery in Stratzing, a small village on a high plateau between Krems and Langenlois, has been family-owned for over 150 years, with Josef Schmid at the helm of the fine estate since 1991. He cultivates his vineyards with great commitment and idealism to vinify wines that are lively, powerful, but also very elegant.

The vineyards are mostly located in Stratzing, on mountain terraces near Senftenberg in Kremstal, and around the city of Krems. This means that Josef Schmid has very diverse terroirs at his disposal. Loess soils and mineral primary rock vineyards enable him to harvest a wide range of white wine grapes - above all Riesling and Grüner Veltliner - in ideal locations. For the winemaker, his top sites are his greatest treasure, and he is firmly convinced that only particularly good and well-suited soils can grow vines that will eventually be reflected in his wines. His approach is confirmed by the numerous awards he has received and the success he has attained.

In 2004, a new cellar extension was completed, which allows for extremely controlled vinification. Pumps have long since become obsolete here, and at least in the cellar Schmid has the desired temperature firmly in hand. The wines, which are surprisingly inexpensive considering their quality, are not only praised by critics, but can also be found on many wine lists throughout Austria's top culinary scene.

(95) Grüner Veltliner ** Ried Kremser Frechau 1ÖTW 2022
14 Vol.-%, cork, wooden barrel, €€€€€

95 Grüner Veltliner ** Krems Ried Kremser Frechau 1ÖTW 2021
Medium greenish yellow, silver glints. Scents of yellow apple, delicate herbal hints, a touch of clementine and guava, and tobacco nuances. Inviting bouquet. Juicy, elegant, tightly woven, subtle expression of fruit, dark mineral reverberations. A multifaceted food accompaniment with potential.

95 Grüner Veltliner ** Ried Kremser Frechau 1ÖTW 2020

(94) Grüner Veltliner ** Ried Kremser Gebling 1ÖTW 2022
13,5 Vol.-%, screwcap, large wooden barrel, €€€€€

93 Grüner Veltliner ** Krems Ried Gebling 1ÖTW 2021

94 Grüner Veltliner ** Ried Kremser Gebling 1ÖTW 2020

WEINGUT JOSEF SCHMID
3552 Stratzing
Obere Hauptstraße 38
T: +43 (2719) 8288
weingut@j-schmid.at
www.j-schmid.at

Winemaker: Josef Schmid
Contact: Josef and Irene Schmid
Production: 120,000 bottles
90 % white, 10 % red, 20 hectares
Fairs: VieVinum
Distribution partners:
BE, DE, NL, CH

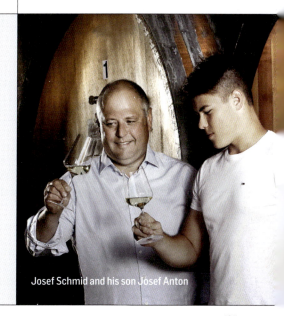

Josef Schmid and his son Josef Anton

* Kremstal DAC   ** Kremstal DAC Reserve

NIEDERÖSTERREICH/LOWER AUSTRIA

(93) Grüner Veltliner ** Alte Reben 2022
13,5 Vol.-%, screwcap, large wooden barrel, €€€€
93 Grüner Veltliner ** Alte Reben 2021
93 Grüner Veltliner ** Alte Reben 2020

91 Grüner Veltliner * Krems Kremser Löss 2022
12,5 Vol.-%, screwcap, steel tank, €€€
91 Grüner Veltliner * Kremser Löss 2019
91 Grüner Veltliner * Kremser Löss 2018

90 Grüner Veltliner * Stratzing 2022
90 Grüner Veltliner * Stratzing 2019

(94) Riesling ** Stratzing Ried Sunogeln 1ÖTW 2022
13,5 Vol.-%, screwcap, steel tank, €€€€
94 Riesling ** Stratzing Ried Sunogeln 1ÖTW 2021
Medium greenish yellow, silver reflections. Somewhat tobacco, a touch of lime, delicate white stone fruit, honey blossom, lemon balm. Complex, juicy, multi-faceted acid structure, apple notes on the finish, mineral touch, tightly meshed, lemony aftertaste, certain ageing potential.
94 Riesling ** Ried Stratzinger Sunogeln 1ÖTW 2020

92 Riesling * vom Urgestein 2022
12,5 Vol.-%, screwcap, steel tank, €€€

92 Riesling * vom Urgestein 2021
92 Riesling * vom Urgestein 2020

92 Riesling K 2022
10 Vol.-%, DIAM, steel tank, €€€

(91) Riesling Ried Pfeiffenberg 2022
12,5 Vol.-%, DIAM, steel tank, €€€

93 Cuvée Heiliger Geist 2020 GV/RR

91 Chardonnay Kerschbaum 2022
13 Vol.-%, screwcap, large wooden barrel, €€€
90 Chardonnay Ried Kerschbaum 2019
90 Chardonnay Ried Kerschbaum 2018

89 Gelber Muskateller Ried Galgenberg 2021
90 Gelber Muskateller Ried Galgenberg 2020
88 Gelber Muskateller Ried Galgenberg 2019

89 Sauvignon Blanc Stratzing 2021
89 Sauvignon Blanc Stratzing 2020

89 Rosé 2020 ZW/CS

90 Cuvée Lena Marie 2017 ZW/CS

WEINGUT STADT KREMS

A unique part of Austrian wine culture has been flourishing in the centre of Krems on the Danube since 1452 - the Weingut Stadt Krems. Historically, it originated from two sources: firstly, from the property of the so-called "Bürgerspitalstiftung" - founded in 1210 by the Babenberg Duke Leopold VI, who bequeathed substantial donations to the hospital, including vineyards - and secondly, from the generous bequests of the Imperial Burgrave of Krems, Ulrich von Dachsberg, who donated vineyards to the city as early as 1452. With more than 550 years of history, Weingut Stadt Krems is one of the oldest wine producers in Austria and Europe. Since 2003, the winery has been run by Fritz Miesbauer, who, together with a young, ambitious team, has turned the friendly but somewhat ossified winery into a model business. Fritz Miesbauer was named "Winemaker of the Year" by Falstaff magazine. As a member of the Austrian Traditional Wine Estates (ÖTW), the estate has the privilege of cultivating Austria's most important vineyards. The 40 hectares of vineyards within the city limits include historical sites such as Weinzierlberg, Schreck, Wachtberg and Grillenparz. These historic vineyards in Stein and Krems are meticulously tended with sensitivity and a hands-on approach. The result is unique wines full of character. Only through careful processing of the grapes and minimalist vinification can the distinctive character of the vineyards be captured. This is also reflected in the range of soils, from the calcareous gravel conglomerate of the Grillenparz site, the slate amphibolite of the Schreck site,

© Robert Herbst

KREMSTAL DAC

WEINGUT STADT KREMS
3500 Krems, Stadtgraben 11
T: +43 (2732) 801441
office@weingutstadtkrems.at
www.weingutstadtkrems.at

Winemaker: Fritz Miesbauer and Peter Rethaller
Contact: Fritz Miesbauer
Production: 100 % white, 40 hectares
Certified: Sustainable Austria
Fairs: Austrian Tasting London, ProWein Düsseldorf, VieVinum, Vinexpo
Distribution partners: AUS, BE, BG, DK, DE, EST, FIN, FR, UK, JP, CDN, LV, LT, NL, NO, PL, RUS, SE, CH, SK, CZ, HU, USA

Ried Grillenparz

the loess terraces, the gneiss of the Wachtberg site to the barren gravel and gneiss of the Weinzierlberg site. It is the combination of the vineyards, with their great diversity of soils, the favourable climate and, last but not least, the winemakers, that produces such a wide range of excellent wines.

(96) Riesling * Ried Schreck 1ÖTW 2022
13 Vol.-%, cork, steel tank, €€€€
96 Riesling * Ried Schreck 1 ÖTW 2021
Medium yellow-green, silver glints. Delicate hints of kumquats, tangerine zest, yellow stone fruit, and a mineral touch. Multifaceted bouquet. Firm, tightly woven, white fruit, a richly refined arc of acidity, precise and fresh, followed by a saline nuanced finish. Exhibiting extreme length and definite ageing potential for many years to come.
95 Riesling * Steiner Ried Schreck 2020

(95) Riesling * Ried Grillenparz 1ÖTW 2022
13 Vol.-%, cork, steel tank, €€€€
95 Riesling * Ried Grillenparz 1ÖTW 2021
94 Riesling * Steiner Ried Grillenparz 1ÖTW 2020

93 Riesling * Stein Schieferterrassen 2020
93 Riesling * Stein Schieferterrassen 2019
92 Riesling * Stein Schieferterrassen 2018

93 Riesling * Stein 2022
13 Vol.-%, screwcap, steel tank, €€€€

93 Riesling * Stein 2021

91 Riesling * Steinterrassen 2022
12,5 Vol.-%, screwcap, steel tank, €€
91 Riesling * Steinterrassen 2021
92 Riesling * Steinterrassen 2020

(94) Grüner Veltliner * Ried Lindberg 1ÖTW 2022
13 Vol.-%, cork, steel tank, €€€€€

(94) Grüner Veltliner * Ried Wachtberg 1ÖTW 2022
13 Vol.-%, cork, steel tank, €€€€€
94 Grüner Veltliner * Ried Wachtberg 1ÖTW 2021
Medium greenish yellow, silver reflections. Somewhat restrained, hints of Golden Delicious apple, soft notes of orange zest, a shy bouquet. Complex, juicy, white apple notes, fine acidity, fruity and good persistency, soft notes of mango on the back palate, has length and certain ageing potential.
94 Grüner Veltliner * Kremser Ried Wachtberg 1ÖTW 2020

(93) Grüner Veltliner * Ried Weinzierlberg 1ÖTW 2022
13 Vol.-%, cork, steel tank, €€€€
93 Grüner Veltliner * Ried Weinzierlberg 1 ÖTW 2021
93 Grüner Veltliner * Ried Weinzierlberg 2020

*Kremstal DAC   **Kremstal DAC Reserve

NIEDERÖSTERREICH/LOWER AUSTRIA

92 Grüner Veltliner * Krems 2022 12,5 Vol.-%, screwcap, steel tank, €€ **92** Grüner Veltliner * Krems 2021 **92** Grüner Veltliner * Krems 2020	**91** Grüner Veltliner * 2022 12,5 Vol.-%, screwcap, steel tank, €€ **91** Grüner Veltliner * 2021 **91** Grüner Veltliner * 2020
(92) Grüner Veltliner * Stein 2022 13 Vol.-%, screwcap, steel tank, €€€€ **92** Grüner Veltliner * Stein 2021 **92** Grüner Veltliner * Stein 2020	**90** Grüner Veltliner Lössterrassen 2021 **90** Grüner Veltliner Lössterrassen 2020 **90** Grüner Veltliner Lössterrassen 2019

WEINGUT STIFT GÖTTWEIG

Weingut Stift Göttweig has been cultivating and producing wine for over 900 years. Fritz Miesbauer took over in 2006 and has brought the winery up to speed and into the premier league of Austrian wine producers. The magnificent Benedictine Abbey is situated opposite the wine town of Krems, on the south bank of the Danube, at the top of the Göttweiger Berg. Built to plans by the famous architect Johann Lukas von Hildebrandt, the complex is famous far beyond the borders of Austria. The imposing Baroque Emperor's Staircase contains a magnificent ceiling fresco by Paul Troger, a miniature version of which appears on the capsule of each bottle of this revived winery. The Benedictines first settled here in 1083, and by the 16th century, the abbey's wines were renowned for their quality and popular with the Austrian aristocracy and imperial troops.

Today, a fresh breeze blows through the ancient walls in the person of Fritz Miesbauer. He is responsible for 26 hectares of the best vineyards on the Göttweiger Berg. Miesbauer is particularly proud of the "Erste Lagen" Gottschelle, Silberbichl and Pfaffenberg. The winery is a member of Traditionsweingüter Österreich and manages several vineyards that are over 1,000 years old. Miesbauer's uncompromising commitment to quality is regularly rec-

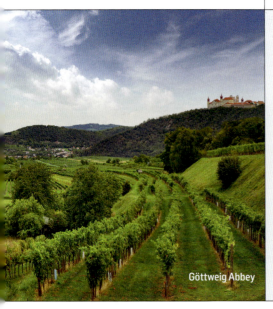

Göttweig Abbey

WEINGUT STIFT GÖTTWEIG
3511 Furth bei Göttweig
Göttweig 1
T: +43 (2732) 801440
office@weingutstiftgoettweig.at
www.weingutstiftgoettweig.at

Winemaker: Fritz Miesbauer and Peter Rethaller
Contact: Fritz Miesbauer and Franz-Josef Gansberger
Production: 90 % white, 10 % red, 26 hectares
Certified: Sustainable Austria ⊘
Fairs: ProWein Düsseldorf, VieVinum, Vinexpo
Distribution partners: AUS, BE, DK, DE, EST, FIN, UK, CDN, NL, NO, PL, RUS, SE, CH, SGP, SK, CZ, HU, USA

© Weingut Müller

KREMSTAL DAC

ognised by the wine world, including being named Falstaff Winemaker of the Year in 2020.

(95) Riesling * Ried Pfaffenberg 1ÖTW 2022
13 Vol.-%, cork, steel tank, €€€€€

95 Riesling * Ried Pfaffenberg 1ÖTW 2021
Bright greenish yellow, silver reflections. Smoky minerality, white tropical fruit, soft notes of white peach, some passion fruit and lime zest, multi-faceted bouquet. Complex, juicy, fine fruity texture, very lively raciness, tight-knit, salty and long lasting, a taut varietal representative, purist, endowed with certain ageing potential.

94 Riesling * Steiner Ried Pfaffenberg 1ÖTW 2020

(94) Riesling * Ried Silberbichl 1ÖTW 2022
13 Vol.-%, cork, steel tank, €€€€

93 Riesling * Ried Silberbichl 1ÖTW 2021

93 Riesling * Further Ried Silberbichl 1ÖTW 2020

91 Riesling * Furth 2022
12,5 Vol.-%, screwcap, steel tank, €€€

91 Riesling * Furth 2021

92 Riesling * Furth 2020

(93) Grüner Veltliner * Ried Gottschelle 1ÖTW 2022
13 Vol.-%, cork, steel tank, €€€€€

94 Grüner Veltliner * Ried Gottschelle 1ÖTW 2021
Medium yellow-green, silver reflections. Delicate pineapple, white pome fruit notes, fresh meadow herbs, a hint of orange zest. Medium-bodied, juicy, white apple fruit, fresh acidity, mineral, underpinned with lemony

Riesling

nuances, tight-knit, good persistency, certain ageing potential.

93 Grüner Veltliner * Further Ried Gottschelle 1ÖTW 2020

90 Grüner Veltliner * Furth 2022
12,5 Vol.-%, screwcap, steel tank, €€€

91 Grüner Veltliner * Furth 2021

92 Grüner Veltliner * Furth 2020

90 Grüner Veltliner Messwein 2021

90 Grüner Veltliner Messwein 2020

90 Grüner Veltliner Messwein 2019

WANDRASCHEK WEINMANUFAKTUR

Since 1970, Krems has been the new residence of Conny and Wolfgang Wandraschek. They worked as architects but soon discovered their passion for wine. Their favourite variety, Cabernet Sauvignon, is grown in the family's personal vineyard. "A barrel for me and my friends," says Wolfgang Wandraschek. The contents of that barrel eventually became the first ‚Falstaff Varietal Winner', followed by three more firsts (1999, 2005 and 2014).

Thus began a passion that has now captured their son Gregor. He has already taken over the family business with just under two hectares - and the trend is upwards. Many people are already talking about the "little piece of Bordeaux in the Kremstal" because the Weinmanufaktur Wandraschek is a boutique winery with exceptional standards. The red wines are aged for two years in French oak barrels, making them harmonious, stable and distinctive. Gregor and his

* Kremstal DAC   ** Kremstal DAC Reserve

NIEDERÖSTERREICH/LOWER AUSTRIA

Stein an der Donau next to Krems

WANDRASCHEK WEINMANUFAKTUR
3500 Krems
Landersdorfer Straße 67
T: +43 (2732) 83645
rotwein@wandraschek.at
www.wandraschek.at

Winemaker/Contact:
Gregor Wandraschek
Production:
13,333 bottles
2 % sparkling, 6 % white, 2 % rosé, 90 % red, 2+0.3 hectares
Fairs: VieVinum
Distribution partners: DE, NL, CH

father, Wolfgang, see themselves as creative craftsmen, using mainly manual labour to produce red wines that are as close to perfection as possible. Recently, in addition to their high quality reds, rosés and sparkling wines, they have begun to produce equally high quality Grüner Veltliner and Riesling from top sites such as Steiner Kögl.
Together with Gregor, Conny Wandraschek is responsible for marketing and sales, and also enjoys organising exclusive wine events and private tastings at the winery.

90   Grüner Veltliner ** Ried Steiner Kögl 2019

90   Riesling ** Ried Windleithen 2020
89   Riesling ** Ried Windleithen 2019
90   Riesling ** Ried Windleithen 2018

91   Cabernet Sauvignon Rose Selection 2021
13 Vol.-%, cork, barrique, €€€€

92   Cabernet Sauvignon Grande Reserve 2020
14 Vol.-%, cork, barrique, €€€€
93   Cabernet Sauvignon Grande Reserve 2019
Deep ruby, purple reflections, broad bright faint ochre rim. Delicate wood spice, dark fruit of forest confit, a bit of cassis, tobacco and some pepper. Juicy, tightly meshed, balanced tannin structure, ripe blackberry on the finish, plum aftertaste, chocolaty finish, sure ageing potential.

93   Cabernet Sauvignon Grande Reserve 2017

93   Merlot 2020
14,5 Vol.-%, cork, barrique, €€€€€
93   Merlot 2019
90   Merlot 2018

92   Pinot Noir 2020
14 Vol.-%, cork, barrique, €€€€
91   Pinot Noir 2019
91   Pinot Noir 2019

92   Cuvée Les Trois 2020 CS/ME/ZW
14 Vol.-%, cork, barrique, €€€
92   Cuvée 2019 CS/ME/ZW
91   Cuvee 2018 CS/ME/ZW

91   Syrah 2018
92   Syrah 2017

91   Blauer Zweigelt 2020
13,5 Vol.-%, cork, barrique, €€€
91   Zweigelt 2019
90   Blauer Zweigelt 2017

© Weingut Mulle

KREMSTAL DAC

SPACE FOR YOUR
WINE NOTES

*Kremstal DAC   **Kremstal DAC Reserve

NIEDERÖSTERREICH/ LOWER AUSTRIA

THERMENREGION

Preisen and Thörlberg in Pfaffstätten

Mitterberg near Baden

HISTORICAL TERROIR, WINES WITH FUTURE

The wine-growing areas Gumpoldskirchen and Bad Vöslau were united in 1985 to create Thermenregion and have a long and rich history. 2,872 vineyard hectares on the foothills of the Vienna Woods stretch from Vienna's city limits into the spa resort Baden. Autochthon grapes like Zierfandler and Rotgipfler are the region's specialties, while St. Laurent and Pinot Noir are the predominant red wine varieties.

Vines were cultivated in the mild climate of this region south of Vienna more than 2000 years ago. Roman legionnaires stationed in Carnuntum and Vindobona brought vines from their homeland and knowledge of wine production to Pannonia. The name "Thermenregion" refers to the sulphurous hot springs of Aquae (Baden). Not only do Thermenregion vines benefit from the balmy summers and dry autumns of the Pannonian-influenced Vienna Basin, but also from an average of 1,800 hours of sunshine every year. Constant air movement ensures that grapes dry rapidly after dew or rain. The region is also geologically quite diverse. Heavy soils comprised of loamy clay, sandy loam and cambisols with high shell limestone content dominate. The weathered rubble and alluvial layers below the surface drain and warm well. In the southeast, Steinfeld has relatively rocky, meagre, gravel soils that offer red wine varieties outstanding conditions.

The rare, typical regional varieties Zierfandler (synonym Spätrot) and Rotgipfler enjoy householder's rights. The blend of the two varieties called Spätrot-Rotgipfler is legendary. The traditional varietal diversity also includes Blauer Portugieser (earlier known as Vöslauer), Neuburger, modern wines from Burgundian grapes, St. Laurent and Zweigelt, yet Merlot and Cabernet Sauvignon also have a deserved place. Red wine centres are Bad

NIEDERÖSTERREICH/LOWER AUSTRIA **THERMENREGION**

Vöslau, Sooß, Tattendorf and Teesdorf. The classic white wines come from Perchtoldsdorf, Gumpoldskirchen, Pfaffstätten, Baden, Guntramsdorf and Traiskirchen.

Nature and culture provide a diversified choice of recreational activities. Visit the Cistercian Heiligenkreuz Abbey's Freigut Thallern, one of the oldest wine estates in Austria, which is currently experiencing an exciting revival. Other highlights include visiting the theatre, operettas, and thermal baths in the culture and spa resort Baden, a road trip on the wine route or hiking in the vineyards along the Vienna Mountain Spring Aqueduct. Follow the water to the excellent food and wine in the local heuriger (winery taverns) and restaurants!

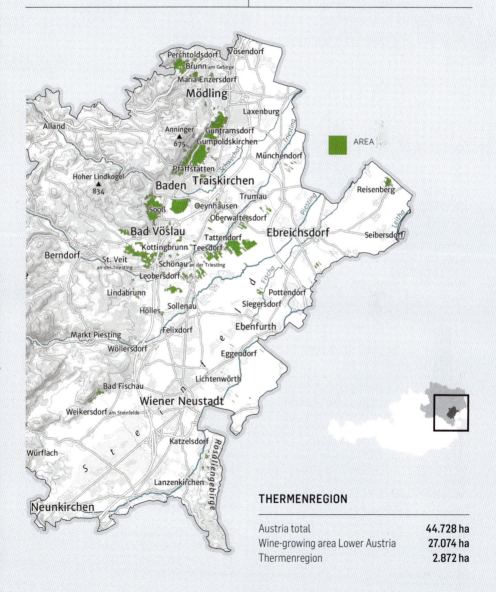

THERMENREGION

Austria total	**44.728 ha**
Wine-growing area Lower Austria	**27.074 ha**
Thermenregion	**2.872 ha**

NIEDERÖSTERREICH/LOWER AUSTRIA

SELECTED WINERIES

★★★★★
Weingut Johanneshof Reinisch, Tattendorf

★★★★
Weingut Stadlmann, Traiskirchen

★★★
Weingut Hartl, Oberwaltersdorf

★★★★

WEINGUT STADLMANN

ORGANIC

The Stadlmann estate has been dedicated to viticulture since 1780. Over the course of eight generations, the know-how of winemaking has been gradually acquired and passed on. Bernhard Stadlmann is one of the few people to have researched the unique conditions and indigenous grape varieties of the Thermenregion. He has deepened his sound academic training through numerous internships abroad and now works with a vast amount of experience and a keen sense of the region's most treasured sites. On the Anninger slopes, Stadlmann masterfully cultivates the predominantly old vines that are deeply rooted in the shell limestone. In the cellar, he deliberately refrains from intervention, giving the wine the time it needs to mature. This allows him to produce authentic wines with enormous ageing potential. The complexity and density of Stadlmann's Zierfandler and Rotgipfler are unparalleled. The winery has always been dedicated to these typical regional grape varieties in all their variations, but Pinot Blanc, Riesling, St. Laurent, and Pinot Noir are also matured to perfection in large wooden barrels. Stadlmann has been a member of Traditionsweingüter Österreich since 2022 and was named Falstaff Winemaker of the Year in 1994.

WEINGUT STADLMANN
2514 Traiskirchen
Wiener Straße 41
T: +43 (2252) 52343
kontakt@stadlmann-wein.at
www.stadlmann-wein.at

Winemaker/Contact:
Bernhard Stadlmann
Production: 85 % white, 13 % red, 2 % sweet, 20 hectares
Certified: Sustainable Austria
Fairs: ProWein Düsseldorf, VieVinum
Distribution partners: BE, DE, FIN, UK, JP, NL, NO, RUS, CH, USA

94 Zierfandler Ried Mandel-Höh 2021
13,5 Vol.-%, cork, large wooden barrel, €€€€€ B

94 Zierfandler Ried Mandel-Höh 2020
Medium golden yellow, silver reflections. Yellow peach fruit underlaid with tangerine zest and blossom honey, a multi-faceted bouquet. Juicy, elegant, fine nuances of yellow fruit, delicate fruit, fresh pineapple, mineral in the background, fine acidity, very harmonious, shows good length, has sure ageing potential.

95 Zierfandler Ried Mandel-Höh 2019

92 Zierfandler Anning 2022
12,5 Vol.-%, screwcap, large wooden barrel, €€€ B
91 Zierfandler Anning 2021
92 Zierfandler Anning 2020

THERMENREGION

93 Zierfandler Ried Igeln 2021 13,5 Vol.-%, cork, large wooden barrel, €€€€ Ⓑ	**92 Rotgipfler Anning 2022** 12,5 Vol.-%, screwcap, large wooden barrel, €€€ Ⓑ
93 Zierfandler Ried Igeln 2020	**91 Rotgipfler Anning 2021**
92 Zierfandler Ried Igeln 2019	**92 Rotgipfler Anning 2020**
94 Rotgipfler Ried Tagelsteiner 2021 13,5 Vol.-%, cork, large wooden barrel, €€€€€ Ⓑ	**94 Rotgipfler Gumpoldskirchen Auslese 2020** 11 Vol.-%, cork, wooden barrel, €€€€€ Ⓑ
93 Rotgipfler Ried Tagelsteiner 2020 Pale yellow gold, silver reflections. Hints of orange, nuances of yellow tropical fruit, a touch of papaya and mango, inviting bouquet. Mineral, taut texture, white pear fruit, discreet acid structure, mineral, salty touch, lingers, good development certain ageing potential.	**94 Zierfandler Traiskirchen Trockenbeerenauslese 2017**
	94 Zierfandler Traiskirchen Auslese 2019
	93 Zierfandler Traiskirchen Auslese 2017
94 Rotgipfler Ried Tagelsteiner 2019	**92 Zierfandler Traiskirchen Eiswein 2018**

WEINGUT JOHANNESHOF REINISCH

ORGANIC

The Reinisch family, now in its fourth generation of winemaking, cultivates vineyards in the most prized locations around the traditional winemaking villages of Tattendorf and Gumpoldskirchen. The unique characteristics of the alluvial brown soils lie in their excellent permeability, which ensures rapid warming and thus favours the ripening process of the grapes. The high lime content imparts a pronounced minerality to the wines and makes the Johanneshof Reinisch soils particularly suitable for cultivating the Pinot varieties.

Pinot Noir, St. Laurent, and Chardonnay are the main varieties grown at the winery, which has been a member of Traditionsweingüter Österreich since 2022. In addition, Rotgipfler and Zier-

WEINGUT JOHANNESHOF REINISCH
2523 Tattendorf
Im Weingarten 1
T: +43 (2253) 81423
office@j-r.at
www.j-r.at

Winemaker/Contact:
The Reinisch famiily
Production: 220,000 bottles
37 % white, 60 % red, 3 % sweet,
40 hectares
Fairs: Millésime Bio, ProWein Düsseldorf, VieVinum, Vinexpo
Distribution partners: AUS, BY, BE, BR, RC, DK, DE, FIN, FR, UK, IRL, JP, CDN, ROK, LU, NL, PL, RUS, CH, SGP, HU, USA, PT

Shoots of the Rotgipfler

NIEDERÖSTERREICH/LOWER AUSTRIA

fandler are cultivated in the nearby village of Gumpoldskirchen on terroir that is well suited to them, where they thrive just as well as the other varieties while retaining their distinctive character. In harmony with the microclimate, about 60 percent of the wines are red, 40 percent white, and sweet, and managed with the utmost attention to detail in the vineyard and cellar. The brothers Johannes, Christian, and Michael Reinisch adhere to the principles of organic farming and viticulture.

91 ❶ Brut Reserve Rosé 2018 PN/SL

93 Zierfandler Gumpolskirchen Ried Spiegel Monopol 2021
14 Vol.-%, cork, large wooden barrel, €€€€€ Ⓑ
93 Zierfandler Ried Spiegel Monopol 2020
94 Zierfandler Ried Spiegel Monopol 2019

94 Zierfandler Rotgipfler Gumpoldskirchen S 2018 ZF/RG
14 Vol.-%, cork, wooden barrel, €€€€€ Ⓑ
94 Zierfandler-Rotgipfler S Gumpoldskirchen 2017 ZF/RG

93 Rotgipfler Gumpoldskirchen Ried Satzing 2021
14 Vol.-%, cork, large wooden barrel, €€€€€ Ⓑ
93 Rotgipfler Ried Satzing 2020
93 Rotgipfler Ried Satzing 2019

92 Rotgipfler 2022
13 Vol.-%, screwcap, steel tank, €€€ Ⓑ
91 Rotgipfler 2021
91 Rotgipfler 2020

95 Chardonnay Ried Kästenbaum 2020
14 Vol.-%, cork, used barriques, €€€€€€ Ⓑ
95 Chardonnay Ried Kästenbaum 2019
Pale golden yellow, silver glints. Fragrantly soft vanilla and caramel notes, yellow tropical fruit, fresh peach, and subtle toasty aromas. Inviting bouquet. Taut, tightly woven, white apple, elegant and persistent, saline-minerality, expressive fruit and ample salinity, excellent length, and good ageing potential.
94 Chardonnay Ried Kästenbaum 2018

94 Chardonnay Ried Lores 2021
14 Vol.-%, cork, barrique, €€€€€ Ⓑ
93 Chardonnay Ried Lores 2020
93 Chardonnay Ried Lores 2019

90 Chardonnay 2022
13 Vol.-%, screwcap, large wooden barrel, €€€ Ⓑ
91 Chardonnay 2021

90 Chardonnay 2020

91 Dialog 2022 SB/CH
12 Vol.-%, screwcap, steel tank, €€ Ⓑ
90 Dialog 2021 SB/CH
90 Dialog 2020 SB/CH

92 Gumpoldskirchner Tradition 2022 ZF/RG
13 Vol.-%, screwcap, steel tank, €€ Ⓑ
90 Gumpoldskirchner Tradition 2021 ZF/RG
90 Gumpoldskirchner Tradition 2020 ZF/RG

90 First 2022 SB/CB
12 Vol.-%, screwcap, steel tank, €€ Ⓑ
89 First 2021 SB/CB
89 First 2020 SB/CB

96 Pinot Noir Ried Kästenbaum 2020
13,5 Vol.-%, cork, barrique, €€€€€€ Ⓑ
95 Pinot Noir Ried Kästenbaum 2019
Strong crimson garnet, purple reflections, faint ochre brightening on the rim. Delicate hints of cloves and vanilla, fine cherry fruit, tobacco minerality but also delicately floral bouquet. Full-bodied, elegant, fine red berry fruit, well-integrated sweet tannins, finesse-rich acidity, saline touch, shows length, has certain ageing potential.
96 Pinot Noir Ried Kästenbaum 2018

(94) Pinot Noir Ried Holzspur 2021
13,5 Vol.-%, cork, barrique, €€€€€ Ⓑ
94 Pinot Noir Ried Holzspur 2020
95 Pinot Noir Ried Holzspur 2019

92 Pinot Noir Gumpoldskirchen 2021
13,5 Vol.-%, cork, wooden barrel, €€€€€ Ⓑ

92 Pinot Noir Gumpoldskirchen Grillenhügel 2020
93 Pinot Noir Grillenhügel 2019
93 Pinot Noir Grillenhügel 2018

91 Pinot Noir 2021
13 Vol.-%, screwcap, large wooden barrel, €€€ Ⓑ
91 Pinot Noir 2020
90 Pinot Noir 2019

(95) St. Laurent Ried Holzspur 2021
13,5 Vol.-%, cork, barrique, €€€€€ Ⓑ
96 St. Laurent Ried Holzspur 2020
Deep ruby garnet, purple glints, faintly lighter at the rim. Delicate nuances of sour cherries and black sweetheart cherries, a hint of wood, underlaid with fresh blackberries. Juicy, complex, ripe cherries, finely fruit forward, savoury, supporting tannins, soft resonating nougat nuances, fresh

and mineral. Exhibits excellent length and great varietal character.

94 St. Laurent Ried Holzspur 2019

94 St. Laurent Ried Frauenfeld 2021
13 Vol.-%, cork, used barriques, €€€€ Ⓑ
93 St. Laurent Ried Frauenfeld 2020
94 St. Laurent Ried Frauenfeld 2019

92 St. Laurent 2021
13 Vol.-%, screwcap, large wooden barrel, €€€ Ⓑ
92 Sankt Laurent 2020
90 Sankt Laurent 2019

91 Sankt Laurent Sommelier Edition 2018
91 St. Laurent Sommelier Edition 2017
90 St. Laurent Sommelier Edition 2016

93 Ried Steingarten 2019 SL/PN
93 Ried Steingarten 2018 SL/PN
93 Ried Steingarten 2017 SL/PN

92 Cabernet Sauvignon - Merlot Reserve 2019
92 Cabernet Sauvignon - Merlot Reserve 2018
92 Cabernet Sauvignon - Merlot Reserve 2017

91 Alter Rebstock 2021 SL/ZW/BF
13 Vol.-%, screwcap, large wooden barrel, €€ Ⓑ
91 Alter Rebstock 2020 SL/ZW/BF
90 Alter Rebstock 2019 SL/BF/ZW

93 Zweigelt Ried Frauenfeld 2021
13,5 Vol.-%, cork, used barriques, €€€€ Ⓑ
92 Zweigelt Ried Frauenfeld 2020
92 Zweigelt Ried Frauenfeld 2019

90 Zweigelt 2021
13 Vol.-%, screwcap, large wooden barrel, €€ Ⓑ
90 Zweigelt 2020
89 Zweigelt 2019

93 Rotgipfler Auslese 2021
93 Rotgipfler Auslese 2018
93 Rotgipfler Auslese 2016

93 Zierfandler Eiswein 2018

92 Roter Eiswein 2021 ME/CS
91 Roter Eiswein 2018 ME/CS
91 Roter Eiswein 2017 ME/CS

★ ★ ★

WEINGUT HARTL

ORGANIC

Heinrich Hartl III and his wife Marie-Sophie run their charming family winery with 16 hectares of vineyards in the Thermenregion wine region south of Vienna. Their training and experience in the wine industry culminated in a focus on achieving the highest quality. Thus, they deliberately decided to remain relatively small in order to focus on their single vineyard sites. The vineyard area is only enlarged when historic vineyards with unique characteristics become available. In a climate where cool and warm influences converge, the talented winemakers produce both white and red wines of great potential: elegant reds from Pinot Noir and Sankt Laurent and old Austrian white varieties such as Rotgipfler, Zierfandler, and Traminer, which have been thriving in this area for centuries. With a sense of modesty and great respect for nature, Marie and Heinrich's top priority is to farm as sustainably as possible. For this reason, production has been certified organic since 2022. Lively, elegant and profound, the Hartl wines are also destined to age. With a modern approach, the two continue to work in harmony with the region's cultural heritage and warmly welcome guests from all over the world to their homestead. Heinrich Hartl has been a "Traditionsweingüter Österreich" member since 2022 and is also chairman of the Regional Wine Committee Thermenregion. He has made it his goal with his colleagues to lead his home region to the forefront of Austria's winegrowing regions once again.

91 ❶ Vom Steinfeld Sekt Austria Niederösterreich g.U. Brut PN/CH

93 Zierfandler maischevergoren 2020

NIEDERÖSTERREICH/LOWER AUSTRIA

Zierfandler

WEINGUT HARTL
2522 Oberwaltersdorf
Trumauer Straße 24
T: +43 (2253) 6289
office@weingut-hartl.at
www.weingut-hartl.at

Winemaker/Contact:
Heinrich Hartl
Production: 5 % sparkling, 42 % white, 2 % rosé, 50 % red, 1 % sweet, 14+2 hectares
Certified: Sustainable Austria
Fairs: VieVinum
Distribution partners: BE, DK, DE, UK, PL, CH, USA

---

90 Zierfandler 2022
13 Vol.-%, screwcap, steel tank, €€€

(92) Skinz 2022 RG/TR/GM
13,5 Vol.-%, cork,screwcap, steel tank, €€€€

(92) Rotgipfler Gumpoldskirchen Ried Kreuzweingarten 2021
13,5 Vol.-%, screwcap, 500-l-barrel, €€€€

92 Rotgipfler Ried Kreuzweingarten 2019
Medium golden yellow, silver reflections. Delicate ripe yellow tropical fruit, soft notes of mango and honey, with underlying candied orange zest. Juicy, elegant, ripe peach, fruity, discreet acidity, harmonious with good persistency, an elegant food wine with ageing potential.

94 Rotgipfler Ried Kreuzweingarten 2018

90 Rotgipfler 2021
14 Vol.-%, screwcap, steel tank, €€€

91 Rotgipfler 2020
92 Rotgipfler 2018

91 Traminer 2020
92 Traminer 2018
91 Traminer 2017

94 Pinot Noir Oberwaltersdorf Ried Graf Weingartl 2020
13,5 Vol.-%, cork,screwcap, barrique, €€€€€

94 Pinot Noir Ried Graf Weingartl 2019
94 Pinot Noir Ried Graf Weingartl 2018

92 Pinot Noir Oberwaltersdorf Ried Kräutergarten 2020
13,5 Vol.-%, cork,screwcap, barrique, €€€€

92 Pinot Noir Reserve Ried Kräutergarten 2019
Strong garnet, purple reflections, faint ochre brightening on the rim. Ripe cherry fruit, soft notes of prunes, fresh orange zest. Juicy, red berry nuances, freshly structured, fine tannins, lively, red cherries on the finish, accessible and easy to drink.

93 Pinot Noir Reserve 2018

(92) St. Laurent Oberwaltersdorf Ried Kräutergarten 2021
12,5 Vol.-%, cork,screwcap, barrique, €€€€

92 St. Laurent Reserve 2020
92 Sankt Laurent Reserve 2019

91 Cabernet Sauvignon 2020
92 Cabernet Sauvignon 2019
92 Cabernet Sauvignon 2018

(90) Merlot 2021
13 Vol.-%, screwcap, barrique, €€€€

91 Merlot 2020
90 Merlot 2018

90 Amicus Cuvée 2019 ZW/CS/ME

93 Grüner Veltliner Eiswein 2022
11,5 Vol.-%, screwcap, steel tank, €€€€

THERMENREGION

SPACE FOR YOUR
WINE NOTES

The Ried Engelreich near Getzersdorf

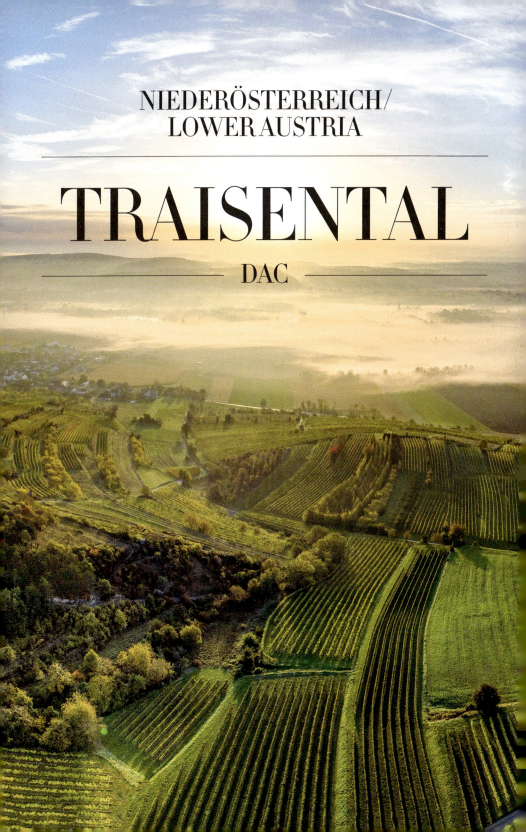

Hochschopf near Nussdorf ob der Traisen

WINES WITH BACKBONE AND FINESSE

Austria's youngest wine-growing area exists in its present form since 1995. Although it is one of the smallest wine areas at just 848 hectares, it certainly excels in one respect: Grüner Veltliner is the star on the stage. Rustic winery taverns are fixtures in the small wine villages, while Traismauer and Herzogenburg offer excursions into the historical past.

Fruity, spicy Grüner Veltliner and crisp, mineral Rieslings with typical regional character are bottled under the Traisental DAC protected designation of origin with the same quality hierarchy as Kremstal DAC wines since the 2006 vintage. In no other region does Grüner Veltliner comprise such a large share of the vineyard area: at 63 % it is the indisputable number one.

Despite this, Riesling is also justifiably considered a specialty in Traisental. Vines grow primarily on tiny terraces with dry, gravelly, very calcareous soils that lend wine a very unique profile with a powerful body and firm backbone. Minerality is also a flavour enhancer that supports acid structure and promotes the ageing capacity of the local wine. Warm, arid Pannonian climate influences converge with cool Alpine air masses resulting in warm days and cool nights that give wines fine aroma and spicy finesse. Proximity to the Danube River also plays a role in regulating temperatures.

Traisental is an attractive destination for wine enthusiasts, hikers, cyclists and fans of culture. Archaeological finds of grape seeds from the early Bronze Age document an ancient wine tradition that existed even before the arrival of the Romans to this region. The neighbouring state capital,

© WSNA

NIEDERÖSTERREICH/LOWER AUSTRIA TRAISENTAL DAC

St. Pölten, offers a versatile, modern cultural program. Multiple trails and roads open to the west and the east from this most southern point of the wine-growing area: from Statzendorf, Unterwölbling and Oberwölbling to Nussdorf, Reichersdorf, Getzersdorf and on to Inzersdorf and Herzogenburg and its splendid abbey.

The uniting element is the congenial wine culture that vintner families share in the numerous cosy winery taverns called "Buschenschanks". They are very conscious of the importance of Grüner Veltliner and Riesling as ambassadors of their region. The winery taverns play an important role in raising awareness for the inimitable style of Traisental wines in a very personal manner by serving them with tasty, regional culinary treats. Visitors should not shy away from exploring other varietal white and red wine specialties.

TRAISENTAL DAC

Austria total	44.728 ha
Wine-growing area Lower Austria	27.074 ha
Traisental DAC	848 ha

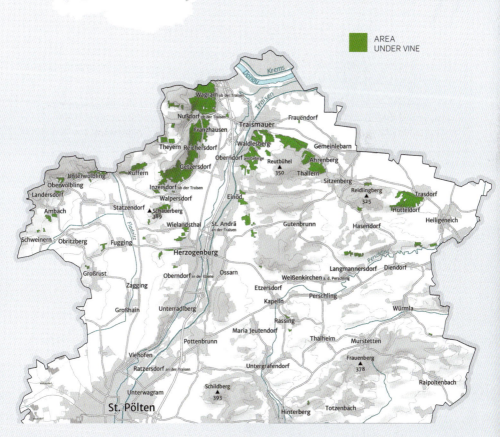

NIEDERÖSTERREICH

SELECTED WINERIES

★★★★
Weingut Markus Huber, Reichersdorf
Weingut Ludwig Neumayer, Inzersdorf ob der Traisen

★★★
Weingut Tom Dockner, Theyern

★★
Nolz Wein, Hilpersdorf
Weingut Thomas Ott, Reichersdorf

★★★

WEINGUT TOM DOCKNER

When rocks and boulders from the Traisen River collide with washed-out limestone, it takes a few millennia for the conglomerate to form - a catch-all term to describe an area that produces excellent Veltliners. Tom Dockner's vines grow on these ancient, glacial soils that have accumulated a wealth of valuable building blocks, namely sedimentary deposits. These, in turn, give his Grüner Veltliners from the Traisental their distinctive character: mineral, complex, expressive, and yet lean. "Conglomerate" is the name given to this unique combination of silt, gravel, calcite, and the elements - wind, and water. These unique vineyard sites are called Theyerner Berg, Pletzengraben, and Hochschopf. Since 2019, the latter two vineyards have been classified as "Erste Lagen 1ÖTW", and the winery is now a member of "Österreichische Traditionsweingüter". Grüner Veltliner and Riesling are undoubtedly the best-known varieties of the Traisental

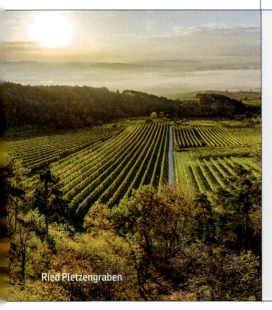
Ried Pletzengraben

WEINGUT TOM DOCKNER
3134 Theyern
Traminerweg 3
T: +43 (664) 5441779
weingut@docknertom.at
www.docknertom.at

Winemaker/Contact:
Thomas Dockner
Production: 90 % white, 10 % red, 23 hectares
Certified: Sustainable Austria
Fairs: VieVinum, MondoVino
Distribution partners: BE, DE, IT, CDN, ROK, NL, NO, PL, SE, CH, CZ

TRAISENTAL DAC

and deservedly Tom Dockner's highlights, but Traminer and Pinot Noir are also just as captivating. The winery's excellent reputation is based on sustainability and natural vineyard management. For Tom Dockner, cellar work means conveying the quality and character of the grapes from the vineyard to the bottle without compromise. This is why meticulous cleanliness and gentle processing are essential. Visitors can sample these unique wines in the bright, spacious tasting room in the heart of the Traisen Valley amid the stunning vineyard landscape.

Traminer

(94) Grüner Veltliner * Neusiedl
Ried Hochschopf 1ÖTW 2022
13 Vol.-%, cork, large wooden barrel, €€€€€ Ⓥ

93 Grüner Veltliner * Neusiedl
Ried Hochschopf 1ÖTW 2021
Medium yellow green, silver reflections. Fine meadow herbs, fresh white apple, delicate underlay of mango and orange zest. Juicy, complex, fine apricot note, fresh acidity, mineral, fruity aftertaste, gently salty on the finish, has length and good aging potential.

93 Grüner Veltliner * Ried Hochschopf 2019

(93) Grüner Veltliner * Inzersdorf
Ried Pletzengraben 1ÖTW 2022
13 Vol.-%, screwcap, large wooden barrel, €€€€€ Ⓥ

92 Grüner Veltliner * Inzersdorf
Ried Pletzengraben 1ÖTW 2021

93 Grüner Veltliner * Ried Pletzengraben 1ÖTW 2020

92 Grüner Veltliner * Nußdorf 2022
91 Grüner Veltliner * Nußdorf 2021
92 Grüner Veltliner * Nussdorf 2020

92 Grüner Veltliner * Ried Theyerner Berg 2022
12,5 Vol.-%, screwcap, steel tank, €€€ Ⓥ

91 Grüner Veltliner * Ried Theyerner Berg 2021
92 Grüner Veltliner * Ried Theyerner Berg 2020

91 Grüner Veltliner * Kalkterrassen 2022
90 Grüner Veltliner * Kalkterrassen 2021
90 Grüner Veltliner * Kalkterrassen 2020

90 Grüner Veltliner * TOM 2022
89 Grüner Veltliner * Tom 2021
91 Grüner Veltliner * Tom 2020

93 Riesling * Inzersdorf
Ried Pletzengraben 1ÖTW 2021
12,5 Vol.-%, screwcap, steel tank, €€€€ Ⓥ

92 Riesling * Inzersdorf Ried Pletzengraben 1ÖTW 2020
Light greenish yellow, silver reflections. Delicate pineapple, papaya and fresh peach, a hint of lime zest, mineral touch. Medium body, fine fruit, white stone fruit, lively structure, delicately salty, good persistency, already drinkable, has good ageing potential.

93 Riesling * Ried Pletzengraben 1ÖTW 2019

92 Riesling * Inzersdorf 2022
92 Riesling * Inzersdorf 2021
92 Riesling * Ìnzersdorf 2020

90 Riesling * Parapluiberg 2022
12 Vol.-%, screwcap, steel tank, €€ Ⓥ

90 Riesling * Parapluiberg 2021
90 Riesling * Parapluiberg 2020

93 Traminer Kalk Konglomerat 2021
13,5 Vol.-%, screwcap, steel tank, €€€€ Ⓥ

90 Traminer Ried Pletzengraben Konglomerat 2020
93 Traminer Ried Pletzengraben 2019

* Traisental DAC   ** Traisental DAC Reserve

NIEDERÖSTERREICH

★★★★
WEINGUT MARKUS HUBER
ORGANIC

Weingut Markus Huber is regarded as the leading winery in Traisental, and its wines are sold in more than 35 countries worldwide. The winemaker and chairman of the Traisental Winegrowers' Association is committed to producing distinctive wines full of character and promoting the Traisental wine region with its unique lime-rich conglomerate soils. Markus Huber's wines have a crystal clean style, with a minerality that reflects the terroir while retaining varietal typicity.

Grüner Veltliner is undoubtedly the main variety. It is produced in four different styles. Depending on the soil type and the potential of the grapes, the wine is aged either in stainless steel tanks or in large wooden barrels. The second main variety is Riesling, followed by Weissburgunder (Pinot Blanc), Sauvignon Blanc, and Gelber Muskateller.

Markus Huber won the SALON Award in 2003, the National Award, the Falstaff Grüner Veltliner Grand Prix four times, the Gold Medal at the London International Wine and Spirit Competition, and the award for "Best White Wine Producer", with outstanding reviews in the Austrian trade media. He was also nominated for the Falstaff "Newcomer of the Year" award. In addition, he was named "Wunderkind" by Decanter magazine: Markus Huber was on the right track at an early stage and has been pursuing it ever since.

With regards to product quality, Markus Huber has also followed a systematic approach: since 2007, the winery has been IFS and BRC certified. No compromise on quality is the top priority for Markus Huber: "Increasing the quality a little every year is my incentive," states the winemaker. Since 2020, all the vineyards have been certified organic. The winery is also a member of the "Traditionsweingüter Österreich" association, and in 2015 Markus Huber was voted "Winemaker of the Year" by Falstaff magazine.

92 ❂ Grüner Veltliner zero dosage Blanc de Blancs NV (Deg. 3/2021)
92 ❂ Grüner Veltliner Blanc de Blancs Zero Dosage NV (Deg. 2020)

(95) Grüner Veltliner * Getzersdorf Ried Berg 1ÖTW 2022
13,5 Vol.-%, cork, large wooden barrel, €€€€€ Ⓑ Ⓥ
95 Grüner Veltliner * Getzersdorf Ried Berg 1ÖTW 2021
Bright greenish yellow, silver glints. Subtle exuberant meadow herbs are underlaid with yellow tropical fruit, nuances of mango and pineapple, hints of mandarin zest, and blossom honey. An inviting bouquet. Juicy and elegant, fruit expressive texture, well-integrated acidity, persistent, yellow apple nuances, and walnut reverberations. Harmonious and with huge future ageing potential. Already accessible.
95 Grüner Veltliner * Getzersdorf Ried Berg 1ÖTW 2020

(94) Grüner Veltliner * Inzersdorf Ried Zwirch 1ÖTW 2022
13,5 Vol.-%, screwcap, large wooden barrel, €€€€ Ⓑ Ⓥ
94 Grüner Veltliner * Ried Zwirch 1ÖTW 2021
94 Grüner Veltliner * Inzersdorf Ried Zwirch 1ÖTW 2020

(93) Grüner Veltliner * Reichersdorf Ried Alte Setzen 1ÖTW 2022
13 Vol.-%, screwcap, large wooden barrel, €€€ Ⓑ Ⓥ
92 Grüner Veltliner * Reichersdorf Ried Alte Setzen 1ÖTW 2021
92 Grüner Veltliner * Reichersdorf Ried Alte Setzen 1ÖTW 2020

92 Grüner Veltliner * Nussdorf Obere Steigen 2022
92 Grüner Veltliner * Nussdorf Obere Steigen 2021
93 Nussdorfer Grüner Veltliner * Obere Steigen 2020

92 Grüner Veltliner * Reichersdorf Ried Kirchweg 2022
92 Grüner Veltliner * Ried Kirchweg 2021

92 Grüner Veltliner * Rosenstock 2022
90 Grüner Veltliner * Rosenweg 2021
91 Grüner Veltliner * Rosenweg 2020

© Weingut Huber

TRAISENTAL DAC

WEINGUT MARKUS HUBER
3134 Reichersdorf
Weinriedenweg 13
T: +43 (2783) 82999
office@weingut-huber.at
www.weingut-huber.at

Winemaker: Markus Huber and Michael Huber
Contact: Markus Huber
Production: 1 % sparkling, 94 % white, 2 % rosé, 2 % red, 1 % sweet, 50 hectares
Certified: Sustainable Austria
Fairs: ProWein Düsseldorf
Distribution partners: AUS, BE, RC, DK, DE, EST, FIN, FR, UK, RI, IRL, IT, JP, CDN, ROK, LU, NL, NO, PL, RUS, SE, CN, SGP, SK, CZ, HU, USA, UAE

Markus Huber

91 Grüner Veltliner * Nussdorf 2022
90 Grüner Veltliner * Nussdorf 2021
91 Grüner Veltliner * Nussdorf 2020

91 Grüner Veltliner * Parapluiberg 2020

90 Grüner Veltliner * Terrassen 2020
90 Grüner Veltliner * Terrassen 2019
89 Grüner Veltliner * Terrassen 2018

91 Grüner Veltliner Metamorphosis 2021
91 Grüner Veltliner Metamorphosis 2020

90 Grüner Veltliner Vision 2020
90 Grüner Veltliner Vision organic 2019

(97) Riesling * Getzersdorf Ried Berg 1ÖTW 2022
13 Vol.-%, cork, steel tank, €€€€€€ B V

96 Riesling * Getzersdorf Ried Berg 1ÖTW 2021
Pale greenish yellow, silver glints. Subtle nuances of yellow fruit, a hint of candied orange zest, delicate blossom honey nuances, and a mineral touch. Taut, tightly woven, subtle vineyard peach, filigree acidity structure, very polished, marked by saline-mineral reverberations and an excellent length. Well-balanced and ethereal, with promising potential for development.

94 Riesling * Getzersdorf Ried Berg 1ÖTW 2020

94 Riesling * Inzersdorf Ried Rothenbart 1ÖTW 2022
13 Vol.-%, screwcap, steel tank, €€€€€ B V

94 Riesling * Inzersdorf Ried Rothenbart 1ÖTW 2021

94 Riesling * Inzersdorfer Ried Rothenbart 1ÖTW 2020

92 Riesling * Getzersdorf Engelsberg 2022
92 Riesling * Getzersdorf Engelsberg 2021
92 Riesling * Getzersdorf Engelsberg 2020

92 Riesling * Parapluiberg 2020

91 Riesling * Nussdorf 2022
90 Riesling * Nussdorf 2021
91 Nussdorfer Riesling * 2020

91 Riesling Terrassen 2021
91 Riesling Terrassen 2020
91 Riesling * Terrassen 2019

94 Chardonnay Ried Spiegeln 2021
13 Vol.-%, cork, 500-l-barrel/barrique, €€€€€ B V

91 Chardonnay 2021
90 Chardonnay 2020

93 Pinot Blanc Alte Reben 2022
13,5 Vol.-%, screwcap, large wooden barrel, €€€ B V

92 Weißburgunder Rosenweg 2021
92 Weißburgunder Rosenweg 2020

* Traisental DAC   ** Traisental DAC Reserve

NIEDERÖSTERREICH

| 92 | Gelber Muskateller Parapluiberg 2020 |

| 92 | Gelber Muskateller 2022 |
12 Vol.-%, screwcap, steel tank, €€ B V
| 91 | Gelber Muskateller 2021 |
| 90 | Gelber Muskateller 2020 |

| (92) | Kontrast 2022 |
12 Vol.-%, DIAM, amphore/large wooden barrel/steel tank, €€€ B O V
| 90 | Kontrast natural wine 2021 |

| 91 | Sauvignon Blanc 2022 |
12,5 Vol.-%, screwcap, steel tank, €€ B V
| 90 | Sauvignon Blanc 2021 |
| 89 | Sauvignon Blanc 2020 |

| 92 | Moments Rosé 2021 BF/ZW/PN/BB/CS/ME/BP |

| 91 | Pinot Noir 2020 |
| 90 | Pinot Noir 2019 |

| 90 | St. Laurent Ried Hochschopf 2018 |
| 90 | St. Laurent Ried Hochschopf 2017 |

★★★★

WEINGUT LUDWIG NEUMAYER

Ludwig Neumayer, for decades the leading oenological star of the Traisental, concentrates exclusively on the production of white wines. The barren, rocky limestone terroir produces wines of exceptional finesse. Grüner Veltliner and Riesling are the most important varieties, but concentrated Weißburgunder and Sauvignon Blanc are also highly regarded. The top wines are called "Der Wein vom Stein" and come from the highest and stoniest Inzersdorf vineyards - Neumayers Stein. In addition, site wines such as "Zwirch", "Rothenbart", and "Rafasetzen" are cultivated here. Outstanding single vineyard wines are also produced under the label "Ikon".

Ludwig Neumayer aims to present an inimitable style of dense wines with plenty of freshness. The pale colour of Neumayer's wines is not due to a lack of ripeness in the grapes but to the unique soils. An additional advantage of the wines is their marked acidity structure. Residual sugars are only tolerated if they suit the style of the wine. Neumayer also uses no animal protein in the winemaking process.

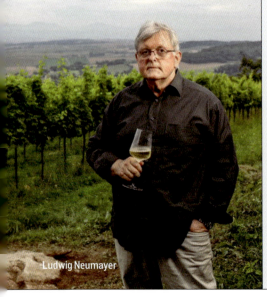
Ludwig Neumayer

WEINGUT LUDWIG NEUMAYER
3131 Inzersdorf ob der Traisen
Dorfstraße 37
T: +43 (2782) 81110
neumayer@weinvomstein.at
www.weinvomstein.at

Winemaker/Contact:
Ludwig Neumayer
Production: 100 % white, 14.5 hectares
Fairs: ProWein Düsseldorf
Distribution partners: USA

TRAISENTAL DAC

Leading Austrian and international restaurateurs have long since discovered these sophisticated wines. Ludwig Neumayer has achieved positions on wine lists that other winemakers can only dream of, such as the star-rated "Astrance" or the "Plaza Athénée" formerly under the management of Alain Ducasse.

(98) Riesling * Inzersdorf Der Wein vom Stein 2022
13 Vol.-%, screwcap, steel tank, €€€€€ Ⓥ

96 Riesling * Inzersdorf Der Wein vom Stein 2021
Pale yellow-green, silver glints. Subtle white tropical fruit, still somewhat reserved, floral fragrance, delicate nuances of vineyard peach and lime zest. Alluring bouquet. Firm, tightly woven, tenderly fruit forward, racy acidity, very salty and persistent, seemingly graceful, marked by its length. Assured ageing potential for many years to come.

95 Riesling ** Inzersdorf Der Wein vom Stein 2019

(95) Riesling * Inzersdorf Ried Rothenbart 1ÖTW 2022
13 Vol.-%, screwcap, steel tank, €€€€€ Ⓥ

95 Riesling * Inzersdorf Ried Rothenbart 1ÖTW 2021
94 Riesling ** Ried Rothenbart 1ÖTW Inzersdorf 2019

(93) Riesling * Inzersdorf Grillenbart 2022
12,5 Vol.-%, screwcap, steel tank, €€€€ Ⓥ

92 Riesling * Inzersdorf Grillenbart 2021
92 Riesling * Inzersdorf Grillenbart 2019

(99) Riesling Steinkapelle 2022
13 Vol.-%, screwcap, steel tank, €€€€€€ Ⓥ

93 Riesling Ried Himmelreich Inzersdorf 2019

97 Grüner Veltliner * Inzersdorf Ikon 2021
95 Grüner Veltliner Ikon Inzersdorf 2018
95 Grüner Veltliner Ikon Inzersdorf 2017

(95) Grüner Veltliner * Inzersdorf Der Wein vom Stein 2022
14 Vol.-%, screwcap, steel tank, €€€€€ Ⓥ

95 Grüner Veltliner * Inzersdorf Der Wein vom Stein 2021
Pale yellow-green, silver glints. Delicately fragrant blossom honey, apricot nuances, a hint of lush apple, tangerine zest, and a touch of minerality. A multifaceted bouquet. Full-bodied, complex, elegant texture, subtly fruit forward at the core, freshly structured, opulent, juicy, and persistent. Excellent length will benefit from bottle ageing.

95 Grüner Veltliner ** Inzersdorf Der Wein vom Stein 2020

(95) Grüner Veltliner * Inzersdorf Ried Rothenbart 2022
14 Vol.-%, screwcap, steel tank, €€€€€ Ⓥ

94 Grüner Veltliner * Inzersdorf Ried Rothenbart 1ÖTW 2021
94 Grüner Veltliner ** Ried Rothenbart Inzersdorf 1ÖTW 2020

(94) Grüner Veltliner * Inzersdorf Ried Zwirch 1ÖTW 2022
13,5 Vol.-%, screwcap, steel tank, €€€€€ Ⓥ

93 Grüner Veltliner ** Ried Zwirch 1ÖTW Inzersdorf 2020
93 Grüner Veltliner * Ried Zwirch 1ÖTW 2019

(92) Grüner Veltliner * Inzersdorf Zwiri 2022
13 Vol.-%, screwcap, steel tank, €€€€ Ⓥ

93 Grüner Veltliner * Inzersdorf Zwiri 2021
93 Grüner Veltliner * Inzersdorf Zwiri 2020

92 Grüner Veltliner * Inzersdorf Ried Rafasetzen 2021
92 Grüner Veltliner * Ried Rafasetzen 2020
92 Grüner Veltliner * Ried Rafasetzen 2019

(91) Grüner Veltliner * Inzersdorf Schieflage 2022
13 Vol.-%, screwcap, steel tank, €€€€ Ⓥ

92 Grüner Veltliner * Inzersdorf Schieflage 2021
91 Grüner Veltliner * Inzersdorf Schieflage 2020

(95) Weißburgunder Inzersdorf Der Wein vom Stein 2022
14 Vol.-%, screwcap, steel tank, €€€€€ Ⓥ

94 Weissburgunder Inzersdorf Der Wein vom Stein 2021
94 Weißburgunder Der Wein vom Stein 2019

94 Sauvignon Blanc Inzersdorf Der Wein vom Stein 2019
93 Sauvignon Blanc Der Wein vom Stein 2018

(92) Sauvignon Blanc Inzersdorf Giess 2022
13 Vol.-%, screwcap, steel tank, €€€€ Ⓥ

93 Sauvignon Blanc Inzersdorf Giess 2021
91 Sauvignon Blanc Inzersdorf Giess 2019

* Traisental DAC   ** Traisental DAC Reserve

NOLZ WEIN

In recent years, a lot has happened at Winzerhof Nolz, in pursuit of their vision: "Producing wines with which one identifies, constantly evolving with our products, and offering our customers the best possible service and advice". Tradition combined with innovative ideas, an uncompromising focus on quality, and a sense of perfect timing are the cornerstones of the young Traisental winemaker's success. The winery is undoubtedly one of the most important contributors to the image of this small wine-growing region. A visit to the Heurigen in the Kellergasse am Eichberg is well worth a detour.

90 ❂ **Gelber Muskateller Sekt 2021**
12 Vol.-%, cork, bottle maturation, €€€

91 ❂ **Gelber Muskateller Sekt 2019**

93 Grüner Veltliner ** Ried Eichberg 2019
Light greenish yellow with silver reflections. A subtle but fragrant nose, mixing Golden Delicious apple and orange zest with hints of vanilla and honeydew melon. The palate is juicy and complex thanks to a delicate woody spice and a touch of caramel on the finish. There's a power to this that makes for a sturdy food companion.

92 Grüner Veltliner * Traismauer Select 2019
91 Grüner Veltliner * Select 2018

91 Grüner Veltliner * Venusberg 2022
12,5 Vol.-%, screwcap, steel tank, €€
91 Grüner Veltliner * Venusberg 2021
91 Grüner Veltliner * Traismauer Venusberg 2020

91 Grüner Veltliner * Ahrenberg Ried Silberboden 2022
13 Vol.-%, screwcap, large wooden barrel, €€
91 Grüner Veltliner * Ahrenberg Ried Silberboden 2021
92 Grüner Veltliner * Ahrenberg Ried Silberboden 2020

90 Grüner Veltliner * Traismauer Ried Hühnerkropf 2022
90 Grüner Veltliner * Ried Hühnerkropf 2021
88 Grüner Veltliner * Hühnerkropf 2020

91 Riesling * 2022
13 Vol.-%, screwcap, steel tank, €€
90 Riesling * 2021
90 Riesling * 2020

89 Weißburgunder 2022
13 Vol.-%, screwcap, steel tank, €€

88 Sauvignon Blanc 2022
12 Vol.-%, screwcap, steel tank, €€
88 Sauvignon Blanc 2020
88 Sauvignon Blanc 2019

89 ❂ **rosa 2021 ZW/CS**

92 Gewürztraminer Auslese 2017

NOLZ WEIN
3133 Hilpersdorf
Dorfstraße 5
T: +43 (664) 73534223
office@nolzwein.at
www.nolzwein.at

Winemaker/Contact:
Josef Nolz
Production: 3 % sparkling, 85 % white, 1 % rosé, 10 % red, 1 % sweet, 8 hectares

TRAISENTAL DAC

WEINGUT THOMAS OTT
3134 Reichersdorf
Obere Ortsstraße 37
T: +43 (664) 5271508
info@ott-traisental.at
www.ott-traisental.at

Winemaker/Contact:
Thomas Ott
Production: 90 % white, 10 % red
Distribution partners: DE

Thomas Ott

WEINGUT THOMAS OTT

Thomas Ott's winery can proudly look back on hundreds of years of winemaking tradition. For him, viticulture has a lot to do with harmony and balance. The aim is to sustain the vineyards and maintain their natural balance, minimizing the need for intervention. The wines also benefit from the unique microclimate of the Traisental: Pannonian influences provide warmth and sunshine. At the same time, Atlantic currents bring cool air that is key to the development of aromas. The terraced vineyards, some of which are very small, are planted mainly with Grüner Veltliner and Riesling. The soil is very calcareous, which conveys minerality and makes the wines truly distinctive. Tip: A local wine tavern with homemade specialities to accompany the wines.

92   Grüner Veltliner * Ried Alte Setzen 2022
13 Vol.-%, screwcap, 500-l-barrel, €€€
91   Grüner Veltliner ** Ried Alte Setzen 2021
Light greenish yellow, silver reflections. Delicate tobacco and herbal spice underlaid with fresh pear fruit, yellow apple, a hint of orange zest. Juicy, finely spicy, some anise and caraway, soft notes of pome fruit, discreet acidity, mineral-salty finish, already developed.
92   Grüner Veltliner ** Ried Alte Setzen 2020

90   Grüner Veltliner * Ried Mitterweg 2022
12,5 Vol.-%, screwcap, steel tank, €€
90   Grüner Veltliner * Einöd
Ried Mitterweg 2021
92   Grüner Veltliner * Ried Mitterweg 2020

90   Grüner Veltliner * Flins 2022
12 Vol.-%, screwcap, steel tank, €€
89   Grüner Veltliner * Flins 2021
90   Grüner Veltliner * Flins 2020

(91) Riesling * Ried Spiegeln 2022
13 Vol.-%, screwcap, steel tank, €€
91   Riesling * Ried Spiegeln 2021
91   Riesling * Ried Spiegeln 2020

91   Riesling * Parapluiberg 2021
90   Riesling * Parapluiberg 2020
90   Riesling * Parapluiberg 2019

90   Blütenmuskateller 2022
12 Vol.-%, screwcap, €€

89   Gemischter Satz Alte Reben 2022
12 Vol.-%, screwcap, steel tank, €€
90   Gemischter Satz Alte Reben 2021
89   Gemischter Satz Alte Reben 2020

---

* Traisental DAC   ** Traisental DAC Reserve

NIEDERÖSTERREICH/ LOWER AUSTRIA

WACHAU
DAC

View from Rührsdorf over the Danube to Weißenkirchen

Spitz an der Donau

STEEP TERRACES, A CULTIVATED HABITAT FOR THE VINES

World cultural heritage and an enchanting feel-good landscape - that is the Wachau. On 1,323 hectares, partly on steep terraces, mainly Grüner Veltliner and Riesling are grown. The wine categories "Steinfeder", "Federspiel" and "Smaragd" represent their natural alcohol content, graded by Vinea Wachau, which will also have DAC status from the 2020 vintage.

The history of the origins of one of Austria's most fascinating wine-growing regions is intriguing: In the post-glacial period, dusty soils settled in the leeward side of the mountains, which became today's loess soils on the one hand and the steeply sloping slopes of Gföhler gneiss on the other. The Danube also contributed by depositing sand, gravel and alluvial loess on the plains. This geology, combined with the terraces created by man as "landscape maintenance" to cultivate the best steep slopes, form the distinctive image of the Wachau. The climate is also exciting, because two strong influences meet here - not head-on, but closely interlocked: the western Atlantic and the eastern continental Pannonian climates. Depending on the slope, exposition, terrain formation and the heat-storing walls and rocks, micro-climatic zones become effective. The hot, dry summers and the harsh winters are balanced by the large water surface of the Danube. The cool downdrafts from the northern Waldviertel cause large fluctuations between day and night temperatures, especially in the months before harvest. From the cooler Spitzer Graben to the warmer Loibenberg, this interplay gives

NIEDERÖSTERREICH/LOWER AUSTRIA **WACHAU DAC**

rise to the grapes' multi-layered aromas. This can be detected in the wines as cool fruit with sometimes exotic hints: from the slender Steinfeder to the elegant Federspiel to the noble Smaragd, defined by an association of winemakers from the wine-growing area known as "Vinea Wachau". And once again, it is exciting to go in search of wine-culinary addresses in the historic ambience of the wine villages. Top vintners and top restaurateurs can be found at every turn in the Wachau, from Spitz to Weißenkirchen, Wösendorf and Joching to Dürnstein and Loiben - although one or two detours to the right bank of the Danube are recommended. Of course, you can also visit numerous traditional wine inns in the Wachau. In addition to the reigning couple Riesling and Grüner Veltliner, which will be available from 2020 as Wachau DAC regional, there are also local and estate wines, Pinot Blanc, Neuburger, Muscat or Sauvignon Blanc. They also guarantee excellent taste experiences as regional and local wines.

WACHAU DAC

Austria altogether	44.728 ha
Wine-growing area Lower Austria	27.074 ha
Wachau DAC	1.323 ha

SELECTED WINERIES

 ★★★★★

Weingut Alzinger, Dürnstein
Weingut Franz Hirtzberger, Spitz an der Donau
Weingut Knoll, Dürnstein
Weingut F. X. Pichler, Dürnstein
Weingut Rudi Pichler, Wösendorf
Weingut Prager, Weißenkirchen/Wachau

 ★★★★

Domäne Wachau, Dürnstein
Weingut Johann Donabaum, Spitz an der Donau
FJ Gritsch – Mauritiushof, Spitz an der Donau
Weingut Josef & Georg Högl, Spitz an der Donau
Weingut Jamek, Joching
Weingut Schmelz, Joching
Weingut Tegernseerhof, Dürnstein

 ★★★

Weingut Atzberg, Spitz an der Donau
Weinhofmeisterei Mathias Hirtzberger, Wösendorf in der Wachau
Weingut Holzapfel, Weißenkirchen
Weingut Hutter Silberbichlerhof, Mautern an der Donau

 ★

Domäne Roland Chan, Wösendorf in der Wachau
Weingut Christoph Donabaum, Spitz
Weingut Ernsthofer, Wösendorf

 ★★★★★

WEINGUT ALZINGER

Leo Alzinger has been one of the stars of the Wachau wine scene since 1983. The vintner, produces Grüner Veltliner and Riesling in his Loibner and Dürnsteiner top vineyards, actively supported by his son of the same name. During my tasting this year, the star sites Loibenberg and Steinertal were, as usual, first class, impressing the jury with their precision and radiance. Alzinger's long-lived wines deserve the undivided attention of wine lovers, because here, once again, an absolute top range has been achieved. It doesn't matter if one turns to the Riesling or to the Grüner Veltliner: one is guaranteed to find what one is looking for in their huge selection. If you have the opportunity to taste more aged wines from this house, you will get to know the true splendour of the Loibner wines. Alzinger's wines, in particular, are often a bit closed in their youth, but develop a strong personality after a few years in bottle. So if you want to get to know the character of a top Veltliner better, you should decant an aged Alzinger wine, give it some time - and then be amazed!

On the occasion of the competition "Exemplary Building in Lower Austria", a renowned tasting panel declared the new concept of the winery building as one of the winning projects in 2017. The tasting panel particularly emphasised that the new winery "represents a further structural development of the Wachau World Heritage Site that is worthy of imitation".

(98) Riesling * Ried Steinertal Smaragd 2022
13 Vol.-%, cork, large wooden barrel
99 Riesling * Ried Steinertal Smaragd 2021
97 Riesling * Ried Steinertal Smaragd 2020

(97) Riesling * Ried Loibenberg Smaragd 2022
13 Vol.-%, cork, large wooden barrel
97 Riesling * Ried Loibenberg Smaragd 2021
Pale greenish yellow, silver glints. Tender yellow tropical fruit, a hint of passion fruit and mango, delicate floral nuances, soft minerality, and a dash of mandarin zest. Juicy, elegant, refined fruit expression, filigree acidic structure, marked by a

WACHAU DAC

WEINGUT ALZINGER
3601 Dürnstein
Unterloiben 11
T: +43 (2732) 77900
weingut@alzinger.at
www.alzinger.at

Winemaker/Contact:
Leo Alzinger
Production: 100 % white,
12 hectares
Fairs: ProWein Düsseldorf,
VieVinum
Distribution partners: AUS, BE, RC, DK, DE, FR, UK, IT, CDN, HR, LU, MV, NZ, NL, PT, RUS, SE, CH, SK, ES, CZ, HU, USA, UAE

Dürnstein

citrus-saline finish. Exhibits excellent length and definite ageing potential for many years ahead.
97   Riesling * Ried Loibenberg Smaragd 2020

(96) Riesling * Ried Höhereck Smaragd 2022
13 Vol.-%, cork, large wooden barrel
96   Riesling * Ried Höhereck Smaragd 2021
94   Riesling * Ried Höhereck Smaragd 2020

(95) Riesling * Ried Hollerin Smaragd 2022
13 Vol.-%, cork, large wooden barrel
95   Riesling * Ried Hollerin Smaragd 2021
95   Riesling * Ried Hollerin Smaragd 2020

94   Riesling * Ried Liebenberg Smaragd 2021
94   Riesling * Ried Liebenberg Smaragd 2020
93   Riesling Smaragd Ried Liebenberg 2019

93   Riesling * Dürnstein Federspiel 2022
12 Vol.-%, screwcap, steel tank
93   Riesling * Dürnstein Federspiel 2021
92   Riesling * Dürnstein Federspiel 2020

(97) Grüner Veltliner * Ried Steinertal Smaragd 2022
13 Vol.-%, cork, large wooden barrel
98   Grüner Veltliner * Ried Steinertal Smaragd 2021
Pale greenish yellow, silver glints. Delicate notions of herbal savouriness, smoky minerality, subtle apple fruit, a hint of mango, as well as tobacco nuances. Multifaceted bouquet. Complex, full-bodied, has traction, luscious white fruit, and a sophisticated structure. Ethereal and balanced. Already very accessible and alluring, with excellent ageing potential.
96   Grüner Veltliner * Ried Steinertal Smaragd 2020

96   Grüner Veltliner * Reserve 2021
95   Grüner Veltliner Reserve 2018

(95) Grüner Veltliner * Loiben Ried Loibenberg Smaragd 2022
13 Vol.-%, cork, large wooden barrel
97   Grüner Veltliner * Ried Loibenberg Smaragd 2020
Pale greenish yellow, silver glints. Finely dusted herbal savoury nuances, meadow herbs, alluring whiffs of white stone fruit, fine orange zest, and a tobacco touch. Juicy, full-bodied, elegant, refined expression of exotic fruit, sophisticated acidity, lovely creamy texture marked by a saline finish. Excellent length, accessible, with promising ageing potential.
95   Grüner Veltliner * Ried Loibenberg Smaragd 2020

(94) Grüner Veltliner * Ried Liebenberg Smaragd 2022
13,5 Vol.-%, cork, large wooden barrel
95   Grüner Veltliner * Ried Liebenberg Smaragd 2021
94   Grüner Veltliner * Ried Liebenberg Smaragd 2020

NIEDERÖSTERREICH/LOWER AUSTRIA

(94) Grüner Veltliner * Ried Mühlpoint Smaragd 2022
13 Vol.-%, screwcap, steel tank
95 Grüner Veltliner * Ried Mühlpoint Smaragd 2021
94 Grüner Veltliner Smaragd Ried Mühlpoint 2019
93 Grüner Veltliner * Ried Mühlpoint Federspiel 2022
12 Vol.-%, screwcap, steel tank
94 Grüner Veltliner * Ried Mühlpoint Federspiel 2021
93 Grüner Veltliner * Ried Mühlpoint Federspiel 2020

93 Grüner Veltliner * Ried Hochstrasser Federspiel 2022
12 Vol.-%, screwcap, steel tank
93 Grüner Veltliner * Ried Hochstrasser Federspiel 2021
92 Grüner Veltliner * Ried Hochstrasser Federspiel 2020

92 Grüner Veltliner * Dürnstein Federspiel 2022
12 Vol.-%, screwcap, steel tank
92 Grüner Veltliner * Dürnstein Federspiel 2021
91 Grüner Veltliner * Dürnstein Federspiel 2020

WEINGUT ATZBERG

The Atzberg lies in the heart of the Wachau, one of the most beautiful cultural landscapes in the world. The "Ärtzberg" was documented as a wine-growing estate as early as 1382. Viticulture on the Atzberg was abandoned in the 1950s due to the difficulty of cultivating these steep vineyards. But the site's unique geology makes the wines so distinct. The renowned Wachau wine expert, pastor Hans Denk (†) attested to the quality of this site, which is unique even in the Wachau, and so from 2008 onwards, this outstanding site was re-cultivated with a lot of manual work and endless steps. The southern orientation, the optimal sun exposure, the cool air flowing down through the Mieslingtal from the Waldviertel, and the immediate proximity to the Danube result in a very unique microclimate. The extremely steep site with slopes of up to 75 percent is painstakingly cultivated entirely by hand. Every year, only two wines are produced, which are among the best in the Wachau in terms of their depth and expressiveness.

WEINGUT ATZBERG
3620 Spitz an der Donau
Mieslingtal 3
T: +43 (650) 7203663
office@atzberg.at
www.atzberg.at

Winemaker: Johann Donabaum
Contact: Paul Kiefer
Production: 100 % white, 2 hectares
Fairs: ProWein Düsseldorf, VieVinum
Distribution partners: DE

(95) Grüner Veltliner * Ried Atzberg Obere Steilterrassen Smaragd 2022
14,5 Vol.-%, cork, large wooden barrel, €€€€€€
95 Grüner Veltliner * Ried Atzberg Smaragd Obere Steilterrassen 2021
Bright golden yellow, green glints. Subtle blossom honey, delicate scents of clementine zest, a little passion fruit, and lush apple, underlaid with meadow herbs. Multifaceted bouquet. Good complexity, powerful, subtle tobacco savouriness, vibrant acidity structure, tightly woven with ripe tropical fruit and mineral reverberations. A sturdy supper accompaniment.
94 Grüner Veltliner * Ried Atzberg Smaragd Obere Steilterrassen 2020

(93) Grüner Veltliner * Ried Atzberg Steilterrassen Smaragd 2022
14 Vol.-%, screwcap, steel tank, €€€€€

94 Grüner Veltliner * Ried Atzberg Smaragd Steilterrassen 2021
Bright golden yellow, silver reflections. Inviting aromas of mango and papaya, underlaid with tangerine zest and soft notes of honeydew melon. Juicy, good complexity, fine spice, balanced acidity, mineral, multi-faceted, yellow tropical fruit on the finish, good food wine with certain ageing potential.

93 Grüner Veltliner * Ried Atzberg Smaragd Steilterrassen 2020

DOMÄNE ROLAND CHAN

Domäne Roland Chan was founded in 2017 by Roland Müksch, a graduate engineer, and his wife, Dr Sharon Chan, which explains the winery's name, which is rather atypical for a Wachau winery. In the first three years, about half a hectare of steep terraces in the Höll and Bach sites were planted. In 2021, vineyard sites in Achleiten and Klaus were acquired, as well as a vintner's house in Sankt Michael. Today, around 9,000 bottles are produced on 2.5 hectares.

Top winemaker Christoph Donabaum is responsible for the vinification, together with Roland Müksch. The steep terraces require three multiple passages to obtain grapes that meet the owner's expectations. Longer macerations before pressing are desired. The wines are then aged for an extended period on fine lees and bottled unfiltered. Domaine Chan's wines are released two years after the harvest.

The wines have already received very high ratings from James Suckling (93 points for the Riesling Ried Bach 2019) and Falstaff (94 points for the Riesling Ried Bach 2020), and the winery is also a two-time trophy winner at the Hong Kong International Wine and Spirits Competition.

94 Riesling * Ried Achleiten Smaragd 2021
14 Vol.-%, cork, steel tank/bottle maturation, €€€€€€

94 Riesling * Ried Klaus Smaragd 2021
13,5 Vol.-%, cork, large wooden barrel/bottle maturation, €€€€€

Harvest in Hoell

DOMÄNE ROLAND CHAN
3610 Wösendorf in der Wachau
Kellergasse 102
T: +43 (660) 8345252
mukschr@yahoo.com
domaene-rolandchan.at

Winemaker: Christoph Donabaum
Contact: Roland Müksch
Production: 10,000 bottles
90 % white, 10 % rosé, 2.3 hectares
Fairs: Vinexpo
Distribution partners: HK, SGP

NIEDERÖSTERREICH/LOWER AUSTRIA

94 Riesling * Ried Höll Smaragd 2021
13,5 Vol.-%, cork, steel tank/bottle maturation, €€€€€

93 Riesling * Ried Bach Smaragd 2021
13,5 Vol.-%, cork, large wooden barrel/bottle maturation, €€€€€

94 Riesling * Ried Bach Wösendorf Smaragd 2020
Light golden yellow, silver reflections. Ripe yellow peach fruit, in the background a touch of blossom honey, plus white blossom aromas, notes of tangerine zest, inviting, multi-faceted bouquet. Juicy on the palate, ripe white stone fruit, racy acidity, mineral, lime in the finish, ripe fruit in the aftertaste, shows length and certain ageing potential.

93 Riesling * Ried Bach Smaragd 2019

93 Grüner Veltliner * Ried Höll Smaragd 2021
13,5 Vol.-%, cork, steel tank/bottle maturation, €€€€€

93 Grüner Veltliner * Ried Bach Federspiel 2022

92 Zweigelt * gleichgepresst »To Hell and Back« 2021
12,5 Vol.-%, cork, steel tank/bottle maturation, €€€€€

DOMÄNE WACHAU

Domäne Wachau has developed into one of Austria's most important wineries with a range of typical Wachau-style wines under the management of Roman Horvath MW and Heinz Frischengruber. World-famous vineyards such as Achleiten, Kellerberg and Singerriedel are only a few examples of top sites vinified by the estate.

One crucial and relevant point not to be overlooked in the famed wines of Domäne Wachau is the work and know-how of the winegrowers.

Generations of families have worked in the steep terraces of the Wachau, passing down the in-depth knowledge of the special characteristics of each parcel. With meticulous manual work and enormous experience, they ensure an ecological balance in the vineyards, promote the diversity of species and plants, and increasingly pursue organic farming. Minimalism at the highest level of craftsmanship, that is wine making in the Wachau. Tradition and innovation are two sides of the same coin. As the production of expressive Rieden wines shows with the Backstage series which highlights new and especially old methods. The harmonious union of provenance, vintage and variety.

The Domäne Wachau was voted one of the World's Best Vineyards by an international tasting panel (No. 1 in Europe & No. 3 worldwide), making it a top destination for wine lovers from all over the world. The quality-oriented event program includes vineyard walks, winery tours, a Kellerschlössel Heuriger (a traditional inn) offering unique gastronomic experiences. Wachau visitors can also stock up at the Domäne Wachau's Vinothek (wine shop) and at Shop 11A in Dürnstein's old town.

96 Grüner Veltliner Ried Achleiten Smaragd »Late release« 2017
13,5 Vol.-%, cork, large wooden barrel, €€€€€€ Ⓥ

95 Grüner Veltliner Ried Achleiten Smaragd Late Release 2016

96 Grüner Veltliner Smaragd Ried Achleiten »Late release« 2015

(95) Grüner Veltliner * Ried Achleiten Smaragd 2022
13,5 Vol.-%, cork, steel tank/large wooden barrel, €€€€€ Ⓥ

95 Grüner Veltliner * Ried Achleiten Smaragd 2021
Medium greenish yellow, silver glints. Fragrant herbal notes, hints of white stone fruit, delicate papaya, and citrus zest. An invigorating dark bouquet. Good complexity, lightly woven, delicate meadow herbs, yellow stone fruit, with a finely savoury finish. A wine with a mineral character, offering potential for development.

© Domäne Wachau

WACHAU DAC

DOMÄNE WACHAU
3601 Dürnstein
Dürnstein 107
T: +43 (2711) 371
office@domaene-wachau.at
www.domaene-wachau.at

Winemaker: Heinz Frischengruber
Contact: Roman Horvath MW
Production: 2,500,000 bottles
90 % white, 4 % rosé, 5 % red,
1 % sweet, 400 hectares
Certified: Sustainable Austria
Fairs: ProWein Düsseldorf,
VieVinum, Vinexpo
Distribution partners: DE, FIN, UK,
CDN, NL, NO, PL, SE, CH, USA

Roman Horvath MW and Heinz Frischengruber

95 Grüner Veltliner * Ried Achleiten Smaragd 2020

(95) Grüner Veltliner * Ried Kellerberg Smaragd 2022
13 Vol.-%, cork, steel tank/large wooden barrel, €€€€€ V
96 Grüner Veltliner * Ried Kellerberg Smaragd 2021
94 Grüner Veltliner * Ried Kellerberg Smaragd 2020

(94) Grüner Veltliner * Ried Axpoint Smaragd 2022
13 Vol.-%, cork, steel tank/large wooden barrel, €€€€€ V
94 Grüner Veltliner * Ried Axpoint Smaragd 2021
93 Grüner Veltliner * Ried Axpoint Smaragd 2020

(94) Grüner Veltliner * Ried Kirnberg Smaragd 2022
13 Vol.-%, cork, steel tank/large wooden barrel, €€€€€ V
95 Grüner Veltliner * Ried Kirnberg Smaragd 2021
93 Grüner Veltliner * Ried Kirnberg Smaragd 2020

(94) Grüner Veltliner * Ried Schön Smaragd 2022
13 Vol.-%, cork, steel tank, €€€€€ V

(93) Grüner Veltliner * Smaragd Himmelstiege 2022
13 Vol.-%, screwcap, steel tank, €€€€ V
93 Grüner Veltliner * Smaragd Himmelstiege 2021
92 Grüner Veltliner * Smaragd Himmelstiege 2020

93 Grüner Veltliner * Weissenkirchen Smaragd 2022
13 Vol.-%, screwcap, steel tank, €€€€ V
93 Grüner Veltliner * Weissenkirchen Smaragd 2021
92 Grüner Veltliner * Weissenkirchen Smaragd 2020

93 Grüner Veltliner * Rossatz Smaragd 2022
13 Vol.-%, screwcap, steel tank, €€€€ V
92 Grüner Veltliner * Rossatz 2021

93 Grüner Veltliner * Dürnstein Smaragd 2022
13 Vol.-%, screwcap, steel tank, €€€€ V
93 Grüner Veltliner * Dürnstein Smaragd 2021
93 Grüner Veltliner * Dürnstein Smaragd 2020

(92) Grüner Veltliner * Spitzer Graben Steinwerk 2022
12,5 Vol.-%, cork, granite, €€€€ V

* Wachau DAC

NIEDERÖSTERREICH/LOWER AUSTRIA

Grüner Veltliner

94 Grüner Veltliner * Steinwerk
    Spitzer Graben 2021
93 Grüner Veltliner Steinwerk
    Spitzer Graben 2019

(93) Grüner Veltliner * Smaragd Terrassen 2022
13 Vol.-%, screwcap, steel tank, €€€€ 🅥
94 Grüner Veltliner * Smaragd Terrassen 2021
93 Grüner Veltliner * Smaragd Terrassen 2020

93 Grüner Veltliner * Ried Loibenberg
    Federspiel 2022
93 Grüner Veltliner * Ried Loibenberg
    Federspiel 2021
92 Grüner Veltliner * Ried Loibenberg
    Federspiel 2020

92 Grüner Veltliner * Ried Kreuzberg
    Federspiel 2022
12,5 Vol.-%, screwcap, steel tank, €€€ 🅥
93 Grüner Veltliner * Ried Kreuzberg
    Federspiel 2021
92 Grüner Veltliner * Ried Kreuzberg
    Federspiel 2020

92 Grüner Veltliner * Ried Kollmitz
    Federspiel 2022
92 Grüner Veltliner * Ried Kollmitz
    Federspiel 2021
93 Grüner Veltliner * Ried Kollmitz
    Federspiel 2020

92 Grüner Veltliner * Ried Kaiserberg
    Federspiel 2022
91 Grüner Veltliner * Ried Kaiserberg
    Federspiel 2021
92 Grüner Veltliner * Ried Kaiserberg
    Federspiel 2020

92 Grüner Veltliner * Ried Liebenberg
    Federspiel 2022
92 Grüner Veltliner * Ried Liebenberg
    Federspiel 2021
92 Grüner Veltliner * Ried Liebenberg
    Federspiel 2020

91 Grüner Veltliner * Dürnstein Federspiel 2022
91 Grüner Veltliner * Dürnstein Federspiel 2021
91 Grüner Veltliner * Dürnstein Federspiel 2020

91 Grüner Veltliner * Ried Pichlpoint
    Federspiel 2022
92 Grüner Veltliner * Ried Pichlpoint
    Federspiel 2021
91 Grüner Veltliner * Ried Pichlpoint
    Federspiel 2020

90 Grüner Veltliner * Weissenkirchen
    Federspiel 2022
90 Grüner Veltliner * Weissenkirchen
    Federspiel 2021
90 Grüner Veltliner * Weissenkirchen
    Federspiel 2020

(96) Riesling * Ried Kellerberg Smaragd 2022
13 Vol.-%, cork, steel tank/large wooden barrel,
€€€€€ 🅥
94 Riesling * Ried Kellerberg Smaragd 2021
Medium greenish yellow, silver reflections. Inviting bouquet, of apricot and guava, underlaid with blossom honey, soft herbs, aniseed, smoky minerality, multi-faceted. Complex, juicy, light on its feet, a bit of citrus and quince on the finish, salty aftertaste, complex food wine.
95 Riesling * Ried Kellerberg Smaragd 2020

(95) Riesling * Ried Achleiten Smaragd 2022
13,5 Vol.-%, cork, steel tank/large wooden barrel,
€€€€€ 🅥
96 Riesling * Ried Achleiten Smaragd 2021
94 Riesling * Ried Achleiten Smaragd 2020

(95) Riesling * Ried Singerriedel Smaragd 2022
13 Vol.-%, cork, steel tank, €€€€ 🅥
96 Riesling * Ried Singerriedel Smaragd 2021
95 Riesling * Ried Singerriedel Smaragd 2020

(95) Riesling * Ried Brandstatt Smaragd 2022
13 Vol.-%, cork, steel tank, €€€€ ⓥ

(94) Riesling * Ried Loibenberg Smaragd 2022
13 Vol.-%, cork, steel tank/large wooden barrel, €€€€€ ⓥ

95 Riesling * Ried Loibenberg Smaragd 2021
93 Riesling * Ried Loibenberg Smaragd 2020

93 **Riesling * Smaragd Terrassen 2022**
13 Vol.-%, screwcap, steel tank, €€€ ⓥ
93 Riesling * Smaragd Terrassen 2021
93 Riesling * Smaragd Terrassen 2020

93 **Riesling * Weissenkirchen Smaragd 2022**
13 Vol.-%, screwcap, steel tank, €€€ ⓥ
93 Riesling * Weissenkirchen Smaragd 2021
92 Riesling * Weissenkirchen Smaragd 2020

92 **Riesling * Ried 1000-Eimer-Berg Federspiel 2022**
93 Riesling * Ried 1000-Eimer-Berg Federspiel 2021
93 Riesling * Ried 1000-Eimer-Berg Federspiel 2020

92 **Riesling * Ried Trenning Federspiel 2022**
12,5 Vol.-%, screwcap, steel tank, €€€ ⓥ

91 Riesling * Ried Bruck Federspiel 2022
92 Riesling * Ried Bruck Federspiel 2021
912 Riesling * Ried Bruck Federspiel 2020

92 Riesling * Ried Loibenberg Federspiel 2022
94 Riesling * Ried Loibenberg Federspiel 2021
92 Riesling * Ried Loibenberg Federspiel 2020

92 Riesling * Ried Steinriegl Federspiel 2022
94 Riesling * Ried Steinriegl Federspiel 2021
92 Riesling * Ried Steinriegl Federspiel 2020

90 Riesling * Dürnstein Federspiel 2022
90 Riesling * Dürnstein Federspiel 2021
91 Riesling * Dürnstein Federspiel 2020

90 Riesling * Weissenkirchen Federspiel 2022
90 Riesling * Weissenkirchen Federspiel 2021
90 Riesling * Weissenkirchen Federspiel 2020

(91) Riesling Amphora 2021
12,5 Vol.-%, cork, amphore, €€€€ ⓘ ⓥ
91 Riesling Amphora 2020

(94) Chardonnay * 20twentyone 2021
13 Vol.-%, cork, small wooden barrel, €€€€€ ⓥ

91 Chardonnay * Reserve 2020
91 Chardonnay Reserve 2019

91 Chardonnay * Federspiel Terrassen 2022
90 Chardonnay * Federspiel Terrassen 2021
91 Chardonnay * Federspiel Terrassen 2020

91 Neuburger * Federspiel Spitzer Graben 2022
91 Neuburger * Federspiel Spitzer Graben 2021
92 Neuburger * Federspiel Spitzer Graben 2020

91 **Roter Traminer * 2022**
13 Vol.-%, cork, steel tank, €€€€ ⓥ
93 Roter Traminer *Reserve 2021
90 Roter Traminer *Reserve 2020

89 Weißburgunder * Federspiel Terrassen 2022
90 Weißburgunder * Federspiel Terrassen 2021
89 Weißburgunder * Federspiel Terrassen 2020

(92) Gemischter Satz * Smaragd Uralt-Reben 2022
13 Vol.-%, cork, wooden barrel, €€€€€ ⓥ
92 Gemischter Satz * Smaragd Uralt-Reben 2020
93 Gemischter Satz Ried Vorderseiber Smaragd Uralt-Reben 2019

(92) Müller Thurgau MTX Extrem 2022
12,5 Vol.-%, screwcap, cement, €€€€ ⓘ ⓥ
92 Müller Thurgau MTX 2021

91 **Rosé * 1805 2022** PN/ZW
13 Vol.-%, screwcap, small wooden barrel, €€€€ ⓥ
91 1805 Rosé * Reserve 2020 PN/ZW

93 Beerenauslese Terrassen 2017 MT/RR/MO/WB

* Wachau DAC

NIEDERÖSTERREICH/LOWER AUSTRIA

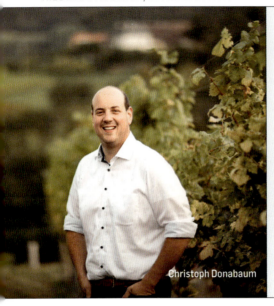
Christoph Donabaum

**WEINGUT
CHRISTOPH DONABAUM**
3620 Spitz
Laaben 16
T: +43 (2713) 2618
office@weindonabaum.at
www.weindonabaum.at

Winemaker/Contact:
Christoph Donabaum
Production: 26,667 bottles
95 % white, 4 % rosé, 1 % sweet,
4+1 hectares
Certified: Sustainable Austria
Fairs: VieVinum
Distribution partners: CZ, USA

WEINGUT CHRISTOPH DONABAUM

Christoph Donabaum took over the winery from his parents, Josef and Herta and since then he has devoted all his time and energy to the winery. The majority of his vineyards are located in the Spitzer Graben. This is a steeply terraced, cooler, and later ripening site of the Wachau wine region. As a result, the grape harvest often extends into November. The steep terraces can only be tended by hand - the same goes for the harvest. Christoph's motivation is to achieve outstanding quality and delicious wines through meticulous selection. It is, therefore, necessary to carry out multiple passages during the harvest to ensure that only the best grapes are selected. In order to produce wines with expression, it is also of utmost importance for the aspiring winemaker to preserve vineyards with old vines. This is confirmed with his Grüner Veltliner Smaragd® Alte Kultur. In addition to Grüner Veltliner, visitors to the winery can also sample the region's renowned Riesling and Neuburger wines. Weather permitting, tasting can take place al fresco in the garden or on the terrace, or in the winery's new tasting room. The Heurige (wine tavern) is open three times a year and Christoph's wines are accompanied by regional snacks.

(94) Grüner Veltliner * Smaragd Alte Kultur 2022
14 Vol.-%, cork, large wooden barrel/steel tank,
€€€€

Light yellow green, silver reflections. Fine yellow apple fruit, a touch of honeydew melon, mineral nuances, a touch of orange zest. Juicy, complex, fine fruit expression, harmoniously structured, balanced finish. Already very gluggable, has certain ageing potential.

93 Grüner Veltliner * Ried Zornberg Smaragd 2022
13,5 Vol.-%, cork, large wooden barrel/steel tank,
€€€€

91 Grüner Veltliner * Federspiel Wachauer Terrassen 2022
12,5 Vol.-%, screwcap, large wooden barrel/steel tank, €€

90 Grüner Veltliner * Federspiel Wachauer Terrassen 2020

© Weingut Christoph Donabaum/Nimo Zimmerhackl

WACHAU DAC

94 **Riesling * Ried 1000-Eimerberg Smaragd 2022**
13,5 Vol.-%, cork, steel tank, €€€€

93 **Riesling * Ried Offenberg Smaragd 2022**
13 Vol.-%, cork, steel tank, €€€€

91 **Riesling * Spitzer Graben Federspiel 2022**
12,5 Vol.-%, screwcap, steel tank, €€€

92 **Riesling * Spitzer Graben 2021**

★★★★

WEINGUT JOHANN DONABAUM

Weingut Johann Donabaum is one of Wachau's up-and-coming wineries. The next generation of Donabaum winemakers is actively supported by his parents in the labour-intensive mountain and terraced vineyards. The estate's wines - Riesling Offenberg and Setzberg, as well as Grüner Veltliner Spitzer Point - can be found on the best-stocked wine lists in the country. The rare Neuburger grape is also grown, and the Smaragd from the Spitzer Biern site is one of the outstanding expressions of this variety. A small bridge over the Spitzer Valley leads to the historic estate, which dates back to the 16th century. The consistent work of the entire family is the key to achieving excellent wines. This results from optimal grapes, which are characterised by the soil, the climate and the winemaker's skill. The winery's greatest success to date came in 2009 at the Decanter World Wine Award in London, the world's largest wine competition: Riesling Smaragd Setzberg 2007 won the international Riesling trophy and was named the best Riesling over £10.

(96) Riesling * Smaragd Limitierte Edition 2022
14,5 Vol.-%, cork, steel tank/large wooden barrel, €€€€€€

96 **Riesling * Limitierte Edition Smaragd 2021**
Bright yellow-green, silver glints. Soft notions of citrus notes underlaid with peach blossoms and white tropical fruit, and a hint of guava. Inviting bouquet. Complex, tightly woven, round, fruit forward reminiscent of apricots, balanced, mineral reverberations, lime nuanced aftertaste, persistent. A complex food accompaniment with potential for development.

95 **Riesling Smaragd Limitierte Edition 2019**

WEINGUT JOHANN DONABAUM

3620 Spitz an der Donau
Laaben 15
T: +43 (676) 9313150
info@weingut-donabaum.at
www.weingut-donabaum.at

Winemaker/Contact:
Johann Donabaum jr.
Production: 73,333 bottles
100 % white, 10 hectares
Fairs: VieVinum
Distribution partners: BE, DK, DE, UK, CDN, NL, PL, RUS, CH, CZ, USA

Johann and Andrea Donabaum

NIEDERÖSTERREICH/LOWER AUSTRIA

(94) Riesling * Ried Setzberg Smaragd 2022
13,5 Vol.-%, screwcap, steel tank, €€€€€ H V
94 Riesling * Ried Setzberg Smaragd 2021
95 Riesling * Ried Setzberg Smaragd 2020

(94) Riesling * Ried Offenberg Smaragd 2022
13,5 Vol.-%, screwcap, steel tank, €€€€ H V
94 Riesling * Ried Offenberg Smaragd 2021
94 Riesling * Ried Offenberg Smaragd 2020

(95) Riesling * Spitz Ried Vogelleithen 2022
13,5 Vol.-%, screwcap, steel tank, €€€€€ H V
95 Riesling * Ried Vogelleithen 2021
94 Riesling Smaragd Ried Vogelleithen 2019

93 Weissenkirchner Riesling * Smaragd 2020
92 Weissenkirchner Riesling Smaragd 2019
92 Weissenkirchner Riesling Smaragd 2018

96 Grüner Veltliner * Limitierte Edition Smaragd 2021
95 Grüner Veltliner Smaragd Limitierte Edition 2019

(95) Grüner Veltliner * Ried Spitzer Point Smaragd 2022
13,5 Vol.-%, screwcap, steel tank, €€€€ H V
95 Grüner Veltliner * Ried Spitzer Point Smaragd 2021
Medium greenish yellow, silver glints. Fragrant meadow herbs are underlain by yellow apple fruit, a hint of orange peel, and delicate quince jelly. A multifaceted bouquet. Good complexity, dark minerality, tightly woven, well-integrated acidity, finely savoury finish, papaya reverberations, and persistence. An all-around food accompaniment.
94 Grüner Veltliner * Ried Spitzer Point Smaragd 2020

(94) Grüner Veltliner * Wösendorf Ried Kirchweg Smaragd 2022
13,5 Vol.-%, screwcap, steel tank, €€€€€ H V
93 Grüner Veltliner * Wösendorf Ried Kirchweg Smaragd 2021
93 Grüner Veltliner * Ried Wösendorfer Kirchweg Smaragd 2020

93 Grüner Veltliner * Ried Zornberg Smaragd 2022
13 Vol.-%, screwcap, steel tank, €€€€ H V
93 Grüner Veltliner * Ried Zornberg Smaragd 2021
93 Grüner Veltliner * Ried Spitzer Zornberg Smaragd 2020

(94) Neuburger * Spitzer Graben Smaragd 2022
13,5 Vol.-%, screwcap, steel tank, €€€€€ H
95 Neuburger Smaragd Spitzer Graben 2019
93 Neuburger Smaragd Spitzer Graben 2017

94 Riesling Auslese Spitzer Graben 2018

WEINGUT ERNSTHOFER

The Ernsthofer winery is located directly on the Danube in the heart of the Wachau. The family vinifies wines typical of the Wachau region, characterised by the climate and soil of this unique cultural landscape. They are proud to make a personal contribution to the preservation of the Wachau World Heritage Site through their challenging work in the steep vineyards. The diverse characteristics of the well-known vineyards such as "Kollmütz", "Steinriegl" or "Hinter der Burg" are reflected in the wines.
Each vintage is an exciting challenge, which is approached with the utmost passion and attention to detail.

(93) Grüner Veltliner * Smaragd Ried Steinriegl 2022
13,5 Vol.-%, screwcap, large wooden barrel, €€€
92 Grüner Veltliner * Ried Steinriegl Smaragd 2021
Medium greenish yellow with silver reflections. An intense and complex nose of apple and papaya, candied clementine zest and floral blossom honey. Nuances of spice lie below the surface. The palate is juicy and elegant, with a fine acid structure, and spiced undertow. Finishes long, on yellow apple fruit - a powerful food companion.
91 Grüner Veltliner Smaragd Ried Steinriegl 2019

WACHAU DAC

WEINGUT ERNSTHOFER
3610 Wösendorf
Winklgasse 52
T: +43 (664) 4598113
weingut@ernsthofer.at
www.ernsthofer.at

Winemaker/Contact:
Georg Ernsthofer
Production: 5 % sparkling,
85 % white, 10 % rosé, 7 hectares
Distribution partners: BE, DE, IT, PL

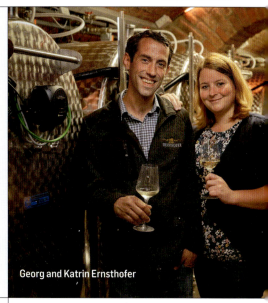

Georg and Katrin Ernsthofer

92 Grüner Veltliner * Weissenkirchen Smaragd 2021

91 Grüner Veltliner * Ried Kollmütz Federspiel 2022
12,5 Vol.-%, screwcap, steel tank, €€€

91 Grüner Veltliner * Ried Hinter der Burg Federspiel 2021

89 Grüner Veltliner * Weißenkirchen Federspiel 2022
12,5 Vol.-%, screwcap, steel tank, €€

90 Grüner Veltliner * Weissenkirchen Federspiel 2021

(93) Riesling * Smaragd Ried Steinriegl 2022
14 Vol.-%, screwcap, steel tank, €€€

92 Riesling * Ried Steinriegl Smaragd 2021

90 Riesling Smaragd Ried Steinriegl 2019

92 Riesling * Ried Gaisberg 2022
12,5 Vol.-%, screwcap, steel tank, €€

91 Riesling * Ried Gaisberg Federspiel 2021

(91) Chardonnay * Reserve 2022
13,5 Vol.-%, screwcap, large wooden barrel, €€€

91 Weißburgunder Smaragd Ried Kollmütz 2018

FJ GRITSCH – MAURITIUSHOF

The FJ Gritsch winery combines the past and present while always focusing on the future. Franz-Josef Gritsch embodies what is already the seventh generation of the family to cultivate vines at the historic Mauritiushof in Spitz on the Danube. Tradition and know-how handed down through the generations are paramount here. However, excellence can only be achieved through continuous development. The "kalmuck" cellar is a prime example, where the wine is produced using state-of-the-art technology. In addition, the ‚Weinerlebnis Mauritiushof' - a complete innovative wine experience: in and around the historic Mauritiushof, an inviting tasting and sales room, complemented by a well-equipped event area with a show kitchen, as well as three stylish and comfortable vacation apart-

NIEDERÖSTERREICH/LOWER AUSTRIA

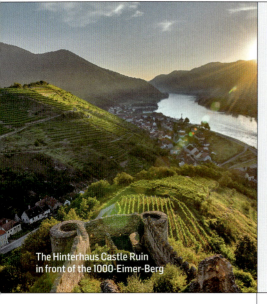

The Hinterhaus Castle Ruin in front of the 1000-Eimer-Berg

FJ GRITSCH – MAURITIUSHOF
3620 Spitz an der Donau
Kirchenplatz 13
T: +43 (2713) 24 50
office@gritsch.at
www.gritsch.at

Winemaker: Franz-Josef Gritsch
Contact: Franz-Josef Gritsch
Production: 14 hectares
Certified: Sustainable Austria
Fairs: Austrian Tasting London, ProWein Düsseldorf, VieVinum
Distribution partners: BE, DE, UK, JP, ROK, CN, CZ, USA

ments, from which you can enjoy a breathtaking view of the famous Singerriedel vineyard. The spacious in-house underground car park rounds off the overall concept.

The link between tradition and the present is also evident in Franz-Josef Gritsch's vineyards: in recent years, he has recultivated countless stone terraces - for example, in the challenging Kalkofen vineyard in the Spitzer Graben, i.e. in the climatic border zone of where viticulture is still feasible. The cultivated Rieslings are characterized by their coolness, elegance, and taut structure. In addition, Gritsch also cultivates the Burgweingarten in Dürnstein, the last of the sizeable vineyards within the historic town walls. The steeply rising stone terraces do not allow any mechanical cultivation - this is the essence of manual labour that is rewarding: the result is a great, multilayered and profound Riesling.

98 Riesling * Ried Kalkofen Smaragd 2022
13,5 Vol.-%, cork, large wooden barrel, €€€€€ V

97 Riesling * Ried Kalkofen Smaragd 2021
Medium greenish yellow, silver glints. Finely scented yellow tropical fruit, with nuances of pineapple and mango, and delicate mineral savouriness. Alluring bouquet. Juicy, elegant, white stone fruit, filigree structure, mineral and taut, remains persistent for a long time, cool stylish structure, fine citrus touch, saline reverberations. Lovely persistent style promising future.

96 Riesling * Ried Kalkofen Smaragd 2020

97 Riesling * Ried Loibenberg Smaragd 2022
13,5 Vol.-%, cork, large wooden barrel, €€€€€

96 Riesling * Ried 1000-Eimerberg Smaragd 2022
13,5 Vol.-%, cork, large wooden barrel, €€€€€ V

96 Riesling * Ried 1000-Eimerberg Smaragd 2021

95 Riesling * Ried 1000-Eimerberg Smaragd 2020

94 Riesling * Ried Setzberg Smaragd 2022
13,5 Vol.-%, screwcap, steel tank, €€€€€ V

94 Riesling * Ried Setzberg Smaragd 2021

94 Riesling * Ried Setzberg Smaragd 2020

93 Riesling * Ried 1000-Eimerberg Federspiel 2022
12,5 Vol.-%, screwcap, steel tank, €€€€ V

92 Riesling * Ried 1000-Eimerberg Federspiel 2021

92 Riesling * Spitz Ried 1000-Eimerberg Federspiel 2021

97 Riesling * Dürnstein Ried Burg Reserve 2022
13,5 Vol.-%, cork, large wooden barrel, €€€€€ V

97 Riesling * Ried Dürnsteiner Burg Reserve 2021
Pale greenish yellow, silver glints. Fine yellow tropical fruit, candied orange zest, delicate blossom honey, and a mineral touch. Complex, juicy, creamy, fine white tropical fruit,

crisp acidity, elegant and persistent, a hint of lime, saline reverberations. Promising future potential.

97 **Riesling * Reserve Ried Dürnsteiner Burg 2020**

97 **Riesling * Reserve Vision 2021**
13 Vol.-%, cork, large wooden barrel, €€€€€

97 **Grüner Veltliner * Ried Singerriedel Smaragd 2022**
14 Vol.-%, cork, large wooden barrel, €€€€€ Ⓥ

97 **Grüner Veltliner * Ried Singerriedel Smaragd 2021**

95 **Grüner Veltliner Smaragd Ried Singerriedel 2019**

95 **Grüner Veltliner * Ried Steinporz Smaragd 2022**
13,5 Vol.-%, screwcap, steel tank, €€€€ Ⓥ

94 **Grüner Veltliner * Ried Steinporz Smaragd 2021**

93 **Grüner Veltliner Smaragd Ried Steinporz 2019**

95 **Grüner Veltliner * Ried Hochrain Smaragd 2022**
13,5 Vol.-%, cork, wooden barrel/large wooden barrel, €€€€€ Ⓥ

95 **Grüner Veltliner * Ried Hochrain Smaragd 2021**

94 **Grüner Veltliner * Ried Hochrain Smaragd 2020**

94 **Grüner Veltliner * Ried Loibenberg Smaragd 2022**
13,5 Vol.-%, cork, large wooden barrel, €€€€€ Ⓥ

96 **Grüner Veltliner * Ried Loibenberg Smaragd 2021**

94 **Grüner Veltliner * Ried Loibenberg Smaragd 2020**

94 **Grüner Veltliner * Ried Klaus Smaragd 2022**
13,5 Vol.-%, cork, large wooden barrel, €€€€€

94 **Grüner Veltliner * Ried Axpoint Federspiel 2022**
12,5 Vol.-%, screwcap, steel tank, €€€€

92 **Grüner Veltliner * Ried Axpoint Federspiel 2021**

92 **Grüner Veltliner Ried Axpoint Federspiel 2019**

Riesling

93 **Grüner Veltliner * Kirchpoint Federspiel 2022**
12,5 Vol.-%, screwcap, steel tank, €€€ Ⓥ

92 **Grüner Veltliner * Federspiel Kirchpoint 2021**

91 **Grüner Veltliner Federspiel Kirchpoint 2019**

93 **Grüner Veltliner * Ried Klaus Federspiel 2021**

93 **Grüner Veltliner * Ried Klaus Federspiel 2020**

93 **Grüner Veltliner Federspiel Ried Klaus 2019**

91 **Grüner Veltliner * Federspiel kalmuck 2022**
12,5 Vol.-%, screwcap, steel tank, €€€ Ⓥ

91 **Grüner Veltliner * Federspiel kalmuck 2021**

91 **Grüner Veltliner Federspiel Kalmuck 2019**

96 **Grüner Veltliner Schwarze Mauritius 2019**

94 **Sauvignon Blanc * Spitz Smaragd 2022**
13,5 Vol.-%, screwcap, large wooden barrel, €€€€€ Ⓥ

94 **Sauvignon Blanc * Spitz Smaragd 2021**

93 **Muskateller * Spitz Federspiel 2022**
12,5 Vol.-%, screwcap, steel tank, €€€€

92 **Gelber Muskateller * Spitz Federspiel 2021**

92 **Gelber Muskateller * Spitz Federspiel 2020**

WEINGUT FRANZ HIRTZBERGER

The Hirtzberger family from Spitz cultivates some of the best sites in the entire Wachau. The terraced sites are famous, such as Singerriedel, which rises directly behind the historic, picturesque winemaker's house and produces a legendary Riesling. But when it comes to Riesling, the Hochrain site is also a fixture in the canon of Austrian Grands Crus. What Singerriedel is to Riesling, Honivogl is to Grüner Veltliner.

Franz Hirtzberger senior and his son Franz junior complement each other perfectly in the vineyard. This is reflected in the entire range of wines. In the wine cellar, Franz junior is now in charge - but not without coordinating the crucial details with his father. Here, too, the wines reflect the harmony of this collaboration.

(100) Riesling * Ried Singerriedel Smaragd 2022
13,5 Vol.-%, cork, steel tank
100 Riesling * Ried Singerriedel Smaragd 2021
Pale greenish yellow, silver glints. Invigorating yellow tropical fruit, hints of mango and passion fruit, subtle white floral nuances, and lime tones. A veritable array of aromas. Juicy, full-bodied, and elegant, subtle stone fruit nuances, filigree structure, finely fruit forward, citrus-mineral finish, prolonged persistence. Resplendent style, with plenty of potential for decades to come.
97 Riesling * Ried Singerriedel Smaragd 2020

98 Riesling * Ried Steinporz Smaragd 2022
13 Vol.-%, cork, steel tank
97 Riesling * Ried Steinporz Smaragd 2021
Pale greenish yellow, silver glints. Fragrant scents of yellow peach, delicate savoury nuances, and minerality. Light and alluring bouquet. Succulent, elegant, finely fruit forward, lovely integrated acidity, mineral, and persistent with a saline finish and peach reverberations. Possesses length and plenty of future potential.
96 Riesling Smaragd Ried Steinporz 2019

(97) Riesling * Ried Hochrain Smaragd 2022
13 Vol.-%, cork, steel tank
98 Riesling * Ried Hochrain Smaragd 2021
97 Riesling Smaragd Ried Hochrain 2019

96 Riesling * Ried Setzberg Smaragd 2022
13 Vol.-%, cork, steel tank
96 Riesling * Ried Setzberg Smaragd 2021
95 Riesling Smaragd Ried Setzberg 2019

95 Riesling * Smaragd Steinterrassen 2020

93 Riesling * Federspiel Steinterrassen 2022
12,5 Vol.-%, cork, steel tank
92 Riesling * Federspiel Steinterrassen 2021
93 Riesling * Federspiel Steinterrassen 2020

98 Grüner Veltliner * Smaragd Honivogl 2022
13,5 Vol.-%, cork, steel tank
99 Grüner Veltliner * Smaragd Honivogl 2021
Pale golden yellow, silver glints. Smoky-tobacco nuances underlaid with delicate mango notes, soft notions of apricot, candied orange zest, and lovely blossom honey. Powerful, juicy, and elegant, with fine nuances of white fruit, well-integrated acidity, and a mineral-saline finish. Already very harmonious and developed, a great food accompaniment with enormous ageing potential.
97 Grüner Veltliner Smaragd Honivogl 2019

WEINGUT FRANZ HIRTZBERGER
3620 Spitz an der Donau
Kremser Straße 8
T: +43 (2713) 2209
weingut@hirtzberger.com
www.hirtzberger.com

Winemaker: Franz Hirtzberger
Contact: Irmgard Hirtzberger
Production: 266,667 bottles
99 % white, 1 % sweet, 35 hectares
Fairs: ProWein Düsseldorf, VieVinum, MondoVino
Distribution partners: AUS, BE, DK, DE, FIN, FR, UK, IT, JP, LU, NZ, NL, NO, SE, CH, SK, CZ, USA

95 Grüner Veltliner * Ried Axpoint
   Smaragd 2022
13 Vol.-%, cork, steel tank
96 Grüner Veltliner * Ried Axpoint
   Smaragd 2021
95 Grüner Veltliner Smaragd
   Ried Axpoint 2019

94 Grüner Veltliner * Smaragd Rotes Tor 2022
13 Vol.-%, cork, steel tank
95 Grüner Veltliner * Smaragd Rotes Tor 2021
95 Grüner Veltliner * Smaragd Rotes Tor 2020

94 Grüner Veltliner * Ried Kirchweg
   Smaragd 2022
13 Vol.-%, cork, steel tank
95 Grüner Veltliner * Ried Kirchweg
   Smaragd 2021
94 Grüner Veltliner * Ried Kirchweg
   Smaragd 2020

93 Grüner Veltliner * Federspiel Rotes Tor 2022
12,5 Vol.-%, cork, stoneware

93 Grüner Veltliner * Federspiel Rotes Tor 2021
93 Grüner Veltliner * Federspiel
   Rotes Tor 2020

95 Chardonnay * Smaragd 2022
13,5 Vol.-%, cork, steel tank
95 Chardonnay * Smaragd 2021
94 Chardonnay * Smaragd 2020

95 Grauburgunder * Smaragd 2022
13,5 Vol.-%, cork, steel tank
94 Grauburgunder * Smaragd 2021
93 Grauburgunder Smaragd 2019

94 Weißburgunder * Smaragd 2022
13 Vol.-%, cork, steel tank
94 Weißburgunder * Smaragd 2021
93 Weißburgunder * Smaragd 2020

94 Neuburger * Smaragd 2021
94 Neuburger Smaragd 2019

WEINHOFMEISTEREI MATHIAS HIRTZBERGER

With his "Weinhofmeisterei", Mathias Hirtzberger has successfully opened a new era in the history of the renowned winemaking family in Wösendorf. A few kilometers away from his parents' Spitzer winery some things are similar but many are different. This is shown by his so-called heraldic wines ("Stab", "Treu", "Greif" and "Zier"), local wines whose names refer to the long history of the Weinhofmeisterei of St. Florian and to the climatic and geological diversity of the municipal vineyards. It gets even more specific in its four single-vineyard Smaragens, which are composed equally of two Veltliners and two Rieslings. Situated at the foot of the slope, the Kollmütz is the basis for a very complex and mineral Grüner Veltliner which finds its counterpoint in a second dark-fruited Veltliner from the loess-rich Spitaler vineyard. Even clearer contrasts can be seen between the Riesling Bach, a steep and warm terraced site,

and the Riesling Kollmitz, a high, barren paragneiss weathered vineyard. The same theory is applied everywhere - meticulous observation and attention in the vineyard, sustainable soil care and targeted manual work will emphasise the characteristics of the variety and yet bring out the subtle voices that make each individualistic vineyard distinctive. Through selective hand-harvesting and the most gentle processes in the cellar, these fine nuances are preserved and can be tasted in a real and impressive way in the wine. You can taste the wines in the newly built winery in Wösendorf.

**(95) Grüner Veltliner * Ried Kollmütz
Smaragd 2022**
13 Vol.-%, cork, steel tank/large wooden barrel, €€€€€€
96 Grüner Veltliner * Ried Kollmütz
   Smaragd 2021
Medium greenish yellow, silver glints. Delicately fragrant herbal savouriness, a hint of honeydew melon, subtle to-

NIEDERÖSTERREICH/LOWER AUSTRIA

Weißenkirchen

WEINHOFMEISTEREI MATHIAS HIRTZBERGER
3610 Wösendorf in der Wachau
Hauptstraße 142
T: +43 (2715) 22 955
buero@weinhofmeisterei.at
www.weinhofmeisterei.at

Winemaker: Mathias Hirtzberger
Contact: Hanna and Mathias Hirtzberger
Production: 100 % white, 9.5 hectares
Fairs: ProWein Düsseldorf, VieVinum
Distribution partners: BE, DE, UK, NL, NO, SE, CH, CZ, USA

bacco nuances, and a smidge of apricot. Complex, tightly woven, nuances of yellow stone fruit, very compact acidity structure, marked by a mineral finish, firm and persistent. Assured ageing potential.

95 Grüner Veltliner * Smaragd Ried Kollmütz 2020

(95) Grüner Veltliner * Joching Smaragd Spitaler 2022
13,5 Vol.-%, cork, steel tank/large wooden barrel, €€€€€

95 Grüner Veltliner * Weißenkirchen Smaragd Spitaler 2021
94 Grüner Veltliner * Smaragd Spitaler 2020

94 Grüner Veltliner * Weißenkirchen Smaragd Greif 2022
13 Vol.-%, cork, steel tank/large wooden barrel, €€€€€

94 Grüner Veltliner * Weißenkirchen Smaragd Greif 2021
93 Grüner Veltliner * Smaragd Greif 2020

92 Grüner Veltliner * Weißenkirchen Federspiel Treu 2022
12,5 Vol.-%, cork, steel tank/large wooden barrel, €€€€

92 Grüner Veltliner * Weißenkirchen Federspiel Treu 2021
92 Grüner Veltliner * Federspiel Treu 2021

91 Grüner Veltliner * Steinfeder Stab 2021
90 Grüner Veltliner * Stab Steinfeder 2020
89 Grüner Veltliner Steinfeder Stab 2015

(95) Riesling * Ried Bach Smaragd 2022
13,5 Vol.-%, cork, steel tank, €€€€€

95 Riesling * Ried Bach Smaragd 2021
94 Riesling * Ried Bach Smaragd 2020

(95) Riesling * Ried Kollmitz Smaragd 2022
13 Vol.-%, cork, steel tank, €€€€€

96 Riesling * Ried Kollmitz Smaragd 2021
Pale yellow-green, silver glints. Yellow tropical fruit, mango, and passion fruit, inviting, delicate tangerine zest, lime, and a floral touch. Tightly woven, very vibrant, white fruit nuances, saline-citrus reverberations, with a mineral finish. Assured development potential - will benefit from bottle ageing.

94 Riesling * Smaragd Ried Kollmitz 2020

92 Riesling * Weißenkirchen Federspiel Zier 2022
12,5 Vol.-%, cork, steel tank, €€€€

93 Riesling Federspiel Zier 2021
92 Riesling * Federspiel Zier 2020

WEINGUT JOSEF & GEORG HÖGL

Authenticity, sustainability and typicity are not just buzzwords but principles by which Josef Högl and his son Georg make their wines in Spitz an der Donau in the Wachau. The speciality of the wines is the Spitzer Graben site, a side valley of the Danube valley and, at the same time, the westernmost and highest part of the Wachau, which stretches from the Waldviertel to Spitz. The Spitz Graben is fascinating not only because of the steepness of its rugged and stony soils but also because of its distinctly cold and inhospitable climate.

Högl's ten hectares of vineyards are all terraced with dry stone walls. The Schön vineyard alone comprises 57 terraces at an altitude of over 130 metres. The Högls' main grape varieties are Grüner Veltliner and Riesling. While the Schön site, with its mica slate soils, is ideal for Grüner Veltliner with depth and minerality, Riesling is grown on the steep stone terraces of the Bruck site, where granodiorite gneiss predominates.

Josef and Georg Högl's philosophy is that the finished wine should reflect the grapes, the soil, the mica slate and gneiss, the site and the character developed by the terroir. Precise and complex wines of the highest quality are created through consistent natural viticulture and the interplay of innovation and tradition. The purest grapes, hand-picked in multiple passages, form the basis of these wines. Högl's Smaragd wines are deep, complex, long-lived wines from old vines.

As a member of the Vinea Wachau Nobilis Districtus, the Högls are committed to the association's strict code of quality, which emphasises the origin, originality and character of the individual Wachau villages and sites.

(97) Riesling * Ried Bruck Smaragd Alte Parzellen 2022
12,5 Vol.-%, cork, steel tank, €€€€€
97 Riesling * Ried Bruck Smaragd Alte Parzellen 2021
Pale greenish yellow, silver glints. Delicate floral notes are underpinned by subtle stone fruit nuances, a hint of peach and mango, and a citrus-mineral touch. An emphatically multidimensional bouquet. Juicy, complex, white peach, fresh acidity, saline touch, lime reverberations, delicately sweet, excellent length. Great ageing potential for years to come.
96 Riesling Smaragd Ried Bruck Alte Parzellen 2019

(97) Riesling * Smaragd Vision 2022
13 Vol.-%, cork, steel tank, €€€€€
94 Riesling * Smaragd Vision 2021
95 Riesling * Smaragd Vision 2020

(96) Riesling * Ried Bruck Smaragd 2022
13 Vol.-%, cork, steel tank, €€€€€
95 Riesling * Ried Bruck Smaragd 2021
96 Riesling * Ried Bruck Smaragd 2020

94 Riesling * Ried Bruck Federspiel 2022
12,5 Vol.-%, screwcap, steel tank, €€€€
93 Riesling * Ried Bruck Federspiel 2021
92 Riesling * Ried Bruck Federspiel 2020

WEINGUT JOSEF & GEORG HÖGL
3620 Spitz an der Donau
Viessling 31
T: +43 (2713) 8458
office@weingut-hoegl.at
www.weingut-hoegl.at

Winemaker: Josef & Georg Högl
Contact: Georg Högl
Production: 60,000 bottles
100 % white, 9.5 hectares
Fairs: VieVinum
Distribution partners: BE, DE, IT, JP, NL, SE, CH, SK, CZ, USA

NIEDERÖSTERREICH/LOWER AUSTRIA

(96) Grüner Veltliner * Ried Schön Smaragd Alte Parzellen 2022
13,5 Vol.-%, cork, steel tank, €€€€€

96 Grüner Veltliner * Ried Schön Smaragd Alte Parzellen 2021
Pale greenish yellow, silver glints. Softly infused tones of white stone fruit, luscious apple, delicate pear, a hint of meadow herbs, and zesty orange peel. An alluring bouquet. Complex, powerful, white fruit, a subtle arc of acidity, mineral, tightly woven, filigree, and persistent, excellent length. Definite ageing potential, and already accessible.

96 Grüner Veltliner Smaragd Ried Schön Alte Parzellen 2019

(95) Grüner Veltliner * Ried Kaiserberg Smaragd 2022
13,5 Vol.-%, cork, steel tank, €€€€

93 Grüner Veltliner * Ried Kaiserberg Smaragd 2021

93 Grüner Veltliner * Ried Kaiserberg Smaragd 2020

(94) Grüner Veltliner * Ried Schön Smaragd 2022
13,5 Vol.-%, cork, steel tank, €€€€

95 Grüner Veltliner * Ried Schön Smaragd 2021

94 Grüner Veltliner * Ried Schön Smaragd 2020

(94) Grüner Veltliner * Ried Brandstatt Smaragd 2022
14 Vol.-%, cork, large wooden barrel, €€€€€

(93) Grüner Veltliner * Ried 1000-Eimerberg Smaragd 2022
13,5 Vol.-%, cork, steel tank, €€€€€

93 Grüner Veltliner * Ried 1000-Eimerberg Smaragd 2021

94 Grüner Veltliner Smaragd Ried 1000-Eimerberg 2019

93 Grüner Veltliner * Ried Schön Federspiel 2022
12,5 Vol.-%, screwcap, steel tank, €€€€

93 Grüner Veltliner * Ried Schön Federspiel 2021

92 Grüner Veltliner * Ried Schön Federspiel 2020

WEINGUT HOLZAPFEL

The Holzapfel Winery is housed in a historic building known as the Lesehof. It was built 700 years ago by the monks of St. Pölten and later given its baroque style by the renowned Austrian architect Jakob Prandtauer. At that time, when the vineyards of the Wachau were largely in the hands of the church and belonged to the surrounding monasteries, the Lesehof was the centre for the pressing of grapes and the administration of wine sales. Today, some 14 hectares of vines are cultivated using traditional methods. These include outstanding sites such as Achleiten, Vorderseiber, Weitenberg, Klaus and Kollmitz. The stony, mineral-rich and chalky slate soils produce high-quality grapes, but it's not just the sites that give these wines their unique character - low yields are also key. The diurnal cycle also plays a key role, creating special climatic conditions and, of course, the different altitudes of the vineyards, all of which contribute to a crisp acidity that ensures freshness and elegance.

Karl Holzapfel's aim is to produce defined, fruity wines full of character for everyday enjoyment. He also produces dry, elegant Smaragd wines with complex aromas and great ageing potential. This is partly due to the fine lees contact after fermentation which results in distinctive wines with style, definition, subtle fruit and a harmonious balance between minerality and freshness. The Holzapfel range includes the three classifications unique to the Wachau: Steinfeder, Federspiel and Smaragd in the Grüner Veltliner, Riesling and Weißburgunder varieties. The "Hippolyt" selection is particularly impressive with its delicious creaminess, elegance and finesse.

(95) Grüner Veltliner * Ried Achleiten Smaragd 2022
14 Vol.-%, screwcap, steel tank, €€€€€ Ⓥ

WACHAU DAC

WEINGUT HOLZAPFEL
3610 Weißenkirchen
Prandtauerplatz 36
T: +43 (2715) 2310
weingut@holzapfel.at
www.holzapfel.at

Winemaker/Contact:
Karl Holzapfel
Production: 95 % white, 5 % red,
14 hectares
Fairs: VieVinum
Distribution partners: SK

Weißenkirchen

95 Grüner Veltliner * Ried Achleiten Smaragd 2021
Bright greenish yellow, silver glints. Subtle tobacco nuances, delicately spicy, lush apples, a tangerine touch, and resonating nuances of blossom honey. Complex, salty, well-integrated acidity structure, saline-minerality, white stone fruit, persistent, and dark reverberations. Assured development potential.

94 Grüner Veltliner * Ried Achleiten Smaragd 2020

(94) Grüner Veltliner * Joching Ried Kollmitz Smaragd 2022
14 Vol.-%, screwcap, steel tank, €€€€ V

93 Grüner Veltliner * Ried Kollmitz Smaragd 2021

93 Grüner Veltliner * Joching Ried Kollmitz Smaragd 2020

92 Grüner Veltliner * Ried Achleiten Federspiel 2022
12,5 Vol.-%, screwcap, steel tank, €€€€ V

92 Grüner Veltliner * Ried Achleiten Federspiel 2021

92 Grüner Veltliner * Ried Achleiten Weissenkirchen Federspiel 2020

90 Grüner Veltliner * Joching Federspiel Zehenthof 2022
12,5 Vol.-%, screwcap, steel tank, €€€ V

91 Grüner Veltliner * Joching Federspiel Zehenthof 2021

91 Zehenthof Grüner Veltliner * Joching Federspiel 2020

(94) Riesling * Ried Vorderseiber Smaragd 2022
13,5 Vol.-%, screwcap, steel tank, €€€€€ V

94 Riesling * Ried Vorderseiber Smaragd 2021
Light greenish yellow, silver reflections. Fine blossom honey, a little apricot, floral, pineapple, tangerine zest, inviting bouquet. Juicy, elegant, tight-knit, mineral, ripe stone fruit, complex, spicy finish, good food wine with certain ageing potential.

94 Riesling * Ried Vorderseiber Smaragd 2020

92 Riesling * Joching Federspiel Zehenthof 2022
12,5 Vol.-%, screwcap, steel tank, €€€€ V

92 Riesling * Federspiel Zehenthof 2021

92 Riesling * Joching Federspiel Zehenthof 2020

NIEDERÖSTERREICH/LOWER AUSTRIA

WEINGUT HUTTER SILBERBICHLERHOF

The family-run Weingut Hutter has about 14 hectares of vineyards in prime locations on both sides of the Danube, in the municipalities of Mautern on the right bank of the Danube and Loiben and Dürnstein on the left bank of the Danube. The seventh generation of the family already manages the traditional Wachau winery. As a member of "Vinea Wachau", they produce white wines of the Wachau wine categories Steinfeder, Federspiel, and Smaragd from the varieties Grüner Veltliner, Riesling, and Grauburgunder (Pinot Gris).

The gastronomic section of the Silberbichlerhof is also available as a venue for weddings, birthday parties, corporate events, and other such gatherings. Depending on the time of day and the weather, there is space for up to 60 people in the vineyard, the wine tavern, or the atrium.

95 Grüner Veltliner * Mautern Ried Süssenberg Smaragd 2021
14,5 Vol.-%, screwcap, steel tank, €€€€
Medium golden yellow, silver reflections. Delicate blossom honey, hints of ripe pear and figs, soft notes of candied orange zest, attractive bouquet. Powerful, juicy, full-bodied, fine ripe yellow fruit, pleasant acidity, very good length, already accessible, a complex food wine, safe future.

94 Grüner Veltliner * Mautern Ried Alte Point Smaragd 2021
14,5 Vol.-%, screwcap, steel tank, €€€€

93 Grüner Veltliner Smaragd Ried Alte Point Mautern 2019

92 Grüner Veltliner * Mautern Ried Süssenberg Federspiel 2022
12,5 Vol.-%, screwcap, steel tank, €€€

91 Grüner Veltliner Federspiel Ried Süssenberg Mautern 2019

91 Grüner Veltliner * Mautern Ried Silberbichl Federspiel 2022
12,5 Vol.-%, screwcap, steel tank, €€€

92 Grüner Veltliner Federspiel Ried Silberbichl Mautern 2019

91 Grüner Veltliner * Mautern Ried Alte Point Federspiel 2022

94 Riesling * Ried Loibenberg Smaragd 2021
14 Vol.-%, screwcap, steel tank, €€€€
Medium chartreuse yellow, with silver reflections. Delicate notes of blood oranges, passion fruit and mango, fine blossom honey, with mineral notes underneath. Juicy, white tropical fruit, a fresh acidity, subtle lychee notes and lime, a salty finish, wonderful length, a lovely food companion.

94 Riesling Smaragd Ried Loibenberg 2015

94 Riesling Smaragd Ried Silberbichl Mautern 2019

91 Riesling * Federspiel 2022
91 Riesling * Federspiel 2021
12,5 Vol.-%, screwcap, steel tank, €€€

WEINGUT HUTTER SILBERBICHLERHOF
3512 Mautern an der Donau
St. Pöltner Straße 385
T: +43 (2732) 83004
info@hutter-wachau.at
www.hutter-wachau.at

Winemaker: Friedrich Hutter IV.
Contact: Friedrich Hutter IV.
Production: 90,000 bottles
97 % white, 2 % rosé, 1 % sweet, 14 hectares
Certified: Sustainable Austria
Fairs: VieVinum
Distribution partners:
BE, DE, NL, CZ

WEINGUT JAMEK

★★★★

Josef Jamek - a name that embodies the cultural landscape of the Wachau and the renaissance of Austrian wine culture like no other. As early as the 1950s, his natural dry wines and vision shaped the style of white wine in the Wachau, and he was the founder of Vinea Wachau, the association that protects the wines of this unique region.

With 25 hectares of vineyards, the winery is one of the most respected private estates in the region, cultivating vineyards on the best terraces of ancient rock. The Klaus vineyard, synonymous with the Jamek winery, is situated on a steep slope with over a hundred stone terraces. This is where Jamek's flagship Wachau Riesling has been produced for decades. The Jamek family has been bottling this wine jewel (which can be seen as a parable of Josef Jamek's great life's work) since 1959. The primary rock terraces of the Achleiten and Liebenberg sites are also renowned for their top-quality Grüner Veltliners, which are characterised by the terroir of the Wachau. The Hochrain and Zweikreuzgarten vineyards in Wösendorf have been cultivated in partnership with the Benedictine Abbey of Melk for over 40 years. Here, the highest quality Pinot Blanc and Grüner Veltliner are grown.

Since 2012, Jamek's granddaughter Julia Jamek and her husband Herwig have continued the winery's tradition. Both are medical doctors and guarantee the sustainable health of the wines! The best place to taste the wines is in the winery's restaurant, run by Johannes Altmann, another grandson of Josef and Edeltraud Jamek. A visit to the Jamek-Altmann estate is a unique and unmissable experience for any visitor to the Wachau region, with the excellent regional cuisine and wines by the glass to be enjoyed in the charming atmosphere of the 100-year-old house and its enchanting garden.

96 Riesling * Ried Klaus Smaragd 2021
14 Vol.-%, cork, large wooden barrel, €€€€€€ V

96 Riesling * Ried Klaus Smaragd 2020
Medium greenish yellow, silver glints. Subtle herbal notes, delicate mango, hints of apricots, kumquat nuances, and resonating lime tones. Complex, elegant, fine acidity structure, saline-minerality, luscious yellow fruit redolent of mango. A superb food accompaniment with definite ageing potential.

96 Riesling Ried Klaus Smaragd 2019

94 Riesling * Smaragd Dürnsteiner Freiheit 2021
13,5 Vol.-%, cork, large wooden barrel, €€€€€ V

95 Riesling * Dürnsteiner Freiheit Smaragd 2020

93 Riesling Smaragd Dürnsteiner Freiheit 2019

93 Riesling * Ried Klaus Federspiel 2022
12,5 Vol.-%, cork, large wooden barrel, €€€€€ V

95 Riesling * Ried Klaus 2021

94 Riesling * Ried Klaus 2020

94 Riesling * Ried Pichl Smaragd 2021
13,5 Vol.-%, screwcap, large wooden barrel, €€€€€ V

94 Riesling * Ried Pichl Smaragd 2020

94 Riesling Smaragd Ried Pichl 2019

WEINGUT JAMEK
3610 Joching
Josef-Jamek-Straße 45
T: +43 (2715) 2235
info@weingut-jamek.at
www.weingut-jamek.at

Winemaker: Volker Mader
Contact: Dr. Herwig Jamek
Production: 3 % sparkling, 90 % white, 3 % rosé, 3 % red, 1 % sweet, 25 hectares
Fairs: ProWein Düsseldorf, VieVinum
Distribution partners: DE, FIN, JP, CDN, NO, RUS, SE, CH, ES, CZ, HU, USA

* Wachau DAC

NIEDERÖSTERREICH/LOWER AUSTRIA

94 Grüner Veltliner * Ried Achleiten Smaragd 2021
14 Vol.-%, cork, wooden barrel, €€€€€

94 Grüner Veltliner * Ried Achleiten Smaragd 2020
Medium green-yellow, silver reflections. Orange zest and pineapple underlaid with dark minerality, a bit of mango, fine touch of citrus, inviting bouquet. Juicy, elegant, fruity, a bit of melon on the finish, well-integrated acidity, persistent, versatile food wine, has ageing potential.

96 Grüner Veltliner Ried Achleiten Smaragd 2019

92 Grüner Veltliner * Dürnstein Ried Liebenberg Smaragd 2021
13,5 Vol.-%, cork, large wooden barrel, €€€€€

94 Grüner Veltliner * Dürnstein Ried Liebenberg Smaragd 2020

94 Grüner Veltliner Smaragd Ried Liebenberg 2019

93 Grüner Veltliner * Ried Achleiten Federspiel 2021

92 Grüner Veltliner * Ried Achleiten Federspiel 2020

92 Grüner Veltliner Federspiel Ried Achleiten 2019

91 Grüner Veltliner * Federspiel Stein am Rain 2021

90 Grüner Veltliner Federspiel Stein am Rain 2017

94 Weißburgunder * Wösendorf Smaragd 2021
13,5 Vol.-%, cork, large wooden barrel, €€€€€

93 Weißburgunder * WösendorfSmaragd 2020

94 Weißburgunder Smaragd Ried Hochrain 2019

97 Riesling Ried Klaus Beerenauslese 2017

WEINGUT KNOLL

Weingut Knoll has produced so many cult wines over the past few decades that a book could be filled with their tasting notes alone. Their St. Urban label also has cult status and has fortunately remained unchanged for decades. However, a lot has happened at the estate itself: In 2014, the new winery building was opened next to the main building, where customers and guests are now welcomed. Emmerich and Monika Knoll run the estate together with their sons Emmerich junior, who has also been chairman of Vinea Wachau since 2012, and August.
They cultivate around 18 hectares, a good third of which is terraced. Grüner Veltliner (45%) is grown on the Kreutles, Trum, Loibenberg and Schütt sites, and Riesling (45%) on the Loibenberg, Kellerberg, Pfaffenberg and Schütt sites. The ‚Vinothekfüllung', a selection of the ripest grapes from different sites, is also made from both varieties, depending on the vintage. The range is complemented by Gelber Muskateller, Chardonnay, Gelber Traminer and Blauburgunder wines. Sweet wines ranging from Auslese to Trockenbeerenauslese are also produced in years with good botrytis. A positive practice at Knoll: The Smaragd and Prädikat wines are not produced until September so that they can mature and develop in the cool cellar over the summer. Knoll wines are considered late starters (which is not entirely true) and very long-lived (which is entirely true).

98 Grüner Veltliner * Loiben Smaragd Vinothekfüllung 2021
14 Vol.-%, cork, large wooden barrel, €€€€€

97 Loibner Grüner Veltliner Vinothekfüllung Smaragd 2019

96 Loibner Grüner Veltliner Smaragd Vinothekfüllung 2018

96 Grüner Veltliner * Ried Schütt Smaragd 2021
13 Vol.-%, cork, large wooden barrel, €€€€

95 Grüner Veltliner * Ried Schütt Smaragd 2020
Pale golden yellow, silver glints. Delicate blossom honey, quince nuances, subtle yellow apple, notes of tobacco, and

WACHAU DAC

WEINGUT KNOLL
3601 Dürnstein
Unterloiben 132
T: +43 (2732) 79355
weingut@knoll.at
www.knoll.at

Winemaker: Emmerich Knoll
Contact: The Knoll family
Production: 98 % white, 1 % red, 1 % sweet, 18 hectares
Fairs: ProWein Düsseldorf, VieVinum
Distribution partners: AUS, BE, DK, DE, EST, FIN, FR, UK, HK, IRL, IT, JP, CDN, ROK, LV, LT, LU, NZ, NL, NO, SE, CH, SGP, SK, ES, TH, CZ, HU, USA, CY

The ruins of Dürnstein Castle

background hints of orange zest. Juicy, subtle stone fruit nuances, silky and balanced, and well developed. An elegant food accompaniment, good ageing potential.

96 Grüner Veltliner Ried Schütt Smaragd 2019

95 Grüner Veltliner * Ried Loibenberg Smaragd 2021
13,5 Vol.-%, cork, large wooden barrel, €€€€€
95 Grüner Veltliner * Ried Loibenberg Smaragd 2020
95 Grüner Veltliner Ried Loibenberg Smaragd 2019

94 Grüner Veltliner * Ried Kreutles Smaragd 2021
13 Vol.-%, cork, large wooden barrel, €€€€€
94 Grüner Veltliner * Ried Kreutles Smaragd 2020
94 Grüner Veltliner Ried Kreutles Smaragd 2019

94 Grüner Veltliner * Ried Kellerberg Federspiel 2020

93 Grüner Veltliner * Ried Kreutles Federspiel 2022
12 Vol.-%, cork, steel tank, €€€€
93 Grüner Veltliner * Ried Kreutles Federspiel 2021
92 Grüner Veltliner * Ried Kreutles Federspiel 2021

93 Grüner Veltliner * Ried Trum Federspiel 2022
12 Vol.-%, cork, steel tank, €€€€€
93 Grüner Veltliner * Ried Trum Federspiel 2021
92 Grüner Veltliner * Ried Trum Federspiel 2020

92 Grüner Veltliner * Loiben Federspiel 2022
12 Vol.-%, cork, steel tank, €€€€
92 Grüner Veltliner * Loiben Federspiel 2021
91 Grüner Veltliner * Loibener Federspiel 2020

92 Grüner Veltliner * Loiben Steinfeder 2022
11 Vol.-%, cork, steel tank, €€€
90 Grüner Veltliner * Loiben Steinfeder 2021
90 Grüner Veltliner * Loiben Steinfeder 2020

96 Grüner Veltliner Loibner Reserve 2018

100 Riesling * Ried Schütt Smaragd 2021
13 Vol.-%, cork, large wooden barrel, €€€€€
97 Riesling * Dürnstein Ried Schütt Smaragd 2020
Medium greenish yellow, silver glints. Luscious apricots, delicate nuances of yellow peach, a little mango, underlaid with orange zest, followed by a mineral touch. Taut, juicy nuances of white stone fruit, elegant and persistent, citrus note, elegant reverberations, and promising ageing potential.
97 Riesling Ried Schütt Smaragd 2019

* Wachau DAC

NIEDERÖSTERREICH/LOWER AUSTRIA

99 Riesling * Loiben Smaragd
   Vinothekfüllung 2021
14 Vol.-%, cork, large wooden barrel, €€€€€

98 Riesling * Loiben Smaragd
   Vinothekfüllung 2020
Pale golden yellow, silver glints. Delicately scented notes of candied orange zest, fine yellow tropical fruit, a slight hint of savoury botrytis, and dark bristling minerality. Robust, sturdy, mineral, taut, vibrant acidic structure, energetic and persistent. Definite ageing potential, designed for a long, flourishing existence.

98 Riesling Loibner Vinothekfüllung
   Smaragd 2019

98 Riesling * Ried Kellerberg Smaragd 2021
13 Vol.-%, cork, large wooden barrel, €€€€€
96 Riesling * Dürnstein Ried Kellerberg
   Smaragd 2020
95 Riesling Ried Kellerberg Smaragd 2019

97 Riesling * Ried Loibenberg Smaragd 2021
13 Vol.-%, cork, large wooden barrel, €€€€€
95 Riesling * Ried Loibenberg Smaragd 2020
94 Riesling Ried Loibenberg Smaragd 2019

95 Riesling * Loiben Smaragd 2021
13 Vol.-%, cork, large wooden barrel, €€€€€
94 Riesling * Loiben Smaragd 2020
93 Loibner Riesling Smaragd 2019

94 Riesling * Ried Loibenberg Federspiel 2022
12 Vol.-%, cork, steel tank, €€€€
94 Riesling * Ried Loibenberg Federspiel 2021
92 Riesling * Ried Loibenberg Federspiel 2020

93 Riesling * Loiben Federspiel 2022
12 Vol.-%, cork, steel tank, €€€€
93 Riesling * Loiben Federspiel 2021
92 Riesling * Loibner Federspiel 2020

98 Riesling Ried Pfaffenberg Selection 2021
13,5 Vol.-%, cork, large wooden barrel, €€€€€
95 Riesling Ried Pfaffenberg Selection 2020
95 Riesling Ried Pfaffenberg Selection 2019

92 Riesling Ried Pfaffenberg 2020
92 Riesling Ried Pfaffenberg Kabinett 2019
93 Riesling Kabinett Ried Pfaffenberg 2018

94 Gelber Muskateller * Loiben Smaragd 2021
13,5 Vol.-%, cork, large wooden barrel, €€€€€
94 Gelber Muskateller * Loiben Smaragd 2020
93 Gelber Muskateller Loibner Smaragd 2019

91 Gelber Muskateller * Loiben
   Federspiel 2022
12 Vol.-%, cork, steel tank, €€€€
91 Gelber Muskateller * Loiben
   Federspiel 2021
90 Gelber Muskateller * Loibner
   Federspiel 2020

94 Traminer * Loiben Smaragd 2021
13 Vol.-%, cork, large wooden barrel, €€€€€
94 Gelber Traminer * Loiben Smaragd 2020
93 Gelber Traminer Loibner Smaragd 2019

94 Chardonnay * Loiben Smaragd 2021
13 Vol.-%, cork, large wooden barrel, €€€€€
93 Chardonnay * Loiben Smaragd 2020
92 Chardonnay Loibner Smaragd 2019

90 Blauer Burgunder * Rosé Federspiel 2022
11,5 Vol.-%, cork, steel tank, €€€€
90 Blauer Burgunder * Rosé Federspiel 2021
89 Rosé * Federspiel 2020

100 Riesling Loiben
    Trockenbeerenauslese 2021
11,5 Vol.-%, cork, €€€€€€

96 Riesling Ried Pfaffenberg
   Beerenauslese 2021
13,5 Vol.-%, cork, €€€€€€

94 Riesling Loiben Auslese 2021
12,5 Vol.-%, cork, €€€€

97 Chardonnay Loiben
   Trockenbeerenauslese 2021
12,5 Vol.-%, cork, €€€€€

95 Gelber Muskateller Loiben
   Beerenauslese 2021
11,5 Vol.-%, cork, €€€€

94 Grüner Veltliner Loiben Beerenauslese 2021
13,5 Vol.-%, cork, €€€€

94 Grüner Veltliner Loiben Auslese 2021
13,5 Vol.-%, cork, €€€€

94 Gelber Traminer Loiben Auslese 2021
13,5 Vol.-%, cork, €€€€€

★★★★★

WEINGUT F. X. PICHLER

The F.X. Pichler winery in Oberloiben has been one of the leading names in the Austrian wine scene for decades. Franz Xaver Pichler Sr. is credited with giving the winery an unmistakable style, which is now enriched by his son Lucas, who runs the estate with his wife, Johanna.

Pichler's Rieslings and Grüner Veltliners are grown in the most famous sites of Loiben and Dürnstein, which stretch from the Steinertal in the east to Loibenberg, Kellerberg and Liebenberg in the west. The Pichler estate has always strived to create wines that are a true reflection of the year, the soil and the unique microclimate of the Wachau. The subtle nuances of each site should be perceptible and palpable in their unique complexity. In this way, tasting the wine series always becomes a "celebration of maturity". Whatever the category, the wines are impressively structured - everything bottled here is exactly as it should be. Anyone attempting to judge these "works of wine" should always bear in mind the time factor, as the full-bodied Smaragd wines need seven or eight years to develop, and the great wines of the house in the "M" or "Infinite" categories even longer.

Since 2009, Lucas Pichler has had the space to realise his ideas in a remarkable new cellar complex in the heart of the vineyards between Dürnstein and Oberloiben.

(100) Riesling * Unendlich 2021
14 Vol.-%, cork, large wooden barrel Ⓥ
99 Riesling * Unendlich 2020
99 Riesling Smaragd Unendlich 2019

(99) Riesling * Ried Kellerberg 2022
13,5 Vol.-%, cork, large wooden barrel Ⓥ
100 Riesling * Ried Kellerberg 2021
Pale yellow-green, silver glints. Delicately floral scents underpin light fruit, white peach, a hint of mandarin, and limes with a mineral touch. Juicy, elegant nuances of white stone fruit, a little passion fruit, opulent, complex, salty, tapering off with immense extract, yet almost ethereal. Excellent length, enormous ageing potential, a wine of tremendous delicacy and finesse.
98 Riesling * Ried Kellerberg 2020

WEINGUT F. X. PICHLER
3601 Dürnstein
Oberloiben 57
T: +43 (2732) 85375
weingut@fx-pichler.at
www.fx-pichler.at

Winemaker: Lucas Pichler
Contact: Johanna Pichler
Production: 100 % white, 20 hectares
Certified: Sustainable Austria Ⓔ
Fairs: ProWein Düsseldorf, VieVinum
Distribution partners: AUS, BE, BG, RC, DK, DE, FIN, FR, GR, IT, JP, CDN, ROK, HR, LV, LT, LU, MV, NZ, NL, RUS, SE, CH, SGP, SK, SLO, ES, TH, CZ, TR

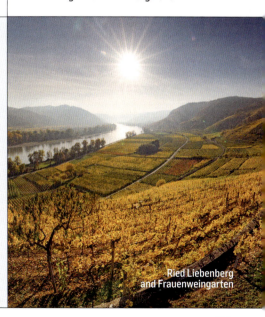

Ried Liebenberg and Frauenweingarten

NIEDERÖSTERREICH/LOWER AUSTRIA

(98) Riesling * Ried Loibenberg 2022
13 Vol.-%, cork, large wooden barrel ⓥ
97 Riesling * Ried Loibenberg 2021
Pale yellow-green, silver glints. Delicate yellow tropical fruit notes, fine stone fruit, yellow peach, a little pineapple, a hint of blossom honey, and orange zest. Juicy, nuances of yellow stone fruit, crispy and vibrant, racy structure, with a succulent-saline touch. Compelling length, remarkably savoury, and promising ageing potential.
96 Riesling * Ried Loibenberg 2020

(97) Riesling * Ried Steinertal 2022
12,5 Vol.-%, cork, large wooden barrel ⓥ
97 Riesling * Ried Steinertal 2021
96 Riesling * Ried Steinertal 2020

95 Riesling * Loiben Ried Burgstall 2022
12,5 Vol.-%, cork, large wooden barrel ⓥ
95 Riesling * Ried Burgstall 2021
93 Riesling * Ried Burgstall 2020

94 Riesling * Ried Trum 2022
12,5 Vol.-%, cork ⓥ
94 Riesling * Ried Trum 2021
94 Riesling Smaragd Ried Trum 2019

93 Riesling * Ried Klostersatz 2022
12,5 Vol.-%, screwcap, steel tank, €€€€€ ⓥ
93 Riesling * Ried Kostersatz 2021

99 Grüner Veltliner * Unendlich 2021
14,5 Vol.-%, cork, large wooden barrel ⓥ
98 Grüner Veltliner Unendlich 2018
100 Grüner Veltiner Unendlich 2017

(98) Grüner Veltliner * Ried Kellerberg 2022
13 Vol.-%, cork, large wooden barrel ⓥ
99 Grüner Veltliner * Ried Kellerberg 2021
Pale yellow-green, silver glints. Delicately fragrant notes of tangerine zest, floral touch, a hint of fresh apple, oranges, limes, and dark minerality. Taut, tightly woven, biting, underpinned with pleasant herbal savouriness, fresh stone fruit, racy structure, and salty minerality. Exhibits tremendous length without any opulence, concise and radiant, assured ageing potential.
97 Grüner Veltliner * Ried Kellerberg 2020

97 Grüner Veltliner Smaragd »M« 2019
97 Grüner Veltliner Smaragd M 2018

(97) Grüner Veltliner * Ried Loibenberg 2022
13 Vol.-%, cork, large wooden barrel ⓥ
96 Grüner Veltliner * Ried Loibenberg 2021
95 Grüner Veltliner * Ried Loibenberg 2020

96 Grüner Veltliner * Ried Liebenberg 2020
95 Grüner Veltliner Smaragd Ried Liebenberg 2019

(95) Grüner Veltliner * Ried Steinertal 2022
12,5 Vol.-%, cork, steel tank ⓥ
95 Grüner Veltliner * Ried Steinertal 2021
94 Grüner Veltliner * Ried Steinertal 2020

94 Grüner Veltliner * Loiben Ried Klostersatz 2022
12,5 Vol.-%, screwcap, steel tank ⓥ
94 Grüner Veltliner * Ried Klostersatz 2021
93 Grüner Veltliner * Ried Klostersatz 2020

94 Grüner Veltliner * Dürnstein 2022
13 Vol.-%, screwcap, steel tank ⓥ
92 Grüner Veltliner * Dürnstein 2021
93 Dürnsteiner Grüner Veltliner * 2020

93 Grüner Veltliner * Ried Frauenweingarten 2022
12,5 Vol.-%, cork ⓥ
94 Grüner Veltliner * Ried Frauenweingarten 2021
93 Grüner Veltliner * Ried Frauenweingarten 2020

93 Grüner Veltliner * Loiben 2022
12,5 Vol.-%, screwcap, steel tank ⓥ
92 Grüner Veltliner * Loiben 2021
92 Loibner Grüner Veltliner * 2020

95 Gelber Muskateller * Dürnstein 2021
94 Dürnsteiner Gelber Muskateller * 2020
94 Dürnsteiner Gelber Muskateller Smaragd 2019

94 Sauvignon Blanc Große Reserve 2019
93 Sauvignon Blanc Grosse Reserve 2018

★★★★★
WEINGUT RUDI PICHLER

Rudi Pichler is one of the most established producers in the Wachau. His vineyards, spread across Joching, Wösendorf and Weißenkirchen, produce white wines brimming with character. In addition to Grüner Veltliner and Riesling, Rudi Pichler cultivates Pinot Blanc and the voluminous Roter Veltliner.

Rudi knows how to breathe a lot of varietal character into each wine style; his Federspiel Grüner Veltliner is always a favourite with connoisseurs as it combines a lively style with classic Wachau varietal expression. With the great Smaragd wines, Pichler and the next generation, Theresa and Rudi Junior, succeed in bringing out the terroir beautifully. After a few years in the bottle, these powerful wines develop their full splendour. Rudi Pichler is not afraid to adapt his winemaking; the fermentation period, which was longer in previous years, has been shortened to better suit the desired style. Maceration times are carefully considered for each variety and wine style. The result is nuanced top wines, each with a very individual character.

The modern winery, inaugurated in 2004, is not only architecturally stunning but also provides the space to press, ferment and age the wines in optimal conditions. Rudi Pichler's characteristic new range is characterised by an immense minerality, tautness and depth of aromas - the different terroirs unfolding in a very precise way. Tasting these remarkable wines, especially the outstanding Grüner Veltliner and the Riesling Achleithen is always a pleasure. The Falstaff editorial team voted Rudi Pichler "Winemaker of the Year" in 2010.

99 Riesling * Ried Achleithen Smaragd 2022
13 Vol.-%, cork, steel tank, €€€€€ 🟢
99 Riesling * Weissenkirchen Ried Achleithen Smaragd 2021
Medium greenish yellow, silver glints. Dark bristling minerality, subtle tropical fruit, a hint of pineapple, multilayered, and very evocative. Powerful, full-bodied, nuances of white fruit, elegant ripe acidity, lingers very long, conveys origin and depth, and will develop more facets with further development. Enormous length, a truly promising future ahead.
97 Riesling * Ried Achleithen Smaragd 2020
98 Riesling * Ried Hochrain Smaragd 2022
13 Vol.-%, cork, steel tank, €€€€ 🟢
97 Riesling * Wösendorf Ried Hochrain Smaragd 2021
96 Riesling * Ried Hochrain Smaragd 2020
96 Riesling * Ried Kirchweg Smaragd 2022
13 Vol.-%, cork, steel tank, €€€€ 🟢
96 Riesling * Wösendorf Ried Kirchweg Smaragd 2021
94 Riesling * Ried Kirchweg Smaragd 2020
94 Riesling * Smaragd Terrassen 2022
12,5 Vol.-%, cork, steel tank, €€€€ 🟢
95 Riesling * Smaragd Terrassen 2021
94 Riesling * Smaragd Terrassen 2020
93 Riesling * Federspiel 2022
12 Vol.-%, cork, steel tank, €€€ 🟢
93 Riesling * Federspiel 2021
93 Riesling * Federspiel 2021

WEINGUT RUDI PICHLER
3610 Wösendorf
Marienfeldweg 122
T: +43 (2715) +43 664 3445742
weingut@rudipichler.at
www.rudipichler.at

Winemaker: Rudi Pichler, Rudi Pichler jr.
Contact: Rudi Pichler, Theresa Pichler
Production: 100 % white, 15 hectares
Fairs: VieVinum
Distribution partners: AUS, BE, RC, DK, DE, FIN, UK, HK, IT, JP, CDN, LV, LT, LU, NL, NO, SE, CH, SRB, SGP, SK, CZ, UA, USA

NIEDERÖSTERREICH/LOWER AUSTRIA

98 Grüner Veltliner * Ried Achleithen Smaragd 2022
13 Vol.-%, cork, steel tank, €€€€€ V

99 Grüner Veltliner * Ried Achleithen Smaragd 2021
Pale greenish yellow, silver glints. Smoky-savoury scents allude to bacon and damp stones, enchantingly mystical, saline nuances, white apple, lime, herbs, and delicately savoury. Firm, elegant, finely nuanced notes of apricot, crisp acidic structure, and persistence superseded by a hint of lime. Possesses ageing potential for years to come.

96 Grüner Veltliner * Ried Achleithen Smaragd 2020

96 Grüner Veltliner * Ried Hochrain Smaragd 2022
13 Vol.-%, cork, steel tank, €€€€€ V

95 Grüner Veltliner * Wösendorf Ried Hochrain Smaragd 2021

94 Grüner Veltliner * Ried Hochrain Smaragd 2020

95 Grüner Veltliner * Ried Kollmütz Smaragd 2022
13,5 Vol.-%, cork, steel tank, €€€€€ V

94 Grüner Veltliner * Wösendorf Ried Kollmütz Smaragd 2021

94 Grüner Veltliner * Ried Kollmütz Smaragd 2020

95 Grüner Veltliner * Smaragd Terrassen 2022
13 Vol.-%, cork, steel tank, €€€€ V

94 Grüner Veltliner * Smaragd Terrassen 2021

93 Grüner Veltliner * Smaragd Terrassen 2020

(93) Grüner Veltliner * Federspiel 2022
12 Vol.-%, cork, steel tank, €€€ V

92 Grüner Veltliner * Federspiel 2021

92 Grüner Veltliner * Federspiel 2020

95 Weißburgunder * Smaragd Terrassen 2022
13,5 Vol.-%, cork, steel tank, €€€ V

94 Weißburgunder * Smaragd Terrassen 2021

93 Weißburgunder * Smaragd Terrassen 2020

95 Roter Veltliner * 2022
13 Vol.-%, cork, steel tank, €€€€ V

95 Roter Veltliner * Smaragd 2021
Light greenish yellow, silver reflections. Delicate pear, yellow tropical fruit, a touch of blossom honey, light nougat, some beeswax. Full-bodied, elegant, fine fruit expression, complex, silky texture, freshly structured, a touch of apricot on the finish, very good length, salty on the aftertaste, good ageing potential.

95 Roter Veltliner Smaragd 2019

WEINGUT PRAGER

"From stone to wine" is Toni Bodenstein's motto. His ambition is to explore the quality and ageing potential of the individual vineyard sites. The goal is to bring unique, archetypal wines into the glass that carry the essence of their provenance. Known as the "Terroirist of the Wachau", the winemaker and chairman of the Regional Wine Committee Wachau has a complex philosophy; history and future, sustainability and authenticity. The work in the vineyard and in the cellar is carried out traditionally but with the necessary innovation, as Toni always strives and searches for the best possible quality. This connection with nature and inspiration is expressed in authentic wines, resulting from a holistic approach combined with sustainable practices. Respect for nature, appreciation of the environment and responsibility towards future generations are the basis for wines that combine elegance and finesse with expression and power. These wines exhibit the great sites of the Wachau, which are among the best in the world.

Numerous international awards confirm the work and philosophy of Ilse and Toni Bodenstein, who run one of Austria's most renowned wineries together. The 2019 vintage brought the ideas and goals of the next generation; son Robert Bodenstein, who wrote his master's thesis on the terroir of Ried Achleiten, has taken on more responsibility and is also fascinated and challenged by the diverse uniqueness of the Wachau terroir.

The estate's vineyards are partly in Weißenkirchen (Steinriegl, Zwerithaler, Klaus and

WACHAU DAC

WEINGUT PRAGER
3610 Weißenkirchen/Wachau
Wachaustraße 48
T: +43 2715 2248
prager@weissenkirchen.at
www.weingutprager.at

Winemaker: Toni Bodenstein
Contact: Ilse Bodenstein, Robert Bodenstein and Sophie-Helen Hinterhölzl
Production: 100 % white, 18.5 hectares
Fairs: VieVinum
Distribution partners: AUS, BE, DK, DE, FR, UK, IT, JP, LT, LU, NL, NO, RUS, SE, CH, SK, TH, CZ, HU, USA

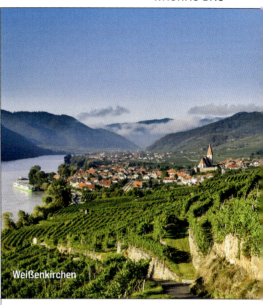

Weißenkirchen

Achleiten) and partly in Dürnstein (Kaiserberg and Liebenberg). The Riesling "Growth Bodenstein", which owes its filigree finesse to the extreme altitude (460 metres), also deserves acclaim. In the case of Grüner Veltliner, it is the "Stockkultur" of Achleiten, where the old vines produce a concentrated, mineral wine that is an absolute pleasure to drink. A particularly characterful Grüner Veltliner comes from the winery's oldest vines at Kammergut (Ried Zwerithaler). In total, there are 18 hectares of vineyards, most of which are planted on steep terraces. For the Bodenstein family, it is both a legacy and a challenge to be able to grow and make wine in this unique region.

(100) Grüner Veltliner * Ried Zwerithaler Kammergut Smaragd 2022
13,5 Vol.-%, cork, steel tank, €€€€€€
100 Grüner Veltliner * Ried Zwerithaler Kammergut Smaragd 2021
Pale yellow-green, silver glints. Delicately savoury, with a hint of meadow herbs, soft aniseed and caraway notions, notes of ripe yellow stone fruit, delicate mango and honeydew melon. Complex, juicy, enormously concentrated, white stone fruit, taut and tightly woven, filigree acidity, salinity and lingers for minutes. Definite ageing potential for decades. A Grüner Veltliner marvel par excellence - will remain unrivalled for a long time.
99 Grüner Veltliner * Ried Zwerithaler Kammergut Smaragd 2020

99 Grüner Veltliner * Ried Achleiten Stockkultur Smaragd 2022
13,5 Vol.-%, cork, steel tank, €€€€€€
98 Grüner Veltliner * Ried Achleiten Stockkultur Smaragd 2021
96 Grüner Veltliner * Ried Achleiten Stockkultur Smaragd 2020

(98) Grüner Veltliner * Wachstum Bodenstein Smaragd 2022
13,5 Vol.-%, cork, steel tank, €€€€€€
95 Grüner Veltliner * Weißenkirchen Wachstum Bodenstein Smaragd 2021
Pale yellow-green, silver glints. Fragrantly pleasant meadow herbs, delicate fresh orange zest, a hint of yellow apple, and mineral facets. Juicy, elegant, silky texture, refined apple fruit, some mango, very finesse, mineral-saline finish, long tapering persistence, and lovely lime nuances. Already well-developed and accessible. Superb ageing potential.
96 Grüner Veltliner * Weißenkirchen Wachstum Bodenstein Smaragd 2020

97 Grüner Veltliner * Ried Achleiten Smaragd 2022
13,5 Vol.-%, cork, steel tank, €€€€€€
97 Grüner Veltliner * Ried Achleiten Smaragd 2021
96 Grüner Veltliner * Ried Achleiten Smaragd 2020

93 Grüner Veltliner * Ried Hinter der Burg Federspiel 2022
12,5 Vol.-%, screwcap, steel tank, €€€€€

NIEDERÖSTERREICH/LOWER AUSTRIA

93 Grüner Veltliner * Ried Hinter der Burg Federspiel 2021
93 Grüner Veltliner * Ried Hinter der Burg Federspiel 2020

(99) Riesling * Wachstum Bodenstein Smaragd 2022
13 Vol.-%, cork, steel tank, €€€€€€
99 Riesling * Wachstum Bodenstein Smaragd 2021
Pale greenish yellow, silver glints. Nuances of light stone fruit, intense whiffs of exotic fruits, a hint of passion fruit, and delicate lime tones. A charming array of nuances. Juicy, complex, very tightly woven, taut, radiant acidity, cool, long-lasting style, great presence, succulent but not cloying. Promising ageing potential for years to come.
97 Riesling * Wachstum Bodenstein Smaragd 2020

(98) Riesling * Ried Klaus Smaragd 2022
13 Vol.-%, cork, steel tank, €€€€€€
98 Riesling * Ried Klaus Smaragd 2021
96 Riesling * Ried Klaus Smaragd 2020

(97) Riesling * Ried Achleiten Smaragd 2022
13 Vol.-%, cork, steel tank, €€€€€€
97 Riesling * Ried Achleiten Smaragd 2021
95 Riesling * Ried Achleiten Smaragd 2020

97 Riesling * Ried Steinriegl Smaragd 2021
95 Riesling Smaragd Ried Steinriegl 2019

93 Riesling * Ried Steinriegl Federspiel 2022
12,5 Vol.-%, screwcap, steel tank, €€€€€
93 Riesling * Ried Steinriegl Federspiel 2021
93 Riesling * Ried Steinriegl Federspiel 2020

98 Riesling Ried Klaus Auslese 2021

★★★★

WEINGUT SCHMELZ

The Schmelz family winery lies in the heart of the Wachau, in Joching. Thomas Schmelz and his wife Bianca run the winery, but Thomas' brother Florian also contributes in many areas, including the vineyard and cellar. The younger generation is actively supported by Monika and Johann Schmelz, who handed over the winery in 2018. The vineyard extends from Wösendorf to Unterloiben (8 km). As a result, the wines are characterised by different soils and climatic factors. Grüner Veltliner is the main variety, followed by Riesling. Gelber Muskateller, Sauvignon Blanc and Pinot Blanc complete the range. Loving work in the vineyards and a careful harvest are the basis for healthy grapes, which are gently processed in the cellar using modern technology. The result is unmistakable, easy-drinking wines with a certain fruitiness. A founding member of the Vinea Wachau association, the Schmelz family's wines have won awards at numerous international and national tastings. In 2005, Johann Schmelz was named "Winemaker of the Year" by Falstaff. Wine tasting is available in a modern setting with stunning views of the vineyards.

96 Riesling * Best of 2021
Medium greenish yellow, silver glints. Soft notions of apricot, blossom honey, a little kumquat, and a floral aroma. Invigorating bouquet. Good complexity, juicy, fruit forward, powerful, yellow tropical fruit, gentle resonating melon, superseded by a slight aftertaste of orange. A multilayered food companion with ageing potential.
96 Best of Riesling * 2020
95 Riesling Smaragd Best Of 2019

95 Riesling * Dürnstein Ried Höhereck Smaragd Dürnsteiner Freiheit 2022
13,5 Vol.-%, screwcap, steel tank, €€€€€
94 Riesling * Ried Höhereck Smaragd Dürnsteiner Freiheit 2021
94 Riesling * Ried Höhereck Smaragd Dürnsteiner Freiheit 2020

94 Riesling * Weißenkirchen Ried Steinriegl Smaragd 2022
13,5 Vol.-%, screwcap, steel tank, €€€€€
95 Riesling * Weißenkirchen Ried Steinriegl Smaragd 2021
94 Riesling * Ried Steinriegl Weißenkirchen Smaragd 2020

© Michael Parak

WACHAU DAC

WEINGUT SCHMELZ
3610 Joching
Joching 14
T: +43 (2715) 2435
info@schmelzweine.at
www.schmelzweine.at

Winemaker/Contact:
Thomas Schmelz
Production: 100 % white,
12 hectares
Fairs: VieVinum
Distribution partners: BE, DE, HK, IT, JP, MAL, NL, PL, RUS, SE, SK, CZ

Thomas Schmelz

---

93 Riesling * Federspiel Stein am Rain 2022
12,5 Vol.-%, screwcap, steel tank, €€€ ⓗ
92 Riesling * Federspiel Stein am Rain 2021
91 Riesling Federspiel Stein am Rain 2018

96 Grüner Veltliner * Smaragd Best of 2022
14 Vol.-%, screwcap, steel tank, €€€€
95 Grüner Veltliner * Smaragd Best of 2021
95 Best of Grüner Veltliner * Smaragd 2020

95 Grüner Veltliner * Joching Ried Kollmitz Smaragd 2022
13,5 Vol.-%, screwcap, steel tank, €€€€ ⓗ
96 Grüner Veltliner * Joching Ried Kollmitz Reserve 2021
Pale greenish yellow, silver glints. Delicate blossom honey, hints of meadow herbs, a pineapple touch, tangerine notes, and lush tropical fruit. An inviting bouquet. Good complexity, subtle fruit expression redolent of apricot, balanced acidity, mineral, and remains very persistent. A complex food accompaniment with ageing potential.

95 Grüner Veltliner * Loiben Ried Steinertal Smaragd 2022
14 Vol.-%, screwcap, steel tank, €€€€ ⓗ
95 Grüner Veltliner * Loiben Ried Steinertal Smaragd 2021
94 Grüner Veltliner * Ried Steinertal Loiben Smaragd 2020

94 Grüner Veltliner * Joching Ried Pichl Point Smaragd 2022
13,5 Vol.-%, screwcap, steel tank, €€€€
94 Grüner Veltliner * Joching Ried Pichl Point Smaragd 2021
94 Grüner Veltliner * Ried Pichl Point Smaragd 2020

94 Grüner Veltliner * Loiben Ried Loibenberg Smaragd 2022
14 Vol.-%, screwcap, steel tank, €€€€€ ⓗ
94 Grüner Veltliner * Loiben Ried Loibenberg Smaragd 2021
93 Grüner Veltliner * Ried Loibenberg Loiben Smaragd 2020

93 Grüner Veltliner * Weißenkirchen Ried Klaus Federspiel 2022
12,5 Vol.-%, screwcap, steel tank, €€€ ⓗ
93 Grüner Veltliner * Weißenkirchen Ried Klaus Federspiel 2021
92 Grüner Veltliner * Ried Klaus Federspiel 2020

93 Grüner Veltliner * Joching Ried Pichl Point Federspiel 2022
12,5 Vol.-%, screwcap, steel tank, €€€ ⓗ
93 Grüner Veltliner * Joching Ried Pichl Point Federspiel 2021
92 Grüner Veltliner * Ried Pichl Point Federspiel 2020

* Wachau DAC

NIEDERÖSTERREICH/LOWER AUSTRIA

91 **Grüner Veltliner * Loiben Federspiel 2022**
12,5 Vol.-%, screwcap, steel tank, €€€ ⓗ
92 **Grüner Veltliner * Loiben Federspiel 2021**
91 **Loibner Grüner Veltliner * Federspiel 2020**

90 **Grüner Veltliner * Wösendorf Federspiel TOM 2022**
12,5 Vol.-%, screwcap, steel tank, €€€ ⓗ
91 **Grüner Veltliner * Wösendorf Federspiel Tom 2021**
91 **Wösendorfer Grüner Veltliner * Federspiel TOM 2020**

90 **Grüner Veltliner * Joching Ried Steinwand Federspiel 2022**
12,5 Vol.-%, screwcap, steel tank, €€€ ⓗ
92 **Grüner Veltliner * Joching Ried Steinwand Federspiel 2021**
90 **Grüner Veltliner * Joching Ried Steinwand Federspiel 2020**

94 **Grüner Veltliner Ried Pichl Point Selection 24 2017**

90 **Gelber Muskateller * Joching Federspiel 2022**
12,5 Vol.-%, screwcap, steel tank, €€€
91 **Gelber Muskateller * Joching Federspiel 2021**
90 **Gelber Muskateller * Joching Federspiel 2020**

90 **Sauvignon Blanc * Joching 2022**
12,5 Vol.-%, screwcap, steel tank, €€€ ⓗ
89 **Sauvignon Blanc * Joching Federspiel 2021**
90 **Sauvignon Blanc * Joching 2020**

91 **Sauvignon Blanc Ried Donaufeld 2019**

★ ★ ★ ★

WEINGUT TEGERNSEERHOF

The history of Tegernseerhof dates back over 1,000 years to the time when Emperor Heinrich II donated ‚two hectares of land' in the Wachau to the Benedictine monastery at Tegernsee. The Tegernseerhof, named after its owner, was built on this land in 1176.

Today, many centuries later, the Tegernseerhof is owned by the sixth generation of the Mittelbach family. The name has been preserved, as has the ancient knowledge of winemaking passed down from generation to generation.

The vineyards of the Tegernseerhof are located on the best sites of the Wachau. They are characterised by steep terraces of solid primary rock, ideally situated to be caressed by the wind and warmed by the sun. As a result, the winery's Smaragd wines display an incredible density and variety of aromas. Whether Grüner Veltliner or Riesling, each wine has a distinct identity and style.

(97) **Riesling * Ried Kellerberg Smaragd 2022**
13 Vol.-%, screwcap, steel tank, €€€€€€
96 **Riesling * Dürnstein Ried Kellerberg Smaragd 2021**
Pale greenish yellow, silver glints. Delicate nuances of yellow fruit, peach, and pineapple, with a hint of tangerine zest and blossom honey. Juicy, tightly woven, white stone fruit with a richly finessed acidity, and a salty-lime touch. Already accessible, assured ageing potential.
95 **Riesling * Ried Kellerberg Smaragd 2020**

(96) **Riesling * Ried Steinertal Smaragd 2022**
13 Vol.-%, screwcap, steel tank, €€€€€€
95 **Riesling * Loiben Ried Steinertal Smaragd 2021**
95 **Riesling * Ried Steinertal Smaragd 2020**

(95) **Riesling * Ried Loibenberg Smaragd 2022**
13,5 Vol.-%, screwcap, steel tank, €€€€€
94 **Riesling * Loiben Ried Loibenberg Smaragd 2021**
94 **Riesling * Ried Loibenberg Smaragd 2020**

WACHAU DAC

WEINGUT TEGERNSEERHOF
3601 Dürnstein
Unterloiben 12
T: +43 (2732) 85362
office@tegernseerhof.at
www.tegernseerhof.at

Winemaker/Contact:
Martin Mittelbach
Production: 97 % white, 3 % rosé, 23 hectares
Fairs: ProWein Düsseldorf, VieVinum
Distribution partners: BE, DK, DE, EST, FIN, UK, IT, JP, CDN, LV, LT, NO, PL, SE, CH, SGP, SK, TH, CZ, HU, USA

Martin Mittelbach

(93) Riesling * Smaragd Bergdistel 2022
13 Vol.-%, screwcap, steel tank, €€€€
93 Riesling * Smaragd Bergdistel 2021
93 Riesling * Smaragd Bergdistel 2020

(96) Grüner Veltliner * Ried Schütt Smaragd 2022
13 Vol.-%, screwcap, steel tank, €€€€€€
95 Grüner Veltliner * Dürnstein Ried Schütt Smaragd 2021
Medium greenish yellow, silver glints. Appealing nuances of papaya and mango, delicate blossom honey, and fresh orange zest. An inviting bouquet. Rich, tightly woven, white stone fruit, filigree structure, mineral on the finish, delicate salinity, and a citrus nuanced aftertaste, promising ageing potential.
94 Grüner Veltliner * Ried Schütt Dürnstein Smaragd 2020

(95) Grüner Veltliner * Ried Höhereck Smaragd 2022
13,5 Vol.-%, screwcap, steel tank, €€€€€€
94 Grüner Veltliner * Dürnstein Ried Höhereck Smaragd 2021
94 Grüner Veltliner * Ried Höhereck Dürnstein Smaragd 2020

(94) Grüner Veltliner * Ried Loibenberg Smaragd 2022
13 Vol.-%, screwcap, steel tank, €€€€
94 Grüner Veltliner * Loiben Ried Loibenberg Smaragd 2021

94 Grüner Veltliner * Ried Loibenberg Loiben Smaragd 2020

(94) Grüner Veltliner * Smaragd Bergdistel 2022
13 Vol.-%, screwcap, steel tank, €€€€€
93 Grüner Veltliner * Smaragd Bergdistel 2021
93 Grüner Veltliner * Smaragd Bergdistel 2020

93 Grüner Veltliner * Ried Kreutles Loiben Federspiel 2020

92 Grüner Veltliner * Dürnstein Federspiel 2021
92 Grüner Veltliner * Dürnstein Federspiel 2020

91 Grüner Veltliner * Dürnstein Ried Superin Federspiel 2021
92 Grüner Veltliner * Ried Superin Dürnstein Federspiel 2020

94 Gemischter Satz * Smaragd 2020

94 Gemischter Satz Ried Weissenkirchner Zwerithaler 2019

The Wagram, here near Großriedenthal, shows a vast terrace of land from prehistoric sediments

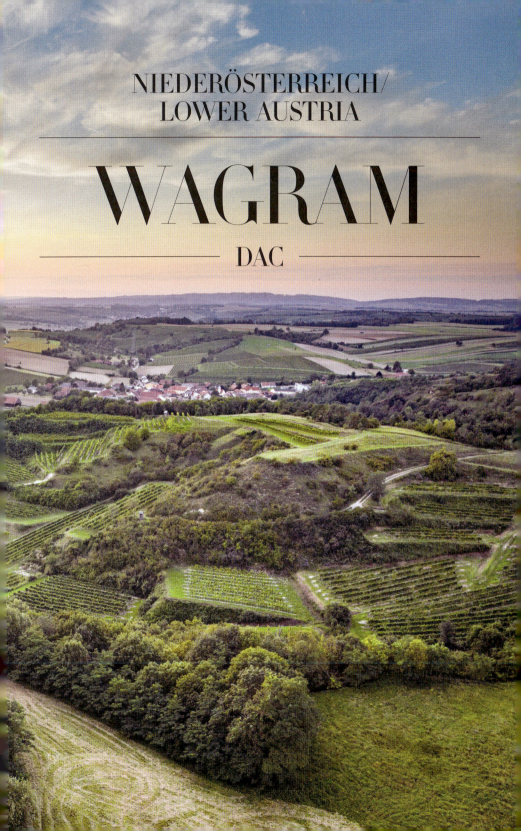

Cellar-lined lane in Feuersbrunn

GRÜNER VELTLINER LUSTS FOR LOESS

Wagram, the official name of this wine-growing region since 2007, has received a DAC classification in 2022, making it the 17th region in Austria with protected origin status. The vast terrain stretches along the left bank of the Danube downstream from Krems for 30 km to the city boundaries of Vienna.

Around 2,459 vineyard hectares are divided between two very different zones in this wine-growing area. The actual "Wagram" is a striking bluff that stretches from the mouth of the Kamp River along the north side of the Danube River. The remaining vineyard area is located south of the Danube in Klosterneuburg and the small wine village Tullnerfeld.

Uniform geological features coupled with consistent weather and climatic patterns make the actual Wagram a model wine region. A deep layer of loess was deposited on the shore of a prehistoric sea forming a unique landscape with soils that are high in fossil and mineral content (the name Wagram comes from "Wogenrain" meaning "shore"). Loess has good water-storage capacities and there is little need for irrigation during the dry growing season. This soil demonstrably lends wines a unique character. The influence of the Pannonian climate provides very warm sunny days that alternate with cool nights. This combination creates wines with pronounced fruit and an elegant, creamy texture. This terroir is exquisitely expressed with the region's main grape variety, Grüner Veltliner. The indigenous speciality Roter Veltliner (not related to Grüner Veltliner) also thrives in these conditions and an increasing number of producers grow and offer it in their wine assortment.

Leading winemakers also produce some of the most opulent, full-bodied red wines in Niederösterreich, especially from Zweigelt and Pinot Noir. Sweet wines, in particular ice wines of exemplary quality, are also produced

© Robert Herbst

NIEDERÖSTERREICH/LOWER AUSTRIA **WAGRAM DAC**

on the Wagram. The tremendous increase in wine quality in past years has raised the status of Wagram and it is certainly no longer considered an insider tip. Places like Feuersbrunn, Fels, Kirchberg, or Großriedenthal have long since established themselves as locations for dedicated wineries, and since the 2021 vintage, the wines typical of the region have been officially under DAC protection.

The wineries of Klosterneuburg, the monastery has been producing wine since 1114, cover a wide range of viticultural activities, from the small, family owned heurigens (winery taverns) to traditional estates of impressive magnitude and sparkling wine producers. The Bundeslehranstalt für Wein und Obstbau (Federal Institute for Viticulture and Pomology), the world's first viticulture and oenology school (founded in 1860), is a leading wine institution with internationally recognised standards for future generations of Austrian winegrowers.

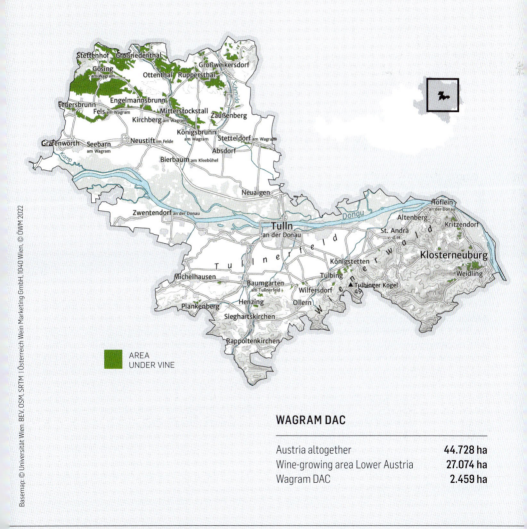

AREA UNDER VINE

WAGRAM DAC

Austria altogether	44.728 ha
Wine-growing area Lower Austria	27.074 ha
Wagram DAC	2.459 ha

NIEDERÖSTERREICH/LOWER AUSTRIA

SELECTED WINERIES

 ★★★★★

Weinberghof Karl Fritsch, Oberstockstall
Weingut Bernhard Ott, Feuersbrunn

 ★★★★

Weingut Anton Bauer, Feuersbrunn
Weingut Ecker – Eckhof, Kirchberg am Wagram
Weingut Josef Fritz, Zaußenberg
Weingut Leth, Fels am Wagram

 ★★★

Weingut Josef Ehmoser, Tiefenthal
Weingut Kolkmann, Fels am Wagram
Weinhof Anton und Elfriede Waldschütz, Sachsendorf

 ★★

Familie Bauer - Bioweingut, Großriedenthal
Weinhof Ehn, Engelmannsbrunn
Weingut Heiderer-Mayer, Großweikersdorf
BIO Weingut Urbanihof – Familie Paschinger, Fels am Wagram

—

Bioweingut Groiß, Kleinwiesendorf

 ★★★★

WEINGUT ANTON BAUER

In 1992, Anton Bauer from Wagram took over his parents' winery with just 3.2 hectares of vineyards. Today, the quality enthusiast manages around 40 hectares of vineyards in Feuersbrunn. He studied at the Krems School of Viticulture, completed an internship in Burgundy - a wine region for which he has a particular passion - and worked for four years as an oenologist at a renowned Lower Austrian winery. After that, Anton Bauer began his journey, the "adventure of being a winemaker". He has been pursuing it ever since with determination and joy.

It is the combination of being deeply rooted and open to new things, of being traditional and experimental, that defines Anton Bauer. From the very beginning, the winemaker has always been a visionary. In addition to the Wagramer classics such as Grüner Veltliner, Roter Veltliner, and Riesling, he started making red wines early on - a bold step that was met with scepticism by many. But Anton Bauer had the courage of his convictions. Today, his Pinot Noir, Cabernet Sauvignon, and legendary Cuvée Legendär are among the top red wines in the country. His varietal and regional white wines are also in the same league. Rosenberg, Spiegel, Kirchthal, and Stiegl are his best sites, from which he vinifies crystal-clear wines with depth year after year.

Anton Bauer attaches great importance to precision and integrated grape production that is friendly to the vineyards' beneficial insects and restrained in its use of pesticides. A healthy soil enriched with humus is the basis for the deep-rooted vines. Summer pruning and selective/cluster berry thinning are further foundations for a qualitatively superior harvest. Once physiologically ripe, the grapes are processed as gently as possible, and 100% manual harvesting is a fundamental part of the process.

(96) Grüner Veltliner * Feuersbrunn Grande Reserve 2022
13,5 Vol.-%, cork, large wooden barrel, €€€€€

94 Grüner Veltliner * Grande Reserve 2021
Medium greenish yellow, silver reflections. Delicate tobacco and herbal savouriness, yellow apple fruit, candied orange zest, delicate hints of honey blossom. Taut, good complexity, powerful, well-integrated acid structure, fine

© Presse&Foto FRANZ GLEISS

WAGRAM DAC

WEINGUT ANTON BAUER
3483 Feuersbrunn
Neufang 42
T: +43 (2738) 2556
office@antonbauer.at
www.antonbauer.at

Winemaker/Contact:
Anton Bauer
Production: 1 % sparkling,
54 % white, 44 % red, 1 % sweet,
40 hectares
Fairs: Austrian Tasting London,
ProWein Düsseldorf, VieVinum
Distribution partners: BE, DK, DE,
UK, IT, NL, RO, CH, USA, CY

Anton Bauer

savoury finish, nuances of yellow fruit in the aftertaste, sturdy food companion with certain ageing potential.
94   Grüner Veltliner Grande Reserve 2020

(95) Grüner Veltliner * Feuersbrunn Private Selection l. E. 2022
13,5 Vol.-%, cork, cement, €€€€€€
94   Grüner Veltliner * Private Selection 2021
93   Grüner Veltliner Private Selection 2020

(95) Grüner Veltliner * Feuersbrunn Ried Rosenberg Alte Rebe 2022
13,5 Vol.-%, screwcap, large wooden barrel, €€€€€
93   Grüner Veltliner * Feuersbrunn Ried Rosenberg Alte Rebe 2021

(94) Grüner Veltliner * Feuersbrunn Ried Spiegel 2022
13,5 Vol.-%, screwcap, large wooden barrel, €€€€€
93   Grüner Veltliner * Ried Spiegel 2021
92   Grüner Veltliner Ried Spiegel 2019

(94) Grüner Veltliner * Feuersbrunn Ried Brenner 2022
13 Vol.-%, screwcap, steel tank, €€€€
91   Grüner Veltliner * Ried Brenner 2021

(93) Grüner Veltliner * Feuersbrunn Ried Kirchthal 2022
13,5 Vol.-%, screwcap, cement, €€€€
92   Grüner Veltliner * Ried Kirchthal 2021
91   Grüner Veltliner Ried Kirchthal 2019

92   Grüner Veltliner * Feuersbrunn Ried Rosenberg 2022
13 Vol.-%, screwcap, steel tank, €€€€
92   Grüner Veltliner * Ried Rosenberg 2021
91   Grüner Veltliner Ried Rosenberg 2019

93   Grüner Veltliner Ried Königsberg Respic 2021
13,5 Vol.-%, screwcap, large wooden barrel, €€€€€

(92) Grüner Veltliner Respic Messwein 2022
12,5 Vol.-%, screwcap, steel tank, €€€

(93) Riesling ** Feuersbrunn Alte Rebe 2022
13,5 Vol.-%, screwcap, cement, €€€€€
93   Riesling * Alte Rebe 2021
92   Riesling Alte Rebe 2020

(93) Chardonnay * Feuersbrunn Reserve 2021
13,5 Vol.-%, cork, barrique, €€€€€
92   Chardonnay Reserve 2020
93   Chardonnay Reserve 2019

(93) Pinot Blanc * Feuersbrunn 2021
13,5 Vol.-%, cork, cement/500-l-barrel, €€€€€
90   Pinot Blanc Ried Kirchthal 2020
91   Pinot Blanc Ried Kirchthal 2019
92   Pinot Blanc Ried Kirchthal 2018

* Wagram DAC

NIEDERÖSTERREICH/LOWER AUSTRIA

(95) Pinot Noir Private Selection L. E. 2020
14 Vol.-%, cork, barrique, €€€€€ 🅱
95 Pinot Noir Private Selection 2019
95 Pinot Noir Private Selection 2018

(93) Pinot Noir * Feuerbrunn Reserve 2021
14 Vol.-%, cork, barrique, €€€€€ 🅱
93 Pinot Noir Reserve Limited Edition 2020
92 Pinot Noir Reserve Limited Edition 2019

(95) Anton Bauer Privat 2020 CS/ME
14 Vol.-%, cork, barrique, €€€€€ 🅱
95 Anton Bauer Privat 2019 CS/ME
Deep dark ruby, purple glints, faintly lighter at the rim. Exuberant damson notes, candied orange peel, balsamic nuances, and a floral touch. Alluring aroma. Juicy, elegant, fine tannin structure, savoury with hints of dark forest berry jam, velvety, fruit forward, tightly woven, and persistent. A complex food accompaniment with ageing potential.
94 Anton Bauer Privat 2018 CS/ME

(95) Cabernet Sauvignon Reserve L. E. 2021
14 Vol.-%, cork, barrique, €€€€€ 🅱
94 Cabernet Sauvignon Reserve Limited Edition 2020
94 Cabernet Sauvignon Reserve Limited Edition 2019

(94) Blaufränkisch Reserve L. E. 2019
14 Vol.-%, cork, barrique, €€€€€ 🅱
93 Blaufränkisch Reserve Limited Edition 2018
92 Blaufränkisch Reserve Limited Edition 2015

93 Merlot Reserve Limited Edition 2020
93 Merlot Reserve Limited Edition 2019
93 Merlot Reserve Limited Edition 2018

(93) Merlot Respic 2021
14 Vol.-%, cork, barrique

94 Grüner Veltliner Eiswein 2017

90 Grüner Veltliner Auslese 2018

FAMILIE BAUER - BIOWEINGUT
ORGANIC

The Bauer family focuses on red: although Grüner Veltliner makes up a large part of the estate's vineyard area. However, the typical Wagram grape variety - the Rote Veltliner - has long been cultivated here with its own selections.

Weingut Großriedenthal is situated in the upper part of Wagram, where gravel and sandy soils dominate alongside the mighty loess formations of the plateaus. Pinot varieties are planted on calcareous loess, while Riesling and Red Veltliner thrive on sandy-gravelly loess. The Bauer organic winery pays particular attention to a living ecosystem - healthy soils, nature and climate. Experience with new Piwi varieties such as Donauriesling and Donauveltliner has been gained in the vineyards and in the vinification process for some time. The three different natural wines are also being sold successfully - mainly on the US market. The Bauer family's sweet wines - Beerenauslese, Trockenbeerenauslese and Eiswein - are also worth highlighting.

92 Grüner Veltliner * Ried Hinterberg 2021
13,5 Vol.-%, screwcap, partial barrique, €€€ 🅱
92 Grüner Veltliner Ried Hinterberg 2020
Medium golden yellow colour with green reflections. Intense bouquet of mango and honeydew melon, candied orange peel, floral touch, some caramel. Juicy, tight, balanced acidity, well-developed, mineral, yellow tropical fruits on the finish, honey in the aftertaste.
92 Grüner Veltliner Ried Hinterberg 2019

91 Grüner Veltliner * Ried Goldberg 2022
13 Vol.-%, screwcap, steel tank, €€ 🅱
91 Grüner Veltliner * Ried Goldberg 2021
90 Grüner Veltliner Ried Goldberg 2020

92 Roter Veltliner * Ried Hinterberg 2021
13,5 Vol.-%, screwcap, partial barrique, €€€ 🅱
92 Roter Veltliner Ried Hinterberg 2020
92 Roter Veltliner Ried Hinterberg 2019

91 Roter Veltliner Urig 2020
13,5 Vol.-%, cork, wooden barrel, €€€€€ 🅱 🅞 🅐
92 Roter Veltliner Urig 2019

© GERALD HOERMANN

FAMILIE BAUER - BIOWEINGUT
3471 Großriedenthal
Hauptstraße 68
T: +43 (2279) 7204
info@familiebauer.at
www.familiebauer.at

Winemaker/Contact:
Josef Bauer
Production: 3 % sparkling,
72 % white, 22 % red, 3 % sweet,
28 hectares
Fairs: ProWein Düsseldorf,
VieVinum, Vinobile Montfort
Distribution partners: DK, DE, JP,
CDN, NL, SE, CH, USA

Eva Maria and Josef Bauer

91 Roter Veltliner Urig 2018

90 Roter Veltliner * Terrassen 2022
12 Vol.-%, screwcap, steel tank, €€ Ⓑ
90 Roter Veltliner * Terrassen 2021
90 Roter Veltliner Wagram Terrassen 2020

92 Weißburgunder * Großriedenthal Reserve 2021
13,5 Vol.-%, screwcap, partial barrique, €€€ Ⓑ
92 Weißburgunder Ried Eisenhut Reserve 2019

WEINGUT ECKER – ECKHOF

Located in the heart of Lower Austria, in Mitterstockstall, Kirchberg am Wagram, Weingut Ecker is a third-generation family business, with the Ecker family spanning over 400 years in the wine industry. The estate is located in the beautiful vine-growing region of Wagram, on that deep loess layer that stretches north of the Danube about 20 kilometers - between Krems and Stockerau - to the east. The climatic profile of this region offers the best conditions for the Grüner and Roter Veltliner varieties. Currently, the winery cultivates 24 hectares of its own vineyards.
Bernhard Ecker produces 80 percent white wine from local varieties. Grüner Veltliner, which is offered in five different variations, as well as Red Veltliner are the most important varieties of the extensive wine assortment. The winery, which has won several national and international awards, has been an integral part of the domestic wine scene for years. Ecker wines are also becoming increasingly popular abroad. Ecker stands for consistent top quality without compromise. The wines, which are appreciated by wine connoisseurs year after year, are characterised above all by clarity, finesse and longevity.
A cosy wine bar spoils the guests with many traditional dishes of the region and the matching glass of wine or Sekt. Furthermore, a modern tasting room is available, where the entire range of wines can be tasted at leisure.

NIEDERÖSTERREICH/LOWER AUSTRIA

Alexandra and Bernhard

WEINGUT ECKER – ECKHOF
3470 Kirchberg am Wagram
Mitterstockstall 25
T: +43 (2279) 2440
weingut@eckhof.at
www.eckhof.at

Winemaker/Contact:
Bernhard Ecker
Production: 80 % white, 20 % red, 24 hectares
Fairs: ProWein Düsseldorf, VieVinum
Distribution partners: BE, DK, DE, UK, IL, NL, PL, CZ, USA

---

(94) Roter Veltliner * Ried Steinberg Große Reserve 2022
13,5 Vol.-%, cork, small wooden barrel, €€€€ Ⓑ

94 Roter Veltliner * Ried Steinberg Große Reserve 2021
Medium golden yellow, silver reflections. Delicate wood spice, a bit of papaya, soft notes of lemon balm, ripe pear fruit, cardamom sounds, attractive bouquet. Juicy, good complexity, well-integrated acidity, pronounced pear fruit, mineral echo, multi-faceted lemony finish, long lasting, good food wine.

95 Roter Veltliner Ried Steinberg Große Reserve 2019

94 Roter Veltliner * Ried Steinberg 2022
13,5 Vol.-%, screwcap, steel tank/large wooden barrel, €€€€

93 Roter Veltliner * Ried Steinberg 2021
93 Roter Veltliner Ried Steinberg 2020

93 Roter Veltliner * Ried Mordthal 2022
13 Vol.-%, screwcap, steel tank, €€€ Ⓑ

90 Roter Veltliner * 2022
12,5 Vol.-%, screwcap, steel tank, €€ Ⓑ

91 Roter Veltliner * Wagram 2021
91 Roter Veltliner Wagram 2020

(94) Grüner Veltliner * Ried Mordthal 2022
14 Vol.-%, screwcap, large wooden barrel, €€€ Ⓑ

93 Grüner Veltliner * Ried Mordthal 2021
Brilliant light greenish yellow, silver reflections. Yellow tropical fruit, subtle spiciness, hints of guava, clementine, some pineapple. Complex, juicy, notes of passion fruit, well-integrated acidity, dark minerality, herbal touch, persistent, a versatile food wine with ageing potential.

93 Grüner Veltliner Ried Mordthal 2020

92 Grüner Veltliner * Ried Schlossberg 2022
13 Vol.-%, screwcap, steel tank, €€€ Ⓑ

92 Grüner Veltliner * Ried Schlossberg 2021
92 Grüner Veltliner Ried Schlossberg 2020

92 Grüner Veltliner * Ried Steinberg 2022
12,5 Vol.-%, screwcap, steel tank, €€ Ⓑ

91 Grüner Veltliner * Ried Steinberg 2021
91 Grüner Veltliner Ried Steinberg 2020

90 Grüner Veltliner * Kirchberg 2021
90 Grüner Veltliner Kirchberg 2020
90 Grüner Veltliner Kirchberg 2019

(93) Grauburgunder * Kalk 2022
13 Vol.-%, screwcap, steel tank/small wooden barrel, €€€€ Ⓑ

93 Grauer Burgunder * 2021

93 Weißburgunder * Kalk 2022
13 Vol.-%, screwcap, steel tank, €€€€ Ⓑ

91 Weißburgunder Ried Schlossberg 2020
92 Weißburgunder Ried Schlossberg 2019
92 Weißburgunder Ried Schlossberg 2018

© Weingut Ecker-Eckhof

90	Weißburgunder * Kirchberg 2021	91	Burgundercuvée von Eckhof 2022 WB/CH
			13 Vol.-%, screwcap, steel tank, €€
93	Riesling * Reserve 2021		
92	Riesling Ried Steinberg Reserve 2018	90	Pinot Noir Reserve Edition Alexandra III 2019
92	Riesling * 2022		13,5 Vol.-%, cork, small wooden barrel, €€€€
	12,5 Vol.-%, screwcap, steel tank, €€	92	Pinot Noir Reserve Edition Alexandra 2018
91	Riesling * Wagram 2021	91	Pinot Noir Reserve Edition Alexandra 2016
91	Riesling Wagram 2020		

WEINGUT JOSEF EHMOSER
ORGANIC

In the eastern part of Wagram, a distinctive mountain range characterised by loess soils, Josef and Martina Ehmoser passionately cultivate premium vineyard sites. Their guiding principles are a hands-on approach passed down through generations and an unwavering commitment to quality. As a member of the Austrian Association of Traditional Wineries, the winery builds on its heritage and focuses on traditional wines - grown in harmony with nature. Each individual bottle is a unique testimony to the Wagram region - with a distinctive charm.

The range is both expressive and comprehensive: the main variety is Grüner Veltliner, which thrives on the characteristic loess soils and is vinified in styles ranging from classic and savoury to powerful and elegant from the two ÖTW Erste Lage sites of Ried Georgenberg and Ried Hohenberg. But the Ehmoser's passion is also evident in their complex Pinot Blanc. Josef Ehmoser demonstrates that Riesling can also develop a wonderful piquancy on loess soils. The reds Zweigelt and St. Laurent matured in large wooden barrels, are also elegantly rich.

Manual labour is very important in the vineyard, and the grapes are harvested exclusive-

Martina and Josef Ehmoser

WEINGUT JOSEF EHMOSER
3701 Tiefenthal
Tiefenthal 9
T: +43 (2955) 70442
office@weingut-ehmoser.at
www.weingut-ehmoser.at

Winemaker: Josef Ehmoser
Contact: Josef and Martina Ehmoser
Production: 80 % white, 20 % red, 17 hectares
Fairs: VieVinum

NIEDERÖSTERREICH/LOWER AUSTRIA

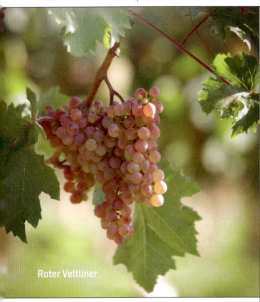
Roter Veltliner

ly by hand. In the cellar, Josef Ehmoser gives his wines time to develop their unique character. He always supports the potential of his wines and emphasises their distinctiveness without forcing them to follow predetermined paths. In this way, nature's power is preserved and can be relished for years to come. Josef Ehmoser's distinctive regional wines are internationally acclaimed. The 2022 vintage was the first certified organic harvest.

95 Grüner Veltliner *
    Ried Georgenberg 1ÖTW 2021
14 Vol.-%, cork, large wooden barrel, €€€€

94 Grüner Veltliner
    Ried Georgenberg 1ÖTW 2020
Medium golden yellow, silver reflections. Fine herbal spice, yellow tropical fruit, nuances of mango, some blossom honey, subtle tobacco notes. Complex, taut, fine nuances of yellow stone fruit, fine acidity, salty minerality, good length, certain ageing potential.

94 Grüner Veltliner
    Ried Georgenberg 1ÖTW 2019

93 Grüner Veltliner *
    Ried Hohenberg 1ÖTW 2021
13,5 Vol.-%, cork, large wooden barrel, €€€€

92 Grüner Veltliner
    Ried Hohenberg 1ÖTW 2020

93 Grüner Veltliner Ried Hohenberg 1ÖTW 2019

90 Grüner Veltliner * Terrassen 2022
12 Vol.-%, screwcap, steel tank, €€ Ⓑ

90 Grüner Veltliner Wagram Terrassen 2021
89 Grüner Veltliner Wagram Terrassen 2020

92 Gemischter Satz * 2021
13 Vol.-%, DIAM, large wooden barrel/cement, €€€

92 Gemischter Satz Unter der Burg 2020
92 Gemischter Satz Unter der Burg 2019

92 Riesling * Grossweikersdorf
    Vom gelben Löss 2022
12,5 Vol.-%, screwcap, steel tank, €€€ Ⓑ

92 Riesling Grossweikersdorf
    Vom gelben Löss 2021

92 Riesling Grossweikersdorf
    Vom gelben Löss 2020

(91) Weißer Burgunder * Grossweikersdorf
    Vom gelben Löss 2022
12,5 Vol.-%, screwcap, large wooden barrel, €€€ Ⓑ

92 Weißburgunder * Grossweikersdorf
    Vom gelben Löss 2021

91 Weißburgunder Grossweikersdorf
    Vom gelben Löss 2020

94 Weisser Burgunder Fassreserve 60 2016
Light yellow green, silver reflections. Delicately nutty underlying fine white pear fruit, a touch of marzipan, subtle tropical fruit in the background, multi-faceted bouquet. Complex, elegant, delicate white nougat, creamy texture, finesse and persistence, nutty touch on the finish, a balanced food wine.

91 Zweigelt Rosé 2022
12 Vol.-%, screwcap, steel tank, €€ Ⓑ

91 Zweigelt Rosé 2021
88 Zweigelt Rosé 2020

93 Gelber Muskateller Auslese 2021

92 Gelber Muskateller Spätlese 2020

WEINHOF EHN

Wagram, with its varied plateaus and slopes, offers the ideal conditions for Gerhard Ehn to produce high-quality wines in conscious harmony with nature. In 2003, the young vintner took over the family business and modernised it step by step, including the construction of a new cellar. The labels were also modified to a sleeker, more expressive look. Gerhard Ehn uses modern cellar techniques and gentle treatment of the grapes to achieve the full potential of his splendid wines. Depending on the variety and vintage, the wines are aged in steel tanks, large wooden barrels or sometimes even in barriques. The main focus of the winemaker is on Grüner Veltliner. Four different vinification methods have made it possible to produce a range of high-quality wines, from the light, spritzy summer wine "Swing" to the full-bodied top Grüner Veltliner from the Mordthal single vineyard, with something for every taste. The varieties Weißburgunder (Pinot Blanc), Chardonnay, Riesling, Frühroter Veltliner and Gelber Muskateller round off the range of white wines. The red wine Zweigelt is vinified both classically and in barriques. The aim of the flourishing winery is to use modern cellar technology and a great deal of respect for nature to produce excellent wines that are simply a pleasure to drink.

93 Grüner Veltliner * Gehnius Große Reserve 2021
13,5 Vol.-%, screwcap, used barriques, €€€€

93 Grüner Veltliner Gehnius Große Reserve 2020
Medium greenish yellow, silver reflections. Fine notes of mango and pineapple, delicate honeydew melon, candied clementine, vanilla touch, tobacco nuances. Juicy, good complexity, tightly meshed, mineral, nice spice, Golden Delicious apple fruit on the finish, honey in the aftertaste, a good food wine with certain ageing potential.

93 Grüner Veltliner Gehnius Große Reserve 2019

92 Grüner Veltliner * Ried Mordthal 2022
13,5 Vol.-%, screwcap, large wooden barrel, €€€

92 Grüner Veltliner * Ried Mordthal 2021

92 Grüner Veltliner Ried Mordthal 2020

91 Grüner Veltliner * Ried Satz 2022
13 Vol.-%, screwcap, steel tank, €€

90 Grüner Veltliner * Ried Satz 2021

WEINHOF EHN
3470 Engelmannsbrunn
Kapellenberg 47
T: +43 (2279) 27377
office@weinhofehn.at
www.weinhofehn.at

Winemaker/Contact:
Gerhard Ehn
Production: 2 % sparkling, 85 % white, 3 % rosé, 10 % red, 10 hectares
Fairs: VieVinum, Weinmesse Innsbruck
Distribution partners: BE, DE, NL

Gerhard Ehn

* Wagram DAC

NIEDERÖSTERREICH/LOWER AUSTRIA

90 Grüner Veltliner Ried Satz 2020	90 Roter Veltliner * 2021
90 Grüner Veltliner * Ried Hochrain 2022 12,5 Vol.-%, screwcap, steel tank, €€	89 Weißburgunder * 2022 13,5 Vol.-%, screwcap, steel tank, €€
91 Grüner Veltliner * Ried Hochrain 2021	90 Weißburgunder * 2021
89 Grüner Veltliner Ried Hochrain 2020	90 Weißburgunder Wagram 2020
91 Roter Veltliner * Ried Bromberg 2022 13 Vol.-%, screwcap, steel tank, €€€	89 Chardonnay Wagram 2020
	89 Chardonnay 2019
	90 Chardonnay 2018

WEINBERGHOF KARL FRITSCH
ORGANIC

For Karl Fritsch, winemaking means focusing on the fundamentals of tradition to determine future decisions because only on the basis of traditional experiences and values, combined with contemporary inspirations, can cultural assets be preserved and new values created.

The 30 hectare estate produces about two-thirds of white wine, mainly Grüner Veltliner and Riesling, and one-third of red wine. The symbiosis of climate and soil in the Wagram provides excellent conditions for Grüner Veltliner. If you are looking for the core talent of the Weinberghof, the best choice is Grüner Veltliner, which is offered here both as a light summer wine and in the subtle style of site specific wines such as Steinberg and Schlossberg. Among the reds, the Foggathal cuvée is one of Austria's best and most renowned, but the juicy Pinot Noir also has an excellent reputation.

Winemaker Karl Fritsch is at the helm of the Weinberghof. He has an excellent reputation among the winemakers of the Wagram region for his innovations and his ability to put them into practice, as evidenced by the growing number of customers and the awards won by his

Vineyards near Oberstockstall

WEINBERGHOF KARL FRITSCH
3470 Oberstockstall
Schlossbergstraße 9
T: +43 (2279) 5037
info@fritsch.cc
www.fritsch.cc

Winemaker/Contact:
Karl Fritsch
Production: 75 % white, 25 % red, 30 hectares
Fairs: Millésime Bio, ProWein Düsseldorf, VieVinum, MondoVino, Summa Margreid
Distribution partners:
DK, DE, IT, PL, CH, CZ, HU, USA

wines. For Karl Fritsch, nature and its resources have been at the forefront of his work since he converted to biodynamics in January 2006. For him, working with nature is not only an obligation but also a privilege. At the end of 2007, the Karl Fritsch winery was accepted into the "Traditionsweingüter Österreich" circle, which underlines its essential role in the Wagram region.

92 ⊖ Purist Pet Nat 2020 RR/GM
92 ⊖ Purist Petnat brut 2019 GM/RR
90 ⊖ Purist Petnat 2018

97 Fritsch & Gottwald Tausend Weiss 2019 CH/WB
12,5 Vol.-%, crown cap, 500-l-barrel, €€€€€ Ⓑ Ⓥ
97 Tausend Weiss 2019 CH/WB
Bright medium golden yellow, green glints. Inviting bouquet of pineapple and tangerine zest, a hint of caramel, delicate fig nuances, underlaid with savoury wood tones. Good complexity, multilayered, tightly woven minerality, soft herbal notes, white tropical fruit on the finish. A complex food accompaniment, marked by nutty reverberations. Good ageing potential.
96 Tausend Weiss 2017 CH/WB

94 Materia Prima 2021 TR/GV
12,5 Vol.-%, cork, cement/large wooden barrel,
€€€€€ Ⓑ Ⓞ
93 Materia Prima 2020 GV/TR
92 Materia Prima 2019 TR/GV

96 Grüner Veltliner
    Ried Schlossberg 1ÖTW 2021
13 Vol.-%, screwcap, steel tank, €€€€€ Ⓑ Ⓥ
96 Grüner Veltliner
    Ried Schlossberg 1ÖTW 2020
Medium greenish yellow, silver glints. Inviting bouquet of apricots and honeydew melon, a hint of orange zest, and delicate hints of guava. Alluring fruity bouquet. Juicy, elegant, well-integrated acidity structure, yellow tropical fruit with a light finish, and mineral backbone. A lovely supper accompaniment with potential.
95 Grüner Veltliner Ried Schlossberg 1ÖTW Oberstockstall 2019

94 Grüner Veltliner * Ried Steinberg 2022
12,5 Vol.-%, screwcap, steel tank, €€€ Ⓑ Ⓥ
92 Grüner Veltliner * Ried Steinberg 2021

93 Grüner Veltliner * Kirchberg 2022
12,5 Vol.-%, screwcap, steel tank, €€€ Ⓑ Ⓥ
92 Grüner Veltliner Kirchberg 2020
91 Grüner Veltliner Kirchberg 2019

93 Grüner Veltliner Geiler Stoff
    by Alexander Fritsch 2021
12,5 Vol.-%, screwcap, large wooden barrel, €€€ Ⓑ Ⓞ

91 Grüner Veltliner Wagram 2020
91 Grüner Veltliner Wagram 2019
89 Grüner Veltliner Wagram 2018

95 Riesling Ried Mordthal 1ÖTW 2021
12,5 Vol.-%, screwcap, steel tank, €€€€ Ⓑ Ⓥ
94 Riesling Ried Mordthal 1ÖTW 2020
94 Riesling Ried Mordthal 1ÖTW 2019

93 Riesling * 2022
12,5 Vol.-%, screwcap, steel tank, €€€ Ⓑ Ⓥ
91 Riesling Wagram 2020
91 Riesling Wagram 2019

94 Roter Veltliner Ried Steinberg 1ÖTW 2021
12,5 Vol.-%, screwcap, steel tank, €€€€ Ⓑ Ⓥ
95 Roter Veltliner Ried Steinberg 1ÖTW 2020
93 Roter Veltliner Ried Steinberg 1ÖTW 2019

92 Roter Veltliner unfiltriert 2018

90 Zweigelt Rosé Wagram 2020
90 Zweigelt Wagram Rosé 2019

96 Pinot Noir P 2019
13 Vol.-%, cork, 500-l-barrel, €€€€€ Ⓑ
95 Pinot Noir P 2018
Strong crimson with garnet and ochre glints, broad and bright at the rim. Ripe red cherry, subtle wild berry, fine nuances of new oak, delicate savoury notes, multi-faceted bouquet. Juicy, taut and finely-meshed, fine acidity, round tannins, chocolatey 'oxidative' touch on the finish, salty finish, very persistent, has class.
94 Pinot Noir P 2017

92 Pinot Noir Ruppersthal 2021
12,5 Vol.-%, screwcap, small wooden barrel, €€€€
Ⓑ Ⓥ
92 Pinot Noir Ruppersthal 2019

93 Pinot Noir Ried Exlberg 2019
91 Pinot Noir Ried Exlberg 2018

93 Foggathal N°23 2017 ZW/CS
92 Foggathal N°22 2016 ZW/CS

93 Riesling Beerenauslese 2017

* Wagram DAC

NIEDERÖSTERREICH/LOWER AUSTRIA

WEINGUT JOSEF FRITZ

Since 2003, Irene and Josef Fritz have been running the Fritz Winery in Zaußenberg near Königsbrunn am Wagram, today with a total of 16 hectares of vineyards. Since 2020, the winery has also been a member of the Austrian Traditional Wine Estates. The Mordthal, Himmelreich, Steinberg and Schlossberg vineyards, with soils of loess, tertiary gravel and sandstone, offer the best conditions for the grape varieties Roter and Grüner Veltliner, Roter Traminer, Pinot Blanc and Riesling, as well as Blauer Zweigelt and St. Laurent, together with the mild climate of the region.

Ecological balance is the be-all and end-all in their vineyards, so that the multifaceted richness of a nature that is as untouched as possible is preserved for the future. For this reason, they limit themselves to minimal plant protection within the framework of the transition to organic viticulture. Wine is understood here as the sum of man, nature and the cultural landscape of the vineyard. Only absolutely ripe and clean grapes are brought into the cellar. This requires a rigorous selection in the vineyard and gentle harvesting by hand. The white wines are fermented cleanly and cool in stainless steel tanks to preserve their fresh and fruity aroma. After the first racking, they are stored in the climatically ideal cellar built into the loess. The lighter wines are stored in stainless steel tanks until bottling, the site wines in wooden barrels.

Since 2019, the restaurant "Josefs Himmelreich" has been existing, named after a Zaußenberg vineyard and equally the vintner. Since the previous year, Marco Gangl from Western Styria, who learned his trade at "Landhaus Bacher" and at the Swedish three-star Frantzén, has been in charge for culinary highlights.

96 Roter Veltliner * Ruppersthal Ried Steinberg 1ÖTW Privat 2021
13,5 Vol.-%, cork, small wooden barrel, €€€€€

96 Roter Veltliner Ruppersthal Ried Steinberg 1ÖTW Privat 2020
Bright golden yellow, silver glints. Exuberant apples underlaid with subtle blossom honey, hints of pineapple, and a tad of tobacco savouriness. Good complexity, juicy, taut, multifaceted acidity, tightly woven, with a mango nuanced finish and fruit forward reverberations followed by a saline

Johannes Fritz

WEINGUT JOSEF FRITZ
3701 Zaußenberg
Ortsstraße 3
T: +43 (2278) 2515
office@weingut-fritz.at
www.weingut-fritz.at

Winemaker: Josef Fritz
Contact: Josef and Irene Fritz
Production: 5 % sparkling, 90 % white, 5 % red, 16 hectares
Certified: Sustainable Austria
Fairs: ÖGW Zürich, ProWein Düsseldorf, VieVinum
Distribution partners: BE, DK, DE, CDN, ROK, LU, NL, PL, CH, SK, CZ, USA

WAGRAM DAC

aftertaste. A complex supper accompaniment with potential.

96 Roter Veltliner Ried Steinberg 1ÖTW Ruppersthal Privat 2019

94 Roter Veltliner * Ruppersthal Ried Mordthal 1ÖTW 2021
13 Vol.-%, cork, large wooden barrel, €€€€

94 Roter Veltliner Ruppersthal Ried Mordthal 1ÖTW 2020

94 Roter Veltliner Ried Mordthal 1ÖTW Ruppersthal 2019

93 Roter Veltliner * Großweikersdorf Ried Steinberg 2022
13 Vol.-%, screwcap, large wooden barrel, €€€

93 Roter Veltliner * Großweikersdorf Ried Steinberg 2021

94 Roter Veltliner Ried Steinberg 2020

90 Roter Veltliner * Terrassen 2022
12,5 Vol.-%, screwcap, steel tank, €€

91 Roter Veltliner * Terrassen 2021

91 Roter Veltliner Wagram Terrassen 2020

97 Roter Veltliner Josef vs. Johannes 2020
13,5 Vol.-%, cork, small wooden barrel, €€€€€€

94 Roter Veltliner Josef vs. Johannes 2019
Medium golden yellow, silver reflections. Delicate honey and mango, a touch of papaya, hints of pear and pineapple, tobacco spice, soft notes of caramel, inviting bouquet. Juicy, tight-knit, well-integrated acidity, Williams pear on the finish, salty aftertaste, balanced, complex food wine, definite ageing potential.

92 Roter Veltliner Gondwana 2021
13 Vol.-%, cork, cement, €€€€€

92 Roter Veltliner Gondwana 2020

93 Grüner Veltliner * Mitterstockstall Ried Schlossberg 1ÖTW 2021
12,5 Vol.-%, cork, large wooden barrel, €€€€

92 Grüner Veltliner Mitterstockstall Ried Schlossberg 1ÖTW 2020

93 Grüner Veltliner Ried Schlossberg 1ÖTW 2019

92 Grüner Veltliner * Zaussenberg Ried Himmelreich 2022
13 Vol.-%, screwcap, steel tank, €€

91 Grüner Veltliner * Zaußenberg Ried Himmelreich 2021

92 Grüner Veltliner Ried Himmelreich 2020

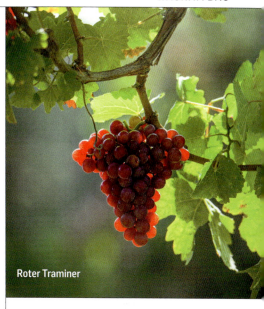

Roter Traminer

91 Grüner Veltliner * Sandstein 2021

90 Grüner Veltliner Sandstein 2019

91 Grüner Veltliner Sandstein 2018

93 Traminer * Große Reserve 2021
13,5 Vol.-%, cork, small wooden barrel, €€€€

92 Roter Traminer Wagram Große Reserve 2020

93 Roter Traminer Wagram Große Reserve 2019

92 Roter Traminer Tertiär T. 2021
13 Vol.-%, cork, small wooden barrel, €€€€ ◐

92 Roter Traminer Tertiär T. 2020

92 Roter Traminer Tertiär T. 2019

93 Chardonnay * Große Reserve 2021
13,5 Vol.-%, cork, small wooden barrel, €€€€

93 Chardonnay Wagram Große Reserve 2020

92 Chardonnay Wagram Große Reserve 2019

93 Sauvignon Blanc Tertiär S. 2020

93 Weißburgunder Wagram Große Reserve 2019

92 Riesling Schaf-Berg-Ei 2021

* Wagram DAC

NIEDERÖSTERREICH/LOWER AUSTRIA

Karin and Herbert Groiß

BIOWEINGUT GROISS
3701 Kleinwiesendorf
Kleinwiesendorf 24
T: +43 (2955) 70 234
office@weingutgroiss.at
weingutgroiss.at/de/

Winemaker: Herbert Groiß
Contact: Karin and Herbert Groiß
Production: 120,000 bottles
5 % sparkling, 70 % white, 25 % red,
15+13 hectares
Distribution partners: DE, USA

BIOWEINGUT GROISS
ORGANIC

Karin and Herbert Groiß are passionate about their work - for the greater good and the sheer joy of it. They work in close harmony with nature, adapting to its needs, embracing its strengths and channelling these energies into their wine.

They are now the third generation to run the winery and have long been organic winemakers at heart, officially since 2019. They farm their vineyards organically because production methods are paramount. They support the natural forces to ensure the vines remain strong and healthy. Plants, organisms, generations of accumulated know-how and the winemaker's touch: All this creates a greater good, hence their motto: "Life is beautiful and we are in the very midst of it".

91 Grüner Veltliner * Ried Steinberg Alte Reben 2021
13 Vol.-%, screwcap, steel tank, €€ B V
Medium yellow green, silver reflections. Candied orange peel, some mango and blossom honey, a hint of guava. Juicy, elegant, fine spice, ripe yellow fruit, well-integrated acidity, mineral, approachable.

90 Grüner Veltliner * Großweikersdorf Ried Steinberg 2022
13 Vol.-%, screwcap, steel tank, €€ B V

91 Riesling * 2022
13 Vol.-%, screwcap, steel tank, €€ B V

90 Roter Veltliner * 2022
13,5 Vol.-%, screwcap, steel tank, €€ B V

89 Chardonnay * 2022
13,5 Vol.-%, screwcap, steel tank, €€ B V

89 Cabernet Sauvignon / Merlot Cuvée 2020 CS/ME
13,5 Vol.-%, screwcap, partial barrique, €€ B

WEINGUT HEIDERER-MAYER

Always in harmony with nature, striving to bring the highest quality from the vine to the bottle - that is the motto of Gabriele and Helmut Mayer's family business. The classified winery of the "Wagramer Selektion" cultivates more than 30 hectares in Baumgarten am Wagram.

The south-facing Löser terraces are destined for white wines, above all for Grüner Veltliner. Fruity Chardonnays and Rieslings of finesse are also convincing with their clear structure. The special love, however, belongs to red wine, for which the grapes thrive in the suitable soils of protected valley locations. In addition to the Zweigelt and St. Laurent varieties, a Cabernet Sauvignon is also vinified. The main focus is on fruity, deep red wines with velvety tannins and beautiful colour intensity. The red wine cuvée called "Legat", matured in barrique, is meant to convey membership of the "European Wine Knighthood". The Pinot Frizzante "Esprit" completes the diverse range.

During a tasting in the cosy dining room, you not only get to know the story of the wines but also have the opportunity to discover the drinking pleasure they give and the very good price-performance ratio.

92 Roter Veltliner * Ried Steinberg 2022
13,5 Vol.-%, screwcap, steel tank/small wooden barrel, €€€€

92 Roter Veltliner * Baumgarten am Wagram Ried Steinberg 2021
Medium greenish yellow, silver reflections. Inviting bouquet, blossom honey notes and meadow herbs, soft notes of melon, a hint of quince jelly, caramel touch, blood orange zest. Juicy, good complexity, powerful, pineapple touch on the finish, well-integrated acidity, mineral, good persistency, fruity food wine.

92 Roter Veltliner Ried Steinberg 2020

(91) Grüner Veltliner * Ried Silberberg 2022
13,5 Vol.-%, screwcap, large wooden barrel, €€€

92 Grüner Veltliner * Ried Silberberg 2021

92 Grüner Veltliner Ried Silberberg 2020

90 Grüner Veltliner * 2022
12,5 Vol.-%, screwcap, steel tank, €€

90 Grüner Veltliner * 2021

91 Grüner Veltliner Wagramer Selektion 2020

WEINGUT HEIDERER-MAYER
3701 Großweikersdorf
Baumgarten am Wagram 25
T: +43 (2955) 70368
office@heiderer-mayer.at
www.heiderer-mayer.at

Winemaker: Reinhard Mayer
Contact: Stefan Mayer
Production: 5 % sparkling, 56 % white, 3 % rosé, 35 % red, 1 % sweet, 30 hectares
Fairs: Alles für den Gast Salzburg, Gast Klagenfurt, ProWein Düsseldorf
Distribution partners: BE, DE, IT, NL, PL, USA

Reinhard and Stefan Mayer

NIEDERÖSTERREICH/LOWER AUSTRIA

- 91 Chardonnay * 2022
  12,5 Vol.-%, screwcap, steel tank, €€
- 89 Chardonnay * 2021
- 89 Chardonnay Wagramer Selektion 2020

- 90 Sauvignon Blanc * 2021
- 89 Sauvignon Blanc Wagramer Selektion 2020
- 88 Sauvignon Blanc Wagramer Selektion 2018

- 89 Riesling * 2021
- 88 Riesling Wagramer Selektion 2017

- 91 Cabernet Sauvignon Barrique 2019
  14,5 Vol.-%, cork, barrique, €€€
- 89 Cabernet Sauvignon 2018
- 89 Cabernet Sauvignon Barrique 2016

- 90 Legat Barrique 2020 ZW/CS/RÖ
  13,5 Vol.-%, screwcap, barrique/used barriques, €€€
- 89 Legat Barrique 2018 ZW/CS/RÖ
- 89 Cuvée Legat Barrique 2017 ZW/CS/RÖ

- 90 Zweigelt Ried Bergthal 2020
- 89 Zweigelt Ried Bergthal 2019

WEINGUT KOLKMANN
ORGANIC

The Kolkmann winery is, in the true sense, a family winery with four generations living and working in harmony. The teamwork and unity within the family are decisive factors for the success of the family winery. The values of authenticity, trust, and reliability are reflected in the wines.

The estate cultivates 60 hectares of vineyards in Fels am Wagram. The fertile loess soil sites are among the best in the region and reflect the taste of the Wagram terroir. The Kolkmann winery is "Sustainable Austria"-certified and has been farming organically since 2021, thus consolidating its future viability for the next generation. Winemakers Horst, Gerhard and Horst Jr. Kolkmann work tirelessly to maintain the natural balance in the vineyards and create vibrant and profound wines. They passionately focus on the Grüner Veltliner and the Roter Veltliner varieties. These wines exemplify the Wagram region more than any other variety. However, the Kolkmann family also values other grape varieties and cultivates and nurtures them with the same attentiveness as the Veltliners. Because at the winery, diversity is a way of life.

The range is well structured, with the Gebietsweine (regional wines) forming the basis. The Grüner Veltliner Fruchtspiel & co offers that fruity temptation to the world of Wagram wines. With the Ortswein (village wines) produced by the Kolkmann family, one can experience the profundity of the loess sites of Fels, with the Grüner Veltliner expressing its spicy character to the full. The single vineyard wines are dominated by the superbly opulent Gruner Veltliner and Roter Veltliner from the top sites of Brunnthal and Scheiben. This is rounded off by a magnificently succulent Riesling from the Fumberg vineyard.

The wines can be sampled and purchased on-site, with a stunning view over the Wagram landscape. The spacious ambience offers a multitude of possibilities to taste all the wines with friendly, competent assistance. The personal touch is the essence of this family-run winery.

- 93 Grüner Veltliner * Ried Brunnthal Reserve 2021
  13,5 Vol.-%, cork, oak barrel, €€€€€
- 93 Grüner Veltliner Ried Brunnthal Reserve 2020
  Medium yellow, green hints, silver reflections. Delicate blossom honey on the nose, some savoury wood notes, a hint of caramel and ripe tropical fruit. Powerful on the palate with subtle savoury notes, balanced acidity, hints of vanilla and apple on the finish. A powerful food companion.
- 93 Grüner Veltliner Reserve Ried Brunnthal 2019
- 91 Grüner Veltliner * Ried Brunnthal 2022
  13,5 Vol.-%, screwcap, steel tank, €€€ Ⓑ
- 91 Grüner Veltliner * Fels am Wagram Ried Brunnthal 2021
- 91 Grüner Veltliner Ried Brunnthal 2020

© KERMER

WAGRAM DAC

WEINGUT KOLKMANN
3481 Fels am Wagram
Kremser Straße 53
T: +43 (2738) 2436
office@kolkmann.at
www.kolkmann.at

Winemaker: Daniel Schön
Contact: Horst and Gerhard Kolkmann
Production: 60 % white, 39 % red, 1 % sweet, 60 hectares
Certified: Sustainable Austria ⓔ
Fairs: ProWein Düsseldorf, VieVinum, Weintage im Museumsquartier
Distribution partners: BE, RC, DE, LT, NL, PL, RUS, CZ

Horst jr., Gerhard and Horst Kolkmann

90 Grüner Veltliner * Fels am Wagram 2022
12,5 Vol.-%, screwcap, steel tank, €€ Ⓑ

89 Grüner Veltliner * Lössmann 2021
90 Grüner Veltliner Lössmann 2020
89 Grüner Veltliner Lössmann 2019

88 Grüner Veltliner * Fruchtspiel 2022
12 Vol.-%, screwcap, steel tank, €€
89 Grüner Veltliner * Fruchtspiel 2021
88 Grüner Veltliner Fruchtspiel 2019

92 Grüner Veltliner Ried Scheiben 2019
92 Grüner Veltliner Ried Scheiben 2017

91 Grüner Veltliner Naturwerk 2020
91 Grüner Veltliner Naturwerk 2018

94 Roter Veltliner * Ried Scheiben Reserve 2021
14 Vol.-%, screwcap, oak barrel, €€€€€ Ⓑ
93 Roter Veltliner Fels am Wagram Ried Scheiben Reserve 2020

Medium green yellow, silver reflections. Fine tobacco vanilla touch, something of blossom honey, ripe tropical fruit, in addition some apricot, an inviting bouquet. Juicy, elegant, multi-faceted acid structure, savoury, delicate hints of citrus, mineral finish, good food companion with certain ageing potential.

92 Roter Veltliner Ried Scheiben Reserve 2019

92 Roter Veltliner * Ried Scheiben 2022
13 Vol.-%, screwcap, steel tank, €€ Ⓑ
91 Roter Veltliner * Fels am Wagram Ried Scheiben 2021
90 Roter Veltliner Ried Scheiben 2020

91 Weißburgunder * Fels am Wagram 2022
13,5 Vol.-%, screwcap, wooden barrel, €€€ Ⓑ
91 Weißburgunder Fels am Wagram Ried Brunnthal 2021
91 Weißburgunder Ried Brunnthal 2020

91 Riesling * Ried Fumberg 2022
13,5 Vol.-%, screwcap, steel tank, €€ Ⓑ
92 Riesling * Fels am Wagram Ried Fumberg 2021
89 Riesling Ried Fumberg 2020

90 * Burgunder vom Löss 2022 CH/WB
13,5 Vol.-%, screwcap, steel tank, €€
89 * Burgunder vom Löss 2021 CH/WB
89 Burgunder vom Löss 2020 CH/WB

90 Zweigelt Rosé Wagram 2021

90 Zweigelt * Perfektion 2021

90 Pinot Noir Reserve 2020
13,5 Vol.-%, screwcap, oak barrel, €€€€
90 Pinot Noir Reserve 2019
90 Pinot Noir Reserve 2019

91 Sämling 88 TBA 2017

WEINGUT LETH
ORGANIC

★★★★

The winery of the Leth family in Fels is located directly on the loess terraces of Wagram. Probably no other wine-growing region in Austria is so terroir-driven like Wagram. The loess significantly characterizes the wines; the Grüner Veltliner expresses superb suppleness, density, and harmony. It is, therefore, no coincidence that more than half of the impressive 52 hectares of vineyards are dedicated to this variety. Five varied Grüner Veltliners are pressed from the south-facing terraced vineyards. Outstanding among these are the two single-vineyard wines from the Brunnthal and Scheiben vineyards, which are classified as "Erste Lagen" of the Traditionsweingüter Österreich. It is not the striking primary fruit in the foreground of these wines but rather the complexity of the aromatics, fine minerality, and excellent potential for long bottle ageing. The fact that the Veltliners from the Leth Winery are among the best in the country is impressively reflected by their first-place rankings in the "Falstaff Grüner Veltliner Grand Prix" as well as in the "SALON Österreich Wein".

In addition to Grüner Veltliner, the winery focuses on the traditional Wagramer variety Roter Veltliner. A highly successful composition of supple fruit notes and succulence demonstrates the high quality potential of this increasingly popular variety, which is vinified in three styles at the Leth Winery.

Thanks to Franz Leth Jr.'s commitment, he gained experience with organic cultivation over a decade ago, and the entire winery was certified organic with the 2021 harvest. Franz Leth Jr. is also uncompromising in all matters relating to quality; despite the extensive vineyard area, harvesting is done 100 per cent by hand, the recently built new press facility has been set up according to the principles for maximum gentle processing, and the estate's top site wines are matured for at least one year in large traditional wooden barrels. The new sparkling wine range under development also focuses only on the two highest quality levels, "Sekt Austria Reserve" and "Sekt Austria Große Reserve".

94 ❂ Blanc de Noirs Sekt Austria Niederösterreich g.U. Große Reserve Brut 2018
12 Vol.-%, cork, bottle fermentation, €€€€€

93 ❂ Blanc de Noirs Sekt g.U. Große Reserve Fels am Wagram Brut 2014

93 ❂ Blanc de Noirs Grosse Reserve 2017

93 ❂ Blanc de Blancs Sekt Austria Große Reserve Niederösterreich g.U. Brut Nature 2018
12 Vol.-%, cork, bottle fermentation, €€€€

92 ❂ Roter Veltliner Brut Reserve Sekt Austria Niederösterreich g.U. 2019
12 Vol.-%, cork, bottle fermentation, €€€€

90 ❂ My Dear! Pet.Nat

94 Grüner Veltliner * Fels Ried Scheiben 1ÖTW 2021
13,5 Vol.-%, screwcap, large wooden barrel, €€€€€ Ⓑ

93 Grüner Veltliner Wagram Ried Scheiben 1ÖTW 2020
Bright medium golden yellow, silver reflections. Inviting bouquet of ripe apple fruit, delicate hints of vanilla and ripe pear, meadow herbs echo, with pineapple underpinnings. Good complexity, tightly meshed, fine tobacco savouriness, delicate honey on the finish, yellow tropical fruit on the back palate, a versatile food companion.

93 Grüner Veltliner Ried Scheiben 1ÖTW 2019

94 Grüner Veltliner * Fels Gigama Grande Reserve 2021
13,5 Vol.-%, screwcap, wooden barrel, €€€€€ Ⓑ

94 Grüner Veltliner Wagram Gigama Grande Reserve 2019

93 Grüner Veltliner Gigama Grande Reserve 2018

93 Grüner Veltliner * Fels Ried Brunnthal 1ÖTW 2021
13 Vol.-%, screwcap, large wooden barrel, €€€€ Ⓑ

92 Grüner Veltliner Wagram Ried Brunnthal 1ÖTW 2020

92 Grüner Veltliner Ried Brunnthal 1ÖTW 2019

WAGRAM DAC

WEINGUT LETH
3481 Fels am Wagram
Kirchengasse 6
T: +43 (2738) 2240
office@weingut-leth.at
www.weingut-leth.at

Winemaker: Franz Leth jr.
Contact: Franz Leth, Franz Leth jr.
Production: 1 % sparkling,
80 % white, 1 % rosé, 18 % red,
52 hectares
Certified: Sustainable Austria ⓔ
Fairs: Austrian Tasting London, ÖGW Zürich, Prodexpo Moskau, ProWein Düsseldorf, VieVinum, Vinexpo
Distribution partners: BE, BG, RC, DK, DE, EST, FIN, UK, HK, IT, JP, CDN, LV, LT, LU, NL, NO, PL, RUS, SE, CH, CZ, HU, USA

Karin and Franz Leth

92 Grüner Veltliner * Fels
 Ried Schafflerberg 2022
12,5 Vol.-%, screwcap, large wooden barrel, €€€ Ⓑ
91 Grüner Veltliner * Ried Schafflerberg 2021
91 Grüner Veltliner Ried Schafflerberg 2020

91 Grüner Veltliner * Fels
 Ried Steinagrund 2022
12,5 Vol.-%, screwcap, steel tank Ⓑ
91 Grüner Veltliner * Ried Steinagrund 2021
91 Grüner Veltliner Ried Steinagrund 2020

93 Roter Veltliner * Fels
 Ried Scheiben 1ÖTW 2021
13,5 Vol.-%, screwcap, large wooden barrel, €€€€ Ⓑ
93 Roter Veltliner Wagram
 Ried Scheiben 1ÖTW 2020
Bright golden yellow, silver reflections. Delicate notes of pear and marshmallow, a hint of candied pineapple, hints of clementine. Juicy, tightly meshed, lively acid structure, nutty, fine oak savouriness, mango notes on the finish, safe certain ageing potential.
94 Roter Veltliner Ried Scheiben 2019

92 Roter Veltliner * Ried Fumberg 2021
92 Roter Veltliner Ried Fumberg 2020

93 Weißburgunder * Fels 2021
93 Weißburgunder Fels Reserve 2020
92 Weißburgunder Reserve 2017

93 Riesling * Fels Ried Schillingsberg 2022
13 Vol.-%, screwcap, large wooden barrel, €€€€ Ⓑ
92 Riesling * Ried Schillingsberg 2021
92 Riesling Ried Schillingsberg 2020

90 Riesling * Fels Ried Brunnthal 1ÖTW 2021
13 Vol.-%, screwcap, wooden barrel, €€€ Ⓑ
93 Riesling Wagram Ried Brunnthal
 1ÖTW 2020
93 Riesling Ried Brunnthal 1ÖTW 2019

93 Chardonnay * Fels Grande Reserve 2021
13,5 Vol.-%, cork,screwcap, used barriques, €€€€ Ⓑ
92 Chardonnay Wagram Fels
 Grande Reserve 2020
93 Chardonnay Fels Grande Reserve 2019

92 Simply Wow! 200 United 2020
92 Simply Wow! 200 United 2019
93 Simply Wow! 200 United 2018

93 Blauer Zweigelt Gigama
 Grande Reserve 2018
93 Blauer Zweigelt Gigama
 Grande Reserve 2017

92 Pinot Noir Reserve 2020
91 Pinot Noir Reserve 2019
92 Pinot Noir Reserve 2018

93 Zweigelt Gigama Grande Reserve 2020
92 Zweigelt Gigama Grande Reserve 2019

* Wagram DAC

NIEDERÖSTERREICH/LOWER AUSTRIA

★★★★★
WEINGUT BERNHARD OTT
ORGANIC

If you want terroir, which fundamentally shapes the wine and its taste, you have to do without human intervention. This is above all a matter of trust: in its own unique potential and in the fact that nature can also develop its own power, if you just let it. Bernhard Ott is convinced of this theory. By switching to biodynamics in 2006, the vintner from Wagram has fully adapted to the rhythm of nature: uncompromising and open to what the respective vintage has in store for him.

Since Bernhard Ott took over his parents' winery in the early 1990's, he has almost exclusively focused on Grüner Veltliner. The deep loess sediment in Wagram and the Kamptal sites is particularly good for this particular grape variety. The cultivation of the vineyards is farmed according to the principles of biodynamics, much is done by hand: the harvest, the biodynamic preparations and the production of organic compost. The ecosystem functions as a whole, gentle soil cultivation with light machinery and spontaneous fermentation by yeasts naturally vivid in the vineyards. Much of the way Bernhard Ott makes his wine today is reminiscent of his ancestors. In the cellar, he has long used hand-operated grape mills and a basket press and macerates the grapes with stems. Bernard Ott uses closed pneumatic presses. The juice is fermented by natural yeasts without temperature control in either stainless steel tanks or Stockinger fuder barrels. They are Ott's greatest homage to tradition, which he carries into the future with respect for the past, but with the knowledge of today. For individual wines, which stand more than ever for uncompromising quality and an unmistakable taste.

Weingut Ott is a member of respekt-BIODYN and the Austrian Traditional Wine Growers Association as well as a partner of the JRE Jeunes Restaurateurs Austria.

98 Grüner Veltliner * Feuersbrunn
Ried Rosenberg 1ÖTW 2021
13 Vol.-%, screwcap, large wooden barrel, €€€€€€ Ⓑ

96 Grüner Veltliner Wagram Feuersbrunn
Ried Rosenberg 1ÖTW 2019
Medium greenish yellow, silver glints. Candied orange zest, Golden Delicious apples, and a dash of honeydew melon. A

Barrel cellar at the Ott winery

WEINGUT BERNHARD OTT
3483 Feuersbrunn
Neufang 36
T: +43 (2738) 2257
bernhard@ott.at
www.ott.at

Winemaker: Günter Weisböck
Contact: Bernhard Ott
Production: 100 % white
Fairs: ProWein Düsseldorf, VieVinum
Distribution partners: BDS

multifaceted, fruity bouquet. Tightly woven, salty, complex, and powerful, well-integrated acidity, mineral finish with resonating yellow tropical fruit nuances, and persistence. A savoury food accompaniment with ageing potential.

95 Grüner Veltliner Ried Rosenberg 1ÖTW Feuersbrunn 2018

96 Grüner Veltliner * Feuersbrunn Ried Spiegel 1ÖTW 2021
13 Vol.-%, screwcap, large wooden barrel, €€€€€ Ⓑ

94 Grüner Veltliner Wagram Feuersbrunn Ried Spiegel 1ÖTW 2019
Medium greenish yellow, silver reflections. Ripe tropical fruit, delicate mango and pineapple, a touch of honey blossom, candied orange zest, floral touch. Complex, juicy, pronounced in fruit of yellow tropical fruit and salted caramel, well-integrated acidic structure, dark minerality on the finish, safe development certain ageing potential.

94 Grüner Veltliner Ried Spiegel 1ÖTW Feuersbrunn 2018

95 Grüner Veltliner * Feuersbrunn Ried Kirchthal 2021
12,5 Vol.-%, screwcap, large wooden barrel, €€€€ Ⓑ

94 Grüner Veltliner Wagram Feuersbrunn Ried Kirchthal Edition JRE 2019
Medium greenish yellow, silver reflections. Delicate apricot notes, some apple fruit, a hint of orange zest, honey blossom, tobacco. Juicy, elegant, well-integrated acid structure, delicate peach, mineral-salty, fine savoury finish, multi-faceted food companion.

93 Grüner Veltliner Ried Feuersbrunner Kirchthal Edition JRE 2017

94 Grüner Veltliner * Feuersbrunn Ried Brenner 2021
13 Vol.-%, screwcap, large wooden barrel, €€€€€ Ⓑ

94 Grüner Veltliner * Gösing Ried Gmirk 2021
13 Vol.-%, screwcap, large wooden barrel, €€€€€ Ⓑ

96 Grüner Veltliner Kamptal DAC Engabrunn Ried Stein 1ÖTW 2021
13 Vol.-%, screwcap, large wooden barrel, €€€€€€ Ⓑ

93 Grüner Veltliner Kamptal DAC Ried Stein 1ÖTW 2020

95 Grüner Veltliner Kamptal DAC Engabrunn Ried Stein 1ÖTW 2019

95 Grüner Veltliner Tausend Rosen® 2018

93 Grüner Veltliner DER OTT® 2019
92 Grüner Veltliner Der Ott® Feuersbrunn 2018

92 Grüner Veltliner Fass 4® 2020
91 Grüner Veltliner Fass 4® 2019
92 Grüner Veltliner Fass 4® Wagram – »Edition 30 Jahre« 2018

★ ★
BIO WEINGUT URBANIHOF FAMILIE PASCHINGER
ORGANIC

The Urbanihof winery in Fels am Wagram, where tradition meets modernity, is run by Sonja and Franz Paschinger, the eleventh generation of the Paschinger family. Jakob and Lisa Paschinger are the "next generation", meaning that the parents are committed to quality and sustainability on a daily basis in order to pass on good practices to their children. This is reflected in the certified conversion to organic viticulture from 2016.

A careful approach to nature and vinification ensures expressive, delicious wines.

92 Grüner Veltliner * Ried Dorner 1598 2021
13,5 Vol.-%, screwcap, small wooden barrel, €€€€ Ⓑ

92 Grüner Veltliner Fels Ried Dorner »1598« 2020
Bright yellow in colour with green reflections. On the nose, aromas of pineapple and papaya are underpinned by blossom honey, subtle meadow herbs, nuances of tobacco and salted caramel. The palate is juicy and powerful with subtle vanilla and notes of yellow tropical fruit on the finish with a nutty aftertaste. Already well developed this is a good food wine.

91 Grüner Veltliner Ried Dorner »1598« 2019

NIEDERÖSTERREICH/LOWER AUSTRIA

BIO WEINGUT URBANIHOF – FAMILIE PASCHINGER
3481 Fels am Wagram
St.-Urban-Straße 3
T: +43 (2738) 234412
weingut@urbanihof.at
www.urbanihof.at

Winemaker/Contact:
Dipl.-HLFL-Ing. Franz Paschinger
Production: 80 % white, 20 % red, 40 hectares
Fairs: ProWein Düsseldorf, VieVinum
Distribution partners: BE, DK, DE, LU, NL, RUS, SE, CH

93 Grüner Veltliner Ried Dorner Grande Reserve 2020
13 Vol.-%, cork, barrique, €€€€ Ⓑ
92 Grüner Veltliner Ried Dorner Grande Reserve 2018
93 Grüner Veltliner Ried Dorner Grande Reserve 2017

91 Grüner Veltliner Ried Brunnthal Wagramer Selektion 2020
12,5 Vol.-%, screwcap, steel tank, €€ Ⓑ
90 Grüner Veltliner Ried Brunnthal Wagramer Selektion 2019
90 Grüner Veltliner Wagramer Selektion 2018

92 Riesling * Fels 2022
13 Vol.-%, screwcap, steel tank, €€€ Ⓑ
91 Riesling * Fels 2021

91 Roter Veltliner * Fels 2021
13,5 Vol.-%, screwcap, small wooden barrel, €€€ Ⓑ

90 Grüner Veltliner * 4U 2022
12,5 Vol.-%, screwcap, steel tank, €€ Ⓑ
90 Grüner Veltliner * 4U 2021
89 Grüner Veltliner 4U 2020

91 Roter Veltliner Ried Dorner 2020
90 Roter Veltliner Ried Dorner 2019
90 Roter Veltliner Ried Dorner 2018

WEINHOF
ANTON UND ELFRIEDE WALDSCHÜTZ

What nature started is continued and perfected with the utmost care at the Waldschütz winery. In doing so, the family relies on 150 years of wine-growing knowledge and a keen instinct. The over 18 hectares of vineyards are on predominantly sunny slopes in the renowned Wagram and Kamptal wine regions. Fruity, elegant wines are produced on primary rock, sandy loam, loess-gravel and deep loam-loess soils. The vineyards are managed with great care to ensure that the vines are well cared for and that the soil remains healthy and vibrant.
Although each vintage has its own characteristics, the Waldschütz family's wine style remains unmistakable. The single-varietal wines of the ‚Hof‘, ‚Gebiet‘ and ‚Ort‘ lines are classically vinified and develop in a particularly fine and distinctive manner. The wines with vineyard site names such as Brunnthal, Anzenthal and Goldberg, with their straightforward style and elegant fruit, do particular credit to their origins. The "Winzer" series shows the passion with which the work is done here.
The family also runs their own wine tavern in Obernholz in the Kamptal, where the wines are served surrounded by vines with local dishes and homemade pastries. The best way to taste and purchase wines is by telephone appointment at the Sachsendorf am Wagram winery and at the TOP-Heurigen in Obernholz.

© Leonhard Hilzensauer

WAGRAM DAC

WEINHOF ANTON UND ELFRIEDE WALDSCHÜTZ
3474 Sachsendorf, Sachsendorf 17
T: +43 (664) 3874076
wein@waldschuetz.at
www.waldschuetz.at
Winemaker: Ralph Waldschütz
Contact: Anton and Elfriede Waldschütz
Production: 1 % sparkling, 70 % white, 7 % rosé, 21 % red, 1 % sweet, 18+10 hectares
Certified: Sustainable Austria
Fairs: Austrian Tasting London, Igeho Basel, ProWein Düsseldorf, London Wine Fair, VieVinum, Vinobile Feldkirch, DAC-Presentations
Distribution partners: AUS, BE, BG, DE, FR, UK, IRL, IT, JP, LU, NZ, NL, PL, CH, SK, CZ, HU

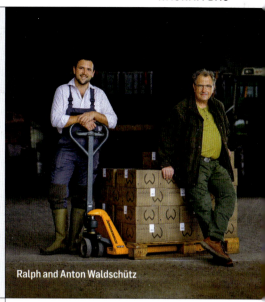

Ralph and Anton Waldschütz

93 Riesling * Fels am Wagram Ried Anzenthal 2021
14 Vol.-%, screwcap, large wooden barrel, €€€€

93 Riesling Fels am Wagram Ried Anzenthal 2020
Medium green yellow, silver reflections. Blossom honey, some greengage plum, apricot fruit, underlaid with lime zest and a hint of papaya. Complex, dark mineral, juicy, multifaceted acid structure, ripe peach notes on the finish, spicy aftertaste, sticks well, secure certain ageing potential.

93 Riesling Ried Anzenthal 2019

91 Riesling Kamptal DAC Strass im Strassertal 2022
12,5 Vol.-%, screwcap, steel tank, €€

91 Riesling Kamptal DAC Strass im Strassertal 2021

90 Riesling Kamptal DAC Strass im Strassertal 2020

95 Grüner Veltliner * Fels am Wagram Ried Scheiben 1ÖTW 2021
14,5 Vol.-%, cork, partial barrique, €€€€€

93 Grüner Veltliner * Fels am Wagram Ried Brunnthal 1ÖTW 2021
14 Vol.-%, cork, partial barrique, €€€€€

92 Grüner Veltliner Fels am Wagram Ried Brunnthal 1ÖTW 2020
Medium greenish yellow in colour with silver reflections. On the nose, aromas of subtle yellow tropical fruits underlaid with blossom honey, a touch of caramel, some pineapple and a dark minerality. The palate is juicy and powerful with well-integrated acidity, finely of vanilla with honeydew melon on the lengthy finish. The wine is already showing signs of development.

92 Grüner Veltliner Ried Brunnthal 1ÖTW 2019

92 Grüner Veltliner * Fels am Wagram 2022
13,5 Vol.-%, screwcap, large wooden barrel, €€€

91 Grüner Veltliner * Fels 2021

90 Grüner Veltliner Fels am Wagram 2020

(92) Roter Veltliner * Gösing Ried Goldberg 2022
13,5 Vol.-%, screwcap, partial barrique, €€€€

92 Roter Veltliner * Gösing Ried Goldberg 2021

91 Roter Veltliner Ried Goldberg 2020

90 Roter Veltliner * von den Wagramer Terrassen 2022
13 Vol.-%, screwcap, steel tank, €€

91 Roter Veltliner * von den Wagramer Terrassen 2021

90 Roter Veltliner von den Wagramer Terrassen 2020

93 Grüner Veltliner Eiswein Ried Hammergraben 2016

* Wagram DAC

NIEDERÖSTERREICH/ LOWER AUSTRIA

WEINVIERTEL
— DAC —

Castle ruins Falkenstein near the Czech border in the north of the Weinviertel

The windmill in Retz is a historic landmark and a symbol of the town's agricultural past

ROMANTIC CELLAR ALLEYS AND PEPPERY GRÜNER VELTLINER

The Weinviertel is an open, inviting and versatile region. Vineyards on gentle rolling hills and cornfields billowing in the wind lie side by side. Extraordinary historic landmarks and gorgeous rows of cellars dot the bucolic landscape.

Nearly half of the region's 13,911 vineyard hectares are planted with the key to its success: Grüner Veltliner, known here in its typical regional style as "Weinviertel DAC". This vast wine region sprawls from the Danube River in the south to the Czech border in the north, and from Manhartsberg in the west to the border of Slovakia in the east.

With 8500 vineyard hectares, Grüner Veltliner is the regional darling that excels with pronounced peppery-fruity bouquet and crisp, refreshing acidity. This specific character profile inspired Austria's first protected geographic designation of origin (DAC), which was established in 2002. "Weinviertel DAC" thus became the pioneer for Austria's new "wine of origin" marketing. Pinot Blanc, known locally as Weissburgunder, thrives alongside Grüner Veltliner in the area surrounding the wine village of Wolkersdorf. Riesling is at home on the slopes of Bisamberg. In Mannersdorf an der March, optimal conditions prevail for Riesling, Traminer and Burgundian varieties, thanks to the influence of the warm Pannonian climate. The winemakers in the northeastern part of the Weinviertel, particularly around Poysdorf, produce mainly Welschriesling in addition to the local hero "GV". Falkenstein,

NIEDERÖSTERREICH/LOWER AUSTRIA **WEINVIERTEL DAC**

on the northern border of the region, focusses on fruit-driven white wines.

Between Retz and Röschitz, in western Weinviertel, Grüner Veltliner and Riesling yield wines of exquisite mineral finesse and a deep spiciness. Due to its dry climate, the red wine enclave of Haugsdorf is an ideal location for rich, fruity Zweigelt.

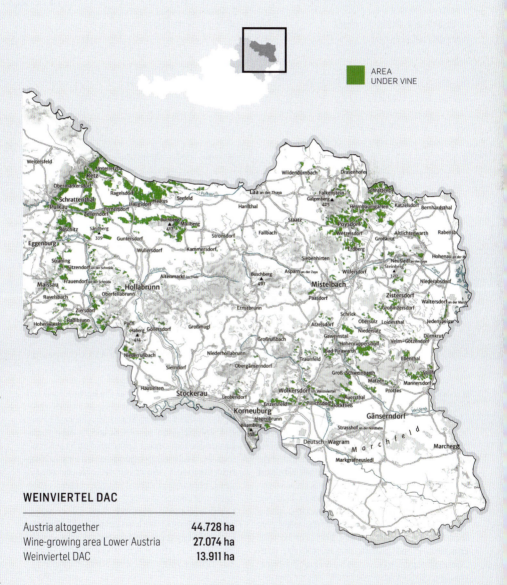

WEINVIERTEL DAC

Austria altogether	44.728 ha
Wine-growing area Lower Austria	27.074 ha
Weinviertel DAC	13.911 ha

NIEDERÖSTERREICH/LOWER AUSTRIA

SELECTED WINERIES

Dürnberg, Falkenstein
Weingut R. & A. Pfaffl, Stetten
Weingut Zull, Schrattenthal

BIO Weingut Gruber Röschitz, Röschitz
Weingut Hagn, Mailberg
Graf Hardegg, Seefeld-Kadolz
Weingut Jordan, Pulkau
Hofkellerei des Fürsten von Liechtenstein, Wilfersdorf

Weingut Wolfgang Seher, Platt
Weingut Sutter, Hohenwarth

Weingut Hirtl, Poysdorf
Weingut Pesau, Falkenstein
Bio-Weingut Schwarz, Schrattenberg
Weingut Zens, Mailberg

—

Weingut Doktor Wunderer, Straning

WEINGUT DOKTOR WUNDERER

Weingut Doktor Wunderer offers a glimpse into the future - and a bright, inspiring, and a responsible one at that. Located in one of the coolest regions of Austria - in the northern Weinviertel and directly bordering the rugged Waldviertel to the west - it takes advantage of the climatic variation and creates wines here that are driven by the freshness and mineral tensity for which Austria wines have become so renowned. Dr. Gerald Wunderer, a doctor by profession, has made his family's dream come true and, together with his partner Matthias Lobner, has developed around ten hectares of vineyards into a sophisticated and sustainable wine project. In this cool region, Sauvignon Blanc and Grüner Veltliner thrive on the primary rock and loess soils to mature into the most exquisite aromas, without ever becoming heavy or overpowering. Winemaker Bernd Karaus creates a fragrant cuvée that, despite its lithe character, boasts impressive complexity and purity, thus raising the term "easy-drinking" to a whole new level. Also fascinating are the Grüner Veltliner single-vineyard site wines, which are characterised by freshness and depth simultaneously and thus radiate a unique appeal. In general, ‚attraction' is an important element at the Doktor Wunderer winery. A special bottle shape was lovingly chosen for the elegant yet fresh style of the reserve wines - and above all a label that reflects the family's medical background with an unmistakable nod towards this: The senses for pleasure and desire as well as the vital physical and emotional instincts are depicted in a pastel blue torso. This refers to the eternal interplay between the cultivated pleasure of wine and the harmonious sensuality of man. Who could know more about these essential interactions than a doctor? From this holistic point of view, it is also very important to the team at the Doktor Wunderer winery that the wines are primarily served as accompaniments to food, which in turn leads to a harmonious ensemble. Incidentally, the winery is managed in accordance with the principles of organic farming (currently in conversion). The construction of a winery with a sustainable concept is currently being planned.

92 Grüner Veltliner ** Ried Steinperz 2021

(91) Grüner Veltliner * Straning 2022
12,5 Vol.-%, screwcap, steel tank, €€€ Ⓑ Ⓥ

WEINVIERTEL DAC

WEINGUT DOKTOR WUNDERER
3722 Straning
Straning 62
T: +43 (2984) 49901
office@doktorwunderer.at
doktorwunderer.at

Winemaker: Bernd Karnaus
Contact: Dr. Gerald Wunderer
Production: 26,667 bottles
100 % white, 4.2 hectares

Dr. Gerald Wunderer and Bernd Klammer

91 Grüner Veltliner * Straning 2021
Light yellow-green with silver reflections. Discreet tropical fruit, a little blossom honey and papaya underlaid with notes of orange zest and hints of cardamom. Light-footed and elegant with apple notes on the finish, finely spiced aftertaste, filigree back taste; a good food companion.

(93) Grüner Veltliner Corpus delicati 2020
14 Vol.-%, cork, steel tank/500-l-barrel, €€€€€

(92) Grüner Veltliner Arena 2022
13,5 Vol.-%, screwcap, wooden barrel, €€€€€ ⓑ ⓘ ⓥ

90 Grüner Veltliner Animus 2022
11,5 Vol.-%, screwcap, steel tank, €€ ⓑ ⓥ

90 Grüner Veltliner Animus 2021

90 Grüner Veltliner Spiritus vitae II 2021
12 Vol.-%, screwcap, used barriques, €€€€

91 Pride 2022 GV/GM/SB/MT
12 Vol.-%, screwcap, steel tank, €€€ ⓑ ⓥ

89 Anima Cuvée 2021 GV/MT/SB

DÜRNBERG

If you are in search of - in the finest sense of the term - an absolutely quintessential representative of the Weinviertel, you will undoubtedly come across Weingut Dürnberg, whose wines embody all the virtues that discerning wine lovers all over the world associate with Austrian wine per se: crystal-clear fruit, with a focus on freshness and elegance. A good half of the vineyards are planted with Grüner Veltliner, which finds the optimal conditions in this region. Another focus is on the Pinot varieties, which can ripen to perfection until the end of October on the particularly lime-rich, barren elevations.

Christoph Körner started out with an inherited small vineyard and the vision of building a leading winery with an international profile in the tradition-steeped Falkenstein. Equipped with a good instinct for the best sites, the areas were steadily expanded, with a focus on taking over well-tended old vineyards. As production took up more and more of their time, it eventually became necessary to set up a professional sales department. This is where

NIEDERÖSTERREICH/LOWER AUSTRIA

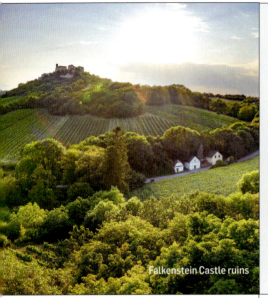
Falkenstein Castle ruins

DÜRNBERG

2162 Falkenstein
Neuer Weg 284
T: +43 (2554) 85355
weingut@duernberg.at
www.duernberg.at

Winemaker: Michael Preyer
Contact: Matthias Marchesani
Production: 4 % sparkling, 82 % white, 8 % rosé, 5 % red, 1 % sweet, 60 hectares
Certified: Sustainable Austria
Fairs: Austrian Tasting London, ProWein Düsseldorf, DAC-Presentations
Distribution partners: AUS, BE, DK, DE, EST, IL, IT, JP, CDN, LV, MT, NL, PL, RO, RUS, SE, CH, CZ, USA

Matthias Marchesani became involved, who contributed with a great deal of passion and has been a tireless ambassador for Dürnberg's wines ever since. For the next necessary step towards modernisation and quality assurance, Georg Klein came on board, contributing valuable know-how in terms of organisation and enabling the necessary expansion of the winery in 2017 by means of crowd-funding. Michael Preyer has brought young momentum to the winery since the beginning of 2020 and has recently been responsible for wines and vineyards as partner and cellar master. He steers the winery with a lot of creativity, supported by Christoph Körner's experience.
The quartet Klein/Marchesani/Preyer/Körner is very dynamically on the move throughout the wine world has the future of one of Austria's most promising wineries firmly in its hands and manages it both professionally and with friendly composure.

94 Grüner Veltliner * Falkenstein Ried Rabenstein Endlos 2021
13,5 Vol.-%, cork, 500-l-barrel, €€€€€

93 Grüner Veltliner * Falkenstein Ried Rabenstein 2021
13,5 Vol.-%, cork, large wooden barrel, €€€€€

93 Grüner Veltliner ** Ried Rabenstein 2020
Medium yellow-green, silver reflections. Fine tobacco oak savouriness, something of meadow herbs, pineapple and anise notes, multi-faceted bouquet. Good complexity, juicy, tightly meshed, fine acid structure, mineral, already easy to drink, a versatile food companion.

93 ** Ried Rabenstein 2019

91 Grüner Veltliner * Falkenstein Tradition 2022
13 Vol.-%, screwcap, partial barrique, €€€€

92 Grüner Veltliner ** Tradition 2021
91 Grüner Veltliner ** Tradition 2020

91 Grüner Veltliner * Alte Reben 2022
12,5 Vol.-%, screwcap, steel tank, €€€

91 Grüner Veltliner * Alte Reben 2021
92 Grüner Veltliner * Alte Reben 2020

90 Grüner Veltliner * Falkenstein 2022
12,5 Vol.-%, screwcap, steel tank, €€

90 Grüner Veltliner * Falkenstein 2021
90 Grüner Veltliner * Falkenstein 2020

94 Grüner Veltliner Endlos Grande Reserve 2020
94 Grüner Veltliner Endlos Grande Reserve 2019
94 Grüner Veltliner Endlos Grande Reserve 2018

92 Grüner Veltliner Elementum 2020

89 Grüner Veltliner Grüner 2020

93 Grauburgunder Reserve 2021
14 Vol.-%, cork, 500-l-barrel, €€€€€

WEINVIERTEL DAC

93	Grauburgunder Reserve 2020

Medium golden yellow, copper reflections. Discreet wood spice, a bit of cardamom, a hint of red apple fruit, some camomile. Juicy, taut, tightly meshed, balanced acidity, passion fruit, long, a good food wine.

93 Grauburgunder Reserve 2019

93 Gemischter Satz Falkenstein
    Ried Kirchberg Reserve 2021

14 Vol.-%, cork, large wooden barrel, €€€€€ Ⓥ

93 Gemischter Satz Ried Kirchberg
    Reserve 2020
92 Gemischter Satz Ried Kirchberg
    Reserve 2018

91 Falkenstein Ortolan Cuvée Prestige
    Reserve 2021 CH/WB/PG

13,5 Vol.-%, cork, 500-l-barrel, €€€€€ Ⓥ

92 Ortolan Cuvée Prestige Reserve 2020
    CH/WB/PG
92 Ortolan Cuvée Prestige Reserve 2019
    CH/WB/PG

92 Traminer Elementum 2020
92 Traminer Elementum 2019

90 Riesling Falkenstein 2020
90 Riesling Falkenstein 2018
90 Riesling Falkenstein 2017

91 Weissburgunder Reserve Falkenstein 2022

13 Vol.-%, screwcap, partial barrique, €€€€ Ⓥ

92 Weißburgunder Falkenstein Reserve 2021
92 Weißburgunder Falkenstein Reserve 2020

89 Chardonnay Falkenstein 2021
89 Chardonnay Falkenstein 2020
89 Chardonnay Falkenstein 2019

(91) Falkenstein Rosé aus der Provinz 2022
     PN/ME/CS

13 Vol.-%, screwcap, 500-l-barrel, €€€€

91 Rosé aus der Provinz 2021 PN/ME/CS
92 Rosé aus der Provinz 2019 PN/ME/CS

90 Zweigelt Blanc de Noir 2021
90 Blanc de Noir Zweigelt 2020
90 Zweigelt Blanc de Noir 2019

91 Merlot Elementum 2019

91 Pinot Noir Ried Kirchberg
    Grande Reserve 2018
91 Pinot Noir Ried Kirchberg
    Grande Reserve 2017
91 Pinot Noir Ried Kirchberg Reserve 2016

93 Grüner Veltliner Eiswein 2020
93 Grüner Veltliner Eiswein 2018

★★★

BIO WEINGUT GRUBER RÖSCHITZ

ORGANIC

Together we can achieve more! We, that's Maria, Ewald and Christian, pulling together, sharing the work and pursuing a common goal: to vinify authentic wines in their home town of Röschitz.

Their grandfather already knew that on the edge of the Weinviertel, in and around Röschitz, there are the best conditions for quality-conscious viticulture. Great primary rock, granite and loess soils and a cool continental climate with little rainfall. The siblings try to convey the characteristics of these soils in their wines, be it the savoury classic Grüner Veltliner, the mineral Riesling or the cool, fruit-driven reds like Sankt Laurent and Pinot Noir. The characteristics of the soil are just as important to them as the drinking pleasure that Gruber wines should convey.

Maria, Ewald and Christian Gruber have been organic farming their many parcels of land for several years. They do this out of conviction! They give nature free rein, promote the self-healing powers of the vines and thus preserve the most valuable resource - the soil of their homeland! As a result, things have changed. The grapes ripen earlier, produce less sugar and alcohol, require less sulphur, and thus produce fresh, long-lasting and uncomplicated wines - wines that the siblings love.

The "wine spirits" that adorn their labels are the result of a consistent strategy of always responding to the ravages of time, bringing the

* Weinviertel DAC   ** Weinviertel DAC Reserve

NIEDERÖSTERREICH/LOWER AUSTRIA

Bioweingut Gruber Röschitz: New location as of January 2024

BIO WEINGUT GRUBER RÖSCHITZ
3743 Röschitz, Winzerstraße 46
T: +43 (2984) 2765
office@gruber-roeschitz.at
www.gruber-roeschitz.at
Winemaker: Ewald Gruber
Contact: Maria Wegscheider
Production: 70 % white, 30 % red
Certified: Sustainable Austria
Fairs: Austrian Tasting London, Forum Vini München, Millésime Bio, Prodexpo Moskau, ProWein Düsseldorf, London Wine Fair, The Shanghai International Wine & Spirits Expo, VieVinum, Vinexpo Bordeaux, Vinitaly, DAC-Presentations, Hong Kong International Wine & Spirits Fair
Distribution partners: BE, DK, DE, FIN, UK, IT, JP, CDN, NL, NO, PL, RUS, SE, CH, SGP, TH, CZ, USA

language of wine to the outside world and working with nature rather than against it. They are micro-organisms that provide natural pest control, break down minerals and stimulate fermentation. The organic process gives them the best possible conditions, which in turn helps the Grubers harvest healthy grapes and create distinctive wines.

92 ⊙ Blanc de Blancs Österreichischer Sekt Reserve Extra Brut 2020 CH
12,5 Vol.-%, cork, bottle fermentation, €€€€€ Ⓑ

91 ⊙ Sekt Cuvée g.U. Reserve 2018 GV/RR

92 Grüner Veltliner ** Ried Mühlberg 2021
13 Vol.-%, screwcap, large wooden barrel, €€€€ Ⓑ
92 Grüner Veltliner ** Ried Mühlberg 2020
Medium yellow, green hints, gold reflections. Subtle savoury wood aromas, a hint of vanilla and papaya with subtle bergamot and a touch of stone fruit. Medium bodied and powerful with some pear notes and honeydew melon on the finish. Already very approachable and easy to drink.
93 ** Ried Mühlberg 2019

92 Grüner Veltliner * Ried Reipersberg 2022
13 Vol.-%, screwcap, steel tank/oak barrel, €€€ Ⓑ
92 Grüner Veltliner * Ried Reipersberg 2021
92 Grüner Veltliner * Ried Reipersberg 2020

92 Grüner Veltliner * Ried Hundspoint 2022
13 Vol.-%, screwcap, steel tank, €€€ Ⓑ

92 Grüner Veltliner * Ried Hundspoint 2021
92 Grüner Veltliner * Ried Hundspoint 2020

90 Grüner Veltliner * 2021
90 Grüner Veltliner * 2020
91 Weinviertel DAC 2019

90 Grüner Veltliner * Klassik 2021
90 Grüner Veltliner * Klassik 2020
90 * Klassik 2019

93 Riesling Black Vintage 2020
12 Vol.-%, cork, steel tank, €€€€€ Ⓑ
95 Riesling Black Vintage 2019
Medium yellow-green, discreet silver reflections. Delicate honeydew melon and candied blood orange, a bit nutty, with spicy nuances underneath, multi-faceted bouquet. Juicy, good complexity, fine herbal notes, tight acidity, peach nuances on the finish, dark minerality on the aftertaste, complex food wine, with definite ageing potential.
93 Riesling Black Vintage 2016

92 Riesling Ried Königsberg 2021
12,5 Vol.-%, screwcap, steel tank, €€€ Ⓑ
92 Riesling Ried Königsberg 2020
92 Riesling Ried Königsberg 2019

91 Riesling 2021
91 Riesling 2020
90 Riesling 2019

© ROBERT HERBST

WEINVIERTEL DAC

93 Chardonnay Black Vintage 2021	90 Pinot Noir Black Vintage 2020
13 Vol.-%, cork, steel tank, €€€€€ Ⓑ	12 Vol.-%, cork, 500-l-barrel, €€€€€ Ⓑ
93 Chardonnay Black Vintage 2016	92 Pinot Noir Black Vintage 2017
91 Gelber Muskateller 2021	91 Sankt Laurent Black Vintage 2021
90 Gelber Muskateller 2019	12,5 Vol.-%, cork, 500-l-barrel, €€€€€ Ⓑ
	92 St. Laurent Black Vintage 2017
90 St. Laurent Rosé 2020	
90 St. Laurent Rosé 2019	91 St. Laurent Ried Galgenberg 2018
92 Cuvée Royale 2017 ZW/ME	

WEINGUT HAGN

The Hagn family has over 300 years of experience in viticulture. The new generation of managers, Leo and Wolfgang, have brought a breath of fresh air to the company. Sustainability and looking to the future are of particular importance to them. This is proven by the recent certification for the processing and production of organic grapes, the in-house photovoltaic system and the electric charging station for guests of the ‚Weindomizil', the Hagns' Restaurant with guest rooms and breathtaking views over the ‚Mailberg Valley'. The wines are some of the best in the Weinviertel. Every year, Weingut Hagn brings numerous awards to Mailberg for its white and red wines and the winery itself. "With our wines we want to offer an incomparable and at the same time completely enjoyable and sustainable experience. By keeping a watchful eye on future developments, we can ensure continuity," explain the cousins.

92 * Green Hunter 2019
89 Grüner Veltliner * 2022
12,5 Vol.-%, screwcap, steel tank, €€

91 Grüner Veltliner Ried Hundschupfen 2022
13 Vol.-%, screwcap, steel tank/wooden barrel, €€
91 Grüner Veltliner Ried Hundschupfen 2021
91 Grüner Veltliner Ried Hundschupfen 2020

91 Grüner Veltliner
    Ried Antlasbergen 2022
13 Vol.-%, screwcap, steel tank, €€

90 Ⓞ Blauer Zweigelt »Juwella« Sekt Rosé
     Brut NV
13 Vol.-%, cork, bottle fermentation, €€€€ Ⓑ

93 Grüner Veltliner ** Green Hunter 2021
13,5 Vol.-%, screwcap, large wooden barrel, €€€€ Ⓑ
93 Grüner Veltliner ** Green Hunter 2020
Bright yellow-green, silver reflections. Fine oak savouriness, a hint of caramel, ripe pineapple and passionfruit, inviting bouquet. Juicy, extract sweet, balanced acidity, a hint of apricot, delicate herbs and white nougat in the aftertaste, a good food companion with safe and certain ageing potential.

WEINGUT HAGN
2024 Mailberg
Hauptstraße 154
T: +43 (2943) 2256
info@hagn-weingut.at
www.hagn-weingut.at

Winemaker: Leo Hagn
Contact: Wolfgang Hagn
Production: 80 % white, 20 % red, 50 hectares
Fairs: Alles für den Gast Salzburg, VieVinum, DAC-Presentations
Distribution partners: BE, RC, DK, DE, UK, ROK, NL, PL, RUS, CH, SK, CZ, USA

* Weinviertel DAC   ** Weinviertel DAC Reserve

NIEDERÖSTERREICH/LOWER AUSTRIA

94 Grüner Veltliner Unique 2021
92 Grüner Veltliner Unique 2018

(92) Riesling Unique 2022
14 Vol.-%, DIAM, large wooden barrel, €€€€€ Ⓑ
92 Riesling Unique 2019
91 Riesling Unique 2018

90 Riesling classic 2022
13 Vol.-%, screwcap, steel tank, €€
90 Riesling classic 2021
90 Riesling classic 2020

(90) Chardonnay unique 2022
14,5 Vol.-%, DIAM, barrique, €€€€€ Ⓑ
92 Chardonnay Unique 2021
Bright yellow-green, silver reflections. Fine tobacco, a bit of passion fruit, a hint of papaya, subtle vanilla notes, orange peel. Complex, juicy, with the fine fruit sweetness of ripe peach, blossom honey, oak, well-integrated tannins, with a promising ageing potential.
91 Chardonnay Unique 2019

90 Roter Traminer Charmeur 2022
13,5 Vol.-%, screwcap, steel tank, €€
90 Roter Traminer Charmeur 2020

89 Sauvignon Blanc 2022
12,5 Vol.-%, screwcap, steel tank, €€
89 Sauvignon Blanc 2020
89 Sauvignon Blanc 2019

88 Welschriesling 2022
12 Vol.-%, screwcap, steel tank, €€

92 Cuvée Colloredo 2020 CS/ME
92 Cuvée Colloredo 2018 ME/CS

90 Cuvée Komptur 2020 PN/ME
91 Cuvée Komptur 2018 ME/PN

90 Blauer Zweigelt 2021
91 Blauer Zweigelt 2019

90 Pinot Noir 2019

★ ★ ★

GRAF HARDEGG

ORGANIC

The 30-hectare Weingut Graf Hardegg vineyard is part of the renowned Hardegg estate in the northern Weinviertel region on the Pulkau river. For the owner, Maximilian Hardegg, the creation of a high-quality ecosystem in a renaturalized cultural landscape is the focus of his endeavours. This holistic approach under the motto "gelebte Artenvielfalt (active biodiversity) is also noticeable on the estate's own vineyard. Thanks to compost from the farm's own recycling system, the barren sandy-rock soils with a high lime content are full of life and thus strengthen the vines. The vineyards are home to countless garden birds, insects and other beneficial insects - even wild bees. Wild herbs and legumes grow. The wine cellars and vineyards are located in the immediate vicinity of Seefeld Castle, the residence of the Hardegg family. The centrepiece is the baroque court cellar dating from 1640 with its impressive vaulted ceilings and branching cellar corridors, which provide information about the century-old wine-growing tradition. Due to the perfect "cellar climate", the Hofkeller is used today for the maturation of top wines and houses the in-house sparkling wine production. The pioneering spirit and dedication of Maximilian Hardegg and his team have proven their worth, as the winery with its exclusive product range has been one of the top Austrian businesses and pioneers for years. Soil, vineyard work, and climate are in harmony here. Especially the markedly continental climate with little rainfall, hot days but cool late summer nights which makes it possible to vinify wines with a lot of elegance, finesse, and a fine acid backbone.

94 ❂ Viognier V Brut Nature 2019
12 Vol.-%, cork, small wooden barrel, bottle fermentation, €€€€€ Ⓑ

92 ❂ Brut Sekt Austria Große Reserve Niederösterreich g.U. 2019 CH/PN
Deg. 12/2020, 12 Vol.-%, cork, large wooden barrel, bottle fermentation, €€€€€ Ⓑ

© R. Herbst

WEINVIERTEL DAC

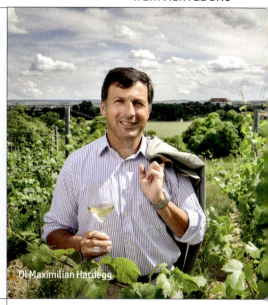

DI Maximilian Hardegg

GRAF HARDEGG
2062 Seefeld-Kadolz
Großkadolz 1
T: +43 (2943) 2203
office@guthardegg.at
www.grafhardegg.at

Winemaker: Andreas Gruber
Contact: DI Maximilian Hardegg and Andreas Gruber
Production: 65 % white, 33 % red, 2 % sweet, 30 hectares
Fairs: VieVinum
Distribution partners: DK, DE, HK, NL, CZ

92 ❂ Graf Hardegg Sekt Austria g.U. brut Große Reserve 2018 CH/PN
Medium yellow-green, silver reflections, fine mousse. Discreet apple fruit, a bit of honey blossom, herbs and quince, kumquats sound. Juicy, elegant, fine acid structure, savoury, passion fruit sounds, fine texture, mineral finish, versatile.

92 ❂ Graf Hardegg Sekt g.U. brut Große Reserve 2015 CH/PN

91 ❂ Graf Hardegg brut 2014
91 ❂ Graf Hardegg brut 2013

93 ❂ Rosé Brut Große Reserve 2019 PN/ZW
12 Vol.-%, cork, large wooden barrel, bottle fermentation, €€€€€ ❸

91 ❂ Graf Hardegg Sekt Austria g.U. rosé brut Große Reserve 2018 PN/ZW
91 ❂ Graf Hardegg Sekt g.U. rosé brut Große Reserve 2016 PN/ZW

93 Riesling Ried Steinbügel 2021
93 Riesling Ried Steinbügel 2020
92 Riesling Ried Steinbügel 2019

92 Riesling Spätlese 2019
89 Riesling Spätlese 2015

(91) Riesling vom Schloss 2022
13 Vol.-%, screwcap, large wooden barrel, €€€ ❸
91 Riesling vom Schloss 2021
92 Riesling vom Schloss 2020

93 Viognier V 2021
13,5 Vol.-%, screwcap, small wooden barrel, €€€€ ❸
93 Viognier V 2020
Pale yellow-green, silver reflections. Fine tobacco savouriness, yellow tropical fruit underlay with some nutty aromas, delicate vanilla, inviting bouquet. Juicy, good complexity, smoky nuances, honeydew melon on the finish, savoury aftertaste, complex, a powerful food companion.
93 V - Viognier 2019

92 Grüner Veltliner Ried Steinbügel 2021
92 Grüner Veltliner Ried Steinbügel 2019
92 Grüner Veltliner Ried Steinbügel 2018

(92) Grüner Veltliner vom Schloss 2022
13,5 Vol.-%, screwcap, large wooden barrel, €€ ❸
91 Grüner Veltliner vom Schloss 2021
92 Grüner Veltliner vom Schloss 2020

90 Grüner Veltliner vom Gut 2022
13 Vol.-%, screwcap, steel tank, €€ ❸
91 Grüner Veltliner vom Gut 2021
90 Grüner Veltliner vom Gut 2020

89 Grüner Veltliner Edition Girlitz 2022
12,5 Vol.-%, screwcap, steel tank, €€ ❸
89 Grüner Veltliner Edition Girlitz 2021

92 Chardonnay Ried Steinbügel 2021
13,5 Vol.-%, screwcap, small wooden barrel, €€€€ ❸
91 Chardonnay Ried Steinbügel 2015

* Weinviertel DAC   ** Weinviertel DAC Reserve

NIEDERÖSTERREICH/LOWER AUSTRIA

92 Roter Veltliner Ried Steinbügel 2021
13,5 Vol.-%, screwcap, large wooden barrel, €€€€€ Ⓑ

90 Rosé Edition Gimpel 2022 PN/ME
12,5 Vol.-%, screwcap, steel tank, €€ Ⓑ

90 Rosé Edition Gimpel 2021 PN/ME

92 Pinot Noir Ried Steinbügel 2018
92 Pinot Noir Ried Steinbügel 2017

91 Pinot Noir vom Schloss 2019
13 Vol.-%, screwcap, small wooden barrel, €€€ Ⓑ

90 Pinot Noir vom Schloss 2018
91 Pinot Noir vom Schloss 2017

88 Blauer Zweigelt Gut Hardegg 2018

93 Blauer Zweigelt Forticus 2015
93 Merlot Forticus - Likörwein 2015

WEINGUT HIRTL

Over the past few years, the name of the Hirtl winery from Poysdorf has been at the forefront of top rankings at national and international wine events. This is not only due to the consistent pursuit of quality by this traditional Lower Austrian winery, but above all due to the natural approach towards winemaking that Andrea and Martin Hirtl have maintained since taking over the business in 2001. Personal contact and exchange with customers are just as important as respect for the natural wealth of a unique wine region. The geological and climatic characteristics of the Weinviertel are combined with know-how, experience, and a great deal of intuition and transferred directly into the bottle. As a result, quality is evident throughout the range of varieties, which includes numerous award-winning examples. All in all, the Hirtl estate is synonymous with fruity, sparkling whites, legendary reds and excellent Prädikat wines that are a pleasure to drink. And, most importantly in times like these, they are not only enjoyable but also affordable.

91 Grüner Veltliner * Ried Kirchberg 2022
12,5 Vol.-%, screwcap, steel tank, €€

89 Grüner Veltliner * Ried Kirchberg 2021
91 Grüner Veltliner * Ried Kirchberg 2020

Martin and Andrea Hirtl

WEINGUT HIRTL
2170 Poysdorf
Brunngasse 72
T: +43 (2552) 2182
office@weingut-hirtl.at
www.weingut-hirtl.at

Winemaker: Martin Hirtl
Contact: Andrea Hirtl
Production: 3 % sparkling, 70 % white, 2 % rosé, 25 % red, 25 hectares
Fairs: ProWein Düsseldorf, VieVinum, Weinmesse München, DAC-Presentations
Distribution partners: BE, DK, DE, FR, UK, NL, PL, CH, SK, CZ

© MICHAEL PEIDINGER

WEINVIERTEL DAC

91 Grüner Veltliner ** 2021 13,5 Vol.-%, screwcap, steel tank, €€€	90 Grüner Veltliner Ried Bürsting 2021 90 Grüner Veltliner Ried Bürsting 2020
90 Grüner Veltliner * Ried Waldberg 2022 12,5 Vol.-%, screwcap, steel tank, €€ 91 Grüner Veltliner * Ried Waldberg 2021 Light greenish yellow. A touch of blossom honey underlaid with meadow herbs, soft notes of pineapple and red apple fruit. Medium body, fine acidity, a bit of lemon balm, apple notes also on the finish, already easy to drink. 91 Grüner Veltliner * Ried Waldberg 2020 90 * Waldberg 2019	90 Weißburgunder Exklusiv 2022 12,5 Vol.-%, screwcap, steel tank, €€ 90 Weißburgunder Exklusiv 2020 89 Riesling Exklusiv 2021 89 Riesling Exklusiv 2019 92 Merlot Reserve Edition Martin Widemann 2019 91 Merlot Reserve 2015
89 Grüner Veltliner * Franz 2022 12,5 Vol.-%, screwcap, steel tank, €€ 90 Grüner Veltliner * Franz 2021 90 Grüner Veltliner * Franz 2020	90 Merlot Exklusiv 2020 89 Merlot Exklusiv 2019
90 Grüner Veltliner Ried Bürsting 2022 12,5 Vol.-%, screwcap, steel tank, €€	89 Zweigelt Exklusiv 2021 90 Zweigelt Exklusiv 2019

WEINGUT JORDAN

Where the Bohemian Massif of the Waldviertel meets the Molasse basin of the Weinviertel, at the foothills of the Manhartsberg, lies the old wine-growing town of Pulkau. Only a stone's throw away, in the small village of Groß-Reipersdorf, is Weingut Jordan. For over 160 years, winemaking has been a tradition here and since 2010 Simone Hiller-Jordan and her partner Hannes have been running the winery with the active support of her parents.

For Simone Hiller-Jordan being a winemaker means capturing the fascination of nature and bringing the best qualities that nature allows in to the cellar. The predominant soils of primary rock as well as loess and loam, coupled with the clash of the harsh Waldviertel winds and the Pannonian climate of the Weinviertel, create wonderful conditions for her expressive wines. The Weinviertel is dominated by white grape production but the Pulkau sites, especially the Ried Haselparz, form an island of red grapes, hence the affinity for red wine at the Jordan Winery. Simone Hiller-Jordan is particularly fond of the old Austrian varieties Zweigelt and St. Laurent. Freely following the motto "wineries are not created overnight, they are made by generations to become what they are today", the young vintner uses the

WEINGUT JORDAN
3741 Pulkau
Groß-Reipersdorf 12
T: +43 (2946) 2464
office@weingut-jordan.at
www.weingut-jordan.at

Winemaker/Contact:
Ing. Simone Hiller-Jordan
Production: 50 % white, 50 % red, 12 hectares
Fairs: ProWein Düsseldorf, VieVinum, Vinobile Feldkirch, DAC-Presentations
Distribution partners: BE, DK, DE, FIN, CDN, NL, CH, CZ, USA

* Weinviertel DAC   ** Weinviertel DAC Reserve

NIEDERÖSTERREICH/LOWER AUSTRIA

knowledge of previous generations, combines it with her own experience and consciously involves nature to press wines with much love and passion.

92 ⓘ Grüner Veltliner Brut Reserve 2020
11,5 Vol.-%, cork, bottle fermentation, €€€€ Ⓥ
92 ⓘ Grüner Veltliner Brut Reserve 2019

92 ⓘ Riesling Brut Große Reserve 2016

90 ⓘ Petillant Naturel 2022
11,5 Vol.-%, crown cap, bottle fermentation, €€€€ Ⓥ

93 Grüner Veltliner ** Ried Reipersberg Alte Reben 2021
13,5 Vol.-%, cork, 500-l-barrel, €€€€ Ⓥ
92 Grüner Veltliner ** Ried Reipersberg Alte Reben 2020
92 ** Ried Reipersberg Alte Reben 2019

93 Grüner Veltliner Große Reserve Steinzeit 2021
13,5 Vol.-%, cork, granite, €€€€€ Ⓥ
93 Grüner Veltliner Reserve Steinzeit 2020
Medium yellow, green hints, silver reflections. Nuances of blossom honey, a hint of meadow herbs, the slightest touch of mango and some quince jelly. Elegant on the palate, fine acidic structure, salty-mineral notes, subtle passion fruit and a lemony finish. A versatile wine.
93 Grüner Veltliner Reserve Steinzeit 2019

90 Grüner Veltliner Simone I. Wine & Queen 2022
12,5 Vol.-%, screwcap, steel tank, €€€ Ⓥ

90 Grüner Veltliner Simone I. Wine & Queen 2021
90 Grüner Veltliner Simone I. Wine & Queen 2019

90 Crushed Chardonnay 2021
12,5 Vol.-%, cork, amphore, €€€€ ⓘ Ⓥ

90 Zweigelt Blanc de Noir 2022
89 Zweigelt Blanc de Noir 2019

92 Zweigelt 42 | Große Reserve 2018
13,5 Vol.-%, cork, barrique, €€€€ Ⓥ
93 Zweigelt Große Reserve 42 2017
Deep ruby, purple glints, faintly lighter ochre hue at the rim. Softly scented with nougat and hardwood, a hint of cloves and vanilla, underlaid with luscious damsons. Succulent, elegant, sweet texture, marked by bourbon vanilla and exhibiting harmony, silky tannins with a chocolate-nuanced finish. Already well-developed and offers versatility in its style.

92 Zweigelt Rubin Reserve 2020
13,5 Vol.-%, cork, barrique, €€€€ Ⓥ
91 Zweigelt Rubin Reserve 2019

90 Cuvée 1858 Memories & Generations 2015

HOFKELLEREI DES FÜRSTEN VON LIECHTENSTEIN

For centuries, the name of the Liechtenstein family has been inextricably linked with viticulture in the northern Weinviertel. Today, Princess Marie is involved in the Hofkellerei together with the innovative and experienced team led by Stefan Tscheppe and Josef Stumvoll.

The wines of the Hofkellerei are closely linked to the distinctive vineyards such as Karlsberg and Johannesbergen and the family's long-standing heritage. Freshness, precision, authenticity and inspiration are the hallmarks of these superb wines. In the centuries-old vaulted cellars, Grüner Veltliner, Riesling, Zweigelt and Merlot mature in small batches to produce wines of fine structure, distinctive vintage characteristics and expressiveness. At the heart of the production, in Wilfersdorf, visitors are guided through the new press house to the cellar vaults, where the vintages from 1957 onwards are stored in the Vinothek. In the modern reception room, wines can be savoured and paired with local delicacies.

WEINVIERTEL DAC

HOFKELLEREI DES FÜRSTEN VON LIECHTENSTEIN
2193 Wilfersdorf
Brünnerstraße 8
T: +43 (2573) 221927
c.fritz@hofkellerei.at
www.hofkellerei.com

Winemaker: Josef Stumvoll
Contact: Stefan Tscheppe
Production: 160,000 bottles
5 % sparkling, 60 % white, 5 % rosé, 30 % red, 35 hectares
Fairs: ProWein Düsseldorf, VieVinum, Vinexpo, DAC-Presentations
Distribution partners: RC, DE, UK, HK, JP, CH, SGP, CZ, USA

Sommelière Princess Marie and Winery Manager Stefan Tscheppe

In the newly designed cellars of the Gartenpalais, the wine shop and bar in Vienna's 9th district, Fürstengasse, set in the magnificent park of the Gartenpalais, the wines are offered for tasting and sale, together with local specialities.

93 ⊙ F.L. Premier Brut 2021 RR/GV
12,5 Vol.-%, cork, bottle fermentation, €€€€
90 ⊙ F.L. Premier Brut 2020 RR/GV

90 Grüner Veltliner * 2019

92 Grüner Veltliner Ried Karlsberg Reserve 2021
12,5 Vol.-%, screwcap, tonneaux barrel, €€€€
92 Grüner Veltliner Ried Karlsberg 2020
92 Grüner Veltliner Reserve Ried Karlsberg 2019

93 Riesling Ried Karlsberg Privat 2021
13 Vol.-%, cork, tonneaux barrel, €€€€
93 Riesling Ried Karlsberg Privat 2020
Medium yellow-green, silver reflections. Floral touch, notes of apricot, underlaid with lime and blossom honey, a touch of meadow herbs. Juicy, elegant, fine acid structure, salty, light-bodied, apple on the finish, a good food companion with maturity and certain ageing potential.
92 Riesling Reserve Ried Karlsberg Privat 2019

91 Riesling Ried Karlsberg 2020

91 Riesling Reserve Ried Karlsberg 2019
91 Riesling Ried Karlsberg Reserve 2017

90 Riesling 2019
90 Riesling 2018

92 Chardonnay Leithaberg DAC 2021
13,5 Vol.-%, cork, tonneaux barrel, €€€€€

91 Herrnbaumgarten 2021 RR/GV
12 Vol.-%, screwcap, steel tank/tonneaux barrel, €€€
92 Herrnbaumgarten Cuvée 2020 RR/GV
Bright golden yellow with silver reflections. Delicate aromas of yellow tropical fruit, notes of meadow herbs, candied tangerine zest and background hints of lychee. Juicy and elegant on the palate, well integrated acidic structure and subtle apple on the finish. A good food companion.

92 Blaufränkisch Leithaberg DAC 2020
13 Vol.-%, cork, tonneaux barrel, €€€€€
92 Blaufränkisch Leithaberg DAC 2019

91 Zweigelt Profundo 2019
91 Zweigelt Profundo 2017
90 Zweigelt Profundo 2016

91 Merlot Ried Karlsberg Anberola 2017
91 Merlot Anberola 2016

92 Grüner Veltliner Eiswein 2018

---

* Weinviertel DAC   ** Weinviertel DAC Reserve

NIEDERÖSTERREICH/LOWER AUSTRIA

WEINGUT PESAU
ORGANIC

Brothers Andreas and Georg Pesau run the family winery which has a tradition dating back more than 300 years. The Pesau name was first mentioned in connection with wine and the town of Falkenstein over 400 years ago. The family's vineyards are located on the hills surrounding the historic town. These hills offers wonderful geological and natural conditions for viticulture: unique soils are characterised by shell limestone which formed about 17 million years ago and have been the basis for mineral wines for centuries. The forested chain of hills around Falkenstein offers the vineyards protection from harsh north and west winds, they also create a balanced microclimate that helps ripen the grapes. In the vineyard, the brothers strive for a sustainable, stable and ecological balance. In order to achieve this, crop cover is managed according to ecological principles allowing beneficial insects to thrive. In the cellar, feeling, experience and time come to the fore. The character of the wines reflects the soil, vintage and grape variety. The signature of the winemaker is decisive: it is characterised by a sensitive approach to nature and careful use of resources.

89 Grüner Veltliner * Falkenstein 2021
90 * Falkenstein 2020
88 * Falkenstein 2019

(93) Grüner Veltliner Falkenstein Unter Brüdern 2020
14 Vol.-%, cork, barrique, €€€€ Ⓥ
93 Grüner Veltliner Unter Brüdern 2019
Medium yellow, green hints and silver reflections. Inviting bouquet with underlying aromas of white stone fruit, subtle caramel notes, a hint of passion fruit and savoury nuances. Juicy on the palate, good complexity, silky, subtle nutty notes and passion fruit on the finish. Developing nicely with definite further ageing potential.
91 Grüner Veltliner Unter Brüdern 2018

(92) Grüner Veltliner Ried Ekartsberg 2022
13 Vol.-%, glass, large wooden barrel, €€€ Ⓥ
92 Grüner Veltliner Ried Ekartsberg 2021
91 Grüner Veltliner Ried Ekartsberg 2020

90 Grüner Veltliner Falkenstein 2022
12 Vol.-%, screwcap, steel tank, €€ Ⓥ
89 Grüner Veltliner Falkenstein 2020
88 Grüner Veltliner Falkenstein 2018

(92) Riesling Ried Rosenberg 2022
13 Vol.-%, glass, large wooden barrel, €€€ Ⓥ
92 Riesling Ried Rosenberg 2021
91 Riesling Ried Rosenberg 2020

91 Riesling Falkenstein 2022
12,5 Vol.-%, screwcap, steel tank, €€€ Ⓑ Ⓥ
91 Riesling Falkenstein 2021
90 Riesling Falkenstein 2020

(92) Weißburgunder Ried Ebersleithen 2022
13 Vol.-%, glass, large wooden barrel, €€€ Ⓥ
91 Weißburgunder Ried Ebersleithen 2021

WEINGUT PESAU
2162 Falkenstein
Wiagasse 253
T: +43 (2554) 6705
office@pesau.at
www.pesau.at

Winemaker: Andreas Pesau
Contact: Georg Pesau
Production: 80,000 bottles
1 % sparkling, 95 % white, 4 % red,
15 hectares
Distribution partners: RC, CZ

WEINGUT R. & A. PFAFFL

When Roman Pfaffl was awarded the title of "Falstaff Winemaker of the Year" in 1996, a dream he had not dared to dream came true. In just under 20 years, with the help of his wife Adelheid, he had turned an agricultural business with 0.75 hectares of vineyards into an ambitious 20-hectare winery. Another 20 years followed, with the next generation also heavily involved - an ensemble that evidently works: The US magazine "Wine Enthusiast" named the winery "European Winery of the Year 2016", the first time this coveted title has been awarded to an Austrian winery. For some 45 years, the Pfaffls have been synonymous with high-quality Grüner Veltliner, Riesling, Chardonnay, Zweigelt, and St. Laurent. The estate's vineyards, which now cover 150 hectares, are spread over thirteen municipalities in the southern Weinviertel and extend as far as Vienna. This distribution brings with it a diversity of soils and microclimates that Roman Josef Pfaffl exploits with great skill. He knows how to bring out the characteristics of each site and present his wines in a variety of styles, from light and playful to dense and powerful. This is especially true of the Grüner Veltliner, which is vinified in no fewer than six variations. But the winery is also very strong in reds. "Some of our vineyards benefit from the mild Pannonian influences that reach here via the Marchfeld region," says Roman Josef Pfaffl, who is passionate about red wines.

90 🍾 Grüner Veltliner Brut
12,5 Vol.-%, cork, bottle fermentation, €€€
91 🍾 Grüner Veltliner brut NV

88 🍾 Secco blanc RR/GM/GV
12,5 Vol.-%, screwcap, steel tank, €€ V
87 🍾 Secco blanc trocken GM/RR/GV

88 🍾 Secco rosé SL/ZW
12,5 Vol.-%, screwcap, steel tank, €€ V
87 🍾 Secco rosé trocken SL/ZW

95 Grüner Veltliner ** Hommage 2022
14,5 Vol.-%, DIAM, large wooden barrel, €€€€€

94 Grüner Veltliner ** Hommage 2021
Medium yellow-green, silver reflections. Yellow apple fruit background with herbal spices and some honey blossom, a hint of bergamot, peach nuances. Juicy, fine acidic structure, mineral, tightly meshed, pronounced tropical fruit, multilayered, remains long lasting, certain ageing potential.
94 ** Hommage 2020

93 Grüner Veltliner ** Golden 2022
14 Vol.-%, DIAM, large wooden barrel, €€€€
93 Grüner Veltliner ** Golden 2021
93 ** Golden 2020

93 Grüner Veltliner ** max. 2022
14 Vol.-%, screwcap, steel tank/large wooden barrel, €€€
93 Grüner Veltliner ** max. 2021
93 ** max. 2020

92 Grüner Veltliner ** Hund 2022
14 Vol.-%, screwcap, large wooden barrel/steel tank, €€€
93 Grüner Veltliner ** Hund 2021
93 ** Hund 2020

91 Grüner Veltliner * Lössdiamant 2022
13 Vol.-%, screwcap, steel tank, €€€
91 Grüner Veltliner * Lössdiamant 2021
92 * Lössdiamant 2020

90 Grüner Veltliner * Selection 2022
13 Vol.-%, screwcap, steel tank, €€
91 Grüner Veltliner * Selection 2021
90 * Selection 2020

90 Grüner Veltliner * Zeisen 2022
13 Vol.-%, screwcap, steel tank, €€
90 Grüner Veltliner * Zeisen 2021
90 * Zeisen 2020

89 Grüner Veltliner * Haiden 2022
13 Vol.-%, screwcap, steel tank, €€
90 Grüner Veltliner * Haiden 2021
92 * Haid 2020

88 Grüner Veltliner vom Haus 2022
12,5 Vol.-%, screwcap, steel tank, €€

---

* Weinviertel DAC   ** Weinviertel DAC Reserve

NIEDERÖSTERREICH/LOWER AUSTRIA

88 Grüner Veltliner vom Haus 2021
89 Grüner Veltliner vom Haus 2020

93 Chardonnay Reserve Vision 2021
14,5 Vol.-%, DIAM, barrique, €€€€€ V
93 Chardonnay Reserve Vision 2020
93 Chardonnay Reserve Vision 2018

91 Chardonnay Exklusiv 2022
14,5 Vol.-%, screwcap, steel tank/barrique, €€€ V
91 Chardonnay Exklusiv 2021
91 Chardonnay Exklusiv 2020

90 Chardonnay Reserve Tribun 2020

89 Chardonnay Selection 2022
13,5 Vol.-%, screwcap, steel tank/barrique, €€

93 Riesling Reserve Passion 2022
13,5 Vol.-%, DIAM, large wooden barrel, €€€€€ V
94 Riesling Reserve Passion 2021
92 Riesling Reserve Passion 2020

92 Riesling Sonne 2022
13,5 Vol.-%, screwcap, steel tank, €€€ V
92 Riesling Sonne 2021
91 Riesling Sonne 2020

91 Riesling Selection 2022
13,5 Vol.-%, screwcap, steel tank, €€
91 Riesling Selection 2021
90 Riesling Selection 2020

89 Riesling Reserve Aurelius 2020

92 Muskateller Reserve Juwel 2022
13,5 Vol.-%, DIAM, large wooden barrel, €€€€€

90 Muskateller Sand 2022
13 Vol.-%, screwcap, steel tank, €€
90 Muskateller Sand 2021
90 Muskateller Sand 2020

89 Muskateller Selection 2022
13 Vol.-%, screwcap, steel tank, €€

92 Weissburgunder Nuss 2022
14 Vol.-%, screwcap, steel tank/large wooden barrel, €€€ V
91 Weissburgunder Nuss 2021
90 Weißburgunder Nuss 2020

91 Grauburgunder La Vita 2022
14 Vol.-%, screwcap, steel tank, €€ V

89 Grauburgunder La Vita 2021
91 Grauburgunder La Vita 2020

90 Sauvignon Blanc Terroir 2022
13,5 Vol.-%, screwcap, steel tank, €€€
91 Sauvignon Blanc Terroir 2021
91 Sauvignon Blanc Terroir 2020

90 Gemischter Satz Harmony 2022
12,5 Vol.-%, screwcap, steel tank, €€ V
89 Gemischter Satz Harmony 2020
90 Gemischter Satz Harmony 2019

89 Wiener Gemischter Satz DAC Selection 2022
12,5 Vol.-%, screwcap, steel tank, €€

88 Wien.1 2022 RR/GV/WB
12,5 Vol.-%, screwcap, steel tank, €€
90 Wien.1 2021 RR/GV/WB
90 Wien.1 2020 RR/GV/WB

88 Ganz Zart 2022 GV/SB/GM
9,5 Vol.-%, screwcap, steel tank, €€
87 Ganz Zart 2021 GV/SB/GM
89 Ganz Zart 2020 GV/SB/GM

88 Junior 2022 MT/GV
12,5 Vol.-%, screwcap, steel tank, €€
88 Junior 2021 MT/GV
88 Junior 2020 GM/SB

92 Rosé La Grande 2022 SL/ZW
13,5 Vol.-%, DIAM, large wooden barrel, €€€
92 Rosé La Grande 2020 SL/ZW
92 Rosé La Grande 2019 SL/ZW

90 Rosé Hasen 2022 ZW/SL
13 Vol.-%, screwcap, steel tank, €€
90 Rosé Hasen 2021 ZW/SL
90 Rosé Hasen 2020 ZW/SL

89 Rosé Selection 2022 ZW/SL
13 Vol.-%, screwcap, steel tank, €€

88 Rosé Ganz Zart 2022 ZW/SL/RÖ
9,5 Vol.-%, screwcap, steel tank, €€
87 Rosé Ganz Zart 2021 ZW/SL/RÖ
89 Ganz Zart Rosé 2020 ZW/SL/RÖ

93 St. Laurent Reserve Alten 2021
14 Vol.-%, DIAM, barrique, €€€€€
92 St. Laurent Reserve Alten 2020

WEINVIERTEL DAC

WEINGUT R. & A. PFAFFL
2100 Stetten
Schulgasse 21
T: +43 (2262) 673423
wein@pfaffl.at
www.pfaffl.at

Winemaker: Roman Josef Pfaffl
Contact: The Pfaffl family
Production: 65 % white, 35 % red, 150 hectares
Certified: Sustainable Austria
Fairs: ProWein Düsseldorf, VieVinum
Distribution partners: AUS, BE, BG, RC, DK, DE, EST, FIN, FR, UK, HK, IT, JP, CDN, HR, LV, LT, LU, MAL, NL, NO, RUS, SE, CH, SGP, SK, ES, TH, CZ, UA

Roman Josef Pfaffl

89 St. Laurent Wald 2022
13,5 Vol.-%, screwcap, steel tank/barrique, €€
90 St. Laurent Wald 2021
90 St. Laurent Wald 2020

88 St. Laurent Granat 2020

88 St. Laurent Selection 2022
13,5 Vol.-%, screwcap, barrique, €€

92 Zweigelt Reserve Burg 2021
13,5 Vol.-%, DIAM, barrique, €€€€
91 Zweigelt Reserve Burg 2020
92 Zweigelt Reserve Burg 2019

90 Zweigelt Sandstein 2022
13,5 Vol.-%, screwcap, barrique/steel tank, €€
90 Zweigelt Sandstein 2021
89 Zweigelt Sandstein 2020

89 Zweigelt Selection 2022
13,5 Vol.-%, screwcap, barrique, €€
90 Zweigelt Selection 2021
89 Zweigelt Selection 2020

88 Zweigelt Reserve Herakles 2019

88 Zweigelt vom Haus 2022
13,5 Vol.-%, screwcap, steel tank/barrique, €€
89 Zweigelt vom Haus 2021
88 Zweigelt vom Haus 2020

91 Excellent Reserve 2021 ZW/ME/CS
14 Vol.-%, DIAM, barrique, €€€€
93 Excellent Reserve 2020 ZW/ME/CS
93 Excellent Reserve 2019 ZW/CS/ME

91 Heidrom Grand Reserve 2020 ME/CS
14,5 Vol.-%, DIAM, barrique, €€€€
94 Heidrom Grand Reserve 2019 ME/CS
Deep dark ruby, purple reflections, soft brightening on the rim. Fine herbal notes, blackberries, some orange zest, soft spiciness, inviting bouquet. Good complexity, velvety, vivid tannins, fine spice, some fine wood notes, ripe cherry fruit on the finish, good persistency, versatile, will benefit from bottle ageing.
93 Heidrom Grand Reserve 2018 ME/CS

91 Cuvée Privat 2021 ME/SL
13,5 Vol.-%, DIAM, barrique, €€€
92 Cuvée Privat 2020 ME/SL
92 Cuvée Privat 2019 ME/SL

89 Wien.2 2022 ZW/PN
13,5 Vol.-%, screwcap, steel tank/barrique, €€
89 Wien.2 2021 ZW/PN
88 Wien.2 2021 ZW/PN

90 Pinot Noir Reserve 2021
14 Vol.-%, DIAM, barrique, €€€€
91 Pinot Noir Reserve 2020
92 Pinot Noir Reserve 2019

---

* Weinviertel DAC   ** Weinviertel DAC Reserve

BIO-WEINGUT SCHWARZ
ORGANIC

Where the Iron Curtain once divided Europe, cross-border tourism now reigns. It is here in Schrattenberg - the most important red wine growing community in the eastern part of the Weinviertel - that the Schwarz family has been making wine for generations. The organic cultivation of the vineyards and the meticulous care of the grapes in the winery form the very essence of the family's approach. This results in very distinctive wines in all categories, year after year: Red, white, rosé, sweet, sparkling, and non-alcoholic. A visit to the Schwarz vineyard offers an insight into the philosophy behind these distinctive wines. Tip: Allow plenty of time to visit the winery, as the range is extensive, and the region has a rich cultural and historical heritage.

92 Chardonnay Premium 2019
92 Chardonnay Premium 2017

91 Riesling Selection 2019

91 Traminer Premium 2021
13,5 Vol.-%, glass, partial barrique, €€€€€ Ⓑ Ⓥ

89 Rosé 2020 ZW/PN/SY/CS/BP
89 Rosé 2019 ZW/BF/BP/CS/PN/ME

92 Cabernet Sauvignon Premium 2017

92 Syrah Premium 2018
13,5 Vol.-%, glass, partial barrique, €€€€€ Ⓑ Ⓥ
92 Syrah Premium 2017

91 Blaufränkisch Premium 2019
13 Vol.-%, glass, partial barrique, €€€€€ Ⓑ Ⓥ

89 Blaufränkisch 2018
89 Blaufränkisch 2017

90 Zweigelt Premium 2019
13 Vol.-%, glass, partial barrique, €€€€€ Ⓑ Ⓥ
91 Zweigelt Premium 2018
91 Zweigelt Premium 2017

90 Pinot Noir Premium 2019
90 Pinot Noir Premium 2018

91 Grande Reserve 2018 CS/ZW/BF/ME
13,5 Vol.-%, glass, barrique, €€€€€€ Ⓑ Ⓥ
92 Grande Reserve 2015 SY/ME/CS/BF
Dark ruby, with purple reflections, subtle brightening on the rim. Inviting, with fine nougat nuances underneath dark berry confit, blackberries, some savoury herbs, subtle orange zest. Juicy, good complexity, ripe cherries, integrated tannins, a salty-mineral finish, enveloping, good ageing potential.
91 Grande Reserve 2012 SY/ME

89 Tradition 2020 BF/SL/ZW
90 Tradition 2018 BF/SL/ZW

92 Riesling Beerenauslese 2018

90 Riesling Auslese 2022
7,5 Vol.-%, screwcap, steel tank, €€€ Ⓑ Ⓥ

89 Traminer Auslese 2019

BIO-WEINGUT SCHWARZ
2172 Schrattenberg
Kleine Zeile 8
T: +43 (2555) 2544
office@schwarzwines.com
www.schwarzwines.com

Winemaker/Contact:
The Schwarz family
Production: 1% sparkling, 23% white, 3% rosé, 72% red, 1% sweet
Fairs: Alles für den Gast Salzburg, Igeho Basel, ÖGW Zürich, ProWein Düsseldorf, VieVinum, Weinmesse München
Distribution partners: DK, DE, IT, HR, NL, CH, CZ, HU, USA

WEINGUT WOLFGANG SEHER

Weingut Seher has been managed by Wolfgang Seher since 2001. The cultivated area of 18 hectares is planted with the white wine varieties Grüner Veltliner, Riesling, Sauvignon Blanc, Pinot Blanc, and Gelber Muskateller, as well as with the red wine varieties Zweigelt, Pinot Noir, Barbera, Merlot, and Cabernet Sauvignon. Despite this diversity, the focus is naturally on Grüner Veltliner. About two-thirds of the vineyards are located in Platt. The most prominent sites are also located here: Kapellenberg, Sandberg, Faustberg, and Kirchleithen. Seven other top sites of the winery are located in: Obermarkersdorf, Feuerberg, Nussberg, Rosenhügel, Geyern, Triftberg, Hochberg, and Hangenstein.

93 Grüner Veltliner ** Ried Kapellenberg 2021
13,5 Vol.-%, cork, 500-l-barrel, €€€
92 Grüner Veltliner ** Ried Platter Kapellenberg 2019
92 Platter ** Ried Kapellenberg 2018

92 Grüner Veltliner ** Ried Feuerberg 2021
13,5 Vol.-%, cork, 500-l-barrel, €€€
93 Grüner Veltliner ** Ried Feuerberg 2019
93 ** Ried Feuerberg 2018

91 Grüner Veltliner * Ried Sandberg 2022
12,5 Vol.-%, screwcap, steel tank, €€
91 Grüner Veltliner * Ried Sandberg 2021
90 Grüner Veltliner * Ried Platter Sandberg 2020

91 Grüner Veltliner * Ried Nussberg 2022
12,5 Vol.-%, screwcap, steel tank, €€
92 Grüner Veltliner * Ried Nussberg 2021
91 Obermarkersdorfer * Ried Nussberg 2019

90 Grüner Veltliner * 2022
12 Vol.-%, screwcap, steel tank, €€
90 Grüner Veltliner * 2021

89 * Platt 28 2019
90 * Platt 28 2018

95 Grüner Veltliner Neue Zeit Nr.6 Reserve 2019
14,5 Vol.-%, cork, 500-l-barrel, €€€€
95 Grüner Veltliner Neue Zeit Nr.5 2018
Bright golden yellow, green glints. Delicate vanilla touch, a bit of blossom honey, soft scents of pineapple and melon, and delicately savoury. Juicy, good complexity, taut, mineral, expressive fruitiness, redolent of mango, and persistent. A complex food companion with potential.
94 Grüner Veltliner Neue Zeit Nr.4 2017

93 Weißer Burgunder Kirchleithen 2021
13,5 Vol.-%, cork, 500-l-barrel, €€€
93 Weißer Burgunder Platt Ried Kirchleithen 2020
Bright golden yellow, silver reflections. Fine blossom honey, discreet lime zest, a bit of bergamot, apple fruit, an inviting bouquet. Juicy, tightly meshed, mineral and salty, well-integrated acid structure, with a pear touch on the nish. It is a good food wine.

90 Weisser Burgunder Mergel 2021
89 Weißer Burgunder Mergel 2020

92 Sauvignon Blanc Faustberg 2021
13,5 Vol.-%, cork, 500-l-barrel, €€€€

WEINGUT WOLFGANG SEHER
2051 Platt
Platt 28
T: +43 (2945) 27138
office@weingutseher.at
www.weingutseher.at

Winemaker/Contact:
Wolfgang Seher
Production: 133,333 bottles
9 % sparkling, 70 % white, 20 % red, 1 % sweet, 18 hectares
Fairs: ProWein Düsseldorf, VieVinum
Distribution partners: AUS

* Weinviertel DAC   ** Weinviertel DAC Reserve

NIEDERÖSTERREICH/LOWER AUSTRIA

92 Sauvignon Blanc Platt Ried Faustberg 2020
92 Sauvignon Blanc Ried Platter Faustberg 2019

92 Sauvignon Blanc Silt 2022
13 Vol.-%, screwcap, steel tank, €€
92 Sauvignon Blanc Silt 2021
91 Sauvignon Blanc Silt 2019

92 Riesling Rosenau 2021
12,5 Vol.-%, screwcap, steel tank, €€€€
91 Riesling Ried Rosenau 2018

90 Riesling Tonstein 2021
89 Riesling Tonstein 2019
89 Riesling Tonstein 2018

88 Rosé Cabernet & Zweigelt 2021 CS/ZW

91 Pinot Noir Ausserm Holz 2018
13,5 Vol.-%, screwcap, barrique, €€€€

90 Merlot Tonmergel 2019
14 Vol.-%, screwcap, barrique, €€

★★★

WEINGUT SUTTER

Doris and Leopold Sutter are already the tenth generation to run their traditional winery in Hohenwarth in the southwestern Weinviertel, where Kamptal borders with Wagram. The wines of grandfather August used to be on the best wine lists in the country. Now, there is new momentum in the business, and it won't take long before they adorn the wine lists of the best restaurants again.

The Sutters' range of wines are as bold and strong as the walls of the winery, which were built in 1671 and lovingly restored. The focus is clearly on Grüner Veltliner, which is available in six varieties: The Weinviertel DAC is a classic regional wine, joined by site wines and a Grüner Veltliner Alte Reben (old vines). Their vines are rooted on gravel, sand, clay and calcareous gravel of the Ur-Donau and provide minerality, which show their clearly defined provenance. Three Red Veltliners, a rare variety cultivated by only a few vintners, and a Frühroter Veltliner also provide the many facets that a Veltliner can have.

WEINGUT SUTTER
3472 Hohenwarth
Weinviertler Straße 6
T: +43 (2957) 200
office@weingut-sutter.at
www.weingut-sutter.at

Winemaker: Leopold Sutter
Contact: Doris Sutter
Production: 20 hectares
Certified: Sustainable Austria
Fairs: ProWein Düsseldorf, VieVinum, Vinexpo, DAC-Presentations
Distribution partners: BE, RC, DE, FR, NL, RUS, SE, CH, TH, CZ, USA

93 Grüner Veltliner * Privat 2019
13 Vol.-%, screwcap, large wooden barrel, €€€€€ V
93 Grüner Veltliner ** Privat 2018
Medium yellow-green, bright reflections. Underlaid with fine savouriness white tropical fruit, dark mineral, a hint of orange zest. Juicy, elegant, powerful, notes of passionfruit, mineral, a sturdy food companion.
94 ** Privat 2017

(92) Grüner Veltliner ** Ried Kellerberg 2022
13 Vol.-%, screwcap, large wooden barrel, €€€€ V
92 Grüner Veltliner ** Ried Kellerberg 2021
92 ** Ried Kellerberg 2020

(91) Grüner Veltliner * Alte Reben 2022
13 Vol.-%, screwcap, large wooden barrel, €€ V
91 Grüner Veltliner * Alte Reben 2021
92 * Alte Reben 2020

91 * Ried Hochstrass Alte Reben 2019
92 ** Ried Hochstrass Alte Reben 2018

WEINVIERTEL DAC

90 Grüner Veltliner * Klassik 2022
12,5 Vol.-%, screwcap, steel tank, €€

89 Grüner Veltliner * Klassik 2021

90 * Klassik 2020

92 Roter Veltliner Privat 2019
13 Vol.-%, screwcap, large wooden barrel, €€€€€

92 Roter Veltliner Privat 2018
Medium yellow-green, silver reflections. Touch of pear underpinned with fine tobacco spice, a hint of baked apple, some anise, inviting bouquet. Juicy, elegant, fine acidity, mineral, white apple on the finish, somewhat restrained finish, will benefit from bottle age.

93 Roter Veltliner Privat 2017

(90) Roter Veltliner Alte Reben 2022
13 Vol.-%, screwcap, large wooden barrel, €€€

91 Roter Veltliner Alte Reben 2021

91 Roter Veltliner Alte Reben 2020

89 Roter Veltliner Ried Hochstrass 2019

89 Pinot Noir Ried Mühlweg 2021
13 Vol.-%, screwcap, steel tank, €€

WEINGUT ZENS

Josef Zens has been instrumental in making the small wine village of Mailberg a little better known than most wine villages in the Weinviertel. As chairman of the "Mailberg Valley", a quality association, he aims to promote the positive potential of the Mailberg basin, with its unique microclimate, to a broader public.

The grapes are grown according to organic principles. The Mailberg soils are very calcareous, covered with loamy sand and loess, and contribute to the individuality of the wines in terms of freshness, flavour and power with a full-bodied structure. In the cellar, too, quality is paramount. Varietal specific ageing in steel tanks or large wooden barrels is a tradition at the estate. Josef Zens produces multilayered white wines, among which the dry Traminer always occupies an interesting position. His powerful wines, known for their longevity, develop very well in the bottle. Great importance is attached to the uniqueness of each vintage. With the remarkable vintages of 2015, 2017 and 2018, powerful "Great Reserves" have been developed alongside the traditional Reserve wines. The 2019, 2020, 2021 and 2022 vintages will focus on fruity and concentrated DAC and Reserve wines. A welcoming vacation accommodation called "Hundschupfen 314" is available to wine lovers and guests all year round.

(91) Grüner Veltliner Ried Hundschupfen Mailberg Reserve 2022
14 Vol.-%, screwcap, steel tank/500-l-barrel, €€

90 Grüner Veltliner Ried Hundschupfen Reserve 2021

92 Grüner Veltliner Ried Hundschupfen Reserve 2020

(90) Grüner Veltliner * Mailberger Bündnis 2022
13 Vol.-%, screwcap, steel tank, €€

WEINGUT ZENS
2024 Mailberg
Holzgasse 66
T: +43 660-5322843, +43 664-805741612
office@weingutzens.at
www.weingutzens.at

Winemaker: Josef Zens
Contact: Josef and Michael Zens
Production: 100 % white, 6 hectares
Fairs: Weintage im Museumsquartier
Distribution partners: SE

* Weinviertel DAC   ** Weinviertel DAC Reserve

NIEDERÖSTERREICH/LOWER AUSTRIA

91 Grüner Veltliner * Ried Alte Bonder
   Mailberger Bündnis 2021
Light yellow-green, silver reflections. Fine tobacco spice, a bit of yellow apple, a touch of lemongrass, soft notes of melon. Juicy, elegant, fine structure, balanced, fruity, apple touch also on the finish, good food wine.

91 Grüner Veltliner * Mailberger Bündnis 2020

(92) Weißburgunder Reserve Mailberg
   Ried Antlasbergen 2022
13 Vol.-%, screwcap, steel tank, €€

92 Weißburgunder Ried Antlasbergen
   Reserve 2020

91 Weißburgunder Ried Antlasbergen
   Reserve 2019

92 Cuvèe Ried Antlasbergen Reserve 2021 CH/WB

(91) Riesling Reserve Mailberg
    Ried Hundschupfen 2022
13 Vol.-%, screwcap, steel tank, €€

90 Riesling Ried Hundschupfen Reserve 2021
91 Riesling Ried Hundschupfen Reserve 2020

(91) Chardonnay Reserve Mailberg
    Ried Antlasbergen 2022
13,5 Vol.-%, screwcap, large wooden barrel, €€

92 Chardonnay Ried Antlasbergen
   Reserve 2020

92 Mailberger Chardonnay
   Ried Antlasbergen Reserve 2019

91 Gewürztraminer Ried Antlasbergen
   Reserve 2020

(88) Gelber Muskateller Mailberg
    Ried Antlasbergen 2022
12,5 Vol.-%, screwcap, steel tank, €€

89 Gelber Muskateller Ried Antlasbergen 2021
89 Gelber Muskateller Ried Antlasbergen 2020

WEINGUT ZULL

No matter where you look: Picturesque vineyards are everywhere, stretching for miles and miles - this is the Weinviertel. In the middle of this idyll, not far from the Czech border, lies Schrattenthal, Austria's smallest wine town. And it is here that you will find the Zull winery, which, with 19 hectares of vineyards, may be small, but it produces great wines. Everything about this winery is a family affair. In the early 1980s, Werner Zull was about to start university when his brother had a fatal accident. The family stuck together during this challenging time, and Werner Zull swapped his studies for work in the vineyard. Since then, the Zull estate has been producing and bottling quality wine.

In the meantime, the small winery has become well-known and famous for its wines. On the one hand, this is due to the area's unique microclimate: heat and sun help the grapes to ripen to perfection, while the nearby Manhartsberg mountain keeps cold winds at bay from the neighbouring Waldviertel region. On the other hand, the deeply rooted vines get the best out of the soil. Last but not least, the Zulls' natural way of working contributes to their wines' unmistakable elegance and complexity. Instead of grand gestures and excessive use of technology, the Zulls rely on intuition, perseverance, patience and the courage to experiment. Son Phillip carries on his father's vision of producing wines with character, brilliance and excellent ageing potential - such as the Grüner Veltliner "Äussere Bergen", the Riesling "Innere Bergen" or the sought-after Pinot Noir.

90 ❂ Rosé Ancestrale 2022 PN/ZW
11 Vol.-%, screwcap, €€€

90 ❂ Ancestrale Rosé 2021 ZW/PN
90 ❂ Ancestrale Rosé 2020 PN/ZW

94 Grüner Veltliner * Ried Äußere Bergen 2021
Medium yellow-green, silver reflections. Discreet apple fruit, a touch of lemon lemon balm, a little peppery, with yellow stone fruit and orange zest underneath. Juicy, elegant, fine acid structure, mineral-salty, mango notes on the finish, persistent, complex food companion with certain ageing potential.

93 ** Ried Schrattenthaler Äußere
    Bergen 2020

WEINVIERTEL DAC

WEINGUT ZULL
2073 Schrattenthal
Schrattenthal 9
T: +43 (2946) 8217
office@zull.at
www.zull.at

Winemaker/Contact:
Phillip Zull
Production: 5 % sparkling, 69 % white, 10 % rosé, 15 % red, 1 % sweet, 19 hectares
Certified: Sustainable Austria
Fairs: Austrian Tasting London, ProWein Düsseldorf, VieVinum, DAC-Presentations
Distribution partners: BE, DK, DE, FR, UK, IRL, IT, JP, CDN, LU, NL, RO, RUS, CN, SK, CZ, HU, USA, CY

Grüner Veltliner

91 Grüner Veltliner * 2022
13 Vol.-%, screwcap, steel tank, €€
91 Grüner Veltliner * 2020
91 Weinviertel DAC 2019

91 Grüner Veltliner * Schrattenthal 2021
91 * Schrattenthal 2019

89 Grüner Veltliner Lust & Laune 2022
12 Vol.-%, screwcap, steel tank, €€
89 Grüner Veltliner Lust & Laune 2021
88 Grüner Veltliner Lust & Laune 2020

94 Riesling Ried Innere Bergen 2022
13,5 Vol.-%, screwcap, steel tank/large wooden barrel, €€€
94 Riesling Ried Innere Bergen 2021
Light yellow-green, silver reflections. Multi-faceted bouquet of white peach, lime zest, a hint of quince, meadow herbs. Juicy, good complexity, taut, elegant, mineral, papaya, lemony finish, certain ageing potential.
94 Riesling Ried Innere Bergen 2020

91 Chardonnay Ried Kalvarienberg 2021
13,5 Vol.-%, screwcap, barrique/amphore, €€€
90 Chardonnay Ried Kalvarienberg 2020
91 Chardonnay Ried Kalvarienberg 2019

91 Weites Land 2022 VI/RR/CH
13 Vol.-%, screwcap, steel tank/large wooden barrel, €€€
90 Weites Land 2021 CH/WR/GM/RR
90 Weites Land 2020 CH/WR/RR/GM

90 NeuLand Gemischter Satz 2019
92 NeuLand Gemischter Satz 2018

88 Rosé Lust & Laune 2022 ZW/PN/ME/CS
12 Vol.-%, screwcap, steel tank, €€
89 Lust & Laune Rosé 2020 CS/PN/ZW
89 Lust & Laune Rosé 2019 ZW/PN

91 Schrattenthal 9 2018 ZW/ME/CS

89 Lust & Laune Rot 2021 ZW/PN
87 Lust & Laune Rot 2019 ZW/PN
88 Lust & Laune Rot 2018 ZW/PN

90 Pinot Noir Zull 2021
13 Vol.-%, screwcap, barrique, €€€€
92 Pinot Noir 2018
92 Pinot Noir 2017

90 Zweigelt 2021
90 Zweigelt 2019

94 Chardonnay Beerenauslese 2017

* Weinviertel DAC   ** Weinviertel DAC Reserve

Jungenberg and Hackelsberg near Jois in the wine-growing region Leithaberg

BURGENLAND

PRIME CONDITIONS FOR GREAT WHITE-, RED-, AND SWEET WINES

Viticulture near Illmitz, Lake Neusiedl

WINE TRILOGY FROM THE LAND OF THE SUN

Under the influence of the Pannonian climate, a total of 11,772 hectares of vineyards in the easternmost federal state produce elegant white wines, full-bodied red wines and world renowned sweet wines. There are differences in the natural conditions that should not be underestimated.

In the very south of Burgenland, for example, the Eisenberg with its special soil and a somewhat cooler climate offers optimal conditions for elegant, delicate Blaufränkisch wines full of character and flanked by the finest minerality. Blaufränkisch grapes also grow on the heavier clay soils of the Mittelburgenland, but also north of the Rosalia Mountains, producing wines with particular depth of fruit and length.

On the Leithaberg, west of Lake Neusiedl, a pronounced mineral note can be detected. In recent years, wines from international grape varieties and cuvées have also achieved the highest recognition. The Leithagebirge with its limestone and slate soils is also a unique terroir for complex white wines, especially Pinot Blanc and Chardonnay, but also Grüner Veltliner. Fine Prädikat wines such as the legendary "Ruster Ausbruch" complete the trinity of Burgenland's wine accomplishments.

East of Lake Neusiedl, Blaue Zweigelt dominates with powerful, juicy red wines, although Blaufränkisch and St. Laurent also deliver excellent results. The Seewinkel in the southern part with its special microclimate is one of the few large sweet wine strongholds in the world. Here, the high humidity due to the numer-

BURGENLAND

ous "zicklacken" (small brackish lakes) in autumn favours the formation of noble rot (Botrytis cinerea). This means that great Beerenauslese and Trockenbeerenauslese wines can be regularly produced here. The great diversity of the soil allows an equally diverse range of grape varieties to thrive. In addition to several other varieties such as Chardonnay, Scheurebe, Muskat Ottonel or Traminer, Welschriesling in particular reaches the highest level of quality in this style, whether with or without the use of wood. With Ruster Ausbruch DAC and the incorporation of the town with the dry wines at Leithaberg DAC as well as with Neusiedlersee DAC for Prädikat wines; show that these DAC wines are now vinified throughout Burgenland.

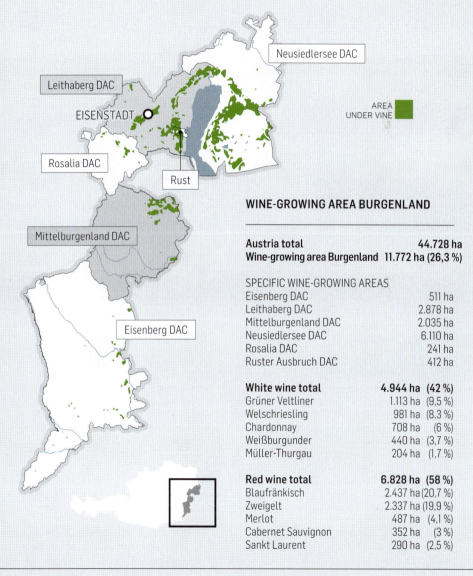

WINE-GROWING AREA BURGENLAND

Austria total	44.728 ha
Wine-growing area Burgenland	11.772 ha (26,3 %)

SPECIFIC WINE-GROWING AREAS

Eisenberg DAC	511 ha
Leithaberg DAC	2.878 ha
Mittelburgenland DAC	2.035 ha
Neusiedlersee DAC	6.110 ha
Rosalia DAC	241 ha
Ruster Ausbruch DAC	412 ha

White wine total	**4.944 ha (42 %)**
Grüner Veltliner	1.113 ha (9,5 %)
Welschriesling	981 ha (8,3 %)
Chardonnay	708 ha (6 %)
Weißburgunder	440 ha (3,7 %)
Müller-Thurgau	204 ha (1,7 %)

Red wine total	**6.828 ha (58 %)**
Blaufränkisch	2.437 ha (20,7 %)
Zweigelt	2.337 ha (19,9 %)
Merlot	487 ha (4,1 %)
Cabernet Sauvignon	352 ha (3 %)
Sankt Laurent	290 ha (2,5 %)

Kleincsaterberg between Kohfidisch and Eisenberg an der Pinka

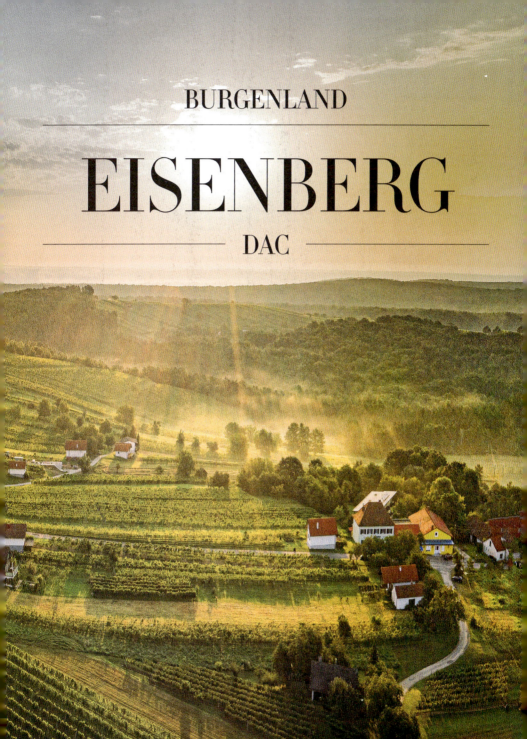

The famous Ried Saybritz

IDYLLIC LANDSCAPE, FIERY BLAUFRÄNKISCH

The idyllic vineyard area of southern Burgenland stretches from the area surrounding Güssing in the far south to Rechnitz in the north and is the most rural landscape of the region. Metamorphic rock dominates the soils in the north, while medium heavy loam, frequently with high iron content, is found in the south. Vineyards cover a total of around 511 hectares.

Eisenberg is of great historic significance and together with the Deutsch Schützen vineyards it comprises the viticultural centre of this wine-growing area. The classic red wines of southern Burgenland are made from Blaufränkisch and are marketed under the "Eisenberg DAC" and "Eisenberg DAC Reserve" protected designations of origin as of the 2009 and 2008 vintages respectively. Next to the classic, fruity varietal representatives, the concentrated Reserve wines are among Austria's greatest typical regional red wines. A unique mineral spice distinguishes these growths. Particularly crisp and fruity Welschriesling and Weissburgunder (Pinot Blanc) are produced in the areas surrounding Rechnitz in the north and Moschendorf in the south. Highly elegant wines are produced in idyllic surroundings on Csaterberg near Kohfidisch and along the Pinkataler wine road from Wintener and over the Kulmer and Gaaser vineyards where one finds numerous historic little wine cellars called "Kellerstöckln". It is a lovely place for

BURGENLAND EISENBERG DAC

a leisurely hike or bicycle tour. In the communities of Heiligenbrunn and Moschendorf at the most southerly point, one encounters a peculiar wine specialty called "Uhudler". These wines are made from the fruit of ungrafted hybrid vines and their pungent fragrance of wild strawberries attracts a surprising number of fans.

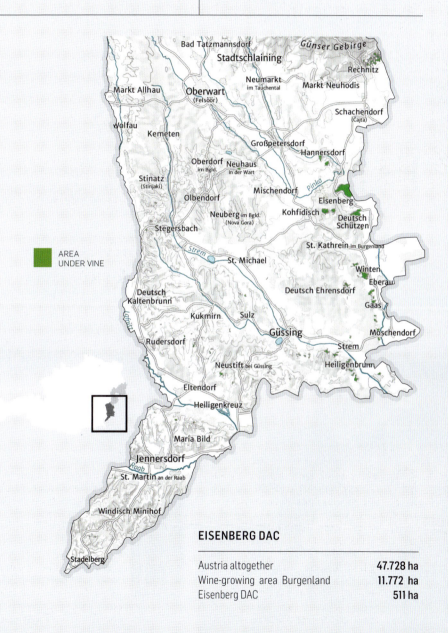

EISENBERG DAC

Austria altogether	47.728 ha
Wine-growing area Burgenland	11.772 ha
Eisenberg DAC	511 ha

BURGENLAND

SELECTED WINERIES

★★★★★
Weingut Krutzler, Deutsch Schützen

★★★★
Weingut Jalits, Badersdorf

★★★★
WEINGUT JALITS

For Mathias Jalits, the Eisenberg is something special, an area with incomparable advantages and characteristics. And that is conveyed in his wines. "You should have the Eisenberg on your palate when you drink our wines" is the philosophy of the South Burgenland winemaker. Sandy, clay, and heavy loam soils and a south-easterly exposure that keeps the icy north winds at bay provide ideal conditions for the powerful mineral Blaufränkisch, the winery's main variety. Cabernet Sauvignon, Pinot Noir, Merlot, Zweigelt, and a small amount of Welschriesling also grow on the slopes of the Eisenberg. The family is now in its fifth generation of winemaking. In 2001, Mathias Jalits took over the winery management, and since then, he has steadily increased the area under vines with a focus on quality and provenance. He does not engage in daring experiments, either in the vineyard or in the cellar: "The regional character should be reflected in my wines. That's who I am, that's Southern Burgenland, and that is conveyed in the wines." The excellent Falstaff ratings show that Mathias Jalits is on the right track with his philosophy. We can look forward to tasting his wines in the years to come.

Blaufränkisch

WEINGUT JALITS
7512 Badersdorf
Untere Dorfstraße 16
T: +43 (664) 3303827
office@jalits.at
www.jalits.at

Winemaker/Contact:
Mathias Jalits
Production: 20 % white, 80 % red, 16 hectares
Fairs: VieVinum, Weinmesse Innsbruck, Weinmesse München, Wein Burgenland Presentations
Distribution partners: DE, CH, SK, USA

EISENBERG DAC

92 Weißburgunder Kalk und Schiefer 2021
14 Vol.-%, cork, used barriques, €€€
93 Weißburgunder Kalk und Schiefer 2020
92 Weißburgunder Kalk und Schiefer 2019

(96) Blaufränkisch ** Ried Reihburg 2021
14 Vol.-%, cork, large wooden barrel, €€€€
98 Blaufränkisch ** Ried Reihburg 2019
Deep ruby garnet, opaque core, purple glints, faintly lighter ochre hue at the rim. Cool bouquet of black berries and traces of graphite, dark minerality, some nougat and background nuances of fresh orange zest. Juicy, elegant, lovely expression of fruit, lush cherry, well integrated, supporting tannins, followed by saline reverberations. Excellent length, very promising.

(94) Blaufränkisch ** Diabas 2021
14 Vol.-%, cork, used barriques, €€€€
97 Blaufränkisch ** Diabas 2019
Deep dark ruby, opaque core, purple glints, faintly lighter ochre hue at the broader rim. Awakening sweetheart cherries, red forest berries, a hint of nougat, and a mineral touch. Multifaceted bouquet. Juicy, fresh sweetheart cherries, subtle expression of fruit, ripe tannins, saline-mineral nuances and persistent. Definite ageing potential.
96 Blaufränkisch ** Diabas 2018

(93) Blaufränkisch ** Ried Fasching 2021
14 Vol.-%, cork, used barriques, €€€€
94 ** Ried Fasching 2019
92 ** Ried Fasching 2018

(92) Blaufränkisch ** Ried Szapary 2021
14 Vol.-%, cork, used barriques, €€€
92 ** Ried Szapary 2020
94 ** Ried Szapary 2019

93 Merlot Reserve 2018

93 Cabernet Sauvignon Reserve 2019
92 Cabernet Sauvignon Reserve 2018

(92) Cuvée Kontur 2021 BF/CS/ME
14 Vol.-%, cork, wooden barrel, €€€€
91 Cuvée Kontur 2020 BF/CS/ME
92 Cuvée Kontur 2019 BF/CS/ME

91 Pinot Noir Ried Szapary 2019
90 Pinot Noir Ried Szapary 2018
91 Pinot Noir Ried Szapary 2017

WEINGUT KRUTZLER

Weingut Krutzler is now run by the fifth generation of the Krutzler family. The first quality wines were bottled in 1966, and to this day, the winery is committed to producing only the best. Traditionally, the family business produces almost exclusively red wines from some 13 hectares of vineyards around Deutsch Schützen and Eisenberg. The focus is on one grape variety in particular, Blaufränkisch. Krutzler's winemaking philosophy is to take advantage of the climate and terroir, not to produce fashionable wines but to find the stylistic soul of the grape variety. The vineyards are all situated in a south-south-east facing basin surrounded by woodland, which creates an ideal microclimate. The soil is rich in minerals, iron and slate. The terroir, long vegetation period and low yields produce wines with originality and character.

The very best vineyards in Deutsch Schützen and on the nearby Eisenberg are the basis for the Eisenberg DAC Reserve; vines that are at least 25 years old, with longer barrel ageing, are the basis for this profound, savoury mineral wine. From a careful selection of the best Blaufränkisch grapes from each vintage, Perwolff Blaufränkisch, the estate's renowned flagship wine, is also aged in oak barrels. This perennial favourite takes its name from the old thirteenth-century name of the site, and as it ages in the bottle, it delights the palate with suppleness and elegance.

92 Welschriesling Ried Ratschen 2021
13,5 Vol.-%, cork, partial barrique, €€€€
93 Welschriesling Ried Ratschen 2020
Light greenish yellow, silver reflections. Delicate toasty hazelnut, some grapefruit in the background, an inviting floral aroma. Medium body, white apple, fine reductive nu-

BURGENLAND

Kellerstöckl in Deutsch Schützen

WEINGUT KRUTZLER
7474 Deutsch Schützen
Winzerstraße 68
T: +43 (664) 1431983
weingut@krutzler.at
www.krutzler.at

Winemaker/Contact:
Reinhold Krutzler
Production:
5 % white, 95 % red, 13 hectares
Certified: Sustainable Austria
Fairs: ProWein Düsseldorf, VieVinum
Distribution partners: BE, DE, UK, JP, CDN, LU, NL, NO, CH, SK, HU, USA

ances of flint and nougat, light on its feet and elegant, a multi-faceted food wine.

93   Welschriesling Ried Ratschen 2019

93   Gemischter Satz Alte Reben 2018

(93) Blaufränkisch ** 2021
13,5 Vol.-%, cork, 500-l-barrel, €€€€€
92   Blaufränkisch ** 2020
93   Eisenberg DAC Reserve 2019

92   Blaufränkisch * Spätfüllung 2018
13,5 Vol.-%, DIAM, large wooden barrel, €€€

91   Blaufränkisch * 2020
91   Eisenberg DAC 2018

(96) Blaufränkisch Perwolff 2021
13,5 Vol.-%, cork, 500-l-barrel, €€€€€€
95   Blaufränkisch Perwolff 2020
Deep ruby, purple glints, faintly lighter at the rim. Subtle nuances of blackberries, black cherries, and a little liquorice, underlaid with sweet spices. A multilayered bouquet. Medium-bodied, red cherries, fine berry fruit, filigree structure, elegant, round tannins, and persistent. A vibrant supper accompaniment with potential for development.
97   Blaufränkisch Perwolff 2019

(95) Merlot 2021
14 Vol.-%, cork, barrique, €€€€€€
94   Merlot 2020
Dark ruby garnet, purple reflections, delicate rim brightening. Ripe black cherries, some blackberries, fine noble wood nuances, some vanilla and orange zest. Juicy, red cherries, some cranberries, fine tannins, salty finish, savoury style, certain ageing potential.
95   Merlot 2019

(94) Alter Weingarten 2021 BF/ZW
13,5 Vol.-%, cork, 500-l-barrel, €€€€€
93   Alter Weingarten 2020 BF/ZW
94   Alter Weingarten 2019 BF/ZW

EISENBERG DAC

SPACE FOR YOUR
WINE NOTES

* Eisenberg DAC ** Eisenberg DAC Reserve

Ried Himmelreich, Leithagebirge near Donnerskirchen

BURGENLAND
LEITHABERG
DAC

Jois marina with a view of the Jungenberg

FULMINANT QUALITY IN WHITE, RED AND SWEET

The Leithagebirge is home to the all-rounders. Hardly any other wine-growing region allows such a variety of wine types as the approximately 2,875 hectares on the western shore of Lake Neusiedl. This is also where the white and red wines with the Leithaberg DAC origin are produced.

The dry wines are characterised by the mineral soils of the Leithagebirge, where primary rock islands repeatedly break through between limestone-rich layers. The wines that are particularly typical of the region are marketed under the name "Leithaberg DAC". The legally defined production area for the Leithaberg DAC includes the district of Eisenstadt and its surrounding area; the Free City of Eisenstadt and the political municipalities of Jois and Winden. White wine with the Leithaberg DAC, Austrian quality wine with a designation of origin may be produced from the varieties Weißburgunder (Pinot Blanc), Chardonnay, Neuburger or Grüner Veltliner. Cuvées from these varieties are also permitted. The red Leithaberg DAC comes from the region's dominant variety Blaufränkisch, although a blend with a maximum of 15 percent Zweigelt, St. Laurent or Pinot Noir is possible. The Leithaberg DACs are always mineral and not overly powerful.

In addition, a great variety of other grape varieties and styles are cultivated in the area west of Lake Neusiedl, most of which are

BURGENLAND **LEITHABERG DAC**

marketed under the name "Burgenland". The area with many renowned wineries is also a wine tourism Mecca. (Wine) culture as a supporting programme is also offered, among others, by the provincial capital Eisenstadt with the enchanting Esterházy Castle, Mörbisch with the Lake Festival, Sankt Margarethen with the Music Festival in the Roman Quarry, the Wine Academy in Rust and the Gourmet Academy in Donnerskirchen.

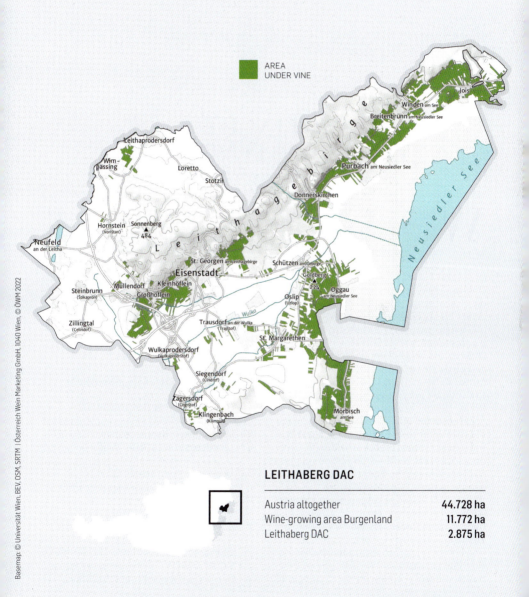

LEITHABERG DAC

Austria altogether	44.728 ha
Wine-growing area Burgenland	11.772 ha
Leithaberg DAC	2.875 ha

SELECTED WINERIES

★★★★★
Weingut Kollwentz, Großhöflein
Weingut Moric, Großhöflein

★★★★
Weingut Markus Altenburger, Jois

★★★★
Weingut Toni Hartl, Reisenberg
Weingut Prieler, Schützen am Gebirge

★★★
Weingut MAD, Oggau

WEINGUT MARKUS ALTENBURGER

ORGANIC

With tremendous dedication and passion, Markus Altenburger has turned the winery into an internationally renowned and one of the most exciting wineries on the Leithaberg within just a few years. A clear focus on low-intervention vinification in combination with grapes from the typical slate and Leithakalk soils in Jois makes his style unmistakable.

The winery's prime red wines are made from Blaufränkisch: the purist site wines from old vines in the Jungenberg and Gritschenberg vineyards are only produced in the best vintages and in small quantities. The perfect introduction is provided by the enjoyable Blaufränkisch vom Kalk, and the vineyard cuvée "Markus Altenburger rot" which indicates the style of the forthcoming years. The Altenburgers are primarily concerned with Chardonnay, Grüner Veltliner and Neuburger. An elegant variant from limestone soils - significantly named "Chardonnay vom Kalk", ‚Kalk' depicting the German word for limestone soils - and a complex site version from the slate-dominated Jungenberg vineyard are vinified.

The love of grape varieties that have become rare is expressed, for example, in the "Neuburger betont" - a play on words, (‚betont' meaning to emphasise and ‚Beton' meaning concrete) since the Neuburger grape variety is matured in an emphatically restrained manner and in egg-shaped concrete tanks. For some years now, a single-vineyard Grüner Veltliner from the limestone-rich Ladisberg vineyard and a natural cuvée of local grape varieties - "Markus Altenburger weiß" - have also been an overall success.

96   121 Brut Nature 2012 (Magnum)
12 Vol.-%, cork, bottle fermentation, €€€€€€

93   Blank. 2015 zero dosage NB/WR/CH

94   Chardonnay * Ried Jungenberg 2021
13 Vol.-%, cork, cement/large wooden barrel, €€€€€ Ⓑ
94   Chardonnay * Ried Joiser Jungenberg 2019
93   Chardonnay * Ried Joiser Jungenberg 2018

92   Chardonnay vom Kalk 2022
12 Vol.-%, DIAM, cement/large wooden barrel/500-l-barrel, €€€ Ⓞ
93   Chardonnay vom Kalk 2020
92   Chardonnay vom Kalk 2019

93   Grüner Veltliner * Ried Joiser Ladisberg 2019
93   Grüner Veltliner * Ried Joiser Ladisberg 2017

LEITHABERG DAC

WEINGUT MARKUS ALTENBURGER
7093 Jois
Untere Hauptstraße 62
T: +43 (2160) 71089
halloservusgriasdi@markusaltenburger.com
www.markusaltenburger.com

Winemaker/Contact:
Markus Altenburger
Production: 5 % sparkling, 30 % white, 65 % red, 2 % sweet, 17 hectares
Fairs: Karakterre
Distribution partners: DE, EST, UK, CDN, ROK, LV, RUS, CH, USA

Jungenberg, Jois

93 Markus Altenburger Weiß Skin and Stones 2022
12,5 Vol.-%, DIAM, cement/500-l-barrel/large wooden barrel, €€€€ 🅑 🅞

92 Markus Altenburger Weiß Skin and Stones 2021

92 Markus Altenburger Weiß Skin and Stones 2020

92 Neuburger betont. 2022
11 Vol.-%, DIAM, cement, €€€€ 🅑 🅞

92 Neuburger betont. 2021

92 Neuburger betont. 2020

96 Blaufränkisch * Ried Gritschenberg 2019
Deep ruby, purple glints, faintly lighter ochre hue at the rim. Delicately fragrant liquorice and cranberry aromas, pleasantly dried herb nuances, tobacco tones, and candied orange zest. Taut, tightly woven, ripe red cherries, elegant, supporting tannins, minerality, and a lovely sweetness on the finish. Remarkable length, assured ageing potential.

95 Blaufränkisch * Ried Gritschenberg 2018
95 Blaufränkisch * Ried Gritschenberg 2017

95 Blaufränkisch Leithaberg DAC Ried Jungenberg Late Release 2013
13 Vol.-%, cork, 500-l-barrel, €€€€€

95 Blaufränkisch * Ried Jungenberg 2019
Deep ruby, purple glints, faintly lighter ochre hue at the rim. Tobacco-herbal savouriness underpinned with red forest berry fruit, preserved cherries, and smoky minerality. Medium complexity, red berry nuances, freshly structured, refined tannins, and a touch salty. Well-developed, elegant style.

96 Blaufränkisch * Ried Joiser Jungenberg 2018
96 Blaufränkisch * Ried Joiser Jungenberg 2017

94 Blaufränkisch * Helden Late Release 2017
12,5 Vol.-%, DIAM, large wooden barrel/500-l-barrel, €€€€ 🅑

93 Blaufränkisch * Rot Helden 2021
12,5 Vol.-%, DIAM, large wooden barrel/500-l-barrel, €€€€ 🅑 🅞

93 Blaufränkisch * Markus Altenburger Rot Helden 2019

93 * Markus Altenburger Rot Helden 2018

91 Blaufränkisch * vom Kalk 2022
13 Vol.-%, DIAM, 500-l-barrel/large wooden barrel, €€€ 🅑

92 Blaufränkisch * vom Kalk 2021
92 Blaufränkisch * vom Kalk 2019

94 Cuvée Altenburger Jois 2018 BF/CS/ME
93 Jois Cuvée Altenburger 2017 CS/BF/ME
93 Jois - Cuvée Altenburger 2015 BF/CS/ME

WEINGUT TONI HARTL
ORGANIC

Weingut Toni Hartl cultivates around 25 hectares of vineyards in two wine-growing regions: the Thermenregion and the Leithaberg. These vineyards produce 50 per cent red wine, 38 per cent white wine (including 10 per cent sparkling wine), 10 per cent rosé and two per cent sweet wine.

The knowledge of the different climatic conditions on either side of the Leithagebirge and the diversity of the vineyard soils in Reisenberg and Purbach allow each variety to be given the optimal site to thrive. One of the main goals of vinification is to bring out the characteristics of each region and its unique identity. New to the range are the natural wines: Amphore Ena, Dyo, Furmint, and Petnat (bottle-fermented sparkling wine). Another sparkling wine from the Brut Classic range is aged on the lees for about two years after the traditional method of fermentation, then riddled and disgorged by hand. In addition to the single vineyard wines, the Reserve range now includes Pinot Noir from the single vineyard Reysenperg in Reisenberg and Chardonnay from the Thenau vineyard in Purbach, both of which are characterised by a high lime content. The wines are only released after three years of ageing and only in exceptionally good years. The Reserve range also includes Blaufränkisch Eisner, which, as its name suggests, comes from vines on one of the top iron-rich sites on the Leithaberg. In optimal interaction with the respective microclimates, the soils form the basis for producing regionally typical, physiologically fully ripe wines. According to the motto "Everything is on loan", the latest ecological knowledge is applied. In order to maintain the biological-organic balance, attention is paid to careful soil management and the targeted conservation of beneficial insects. The winery has been certified organic since 2010 and is a founding member of the Leithaberg DAC association. The winery has been Demeter certified since 2021.

92 ⊕ **Petnat Rosé 2019 PN/CH/SY**

91 ⊕ **Hartl Klassik Sekt g.U. extra brut NV CH/PN/SY**

(94) **Chardonnay * 2020**
13,5 Vol.-%, cork, large wooden barrel, €€€€ ⓑ
93 **Chardonnay * 2019**
92 **Chardonnay * 2018**

(95) **Chardonnay Purbach Ried Thenau 2019**
13,5 Vol.-%, cork, large wooden barrel, €€€€€€ ⓑ
95 **Chardonnay Ried Thenau 2018**
Bright medium golden yellow, silver reflections. Delicate nuances of flint, yellow peach, a hint of mango, delicate notes of tangerine zest, multi-faceted bouquet. Full-bodied, white stone fruit, fine acidity, tightly-meshed and persistent, delicately nutty on the finish, still somewhat underdeveloped, will benefit from bottle ageing.
94 **Chardonnay Ried Thenau 2017**

92 **Chardonnay 2021**
13,5 Vol.-%, screwcap, large wooden barrel, €€ ⓑ
90 **Chardonnay 2018**
91 **Chardonnay 2017**

WEINGUT TONI HARTL
2440 Reisenberg
Florianigasse 7
T: +43 (2234) 80636
wine@toni-hartl.at
www.toni-hartl.at

Winemaker: Toni Hartl
Contact: Toni Hartl, Moni Eder
Production: 10 % sparkling, 28 % white, 10 % rosé, 50 % red, 2 % sweet, 25 hectares
Fairs: Millésime Bio, ProWein Düsseldorf, VieVinum, DAC-Presentations, Wein Burgenland Presentations
Distribution partners: BE, DK, DE, FIN, FR, IT, JP, LU, NL, NO, PL, RO, SE, CH, SK, SLO, ES, CZ, HU

93 Furmint 2020
13,5 Vol.-%, cork, amphore, €€€€ Ⓑ Ⓘ Ⓥ

**93 Blaufränkisch * Purbach
Ried Rosenberg 2020**
13,5 Vol.-%, cork, 500-l-barrel, €€€€ Ⓑ

**93 Blaufränkisch * Purbach
Ried Rosenberg 2019**

97 Blaufränkisch Ried Eisner 2019
14 Vol.-%, cork, wooden barrel, €€€€€ Ⓑ

99 Blaufränkisch Ried Eisner 2017
Dark ruby colour, opaque core, purple reflections, subtle brightening on the rim. Fresh cherries, hints of liquorice and sea buckthorn, nuances of fine oak, mineral touch. Complex on the palate, fine red berryish fruit, well-integrated tannins, salty minerality, pleasant freshness in the aftertaste. Seems light-footed, remains long lasting; a varietal representative full of finesse and with certain ageing potential.

92 Blaufränkisch Ried Edelberg 2020
92 Blaufränkisch Ried Edelberg 2019

(94) Pinot Noir Ried Reysenperg 2020
13,5 Vol.-%, cork, 500-l-barrel, €€€€€ Ⓑ
94 Pinot Noir Ried Reysenperg 2019
93 Pinot Noir Ried Reysenperg 2018

92 Pinot Noir Ried Goldberg 2019
92 Pinot Noir Ried Goldberg 2018

94 Cabernet Sauvignon Ried Felsenstein 2020

(93) Syrah Purbach Ried Thenau 2020
14 Vol.-%, cork, small wooden barrel, €€€€€ Ⓑ
94 Syrah Ried Thenau 2019

94 Inkognito 2020 BF/CS/SY
14 Vol.-%, cork, small wooden barrel, €€€€ Ⓑ

WEINGUT KOLLWENTZ

What defines a truly great winemaker? Whether it's a small vintage or a great one, you can always count on them to create a superb wine. And the Kollwentz family has been a force to be reckoned with at every tasting for years, no matter what the vinification method or variety. At the Falstaff magazine's annual summer tasting of white Pinot and Chardonnay, the tasters are always in complete agreement. Not only is the classically vinified Chardonnay Leithakalk one of the best year after year, but the two Chardonnays from the Tatschler and Neusatz vineyards have also won the Burgunder-Barrique-Trophy (white Pinot varieties and Chardonnay barrique trophy) many times. And the Chardonnay Gloria won the Reserve Trophy. The Sauvignon Blanc from the Steinmühle vineyard also deserves special attention, as its flinty soil is ideal for this piquant variety. The results for the reds are no different from those for the whites: While Cabernet Sauvignon won in its category with the 2009 and 2011 vintages, the jury chose the Cuvée Steinzeiler 2008 as the winner. The Blaufränkisch Point 2015 scored an astounding 98 points, and the Cabernet Sauvignon 2018 received the top score of 100 points. Anton Kollwentz, senior, is the pioneer of Cabernet Sauvignon in Austria and started a real Cabernet boom with his Falstaff wins in 1984 and 1985. Andi Kollwentz junior is the decathlete of Austria's winemakers, mastering a wide range of disciplines and ranking among the best in every category. He is supported by his wife, Heidi, their two daughters, Barbara and Christina, and a well-coordinated team whose members have been working at the winery for over 25 years. The Kollwentz family's success is rooted not only in their meticulous nurturing of the vines but also in their 25 hectares of vineyard sites. Situated on the southern slopes of the Leithagebirge, the vineyards bear names such as Steinzeiler, Point, Setz, Dürr, Steinmühle, Neusatz, Tatschler, Katterstein, and Gloria. They are among the most historic and prestigious in the country. The vineyards are situated between 170 and 325 metres above sea level. The warmest sites are dominated by Blaufränkisch. The Point and Setz vineyards form the core of Großhöflein's red vineyards, from which the Blaufränkisch grapes for Steinzeiler, the win-

BURGENLAND

The Kollwentz family

WEINGUT KOLLWENTZ
7051 Großhöflein
Hauptstraße 120
T: +43 (2682) 65158
kollwentz@kollwentz.at
www.kollwentz.at

Winemaker: Andi Kollwentz
Contact: Heidi Kollwentz
Production:
54 % white, 5 % rosé, 40 % red,
1 % sweet, 25 hectares
Certified: Sustainable Austria
Fairs: ProWein Düsseldorf,
VieVinum, véritable St.Martin
Distribution partners: BY, BE, DE, UK, LU, NL, NO, PL, CH, SRB, SK, SLO, CZ, PT

ery's top wine, come. At over 200 metres above sea level, the realm of the Chardonnay begins. The altitude and the influence of the forests flanking the highest peaks of the Leithagebirge create a cool microclimate, which is reflected in the finesse of the aromas and the intensity of the flavours. The Chardonnay Crus "Gloria", "Tatschler", "Katterstein", and "Neusatz" thrive here on limestone soils, as does the Pinot Noir in the Dürr vineyard.

98 Chardonnay Gloria 2021
14 Vol.-%, cork, small wooden barrel, €€€€€€

96 Chardonnay Gloria 2020
Pale yellow-green, silver glints. Gently aromatic nuances of yellow tropical fruit redolent of pineapple and fresh mango, a hint of vanilla and blossom honey, as well as lychees and papaya. Complex, full-bodied, white peach, elegantly structured, silky and mineral, ethereal and persistent, superseded by resonating nuances of yellow apple. Definite ageing potential.

96 Chardonnay Gloria 2019

97 Chardonnay Ried Tatschler 2021
14 Vol.-%, cork, small wooden barrel, €€€€€€

95 Chardonnay Ried Tatschler 2020
95 Chardonnay Ried Tatschler 2019

96 Chardonnay Ried Katterstein 2021
14,5 Vol.-%, cork, small wooden barrel, €€€€€€

96 Chardonnay Ried Katterstein 2020
98 Chardonnay Ried Katterstein 2019

94 Chardonnay Ried Neusatz 2021
13,5 Vol.-%, cork, small wooden barrel, €€€€€€

94 Chardonnay Ried Neusatz 2020
94 Chardonnay Ried Großhöfleiner Neusatz 2019

93 Chardonnay Leithakalk 2022
13,5 Vol.-%, cork, large wooden barrel, €€€€

92 Chardonnay Leithakalk 2021
93 Chardonnay Leithakalk 2020

96 Sauvignon blanc Ried Steinmühle Methusalemreben 2021
13,5 Vol.-%, cork, used barriques, €€€€€

95 Sauvignon Blanc Ried Steinmühle Methusalemreben 2020
95 Sauvignon Blanc Ried Steinmühle Methusalemreben 2017

94 Sauvignon blanc Ried Steinmühle 2022
13 Vol.-%, cork, large wooden barrel, €€€€€

94 Sauvignon Blanc Ried Steinmühle 2021
94 Sauvignon Blanc Ried Eisenstädter Steinmühle 2020

96 Blaufränkisch Ried Point 2020
14 Vol.-%, cork, barrique, €€€€€€

97 Blaufränkisch Ried Point 2019
Deep ruby, purple glints, faintly lighter at the rim. Delicate aromas of hardwood, lovely dark cherry notes, a touch of blackberry, and delicate tobacco nuances. Multifaceted, youthful bouquet. Juicy, elegant, ripe sweetheart cherries,

© ©Bernhard Angerer / Wien

LEITHABERG DAC

delicately expressive, supporting tannins, mineral, and compellingly persistent. Definite potential for development.
97 Blaufränkisch Ried Point 2018

95 Blaufränkisch Ried Setz 2020
14 Vol.-%, cork, barrique, €€€€€
96 Blaufränkisch Ried Setz 2019
96 Blaufränkisch Ried Setz 2018

93 Blaufränkisch Leithakalk 2020
14 Vol.-%, cork, barrique, €€€€
93 Blaufränkisch Leithakalk 2019
92 Blaufränkisch Leithakalk 2017

96 Steinzeiler 2020 BF/CS/ZW
14 Vol.-%, cork, barrique, €€€€€
96 Steinzeiler 2019 BF/ZW/CS
Deep ruby, purple glints, faintly lighter at the rim. Fragrantly floral and underpinned with dark sweetheart cherries, subtle savoury wood tones, and soft notions of vanilla and nougat. Inviting bouquet. Juicy, elegant, ripe sweetheart cherries, fine tannins, balanced and long-lasting, with an ethereal impression and sweet reverberations. A very versatile food accompaniment, already accessible.
96 Steinzeiler 2018 BF/ZW/CS

94 Eichkogel 2020 BF/ZW
14 Vol.-%, cork, barrique, €€€€€
93 Eichkogel 2019 BF/ZW
94 Eichkogel 2018 BF/ZW

95 Cabernet Sauvignon 2020
14 Vol.-%, cork, barrique, €€€€€
95 Cabernet Sauvignon 2019
100 Cabernet Sauvignon 2018

94 Pinot Noir Ried Dürr 2021
13 Vol.-%, cork, barrique, €€€€
94 Pinot Noir Ried Dürr 2019
93 Pinot Noir Ried Großhöfleiner Dürr 2018

92 Zweigelt Leithakalk 2021
13,5 Vol.-%, cork, large wooden barrel, €€€
92 Zweigelt Leithakalk 2019
92 Zweigelt Leithakalk 2018

95 Chardonnay Beerenauslese 2020
97 Chardonnay Trockenbeerenauslese 2018
96 Chardonnay TBA 2007

94 Scheurebe Beerenauslese 2017
94 Scheurebe Beerenauslese 2016

★★★

WEINGUT MAD

Deeply rooted - and, as the winery's name suggests, a little crazy - the Weingut Mad has been in existence for 235 years and is now in its eighth generation of winemaking. Located in Oggau, in one of the world's most beautiful wine-growing regions between Leithaberg and Lake Neusiedl, the work of the extended family has always been defined by visions that seem a little crazy and challenging to realise. They are future-oriented but without forgetting tradition and craftsmanship.
The focus is always on quality. Sebastian and Tobias Siess took over the 34-hectare estate in 2018 and are dedicated, with the whole family's support, to produce wines with character and depth, which reflect the climate, the soil, and the people who make them. The brothers believe that great wine is alive, constantly changing, and needs time to mature.

92 Pinot Blanc * 2020
90 Pinot Blanc * Oggau 2019

91 Chardonnay * Oggau 2020
91 Chardonnay * Oggau 2019

90 Grüner Veltliner * 2020
89 Grüner Veltliner * Oggau 2019
90 Grüner Veltliner * Oggau 2018

89 Grüner Veltliner Seestern 2021

(92) * Hochenperg 2021 CH/NB/WB
13,5 Vol.-%, cork, barrique/used barriques, €€€€€
92 * Hochenperg 2020 CH/NB/WB
Pale golden yellow, silver reflections. Subtle background to-

*Leithaberg DAC

BURGENLAND

Merlot

WEINGUT MAD
7063 Oggau
Antonigasse 1
T: +43 (2685) 7207
office@weingut-mad.at
www.weingut-mad.at

Winemaker: Tobias Siess
Contact: Sebastian Siess
Production: 1 % sparkling, 34 % white, 4 % rosé, 60 % red, 1 % sweet, 34 hectares
Certified: Sustainable Austria
Fairs: Forum Vini München, ÖGW Zürich, ProWein Düsseldorf, VieVinum, DAC-Presentations, Wein Burgenland Presentations
Distribution partners: BE, RC, DE, NL, PL, SE, CH, USA

bacco aromas, yellow apple nuances, hints of pear and orange zest. Juicy on the palate with fine fruit expression, mineral, freshly structured and a salty-lemon finish. Already developing well with definite further ageing potential.

92 * Hochenperg 2019 CH/NB/WB

91 Blaufränkisch Ried Marienthal Rosé 2021

89 Pink Bliss 2021 BF/SL/PN/CF
88 Pink Bliss 2017 SL/PN/CS/BF/ME/ZW/CF

95 Blaufränkisch * Oggau Ried Marienthal M 56 2018
14,5 Vol.-%, cork, small wooden barrel, €€€€€

94 Blaufränkisch * Oggau Ried Marienthal 2019
14 Vol.-%, cork, barrique/used barriques, €€€€€
94 Blaufränkisch * Ried Marienthal 2018
Dark ruby with purple reflections, brightening at the rim. A hint of liquorice and herbs, with background notes of dark forest berries and a touch of orange zest, along with mineral appeal. Juicy, elegant, and balanced, with ripe cherry fruit, fresh structure, and a long, savoury finish. Already approachable, it has certain ageing potential.
94 * Ried Marienthal 2017

91 Blaufränkisch * 2019
92 Blaufränkisch * 2018
91 Blaufränkisch * Oggau 2017

92 Cabernet Franc Ried Neugebirge 2019
14 Vol.-%, cork, barrique, €€€€€
93 Cabernet Franc Ried Neugebirge 2018

92 Cabernet Sauvignon Merlot Ried Neugebirge 2020 ME/CS
92 Cabernet-Merlot Ried Neugebirge 2019 ME/CS/CF
93 Cabernet-Merlot Ried Neugebirge 2018 CS/ME/CF

91 Merlot Ried Loisland 2021
14 Vol.-%, screwcap, used barriques/barrique, €€€
91 Merlot Ried Loisland 2020
91 Merlot Ried Loisland 2019

89 Zweigelt Seestern 2021
89 Zweigelt Seestern 2020
89 Zweigelt Seestern 2019

92 Furioso 2019 BF/CS/ME/SY/CF
14 Vol.-%, cork, barrique/used barriques, €€€€€
93 Furioso 2018 BF/CS/ME/CF
92 Furioso 2017 BF/CS/ME/ZW

WEINGUT MORIC

Few other winemakers have generated as much public interest in recent years as Roland Velich. He has set himself the goal of giving Blaufränkisch a new, individual profile that will enable this typically Austrian grape variety to join the ranks of the world's great red wines. Velich believes that Burgenland has the same excellent conditions for producing great red wines as Burgundy or the northern Rhône Valley. He does not strive for stylistic copies but would rather portray his wines' "cool climate" character. He has complete confidence in the strengths of Burgenland and tries to exploit the guaranteed ageing potential of the Blaufränkisch variety and the varied soils. Roland Velich found suitable plots for his concept in central Burgenland. In Neckenmarkt and Lutzmannsburg, he discovered old vineyards, some over a hundred years old, planted at high densities of up to 8,000 vines per hectare. Here, with ideal exposure and terroir, the small-berried grapes that form the basis of the Moric line grow. The Lutzmannsburg site produces a fine mineral wine with floral nuances, while the neighbouring Neckenmarkt site produces a savoury Blaufränkisch, darkened by the slate soils. Small yields in the vineyard, extremely restrained processing, and long ageing in used 500 and 1,000-litre wooden barrels allow the distinct varietal and the soil character of the individual terroirs to come to the fore. A fine, full-bodied Grüner Veltliner is also produced in small quantities in St. Georgen near Eisenstadt.

In recent years, the old Blaufränkisch parcels in Lutzmannsburg have come increasingly into focus, fulfilling a long-held desire of Velich, starting with the 2019 vintage. He has bottled several different terroir wines individually and can now express the diversity and nuances of Blaufränkisch even more precisely. The 'Old Vines' from Lutzmannsburg are crowned at the top of the range, offering the best grapes a vintage has to offer from this exceptional winemaker. More Blaufränkisch is not possible. The international secondary market has already taken this into account: No other Austrian red wine producer enjoys greater demand, as the latest figures from the London wine exchange Liv-ex show.

96 Grüner Veltliner Sankt Georgen Ried Krainer 2021
13 Vol.-%

95 Grüner Veltliner Sankt Georgen Ried Krainer 2020

94 Grüner Veltliner Sankt Georgen 2021
13 Vol.-%

94 Grüner Veltliner Sankt Georgen 2020

92 Hausmarke weiß 2021
13,5 Vol.-%

(100) Blaufränkisch Lutzmannsburg Alte Reben 2021
13,5 Vol.-%

99 Blaufränkisch Lutzmannsburg Alte Reben 2019
Intense garnet core brightening to purple at the rim. Fine red cherries, red berries, a touch of liquorice, delicate tobacco and mineral notes in the background with a hint of bergamot. Complex, juicy, red berry fruit, taut tannins, finessed, richly structured, balanced, mineral, salty finish, exceptional length which is subtle and nuanced, very good ageing potential; surely a blueprint for great Blaufränkisch.

WEINGUT MORIC
7051 Großhöflein
Kirchengasse 3
T: +43 (664) 4003231
office@moric.at
www.moric.at

Winemaker/Contact:
Roland Velich
Production:
5 % white, 95 % red

BURGENLAND

98 Blaufränkisch Lutzmannsburg
   Ried Maissner 2021
13,5 Vol.-%

97 Blaufränkisch Lutzmannsburg
   Ried Maissner 2019

97 Blaufränkisch Lutzmannsburg
   Ried Kirchberg 2021
13,5 Vol.-%

96 Blaufränkisch Lutzmannsburg
   Ried Kirchberg 2019

Intense ruby with purple at the narrow rim. Elegant red berry notes are underscored with red cherries, a hint of raspberries, delicate notes of kumquats; a multi-faceted bouquet. Substantial, tightly textured, red berry fruit, fine tannins, lemony and fresh on the finish; a lively style with very good length and excellent ageing potential.

97 Blaufränkisch Lutzmannsburg
   Ried Schwemmer 2021
13,5 Vol.-%

96 Blaufränkisch Lutzmannsburg
   Ried Schwemmer 2019

Intense garnet with purple hues at the narrow rim. Fine nuances of dark cherries, a touch of liquorice, raspberries, candied orange zest, red berry notes, tobacco spiciness. Juicy, red berry fruit, mineral, fine well-integrated tannins, salty, very persistent, lovely red fruited finish.

95 Blaufränkisch Zagersdorf Krcsi 2012

(95) Blaufränkisch Moric Reserve 2021
13,5 Vol.-%

94 Blaufränkisch Moric Reserve 2019
94 Blaufränkisch Moric Reserve 2017

94 Blaufränkisch Raiding Ried Raga 2011

94 Blaufränkisch Burgenland 2021
12,5 Vol.-%

93 Blaufränkisch Burgenland 2020

93 Hausmarke rot S21
12,5 Vol.-%

93 Hausmarke rot Solera 2020

WEINGUT PRIELER
ORGANIC

"Wine is poetry in bottles". There is no better way to describe the wines of this small but fine family winery. Most of the estate is located in Schützen am Gebirge, but a significant portion of the vineyards are in the neighbouring village of Oggau. There are different soil compositions at every point of the compass, so it is easy to explain why the best sites were chosen for the specific varieties. Georg Prieler, the young oenologist with experience from abroad, has this talent. He always makes his decisions intuitively, which is fortunate because his wines are truly memorable. Soil and terroir also play a key role for the Prielers: the Seeberg and Sinner vineyards, which face Lake Neusiedl and produce the grapes for the great white wines, have limestone soils. Ungerbergen has sandy loam with gravel and is ideal for late-ripening varieties such as Cabernet Sauvignon. Goldberg, the undisputed best site of the estate, offers barren mica slate and is predestined for Blaufränkisch, the most traditional and important variety. The Prieler family always orientates itself on the characteristics of the respective site when vinifying the wines. The Pinot Blanc Seeberg, for example, is fermented exclusively in stainless steel tanks after an extensive maceration period to preserve its finesse and freshness. Blaufränkisch Johanneshöhe, on the other hand, is ‚nurtured' in large wooden barrels. And the very famous Blaufränkisch Goldberg acquires its incredible suppleness during a period of up to 26 months in 500-litre barrels. The latter Blaufränkisch Goldberg is a wine of superlatives, which has already won the "Falstaff Reserve Trophy" twice - in 2005 and 2008. The Prielers have also won the Falstaff Pinot Trophy with their white wines: two trophies for the Pinot Blanc Seeberg 2004 and the exceptionally mature Chardonnay Seeberg 2001. No wonder the family was honoured as "Winemaker of the Year" in 2009.

LEITHABERG DAC

WEINGUT PRIELER
7081 Schützen am Gebirge
Hauptstraße 181
T: +43 (2684) 2229
weingut@prieler.at
www.prieler.at
Winemaker/Contact:
Georg Prieler
Production: 40 % white, 60 % red,
23 hectares
Fairs: Austrian Tasting London,
ProWein Düsseldorf, VieVinum,
DAC-Presentations, MondoVino,
véritable St.Martin, Wein
Burgenland Presentations
Distribution partners: AUS, BE,
BR, RC, DE, UK, IRL, CDN, LV, NL, NO,
PL, RUS, SE, CH, ES, HU, US

(95) Pinot Blanc * Ried Steinweingarten 2021
13,5 Vol.-%, cork, wooden barrel, €€€€€ Ⓑ
95 Pinot Blanc * Ried Steinweingarten 2020
Medium yellow-green, silver reflections. Dark minerality, a touch of slate underlaid with soft yellow tropical fruit, some lime, fine blossom honey, multi-faceted bouquet. Full-bodied, elegant and balanced, a touch of fruit, fine acidity, soft caramel notes on the finish, persistent, definite ageing potential, a light-footed food wine with great depth.
95 Pinot Blanc * Ried Steinweingarten 2019

(94) Pinot Blanc * Ried Haidsatz 2021
13,5 Vol.-%, cork, oak barrel, €€€€ Ⓑ
94 Pinot Blanc * Ried Haidsatz 2020
95 Pinot Blanc * Ried Haidsatz 2019

(93) Pinot Blanc * Alte Reben 2021
13,5 Vol.-%, cork, wooden barrel, €€€€€ Ⓑ
93 Pinot Blanc * 2020
94 Pinot Blanc * 2019

92 Pinot Blanc Ried Seeberg 2022
13 Vol.-%, screwcap, steel tank, €€€ Ⓑ
92 Pinot Blanc Ried Seeberg 2021
91 Pinot Blanc Ried Seeberg 2020

92 Chardonnay Schützen am Gebirge Sinner® 2022
13,5 Vol.-%, screwcap, steel tank, €€€ Ⓑ
92 Chardonnay Sinner 2021
92 Chardonnay Sinner 2020

91 Rosé vom Stein 2022
12,5 Vol.-%, screwcap, steel tank, €€€ Ⓑ
90 Rosé vom Stein 2021

97 Blaufränkisch * Schützen am Gebirge Ried Goldberg 2019
96 Blaufränkisch * Ried Goldberg 2018
98 Blaufränkisch * Ried Goldberg 2017

95 Blaufränkisch * Ried Marienthal 2020
13,5 Vol.-%, cork, wooden barrel, €€€€€ Ⓑ
99 Blaufränkisch * Ried Marienthal 2019
Deep dark ruby, deep core, purple reflections, a subtle ochre lightening on the rim. Fine fresh herbs, red sour cherries, some cassis and tobacco, dark mineral notes, hints of lime zest and red pepper. Taut, elegant, ripe red cherries, fresh red berries, fine tannins, salty and enveloping, chalky nuances, an elegant food companion, with great ageing potential.
98 Blaufränkisch * Ried Marienthal 2018

(94) Blaufränkisch * Ried Pratschweingarten 2020
13,5 Vol.-%, cork. wooden barrel, €€€€ Ⓑ
94 Blaufränkisch * Oggau Ried Pratschweingarten 2019

92 Blaufränkisch Johanneshöhe 2018
91 Blaufränkisch Johanneshöhe 2017

94 Merlot Schützner Stein® 2020
14,5 Vol.-%, cork, barrique, €€€€€ Ⓑ
93 Merlot Schützner Stein 2019
93 Merlot Schützner Stein 2018

92 St. Laurent 2019
90 St. Laurent 2018

* Leithaberg DAC

The Neckenmarkter Hochberg is one of the most valuable red wine sites in Austria

BURGENLAND

MITTEL-BURGENLAND

DAC

Ried Gartenäcker, Deutschkreutz

BLAUFRÄNKISCH WITH CHARACTER

Blaufränkisch is the leading grape in the 2,035 hectares of vineyards in Mittelburgenland. "Mittelburgenland DAC" represents the ideal regional typicity of this variety. Four communities set the tone: Deutschkreutz, Horitschon, Lutzmannsburg and Neckenmarkt. Two modern cooperatives #prove that size can indeed translate to the highest quality.

Austrians have affectionately called central Burgenland, south of Lake Neusiedl on the Hungarian border, "Blaufränkischland" for decades. It was logical that the predominant variety of the 2,104 hectares of vineyards be the basis for its protected designation of origin. It was also logical that the regional name, which was already so strongly identified with Blaufränkisch, serve as the name for the region's DAC from the year 2005 onwards.

The Mittelburgenland DAC comes in three categories. Mittelburgenland DAC stands for fruit-driven Blaufränkisch vinified in traditional large wooden casks or stainless steel tanks. Single-vineyard Mittelburgenland DAC wines also bear the name of the vineyard in which they grew and are often matured in used small oak barrels.

The premium Blaufränkisch wines that are harvested late and are fuller in body, mature in small oak barrels and appear under the Mittelburgenland DAC Reserve protected designation of origin label.

From a geological point of view, central Burgenland belongs to the Oberpullendorf Basin. Its clayey marl, sand and gravel soils are occasionally interspersed with ancient coral banks. The protection of three mountain ranges in the north, south and west with an opening to the east, fully fosters the influence of the Pannonian climate.

BURGENLAND MITTELBURGENLAND DAC

There is an average of over 300 sunny days and as little as 600 mm rainfall annually. The regional soils' excellent capacity to store moisture has proven ideal for the late-ripening Blaufränkisch in such an arid climate.

Alongside Blaufränkisch, the red wine varieties Zweigelt, Cabernet Sauvignon and Merlot display ample body and supple structure, and perform very well both as varietal wines and blends. Dry white and rosé wines are also produced. These wines appear under the Burgenland protected geographical indication.

Mittelburgenland has become an attractive destination for tourists, not just for wine, but also for the thermal spas that have mushroomed in the past years. A varied recreational program for people of all ages adds to the appeal of this hospitable region.

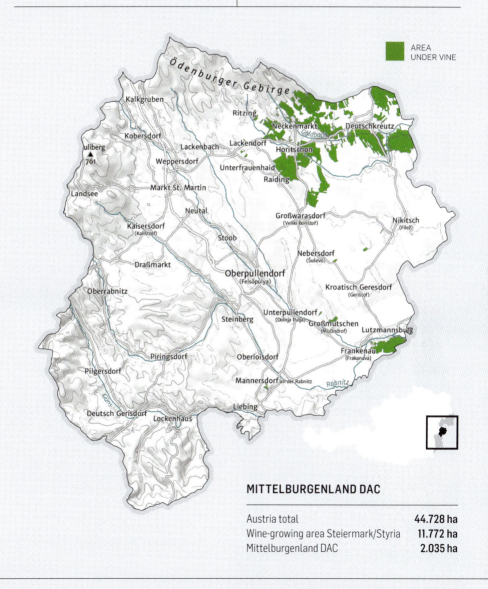

MITTELBURGENLAND DAC

Austria total	44.728 ha
Wine-growing area Steiermark/Styria	11.772 ha
Mittelburgenland DAC	2.035 ha

BURGENLAND

SELECTED WINERIES

★★★★★
Weingut Gesellmann, Deutschkreutz

★★★★
Weingut Gager, Deutschkreutz
IBY Rotweingut Bio, Horitschon

Weingut Josef Tesch, Neckenmarkt
Weingut Wellanschitz, Neckenmarkt

★★★
Weingut Ernst, Deutschkreutz

WEINGUT ERNST

The importance of being earnest has literally applied to Bernhard Ernst since he started in 2005. Even in the early days, he aimed to make serious and authentic wines. However, the process was more improvised and experimental in his parent's garage.
Everything has since stayed the same in his aim to make serious wines. What has changed are the circumstances: A modern new winery and a wife who "now shares his vision". Structure, order, and a touch of feminine elegance and flair were introduced. Sylvia Ernst, from Vorarlberg, decided to live in the east of Austria instead of the west and devote all her energy to this new task.
Together, the two live their daily lives as winemakers with one goal: to reflect their region in their wines. "Origin counts" is both their motto and their mission. In their three flagship site wines, the Blaufränkisch Fabian, Goldberg, and Hochberg, as well as in the two cuvées ZION and La Mission, you can clearly sense their origin - Deutschkreutz in Mittelburgenland - and their mission.

93 Blaufränkisch ** Ried Hochberg 2020
14,5 Vol.-%, cork, 500-l-barrel, €€€€
92 Blaufränkisch Reserve Ried Hochberg 2019
92 Blaufränkisch Ried Hochberg Reserve Deutschkreutz 2019

93 Blaufränkisch Ried Goldberg Reserve 2020
14,5 Vol.-%, cork, 500-l-barrel, €€€€
93 Blaufränkisch Ried Goldberg Reserve Deutschkreutz 2019
Deep dark ruby, opaque core, purple reflections, delicate bright rim. Cedar, graphite, ripe blackberry fruit, black cherry, some liquorice and tangerine zest. Full-bodied, red cranberry fruit, ripe tannins, elegant and mineral, pleasant freshness, shows length, good ageing potential, a juicy food wine.
93 Blaufränkisch * Ried Goldberg 2018

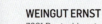

WEINGUT ERNST
7301 Deutschkreutz
Neubaugasse 21
T: +43 (664) 3860220
info@weinguternst.at
www.weinguternst.at

Winemaker/Contact:
Bernhard Ernst
Certified: Sustainable Austria
Fairs: VieVinum, Vinobile Feldkirch, Weinmesse Innsbruck
Distribution partners: BE, DE, UK, CH

MITTELBURGENLAND DAC

92 Blaufränkisch Ried Fabian Reserve 2020
14,5 Vol.-%, cork, 500-l-barrel, €€€€

92 Blaufränkisch Ried Fabian Reserve 2019

91 Blaufränkisch Deutschkreutz 2021
14 Vol.-%, screwcap, large wooden barrel, €€

90 Blaufränkisch Deutschkreutz 2020

91 Blaufränkisch Deutschkreutz 2019

94 La Mission 2020 ME/CS
15 Vol.-%, cork, barrique, €€€€€

94 La Mission 2019 ME/CS
Dark ruby garnet, black core, purple reflections, delicate rim brightening. Fine wood savouriness, tobacco, some cassis, liquorice notes, a touch of Valrhona chocolate, mineral touch. Juicy, taut, fine nougat notes, lemony touch, velvety tannin that carries well, fine blackberry notes, persistent, toasted nuances in the finish, a savoury food companion with certain ageing potential.

93 La Mission 2018 ME/CS

92 Zion 2020 BF/ZW/ME/CS
14,5 Vol.-%, cork, barrique, €€€€

91 Zion 2019 BF/ZW/ME/CS

90 Zion 2018 BF/ZW/ME/CS

WEINGUT GAGER

Perfection is the goal of the Gager winery in Deutschkreutz, Burgenland. Like a square with four equal and perfect sides, the square being the operative word here, as it has been used on the labels of Gager wines since the very beginning. Everything is done to achieve this figuratively speaking square: perfection in wine. What began as a hobby for his parents in the 1980s is now being pursued by Horst Gager in the second generation, and the future seems secure, with son Jonas, a student at the Klosterneuburg School of Viticulture, already helping out in the family business. With its exclusive red wine production, the Gager winery has already positioned itself as a red wine specialist far beyond Austria's borders. However, Gager does not have to look far when it comes to sourcing raw materials, as everything is close at hand - in the form of perfect grapes. And because of the winery's commitment to regionalism and conservation, it has already been certified as 'sustainable'. The company currently cultivates 38

WEINGUT GAGER
7301 Deutschkreutz
Karrnergasse 2 und 8
T: +43 (2613) 80385
info@weingut-gager.at
www.weingut-gager.at
Winemaker: Josef Gager, Horst Gager, Manuel Wieder
Contact: Josef and Paula Gager, Ing. Horst Gager, Daniela Dostal
Production: 100 % red, 38 hectares
Certified: Sustainable Austria
Fairs: ÖGW Zürich, ProWein Düsseldorf, VieVinum, Vinobile Feldkirch, Weinmesse Berlin/ Innsbruck/ München/ Salzburg, Weintage im Museumsquartier, Wein Burgenland Presentations
Distribution partners: BE, DE, LU, NL, CH

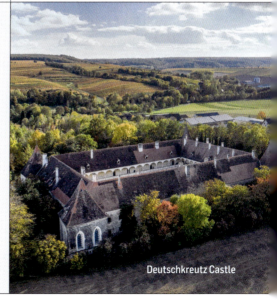

Deutschkreutz Castle

*Mittelburgenland DAC **Mittelburgenland DAC Reserve

BURGENLAND

hectares of vineyards. A total of eight grape varieties are grown, including the main regional variety and the Gagers' signature grape: Blaufränkisch. In addition to the region's leading variety, Zweigelt, Cabernet Sauvignon, and Merlot are also highlights. As well as their deep, dark colour, Gager wines are characterised by their compact structure and exceptional ageing potential - qualities that have earned them a long list of accolades.

(94) Blaufränkisch ** Ried Mitterberg 2021
14,5 Vol.-%, cork, barrique, €€€€€
95 Blaufränkisch * Ried Mitterberg 2020
97 Blaufränkisch ** Ried Mitterberg 2019

(96) Blaufränkisch BFG 2020
14,5 Vol.-%, cork, barrique, €€€€€
96 Blaufränkisch BFG 2019
Deep dark ruby, opaque core, purple glints, faintly lighter ochre hue at the rim. Sweet spices, a hint of cedar and bourbon vanilla, exuberant sweetheart cherries, blackberries, damsons, candied orange zest and a dash of nougat. Juicy, velvety, powerful, sweet berries, vivid, well-integrated tannins, saline-mineral finish. Still a little underdeveloped but will benefit from bottle ageing.
95 Blaufränkisch BFG 2017

(92) Blaufränkisch Ried Fabian 2021
14 Vol.-%, screwcap, used barriques, €€€
92 Blaufränkisch Ried Fabian 2020

92 Blaufränkisch Ried Fabian 2019

(94) Tycoon 2020 BF/TA/CS
14,5 Vol.-%, cork, barrique, €€€€€
94 Tycoon 2019 BF/CS/TA
Deep dark ruby, opaque core, purple reflections, delicate bright ochre rim. Spicy, tobacco, black berry, dark cherry, fine oak nuances, mineral touch, some vanilla in the background. Powerful, chocolaty, vivid somewhat demanding tannins, subtle fruit, persistent, port-like flavours of dried plum on the finish, shows length, still needs time.
94 Tycoon 17 2017 BF/TA/CS

(95) Cablot 2021 CS/ME/CF
14,5 Vol.-%, cork, barrique, €€€€
93 Cablot 2020 CS/ME/CF
95 Cablot 2019 CS/ME/CF

(93) Quattro 2021 BF/CS/ZW/ME
14,5 Vol.-%, cork, screwcap, used barriques, €€€€
92 Quattro 2020 BF/CS/ZW/ME
93 Quattro 2019 CS/BF/ME/ZW

(92) Q2 2021 BF/CS/SY
14,5 Vol.-%, screwcap, used barriques, €€€
91 Q2 2020 BF/CS/SY
92 Q2 2019 BF/CS/SY

92 T^nn^t 2018

93 Merlot 2017

WEINGUT GESELLMANN
ORGANIC

"In harmony with nature, we want to create wines that are rich in character and typical of the region every year." This guiding principle has accompanied Albert Gesellmann for years. With the 2015 vintage, the conversion was completed, and the first organically certified wines went on sale. The estate's 50 hectares are an exclusive size specifically designed to supply wine lovers worldwide with limited quantities rather than the world market.

At the Gesellmann winery, the focus is primarily on local red wine varieties. The "Opus Eximium", which combines the autochthonous varieties Blaufränkisch, Zweigelt, and St. Laurent to create an ideal food companion, is the winery's benchmark. The "G" cuvée also plays a key role: vinified from the Blaufränkisch and St. Laurent varieties. It captivates with its precise clarity, which is deeply enhanced by ninety-year-old vines. Since 2005, the "hochberc" has been vinified, a single-varietal Blaufränkisch that combines winemaker, variety, and region with great finesse. Another top cuvée is the "Bela Rex", a blend of Merlot and Cabernet Sauvignon, in which the winemaker demonstrates his skills with international grape varieties.

The Gesellmanns' vineyards also offer the best

© Photo credits: by Weingut Gesellmann

MITTELBURGENLAND DAC

WEINGUT GESELLMANN
7301 Deutschkreutz
Langegasse 65
T: +43 (2613) 80360
weingut@gesellmann.at
www.gesellmann.at

Winemaker: Albert Gesellmann
Contact: Albert and Silvia Gesellmann
Production: 9 % white, 90 % red, 1 % sweet, 50 hectares
Certified: Sustainable Austria
Fairs: VieVinum, Vinexpo, DAC-Presentations, MondoVino, Wein Burgenland Presentations
Distribution partners: AUS, BE, DK, DE, UK, JP, CDN, LU, NL, NO, SE, CH, CZ

Albert Gesellmann

conditions for the creation of white wine gems: The Chardonnay Steinriegel offers an exciting variety of aromas with fine mineral tones, and the classically vinified Chardonnay also reflects the winemaker's talent.

95 Chardonnay Ried Steinriegel 2021
14 Vol.-%, screwcap, small wooden barrel, €€€€€

94 Chardonnay Ried Steinriegel 2020
Light golden yellow, silver reflections. Delicate flint and grapefruit zest, hints of honeydew melon and vanilla, multi-faceted bouquet. Full-bodied, powerful, white tropical fruit, nashi pear and caramel, mineral finish, salty-lemony aftertaste.

94 Chardonnay Ried Steinriegel 2019

91 Chardonnay 2022
13 Vol.-%, screwcap, used barriques, €€€

92 Chardonnay 2021
91 Chardonnay 2020

93 Gemischter Satz hochberc weiss 2021
14 Vol.-%, screwcap, used barriques, €€€€
93 Gemischter Satz hochberc weiß 2020
92 Gemischter Satz hochberc weiss 2019

92 Sauvignon Blanc 2021
91 Sauvignon Blanc 2020
91 Sauvignon Blanc 2019

94 Blaufränkisch ** Creitzer 2021
14 Vol.-%, screwcap, used barriques, €€€€

93 Blaufränkisch ** Creitzer 2020
94 Blaufränkisch ** Creitzer 2019

(98) Blaufränkisch hochberc 2020
14,5 Vol.-%, cork,screwcap, 500-l-barrel, €€€€€

98 Blaufränkisch hochberc 2019
Dark ruby colour with opaque core, purple reflections, delicate brightening on the rim. Black forest berries, blackberries and liquorice, hints of cedar and vanilla, subtle hint of leather, dark minerality. Juicy, ripe heart cherries, nuances of red berries, ripe, structured tannins, fine acidity, mineral on the finish, already shows great length, salty touch in the aftertaste, good ageing potential.

97 Blaufränkisch hochberc 2018

97 Blaufränkisch hochberc Stockkultur 2018
98 Blaufränkisch hochberc Stockkultur 2017
97 Blaufränkisch hochberc Stockkultur 2016

93 Blaufränkisch vom Lehm 2021
14 Vol.-%, screwcap, large wooden barrel, €€€
91 Blaufränkisch vom Lehm 2020
92 Blaufränkisch vom Lehm 2019

(100) G 2019 BF/SL
14,5 Vol.-%, cork,screwcap, small wooden barrel, €€€€€€

97 G 2018 BF/SL
Deep ruby, purple glints, faintly lighter at the rim. Subtly fragranced wood nuances, delicate blackberry, blueberry, and a hint of liquorice, with resonating tones of nougat and orange zest. A multifaceted bouquet. Complex, luscious red sweet-

*Mittelburgenland DAC   ** Mittelburgenland DAC Reserve

BURGENLAND

heart cherries, subtle tannins, filigree structure, with a subtly sweet finish, mineral and persistent. Great ageing potential.
98 G 2017 BF/SL

(95) Bela Rex 2020 CS/ME
14,5 Vol.-%, cork,screwcap, small wooden barrel, €€€€€ Ⓑ
96 Bela Rex 2019 CS/ME
97 Bela Rex 2018 ME/CS

93 Opus Eximium No 33 2020 BF/SL/ZW
14,5 Vol.-%, cork,screwcap, oak barrel, €€€€€ Ⓑ
94 Opus Eximium No 32 2019 BF/ZW/SL
93 Opus Eximium No 31 2018 BF/SL/ZW

96 Merlot 2017
95 Merlot 2015

94 Syrah 2019
93 Syrah 2017

92 Pinot Noir Ried Siglos 2020
14 Vol.-%, cork,screwcap, 500-l-barrel, €€€€€ Ⓑ
93 Pinot Noir Ried Siglos 2019
92 Pinot Noir Ried Siglos 2018

94 Beerenauslese 2014 CH/SÄ

94 Sämling TBA 2015
95 Sämling 88 TBA 2013

★★★★

IBY ROTWEINGUT BIO
ORGANIC

The Iby family from Horitschon has been cultivating vines since 1884 and converted to organic farming more than ten years ago. The Ibys' main goal is to achieve the highest possible quality: "We can only achieve this with organic farming. For me, quality also means sustainability," says Anton M. Iby. "We are a normal family, with lively children, caring mothers and grandmothers, and self-confident fathers and grandfathers who naturally follow their wives' advice." However, two things set the Iby household apart from other families: Blaufränkisch and the name Anton. Anton Iby I founded the wine dynasty in Horitschon more than 100 years ago. Generation after generation, from Anton I to Anton V, have passed on their love of wine, craft and experience. Anton Iby IV paved the way for the breakthrough of the Blaufränkisch variety. Meanwhile, Anton M. Iby V continues to make wine with the know-how of his ancestors. "The beauty of observing the vine is that you use all your senses and possibilities to try to grasp what is happening - every year, every moment," he says.

The Ibys are proud of their Dürrau, Hochäcker, Gfanger and Rager vineyards, which could not be more different in composition. And just as a mother loves each of her children equally, they cherish each of their sites. They have a very clear idea of what they want from the vine and what they do not. They benefit from an in-depth knowledge of their soils, so they know how much nurturing the vines need in the vineyard and later in each of their wines. "We literally get to the bottom of Blaufränkisch because we live Blaufränkisch," says Eva M. Iby. The result is fruity, supple, elegant and highly refined red wines that captivate from the first sip.

IBY ROTWEINGUT BIO
7312 Horitschon
Am Blaufränkischweg 3
T: +43 (2610) 42292
weingut@iby.at
www.iby.at

Winemaker: Ing. Anton M. Iby
Contact: Ing. Eva M. Iby
Production: 180,000 bottles
100 % red, 40 hectares
Fairs: ProWein Düsseldorf, VieVinum, Wein Burgenland Presentations
Distribution partners: AUS, BE, RC, DE, HK, LU, NL, CH, CZ, HU, USA

MITTELBURGENLAND DAC

88 Blaufränkisch Rosé 2020	92 Blaufränkisch ** Ried Hochäcker 2019
89 Blaufränkisch Rosé 2019	
90 Blaufränkisch Rosé 2018	90 Blaufränkisch Classic 2021

95 Blaufränkisch ** Ried Dürrau 2018
14 Vol.-%, glass, barrique/large wooden barrel, €€€€€ Ⓑ Ⓕ Ⓗ Ⓢ Ⓥ

94 Blaufränkisch ** Horitschon
Ried Dürrau 2017

Dark garnet, purple reflections, faint ochre brightening on the rim. An inviting bouquet with hints of blackberry confit and ripe plums underlaid with pleasant herbal spice, spicy nougat touch, some leather. Juicy, elegant, red cherries, good fruit expression, fine, well-integrated tannins, freshly structured, salty minerality on the finish, shows length, good ageing potential.

94 Blaufränkisch ** Ried Dürrau 2015

94 Blaufränkisch ** Quintus 2019
94 Blaufränkisch ** Quintus 2017
93 Blaufränkisch ** Quintus 2016

(93) Blaufränkisch ** Chevalier 2021
13,5 Vol.-%, glass, barrique, €€€€ Ⓑ Ⓕ Ⓗ Ⓢ Ⓥ
93 Blaufränkisch ** Chevalier 2020
93 Blaufränkisch ** Chevalier 2019

92 Blaufränkisch ** Ried Hochäcker 2021
13 Vol.-%, glass, used barriques, €€€ Ⓑ Ⓕ Ⓗ
92 Blaufränkisch ** Horitschon
Ried Hochäcker 2020

92 Zweigelt Reserve 2020
91 Zweigelt Reserve 2019
91 Zweigelt Reserve 2018

89 Zweigelt Classic 2021
90 Zweigelt Classic 2017

(94) Vin Anton 2021 BF/ME
14 Vol.-%, glass, partial barrique, €€€€€ Ⓑ Ⓕ Ⓗ Ⓢ Ⓥ
93 Vin Anton 2019 BF/ME

Dark ruby, purple reflections, subtle ochre rim brightening. Delicately tobacco, black forest berries, a touch of liquorice, nuances of orange zest, delicate cassis. Powerful, dark wild berries, freshly structured, well-integrated tannins, mineral-salty finish, will benefit from bottle age.

93 Vin Anton 2018 BF/ME

91 Big Blend 2021 ZW/ME
13,5 Vol.-%, glass, used barriques, €€€ Ⓑ Ⓕ Ⓗ
91 Big Blend 2020 ZW/ME
91 Big Blend 2018 ZW/ME

(93) Merlot 2021
14,5 Vol.-%, glass, barrique, €€€€ Ⓑ Ⓕ Ⓗ Ⓢ Ⓥ
94 Merlot Reserve 2020
93 Merlot Reserve 2019

★ ★ ★ ★
WEINGUT JOSEF TESCH

The Tesch family has made it their profession and mission to produce excellent wines. Neckenmarkt in central Burgenland, with its deep, loamy soils, offers the best natural conditions for this. But it is not only the terroir and climate that determine the quality of a wine. It also takes a harmonious combination of winemaking knowledge, experience and hard work to produce wines of the highest quality. For the Tesch family, this "art of winemaking" is more than "just" work. For them, it is an expression of joie de vivre and a way of life that can be tasted and appreciated in the excellent wines that have been "liquefied" to reflect the unique character of the region and the grape.

The Tesch family's vineyards cover some 26 hectares in the foothills of the Ödenburg Mountains. Vines up to 70 years old and typical regional varieties thrive on the Hochberg, Weissen Weg and other prime sites. The soil composition is complex, and each vineyard has its own microclimate and unique characteristics. It is these differences and characteristics that are brought out in Tesch's wines through varietal distinctions and clear vinification. Blaufränkisch is the main variety in the Tesch's vineyards, accounting for around 60% of the total. Natural farming methods, limited yields to achieve the best quality, and care-

BURGENLAND

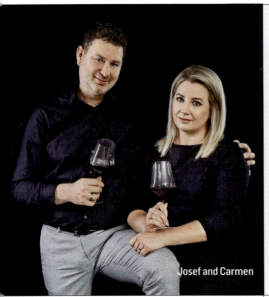

Josef and Carmen

WEINGUT JOSEF TESCH
7311 Neckenmarkt
Herrengasse 26
T: +43 (2610) 43610
titan@tesch-wein.at
www.tesch-wein.at

Winemaker: Josef Christian Tesch
Contact: Josef, Carmen and Helene Tesch
Production: 3 % white, 97 % red, 26 hectares
Certified: Sustainable Austria
Fairs: ProWein Düsseldorf, VieVinum, DAC-Presentations, Wein Burgenland Presentations
Distribution partners: RC, DK, DE, NO, RUS, SE, CH

ful hand harvesting are the basis of their first-class wines. For some years now, the Tesch name and especially the house wines have been the talk of the town. Tesch is committed to the Mittelburgenland region and focuses on authenticity in the development of its wines. The result is wines in which you can taste the deep affinity with the region.

89   Chardonnay 2020
89   Chardonnay 2019

90   Rosé 2022 BF/ZW

94   Blaufränkisch ** 2019
93   Mittelburgenland DAC Reserve 2017

91   Blaufränkisch * Neckenmarkt
     Ried Hochberg 2020
91   Blaufränkisch * Ried Hochberg 2019
91   * Ried Hochberg 2018

92   Blaufränkisch * Classic 2021
89   * Classic 2018
89   * Neckenmarkt Classic 2017

(97) Blaufränkisch Patriot 2019
14 Vol.-%, cork, barrique, €€€€€   V
95   Blaufränkisch Patriot 2018
Deep ruby garnet, purple glints, faintly lighter at the rim. Elegant wood notes, subtle vanilla, black forest berries, and a gentle cherry touch. A multifaceted bouquet. Good complexity, nougat touches, ripe tannins, and a vibrant structure marked by a cocoa finish. Offers promising ageing potential.
96   Blaufränkisch Patriot 2017

(93) Blaufränkisch Ried Bergleiten 2021
14 Vol.-%, cork, 500-l-barrel, €€€€€   V
93   Blaufränkisch Selection 2019
93   Blaufränkisch Selection 2018

(95) Titan 2021 BF/CS/ME
14 Vol.-%, cork, barrique, €€€€€   V
95   Titan 2020 BF/ME/CS
Dark ruby, purple reflections, soft brightening on the rim. Fine wood nuances, some vanilla and nougat, black cherries, ripe blackberries, soft notes of cassis and orange zest. Complex, juicy, sweet cherry fruit, taut, supporting tannins, good freshness, still very young and very promising, shows good length and certain ageing potential.
96   Titan 2019 BF/CS/ME

(94) Jana Paulina 2021 ME/CS
14 Vol.-%, cork, 500-l-barrel, €€€€€
93   Jana Paulina 2018 CS/ME
94   Jana Paulina 2017 ME/CS

92   Kreos 2019 BF/SY/ME/ZW
92   Kreos 2018 SY/BF/ME/ZW
92   Kreos 2017 SY/BF/ME/ZW

(90) Joe Nr.5 2020 BF/ZW/ME
13,5 Vol.-%, screwcap, 500-l-barrel, €€   V

MITTELBURGENLAND DAC

91 Cuvée 2020 BF/ZW/ME	(91) Zweigelt Ried Hochberg 2021
90 Carpo-Cuvée 2019 BF/ZW/ME	13,5 Vol.-%, screwcap, 500-l-barrel, €€€
90 Carpo 2018 BF/ZW/ME	91 Zweigelt Ried Hochberg 2019
	91 Zweigelt Ried Hochberg 2017
88 BZ Cuvée 2019 BF/ZW	
89 BZ - Cuvée 2018 BF/ZW	90 Zweigelt Classic 2021
	89 Zweigelt Classic 2019
(94) Merlot Enya Valea 2021	
14 Vol.-%, cork, 500-l-barrel, €€€€	(91) Pinot Noir Ried Hochäcker 2021
94 Merlot Enya 2020	13 Vol.-%, cork, used barriques, €€€€
95 Merlot Enya Valea 2019	91 Pinot Noir Ried Hochäcker 2020
92 Cabernet Sauvignon Tabea 2019	

★★★★

WEINGUT WELLANSCHITZ

ORGANIC

Few winemaking families have demonstrated as impressively as the Wells how to successfully steer a small family winery into the future without abandoning tradition and reverence for the precious terroir they cultivate. Since taking over from their parents and grandparents, they have carefully expanded the estate, following a philosophy mainly based on allowing the land of mica schist, granite gneiss, barren limestone and clay to shape their wines. Organic farming (certification completed) and a clear commitment to minimal intervention in the cellar are fundamental elements of the Wellanschitz wines. The vineyards are located in the foothills of the Alps, in the Ödenburg Mountains, on the border with Hungary. The high altitude vineyards (up to 480 metres above sea level) are a unique feature of Mittelburgenland and enable the production of complex wines. The Wellanschitz family's extensive range of Blaufränkisch wines

WEINGUT WELLANSCHITZ
7311 Neckenmarkt
Lange Zeile 28
T: +43 (2610) 42302
info@wellanschitz.at
www.wellanschitz.at

Winemaker: Stefan Wellanschitz, Georg Wellanschitz
Contact: The Wellanschitz family
Production: 1 % sparkling, 10 % white, 90 % red, 35 hectares
Fairs: VieVinum
Distribution partners: AUS, RC, DE, IRL, CDN, NL, CH, CZ, UA

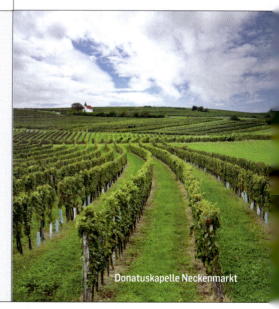
Donatuskapelle Neckenmarkt

* Mittelburgenland DAC   ** Mittelburgenland DAC Reserve

BURGENLAND

Blaufränkisch

showcase the differences between the individual sites in Mittelburgenland and make a valuable contribution to the preservation of the region's Blaufränkisch tradition. The Wellanschitz estate is known for its single vineyard Blaufränkisch from Hochberg, Sonnensteig, Hussi and Alter Weingebirge, as well as the Blaufränkisch Well Alte Reben from the family's oldest vineyard. The Rüsselgrund site guarantees perfectly ripe Cabernet Sauvignon, and the Fraternitas cuvée illustrates the collaboration between the Wellanschitz brothers, Stefan Paul and Georg.

99 Blaufränkisch Ried Sonnensteig 2019
13,5 Vol.-%, cork, 500-l-barrel, €€€€€€ B
98 Blaufränkisch Ried Sonnensteig 2018
Deep ruby, opaque core, purple glints, faintly lighter at the rim. Intense fresh dark berry fruit, sweetheart cherries, blackberries, a hint of liquorice, gentle herbal savoury nuances, and resonating zesty tones. A multifaceted bouquet. Succulent, fine fruit expression, elegant, balanced, silky tannins, pleasant freshness, and superbly developed. A seamless wine with great length and precision, saline reverberations.
97 Blaufränkisch Ried Sonnensteig 2017

94 Blaufränkisch Well Alte Reben 2020
96 Blaufränkisch Well Alte Reben 2019
13,5 Vol.-%, cork, 500-l-barrel, €€€€ B
Dark ruby, purple reflections, subtle brightening on the rim. Delicate herbal notes, tobacco, a touch of cherries, plums, candied orange zest. Juicy, elegant, plum fruit, red

cherries, fresh structure, well-integrated tannins, mineral, slightly salty finish, elegant with good persistency, complex food wine with ageing potential.
94 Blaufränkisch Well Alte Reben 2018

94 Blaufränkisch Neckenmarkter Ried Hussi 2019
93 Blaufränkisch Neckenmarkter Ried Hussi 2018
93 Blaufränkisch Neckenmarkter Ried Hussi 2017

94 Blaufränkisch Ried Burgstall 2021
13 Vol.-%, cork, 500-l-barrel, €€€€ B

94 Blaufränkisch Private Fass Selektion 2019

93 Blaufränkisch Neckenmarkter Fahnenschwinger 2021
13,5 Vol.-%, cork, large wooden barrel, €€€€ B V
92 Blaufränkisch Neckenmarkter Fahnenschwinger 2019
92 Blaufränkisch Neckenmarkter Fahnenschwinger 2017

(92) Blaufränkisch Central Schiefer & Lehm 2021
13,5 Vol.-%, screwcap, wooden barrel, €€€ B V
91 Blaufränkisch Central Schiefer & Lehm 2020
91 Blaufränkisch Central 2019

93 Fraternitas 2019 BF/CS/ZW
93 Fraternitas 2018 BF/CS/ZW
93 Fraternitas 2017 BF/CS/ZW

91 HA5NG 2021 BF/ZW/ME/CS
13,5 Vol.-%, screwcap, partial barrique, €€€ B
92 HA5NG 2020 BF/ZW/ME/CS

91 Cuvée vom Hotter 2021 BF/ZW/ME/SY/CS
13,5 Vol.-%, screwcap, wooden barrel, €€€ B V
91 Cuvée vom Hotter 2020 ME/ZW/CS/SY
90 Rote Cuvée vom Hotter 2019 ME/ZW/CS/SY

92 Cabernet Sauvignon Ried Rüsselsgrund 2019
93 Cabernet Sauvignon Ried Rüsselsgrund 2017

93 Syrah Orthogneis 2020
93 Syrah Orthogneis 2019
94 Syrah Orthogneis 2018

MITTELBURGENLAND DAC

SPACE FOR YOUR
WINE NOTES

* Mittelburgenland DAC   ** Mittelburgenland DAC Reserve

The region north and east of Lake Neusiedl owes its name to Europe's second largest steppe lake and offers perfect growing conditions for red and sweet wines

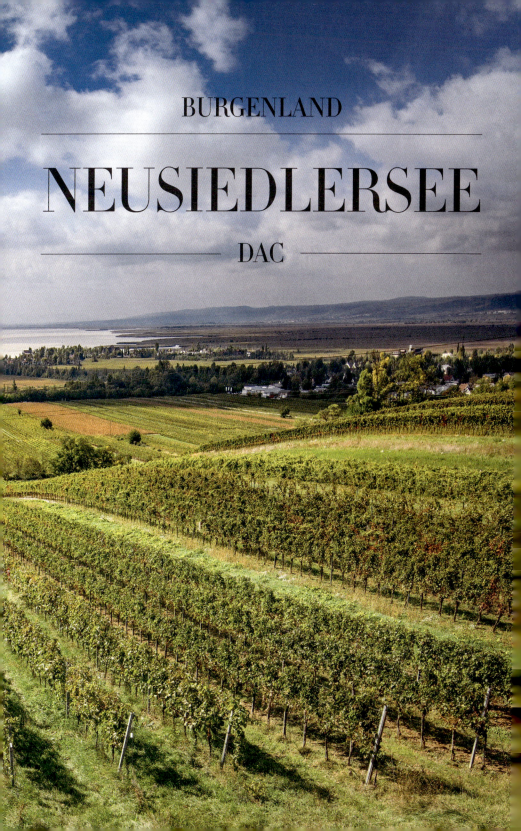

Ried Salzgründe, Lange Lacke near Apetlon

VARIETY OF ZWEIGELT AND GREAT SWEET WINES

On 6,110 hectares of vineyards, a variety of white, red and sweet wines ripen on the shores of the shallow steppe lake - from fresh wines to full-bodied and aromatic wines to the world-famous sweet wines, which will be allowed to bear the designation Neusiedlersee DAC from the 2020 vintage onwards. In recent years, the diversity of the Zweigelt in particular has come more and more to the fore, which has been allowed to be called Neusiedlersee DAC since 2012.

With 1,812 hectares, Zweigelt is the main variety here. For the classic Neusiedlersee DAC, which is brought to market a few months after the harvest; for the reserve category, ageing takes place in wood and the wine is bottled at least one year later. The vines are capable of storing pure sunshine in the extensive enclosed vineyards. The fully effective continental Pannonian climate with its hot, dry summers and cold winters, together with Lake Neusiedl as a temperature regulator, ensures a long growing season. High humidity and autumnal fog favour the noble rot (Botrytis cinerea) that regularly occurs here as the basis for the highest Prädikat wines such as Beerenauslesen and Trockenbeerenauslesen. These specialities have contributed significantly to the fact that the Seewinkel, which is still relatively young compared to more traditional Austrian wine-growing regions, has become known all over the world. Starting with the 2020 vintage, this reputation will be taken into account with the introduction into the DAC pyramid. The very differentiated soil structure - from loess and black earth to gravel and sand - allows an equally diverse range of grape varieties to flourish. In the white wine segment, it is mainly Pinot Blanc and Chardonnay as well as aromatic varieties, in addition to the leading variety Welschriesling, while in the red segment the Blaue Zweigelt

BURGENLAND **NEUSIEDLERSEE DAC**

is at the top, accompanied by Blaufränkisch, St. Laurent and Pinot Noir as well as international varieties. Whether they have been developed with fruit expression, matured in wooden barrels or barriques, or single-varietal or cuvée: the red wines from Lake Neusiedl are clearly on the road to success. The regional gastronomy has also started a campaign of charming eateries and food specialities, scoring points with an exciting combination of creative, modern cuisine and down-to-earth products. Vegetable specialities, fish or old breeds of cattle enrich the menus, congenially accompanied by suitable wines for every taste. As a balance to the wine and culinary indulgence programme, cycling tours, horseback riding or water sports are offered. The selection of guest rooms in every category also leaves nothing to be desired - from Neusiedl am See, Gols and Mönchhof on the north shore to Podersdorf, Illmitz, Apetlon and Pamhagen in the south and Wallern, Tadten, St. Andrä, Andau or Frauenkirchen in the east of the area.

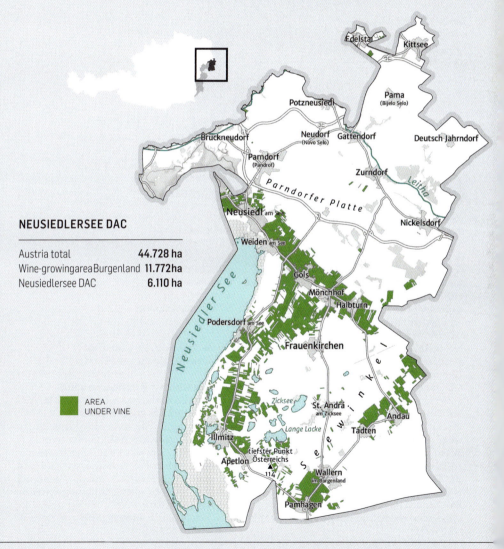

NEUSIEDLERSEE DAC

Austria total	44.728 ha
Wine-growing area Burgenland	11.772 ha
Neusiedlersee DAC	6.110 ha

SELECTED WINERIES

Weingut Paul Achs, Gols
Weingut Gernot und Heike Heinrich, Gols
Weinlaubenhof Kracher, Illmitz
Weingut Pöckl, Mönchhof
Weingut Tschida - Angerhof, Illmitz
Weingut Velich, Apetlon

Weingut Scheiblhofer, Andau
Weingut Schwarz, Andau

Allacher Vinum Pannonia, Gols
Weingut Jacqueline Klein, Andau
Weingut Münzenrieder, Apetlon
Weingut PMC Münzenrieder, Apetlon
Weingut Gebrüder Nittnaus, Gols
Weingut Hannes Reeh, Andau
Weingut Salzl – Seewinkelhof, Illmitz

Weingut Amsee, Gols
Nestor, Halbturn

WEINGUT PAUL ACHS

ORGANIC

Golser 'Pannobile' winemaker Paul Achs joined his parents' business full-time with the 1991 harvest and just four years later was named Falstaff Winemaker of the Year. Since then, the winery, which was once dedicated to white wines and combined tradition with modern cellar technology, has become a producer of excellent red wines. Red wine now accounts for 90 per cent of the estate's production. Paul Achs produces elegant wines with an eye for detail. Most of the wines are aged in barriques. This applies to Chardonnay and Sauvignon Blanc as well as the red wine specialities - from Pinot Noir to Blaufränkisch "Ungerberg" and the cuvée "Pannobile". A strict harvest limit of 3,000 kilograms of grapes per hectare is considered a prerequisite for top quality - an effort that has long since paid off, as Paul Achs' wines are among the best on the Austrian red wine scene, as the annual Falstaff Red Wine Awards attest.

97 Chardonnay Alte Reben 2021
14 Vol.-%, cork, 500-l-barrel, €€€€€ Ⓑ Ⓗ
94 Chardonnay Alte Reben 2020
Light yellow-green, silver reflections. Delicate nuances of yellow fruit, hints of apple and mango, fine nutty aromas, a touch of candied orange zest. Juicy, elegant, tightly structured, seems very delicate despite power, salty, a touch of walnut and lemon on the finish, a sophisticated food wine with ageing potential.
93 Chardonnay Alte Reben 2018

92 Chardonnay 2022
13 Vol.-%, screwcap, steel tank/wooden barrel, €€€
Ⓑ Ⓗ
92 Chardonnay 2021
91 Chardonnay 2020

90 Rosé 2021 BF/SL
90 Rosé 2020 BF/SL

97 Blaufränkisch Ried Altenberg 2020
14 Vol.-%, cork, used barriques, €€€€€€ Ⓑ Ⓗ
96 Blaufränkisch Altenberg 2019
Deep ruby, purple glints, delicate ochre hue at the rim. Delicately fragrant black forest berries, nuances of blackberries, and liquorice, a hint of cassis, as well as mineral undertones. Juicy, full-bodied, dark fruit, freshly structured, ripe, well-integrated tannins, mineral, and persistent. Promising ageing potential, a complex food accompaniment.
95 Blaufränkisch Altenberg 2017

NEUSIEDLERSEE DAC

WEINGUT PAUL ACHS
7122 Gols
Neubaugasse 13
T: +43 (2173) 2367
office@paul-achs.at
www.paul-achs.at

Winemaker/Contact:
Paul Achs
Production: 100,000 bottles
20 % white, 80 % red, 27 hectares
Fairs: ProWein Düsseldorf, VieVinum
Distribution partners: BE, DE, FR, NL, CH, USA

View of Lake Neusiedl near Gols

95 Blaufränkisch Ried Ungerberg 2021
13,5 Vol.-%, cork, used barriques, €€€€€€ Ⓑ Ⓗ
94 Blaufränkisch Ungerberg 2020
95 Blaufränkisch Ried Golser Ungerberg 2019

95 Blaufränkisch Reserve 2017
13 Vol.-%, cork, large wooden barrel, €€€€€ Ⓑ Ⓗ

94 Blaufränkisch Ried Spiegel 2021
13,5 Vol.-%, cork, used barriques, €€€€€€ Ⓑ Ⓗ
94 Blaufränkisch Spiegel 2020
94 Blaufränkisch Ried Golser Spiegel 2019

94 Blaufränkisch Ried Seufertsberg 2017

(92) Blaufränkisch Edelgrund 2022
13 Vol.-%, screwcap, used barriques, €€€€ Ⓑ Ⓗ
92 Blaufränkisch Edelgrund 2021
93 Blaufränkisch Edelgrund 2020

92 Blaufränkisch Heideboden 2019
90 Blaufränkisch Heideboden 2018

95 Pinot Noir Reserve Selektion P 2021
13,5 Vol.-%, cork, used barriques, €€€€€€ Ⓑ Ⓞ
94 Pinot Noir Reserve Selektion P 2020
Strong crimson garnet, purple reflections, broad ochre rim lightening. Red wild berries, floral nuances, a touch of bergamot, in the background with currant. Medium-bodied, fine cherry fruit, delicate, ripe tannins, light-bodied, light style, mineral on the finish, lingers well, certain ageing potential.

94 Pinot Noir Reserve Selektion P 2019

(93) Syrah 2021
13 Vol.-%, cork, used barriques, €€€€€ Ⓑ Ⓗ
93 Syrah 2020
94 Syrah 2019

(94) Pannobile Reserve 2021 BF/ZW
13 Vol.-%, cork, used barriques, €€€€€ Ⓑ Ⓗ
93 Pannobile Reserve 2020 BF/ZW
94 Pannobile Reserve 2019 BF/ZW

89 Lust & Leben 2019 BF/ZW/SL
90 Lust & Leben 2018 ZW/BF/SL

(93) Zweigelt Alte Reben 2022
13 Vol.-%, screwcap, used barriques, €€€ Ⓑ Ⓗ
91 Zweigelt Alte Reben 2021
92 Zweigelt Alte Reben 2020

(92) Zweigelt 2022
13 Vol.-%, screwcap, large wooden barrel, €€€ Ⓑ Ⓗ
90 Zweigelt 2021
90 Zweigelt 2020

91 St. Laurent 2021
91 St. Laurent 2019
91 St. Laurent 2018

* Neusiedlersee DAC   ** Neusiedlersee DAC Reserve

The Allacher family

ALLACHER VINUM PANNONIA
7122 Gols
Salzbergweg 4
T: +43 (2173) 3380
wein@allacher.com
www.allacher.com

Winemaker/Contact:
Michael Allacher
Production: 40 % white, 60 % red, 37 hectares
Fairs: Dornbirner Frühjahrs- und Herbstmesse, fafga Innsbruck, ProWein Düsseldorf, VieVinum, Vinobile Feldkirch, Weinmesse Innsbruck, Wein Burgenland Presentations
Distribution partners: BDS, DE, CH

ALLACHER VINUM PANNONIA

The vine has stood the test of time. The Allacher family has always worked in harmony with nature, trying not to tame the elements but to live with them and make the most of them to ensure the longevity of the vine. To make wine, you have to love nature with all its vagaries. The seasons mark the course of life and remind us of the transience of being. The joy of wine, creating something so wonderful and unique, motivates the Allachers to spend every day in the vineyards tending the vines. They see the harvest as nature's way of thanking humankind for all it has tended and nurtured over the year. The grape gives rise to unique creations and never ceases to inspire. Numerous awards confirm the success of the winery. The Allachers produce a wide range of wines - from dry whites to reds and sweet dessert wines. The Golser winery has made a name for itself with its red wines; the Zweigelt from the top Salzberg vineyard, for example, is constantly ranked among the best.

(92) Chardonnay Ried Altenberg 2022
13,5 Vol.-%, glass, barrique, €€€
92 Chardonnay Reserve 2020
Pale chartreuse yellow, silver reflections. Delicate notes of vanilla and pineapple, a touch of blossom honey, with subtle notes of wood in the background. Juicy, elegant, honeydew melon, a gentle acidity, harmonious and balanced, subtle caramel in the aftertaste, a versatile food companion.
92 Chardonnay Reserve Ried Altenberg 2019

90 Chardonnay 2022
13 Vol.-%, screwcap, steel tank, €€
90 Chardonnay 2021
90 Chardonnay 2020

90 Sauvignon Blanc 2022
12,5 Vol.-%, screwcap, steel tank, €€
90 Sauvignon Blanc 2021
91 Sauvignon Blanc 2020

89 Weissburgunder 2022
13 Vol.-%, screwcap, steel tank, €€ ⓗ
90 Weissburgunder 2021

(93) Blauer Zweigelt ** Ried Salzberg 2021
14,5 Vol.-%, glass, barrique, €€€€€
92 Blauer Zweigelt ** Ried Salzberg 2020
93 Blauer Zweigelt ** Ried Salzberg 2019

NEUSIEDLERSEE DAC

93 Blaufränkisch Ried Salzberg 2020
14 Vol.-%, glass, barrique, €€€€

93 Blaufränkisch Ried Eroffäcker 2017

(94) Imperium 2020 ME/CS
14,5 Vol.-%, glass, barrique, €€€€
93 Imperium 2019 ME/CS
93 Imperium 2018 ME/CS

(92) Cuvée Gérard 2021 ZW/BF/CS
14,5 Vol.-%, glass, barrique, €€€
90 Cuvée Gérard 2019 ZW/BF
90 Cuvée Gérard 2018 ZW/BF

(93) Ried Altenberg 2021 SL/ME/CS
14,5 Vol.-%, glass, barrique, €€€€
93 Ried Altenberg 2019 CS/SL/ME
Deep dark ruby, opaque core, purple reflections and delicate rim brightening. Underlaid with delicate smoky nuances, black forest berry confit, cassis, savoury nuances and orange zest. Juicy, fine tannic structure, oak savouriness, ripe plums, powerful, nougat on the finish, long lasting, will benefit from bottle age.

92 Altenberg 2018 CS/SL/ME

92 All Red 2021 ZW/ME
91 All Red 2020 ZW/ME
90 All Red 2019 ZW/ME

(92) St. Laurent Ried Apfelgrund 2021
14,5 Vol.-%, glass, barrique, €€€
91 St. Laurent Apfelgrund 2020
91 St. Laurent Ried Apfelgrund 2019

(91) Merlot 2021
14,5 Vol.-%, glass, barrique, €€€
92 Merlot 2019
92 Merlot 2018

WEINGUT AMSEE

Franz Pirker, a new winemaker and former manager in the field of electric mobility and a long-time winemaking friend, Helmut Preisinger, had a dream to produce their own wine. This dream was realised in 2012, and since then, the winery has won many awards and is an insider tip for wine lovers. Under the motto "Freude am Wein und Genuss" (Joy of Wine and Enjoyment), only high-quality single-varietal wines are produced with distinctive fruit notes. Only selected sites with the most suitable grape varieties are chosen to achieve this, as the site and the vine must be in harmony to achieve the desired characteristics. All grapes are selected, hand-picked and gently processed. The elaborate production methods contribute significantly to the distinctive fruity taste of the wines. Luscious notes like cherry, blackcurrant, banana vanilla and chocolate can be detected in these fruity wines.

90 Chardonnay 2022
12,5 Vol.-%, glass, steel tank, €€€
90 Chardonnay 2019
91 Chardonnay 2018

(94) Cabernet Sauvignon Alter Satz 2020
14 Vol.-%, glass, barrique, €€€€€
93 Cabernet Sauvignon Alter Satz 2019
Deep dark ruby, purple reflections, opaque core, delicate

WEINGUT AMSEE
7122 Gols
Neubaugasse 19
T: +43 (664) 75038676
office@wein-amsee.at
www.wein-amsee.at

Winemaker: Helmut Preisinger
Contact: Franz Pirker and Helmut Preisinger
Production: 5 % white, 95 % red
Distribution partners: DE

* Neusiedlersee DAC   ** Neusiedlersee DAC Reserve

BURGENLAND

bright rim. Fine tobacco spice, ripe plum, black olive, fine cassis nuances, floral touch. Juicy, tight, sweet tannins, blackberry confit on the finish, salty aftertaste, nougat and wood spice on the back palate, sure ageing potential.
93 Cabernet Sauvignon Alter Satz 2018

(93) Blaufränkisch V36 2020
14 Vol.-%, glass, partial barrique, €€€€€
94 Blaufränkisch V36 2019

93 Blaufränkisch V36 2018

91 Cabernet Franc 2019
92 Cabernet Franc 2018

(89) Zweigelt 2022
13,5 Vol.-%, glass, used barriques, €€€
91 Blauer Zweigelt 2020
91 Zweigelt 2019

WEINGUT GERNOT UND HEIKE HEINRICH

ORGANIC

Insightful observation of nature, biodynamic farming, and the untamed biodiversity above and below ground: Gernot and Heike Heinrich's idea of terroir-driven wines are based on a deep understanding of the diverse environmental habitats within their vineyards. The aim is to create a natural balance in which vines, people, and animals live in symbiosis, and the essential elements form a greater whole. The natural conditions for this are the cool limestone slopes of the Leithaberg, a modulated topography with a warmer climate around the winery in Gols, and a handful of autochthonous grape varieties led by Blaufränkisch. Undogmatic, artisanal vinification allows the wines to reveal their origins in an unadulterated and distinctive way. They lay the foundations for eternal evolution. The exchange with friends from Pannobile, Demeter, and the Respect Biodyn association opens up new perspectives. The result is vibrant and vital wines that reveal the essence of their place of origin in a purist and characterful way, whether on the Leithaberg or around Gols.

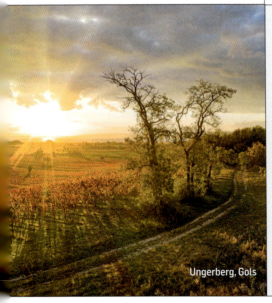

Ungerberg, Gols

WEINGUT GERNOT UND HEIKE HEINRICH
7122 Gols, Baumgarten 60
T: +43 (2173) 3176
weingut@heinrich.at
www.heinrich.at
Winemaker: Gernot Heinrich and Harald Lehner
Contact: Heike Heinrich
Production: 15 % white, 85 % red, 100 hectares
Fairs: Austrian Tasting London, Millésime Bio, ProWein Düsseldorf, London Wine Fair, VieVinum, DAC-Presentations, Summa Margreid, Karakterre, 501 Bio-Dyn
Distribution partners: BY, BE, BR, RC, DK, DE, EST, FIN, FR, UK, HK, IS, IT, JP, CDN, LV, LT, LU, NL, NO, PE, PL, PT, RUS, SE, CH, SGP, ES, ZA, TH, UA, USA, UAE, PT

94 Roter Traminer Freyheit 2021
92 Roter Traminer Freyheit 2019
94 Roter Traminer Freyheit 2018

91 Graue Freyheit 2021 WB/PG/CH/NB
12,5 Vol.-%, cork, large wooden barrel/amphore, €€€€€ Ⓑ Ⓘ Ⓥ
93 Graue Freyheit 2020 WB/PG/CH/NB
Bright light copper red, orange reflections. Delicate bouquet, fresh red fruit of the forest, some pear, nuances of black tea, a touch of orange zest. Elegant, white stone fruit, fresh acidity, mineral salty finish, nice citrus touch, a lively food wine.
94 Graue Freyheit 2018 WB/PG/CH

92 Muskat Freyheit 2017

92 Weißburgunder Ried Salzberg 2019

(97) Blaufränkisch Leithaberg DAC
 Ried Alter Berg 2019
13,5 Vol.-%, glass, 500-l-barrel/amphore, €€€€€€ Ⓑ Ⓥ
96 Blaufränkisch Leithaberg DAC Winden
 Ried Alter Berg 2018
Deep ruby, purple tinges, faintly lighter ochre hue at the rim. Soft spicy notions, candied orange zest, dark berries, and black cherries. A multifaceted, attractive bouquet. Juicy nuances of red fruit, mineral, silky tannins, freshly structured, marked by cherry reverberations and a saline finish. Already accessible, good ageing potential.
97 Blaufränkisch Leithaberg DAC
 Ried Alter Berg 2017

(95) Blaufränkisch Leithaberg DAC
 Breitenbrunn Ried Edelgraben 2019
13,5 Vol.-%, glass, 500-l-barrel/amphore, €€€€€€ Ⓑ Ⓥ
95 Blaufränkisch Leithaberg DAC Breitenbrunn Ried Edelgraben 2018
Deep dark ruby, purple glints, faintly lighter at the rim. Black forest berries, blackberry confit, a hint of tobacco, and subtle toasty notes. Inviting bouquet. Juicy, elegant, lush cherry fruit, silky tannins, mineral, and persistent marked by resonating sweet cherry nuances. A harmonious food accompaniment, very good ageing potential.
95 Blaufränkisch Leithaberg DAC
 Ried Edelgraben 2017

(93) Blaufränkisch Leithaberg DAC 2019
13 Vol.-%, glass, 500-l-barrel/amphore, €€€€€ Ⓑ Ⓥ
93 Leithaberg DAC 2017

97 Ried Salzberg 2018 BF/ME
98 Ried Salzberg 2017 BF/ME

94 Ried Gabarinza 2018 ZW/ME/BF
94 Ried Gabarinza 2017 BF/ME/ZW

94 Pannobile 2019 ZW/BF
13 Vol.-%, glass, 500-l-barrel/amphore, €€€€€ Ⓑ Ⓥ
94 Pannobile 2018 ZW/BF
93 Pannobile 2017 ZW/BF

WEINGUT JACQUELINE KLEIN

The concentrated power of the sun in every grape is what Jacqueline Klein captures in her wines. In northern Burgenland, surrounded by windmills, farmland, and the picturesque countryside around Andau, the hottest place in Austria, are the winemaker's sustainably cultivated vineyards. Here, her vines flourish to produce exquisite, full-bodied wines of exceptional style. This terroir is made for red wine!

The leading grape variety is the autochthonous Zweigelt, which is used both as a single variety and as a cuvée. Due to climate change, the trend is towards international grape varieties such as Cabernet Sauvignon, Merlot, Syrah, and Cabernet Franc. This is also reflected in the restructuring of the vineyard, where in recent years, more Cabernet varieties have been planted, which are better able to cope with prolonged drought due to their small, loose berry clusters and robust skin.

The reds are mostly matured in French oak barrels, where a variety of toasting variants are carefully selected depending on the vintage and maturity. This is how Klein makes wine.

(91) Chardonnay 2022
14,5 Vol.-%, screwcap, barrique, €€
90 Chardonnay 2021
91 Chardonnay 2020

BURGENLAND

Vines near Andau

WEINGUT JACQUELINE KLEIN
7163 Andau
Baumhöhäcker 10
T: +43 (664) 75124505
info@klein-wein.at
www.klein-wein.at

Winemaker/Contact:
Jacqueline Klein
Production: 15 % white, 85 % red, 42 hectares
Certified: Sustainable Austria
Fairs: VieVinum, Vinobile Feldkirch, DAC-Presentations, Wein Burgenland Presentations
Distribution partners: BE, RC, DE, LU, PL, CH, CZ

---

93 Neusiedlersee DAC Reserve 2017

90 Zweigelt * 2019
90 Neusiedlersee DAC 2018

92 Zweigelt Exklusiv 2021
14 Vol.-%, cork, barrique, €€€
92 Zweigelt Exklusiv 2020
Dark ruby garnet colour with opaque core, purple reflections, delicate ochre brightening on the rim. Black forest berries, hints of figs, dried plums, nougat, candied orange zest. Juicy, ripe heart cherries, fresh acidity, elegant and balanced, fine savoury finish, fine nougat in the aftertaste, a textured food wine.
92 Zweigelt Exklusiv 2019

94 Cabernet Franc Reserve 2020
15 Vol.-%, cork, barrique, €€€€€

92 Cabernet Franc 2019
93 Cabernet Franc 2018

94 Alius 2020 ME/SY
15 Vol.-%, cork, barrique, €€€€
92 Alius 2019 ME/SY
Dark ruby colour, deep core, purple reflections, subtle ochre lightening on the rim. Ripe plums, nougat, tobacco and some old wood spice, a hint of figs in the background. Juicy, fine nougat, freshly structured with integrated, firm tannins, ripe fruit with plums, a chocolatey finish, good ageing potential.
92 Alius 2018 ME/SY

91 Tribus 2020 ZW/ME/CS
92 Tribus 2019 ZW/ME/CS
92 Tribus 2018 ZW/ME/CS

91 Aridus 2019 ZW/SY

90 Crassus 2020 CF/ZW/SY
91 Crassus 2019 CF/ZW/SY
92 Crassus 2018 CF/ZW/SY

92 Cabernet Sauvignon 2020
91 Cabernet Sauvignon 2018

92 Merlot Reserve 2017

90 Merlot 2020
92 Merlot 2019

92 Syrah 2019
92 Syrah 2018

WEINLAUBENHOF KRACHER

⭐⭐⭐⭐⭐

In 1981, when Alois Kracher had just taken over the vinification from his father, the next promising generation of the Burgenland winemaking family was already born with Gerhard Kracher. After completing an apprenticeship in business administration, Gerhard began to actively work in the winery, to establish contacts and to contribute and implement his ideas and conceptions. Together with his father he planned and carried out the rebuilding of the winery, step by step he took over responsibility in specific markets, represented the winery at various events worldwide and gained important experience with the distribution partner in the USA. The good contacts of his father Alois contributed significantly to Gerhard Kracher quickly finding the right contacts in the wine scene. Thus, he was able to acquire a profound wine knowledge very quickly and found the opportunity to train his palate and to taste and learn to distinguish between the different wines and wine styles. Today, he manages the winery with the support of his wife Yvonne.

The Kracher name no longer stands for sweet wine alone. Together with producer friends, Alois Kracher has created a whole range of products for upscale enjoyment. Gerhard Kracher continues these successful cooperations. It is an exciting legacy that the 40-year-old is carrying on. It does not only include a world-famous winery, sought-after wines with top ratings and the responsibility to continue this, but also character traits like the spirit, the strength and the indomitable will that Gerhard inherited from his famous father.

93 **Muskat Ottonel Auslese 2021**
10 Vol.-%, screwcap, steel tank, €€€
93 **Muskat-Ottonel Auslese 2020**
92 **Muskat Ottonel Auslese 2019**

94 **Cuvée Auslese 2022 WR/CH**
10 Vol.-%, screwcap, steel tank, €€€
93 **Auslese Cuvée 2021**
91 **Auslese Cuvée 2017 CH/WR**

92 **Traminer Auslese 2018**
90 **Traminer Auslese 2017**

93 **Cuvée Spätlese 2022 CH/WB/WR**
8 Vol.-%, screwcap, steel tank, €€€
92 **Spätlese Cuvée 2021 WR/WB/CH**
91 **Spätlese Cuvée 2020 CH/WB/WR**

94 **Cuvée Beerenauslese 2020 WR/CH**
11 Vol.-%, cork, steel tank/barrique, €€€€
93 **Beerenauslese Cuvée 2018 WR/CH**
93 **Beerenauslese Cuvée 2017 CH/WR**

93 **Zweigelt Auslese 2022**
10,5 Vol.-%, cork, barrique, €€€
91 **Zweigelt Auslese 2020**

92 **Zweigelt Spätlese Rot 2020**

94 **Zweigelt Beerenauslese 2021**
11 Vol.-%, cork, barrique, €€€€
92 **Zweigelt Beerenauslese 2019**
91 **Zweigelt Beerenauslese 2018**

92 **Merlot Spätlese Rosé 2022**
9 Vol.-%, screwcap, steel tank, €€€
90 **Merlot Spätlese Rosé 2021**
92 **Merlot Spätlese Rosé 2020**

WEINLAUBENHOF KRACHER
7142 Illmitz
Apetloner Straße 37
T: +43 (2175) 3377
office@kracher.at
www.kracher.at

Winemaker/Contact:
Gerhard Kracher
Production: 15 % white, 15 % red, 70 % sweet, 33 hectares
Fairs: ProWein Düsseldorf, Vinexpo
Distribution partners: AUS, BE, BR, BG, RC, DK, DE, EST, FIN, FR, UK, HK, RI, IRL, IL, IT, JP, CDN, HR, LV, LT, LU, NL, NO, PL, PT, RO, RUS, SE, CH, SGP, SK, ES, TH, CZ, UA, HU, USA, UAE, PT

BURGENLAND

Illmitz

94 Rosenmuskateller Beerenauslese
    Red Roses 2020
11 Vol.-%, cork, barrique, €€€€€

93 Rosenmuskateller Beerenauslese
    »Red Roses« 2018

97 Welschriesling 60 Years Anniversary
    TBA 2017

KRACHER COLLECTIONS

VINTAGE 2020

94 TBA No. 1 Zweigelt Nouvelle Vague
10,5 Vol.-%, cork, barrique, €€€€€€
95 TBA No. 2 Traminer Nouvelle Vague
11 Vol.-%, cork, barrique, €€€€€€
96 TBA No. 3 Scheurebe Zwischen den Seen
9 Vol.-%, cork, steel tank, €€€€€
97 TBA No 4. Grande Cuvée Nouvelle Vague
    WR/CH
10 Vol.-%, cork, wooden barrel/barrique, €€€€€€
97 TBA No. 5 Rosenmuskateller
    Zwischen den Seen
9 Vol.-%, cork, barrique
98 TBA No. 6 Welschriesling
    Zwischen den Seen
8,5 Vol.-%, cork, steel tank

VINTAGE 2019

94 TBA No. 1 Traminer Nouvelle Vague
10 Vol.-%, cork, barrique, €€€€€€
96 TBA No. 2 Muskat Ottonel Zwischen den Seen
10 Vol.-%, cork, steel tank, €€€€€€
Strong golden yellow, silver reflections. White tropical fruit, some nutmeg, subtle herbal spice, a touch of blossom honey. Medium-bodied, balanced, peach, fine acidity, mineral and taut, delicate stone fruit nuances on the finish, full of tension, freshness and fruit, like from a picture book.
94 TBA No. 4 Zweigelt Nouvelle Vague
9 Vol.-%, cork, barrique, €€€€€€
98 TBA No. 5 Grande Cuvée Nouvelle Vague
10 Vol.-%, cork, barrique, €€€€€€
Strong golden yellow, silver reflections. Fine wood nuances, OF cardamom and vanilla, background of ripe yellow tropical fruit, fine dried fruit nuances, savoury botrytis touch, candied orange zest. Juicy, ripe yellow tropical fruit, mango and papaya, elegant and already very well developed, a particularly coherent and easy-to-drink wine with certain ageing potential.
98 TBA No. 6 Welschriesling
    Zwischen den Seen
9,5 Vol.-%, cork, steel tank, €€€€€€
Strong golden yellow, silver reflections. Delicate herbal savouriness, fine stone fruit nuances, a touch of dried fruit, discreet nougat, candied orange zest, multi-faceted bouquet. Complex, tightly meshed, fine fruit sweetness, underpinned with a pleasant acid structure, mineral and long lasting, already very well developed, still some baby fat, elegant wine, certain ageing potential.
98 TBA No. 7 Rosenmuskateller
    Zwischen den Seen
10,5 Vol.-%, cork, barrique, €€€€€

VINTAGE 2018

93 TBA No. 1 Zweigelt Nouvelle Vague
93 TBA No. 2 Welschriesling Zwischen den Seen
94 TBA No. 3 Scheurebe Zwischen den Seen
94 TBA No. 4 Rosenmuskateller
    Nouvelle Vague
96 TBA No. 5 Grande Cuvée Nouvelle Vague
    WR/CH
94 TBA No. 6 Traminer Nouvelle Vague
95 TBA No. 7 Scheurebe Zwischen den Seen
96 TBA No. 8 Welschriesling
    Zwischen den Seen
98 TBA No. 9 Welschriesling
91 TBA No. 10 Traminer Nouvelle Vague

WEINGUT MÜNZENRIEDER

Weingut Münzenrieder is located in Apetlon, in the immediate vicinity of numerous salt lakes that are highly typical of this area. Today, this winery is far from unknown, especially regarding its Prädikat wines, the balance of which is one of the winemaker's most important concerns. The typical character of the terroir is reflected in the wines of this dedicated winemaking family. Johannes Münzenrieder, who took over the winery in 2005, has given it a new lease of life with his red wine cuvée "Mavie" and the reconstruction of the cellar and the new sales room. The fruitiness and concentration of the Sämling, Welschriesling, and Grüner Veltliner grape varieties make them ideal for producing Beerenauslese, Trockenbeerenauslese, and Icewines typical of the region, which is characterised by a harmonious combination of sweetness and acidity with the fruity components of the wine. Zweigelt, Blaufränkisch and cuvées of Zweigelt, Cabernet Franc and Merlot are also produced. However, the Münzenrieder family is also devoting more and more energy to dry white wines, which are vinified in steel tanks as well as small wooden barrels. International awards and frequent inclusion in the Austrian Wine Salon are testimony to the quality of the wines, as are export successes overseas.

93 Chardonnay Ried Salzgründe Reserve 2020
13,5 Vol.-%, cork, 500-l-barrel, €€€

91 Chardonnay Heideboden 2022
13,5 Vol.-%, screwcap, partial barrique, €€
90 Chardonnay Heideboden 2021
90 Chardonnay Heideboden 2020

91 Chardonnay Reserve C14 2020
91 Chardonnay Reserve C13 2019
92 Chardonnay Reserve C12 2018

90 Sauvignon Blanc Reserve 2019
91 Sauvignon Blanc Reserve 2018

89 Sauerstoff 2021 GV/GM/SB/CH
90 Sauerstoff 2020 GV/SB/GM

92 Blauer Zweigelt ** Ried Römerstein 2020
14 Vol.-%, cork, barrique, €€€
91 Zweigelt ** Ried Römerstein 2019
91 * Ried Illmitzer Römerstein 2018

(93) Zweiglas 2020 ME/CF/ZW
14,5 Vol.-%, cork, barrique, €€€€
93 Zweiglas 2019 ME/CF/ZW
93 Zweiglas 2018 ZW/CF/ME

92 Mavie 2020 ME/ZW/CF
14,5 Vol.-%, cork, barrique, €€€€
92 Mavie 2019 ME/CF
Opaque ruby core, purple reflections, subtle brightening on the rim. Elegant aromas of blackberries and delicate savoury notes of wood spices, garden herbal and bergamot. Good complexity, juicy, concentrated black cherries, saline notes and rich plums on the finish. Offering very good ageing potential.
92 Mavie 2018 ME/CF/ZW

89 Grande Cuvée Reserve 2020 ZW/ME
90 Grande Cuvée Reserve 2019 ZW/ME

91 Merlot Reserve 2020
14,5 Vol.-%, screwcap, barrique, €€€
92 Merlot Reserve 2019

WEINGUT MÜNZENRIEDER
7143 Apetlon
Wallerner Straße 27
T: +43 (2175) 2259
info@muenzenrieder.at
www.muenzenrieder.at

Winemaker/Contact:
Johannes Münzenrieder
Production: 30 % white, 5 % rosé, 60 % red, 5 % sweet, 33+15 hectares
Certified: Sustainable Austria
Fairs: VieVinum
Distribution partners: BE

* Neusiedlersee DAC   ** Neusiedlersee DAC Reserve

BURGENLAND

91 Merlot Reserve 2018	94 Welschriesling Siddhartha TBA 2017
91 Cabernet Franc Reserve 2020	96 Welschriesling TBA Siddhartha 2015
14,5 Vol.-%, screwcap, barrique, €€€	
90 Cabernet Franc Reserve 2018	94 Sämling TBA 2020
91 Cabernet Franc Reserve 2017	9 Vol.-%, cork, steel tank, €€€
	92 Sämling TBA 2018
94 Welschriesling ** Siddhartha TBA 2018	94 Sämling TBA 2017
Deep golden yellow, silver reflections. Delicate botrytis nuances, orange zest, subtle wood spice, underpinned with yellow tropical fruit and a honey touch. Juicy, ripe yellow apple, well-integrated fruit, fine acidity, balanced and developed, a versatile sweet wine with definite ageing potential.	93 Blauer Zweigelt Beerenauslese 2020
	93 Grüner Veltliner Eiswein 2018
	93 Beerenauslese Cuvée 2017 WR/SÄ/GV

WEINGUT PMC MÜNZENRIEDER

Weingut Münzenrieder winery is located in Apetlon, in the immediate vicinity of numerous salt lakes of the National Park Lake Neusiedl - Seewinkel, and is owned by brothers Peter and Christoph Münzenrieder. The management has an eye for design and flair, as is evident from the winery's design and memorable wine labels. The tasting rooms offer a glimpse into the impressive barrique cellar, where the site's wines mature at optimal temperatures. The brothers are right on target with their viticultural philosophy and sense of terroir. Four wines deserve special mention from the single vineyard sites: Pinot Noir and Chardonnay, which are grown on the best sites in Apetlon and the ideal location for the Sauvignon Blanc as well as the Zweigelt from Neubruch. Their main variety is Zweigelt. It is particularly at home in the Lake Neusiedl region and is rewarded with excellent qualities. The winery's top cuvées - "Diabolus", the red devil, and "Auratum TBA", liquid gold - are blended

Christoph and Peter Münzenrieder

WEINGUT PMC MÜNZENRIEDER
7143 Apetlon
Triftgasse 31
T: +43 (2175) 26700
office@weingut-pmc.at
www.weingut-pmc.at

Winemaker: Christoph Münzenrieder
Contact: Peter Münzenrieder
Production: 30 % white, 50 % red, 20 % sweet, 26 hectares
Certified: Sustainable Austria
Fairs: VieVinum
Distribution partners: NZ

NEUSIEDLERSEE DAC

and bottled only after extensive ageing in French barriques. Some of the best sweet wine producers in the world come from the Seewinkel. And the two brothers are definitely among the best, with countless international gold medals and other prestigious awards for their white and red Prädikat wines. PMC Münzenrieder wines can be found on the wine lists of many of the world's finest restaurants.

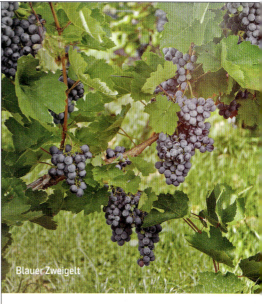
Blauer Zweigelt

(93) Chardonnay Apetlon Ried Neubruch 2021
14 Vol.-%, DIAM, 500-l-barrel, €€€€€
92 Chardonnay Ried Neubruch 2020
Bright yellow gold, silver reflections. Fine tropical fruit, delicate notes of mango and papaya, hints of caramel and vanilla, candied orange zest. Juicy, nuances of yellow fruit, ripe peach, honey notes on the finish, a sturdy, powerful food companion.
92 Chardonnay Ried Neubruch 2019

(92) Sauvignon Blanc Apetlon Ried Neubruch 2021
13,5 Vol.-%, DIAM, 500-l-barrel, €€€€€
92 Sauvignon Blanc Ried Neubruch 2020
92 Sauvignon Blanc Ried Neubruch 2019

91 Zweigelt ** Ried Neubruch 2020
92 Zweigelt Ried Neubruch 2019
90 Zweigelt Ried Neubruch 2018

(93) Blaufränkisch Glimmerschiefer und Kalk 2021
14 Vol.-%, DIAM, 500-l-barrel, €€€€€

(92) Apetlon ME-CF 2021 ME/CF
14 Vol.-%, DIAM, 500-l-barrel, €€€€€

91 Diabolus 2021 ME/ZW/CF
14 Vol.-%, DIAM, 500-l-barrel, €€€
90 Diabolus 2020 ZW/ME/BF
90 Diabolus 2019 ZW/ME/BF

92 Merlot 2020
93 Merlot 2019
92 Merlot 2018

(91) Pinot Noir Ried Neubruch 2021
14 Vol.-%, cork, 500-l-barrel, €€€€€
91 Pinot Noir Ried Neubruch 2020
91 Pinot Noir Ried Neubruch 2019

(96) Chardonnay TBA 2021
8,5 Vol.-%, DIAM, oak barrel, €€€€

95 Chardonnay TBA 2020
Medium golden yellow, silver glints. Delicate yellow peach, ripe apple, subtle honey touch, and caramel nuances. Inviting bouquet. Juicy, complex, subtle notes of dried figs, a hint of nougat, elegant, persistent, and accessible.
95 Chardonnay TBA 2018

96 Welschriesling TBA 2020
94 Welschriesling TBA 2018
95 Welschriesling TBA 2017

(95) Muskat Ottonel TBA 2020
9,5 Vol.-%, DIAM, steel tank, €€€€

94 Scheurebe ** TBA 2021
8,5 Vol.-%, DIAM, steel tank, €€€€
94 Scheurebe ** TBA 2020
94 Scheurebe TBA 2018

94 Sauvignon Blanc TBA 2017

94 Traminer TBA 2018

94 Sämling 88 TBA 2017

93 Grüner Veltliner TBA 2019

93 Auratum TBA 2018 CH/WR/SÄ

92 Beerenauslese Cuvée 2017 CH/WR/SÄ/SB

* Neusiedlersee DAC   ** Neusiedlersee DAC Reserve

NESTOR

Since the 2019 harvest, Günther Neukamp and Thomas Stadler have been bottling single vineyard Chardonnay, Cabernet Franc, and Pinot Gris wines under the brand names "NESTOR" and "NEUKAMP & STADLER". The 39 hectares of vineyards surrounding Halbturn have yielded excellent grapes for over 40 years. The best sites produce wines under the "NESTOR" brand. A conscious reduction in the number of vines planted in these sustainably cultivated sites, careful selection during harvest, and elaborate and technically demanding vinification processes create exceptional wines with a unique character that will age well.

Almost all premium wines are aged on fine lees in limited quantities of 3,000 to 4,000 bottles per variety in French barriques and 500-litre oak casks from renowned cooperages. Batonnage and 12 (white) or 18 (red) months of barrel ageing create elegant wine rarities that open their drinking window just two years after harvest. Vintage and varietal typicity determine the characteristics of the "NESTOR" wines. In particular, the vineyard area under Cabernet Franc and Pinot Gris has increased since 2019 in response to strong demand.

94 Pinot Gris Ried Lehendorf Nestor Reserve 2021
13,5 Vol.-%, cork, 500-l-barrel/bottle maturation, €€€€€

93 Nestor Pinot Gris Ried Lehendorf 2020
Medium golden yellow, silver reflections. Delicate oak savouriness, fine notes of yellow stone fruit, delicate nougat and caramel, attractive bouquet. Juicy, complex, elegant texture, fine acidity, yellow fruit in the aftertaste, already harmonious and easy to drink, a sturdy food companion.

91 Pinot Gris Reserve Ried Lehendorf 2019

93 Chardonnay Ried Lehendorf Nestor 2020
13,5 Vol.-%, cork, 500-l-barrel, €€€€€

90 Chardonnay Reserve Ried Kaiserberg 2019

93 Gelber Muskateller Orangewein Nestor 2021
12,5 Vol.-%, cork, used barriques, €€€€

93 Cabernet Franc Ried Kaiserberg Nestor 2020
93 Cabernet Franc Reserve Ried Kaiserberg 2019

93 Cuvée Nestor 02 Reserve 2020 ME/CF/SY
92 Cuvée Nestor 01 Reserve Neukamp & Stadler 2019 ME/CF/ZW

Thomas Stadler and his wife Victoria, Evangeline Adler and her husband Günther Neukamp

NESTOR
7131 Halbturn
Frauenkirchner Straße 8
T: +43 (1) 9418333
mail@nestor.wine
www.nestor.wine

Winemaker: Thomas Stadler (Weingut Stadler)
Contact: Günther Neukamp (Nestor Weine)
Production: 38 % white, 60 % red, 2 % sweet, 39 hectares
Certified: Sustainable Austria
Fairs: Austrian Tasting London, ÖGW Zürich, ProWein Düsseldorf, VieVinum, DAC-Presentations, Wein Burgenland Presentations, WeinMüchen
Distribution partners: UK, JP, CDN, ROK, NL, CH

WEINGUT GEBRÜDER NITTNAUS

Weingut Gebrüder Nittnaus in Gols on Lake Neusiedl is synonymous with excellent wine quality, long-term commitment to sustainability and reliability. For decades, the family winery has focused on the potential and diversity of the vineyards surrounding Lake Neusiedl. These limestone-rich, fertile sites and the unique climatic conditions produce fruity wines that are characteristic of the Burgenland region. In this way, the Nittnaus brothers exemplify the excellence of their red, white and sweet wines.

92 Grüner Veltliner Reserve 2021
91 Grüner Veltliner Reserve 2019

92 Sauvignon Blanc Reserve Edition Hans 2018
91 Sauvignon Blanc Reserve Edition Hans 2017

90 Sauvignon Blanc Obere Heide 2021

90 Sauvignon Blanc Obere Wies 2019

89 Sauvignon Blanc 2020
90 Sauvignon Blanc 2019
88 Sauvignon Blanc 2018

90 Chardonnay Reserve 2022
13,5 Vol.-%, DIAM, partial barrique, €€€
92 Chardonnay Reserve 2021
Pale yellow gold, silver reflections. Delicate yellow apples, hints of vanilla and blossom honey, ripe pineapple, an inviting bouquet. Juicy, elegant, yellow peaches, a touch of cloves, a subtle honeyed touch, long lasting, juicy.
91 Chardonnay Reserve 2018

90 Chardonnay Selection 2020
90 Chardonnay Selection 2019
90 Chardonnay Selection 2018

88 Chardonnay Exquisit 2022
13,5 Vol.-%, screwcap, steel tank, €€
89 Chardonnay Exquisit 2020
89 Chardonnay Exquisit 2019

88 Gelber Muskateller Exquisit 2020
89 Gelber Muskateller Exquisit 2018

(93) Blauer Zweigelt ** Luckenwald 2021
13,5 Vol.-%, DIAM, barrique, €€€€
92 Blauer Zweigelt ** Ried Luckenwald 2020
Deep ruby, purple glints, faintly lighter ochre hue at the rim. Subtly refined scents of spiced wood, lush sweetheart cherries, red forest berry medley, and tobacco nuances. Juicy, elegant, fresh acidity, subtle tannins, delicate nougat, red cherry finish, balanced and accessible.
93 Blauer Zweigelt ** Ried Luckenwald 2019

92 Blauer Zweigelt ** Ried Goldberg 2020
92 Zweigelt ** Ried Goldberg 2019

(90) Blauer Zweigelt * 2022
13 Vol.-%, screwcap, steel tank, €€
90 Blauer Zweigelt * 2021
13 Vol.-%, screwcap, steel tank, €€
90 Zweigelt * 2020

(88) Zweigelt Exquisit 2022
13 Vol.-%, screwcap, steel tank, €€
90 Zweigelt Exquisit 2021
90 Zweigelt Exquisit 2020

92 Pinot Noir Reserve 2021
13 Vol.-%, DIAM, partial barrique, €€€

WEINGUT GEBRÜDER NITTNAUS
7122 Gols
Untere Hauptstraße 105
T: +43 (2173) 2186
weingut@nittnaus.net
www.nittnaus.net

Winemaker: Hans Michael Nittnaus
Contact: Andreas and Hans Michael Nittnaus
Production: 30 % white, 60 % red, 10 % sweet, 50 hectares
Certified: Sustainable Austria
Fairs: ProWein Düsseldorf, VieVinum, DAC-Presentations
Distribution partners: BE, RC, DK, DE, FIN, FR, UK, IT, LU, NL, NO, RUS, SE, CH, CZ, USA

* Neusiedlersee DAC   ** Neusiedlersee DAC Reserve

BURGENLAND

90 Pinot Noir Reserve 2020	93 Weißburgunder TBA Grand Selection 2015
90 Pinot Noir Reserve 2018	
	91 Trockenbeerenauslese Exquisit 2021
(91) Blaufränkisch Ried Altenberg Reserve 2021	8,5 Vol.-%, DIAM, steel tank, €€€
13,5 Vol.-%, DIAM, barrique, €€€€	93 Trockenbeerenauslese Exquisit 2018
92 Blaufränkisch Ried Altenberg Reserve 2020	WR/GV/SÄ/WB
91 Blaufränkisch Ried Altenberg Reserve 2019	
	(92) Beerenauslese Exquisit 2021 GV/WR/SÄ
(90) Blaufränkisch Exquisit 2022	9 Vol.-%, screwcap, steel tank, €€
13 Vol.-%, screwcap, steel tank, €€	91 Beerenauslese Exquisit 2020
89 Blaufränkisch Exquisit 2021	WB/CH/GV/SÄ
88 Blaufränkisch Exquisit 2020	93 Exquisit Beerenauslese 2018
	SÄ/WR/GV/MO/SB
(89) Heideboden Prestige 2021 ZW/ME/BF/CS	
13,5 Vol.-%, screwcap, partial barrique, €€	91 Eiswein Exquisit 2021
90 Heideboden Premium 2020 ZW/CS/ME/BF	9 Vol.-%, DIAM, steel tank, €€€€
91 Heideboden Premium 2019 ZW/CS/ME/BF	
	(90) Eiswein Exquisit Rosé 2021 ZW/CS
95 Scheurebe TBA Grand Selection 2015	10 Vol.-%, DIAM, steel tank, €€€€
93 Scheurebe Reserve TBA 2018	
	90 Muskat Ottonel * Spätlese 2021
94 Chardonnay TBA Grand Selection 2015	91 Muskat Ottonel Spätlese 2018
94 Chardonnay Reserve TBA 2018	

★★★★★

WEINGUT PÖCKL

Red wine is the passion of René and Eva Pöckl. Their aim is to constantly improve the quality and produce the best possible Pöckl wine. In the vineyard, they work in harmony with nature. The soils have a permanent cover crop, and the vines have a double guyot training system, which results in small-berried, concentrated grapes. These form the perfect basis for the unique, long-lasting Pöckl wines. The history of the Pöckl winery dates back to 1910 when Albert Pöckl returned to Austria from the USA and laid the foundations for the winery. Over the years, the Pöckl family has specialised in viticulture, with a particular focus on red wine. Their success has proven them right, as the area around Mönchhof offers the ideal terroir for Zweigelt and St. Laurent, as well as international varieties such as Merlot, Cabernet Sauvignon and Syrah. Two quotes from Josef and his son René Pöckl, who died much too young, sum up the winery's philosophy: "A winemaker who does not know his soil, his vines and his climate very well can never make a great wine. And: "If you don't get it right in the vineyard, you can't make up for it in the cellar. Consumers can recognise this too because Pöckl wines show the regional typicity, the climate, the location and the dedication to work in the vineyard and in the cellar. René Pöckl was already in the limelight as a young man with his 'Rêve de Jeunesse' and has won several Falstaff red wine awards as well as the multi-award winning 'Admiral', one of the estate's top wines. Another quality wine in the range is the Pinot Noir, which has been a podium performer at the Falstaff Awards. Produced in small quantities, it is one of the Pöckl's favourites because of the viticultural challenges it presents. In addition, the winery never ceases to surprise with new wine concepts, often demonstrating a good working relationship with its partners. Its most famous niche wine is 'Mystique', which can certainly compete with the greats of the wine world. Mystique is actually a research wine used by the winery to explore the possibilities of the vineyard and vinification. The lessons learnt are then applied to the production of the whole range. This

© Hayder Steve

NEUSIEDLERSEE DAC

WEINGUT PÖCKL
7123 Mönchhof
Zwergäcker 1
T: +43 (2173) 80258
info@poeckl.com
www.poeckl.com

Winemaker: René Pöckl
Contact: Eva Pöckl
Production: 1 % white, 99 % red, 42 hectares
Fairs: ProWein Düsseldorf, VieVinum, DAC-Presentations, Wein Burgenland Presentations
Distribution partners: BE, RC, DK, DE, LT, LU, CH, SGP, CZ

René Pöckl

is one of the reasons why the potential of Pöckl's great wines can hardly be surpassed and why, with some bottle ageing, they offer the ultimate drinking experience. Pöckl's Solo Rosso, the Zweigelt Classique or the Rosso e Nero Cuvée for the more discerning palate are also great delights. In good years, excellent Prädikat wines are also produced. Thanks to many years of consistent excellence and a constant drive to produce even more sophisticated wines, the winery has been awarded five stars, making it one of the top wineries in the world.

92   Chardonnay 2019
92   Chardonnay 2018

(96) Blauer Zweigelt ** 2021
15,5 Vol.-%, cork, barrique, €€€€€€
95   Blauer Zweigelt ** 2020
Deep dark ruby, opaque core, purple glints, faintly lighter at the rim. Delicate nougat, lush plums, blackberry jam, and caramel, with soft undertones of vanilla. Juicy, complex and sweet, ripe fig notes, well-integrated tannins, mineral with a luscious sweetheart cherry aftertaste, and excellent length. Good ageing potential.
95   Zweigelt ** 2019

93   Zweigelt Classique 2021
12,5 Vol.-%, cork, barrique, €€€
90   Zweigelt Classique 2018
90   Blauer Zweigelt Classique 2017

(97) Rêve de Jeunesse 2021 CS/ME/SY/ZW
15 Vol.-%, cork, barrique, €€€€€€ Ⓥ
97   Rêve de Jeunesse 41 2020 CS/ME/SY/ZW
Deep dark ruby, opaque core, purple glints, with a faint watery rim. Delicate savoury herbal scents, liquorice, an array of black berries, candied oranges, and vanilla, followed by gentle hints of sweet plum and tobacco nuances. Full-bodied, chocolatey, ripe, round tannins, delicate figs, sweet reverberations, nougat nuances, very balanced, good length, and lovely crispness. Already accessible, a multifaceted food companion with excellent development potential.
97   Rêve de Jeunesse 40 2019 ME/CS/SY/ZW

(96) Admiral 2021 ZW/ME/CS
14,5 Vol.-%, cork, barrique, €€€€€€
96   Admiral 2020 ZW/CS/ME/CF
Deep ruby, opaque core, purple tinges, faint watery rim. Soft nutty notions underlaid with an array of black berries, dark cherries, lush plums, fresh orange zest, a touch of nougat, and hardwood underlaid with herbal savouriness. Juicy, complex, lush forest berries, well-integrated, ripe tannins, substance, lovely plum fruit, mineral, and persistent. Sweet reverberations, excellent potential.
96   Admiral 2019 ZW/ME/CS

(94) Rosso e Nero 2021 ZW/CS/ME/BF
13,5 Vol.-%, cork, barrique, €€€€€
93   Rosso e Nero 2020 ZW/CS/ME/BF
93   Rosso e Nero 2019 ZW/CS/ME/BF

92   Solo Rosso 2019 BF/ME/CS
91   Solo Rosso 2018 BF/ME/PN

* Neusiedlersee DAC   ** Neusiedlersee DAC Reserve

BURGENLAND

93 Pinot Noir Reserve 2020	92 Blaufränkisch Classique 2021
94 Pinot Noir Reserve 2019	13 Vol.-%, cork, barrique, €€€
93 Pinot Noir Reserve 2018	91 Blaufränkisch Classique 2019
92 St. Laurent Classique 201	

★★★

WEINGUT HANNES REEH

"It has to be a passion, not a science", Hannes Reeh likes to say when talking about wine. The winemaker combines a long family tradition and the authenticity of a true Burgenländer with time spent in the New World. The result of his work: accessible wines that convince both novices and confirmed connoisseurs. It's good to live under the Andau sun - for people and vines. With around 2,400 hours of sunshine a year, Andau is the sunniest place in Austria - but with less than 500 millimetres of annual rainfall, it is one of the driest places in the country. The Pannonian climate is ideal for good wine, producing exceptionally ripe grapes and wines of elegance, power, and structure. As you would expect from the Pannonian steppe, the soils of Hannes Reeh's vineyards are mostly barren and gravelly. All Hannes Reeh wines have a few things in common: they are streamlined, strong in character, and reflect the terroir in the bottle. And yet each variety has its own unique characteristics. The Andau winemaker's wines are divided into four groups: The "Haus und Hof" wines are single-varietal, enjoyable, and uncomplicated; they are simply the classics of the estate. The "Heideboden" wines combine aromatics and density with a delightful freshness. On the other hand, the ‚Unplugged' wines are no-frills, with no fining or adulteration. And the new ‚In Bloom' range is intense and complex, just like Nirvana's song ‚In Full Bloom'.

92 Chardonnay Unplugged 2020
14 Vol.-%, screwcap, barrique, €€€€
92 Chardonnay Unplugged 2019
92 Chardonnay Unplugged 2018

Hannes Reeh

WEINGUT HANNES REEH
7163 Andau
Augasse 11a
T: +43 (2176) 27011
wein@hannesreeh.at
www.hannesreeh.at

Winemaker: Hannes Reeh, Herbert Götzinger, Daniel Tschida
Contact: Marina Würz
Production: 18 % white, 2 % rosé, 80 % red, 80+40 hectares
Certified: Sustainable Austria
Fairs: ProWein Düsseldorf, VieVinum, Weinmesse Innsbruck, Weinmesse München, Weinmesse Salzburg
Distribution partners: RC, DE, NL, CH

NEUSIEDLERSEE DAC

91 Heideboden Cuvée weiss 2022 SB/WB/CH
13,5 Vol.-%, screwcap, steel tank, €€€
91 Heideboden Cuvée weiss 2021 WB/SB/GV/CH
90 Heideboden Cuvée weiss 2020 SB/WB

91 In Bloom Rosé 2021 BF/CS
90 In Bloom Rosé 2020 BF/CS

90 Blauer Zweigelt * 2021
90 Zweigelt * 2020
90 Neusiedlersee DAC 2019

93 Zweigelt Unplugged 2021
14 Vol.-%, cork, barrique, €€€€
93 Zweigelt Unplugged 2020
Deep dark ruby, opaque core, purple glints, faintly lighter at the rim. Finely savoury, black forest berry medley, tobacco, nuances of cassis, and luscious damsons. Complex, juicy, blackberries, vivid tannins, mineral, and red cherries, with a hint of figs on the finish and a saline aftertaste.
92 Zweigelt Unplugged 2019

94 Merlot Unplugged 2020
14,5 Vol.-%, cork, barrique, €€€€€
92 Merlot Unplugged 2019
93 Merlot Unplugged 2018

(94) Unplugged X Cuvée rot 2020 ME/CS/CF
14 Vol.-%, cork, barrique, €€€€€
94 Unplugged Cuvée X 2019 ME/CS/CF/ZW
Deep dark ruby colour with opaque core, purple reflections, delicate brightening on the rim. Ripe plums, spices, dark heart cherries, subtle hints of figs, nougat and candied orange zest. Powerful, complex, notes of dark berries, vivid tannins, savoury on the finish, chocolatey, mineral and salty on the finish, will benefit from bottle ageing.
94 Unplugged Cuvée X 2017 CF/CS/ME

90 Heideboden Cuvée rot 2020 ZW/CS/ME/SL
13,5 Vol.-%, screwcap, used barriques, €€€
91 Heideboden Cuvée Rot 2019 ZW/CS/SL/ME
91 Heideboden Cuvée rot 2018 ZW/CS/SL/ME

93 Cabernet Franc Unplugged 2019
14,5 Vol.-%, cork, barrique, €€€€€
93 Cabernet Franc Unplugged 2018
93 Cabernet Franc Unplugged 2017

92 Cabernet Sauvignon Unplugged 2020
14,5 Vol.-%, cork, barrique, €€€€€
93 Cabernet Sauvignon Unplugged 2019
92 Cabernet Sauvignon Unplugged 2018

WEINGUT SALZL – SEEWINKELHOF

Weingut Salzl in Illmitz, Burgenland, is located on the shores of Lake Neusiedl and in the Seewinkel National Park, which is a World Heritage Site and where their vines are also planted.
For Christoph Salzl, this is a lifelong commitment, a mission, and an honour at the same time because, for the Salzl family, home means not only residing here but also cherishing and protecting this privilege passionately.
Three generations of the Salzl family have put their experience and joie de vivre into crafting good wine. Their flagship wine is the region's favourite, Zweigelt, with other national and international white, red, and sweet varieties complementing the portfolio.
If you want to taste these delightful wines, book a tasting. If you want to ‚taste' a little more of this extraordinary region, consider staying at the attached four-star guesthouse.

92 Chardonnay Premium 2020
92 Chardonnay Premium 2017

91 Graburgunder Reserve 2019
90 Graburgunder Reserve 2018

92 Blauer Zweigelt ** Ried Lüss Sacris 2019
14 Vol.-%, DIAM, barrique, €€€€€ ⓗ
93 Zweigelt ** Ried Lüss Sacris 2018
93 ** Ried Lüss Sacris 2017

91 Zweigelt Reserve 2019
91 Zweigelt Reserve 2018
91 Zweigelt Reserve 2017

93 3-5-8 Premium 2019 CS/ME
14 Vol.-%, DIAM, barrique, €€€€€ ⓗ
93 3-5-8 Premium 2018 CS/ME
Deep dark ruby red, opaque core with purple reflections at the narrow rim. Intense aroma of ripe cherries, dark forest

* Neusiedlersee DAC ** Neusiedlersee DAC Reserve

BURGENLAND

WEINGUT SALZL – SEEWINKELHOF
7142 Illmitz, Zwischen den Reben 1
T: +43 (2175) 24342
weingut@salzl.at
www.salzl.at

Winemaker/Contact:
Christoph Salzl
Production: 1 % sparkling, 25 % white, 2 % rosé, 70 % red, 2 % sweet, 30+70 hectares
Certified: Sustainable Austria
Fairs: Austrian Tasting London, ProWein Düsseldorf, VieVinum, DAC-Presentations, Wein Burgenland Presentations
Distribution partners: DK, DE, NL, PL, SE, CZ

93 Pannoterra 2019 ZW/ME/CS
14 Vol.-%, DIAM, barrique, €€€€€
92 Pannoterra 2018 ZW/ME/CS
92 Pannoterra 2017 ZW/ME/BF/CS

91 Josanna 2019 ZW/ME/CS

91 Grande Cuvée 2018 ZW/ME/CS

92 Cabernet Franc Premium 2019
14 Vol.-%, DIAM, barrique, €€€€€
94 Cabernet Franc Premium 2018
Deep dark ruby, opaque core, purple glints, faintly lighter at the rim. Fine vegetal nuances, delicate cassis, fresh figs, herbal nuances, underlaid with fine savoury hardwood. Juicy, tightly knit, complex, pleasant blueberry tones, vivid tannins, chocolatey aftertaste, nutty finish. Will benefit from bottle ageing.
92 Cabernet Franc Premium 2017

91 Cabernet Sauvignon Reserve 2019
91 Cabernet Sauvignon Reserve 2018
90 Cabernet Sauvignon Reserve 2017

91 Syrah Reserve 2019

90 Merlot Reserve 2019
91 Merlot Reserve 2018

93 Goldene Finesse TBA 2017

berry compote, underscored with dark chocolate and wood savouriness. Taut, complex, well-integrated tannins, dark fruit on the finish, savoury notes and blackcurrants on the back palate; seems light on its feet, certain ageing potential.
93 3-5-8 Premium 2017 CS/ME

WEINGUT SCHEIBLHOFER

Weingut Scheiblhofer is located in Andau, in the region of Neusiedl am See, and is one of the largest wineries in Burgenland, with 85 hectares of vineyards. The winery, known for its renowned Big John red wine, was founded by Johann Scheiblhofer and taken over by his son Erich in 2000. In addition to the production of high-quality wines, the family business is characterised by modernity, innovation, sustainability, and social competence. In 2017, Scheiblhofer was the first winemaker in Austria to be awarded the "Leitbetriebe Austria" (leading Austrian company) award. But that was not all: in May 2017, the winery, together with Bankhaus Spängler, BDO Austria, and the Austrian Chamber of Notaries, was named the best family business in Burgenland by the national

daily newspaper "Die Presse", as well as "Winery of the Year" in the "Best of Burgenland" wine awards of the Burgenland Chamber of Agriculture. Erich Scheiblhofer was also named "Winemaker of the Year 2021" by Falstaff.
Scheiblhofer is a pioneer in the field of sustainability and has been distinguished for years by its energy-autonomous wine production. This is made possible by its own photovoltaic system, the largest privately operated in Burgenland. In the spring of 2020, the system was expanded to a total of 668 kWp. In the future, the mobile transport of employees will also be energy-efficient. Electric vehicles have already been purchased, and a charging station has been installed. Situated in one of the best wine-growing areas in Austria and with the country's largest number of

NEUSIEDLERSEE DAC

WEINGUT SCHEIBLHOFER
7163 Andau
Halbturner Straße 1a
T: +43 (2176) 2610
office@scheiblhofer.at
www.scheiblhofer.at

Winemaker/Contact:
Erich Scheiblhofer
Production: 25 % white, 75 % red, 85 hectares
Certified: Sustainable Austria 🌿
Fairs: ProWein Düsseldorf, VieVinum, DAC-Presentations, ProWine China, Wein Burgenland Presentations
Distribution partners: BE, RC, DK, DE, LU, PL, CH, CZ

Erich Scheiblhofer

barrique barrels, Scheiblhofer is an important employer in the region and a supporter and promoter of social projects.
The winery is known far beyond Austria's borders as a place of relaxation and tranquillity, and with the recent opening of "The Resort", a spa hotel of superlatives, there is finally more space for the winery's many visitors. Of course, the winery's success is no accident: It is only through the tireless efforts of all the staff and the tremendous family cohesion that all this has been possible.

92 **The Chardonnay 2021**
13 Vol.-%, DIAM, barrique, €€€ ⓗ
92 **The Chardonnay 2020**
92 **The Chardonnay 2019**

90 **Chardonnay Classic 2022**
12,5 Vol.-%, screwcap, steel tank, €€ ⓗ
90 **Chardonnay Classic 2021**
90 **Chardonnay Classic 2020**

92 **Big John White 2022 CH/SB**
13,5 Vol.-%, screwcap, partial barrique, €€ ⓗ
89 **Big John White 2021 CH/SB**
90 **Big John White 2020 CH/SB**

89 **Gelber Muskateller 2022**
12 Vol.-%, screwcap, steel tank, €€ ⓗ
89 **Gelber Muskateller 2021**
89 **Sauvignon Blanc 2022**
12 Vol.-%, screwcap, steel tank, €€ ⓗ

89 **Sauvignon Blanc 2021**

90 **Zweigelt * 2022**
13,5 Vol.-%, screwcap, used barriques, €€ ⓗ
92 **Blauer Zweigelt * 2021**
92 **Zweigelt * 2020**

93 **The Zweigelt Ried Prädium 2021**
14,5 Vol.-%, DIAM, barrique, €€€€ ⓗ
93 **The Zweigelt Ried Prädium 2020**
Deep dark ruby, opaque core, purple reflections, subtle rim brightening. Delicate herbal savouriness, some oak, blackberry fruit, a fine hint of cardamom and liquorice. Juicy, savoury and well lasting, cloves, nougat, elegant and endowed with length, a powerful red for BBQ.
93 **The Zweigelt Ried Prädium 2019**

91 **Zweigelt Selection Heideboden 2022**
13,5 Vol.-%, screwcap, used barriques, €€ ⓗ
91 **Zweigelt Heideboden Selection 2020**
91 **Zweigelt Heideboden Selection 2018**

(95) **Praittenbrunn 2019 CS/ME**
15 Vol.-%, DIAM, barrique, €€€€€ ⓗ
95 **Praittenbrunn 2017 CS/ME**

94 **The Great Bustard 2021 ME/CS/ZW**
14,5 Vol.-%, DIAM, barrique, €€€€€ ⓗ ⓥ
94 **The Great Bustard 2019 ME/CS/ZW**
94 **The Great Bustard 2018 ME/CS/ZW**

* Neusiedlersee DAC   ** Neusiedlersee DAC Reserve

BURGENLAND

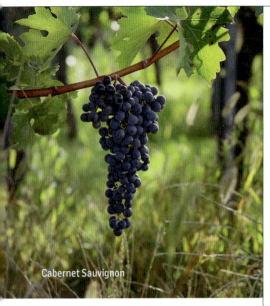
Cabernet Sauvignon

(93) The Peak of Glory 2021 ZW/ME/CS
14 Vol.-%, DIAM, barrique, €€€€ ⓗ
94 The Peak of Glory 2020 ZW/ME/CS
Deep dark ruby, opaque core, purple reflections, subtle rim brightening. Nuances of blueberry and black cherry, delicate hints of nougat and vanilla, fine herbal savouriness, candied orange zest. Juicy, sweet wild berries, ripe cherry, round tannins, pleasant freshness, elegant and lasting, shows length, already easy to drink, endowed with maturity and certain ageing potential.
93 The Peak of Glory 2019 ZW/ME/CS

93 Mordor 2021 BF/CS/ME/SY
14 Vol.-%, DIAM, barrique, €€€€ ⓗ
92 Mordor 2020 BF/CS/ME/SY
92 Mordor 2019 BF/CS/ME/SY

92 Big John 2021 ZW/CS/PN
14 Vol.-%, DIAM, barrique, €€€ ⓗ
91 Big John Cuvée Reserve 2020 ZW/CS/PN
92 Big John Cuvée Reserve 2019 ZW/CS/PN

92 The Legends 2021 CS/ME
14 Vol.-%, DIAM, barrique, €€€ ⓗ
91 The Legends 2020 CS/ME
92 The Legends 2019 CS/ME

91 Premium Cuvée 2022 ZW/CS/ME
13,5 Vol.-%, screwcap, used barriques, €€ ⓗ
91 Premium Cuvée 2021 ZW/CS/ME
91 Premium Cuvée 2020 ZW/CS/ME

(94) The Cabernet Franc 2021
14,5 Vol.-%, DIAM, barrique, €€€€€ ⓗ
93 The Cabernet Franc 2019
93 The Cabernet Franc 2018

94 The Shiraz 2021
14,5 Vol.-%, DIAM, barrique, €€€€€ ⓗ ⓥ
93 The Shiraz 2019
94 The Shiraz 2018

92 Syrah Selection 2021
14 Vol.-%, DIAM, partial barrique, €€€ ⓗ
91 Syrah Selection 2020
92 Syrah Selection 2019

(93) The Merlot 2021
14,5 Vol.-%, DIAM, barrique, €€€€€ ⓗ
92 The Merlot 2020
93 The Merlot 2019

92 Merlot Selection 2021
14 Vol.-%, DIAM, partial barrique, €€€ ⓗ
90 Merlot Selection 2020

93 The Cabernet Sauvignon 2021
14,5 Vol.-%, DIAM, barrique, €€€€€ ⓗ
93 The Cabernet Sauvignon 2020
92 The Cabernet Sauvignon 2019

91 Cabernet Sauvignon Selection 2022
14 Vol.-%, screwcap, used barriques, €€ ⓗ
91 Cabernet Sauvignon Selection 2021
92 Cabernet Sauvignon Selection 2020

92 Blaufränkisch Jois 2020
14,5 Vol.-%, DIAM, barrique, €€€€€ ⓗ
91 Blaufränkisch Jois 2019
92 Blaufränkisch Jois 2018

91 Blaufränkisch Classic 2022
13,5 Vol.-%, screwcap, used barriques, €€ ⓗ
90 Blaufränkisch 2021
90 Blaufränkisch Classic 2020

91 The Pinot Noir 2020
92 The Pinot Noir 2018

89 Pinot Noir 2022
14 Vol.-%, screwcap, used barriques, €€ ⓗ
89 Pinot Noir 2021

WEINGUT SCHWARZ

About twenty years ago, Hans Schwarz, a skilled butcher from Andau, dared to do something different; he switched professions, from professional butcher to winemaker, and has never looked back. Andau, the warmest wine-growing region in Austria, offers the best conditions for making great wines, and Hans Schwarz has proved, with his often unorthodox methods, that wines from Andau can reach cult status. Schwarz relied on the autochthonous Zweigelt grape, which to this day is praised by wine lovers, wine critics, and gastronomes as "Schwarz-Rot". The line "The Butcher" is a homage to his previous profession. But not forgetting the future, Michael Schwarz, who has been running the day-to-day business since 2018, is now expanding the "The Butcher" range to include international grape varieties.

Michael has returned from several internships abroad to continue his father's work. He is planning two new lines in the premium and basic ranges. The winery is being expanded to include a cosy tasting room where you can sample the cult wines and pair them with Burgenland delicacies such as homemade bacon or Hans' famous chilli-cheese-style sausages. Hans Schwarz believes that food and drink go hand in hand. Michael tries to achieve what all young winemakers strive for, to do everything like his father - and yet be completely different.

(93) Schwarz Weiss 2021 CH/GV
14 Vol.-%, DIAM, barrique/used barriques, €€€€€
93 Schwarz Weiß 2020 CH/GV
Bright medium golden yellow, silver reflections. Delicate orange zest, fine oak savouriness, ripe yellow tropical fruit, hints of mango and papaya, delicate blossom honey. Complex, white peach, finesse-rich structure, salty lemon finish, sticks well, has very good certain ageing potential.
93 Schwarz Weiß 2019 CH/GV

(92) Kumarod Cuvée Weiss 2022 SÄ/WR
12 Vol.-%, screwcap, steel tank, €€
90 Kumarod Cuvée Weiss 2021 SÄ/WR
90 Kumarod Weiss 2019 SÄ/WR/MO

91 The Butcher Cuvée Weiss 2022 GV/WR/SB
12,5 Vol.-%, screwcap, steel tank, €€ Ⓥ
90 The Butcher Cuvée Weiss 2021 GV/WR/SB
90 The Butcher Cuvée Weiss 2020 GV/WR/SB

(91) Chardonnay The Butcher 2022
13 Vol.-%, screwcap, steel tank/small wooden barrel, €€ Ⓥ
91 Chardonnay The Butcher 2021
90 Chardonnay The Butcher 2020

90 Zweigelt * 2020
13 Vol.-%, screwcap, partial barrique, €€
90 Blauer Zweigelt * 2020
90 Zweigelt * 2019

(96) Zweigelt Schwarz Rot 2021
13,5 Vol.-%, DIAM, barrique/used barriques, €€€€€€
94 Zweigelt Schwarz Rot 2020
Dark ruby, purple reflections, delicate bright rim. Fine oak spice, black berry and fresh cherry, subtle floral underlay, a multi-faceted bouquet. Juicy, elegant, discreet fruit, delicate spicy underlay, blackberry fruit, orange zest, balanced and long, tobacco nuances on the finish, compared to previous years a rather light-footed style.
93 Zweigelt Schwarz Rot 2019

WEINGUT SCHWARZ
7163 Andau
Hauptgasse 21
T: +43 (2176) 3231
office@schwarz-weine.at
www.schwarz-weine.at

Winemaker/Contact:
Michael Schwarz
Production: 29 hectares
Certified: Sustainable Austria ☺
Fairs: ProWein Düsseldorf, VieVinum
Distribution partners: BE, RC, DK, DE, FIN, FR, IT, LU, NL, NO, PL, RUS, SE, CH, SGP, CZ, USA

* Neusiedlersee DAC   ** Neusiedlersee DAC Reserve

BURGENLAND

90 Zweigelt The Butcher 2020
12,5 Vol.-%, screwcap, used barriques, €€ V
91 Zweigelt The Butcher 2018

93 The Butcher Cuvée 2020 ZW/BF/ME
13,5 Vol.-%, DIAM, barrique/used barriques, €€€€
92 Cuvée The Butcher 2019 ZW/BF/ME
92 The Butcher Cuvée 2018 ZW/BF/ME

92 Cuvée Tiefschwarz 2020 ZW/BF
13,5 Vol.-%, DIAM, used barriques, €€€€
92 Tiefschwarz Cuvée 2019 ZW/BF

90 Kumarod Rot 2020 ZW/CS/ME
13,5 Vol.-%, screwcap, used barriques, €€€
91 Kumarod Rot 2018 ZW/CS/ME
90 Kumarod Rot 2017 ZW/CS/ME

92 Blaufränkisch The Butcher 2020
13,5 Vol.-%, DIAM, large wooden barrel, €€€
90 Blaufränkisch The Butcher 2019

(91) Pinot Noir The Butcher 2021
13 Vol.-%, DIAM, large wooden barrel, €€€ V
90 Pinot Noir 2020
91 Pinot Noir The Butcher 2019

97 Muskat Ottonel Schwarz Gold 2020
10 Vol.-%, DIAM, barrique, €€€€€€
96 Muskat Ottonel Schwarz Gold 2019
96 Muskat Ottonel Schwarz Gold Strohwein 2018

96 Zweigelt Schwarz Schwarz 2020
12 Vol.-%, DIAM, barrique, €€€€€€
95 Zweigelt Schwarz Schwarz 2019
95 Zweigelt Schwarz Schwarz Strohwein 2018

★★★★★

WEINGUT TSCHIDA – ANGERHOF

Some of the world's best sweet wine producers come from Burgenland, and one of them is Hans Tschida from Illmitz. His striving for quality in grape production and his subtle intuition in the cellar determine his wines, which have won many awards. Seventy percent of his wine production is in the Prädikatswein range. The climate at Lake Neusiedl helps him because it could hardly be better for the production of botrytis wines. When the grapes already have a sufficiently high sugar gradation in autumn and the early mists set in, the berries are attacked almost overnight by the desired noble mould - a nightmare for the red wine vintners in northern Burgenland, a gift of nature to the sweet wine producers.
Stylistically, the wines from Angerhof are captivating due to their varietal typicity and elegance. They tend to be reductive, and in terms of sugar levels, Hans Tschida usually prefers the lower range - thick, syrupy essences are not his style. The consistency and palatability of his products are of utmost importance to him. His wines are never cloying, and he is a fan of the Lüss site because the wines from there usually have an acidity level of one per mille higher. The Sämling is the variety with which the winery has earned an

excellent reputation. But he is also particularly fond of his Spät- and Auslese wines. They are in the true sense of the meaning - sweet starter wines for those who want to accustom themselves to the world of sweet perfection.

90 Grand Select 2017 CS/ZW

95 Sauvignon Blanc Beerenauslese 2017

89 Spätlese 2022 CH/WR/MO
8 Vol.-%, screwcap, steel tank, €€
91 Spätlese 2021 SÄ/GV/WR/CH
90 Spätlese 2020 WR/CH/SÄ/TR

93 Auslese 2022 SB/BO/WR/CH
8 Vol.-%, screwcap, steel tank, €€
91 Auslese 2018 WR/CH/TR

92 Welschriesling Auslese 2019

89 Spätlese Merlot 2018
91 Merlot Spätlese 2017

93 Chardonnay Beerenauslese 2021
8,5 Vol.-%, glass, steel tank, €€€
94 Chardonnay Beerenauslese 2017

NEUSIEDLERSEE DAC

WEINGUT TSCHIDA – ANGERHOF
7142 Illmitz
Angergasse 5
T: +43 (2175) 3150
weingut@angerhof-tschida.at
www.angerhof-tschida.at

Winemaker: Hans Tschida
Contact: Hans and Lisa Tschida
Production:
20 % red, 80 % sweet, 35 hectares
Fairs: ProWein Düsseldorf, VieVinum

Hans Tschida

96 Muskateller Eiswein 2020
96 Gelber Muskateller Eiswein 2019
94 Gelber Muskateller Eiswein 2018

94 Muskat Ottonel Auslese 2022
8 Vol.-%, screwcap, steel tank, €€€
94 Muskat Ottonel Auslese 2021
Medium golden yellow, silver reflections. Delicate notes of passion fruit, lychees and nutmeg, juicy tropical fruit, grapey nuances. Full-bodied and sweet, lively acidity, white peach, good balance and length, mineral underpinnings on the finish, certain ageing potential, offers easy drinking pleasure.
93 Muskat Ottonel Auslese 2019

95 Muskat Ottonel Beerenauslese 2021
8 Vol.-%, glass, steel tank, €€€

97 Muskat Ottonel Schilfwein 2021
8 Vol.-%, glass, steel tank, €€€€€
98 Muskat Ottonel Schilfwein 2019
Medium yellow gold, silver glints. Refreshingly zesty, white tropical fruit, lime oil, a hint of nutmeg, complex, multifaceted bouquet. Floral and attractive. Juicy, ripe vineyard peach, substantial sweetness, fine acid structure, silky and elegant, ethereal, persists for a long time. Already well-developed, delicate grapey reverberations. A superb accompaniment to a dessert.

96 Sämling 88 ** TBA Ried Lüss 2020
8,5 Vol.-%, glass, steel tank, €€€€€
97 Sämling 88 ** Ried Lüss TBA 2019
Medium yellow gold, silver glints. Delicate yellow tropical fruit, a hint of passion fruit, yellow peach, candied tangerine zest, and fine honey. Medium complexity, silky and elegant, a fine arc of acidity, citrus nuances, good length. Already developed, good ageing potential.

96 Sämling TBA 2017

94 Sämling Domkapitel Beerenauslese 2017

95 Sämling 88 Beerenauslese 2017

95 Sämling Domkapitel TBA 2017

92 Sämling 88 Illmitz Spätlese 2022
8 Vol.-%, screwcap, steel tank, €€
92 Sämling 88 Illmitz Spätlese 2021
91 Illmitzer Spätlese 2020

94 Sämling 88 Beerenauslese 2019
8,5 Vol.-%, glass, steel tank, €€€

94 Grüner Veltliner Beerenauslese 2018
93 Grüner Veltliner Beerenauslese 2017

94 Grüner Veltliner Eiswein 2020

95 Welschriesling Beerenauslese 2017

96 Welschriesling ** TBA Ried Domkapitel 2021
8 Vol.-%, glass, steel tank, €€€€€

94 Blaufränkisch Eiswein 2020

* Neusiedlersee DAC   ** Neusiedlersee DAC Reserve

WEINGUT VELICH

★★★★★

The Velich family winery is located in the heart of the Lake Neusiedl - Seewinkel nature reserve in Apetlon. The village is surrounded by numerous lakes - called Lacken. Heinz Velich currently cultivates twelve hectars of vineyards planted exclusively with white wine varieties. Chardonnay accounts for 45 percent, Welschriesling for about a quarter of the area, and Muskat-Ottonel and Bouvier share the rest. The light, fruity wines like Welschriesling and Muskat-Ottonel are vinified in steel tanks. Chardonnay is expressive - yet opulently finesse and is preferably fermented and matured in barrique. The Chardonnay with the name "Tiglat" has been considered one of the best varietal exponents in the country for years. It is accompanied by the second dry Chardonnay of the house, the "Darscho", and a cuvée produced from Chardonnay, Welschriesling and Sauvignon Blanc called "TO" (which means "lake" in Hungarian). Sweet wines are only vinified in favourable years and for the most part in barriques.

The winery attaches particular importance to a high degree of maturation and the regional typicity of the wines. Falstaff magazine named Heinz Velich "Winemaker of the Year 2012".

WEINGUT VELICH
7143 Apetlon
Seeufergasse 12
T: +43 (2175) 3187
weingut@velich.at
www.velich.at

Winemaker/Contact:
Heinz Velich
Production: 50,000 bottles
80 % white, 20 % sweet,
12+6 hectares
Fairs: ProWein Düsseldorf, Summa Margreid
Distribution partners: AUS, BE, RC, DK, DE, FR, UK, IT, HR, NZ, NL, PE, PL, PT, RUS, CH, SK, SLO, ES, CZ, HU, USA

97 Chardonnay Tiglat 2020
13,5 Vol.-%, DIAM, wooden barrel, €€€€€
97 Chardonnay Tiglat 2019
Medium golden yellow, silver glints. Pleasantly scented with candied tangerine zest, a hint of yellow tropical fruit, delicate grounded hazelnut, and notes of blossom honey, underpinned with white peach. Juicy, elegant, fine stone fruit nuances, filigree structure, mineral, and long-lasting. Well-posed, excellent length, and has superb potential for further development.
96 Chardonnay Tiglat 2018

95 Chardonnay Darscho 2020
13,5 Vol.-%, DIAM, wooden barrel, €€€€
96 Chardonnay Darscho 2019
Medium greenish yellow, silver glints. Delicate savoury wood nuances, a hint of meadow herbs, followed by a faint nutty reduction note underlaid with lime zest. Succulent, white peach fruit, compact and taut, underpinned by citrus minerality, the Puligny-Montrachet of Burgenland, marked by a silky-saline finish. Already accessible, a multifaceted food accompaniment.
95 Chardonnay Darscho 2018

93 TO 2020 CH/WR/SB
13 Vol.-%, DIAM, wooden barrel, €€€€
93 TO 2019 CH/SB/WR
92 TO 2018 CH/SB/WR

93 Welschriesling Alte Reben 2021
12,5 Vol.-%, DIAM, wooden barrel, €€€€
93 Welschriesling Alte Reben 2020
Bright medium golden yellow, silver reflections. A delicate bouquet, hints of ripe yellow tropical fruit, nuances of tangerine zest, very reserved. Medium-bodied, fine yellow apple fruit, refined ripe acidity, mineral and persistent, subtle citrus component on the finish. It is an elegant food wine.
92 Welschriesling Alte Reben 2018

93 Muskat Ottonel 2021
13 Vol.-%, DIAM, steel tank, €€
92 Muskat Ottonel 2020
91 Muskat Ottonel 2018

97 SW Beerenauslese 2017 WR/SÄ/MO
13,5 Vol.-%, cork, wooden barrel, €€€€
97 Welschriesling TBA 2009
97 Sämling TBA 2009
94 SW Chardonnay Beerenauslese 2014

NEUSIEDLERSEE DAC

SPACE FOR YOUR
WINE NOTES

*Neusiedlersee DAC   **Neusiedlersee DAC Reserve

Eckberg near Glanz in the wine-growing region Südsteiermark

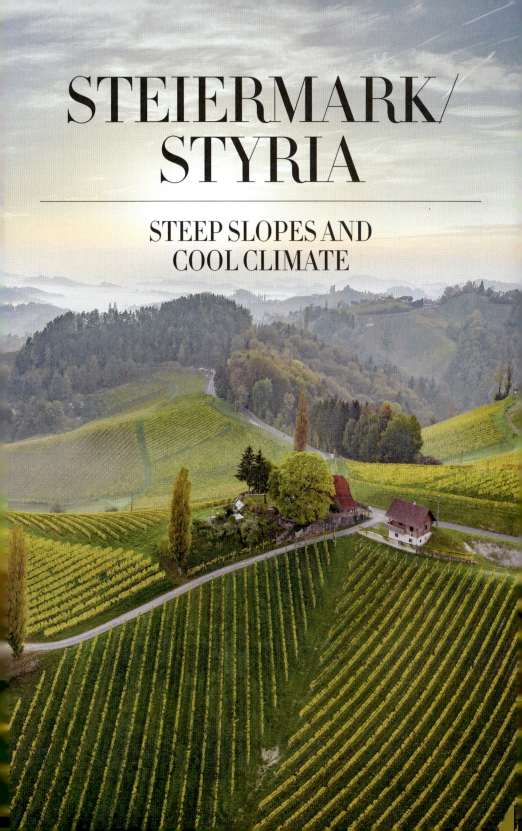

STEIERMARK/ STYRIA

STEEP SLOPES AND COOL CLIMATE

Klöchberg, Vulkanland Steiermark

THE MECCA OF CRISP WHITES

There are certainly wine-growing areas where richer wines with higher alcohol ripen, but nowhere in the world are there fresher, more brilliant wines that so elegantly express regional typicity than in Southern Styria. The three Styrian wine-growing areas with their incomparable specialties cover 5,086 vineyard hectares in the southern part of the state.

In Western Styria one finds a picturesque, hilly landscape where "Schilcher" reigns, a spicy rosé with slate-like minerality that is one of the most distinctive terroir wines in the country. In Sausal and on the Südsteirische Weinstrasse (Southern Styrian Wine Route), Sauvignon Blanc and Muskateller (Muscat) set the tone. Next to Burgundian varieties and Sauvignon Blanc in Vulkanland to the southeast, Traminer is a glittering jewel for connoisseurs. The ubiquitous Welschriesling, whose green apple bouquet has many devotees, is the stuff of dreams.

Those seeking fuller bodied wines are in good hands with the Pinot family in Styria. The Weissburgunder (Pinot Blanc) achieves a refined minerality and distinguished character in calcareous soils. Chardonnay, known by its old local name "Morillon", attains weighty firmness and power without sacrificing its pristine freshness and, like the best Grauburgunder (Pinot Gris) from this region, benefits from extended bottle maturation.

Beginning with the 2018 vintage, a new system of Protected Designation of Origin will take effect in Styria. This system classifies the three wine-growing areas as Südsteiermark DAC (Southern Styria), Vulkanland Steiermark DAC, and Weststeiermark DAC (Western Styria.) Within the wine-growing areas, the wines are divided into a pyramid made up of Gebietsweinen (regional wines), Ortsweinen (local or village wines), and Riedenweinen (single-vineyard wines), which define both the grape variety and the first release date. For all levels of DAC wine, hand-picked grapes are compulsory!

From gourmet restaurants to rustic winery taverns set in the enchanting landscape, Styria has plenty to offer. In the past few years ever more hotels and guesthouses of a very high quality have appeared, guaranteeing a wonderful holiday. At www.gutfinden.at you can find many locations that make Steiermark a highly attractive destination for connoisseurs.

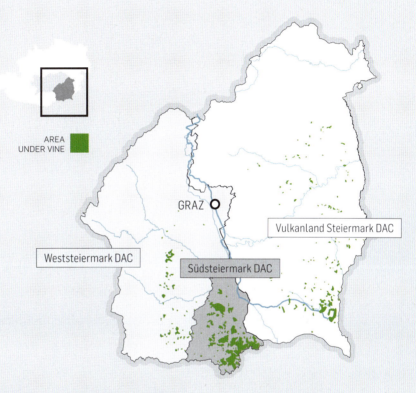

WINE-GROWING AREA STEIERMARK/STYRIA

Austria altogether	44.728 ha	SPECIFIC WINE-GROWING AREAS		
Wine-growing area		Südsteiermark DAC		2.788 ha
Steiermark/Styria	5.086 ha (11,4 %)	Vulkanland Steiermark DAC		1.657 ha
		Weststeiermark DAC		641 ha
White wine altogether	4.069 ha (80 %)	**Red wine altogether**	1.017 ha	(20 %)
Sauvignon Blanc	929 ha (18,3 %)	Blauer Wildbacher	518 ha	(10,2 %)
Welschriesling	773 ha (15,2 %)	Zweigelt	296 ha	(5,3 %)
Weißburgunder	690 ha (13,6 %)	Merlot	21 ha	(0,4 %)
Muskateller	549 ha (10,8 %)	Pinot Noir	20 ha	(0,4 %)
Chardonnay	385 ha (7,6 %)	Blaufränkisch	9 ha	(0,2 %)

STEIERMARK/STYRIA

SÜD-STEIERMARK

DAC

Southern Styria is often referred to as the »Styrian Tuscany«, steep hills, here at Heimschuh, characterize the landscape

Eichberg-Trautenburg, Oberer Zotzel

SAUVIGNON BLANC & CO FROM THE SOUTHERN HILLS

Südsteiermark is known for its classy, crisp, highly aromatic wines, in particular from its leading grape, Sauvignon Blanc. 2,788 vineyard hectares also provide splendid opportunities for a broad varietal spectrum ranging from Welschriesling to Morillon and Muskateller to Traminer. Although one of the most charming vineyard landscapes in Europe, grape growing on extremely steep slopes demands painstaking labour.

Just as diverse as the grape varieties are the soils of Südsteiermark, which include sand, shale, schist, marl and shell limestone. The warm, humid Mediterranean climate determines the vegetation cycle. Cool nights enhance nuanced aromatic intensity and noble character of the white wines. From the lean, fruity young wines called "Junker" that herald each new vintage, to the elegant "Klassik" wines to the mature, richly extracted single-vineyard wines, vintners demonstrate the full potential of the region throughout.

In the wide-ranging palette of regionally typical DAC wines, Sauvignon Blanc from Südsteiermark has achieved international recognition as one of the world's very best examples of the variety thanks to continual development of a unique, terroir-driven style. Open-minded winegrowers ensure that the high standards and quality are maintained by bringing home knowledge and know-how from trips and work experience abroad. There is also an excellent viticultural school in Silberberg that continues to prepare new winegrowers with skills and experience through theoretical and practical courses.

No matter the season, it is always well worth getting to know Südsteiermark. Highly rec-

© WSNA

STEIERMARK/STYRIA **SÜDSTEIERMARK DAC**

ommended is an autumn journey along the wine routes that hug the Slovenian border, wind through the Sausal Valley and continue west of Leibnitz. Be sure to leave sufficient time for visiting the towns of Ehrenhausen, Gamlitz, Leutschach and Kitzeck. Vineyard sites including Czamillonberg, Grassnitzberg, Kittenberg, Nussberg, Obegg, Sernauberg, and Zieregg are just as impressive to see as their wines are to drink. Not only have these wines established a fixed place on the tables of regional restaurants, but they have gained international favour as well. Archduke Johann of Austria, grandson of Empress Maria Theresia and visionary winegrowing pioneer would be proud of the spirit that continues in "his" winegrowers in Südsteiermark.re stolz auf seine südsteirischen Winzer.

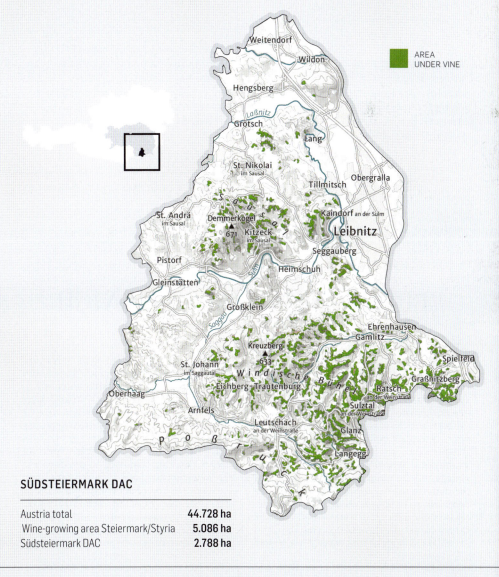

SÜDSTEIERMARK DAC

Austria total	44.728 ha
Wine-growing area Steiermark/Styria	5.086 ha
Südsteiermark DAC	2.788 ha

SELECTED WINERIES

Weingut Gross, Ehrenhausen
Weingut Lackner-Tinnacher, Gamlitz
Weingut Erwin Sabathi,
Leutschach an der Weinstraße
Familienweingut Sattlerhof, Gamlitz
Familienweingut Tement, Ehrenhausen

Weingut Kodolitsch, Leibnitz
Weingut Wolfgang Maitz,
Ehrenhausen an der Weinstraße
Weingut Muster.gamlitz, Gamlitz
Weingut Polz, Strass in der Steiermark
Weingut Hannes Sabathi, Gamlitz
Weingut Skoff Original – Walter Skoff, Gamlitz
Weingut Wohlmuth, Kitzeck im Sausal
Ewald Zweytick Wein, Ratsch an der Weinstraße

Domaines Kilger, Gamlitz
Weingut Masser, Leutschach
Weingut Regele, Ehrenhausen an der Weinstraße
Weingut Peter Skoff – Domäne Kranachberg, Gamlitz

Weingut Buschenschank Firmenich, Ehrenhausen
Weingut Kögl, Ratsch an der Weinstraße
Landesweingut Silberberg, Leibnitz
Sanfter Weinbau Maria und Johannes Söll, Gamlitz
Weingut Strauss Gamlitz, Gamlitz

Weingut Wruss, Gamlitz

WEINGUT BUSCHENSCHANK FIRMENICH

Weingut Firmenich, located in the picturesque village of Steinberg, is a family-run winery with a wine tavern called the Steinberghof, situated on the South Styrian wine route. Beech trees flank the winery's driveway, and from the winery, one can savour a panoramic view of the vineyards and the eastern Styrian countryside.

Sustainable agriculture, manual labour, low yields and uncompromising quality standards are the cornerstones of the estate's elegant wines. The grapes are sourced exclusively from the estate's own vineyards, which lie at an altitude of 400 to 500 metres above sea level. The geology of the area is characterised by coral limestone and opok, a fine-grained calcareous soil type, resulting in vibrant and mineral wines. The main grape varieties are Sauvignon Blanc, which is the most widely grown, as well as Gelber Muskateller, Welschriesling and Morillon. White wine varieties account for over 90 per cent of the cultivated area.

The South Styrian regional wines form the basis of the range and are an expression of the South Styrian spirit: fresh and fruity, lively but with a hint of minerality. For the local wines, the focus is on the soil and its composition. The estate wines are made exclusively from grapes of optimal ripeness from the vineyards of Steinberg and Grassnitzberg.

SÜDSTEIERMARK DAC

WEINGUT BUSCHENSCHANK FIRMENICH
8461 Ehrenhausen
Wielitsch 57
T: +43 (3453) 2435
weingut@firmenich.at
www.firmenich.at

Winemaker/Contact:
Johannes Firmenich
Production: 10 % sparkling, 80 % white, 5 % rosé, 5 % red, 5.5 hectares
Distribution partners: DE

Johannes Firmenich

These are bold and distinctive wines with long ageing potential. They epitomise origin and craftsmanship.

The Steinberghof's lovingly decorated wine tavern serves regional cuisine in a cosy atmosphere. In addition to traditional Styrian delicacies, the menu includes a variety of more unusual dishes, as well as vegetarian and vegan delicacies. The perfect place to indulge your taste buds. Insider tip: Steinberghof is also the home of STIN - Styrian Gin.

93 Sauvignon Blanc Ried Zieregg 2019
13,5 Vol.-%, glass, used barriques, €€€€€€

94 Sauvignon Blanc Ried Zieregg Reserve 2017
13,5 Vol.-%, glass, used barriques, €€€€€€

92 Sauvignon Blanc Ried Steinberg 2019
13,5 Vol.-%, glass, steel tank, €€€€

92 Sauvignon Blanc * Ried Steinberg 2018
91 Sauvignon Blanc * Ried Steinberg 2017

92 Sauvignon Blanc * Ried Grassnitzberg 2018
93 Sauvignon Blanc Ried Grassnitzberg Reserve 2017
Medium yellow-green, silver reflections. Delicate blossom honey, white currants, delicate smoky herbal touch, underlaid with nuances of grapefruit. Juicy, elegant, white peach, mineral texture, fresh and lemony, appears very youthful, a savoury food wine, further certain ageing potential guaranteed.

92 Sauvignon Blanc Ried Grassnitzberg Reserve 2015

89 Sauvignon Blanc * 2021
89 Sauvignon Blanc * 2020
89 Sauvignon Blanc * 2019

93 Morillon Ried Steinberg 2020
13,5 Vol.-%, glass, used barriques, €€€€€

91 Chardonnay * Ried Steinberg 2019
91 Morillon * Ried Steinberg 2018

92 Welschriesling * Ried Steinberg 2019

91 Gelber Muskateller 2022
11,5 Vol.-%, screwcap, steel tank, €€€
90 Gelber Muskateller * 202
89 Gelber Muskateller * 2020

89 Roter Muskateller 2020
90 Roter Muskateller 2019

* Südsteiermark DAC

★★★★★

WEINGUT GROSS

"Focus!" is the motto of Martina and Johannes Gross - primarily on outstanding wines in the entry-level segment as well as on single vineyard wines that are allowed to age for a long time in their cellar. Their South Styrian regional wines, such as Sauvignon Blanc and Gelber Muskateller, owe that certain something to their attentive, hands-on approach. Their wines all derive from the family's own vineyards, which are tended with dedication.

The Welschriesling from Weingut Gross is an entirely new and progressive style. The winemakers call it "Welschriesling Pro" and show what this variety is capable of. The reduced grape yield and the more extended maturation period make it an excellent companion for supper. In the area of the Rieden (single vineyard site) wines, Weingut Gross was the first white wine estate in Austria to take a bold step: all Rieden wines are allowed to "mature" at their own pace. They are allowed to mature and age for at least four years before being released. It is evident how well the wines benefit from being allowed to age and mature in the best possible conditions.

91 🅑 Gross & Gross Fortuna Minor zero dosage Ein Quäntchen Glück 2019 WR/SÄ

(96) Sauvignon Blanc * Ried Sulz 1STK 2019
13,5 Vol.-%, cork, large wooden barrel, €€€€€ 🅑
94 Sauvignon Blanc * Ried Sulz 1STK 2018
94 Sauvignon Blanc Ried Sulz 1 STK 2017

(96) Sauvignon Blanc *
Ried Nussberg GSTK 2019
13,5 Vol.-%, cork, large wooden barrel, €€€€€€ 🅑
95 Sauvignon Blanc *
Ried Nussberg GSTK 2018
Light yellow-green, silver reflections. Delicate tropical fruit, ripe gooseberry, a hint of yellow tropical fruit, hints of guava, discreet candied orange zest. Taut, tight-knit, white fruit, finesse, bright acidity, lemony-salty finish. Plenty of development potential.
96 Sauvignon Blanc Ried Nussberg G STK 2017

94 Sauvignon Blanc * Ried Obere Ranz 2019

94 Sauvignon Blanc * Ehrenhausen 2021
13 Vol.-%, DIAM, large wooden barrel, €€€€ 🅑
94 Sauvignon Blanc * Ehrenhausen 2020
93 Sauvignon Blanc * Ehrenhausen 2019

93 Sauvignon Blanc * Gamlitz 2020
93 Sauvignon Blanc * Gamlitz 2019
93 Sauvignon Blanc * Gamlitz 2018

92 Sauvignon Blanc * 2022
12,5 Vol.-%, screwcap, steel tank, €€€ 🅑
93 Sauvignon Blanc * 2021
92 Sauvignon Blanc * 2020

91 Sauvignon Blanc * Gross & Gross Jakobi 2019
91 Sauvignon Blanc * Gross & Gross Jakobi 2018

98 Sauvignon Blanc Privat FR 2017

(97) Sauvignon Blanc Wi.He.Be. Historischer Doppelbesitz 2019
13,5 Vol.-%, cork, large wooden barrel, €€€€€€ 🅑
97 Sauvignon Blanc Witscheiner Herrenberg FR Historischer Doppelbesitz 2017
Pale golden yellow, silver glints. Scented nuances of orange blossom, fine gooseberry notes, pleasant herbal savouriness, air contact a little cassis, St. John's wort, and dark bristling minerality. Complex, full-bodied, fruit-forward core, nuances of blood oranges, salinity, refined acidic core, saline reverberations - exhibiting excellent length and potential. Unique character.

97 Sauvignon Blanc Ried Nussberg GSTK FR 2017
Pale golden yellow, silver glints. Delicately scented floral nuances, very delicate yellow tropical fruit, a hint of ripe gooseberries, candied orange zest, and smoky minerality. Juicy, complex, tightly woven, fine, silky texture, filigree structure, subtle minerality, followed by pleasantly resonating expression of fruit. Excellent length, calm, already accessible, and definite ageing potential.

97 Sauvignon Blanc Witscheiner Herrenberg 2017

95 Sauvignon Blanc Ried Sulz 1STK FR 2017

92 Sauvignon Blanc Alte Reben 2020

© LUPI SPUMA Fine Photography

SÜDSTEIERMARK DAC

WEINGUT GROSS
8461 Ehrenhausen
Ratsch an der Weinstraße 26
T: +43 (3453) 2527
weingut@gross.at
www.gross.at

Winemaker: Johannes Gross
Contact: Martina and Johannes Gross
Production: 131,600 bottles
99 % white, 1 % sweet, 37 hectares
Certified: Sustainable Austria
Fairs: VieVinum
Distribution partners: BE, RC, DK, DE, FIN, FR, UK, HK, IT, JP, CDN, HR, NL, NO, PL, RUS, SE, CH, SGP, SLO, CZ, HU, USA

Martina and Johannes Gross

(95) Weißburgunder * Ried Nussberg Stauder GSTK 2019
12,5 Vol.-%, cork, large wooden barrel/bottle fermentation, €€€€€ B
95 Weißburgunder * Ried Nussberg "Stauder" GSTK 2019
95 Weißburgunder * Ried Nussberg GSTK Stauder 2018

(94) Weißburgunder * Ried Kittenberg 1STK 2019
12,5 Vol.-%, cork, large wooden barrel/bottle maturation, €€€€ B
94 Weißburgunder * Ried Kittenberg 1STK 2018
94 Weißburgunder Ried Kittenberg 1STK FR 2017

(92) Weißburgunder * Ehrenhausen 2021
12,5 Vol.-%, DIAM, large wooden barrel, €€€ B
93 Weißburgunder * Ehrenhausen 2020
93 Weißburgunder * Ehrenhausen 2019

(94) Morillon * Ried Nussberg Preschnigg GSTK 2019
13,5 Vol.-%, cork, large wooden barrel, €€€€€ B
94 Morillon * Ried Nussberg "Pretschnigg" GSTK 2019
94 Morillon Ried Nussberg – Pretschnigg G STK 2017

(92) Morillon * Ehrenhausen Startin 2021
13 Vol.-%, DIAM, large wooden barrel, €€€ B
93 Morillon * Ehrenhausen Startin 2019
93 Morillon * Ehrenhausen Startin 2018

93 Gelber Muskateller * Gamlitz 2020
92 Gelber Muskateller * Gamlitz 2019
92 Gelber Muskateller * Gamlitz 2018

92 Gelber Muskateller * Ried Perz 1STK 2020
11,5 Vol.-%, cork, large wooden barrel, €€€€€ B
94 Gelber Muskateller * Ried Perz 1STK 2019
94 Gelber Muskateller * Ried Perz 1STK 2018

91 Gelber Muskateller * 2022
11 Vol.-%, screwcap, steel tank, €€€ B
92 Gelber Muskateller * 2021
91 Gelber Muskateller * 2020

90 Gelber Muskateller * Gross & Gross Mitzi 2019
90 Gelber Muskateller * Gross & Gross Mitzi 2018

92 Welschriesling Pro. 2021
12,5 Vol.-%, DIAM, large wooden barrel, €€€ B
91 Welschriesling * Pro. 2020
92 Welschriesling * 2019

92 * Bergwein 2021 SB/WR
13,5 Vol.-%, DIAM, large wooden barrel/steel tank, €€€ B
92 * Bergwein 2020 SB/WR
91 * Bergwein 2019 SB/WR

96 Sauvignon Blanc Beerenauslese 2017
95 Sauvignon Blanc TBA 2017
95 Welschriesling TBA 2017
94 Chardonnay TBA 2017

* Südsteiermark DAC

DOMAINES KILGER

Domaines Kilger is a winery that vinifies fine wine specialities from three Austrian wine-growing regions: From western Styria come the Blauer Wildbacher grapes for the Domaines' characterful rosé and sparkling wines. In southern Styria, the Sonneck vineyard, with Sauvignon Blanc vines dating back to 1842, and the Kranachberg vineyard, with 25-year-old vines, produce fascinating, elegant Sauvignon Blancs, and on the Eisenberg in southern Burgenland the Blaufränkisch and Merlot grapes grow for grandiose red wines.

What all of these wines have in common is that they unmistakably display their provenance and terroir, while being characterised by the utmost elegance. The philosophy of Domaines Kilger is to produce wines that are pure and unadulterated and to get the best possible out of everything.

91 ⊙ Rosé Brut Reserve Sekt Steiermark g.U. 2015

(95) Sauvignon Blanc * Ried Kranachberg Obere Kapelle Reserve 2021

(95) Sauvignon Blanc * Ried Sonneck Alte Reben 2021
14 Vol.-%, screwcap

95 Sauvignon Blanc * Ried Kranachberg Reserve 2020
Light green-yellow, silver reflections. Delicate blossom honey, white tropical fruit, fresh peach, subtle hints of grapefruit. Taut, elegant, tight-knit, lively structure, salty-citrusy finish, clear as a mountain stream, has ageing potential.

94 Sauvignon Blanc * Ried Kranachberg Reserve 2019

94 Sauvignon Blanc Ried Kranachberg Reserve 2018

(94) Sauvignon Blanc * Ried Sonneck 2021
13,5 Vol.-%, cork

93 Sauvignon Blanc * Ried Sonneck 2020

91 Sauvignon Blanc Ried Sonneck 2018

(94) Sauvignon Blanc * Ried Kranachberg 2021
13,5 Vol.-%, cork

92 Sauvignon Blanc * Ried Kranachberg 2020

93 Sauvignon Blanc * Ried Kranachberg 2019

93 Sauvignon Blanc * Gamlitz 2021
13,5 Vol.-%, screwcap, large wooden barrel, €€€€

93 Sauvignon Blanc * Gamlitz 2020

93 Sauvignon Blanc * Ehrenhausen 2021
13 Vol.-%, screwcap

92 Sauvignon Blanc * Ehrenhausen 2021

92 Sauvignon Blanc * »Hans & Walter« 2022
13 Vol.-%, screwcap

91 Sauvignon Blanc * Hans & Walter 2021

(94) Chardonnay * Ried Kranachberg 2021
13,5 Vol.-%, cork

93 Chardonnay Ried Kranachberg Reserve 2018
Medium golden yellow, silver reflections. Candied orange, ripe golden delicious apple, delicate pear, a hint of light nougat. Medium complexity, white stone fruit, mineral core, nice fruit in the finish, discreet caramel touch in the aftertaste, already well developed, a multi-faceted food wine.

DOMAINES KILGER
8462 Gamlitz
Eckberger Weinstraße 32
T: +43 (3453) 2363-11
wein@domaines-kilger.com
www.domaines-kilger.com

Winemaker: Walter Polz
Contact: Alexandra Herrmann
Production: 533,333 bottles
15 % sparkling, 63 % white, 2 % rosé, 20 % red, 60+30 hectares
Certified: Sustainable Austria
Fairs: ProWein Düsseldorf, VieVinum
Distribution partners: DE

SÜDSTEIERMARK DAC

93 Chardonnay Reserve
    Ried Kranachberg 2018

93 Chardonnay * Gamlitz 2021
13,5 Vol.-%
92 Chardonnay * Gamlitz 2020

93 Chardonnay * Leutschach 2021
14 Vol.-%, screwcap, large wooden barrel, €€€€

92 Welschriesling * Alte Reben 2021
13 Vol.-%

91 Weißburgunder * 2022
12,5 Vol.-%, screwcap
92 Weißburgunder * 2021
90 Weißburgunder 2018

91 Gelber Muskateller * 2021

91 Muskateller Ried Sonneck 2019

91 Blauer Wildbacher Rosé Reserve 2017
91 Blauer Wildbacher Rosé Reserve 2015

94 Blaufränkisch Ried Königsberg 2017

92 Cuwe 2018 BF/ME
93 Cuvée Private Reserve 2017 BF/ME

91 Blaufränkisch Burgenland 2018

92 Zweigelt Burgenland Reserve 2019

★★★★

WEINGUT KODOLITSCH

For centuries - more than 300 years, to be precise - the Kodolitsch family has been running the estate. The current owners, Christa and Nikolaus Kodolitsch, took over the winery in 1993 and developed it into a landmark winery synonymous with premium quality wines.

Today, Mario Weber is responsible for the vinification, which is undertaken with great sensitivity and in harmony with nature. The distinctive features of the terroirs of the Rosengarten and Kogelberg sites are expressed by Mario Weber with endless nuances of intricacies. The grapes are harvested ex-

WEINGUT KODOLITSCH
8430 Leibnitz
Kodolitschweg 9
T: +43 (664) 4225919
weingut@kodolitsch.at
www.kodolitsch.at

Winemaker/Contact:
Mario Weber
Production: 100 % white, 16+2,5 hectares
Certified: Sustainable Austria
Fairs: VieVinum
Distribution partners: DE, SK

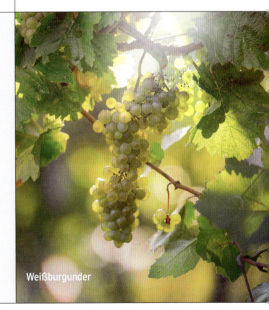

Weißburgunder

* Südsteiermark DAC

STEIERMARK/STYRIA

clusively by hand and then carefully processed with great expertise and sensitivity.
The pursuit of perfection and the passion for wine are the reasons for the many awards the estate has received in recent years.

95 Sauvignon Blanc * Ried Rosengarten T.M.S. 2020
13,5 Vol.-%, cork, wooden barrel, €€€€€€

97 Sauvignon Blanc * Ried Rosengarten T.M.S 2019
Pale greenish yellow, silver glints. Smoky-herbal savoury nuances are underlaid with cassis, delicate hints of gooseberries and grapefruit, and a dash of yellow tropical fruit. Complex, juicy, well-balanced, fine yellow peach, filigree arc of acidity, saline-minerality, prolonged persistence with resonating lime notes. Promising ageing potential.

96 Sauvignon Blanc * Ried Rosengarten T.M.S. 2018

94 Sauvignon Blanc * Ried Kogelberg Alte Reben 2020
13,5 Vol.-%, cork, wooden barrel, €€€€€€

95 Sauvignon Blanc * Ried Kogelberg Alte Reben 2019

93 Sauvignon Blanc * Ried Rosengarten 2021
13,5 Vol.-%, cork, large wooden barrel, €€€€

93 Sauvignon Blanc * Ried Rosengarten 2020
94 Sauvignon Blanc * Ried Rosengarten 2018

93 Sauvignon Blanc * Gamlitz 2022
13,5 Vol.-%, screwcap, steel tank, €€€€

92 Sauvignon Blanc * 2022
12,5 Vol.-%, screwcap, steel tank, €€€

90 Sauvignon Blanc * 2021
92 Sauvignon Blanc * 2020

95 Chardonnay * Ried Kogelberg Alte Reben 2019
Bright golden yellow, silver glints. Lovely herbal savoury scents, soft notions of delicate vanilla, yellow apple, and a hint of new wood. A Burgundian-styled character. Juicy, elegant, white fruit, filigree arc of acidity, saline-minerality, persistence, citrus finish. Assured ageing potential.

93 Chardonnay * Ried Kogelberg Alte Reben 2018

94 Chardonnay Ried Kogelberg Alte Reben 2017

94 Chardonnay * Ried Rosengarten Alte Reben 2020
13,5 Vol.-%, cork, small wooden barrel, €€€€€€

94 Chardonnay * Ried Rosengarten Alte Reben 2019

94 Chardonnay * Ried Rosengarten Alte Reben 2018

93 Weißburgunder * Ried Rosengarten 2021
13,5 Vol.-%, cork, wooden barrel, €€€€

92 Weißburgunder * Ried Rosengarten 2020
92 Weißburgunder * Ried Rosengarten 2019

91 Weißburgunder * 2022
12,5 Vol.-%, screwcap, steel tank, €€

91 Weißburgunder * 2021

93 Riesling * Ried Kogelberg 2021
12,5 Vol.-%, cork, 500-l-barrel, €€€€

92 Riesling * Ried Kogelberg 2020

92 Riesling * Kitzeck-Sausal 2021
12,5 Vol.-%, cork, 500-l-barrel, €€€

93 Gelber Muskateller * Ried Rosengarten 2021
12,5 Vol.-%, cork, large wooden barrel, €€€€

92 Gelber Muskateller * 2021
90 Gelber Muskateller * 2019

92 Welschriesling * Ried Rosengarten Alte Reben 2020
13,5 Vol.-%, cork, 500-l-barrel, €€€€

SÜDSTEIERMARK DAC

WEINGUT KÖGL
8461 Ratsch an der Weinstraße
Ratsch an der Weinstraße 59
T: +43 (3453) 4341
info@weingut-koegl.com
www.weingut-koegl.com

Winemaker/Contact:
Tamara Kögl
Production: 33,333 bottles
10 % sparkling, 85 % white, 5 % red,
10 hectares
Fairs: VieVinum, Vinobile Feldkirch,
DAC-Presentations, Bio Österreich
Distribution partners: DE, USA

Riesling

WEINGUT KÖGL
ORGANIC

Tamara and Robert Kögl-Rettenbacher vinify inimitable, characterful wines that undoubtedly reflect their origins in southern Styria. With their biodynamic approach, the two live their vision of nurturing resolute sustainable viticulture, characterised by respect and appreciation for nature and the search for harmony. "The vine provides us with everything we need for our wine. We create a good environment and protection. Subsequently the grape carries the energy required for the wine. Observed with a watchful eye, with patience and minimal intervention, the wine develops into a dynamic phenomenon," explains the couple with absolute conviction.

92 ❂ Pet Nat »Under Pressure« 2022 WB/WR
12,5 Vol.-%, crown cap, steel tank/bottle fermentation,
€€€€ B

Light yellow-green, silver reflections, lively mousse. Fresh white pear fruit, floral nuances, a hint of lime. Medium body, white stone fruit, fresh and lively, lemony-salty finish, animating alternative to classic flint wine.

93 ❂ 2020 »Under Pressure« WB/WR

90 ❂ 2020 »Forever Young« GM/WR

92 Morillon * Ehrenhausen 2020
12 Vol.-%, screwcap, steel tank, €€€€ B V

91 Morillon * Ehrenhausen 2018

91 Welschriesling * Ried Stermetzberg 2019

91 Welschriesling * Ehrenhausen 2019

89 Welschriesling Alte Reben 2017

90 Muskateller * Ehrenhausen 2019

90 Muskateller Herrschaft NV
13 Vol.-%, cork, steel tank, €€€€€ B V

90 Sauvignon Blanc * 2019
90 Sauvignon Blanc * Gamlitz 2019

93 Sauvignon Blanc Meierei NV
14,5 Vol.-%, cork, 500-l-barrel, €€€€ B V

(92) Sauvignon Blanc Kalkmergel 2021
14 Vol.-%, cork, screwcap, steel tank, €€€€ B V

94 Grauburgunder Ried Stermetzberg 2017

* Südsteiermark DAC

STEIERMARK/STYRIA

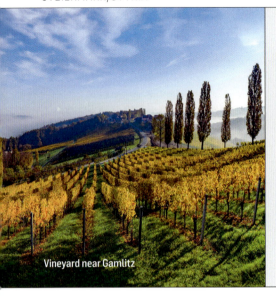
Vineyard near Gamlitz

WEINGUT LACKNER-TINNACHER
8462 Gamlitz
Steinbach 12
T: +43 (3453) 2142
weingut@tinnacher.at
www.tinnacher.at

Winemaker/Contact:
Katharina Tinnacher
Production: 97 % white, 1 % red, 2 % sweet, 28 hectares
Certified: Sustainable Austria
Fairs: ProWein Düsseldorf, VieVinum
Distribution partners: BE, DE, FR, LU, NL, NO, RUS, SE, CH, SK, CZ, USA

★★★★★

WEINGUT LACKNER-TINNACHER
ORGANIC

Weingut Lackner-Tinnacher is located in the midst of vineyards on a ridge of hills in Steinbach near Gamlitz. Viticulture has been practised on the estate for centuries; as early as 1787, four vineyard parcels were described in detail in the Josephinian cadastre. Today the estate is run by Katharina Tinnacher. Approximately 28 hectares of vineyards are located at ideal climatic altitudes of 400 to 500 metres on the best steep slopes in the wine-growing villages of Gamlitz and Kitzeck-Sausal.

The vineyards are the focus of Katharina Tinnacher's attention. They are cultivated carefully and organically. The vines are carefully trained by hand to achieve a higher degree of ripeness. Harvesting is usually late, with particular attention paid to optimum harvesting times by hand. It is also common practice for the grapes to reach the press quickly and intact and to be pressed gently. For many years, traditional and meticulous vinification has been the hallmark of the winery's timeless, elegant line.

The wines are always finely structured, infused with depth of fruit and shaped by the soil, climate and vintage. All the estate's wines are sourced from the estate's own vineyards. The individual sites and vineyards have different soil conditions, and Katharina Tinnacher is keen to show these fine structural differences in the wine. The main variety is Sauvignon Blanc, with the grapes for the local Gamlitz Sauvignon Blanc growing on predominantly sandy-gravelly soils. The Sauvignon Blanc Ried Welles has a stony, mineral-rich gravel conglomerate subsoil and a topsoil of red and grey sands. The winery also focuses on Pinot varieties: Pinot Blanc Ried Eckberg and Morillon Ried Eckberg are grown on limestone marl soils, while Pinot Blanc Ried Steinbach and Pinot Gris Ried Steinbach thrive on sandy and gravelly soils. In addition, Welschriesling, Gamlitz Gelber Muskateller and Gelber Muskateller Ried Gamitz are pressed from over fifty years old vines.

At the beginning of 2008, the winery was expanded to include vineyards in the Ried Flamberg in the municipality of St. Nikolai im Sausal. The five hectares of south-southwest facing, basin-shaped slopes offer a unique terroir characterised by coral limestone soils, providing an exciting contrast to the Steinbach sites. Not surprisingly, Flamberg is now the focus of Kathar-

SÜDSTEIERMARK DAC

ina Tinnacher, who studied the interaction of vine, soil and climate during her studies at the University of Natural Resources and Applied Life Sciences. In addition to preserving the valuable old vines, she is focusing on the cultivation of Sauvignon Blanc and Pinot varieties at Flamberg. As of the 2016 vintage, all wines are certified organic.

97 Sauvignon Blanc * Ried Welles GSTK 2020
13 Vol.-%, glass, large wooden barrel, €€€€€ B V

96 Sauvignon Blanc * Ried Welles GSTK 2019
Bright golden yellow with silver reflections. Some blossom honey on the nose with a background of tobacco savouriness, a breath of caramel and some ripe gooseberry, this is an inviting bouquet. Juicy, elegant, good complexity, some lychee and ripe fruit exoticism with some citrus nuances, lasts well this is complex with good ageing potential.

96 Sauvignon Blanc * Ried Welles GSTK 2018

97 Sauvignon Blanc Ried Welles GSTK Reserve 2017
Medium yellow-green, silver glints. Dark savouriness, awakening grapefruit zest, tobacco nuances, white stone fruit, a hint of yellow pepper, and a herb touch. Full-bodied, elegant white fruit nuances, exhibits excellent depth, minerality, and persistence superseded by saline reverberations. Superb future potential.

95 Sauvignon Blanc * Ried Flamberg GSTK 2020
12,5 Vol.-%, glass, large wooden barrel, €€€€€ B V

95 Sauvignon Blanc * Ried Flamberg GSTK 2019

94 Sauvignon Blanc * Ried Steinbach 1STK 2021
13 Vol.-%, glass, large wooden barrel, €€€€€ B V

93 Sauvignon Blanc * Ried Steinbach 1STK 2020
94 Sauvignon Blanc * Ried Steinbach 1STK 2019

92 Sauvignon Blanc * Kitzeck-Sausal 2021
12,5 Vol.-%, glass, steel tank, €€€€ B V
93 Sauvignon Blanc * Kitzeck-Sausal 2019

93 Sauvignon Blanc * Gamlitz 2021
92 Sauvignon Blanc * Gamlitz 2020
92 Sauvignon Blanc * Gamlitz 2019

95 Morillon * Ried Welles GSTK 2020
13 Vol.-%, glass, 500-l-barrel, €€€€€ B V

94 Morillon * Ried Steinbach 1STK 2021
13 Vol.-%, glass, large wooden barrel, €€€€€ B V
93 Morillon * Ried Steinbach 1STK 2020

94 Morillon * Ried Steinbach 1STK 2019
94 Morillon * Ried Eckberg STK 2021
12,5 Vol.-%, glass, large wooden barrel, €€€€ B V
93 Morillon * Ried Eckberg 2019

94 Morillon * Ried Flamberg GSTK 2020
95 Morillon * Ried Flamberg GSTK 2019
94 Morillon Ried Flamberg G STK 2017

95 Grauburgunder Reserve * Ried Steinbach 1STK 2019
Pale golden yellow, silver glints. Delicately fragrant grapefruit notes, floral touches, white stone fruit nuances, tobacco-herbal savouriness, and a subtle caramel touch. Powerful, juicy, very complex, taut texture, fine expression of fruit, a hint of pear on the finish, as well as lovely nougat nuances, huge length, minerality, and soft saline reverberating notions. Already accessible, good ageing potential.

94 Grauburgunder * Ried Steinbach 1STK 2021
13 Vol.-%, glass, large wooden barrel, €€€€€ B V
94 Grauburgunder * Ried Steinbach 1STK 2019
94 Grauburgunder * Ried Steinbach 1STK 2018

94 Weißburgunder * Ried Steinbach 1STK Kogel 2021
13 Vol.-%, glass, large wooden barrel, €€€€€ B V
94 Weißburgunder * Ried Steinbach 1STK 2020
93 Weißburgunder * Ried Steinbach 1STK 2019

92 Weißburgunder * Ried Eckberg STK 2021
12,5 Vol.-%, glass, steel tank, €€€€ B V
92 Weißburgunder * Ried Eckberg 2020
93 Weißburgunder * Ried Eckberg 2019

94 Roter Traminer * Ried Türken 2019

93 Welschriesling * Franz Lackner 2020
12,5 Vol.-%, glass, large wooden barrel, €€€€€ B V
92 Welschriesling * Franz Lackner 2019

(92) Gelber Muskateller * Gamlitz 2022
11,5 Vol.-%, cork, steel tank, €€€ B V
91 Gelber Muskateller * Gamlitz 2020
92 Gelber Muskateller * Gamlitz 2019

95 Welschriesling TBA 2017
11,5 Vol.-%, glass, steel tank, €€€€€ B V

95 Sauvignon Blanc Beerenauslese 2017

94 Morillon Beerenauslese 2017

*Südsteiermark DAC

WEINGUT MUSTER.GAMLITZ

★★★★

Reinhard Muster and his family believe that good wine is made with love. They have followed this formula for years. They are committed to craftsmanship out of conviction. The wines are consistently well-balanced in taste, yet traditional in the sense of time-honoured. In southern Styria, in the lee of the Alps, the Illyrian climate determines the weather. Contrasting weather conditions with Mediterranean hours of sunshine, large temperature fluctuations and abundant rainfall are not uncommon, but the norm. The Muster family is aware of these unique advantages and produces naturally good wine with composure and serenity.

Should the first or the last glass of a bottle of wine give the greatest pleasure? This fundamental question determines what is done in the cellar. "We are resolutely committed to the last glass," says Reinhard Muster. Since the 1990s, local winegrowers have changed the way they make their wines. In the past, work in the cellar was central and had a major influence on the wine. In a sense, the wine was 'made' then; now the wines are 'allowed to develop'. From the grape to the bottle, the work in the cellar is the necessary foundation. The wine evolves: one observes quietly in the background. Of course, the winemaker still has a marked influence on the characteristics and quality, but in a targeted, deliberate and rational way. The last glass of each bottle is therefore very rewarding.

Reinhard Muster is the down-to-earth and open-minded head of the winery.

He is the creative mind of the winery and goes about his daily routine with diligence, no matter what the situation may be. Miriam and Laurenzia are the whirlwinds of the winery, always in high spirits. A colourful team works here, taking on tasks beyond their scope and performing small miracles every day with diligence and flair.

The classic wines showcase the diversity of South Styrian grape varieties and their very distinctive flavours. They are mostly vinified in stainless steel tanks to preserve the typical character of the grape varieties. The wines are fruity and approachable and are usually drunk young.

The temperamental Illyrian weather has always brought out the characteristics of each grape variety in the bottle. The label also pays homage to the weather, and the "Reverence" series is now called "Illyr". The ripest grapes, those most affected by the weather during the year, are aged in various wooden barrels and stainless steel tanks until they begin to mature, and then bottled the year after the harvest.

Europe - Austria - South Styria - Gamlitz - Grubthal: The more unique the origin, the higher the demand for quality. At the top of the quality pyramid are the Grosses Gewächse from the Grubthal vineyard. This can be quite a challenge, which is why these wines are only made in exceptional vintages. For these wines, cellar management is only a means to an end. The grapes are fermented and matured for 20 to 30 months in new and old oak barrels. Complexity, structure and saline minerality characterise these wines. They reach their optimum maturity after three to four years and have a cellaring potential of at least 10 to 15 years.

94 Sauvignon Blanc * Ried Grubthal 2020
13,5 Vol.-%, glass, barrique, €€€€€€

95 Sauvignon Blanc * Ried Grubthal 2019
Medium yellow-green, silver reflections. Intense bouquet, hints of lime, grapefruit, fresh guava and herbs, backed by fine wood spice, mineral touch. Juicy, elegant, nuances of essential oils, some eucalyptus, fine and balanced, mineral, taut, great length and finesse.

95 Sauvignon Blanc * Ried Grubthal 2018

94 Sauvignon Blanc * Ried Grubthal Privatarchiv 2017

93 Sauvignon Blanc Grubthal Privatarchiv 2016
13 Vol.-%, glass, barrique, €€€€€€

94 Sauvignon Blanc Ried Grubthal Privatarchiv 2015

© Anna Stöcher

SÜDSTEIERMARK DAC

WEINGUT MUSTER.GAMLITZ
8462 Gamlitz
Grubtal 14
T: +43 (3453) 2300
weingut@muster-gamlitz.at
www.muster-gamlitz.at

Winemaker: Reinhard Muster
Contact: The Muster family
Production: 100 % white,
58 hectares
Fairs: ProWein Düsseldorf
Distribution partners: DE

Reinhard Muster

92 Sauvignon Blanc Illyr 2021
13,5 Vol.-%, glass, barrique, €€€€
93 Sauvignon Blanc * Reverenz 2020
93 Sauvignon Blanc * Gamlitz Reverenz 2019

91 Sauvignon Blanc Klassik 2022
12,5 Vol.-%, screwcap, steel tank, €€€
92 Sauvignon Blanc * Klassik 2021
91 Sauvignon Blanc * Klassik 2020

94 Chardonnay * Ried Grubthal 2020
13,5 Vol.-%, glass, barrique, €€€€
95 Chardonnay * Ried Grubthal 2019
Pale golden yellow, faint brass tinges. Delicately scented savoury wood nuances, sweet spices, a floral touch, and peppermint tones. Juicy, elegant, silky texture, a hint of light caramel, fine acidity structure, complex and multifaceted, with nuances of yellow tropical fruit, toasty reverberations and shows length. Will benefit from bottle ageing.
94 Chardonnay * Ried Grubthal 2018

92 Chardonnay * Marienkreuz 2020

94 Chardonnay Ried Grubthal
    Privatarchiv 2015
93 Chardonnay Grubthal Privatarchiv 2013
13 Vol.-%, glass, barrique, €€€€€
94 Chardonnay Grubthal Privat Reserve 2013

91 Chardonnay Illyr 2021
13 Vol.-%, screwcap, barrique, €€€

92 Grauburgunder Illyr 2021
13 Vol.-%, glass, barrique, €€€€
92 Grauburgunder * Reverenz 2020
92 Grauburgunder * Reverenz 2019

91 Weißburgunder * Klassik 2021

92 Weissburgunder Illyr 2021
13,5 Vol.-%, glass, barrique, €€€€
93 Weißburgunder * Reverenz 2020
91 Weißburgunder * Reverenz 2019

90 Welschriesling * Retro 2021
90 Welschriesling * Retro 2020

92 Gelber Muskateller Klassik 2021

90 Gelber Muskateller Illyr 2021
12,5 Vol.-%, glass, barrique, €€€
90 Gelber Muskateller Reverenz
    Steiermark 2020
92 Gelber Muskateller Reverenz
    Steiermark 2018

91 Rosé Illyr 2021 BW/ZW
13 Vol.-%, glass, barrique, €€€€

* Südsteiermark DAC

WEINGUT WOLFGANG MAITZ

Origin is grounded, is the motto of winemaker Wolfgang Maitz. His ten-hectare estate produces only wines with a distinct character and provenance. These wines are 100 per cent South Styrian and 100 per cent hand-harvested. Wines are produced with the provenance Südsteiermark DAC, the local wines "Ehrenhausen" and single vineyard wines from Sulz, Krois 1STK, Schusterberg 1STK and the top vineyard Hochstermetzberg GSTK. Careful work with nature and serenity in the cellar guarantee expressive wines of provenance with an artisan character. The winery is a member of the Association of Styrian Terroir and Classic Wine Estates. Attached to the winery is a guesthouse with a wine hotel, which is an ideal starting point for wine tours.

92 ❂ Zweigelt extra brut Blanc de Noirs 2017

95 Sauvignon Blanc * Ried Hochstermetzberg GSTK 2020
13 Vol.-%, screwcap, wooden barrel, €€€€€€

94 Sauvignon Blanc * Ried Hochstermetzberg GSTK 2019
Medium yellow-green with silver reflections. Ripe gooseberry underlaid by fine blossom honey, a little ripe mango and a breath of caramel – a powerful bouquet. Complex, juicy, elegant, fine acid structure, mineral, savoury, and fruity on the finish. The wine is already well developed and has further ageing potential.

95 Sauvignon Blanc * Ried Hochstermetzberg GSTK 2018

(94) Sauvignon Blanc * Ried Schusterberg 1STK 2021
13,5 Vol.-%, screwcap, large wooden barrel, €€€€€

94 Sauvignon Blanc * Ried Schusterberg 1STK 2020

94 Sauvignon Blanc * Ried Schusterberg 1STK 2019

(93) Sauvignon Blanc * Ehrenhausen 2021
13 Vol.-%, screwcap, large wooden barrel, €€€€

93 Sauvignon Blanc * Ehrenhausen 2020
91 Sauvignon Blanc * Ehrenhausen 2019

92 Sauvignon Blanc * 2022
12 Vol.-%, screwcap, steel tank, €€€

92 Sauvignon Blanc * 2021
91 Sauvignon Blanc * 2020

94 Morillon * Ried Schusterberg 1STK 2020
Light yellow-green, silver reflections. Very delicate wood nuances, fine notes of pear and mango, herbal savouriness, a touch of tangerine zest. Taut, tightly meshed and very lively structure, seems incredibly light on its feet, white stone fruit, limes on the finish, animating, cool style, certain ageing potential for aging.

94 Morillon Ried Schusterberg 1STK 2017

92 Morillon * Ehrenhausen 2019
92 Morillon Ehrenhausen 2017

94 Gewürztraminer * Ried Krois 1STK 2020
94 Gewürztraminer * Ried Krois 1STK 2019

93 Traminer * Ried Sulz Granbarrel 2018

93 Gelber Muskateller * Ried Krois 1STK 2020
11 Vol.-%, screwcap, large wooden barrel, €€€€

92 Gelber Muskateller * Ried Krois 1STK 2019
92 Gelber Muskateller Ried Krois 1 STK 2017

WEINGUT WOLFGANG MAITZ
8461 Ehrenhausen an der Weinstraße
Ratsch 45
T: +43 (3453) 2153
weingut@maitz.co.at
www.maitz.co.at

Winemaker/Contact:
Wolfgang Maitz
Production: 2% sparkling, 94% white, 2% red, 2% sweet, 10+1 hectares
Certified: Sustainable Austria
Fairs: ProWein Düsseldorf, VieVinum
Distribution partners: DE, NL, CH

SÜDSTEIERMARK DAC

- 90 Gelber Muskateller * 2020
- 90 Gelber Muskateller * 2019
- 91 Gelber Muskateller * 2018

(92) Welschriesling * Ried Sulz STK 2021
12,5 Vol.-%, screwcap, large wooden barrel, €€€€€
- 92 Welschriesling * Ried Sulz 2020
- 92 Welschriesling * Ried Sulz 2019

- 91 Riesling * Ried Hochstermetzberg GSTK 2019
- 93 Grauburgunder Ried Schusterberg 1STK 2017
- 93 Riesling Beerenauslese Südsteiermark 2017

WEINGUT MASSER

Peter Masser's winery in Fötschach, not far from Leutschach, is renowned among gourmets not only for its wines but also for its second mainstay, the breeding of Scottish Highland cattle. Close to the South Styrian Wine Road, the Massers find perfect conditions for the production of quality wine. The vineyards of Sernauberg, Oberglanz and Schlingelberg, with slopes of up to 50 degrees, provide ideal conditions for the vines. The range includes the typical South Styrian grape varieties; crisp Welschriesling, Morillon, various Pinot Noirs and Sauvignon Blanc, as well as Muskateller. In good years, sweet wines (Eiswein, Ausbruch, Trockenbeerenauslese) are also produced. "Stock" is a fresh, fruity, invigorating, light wine with a distinctive varietal character. "Bod'n" is the classic reflection of the provenance and typicality of the vineyards - these are wines of great character and elegant richness. Zeit+Ruh" are very special wines, slowly matured in small wooden barrels to develop their full ageing potential. Since 2016, Florian and Peter Masser have been working as pioneers in the field of fungus resistant grape varieties and they now cultivate the largest organic vineyard of new grape varieties in Austria. However, the father-son duo's love of experimentation doesn't stop there, four amphora are also owned by the Massers confirming their commitment to exciting wine styles with great ageing potential.

- 92 ⓘ Sauvignon blanc Sekt g.U. Reserve 2018
- 92 ⓘ Sauvignon Blanc Sekt Selektion Brut
- 91 ⓘ Chardonnay Sekt g.U. Klassik Brut NV

- 90 ⓘ PetNat Brut nature 2019

- 94 Sauvignon Blanc * Ried Schlingelberg Dachstein 2019
13 Vol.-%, cork, used barriques, €€€€€
- 95 Sauvignon Blanc * Ried Schlingelberg Dachstein 2018

- 94 Sauvignon Blanc * Ried Schlingelberg Fuhreg 2020
13,5 Vol.-%, cork, barrique/bottle maturation, €€€€€
- 94 Sauvignon Blanc * Ried Schlingelberg Fuhreg 2019

Medium yellow-green, silver reflections. Tropical fruit, delicate candied tangerine zest, a hint of yellow pepper and mead-

WEINGUT MASSER
8463 Leutschach
Fötschach 41
T: +43 (3454) 467
weingut@masser.cc
www.masser.cc

Winemaker: Peter & Florian Masser
Contact: Peter Masser
Production: 160,000 bottles
83 % white, 15 % red, 2 % sweet, 25 hectares
Fairs: VieVinum, DAC-Presentations
Distribution partners: DE, HR, CH, SK, SLO, CZ

* Südsteiermark DAC

STEIERMARK/STYRIA

ow herbs. Juicy and fruity-sweet on the palate with fine acidity, powerful, mango touch with a long salty finish. Versatile.

93 Sauvignon Blanc Ried Schlingelberg Fuhreg Zeit & Ruh 2018

94 Sauvignon Blanc * Ried Schlingelberg IC® Zeit&Ruh 2020
13 Vol.-%, cork, used barriques/bottle maturation, €€€€€

94 Sauvignon Blanc * Ried Schlingelberg IC® Zeit&Ruh 2019

94 Sauvignon Blanc * Ried Schlingelberg IC® Zeit & Ruh 2018

92 Sauvignon Blanc * Ried Sernauberg Steinfass 2019

92 Sauvignon Blanc Ried Sernauberg Steinfass® Zeit & Ruh 2018

92 Sauvignon Blanc * Gamlitz 2020
91 Sauvignon Blanc * Gamlitz 2019
90 Sauvignon Blanc * Gamlitz 2018

89 Sauvignon Blanc * Stock 2020
89 Sauvignon Blanc * Stock 2019

94 Weißburgunder * Ried Sernauberg Privat 2020
13 Vol.-%, cork, used barriques, €€€€€

94 Weißburgunder * Ried Sernauberg Privat 2019

89 Weißburgunder * Stock 2020
89 Weisser Burgunder * Stock 2019

93 Grauburgunder * Ried Schlingelberg Alte Reben 2020
13,5 Vol.-%, cork, used barriques, €€€€€

93 Grauburgunder * Ried Schlingelberg Alte Reben 2018

92 Grauburgunder * Leutschach 2021
13 Vol.-%, screwcap, steel tank, €€€€

93 Grauburgunder * Leutschach 2020
Medium golden yellow, silver reflections. Fine meadow herbs, a touch of white flowers, delicate nashi pear, orange zest in the background. Juicy, nuances of white stone fruit, very racy acidity, lime on the finish, salty and long, a very lively example of the variety, good ageing potential.

91 Grauburgunder * Leutschach 2019

93 Chardonnay * Ried Czamillonberg 2019
93 Chardonnay Ried Schlingelberg Dachstein 2017

92 Chardonnay * Ried Schlingelberg Steinfass 2019
92 Chardonnay Ried Schlingelberg Steinfass® Zeit & Ruh 2017

90 Morillon * Leutschach 2020
91 Chardonnay * Leutschach 2019
90 Morillon * Leutschach 2018

90 Chardonnay * Stock 2020
88 Morillon * Stock 2019

93 Riesling * Ried Oberglanz 2020
12,5 Vol.-%, cork, used barriques, €€€€€

(93) Welschriesling * Ried Sernauberg Wetterschütz® IC® Zeit & Ruh 2021
13 Vol.-%, cork, used barriques, €€€€€

93 Welschriesling * Ried Sernauberg Wetterschütz® IC® Zeit & Ruh 2020

93 Welschriesling Ried Sernauberg »IC« Wetterschütz 2019

88 Welschriesling * Stock 2020
88 Welschriesling * Stock 2019

89 Welschriesling * Gamlitz 2020

(93) Gelber Muskateller * Ried Oberglanz Zeit & Ruh 2021
13 Vol.-%, cork, used barriques, €€€€€

93 Gelber Muskateller * Ried Oberglanz 2020
93 Gelber Muskateller * Ried Oberglanz 2019

92 Gelber Muskateller * Leutschach 2020
90 Gelber Muskateller * Leutschach 2019

90 Gelber Muskateller * Stock 2020
90 Gelber Muskateller * Stock 2019

(93) Kompromisslos 2021 SC/MS/SOG
13 Vol.-%, screwcap, steel tank, €€€€ Ⓑ Ⓘ

92 50:50 BMxTR 2019 BLM/TR

92 Souvignier gris Sturmkogl 2020
91 Souvignier Gris Sturmkogl® BIO 2019

88 Sauvignac 604 Sturmkogl® 2019 SC

91 Muscaris Sturmkogl 2020
90 Muscaris Sturmkogl® 2019

SÜDSTEIERMARK DAC

WEINGUT POLZ
8472 Strass in der Steiermark
Am Grassnitzberg 39
T: +43 (3453) 2301
weingut@weingutpolz.at
www.weingutpolz.at

Winemaker: Christoph Polz
Contact: Erich Polz jr.
Production: 95 % white, 5 % red, 75 hectares
Certified: Sustainable Austria
Fairs: ProWein Düsseldorf, VieVinum
Distribution partners: AUS, BE, BG, DE, FIN, UK, NL, RUS, SE, CH, SK, SLO, CZ, USA

Erich Polz

WEINGUT POLZ

The Polz Winery is redefining itself and returning to its origins of 1912. Already in its fourth generation, the family is dedicated to delivering its vision of excellence to the glass.

Since 2020, Erich Polz Jr. has been running the business with the vision of leading the enormous potential and valuable know-how of his family's long winemaking tradition into a fruitful and healthy future. Erich junior and his brother Christoph Polz are responsible for the cellar and vinification - with great faith in every bunch of grapes. The brothers are passionate about their craft, which stems directly from their origins in southern Styria, a unique terroir.

They are committed to sustainability, whether it be through gentle pruning, the renunciation of insecticides and glyphosates, or the conversion of the vineyards to organic farming, which is already in progress.

In the words of Erich Polz Jr: "Our invaluable know-how has been passed on from generation to generation for 111 years. We work with vigorous vines on healthy soils. We strive for balance and excellence in our wines. And now, we are exploring new paths because nothing is riskier than not taking risks.

95 Morillon * Ried Obegg GSTK Aeon 2021
cork, large wooden barrel, €€€€€€
95 Morillon * Ried Obegg GSTK 2020
Bright medium green-yellow, silver reflections. Fine nuances of grapefruit zest, a touch of vanilla, white peach, mineral touch, delicate notes of spice. Medium complexity, white apple fruit, fine acidity, subtle wood spice, salty-mineral aftertaste, lingers long on the finish, very balanced, a multi-faceted food wine with ageing potential.
95 Chardonnay * Ried Obegg GSTK 2019

(94) Morillon * Ried Grassnitzberg 1STK Licht 2021
13,5 Vol.-%, cork, large wooden barrel, €€€€€
93 Morillon * Ried Grassnitzberg 2020
93 Chardonnay * Ried Grassnitzberg 2019

93 Chardonnay * Ried Theresienhöhe 1STK 2020
93 Chardonnay * Ried Theresienhöhe 1STK 2019
94 Chardonnay * Ried Theresienhöhe 1STK 2018

* Südsteiermark DAC

STEIERMARK/STYRIA

92 Morillon * 2021
91 Morillon * 2020
92 Morillon * 2019

92 Morillon * Ehrenhausen 2020

(96) Sauvignon Blanc * Ried Hochgrassnitzberg GSTK 2021
cork, large wooden barrel, €€€€€
95 Sauvignon Blanc * Ried Hochgrassnitzberg GSTK 2020
Medium greenish yellow, silver reflections. Fresh herbal spice, a touch of grapefruit zest and cassis, light minerality, multi-faceted aromatics. Juicy, spicy, white apple, some peach, lively acidity, lime on the finish, shows good length, taut, certain ageing potential.
94 Sauvignon Blanc * Ried Hochgrassnitzberg GSTK 2019

(95) Sauvignon Blanc * Ried Grassnitzberg 1STK Licht 2021
cork, large wooden barrel, €€€€
94 Sauvignon Blanc * Ried Grassnitzberg 1STK 2020
95 Sauvignon Blanc * Ried Grassnitzberg 1STK 2019

95 Sauvignon Blanc * Reserve Ried Theresienhöhe 1STK 2020
12,5 Vol.-%, cork, large wooden barrel, €€€€€

94 Sauvignon Blanc * Ried Theresienhöhe Therese 1STK 2021
13 Vol.-%, screwcap, steel tank, €€€€€
94 Sauvignon Blanc * Ried Theresienhöhe 1STK Therese 2020
93 Sauvignon Blanc * Ried Theresienhöhe 1STK Therese 2019

94 Sauvignon Blanc * Ried Czamillonberg 2019
94 Sauvignon Blanc * Ried Czamillonberg 2018

93 Sauvignon Blanc * Ehrenhausen 2021
13 Vol.-%, screwcap, large wooden barrel, €€€€
93 Sauvignon Blanc * Ehrenhausen 2020
93 Sauvignon Blanc * Ehrenhausen 2019

93 Sauvignon Blanc * Ried Pössnitzberg 2019
93 Sauvignon Blanc * Ried Pössnitzberg 2018

93 Sauvignon Blanc * Ried Witscheiner Herrenberg 2020
13 Vol.-%, screwcap, large wooden barrel, €€€€

94 Sauvignon Blanc * Ried Witscheiner Herrenberg 2019
93 Sauvignon Blanc * Ried Witscheiner Herrenberg 2019

(93) Sauvignon Blanc * Kitzeck-Sausal 2022
13 Vol.-%, screwcap, steel tank, €€€€
93 Sauvignon Blanc * Kitzeck Sausal 2021
92 Sauvignon Blanc * Kitzeck Sausal 2020

92 Sauvignon Blanc * 2022
12 Vol.-%, screwcap, steel tank, €€€
92 Sauvignon Blanc * 2021
92 Sauvignon Blanc * 2020

94 Weißburgunder * Ried Grassnitzberg 2020

91 Weißburgunder * 2021
90 Weißburgunder * 2020
91 Weißburgunder * 2019

93 Welschriesling Licht * Ried Grassnitzberg 1STK 2021
13 Vol.-%, cork, large wooden barrel, €€€€€
92 Welschriesling * Ried Hochgrassnitzberg 2018
92 Welschriesling Ried Hochgrassnitzberg 2017

91 Welschriesling * 2021
89 Welschriesling * 2020
90 Welschriesling * 2019

(93) Riesling * Ried Hochgrassnitzberg STK 2021
13 Vol.-%, cork, large wooden barrel, €€€€€
92 Riesling * Ried Hochgrassnitzberg 2018

92 Grauburgunder * 2019
93 Grauer Burgunder * 2018

92 Gelber Muskateller * Leutschach 2018

91 Gelber Muskateller * 2021
90 Gelber Muskateller * 2020
91 Gelber Muskateller * 2019

94 Beerenauslese Ried Hochgrassnitzberg 2017

SÜDSTEIERMARK DAC

WEINGUT REGELE

The Regele family runs one of the most traditional wineries in southern Styria. Founded in 1830, today Georg and Ingrid Regele, with their son Franz are responsible for the renowned winery. Georg Regele likes to compare the remarkable success story with his vines - because only strong roots guarantee healthy development and a constant increase in quality.

About 25 hectares of vines are cultivated, all harvested by hand. Oberglanzberg, Sulz, and the sizeable vineyard Zoppelberg are outstanding vineyards, first documented in the 13th century. The resulting DAC Rieden wines enjoy the highest acclaim, and their minerality, which is influenced by the terroir, is truly captivating, as is the balance. With the production of richly finesse sparkling wines, one is in pursuit of the myth of the perfect mousse. Classified in the fastidious Austrian sparkling wine pyramid with a protected designation of origin, their sparkling wine consistently receives top national and international ratings. Viticulture is not only a field rich in tradition but also an incredibly innovative one. In recent years, it has changed dramatically in its diversity, scope, jurisdiction, orientation, and importance. Franz Regele Junior possesses the necessary credentials after graduating from the HBLA Klosterneuburg College in viticulture and winemaking. He successfully acts responsibly and pragmatically with new innovations and consolidates past proven concepts. "The more concise the technical progress becomes, the more the environment in which all this happens plays a role," says Franz Regele. Exciting fields of innovation for him also include the ageing of his wines in amphorae or concrete eggs and the cultivation of (fungus-resistant) PIWI grape varieties such as Souvignier Gris. However, the prerequisite for innovative work in viticulture is the consistent, sustainable cultivation of the vineyards - and always keeping in harmony with nature. "In every passing season, this is not only a challenge for me, but constant motivation."

93 ⊙ Blanc de Blancs Chardonnay Sulztaler Sulz Steiermark g.U. Grosse Reserve 2017
12,5 Vol.-%, cork, bottle maturation, €€€€€

93 ⊙ Blanc de Blancs Chardonnay Sulztaler Sulz Steiermark g.U. Grosse Reserve 2012

WEINGUT REGELE
8461 Ehrenhausen an der Weinstraße
Ewitsch 34
T: +43 (3453) 2426
office@regele.com
www.regele.com

Winemaker/Contact:
Ing. Georg Regele
Production: 10 % sparkling, 79 % white, 10 % red, 1 % sweet, 25 hectares
Certified: Sustainable Austria ⊙
Fairs: VieVinum, DAC-Presentations
Distribution partners: DE

Franz Regele

STEIERMARK/STYRIA

92 ❂ Blanc de Noirs Brut Nature g.U. Steiermark Klassik

92 ❂ Brut Rosé Reserve Sekt g.U. Steiermark
Deg. 2023, 12,5 Vol.-%, cork, bottle fermentation, €€€€

93 ❂ Brut Rosé Reserve Sekt g.U. Steiermark
92 Brut Rose Reserve Sekt g.U.

(93) Sauvignon Blanc * Ried Sulztaler Zoppelberg Unfiltriert 2021
13 Vol.-%, cork, large wooden barrel/steel tank, €€€€

92 Sauvignon Blanc * Ried Sulztaler Zoppelberg 2020
90 Sauvignon Blanc * Ried Sulztaler Zoppelberg 2019

(93) Sauvignon Blanc * Ried Sulztaler Sulz Unfiltriert 2021
13 Vol.-%, cork, steel tank, €€€

91 Sauvignon Blanc * Ried Sulztaler Sulz 2020
91 Sauvignon Blanc * Ried Sulz 2019

92 Sauvignon Blanc * Ehrenhausen 2021
13 Vol.-%, screwcap, steel tank, €€€

91 Sauvignon Blanc * Ehrenhausen Die Sieme 2021
91 Sauvignon Blanc * Ehrenhausen Sieme 2020

91 Sauvignon Blanc * 2022
12,5 Vol.-%, screwcap, steel tank, €€

93 Weißburgunder * Ried Oberewitsch Unfiltriert 2021
13 Vol.-%, cork, steel tank/used barriques, €€€€€

93 Weißburgunder * Unfiltriert 2020
Delicately cloudy pale yellow green, silver reflections. Delicate nuances of meadow herbs, white pear fruit, a hint of lime zest, a mineral touch. Juicy, elegant, fine sweet tropical fruit, refined acidity, orange on the finish, with a salty mineral aftertaste, good length. It is a fine food wine.

90 Weißburgunder * Ehrenhausen 2020

90 Weißburgunder * Privat 2018

92 Grauburgunder * Ried Sulztaler Zoppelberg Unfiltriert 2021
13 Vol.-%, cork, used barriques/steel tank, €€€€€

91 Grauburgunder * Ried Sulztaler Zoppelberg 2018

92 Chardonnay * Ried Sulz Fassreserve 2020
Pale chartreuse yellow, silver reflections. Delicate nuances of white fruit, coconut, a touch of gooseberry, nuances of grapefruit and lime zest. Taut, tightly meshed, notes of cassis, juicy white tropical fruit, a fresh structure, notes of lime zest on the palate as well, lively and salty, a multi-faceted food companion.

91 Chardonnay * Ehrenhausen 2021

93 Chardonnay unfiltriert 2018

92 Gelber Muskateller * Ried Oberglanz 2021
89 Gelber Muskateller * Ried Oberglanzberg 2020
90 Gelber Muskateller * Ried Oberglanzberg 2019

90 Gelber Muskateller * 2022
12 Vol.-%, screwcap, steel tank, €€

90 Welschriesling * Ried Zoppelberg 2019
90 Welschriesling * Ried Sulztaler Zoppelberg 2019
89 Welschriesling * Ried Zoppelberg 2018

90 Souvignier Gris 2021
91 Souvignier Gris 2019

Gelber Muskateller

SÜDSTEIERMARK DAC

WEINGUT ERWIN SABATHI
8463 Leutschach an der Weinstraße
Pössnitz 48
T: +43 (3454) 265
weingut@sabathi.com
www.sabathi.com

Winemaker: Erwin Sabathi
Contact: The Erwin Sabathi family
Production: 97 % white, 3 % red,
54 hectares
Certified: Sustainable Austria
Fairs: ProWein Düsseldorf,
VieVinum, MondoVino
Distribution partners: BE, DK, DE,
UK, IT, CDN, NL, NO, SE, CH, USA

Patrizia and Erwin Sabathi

WEINGUT ERWIN SABATHI
ORGANIC

There has been a tradition for viticulture in the Sabathi family since 1650. The great upswing began in 1992 when Erwin Sabathi Jr. joined his parents' business. Today the family winery is in the hands of Erwin and his wife Patrizia. The winery is an organically-certified operation. Patrizia and Erwin Sabathi's philosophy is based on the provenance of the wine and the work of nature: All grapes are hand-picked - due to the nature of the vineyards alone (extremely steep slopes), only traditional manual harvesting is possible. However, another and much more important argument for the winemaking couple is the quality: Here they deliberately rely on hand harvesting.

The most important grape varieties are Sauvignon Blanc and Chardonnay; these enjoy the highest international standing. His Sauvignon Blancs and Chardonnays from the Ried Pössnitzberg (Große STK Ried) are on a par with the very great white wines of the world - and thus at the very top. The Sauvignon Blanc Ried Pössnitzberg Alte Reben and the Chardonnay Ried Pössnitzberg Alte Reben are considered to be absolute rarities: The meticulously selected grapes for these wines come from the oldest vines on the Pössnitzberg. The Chardonnay Ried Pössnitzberger Kapelle and the Sauvignon Blanc Ried Pössnitzberger Kapelle are considered extremely precise world-class wines.

In 2016, Falstaff voted Erwin Sabathi "Winemaker of the Year". One of the reasons for this was his excellence with the Chardonnay grape variety. The Chardonnay Ried Pössnitzberg Alte Reben GSTK is awarded high points year after year. If you are looking for a definite ageing potential upgrade to this wine, look out for the grandiose Chardonnay Ried Pössnitzberger Kapelle, the rarest wine in Sabathi's range. The search is worthwhile: The Alpine republic currently has hardly any "more" Chardonnay to offer.

93 Chardonnay Brut Zero Dosage 2015

92 Chardonnay Brut 2019
93 Chardonnay brut 2013

(98) Chardonnay * Ried Pössnitzberg GSTK
Alte Reben 2021
13,5 Vol.-%, cork, 500-l-harrel, €€€€€€

STEIERMARK/STYRIA

Lubekogel, Leutschach

97 Chardonnay * Ried Pössnitzberg GSTK Alte Reben 2020
Medium greenish yellow, silver glints. Herbaceous savoury notes, a hint of dark nougat, flint nuances, a touch of grapefruit, white tropical fruit, peach, and candied orange zest. Full-bodied, complex, lush honeydew melon, filigree acidity, saline-citrus finish followed by gentle resonating expression of fruit. Excellent length, well-balanced, definite ageing potential.

98 Chardonnay * Ried Pössnitzberger Kapelle GSTK 2020
13 Vol.-%, cork, 500-l-barrel, €€€€€ B

98 Chardonnay * Ried Pössnitzberger Kapelle GSTK 2019
Pale greenish yellow, silver glints. Exquisite aroma of grounded hazelnuts, yellow tropical fruit, notes of guava, and lush gooseberries, pervaded by alluring woody savoury nuances. Juicy, white peach, well-integrated acidity structure that imparts vibrancy and raciness to the wine, marked by a salty finish. Ethereal and persistent with a lime aftertaste and promising ageing potential, equally on par with a Grand Cru.

97 Chardonnay * Ried Pössnitzberger Kapelle GSTK 2018

(96) Chardonnay * Ried Pössnitzberg GSTK 2021
13,5 Vol.-%, cork, 500-l-barrel, €€€€ B
95 Chardonnay * Ried Pössnitzberg GSTK 2020
95 Chardonnay * Ried Pössnitzberg GSTK 2019

(94) Chardonnay * Ried Oberpössnitz STK 2021
13,5 Vol.-%, screwcap, small wooden barrel, €€€€€ B

94 Chardonnay * Ried Saffran STK 2021
13,5 Vol.-%, cork, 500-l-barrel, €€€€€ B
94 Chardonnay * Ried Saffran 2020
94 Chardonnay * Ried Saffran 2019

(93) Chardonnay * Leutschach 2022
12,5 Vol.-%, screwcap, large wooden barrel, €€€€ B
93 Chardonnay * Leutschach 2021
93 Chardonnay * Leutschach 2020

98 Sauvignon Blanc * Ried Pössnitzberger Kapelle GSTK 2020
13 Vol.-%, cork, large wooden barrel, €€€€€€ B
98 Sauvignon Blanc * Ried Pössnitzberger Kapelle GSTK 2019
Pale yellow-green, silver glints. Candied tangerine zest, soft exuberant tropical fruit tones, a hint of yellow gooseberries, floral touch, white flowers, and a dash of mint and lime. Complex, tightly woven, juicy, lovely fruit expression, elegant, refined structure, saline reverberations, prolonged persistence, developing tremendous tension, with an aftertaste of delicate tropical fruit. Excellent ageing potential for years to come.

98 Sauvignon Blanc Ried Pössnitzberger Kapelle GSTK 2017

(97) Sauvignon Blanc * Ried Pössnitzberg GSTK Alte Reben 2021
13 Vol.-%, cork, large wooden barrel, €€€€€€ B
96 Sauvignon Blanc * Ried Pössnitzberg GSTK Alte Reben 2020
96 Sauvignon Blanc * Ried Pössnitzberg GSTK Alte Reben 2019

(95) Sauvignon Blanc * Ried Pössnitzberg GSTK 2021
13 Vol.-%, cork, large wooden barrel, €€€€ B
95 Sauvignon Blanc * Ried Pössnitzberg GSTK 2020
96 Sauvignon Blanc * Ried Pössnitzberg GSTK 2019

(94) Sauvignon Blanc * Ried Poharnig 1STK 2022
13 Vol.-%, screwcap, large wooden barrel, €€€€€ B
94 Sauvignon Blanc * Ried Poharnig 1STK 2021
94 Sauvignon Blanc * Ried Poharnig 1STK 2020

(93) Sauvignon Blanc * Leutschach 2022
13 Vol.-%, screwcap, large wooden barrel, €€€€ B
94 Sauvignon Blanc * Leutschach 2021
93 Sauvignon Blanc * Leutschach 2020

SÜDSTEIERMARK DAC

91	Sauvignon Blanc * 2022	
12,5 Vol.-%, screwcap, steel tank, €€€€ Ⓑ		
92	Sauvignon Blanc * 2021	
92	Sauvignon Blanc * 2020	

(94) Gelber Muskateller * Ried Krepskogel 1STK 2022
12,5 Vol.-%, screwcap, large wooden barrel, €€€€€ Ⓑ
95 Gelber Muskateller * Ried Krepskogel 1STK 2021
94 Gelber Muskateller * Ried Krepskogel 1STK 2020

92 Gelber Muskateller * 2022
11,5 Vol.-%, screwcap, steel tank, €€€ Ⓑ
93 Gelber Muskateller * 2021
91 Gelber Muskateller * 2020

(93) Weißburgunder * Ried Jägerberg 1STK 2022
13 Vol.-%, screwcap, large wooden barrel, €€€€€ Ⓑ
93 Weißburgunder * Ried Jägerberg 1STK 2021
93 Weißburgunder * Ried Jägerberg 1STK 2019

91 Weißburgunder * 2022
12 Vol.-%, screwcap, steel tank, €€€ Ⓑ
92 Weißburgunder * 2021

92 Weißburgunder * 2020

(93) Grauburgunder * Ried Jägerberg 1STK 2022
13 Vol.-%, screwcap, large wooden barrel, €€€€€ Ⓑ
93 Grauburgunder * Ried Jägerberg 1STK 2021
93 Grauburgunder * Ried Jägerberg 1STK 2019

90 * Sabathini 2022 WR/SB
11,5 Vol.-%, screwcap, steel tank, €€ Ⓑ
91 * Sabathini 2021 WR/SB
90 * Sabathini 2020 WR/SB

89 Welschriesling * 2022
11,5 Vol.-%, screwcap, steel tank, €€ Ⓑ
92 Welschriesling * 2021
90 Welschriesling * 2020

90 Sabathini Rosé 2022 ZW/CS/ME
11,5 Vol.-%, screwcap, steel tank, €€ Ⓑ
90 Sabathini Rosé 2020 CS/ZW/ME
90 Sabathini Rosé 2019 ZW/PN

96 Sauvignon Blanc TBA Ried Pössnitzberg 2017

95 Sauvignon Blanc Auslese 2019

WEINGUT HANNES SABATHI

Hannes Sabathi is passionate about the soil because it gives the wine its distinctive character. "This is what fascinates me, and, for me, this is where the truth in wine lies," says the winemaker. Or, in other words: "Great soil, great wine", as Sabathi likes to put it. His wines always show clarity and depth, precise soil characteristics and the individuality of the vintage. You can tell that this is a winemaker who not only knows his craft brilliantly but also knows how to take a step back. Sabathi creates his wines with a keen sense of the interplay between soil, grape variety and weather, which varies from year to year: "I don't think of myself as a winemaker because I don't make wine. The soil and the vintage make the wine," he explains.

A winemaker like Hannes Sabathi, who believes that "less is more", needs a lot of experience, trust in nature and, above all, patience. His dream has always been to create wines from different soils because each site has a very specific geological and mineral history that needs to be understood. Sabathi wants this individual character to live on in the wines. To achieve this, he intervenes as little as possible and lets nature take its course. Whether it be wines with the saline elegance of the Kranachberg, the dense minerality of the Jägerberg, the deep substance of the Ried Loren or the cool savouriness of the Kehlberg: What they all have in common, year after year, is their unique terroir. Only a soil expert like Hannes Sabathi can achieve this.

96 Sauvignon Blanc * Ried Kranachberg GSTK Reserve 2019

Pale golden yellow, silver glints. Delicate wood savouriness, hints of vanilla and caramel, white tropical fruit, soft notions of guava, white peach, and luscious gooseberry notes. Powerful and complex, a touch of nougat, saline-mineral texture,

STEIERMARK/STYRIA

Kranachberg

WEINGUT HANNES SABATHI
8462 Gamlitz, Sernau 48
T: +43 (3453) 2900
office@hannessabathi.at
www.hannessabathi.at

Winemaker/Contact:
Hannes Sabathi
Production: 2% sparkling, 96% white, 1% rosé, 1% sweet, 65 hectares
Certified: Sustainable Austria
Fairs: Austrian Tasting London, ÖGW Zürich, ProWein Düsseldorf, VieVinum, DAC-Presentations, Hong Kong International Wine & Spirits Fair
Distribution partners: BE, BR, BG, RC, DK, DE, FIN, HK, JP, NL, NO, PL, RUS, SE, CH, SGP, CZ, USA

and yellow tropical fruit on the finish shows excellent concentration and, at the same time, astonishing vitality. Superbly accessible with length and potential.

96 Sauvignon Blanc * Ried Kranachberg GSTK Reserve 2017
95 Sauvignon Blanc Ried Kranachberg Reserve GSTK 2016

95 Sauvignon Blanc * Ried Kranachberg GSTK 2020
95 Sauvignon Blanc * Ried Kranachberg GSTK 2019
95 Sauvignon Blanc * Ried Kranachberg GSTK 2018

95 Sauvignon Blanc * Alte Reben 2019
14,5 Vol.-%, glass, wooden barrel, €€€€€

94 Sauvignon Blanc * Ried Loren 2020
95 Sauvignon Blanc * Ried Loren 2019
94 Sauvignon Blanc * Ried Loren 2018

(93) Sauvignon Blanc * Ried Dirnbeck STK 2021
13 Vol.-%, glass, steel tank, €€€€
92 Sauvignon Blanc * Ried Dirnbeck 2020

93 Sauvignon Blanc * Leutschach 2021
13,5 Vol.-%, glass, steel tank, €€€€
93 Sauvignon Blanc * Leutschach 2019
92 Sauvignon Blanc * Leutschach 2018

93 Sauvignon Blanc * Gamlitz 2021
92 Sauvignon Blanc * Gamlitz 2020
92 Sauvignon Blanc * Gamlitz 2019

91 Sauvignon Blanc * 2022
12,5 Vol.-%, screwcap, steel tank, €€€
92 Sauvignon Blanc * 2021
91 Sauvignon Blanc * 2020

(93) Sauvignon Blanc Falter Ego Weststeiermark DAC Ried Kehlberg STK 2021
13,5 Vol.-%, glass, large wooden barrel, €€€€€
93 Sauvignon Blanc Weststeiermark DAC Ried Kehlberg Falter Ego 2020
94 Sauvignon Blanc Weststeiermark DAC Ried Kehlberg Falter Ego 2019

93 Sauvignon Blanc Weststeiermark DAC Graz Falter Ego 2021
92 Sauvignon Blanc Weststeiermark DAC Graz Falter Ego 2020
93 Sauvignon Blanc Weststeiermark DAC Falter Ego Graz 2019
91 Sauvignon Blanc Weststeiermark DAC Graz 2018
92 Sauvignon Blanc Grazer Stadtwein 2017

(94) Chardonnay * Ried Jägerberg 1STK 2021
13 Vol.-%, glass, large wooden barrel, €€€€
93 Chardonnay * Ried Jägerberg 1STK 2020
Light golden yellow, silver reflections. Delicate peach and mango, hints of blossom honey and candied citrus zest. El-

SÜDSTEIERMARK DAC

egant, displays good drive, white apple, fine acidity, lemony salty aftertaste, well balanced and already easy to drink, has definite ageing potential.

94 Chardonnay * Ried Jägerberg 1STK 2019

94 Chardonnay * Ried Loren 2019
93 Chardonnay * Ried Loren 2018

92 Chardonnay * Gamlitz 2020
13 Vol.-%, glass, large wooden barrel, €€€
92 Chardonnay * Gamlitz 2019
92 Chardonnay * Gamlitz 2018

(93) Grauburgunder * Ried Jägerberg 1STK 2021
13,5 Vol.-%, glass, large wooden barrel, €€€€
93 Grauburgunder * Ried Jägerberg 1STK 2020
93 Grauburgunder * Ried Jägerberg 1STK 2019

(94) Grauburgunder Falter Ego Weststeiermark DAC Ried Kehlberg STK 2021
13,5 Vol.-%, glass, large wooden barrel, €€€€
93 Grauburgunder Weststeiermark DAC Ried Kehlberg Falter Ego 2020
92 Grauburgunder Weststeiermark DAC Ried Kehlberg Falter Ego 2019

92 Grauburgunder * Gamlitz 2021

93 Gelber Muskateller * Ried Graf Woracziczky 2021
13 Vol.-%, glass, steel tank, €€€€€

92 Gelber Muskateller * Gamlitz 2019
91 Gelber Muskateller * Gamlitz 2018

91 Gelber Muskateller * 2022
12 Vol.-%, screwcap, steel tank, €€€
90 Gelber Muskateller * 2021
90 Gelber Muskateller * 2020

91 Gelber Muskateller Weststeiermark DAC Graz Falter Ego 2021
91 Gelber Muskateller Weststeiermark DAC Graz Falter Ego 2020
92 Gelber Muskateller Weststeiermark DAC Graz Falter Ego 2019

(93) Welschriesling * Ried Czamillonberg 2021
13 Vol.-%, glass, large wooden barrel, €€€€

93 Welschriesling * Ried Kranachberg 2020
93 Welschriesling * Ried Kranachberg GSTK 2019

90 Welschriesling * 2022
11,5 Vol.-%, screwcap, steel tank, €€
90 Welschriesling * 2021
90 Welschriesling * 2019

92 Weißburgunder * Gamlitz 2021
12,5 Vol.-%, glass, large wooden barrel, €€€€
92 Weißburgunder * Gamlitz 2020
92 Weißburgunder * Gamlitz 2019

91 Weißburgunder * 2022
12 Vol.-%, screwcap, steel tank, €€
91 Weißburgunder * 2021
91 Weißburgunder * 2020

94 Weißburgunder Ried Kranachberg GSTK 2017

90 MeinSatz 2020 SB/SÄ/WB/WR/GM
90 MeinSatz 2019 WR/WB/CH/SV

90 Stadtblick 2020 SB/GM/PG

89 Scheurebe 2020

89 OZ magic Rosé 2022 ZW/CS
11 Vol.-%, screwcap, steel tank, €€

97 Sauvignon Blanc TBA Ried Kranachberg 2017

92 Riesling Spätlese 2021
9,5 Vol.-%, glass, steel tank, €€€€

Welschriesling

FAMILIENWEINGUT SATTLERHOF

★★★★★

ORGANIC

Surrounded by steep slopes, the family winery has been perched on a hill near Gamlitz since 1887. Since 2020, the 35-hectare estate has been one of the 100 best wineries in the world, according to the US wine magazine "Wine & Spirits". This distinction is not only due to the biodynamic agricultural approach to flourishing vineyards introduced by Andreas and Alexander Sattler but also to the many years of accumulated experience of their parents Maria and Willi Sattler.

Perfect physiological ripeness of the grapes, selective hand harvesting and puristic vinification are some of the artisanal steps with which the family has kept the quality of the wines at such high standards for decades. The aim of the meticulous working method is to allow the character of the excellent vineyards Kranachberg, Pfarrweingarten, Sernauberg, and Kapellenweingarten to evolve. With vines up to 55 years old on extremely steep slopes, the vineyards are characterised by quartz, limestone, and gravel. It is probably also due to the interplay of the gentle farming methods of the young generation and the experience of the parents that the premium wines from the Sattlerhof winery continue to become even more distinctive, long-lived, and authentic every year.

99 Sauvignon Blanc Ried Trinkaus GSTK 2019
99 Sauvignon Blanc Trinkaus Kellerreserve Ried Kranachberg GSTK 2017

(98) Sauvignon Blanc * Ried Alter Kranachberg GSTK 2021
13,5 Vol.-%, glass, steel tank, €€€€€€ B V

97 Sauvignon Blanc * Ried Kranachberg GSTK 2020
Pale yellow-green, silver glints. Refreshing redcurrant fragrance, pleasant herbal savouriness, smoky nuances, white tropical fruit, a hint of grapefruit, walnut, and a smidge of blossom honey. Juicy, elegant, exquisite complexity, nuances of white stone fruit, filigree acidity, salinity, and crisp reverberations. Exhibits excellent length and will most definitely benefit from bottle ageing.

97 Sauvignon Blanc * Ried Kranachberg GSTK 2019

97 Sauvignon Blanc * Privat 2019
13,5 Vol.-%, glass, wooden barrel, €€€€€€ B
98 Sauvignon Blanc Privat 2015

95 Sauvignon Blanc * Ried Pfarrweingarten GSTK 2021
13,5 Vol.-%, glass, steel tank, €€€€€€ B
95 Sauvignon Blanc * Ried Pfarrweingarten GSTK 2020
96 Sauvignon Blanc * Ried Pfarrweingarten GSTK 2019

95 Sauvignon Blanc * Ried Grassnitzburg STK 2020
13,5 Vol.-%, glass, steel tank, €€€€€€ B
96 Sauvignon Blanc * Ried Grassnitzburg 2018
95 Sauvignon Blanc Grassnitzburg 2017

95 Sauvignon Blanc * Ried Grassnitzburg Reserve 2017

FAMILIENWEINGUT SATTLERHOF
8462 Gamlitz
Sernau 2
T: +43 (3453) 2556
weingut@sattlerhof.at
www.sattlerhof.at

Winemaker: Willi, Alex and Andreas Sattler
Contact: Alex and Andreas Sattler
Production: 95 % white, 3 % red, 2 % sweet, 35 hectares
Certified: Sustainable Austria
Fairs: ProWein Düsseldorf, VieVinum, DAC-Presentations
Distribution partners: BE, BG, RC, DK, DE, FIN, FR, UK, HK, IS, IT, JP, CDN, ROK, HR, LT, LU, MT, NL, NO, PT, SE, CH, SGP, SK, CZ, USA, PT

SÜDSTEIERMARK DAC

(94) Sauvignon Blanc *
Ried Kapellenweingarten STK 2021
12,5 Vol.-%, glass, large wooden barrel, €€€€€ Ⓑ Ⓥ
94 Sauvignon Blanc
Ried Kapellenweingarten 2020
94 Sauvignon Blanc *
Ried Kapellenweingarten 2019

(94) Sauvignon Blanc * Ried Sernauberg 1STK 2021
13 Vol.-%, glass, steel tank, €€€€ Ⓑ Ⓥ
94 Sauvignon Blanc * Ried Sernauberg 1STK 2020
94 Sauvignon Blanc * Ried Sernauberg
1STK 2019

94 Sauvignon Blanc * Ried Marein 2020
93 Sauvignon Blanc * Ried Marein 2019

(94) Sauvignon Blanc * Gamlitz 2022
13 Vol.-%, glass, steel tank, €€€ Ⓑ Ⓥ
94 Sauvignon Blanc * Gamlitz 2021
93 Sauvignon Blanc * Gamlitz 2020

93 Sauvignon Blanc * Eichberg 2019
93 Sauvignon Blanc Eichberg 2017

92 Sauvignon Blanc * 2022
13 Vol.-%, screwcap, steel tank, €€€ Ⓑ
92 Sauvignon Blanc * 2021
92 Sauvignon Blanc * 2020

96 Morillon * Ried Pfarrweingarten GSTK 2021
13,5 Vol.-%, glass, steel tank, €€€€€€ Ⓑ Ⓥ
95 Morillon * Ried Pfarrweingarten GSTK 2020
Light greenish yellow, silver reflections. Delicate grapefruit notes, white stone fruit, a touch of apple, a tiny bit of reduction, hints of caramel and vanilla. Juicy, white stone fruit, finesse-rich acidity, lime touch on the finish, spicy, balanced, saline finish, a multi-faceted food wine.
96 Morillon * Ried Pfarrweingarten GSTK 2019

(94) Morillon * Ried Kapellenweingarten STK 2021
12,5 Vol.-%, glass, large wooden barrel, €€€€€ Ⓑ Ⓥ
94 Morillon * Ried Kapellenweingarten 2020
95 Morillon * Ried Kapellenweingarten 2019

(93) Morillon * Gamlitz 2022
13 Vol.-%, glass, large wooden barrel, €€€€ Ⓑ Ⓥ
93 Morillon * Gamlitz 2019
92 Morillon * Gamlitz 2018

95 Weißburgunder * Ried Pfarrweingarten
GSTK 2020
Light yellow-green, silver reflections. Delicate wood nuances, a hint of Good Luise pear, fine vanilla touch, lime zest in the background. Full-bodied, white apple, a hint of pear on the palate, delicate fruit expression, very lively, mineral and salty finish, nutty with lemony nuances and fine blossom honey on the aftertaste.
94 Weißburgunder * Ried Pfarrweingarten
GSTK 2019
94 Weißburgunder * Ried Pfarrweingarten
GSTK 2018

93 Weißburgunder * Gamlitz 2019
92 Weißburgunder Gamlitz 2017

94 Gelber Muskateller * Ried Marein STK 2021
12 Vol.-%, glass, steel tank, €€€€€ Ⓑ Ⓥ

93 Gelber Muskateller * Ried Sernauberg
1STK 2019

92 Gelber Muskateller * Eichberg 2021
93 Gelber Muskateller * Eichberg 2020
93 Gelber Muskateller * Eichberg 2019

92 Gelber Muskateller * Gamlitz 2019
92 Gelber Muskateller * Gamlitz 2018

91 Gelber Muskateller * 2019

93 Welschriesling * Alte Reben 2021
12,5 Vol.-%, screwcap, wooden barrel, €€€€ Ⓑ
93 Welschriesling Alte Rebstöcke 2020
92 Welschriesling Alte Rebstöcke 2015

92 Welschriesling * 2019
91 Welschriesling * 2018

92 Welschriesling Gamlitz 2017

96 Gemischter Satz Fassreserve
Pfarrweingarten 2017
13 Vol.-%, glass, small wooden barrel, €€€€€€ Ⓑ

94 Blauburgunder Alte Reben 2020
12,5 Vol.-%, screwcap, wooden barrel, €€€€€ Ⓑ

93 Pinot Noir Freude am Leben 2019
93 Pinot Noir 2017

98 Sauvignon Blanc TBA 2017

94 Sauvignon Blanc Beerenauslese 2021
11,5 Vol.-%, glass, steel tank, €€€€ Ⓑ Ⓥ
93 Sauvignon Blanc Beerenauslese 2020
96 Sauvignon Blanc Beerenauslese 2017

* Südsteiermark DAC

STEIERMARK/STYRIA

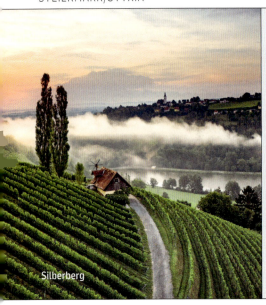

Silberberg

LANDESWEINGUT SILBERBERG
8430 Leibnitz
Silberberg 1
T: +43 (3452) 82339 45
weinkeller.lfssilberberg@stmk.gv.at
www.silberberg.at

Winemaker: Klaus Fischer
Contact: Klaus Fischer and Karl Menhart
Production: 1 % sparkling, 92 % white, 6 % red, 1 % sweet, 35 hectares
Certified: Sustainable Austria
Fairs: VieVinum, DAC-Presentations
Distribution partners: DE, IT, HR, SE, CH

LANDESWEINGUT SILBERBERG

For 120 years, Silberberg has been at the forefront of innovation and enthusiastically motivating the next generation of Styrian winemakers: this is what the Silberberg Winemaking Training Centre is known for. Here, training is combined with the solid craftsmanship of the Landesweingut. Since 2014, Klaus Fischer, a young, dynamic, cosmopolitan cellar master, has been responsible for the wines. In 2019, master winemaker Gernot Lorenz took over the management of the vineyards, which are spread over several locations in southern Styria. In 2020 the former oenologist Ing. Reinhold Holler assumed the winery's management, and Karl Menhart has brought a breath of fresh air as his successor. Together they work tirelessly on new impulses, leaving no creative idea untested.

In the vineyards, they have abandoned the use of herbicides; the Schlossberg/Leutschach site is entirely certified organic, and more than three-quarters of the area is protected by hail nets. Modern technology is used to process the grapes in the cellar, and spontaneous fermentation is increasingly being used.

Even before the introduction of the Südsteiermark DAC quality label, Silberberg wines were clearly structured in their designation of origin. Local wines from Leutschach and Kitzeck complement a perfect range of regional wines. Wines from Trebien, Steinbruch and Annaberg come from the slate soils of the Sausal. Riesling, a highlight, is lovingly cultivated in Kitzeck. The wines from the Opok soils of Leutschach an der Weinstrasse are all certified organic. In the cellar, these wines are spontaneously fermented and, where possible, aged in wooden barrels. This distinguishes these wines even more from the wines of the Sausal.

94 Sauvignon Blanc * Ried Trebien B.O.S. Best of Silberberg 2020
Bright golden yellow with silver reflections. Fine herbal savouriness, light caramel, pleasant aromas of yellow tropical fruit, and subtle oak nuances. Complex, juicy, fine mango/apple fruit, mineral, discreet acidity, with a salty finish and lime on the aftertaste. Already well matured, a powerful, elegant food companion.

93 Sauvignon Blanc * Ried Trebien B.O.S. 2018

93 Sauvignon Blanc B. O. S.
Best of Silberberg 2017
94 Sauvignon Blanc * Ried Meletin 2020
13,5 Vol.-%, cork, small wooden barrel/bottle maturation, €€€€€ Ⓑ Ⓥ
92 Sauvignon Blanc * Ried Meletin 2019

93 Sauvignon Blanc * Ried Steinbruch 2021
14 Vol.-%, glass, large wooden barrel, €€€€€ Ⓥ
93 Sauvignon Blanc * Ried Steinbruch 2020
92 Sauvignon Blanc * Ried Steinbruch 2019

90 Sauvignon Blanc * 2019
90 Sauvignon Blanc * 2018

92 Chardonnay * Ried Trebien 2020
13 Vol.-%, cork, small wooden barrel, €€€€€ Ⓥ
93 Chardonnay * Ried Trebien 2019
92 Chardonnay * Ried Trebien 2017

93 Weißburgunder * Ried Annaberg 2021
13,5 Vol.-%, screwcap, large wooden barrel, €€€ Ⓥ

91 Weißburgunder * Ried Annaberg 2019
92 Weißburgunder * Ried Annaberg 2018

92 Riesling * Kitzeck-Sausal 2021
12 Vol.-%, screwcap, large wooden barrel, €€€ Ⓥ
90 Riesling * Kitzeck-Sausal 2020
90 Riesling * Kitzeck-Sausal 2019

92 Welschriesling Schiefer-Terrassen 2021
13 Vol.-%, cork, 500-l-barrel, €€€€ Ⓥ

92 Welschriesling * Kitzeck-Sausal
Ried Trebien 2020
89 Welschriesling * Ried Trebien
Kitzeck-Sausal 2018

91 Grauburgunder * Leutschach Bio 2019
90 Grauburgunder * Leutschach 2018

91 Gelber Muskateller * Kitzeck- Sausal 2018

89 Gelber Muskateller * 2018

WEINGUT SKOFF ORIGINAL
WALTER SKOFF

Walter Skoff is the fourth generation to run the family winery SKOFF ORIGINAL, which cultivates an area of around 60 hectares. The unique climate and fertile soils of southern Styria create the perfect conditions for premium wines, which have received much positive attention from international wine critics. In this part of Styria, the diversity of different vineyard sites with a wide range of terroirs at the winery's disposal is particularly exceptional. As a result, Gamlitzer Eckberg produces wines with character and international standing.

Over the past 35 years, Walter Skoff's wines have won many awards. In 2017, they were honoured at the Concours Mondial du Sauvignon Blanc, one of the world's most important white wine competitions. They were also awarded the "Denis Dubourdieu Trophy" for the Sauvignon Blanc Kranachberg (2015 vintage) from among 867 international wines submitted. This is awarded to the wine with the purest and most refined Sauvignon character and is considered the ultimate world championship title in the wine scene.

He is a master of his craft, and it is his passion for viticulture that drives him on a daily basis, whether it is planting a new vineyard with great attention to detail and love or orchestrating the work in the vineyard to the exact rhythm of nature through the seasons. In addition to his intuitive sense of the soil and climate and his enormous expertise, he is supported by his team: long-serving employees with an equal amount of passion and drive for wine. As well as following traditional and well-established methods, innovative approaches - from ageing in granite barrels to organic vinification - have their niche at his winery.

STEIERMARK/STYRIA

Grassnitzberg

94 Sauvignon Blanc * Ried Obegg 2020
13,5 Vol.-%, screwcap, large wooden barrel/barrique, €€€€€
93 Sauvignon Blanc * Ried Obegg 2019
94 Sauvignon Blanc * Ried Obegg 2018

93 Sauvignon Blanc * Ried Obegg-Stani 2021
13,5 Vol.-%, DIAM, large wooden barrel, €€€€€ Ⓑ
91 Sauvignon Blanc * Ried Obegg-Stani 2020

94 Sauvignon Blanc * Ried Kranachberg 2021
13,5 Vol.-%, screwcap, steel tank/large wooden barrel, €€€€€
94 Sauvignon Blanc * Ried Kranachberg 2020
93 Sauvignon Blanc * Ried Kranachberg 2019

94 Sauvignon Blanc *
Ried Oberkranachberg 2020
13,5 Vol.-%, DIAM, large wooden barrel, €€€€€
94 Sauvignon Blanc *
Ried Oberkranachberg 2019

93 Sauvignon Blanc * Ried Hochsulz 2021
13,5 Vol.-%, screwcap, large wooden barrel, €€€€€
93 Sauvignon Blanc * Ried Hochsulz 2020
93 Sauvignon Blanc * Ried Hochsulz 2019

93 Sauvignon Blanc * Ried Sulz 2021
13,5 Vol.-%, screwcap, large wooden barrel, €€€€
92 Sauvignon Blanc * Ried Sulz 2020
92 Sauvignon Blanc Ried Sulz 2018

93 Sauvignon Blanc * Ried Grassnitzberg 2021
13,5 Vol.-%, screwcap, steel tank, €€€€
92 Sauvignon Blanc * Ried Grassnitzberg 2020
92 Sauvignon Blanc * Ried Grassnitzberg 2019

92 Sauvignon Blanc * Gamlitz 2022
13 Vol.-%, screwcap, steel tank, €€€€
91 Sauvignon Blanc * Gamlitz 2021
92 Sauvignon Blanc * Gamlitz 2020

(92) Sauvignon Blanc * Privat Selektion 2022
13,5 Vol.-%, screwcap, large wooden barrel, €€€€
92 Sauvignon Blanc * Privat Selektion 2020
92 Sauvignon Blanc * Privat Selektion 2019

92 Sauvignon Blanc * Eichberg 2019

91 Sauvignon Blanc * 2022
13 Vol.-%, screwcap, steel tank, €€€ Ⓑ
90 Sauvignon Blanc * BIO 2021

90 Sauvignon Blanc * 2022
12,5 Vol.-%, screwcap, steel tank, €€€
90 Sauvignon Blanc * 2021

95 Sauvignon Blanc Royal 2020
14 Vol.-%, DIAM, barrique, €€€€€
95 Sauvignon Blanc * Royal 2019
Medium greenish yellow, silver reflections. Fine nuances of roasted aromas and caramel, soft notes of cassis, white tropical fruit, ripe gooseberries, candied grapefruit zest, attractive bouquet. Juicy, good complexity, well-integrated wood spice, white fruit on the finish, soft hints of cloves and honey, good length and ageing potential.
95 Sauvignon Blanc * Royal 2018

95 Sauvignon Blanc Stoan 2020
13,5 Vol.-%, DIAM, granite, €€€€€€
94 Sauvignon blanc Stoan 2019
92 Sauvignon Blanc Stoan 2015

94 Chardonnay Royal 2021
14 Vol.-%, DIAM, barrique, €€€€€
94 Chardonnay * Royal 2019
Medium green-yellow, silver reflections. Fine yellow tropical fruit, soft hints of pineapple and mango, a touch of ripe passion fruit, light caramel, fine wood nuances, inviting bouquet. Powerful, some nougat, yellow peach, fine acidity, subtle sweetness on the finish, balanced and persistent, pear on the aftertaste, a sturdy food wine.
95 Chardonnay Royal 2017

SÜDSTEIERMARK DAC

WEINGUT SKOFF ORIGINAL – WALTER SKOFF
8462 Gamlitz
Eckberg 16
T: +43 (3453) 4243
office@skofforiginal.com
www.skofforiginal.com

Winemaker/Contact:
Walter Skoff
Production: 90 % white, 8 % red, 2 % sweet
Certified: Sustainable Austria
Fairs: ProWein Düsseldorf, VieVinum
Distribution partners: BE, RC, DE, JP, NL, CH, HU, CY

Eva Skoff-Liebau and Walter Skoff

92 Morillon * Ried Grassnitzberg 2020
13,5 Vol.-%, screwcap, large wooden barrel/barrique, €€€€
92 Morillon * Ried Grassnitzberg 1STK 2019
93 Morillon Grassnitzberg Skoff Original 2017

90 Morillon * 2022
13 Vol.-%, screwcap, steel tank, €€€
90 Morillon * 2021
91 Morillon * 2020

93 Gelber Muskateller * Ried Hohenegg 2021
12,5 Vol.-%, screwcap, steel tank, €€€€
92 Gelber Muskateller * Ried Hohenegg 2020
92 Gelber Muskateller Ried Hohenegg 2018

92 Gelber Muskateller * 2022
12,5 Vol.-%, screwcap, steel tank, €€€
91 Gelber Muskateller * 2021
90 Gelber Muskateller * 2020

91 Gelber Muskateller * Eichberg 2019

94 Gelber Muskateller Reserve 2021
13 Vol.-%, DIAM, large wooden barrel, €€€€€

93 Grauburgunder * Ried Kranach 2022
13,5 Vol.-%, screwcap, large wooden barrel, €€€€
92 Grauburgunder * Ried Kranach 2021

91 Grauburgunder * 2020
91 Grauburgunder * 2019

92 Souvignier Gris 2022
13,5 Vol.-%, screwcap, large wooden barrel, €€€ Ⓑ

90 Weißburgunder * 2022
12,5 Vol.-%, screwcap, steel tank, €€€
90 Weißburgunder * 2021
91 Weißburgunder * 2020

89 Gewürztraminer Steiermark 2021
91 Gewürztraminer * Ried Kranach 2020
92 Gewürztraminer * Ried Kranach 2018

89 Zweigelt Rosé 2021
89 Rosé 2017 ME/ZW

91 Zweigelt Barrique 2019
92 Zweigelt Barrique 2018

* Südsteiermark DAC

STEIERMARK/STYRIA

★★★

WEINGUT PETER SKOFF DOMÄNE KRANACHBERG

The winery of the Peter Skoff family is one of the top addresses in the South Styrian wine scene. Sauvignon Blanc, the winery's superstar, has won several recent tasting awards, including "Austria's Best Sauvignon 2021" (Concours Mondial). Satisfied wine customers and numerous other awards confirm the uncompromising strive for quality. The winery is located in the middle of the very high vineyards on the Kranachberg with a wonderful panoramic view over the Südsteiermark Nature Park.

Peter Skoff and his two sons, Markus and Peter junior, cultivate about 30 hectares of vineyards in one of the best wine-growing areas of the country. The wines with their mineral character score points for, above all, their harmonious drinking pleasure and as perfect accompaniments to food. Connoisseurs can taste the wine in the popular Buschenschank (wine tavern) and then make themselves comfortable in one of the five cosy guest rooms. Since the 2014 vintage, certified organic wines have also been available under the "Peter Skoff - Gut Kaspar" label.

95 Sauvignon Blanc * Ried Kranachberg »Ex Baca« 2020
Bright medium golden yellow, silver reflections. Fresh nuances of yellow gooseberries, some lychee, hints of guava and tangerine zest, fine floral honey, intense bouquet. Taut, pithy and mineral, fine tannic nuances, fresh structure, white apple fruit, salty and persistent, an IZ style (intercellular fermentation) for the advanced connoisseur.

95 Sauvignon Blanc * Ried Kranachberg Rottriegl 2019
14 Vol.-%, screwcap, small wooden barrel, €€€€€

94 Sauvignon Blanc * Ried Kranachkogl Finum 2021
14 Vol.-%, screwcap, steel tank, €€€€

94 Sauvignon Blanc * Ried Kranachkogl Finum 2019

93 Sauvignon Blanc * Ried Kranachkogel Finum 2018

94 Sauvignon Blanc * Ried Hoch Kranachberg 2021
13,5 Vol.-%, screwcap, large wooden barrel, €€€€€

Peter and Markus Skoff

WEINGUT PETER SKOFF – DOMÄNE KRANACHBERG
8462 Gamlitz
Kranachberg - Sauvignonweg 50
T: +43 (3454) 6104
weingut@peter-skoff.at
www.peter-skoff.at

Winemaker/Contact:
Peter and Markus Skoff
Production: 1 % sparkling, 95 % white, 2 % red, 1 % sweet, 30 hectares
Fairs: Gast Klagenfurt, ÖGW Zürich, VieVinum, Weintage im Museumsquartier
Distribution partners: BE, DE, PL, CH, CZ

SÜDSTEIERMARK DAC

94 Sauvignon Blanc * Ried Jägerberg 2021
13 Vol.-%, screwcap, steel tank, €€€€
93 Sauvignon Blanc * Ried Jägerberg 2020
93 Sauvignon Blanc * Ried Jägerberg 2019

93 Sauvignon Blanc * Ried Kranachberg 2020
93 Sauvignon Blanc * Ried Kranachberg 2019
12,5 Vol.-%, screwcap, large wooden barrel, €€€€€ ❺

(93) Sauvignon Blanc * Gamlitz 2022
13 Vol.-%, screwcap, steel tank, €€€ ❶
92 Sauvignon Blanc * Gamlitz 2021
91 Sauvignon Blanc * Gamlitz 2020

93 Sauvignon Blanc * Gamlitz
   Gut Kaspar 2022
13 Vol.-%, screwcap, steel tank, €€€ ❺
91 Sauvignon Blanc * Gamlitz
   »Gut Kaspar« 2020
92 Sauvignon Blanc Natural
   »Gut Kaspar« 2019

(92) Sauvignon Blanc * Ried Jungfernhang 2022
13 Vol.-%, screwcap, steel tank, €€€
92 Sauvignon Blanc * Ried Jungfernhang 2021
92 Sauvignon Blanc * Ried Jungfernhang 2020

92 Sauvignon Blanc * Klassik 2022
12 Vol.-%, screwcap, steel tank, €€€
90 Sauvignon Blanc * Klassik 2021
90 Sauvignon Blanc * Klassik 2020

91 Sauvignon Blanc * Ried Kranachberg
   »Gut Kaspar« Natural 2019
92 Sauvignon Blanc * Ried Kranachberg
   »Gut Kaspar« 2018

92 Bio Natural 2021 SB
13 Vol.-%, cork, wooden barrel, €€€€ ❺ ❶
93 Natural 2020 SB/CB

94 Morillon * Ried Kranachberg Rottriegl
   Reserve 2019
14 Vol.-%, screwcap, small wooden barrel, €€€€€
94 Morillon * Ried Kranachberg Reserve 2018
Bright greenish yellow, silver reflections. Fine wood savouriness, yellow tropical fruit, nuances of mango and papaya, delicate honey blossom, inviting bouquet, tangerine zest. Juicy, elegant, white pear fruit, fine minerality, soft acidity, shows good length, fruit sweetness in the finish, a balanced food companion.
93 Morillon * Reserve Ried Kranachberg 2017

93 Morillon * Ried Kranachberg 2019

(91) Morillon * Klassik 2022
12 Vol.-%, screwcap, wooden barrel, €€
90 Morillon * Gamlitz 2021
91 Morillon * Gamlitz 2020

93 Weißburgunder * Klassik 2022
12 Vol.-%, screwcap, steel tank, €€
89 Weißburgunder * Klassik 2021
90 Weißburgunder * Klassik 2020

92 Weißburgunder * Ried Kranachberg 2020
92 Weißburgunder Ried Kranachberg 2017

92 Gewürztraminer * Gamlitz 2020
91 Gewürztraminer * Gamlitz 2019
92 Gewürztraminer Gamlitz 2017

93 Gewürztraminer Ried Kranachberg
   Reserve 2017

92 Gelber Muskateller *
   Ried Kranachberg 2021
13 Vol.-%, screwcap, large wooden barrel, €€€€
91 Gelber Muskateller Ried Kranachberg 2017

91 Gelber Muskateller * Gamlitz 2022
12,5 Vol.-%, screwcap, steel tank, €€€
89 Gelber Muskateller * Gamlitz 2018

92 devilORANGEl 2019 SOG
12,5 Vol.-%, screwcap, large wooden barrel, €€€€ ❶
92 devilORANGEl 2017 MS/TR
93 devilORANGEl 2015 TR/GM

91 Souvignier Gris Gut Kaspar BIO 2022
12,5 Vol.-%, screwcap, large wooden barrel, €€ ❺
90 Souvignier Gris 2020
90 Souvignier Gris »Gut Kaspar« 2019

91 Welschriesling * Klassik 2022
11,5 Vol.-%, screwcap, steel tank, €€
89 Welschriesling * Klassik 2021
89 Welschriesling * Klassik 2020

94 Gewürztraminer TBA 2018

96 Sauvignon Blanc TBA 2017

96 Vergissmeinnicht TBA 2017
   SB/CH/TR/WB/WR

* Südsteiermark DAC

STEIERMARK/STYRIA

The Strauss family: Karl with Sabine and Gustav with Bettina

WEINGUT STRAUSS GAMLITZ
8462 Gamlitz
Steinbach 16
T: +43 (664) 4424128
office@weingut-strauss.at
www.weingut-strauss.at

Winemaker: Gustav Strauss
Contact: Karl and Gustav Strauss
Production: 5 % sparkling, 80 % white, 5 % rosé, 9 % red, 1 % sweet, 30 hectares
Certified: Sustainable Austria
Fairs: Tag des Steirischen Weines im Museumsquartier, VieVinum
Distribution partners: DE, PL, CH, USA

★★

WEINGUT STRAUSS GAMLITZ

The wines of the brothers Karl and Gustav Strauss from Gamlitz impressively reflect Southern Styria: on the one hand, elegant and harmonious, on the other, a bit wild, intense and full of contrasts. All of the growths have one thing in common: they combine power with fruit, freshness with a lot of elegance and they are all very drinkable.

Every wine-growing region in the world has its own charm - Southern Styria has a very special one. Here Gustav Strauss presses a wide range of quality wines: From the fruity-fresh regional wines Südsteiermark DAC (Welschriesling, Pinot Blanc, Morillon, Sauvignon Blanc and Gelber Muskateller) to the fruity-full local wines "Gamlitz" (mainly from the varieties Sauvignon Blanc and Muskateller) to the Riedenweine of the sites Gamlitzberg and Hundsberg, which are aged in large neutral oak barrels and in the "Betonei" (concrete egg). In particularly good years, the "Strauss Reserve Line" from the Gamlitzberg vineyard is pressed; these grapes ripen for up to 24 months in barrique barrels towards perfection. Sauvignon Blanc, Gelber Muskateller, Pinot Gris and Chardonnay are bottled with a great ageing potential.

The winery has been family-owned since 1810 and offers visitors cellar tours and tastings with a great view of the Gamlitzberg. In addition to the main house, a second building was also opened in 2019: "sleep | eat | drink" in the "Weinschmiede 18". The Strauss family is happy about every visit.

94 Sauvignon Blanc * Ried Gamlitzberg Grande Reserve 2019
13,5 Vol.-%, screwcap, barrique, €€€€€ Ⓥ
Light greenish yellow, with silver reflections. Inviting white tropical fruit, ripe gooseberry aromas, a hint of fresh guava: an attractive bouquet. Juicy, elegant, with white peach, a finesse-rich structure, a salty-lemon finish and good length - a fine food companion with ageing potential.

93 Sauvignon Blanc Ried Gamlitzberg Reserve 2017

92 Sauvignon Blanc * Ried Gamlitzberg 2022
13 Vol.-%, screwcap, wooden barrel, €€€ Ⓥ

92 Sauvignon Blanc * Ried Gamlitzberg 2021
92 Sauvignon Blanc * Ried Gamlitzberg 2020

91 Sauvignon Blanc * 2020
90 Sauvignon Blanc * Klassik 2019

© Weingut Strauss

SÜDSTEIERMARK DAC

91 Sauvignon Blanc * Ried Hundsberg 2018	89 Morillon * Klassik 2021
92 Sauvignon Blanc Ried Hundsberg 2017	
	91 Weißburgunder * Gamlitz 2022
93 Chardonnay * Ried Gamlitzberg Grande Reserve 2019	12,5 Vol.-%, screwcap, steel tank, €€ 🅗 🅥
13 Vol.-%, screwcap, barrique, €€€€€ 🅥	90 Graubugunder * Ried Gamlitzberg 2021
92 Chardonnay * Ried Gamlitzberg Reserve 2019	92 Graubugunder * Ried Gamlitzberg 2020
93 Chardonnay Reserve Ried Gamlitzberg 2017	90 Graubugunder Ried Gamlitzberg 2017
	90 Gelber Muskateller * Ried Gamlitzberg 2022
91 Chardonnay * Ried Gamlitzberg 2022	12,5 Vol.-%, screwcap, wooden barrel, €€€ 🅗 🅥
13 Vol.-%, screwcap, wooden barrel, €€€ 🅥	91 Gelber Muskateller * Ried Gamlitzberg 2021
91 Chardonnay * Ried Gamlitzberg 2018	91 Gelber Muskateller Ried Gamlitzberg 2017
90 Chardonnay Ried Gamlitzberg 2017	
	90 Gelber Muskateller * 2020
91 Chardonnay * Ried Hundsberg 2018	89 Gelber Muskateller * Klassik 2019
92 Chardonnay Ried Hundsberg 2017	
	90 Rosé Mischsatz Steiermark 2022 BW/ZW

SANFTER WEINBAU
MARIA UND JOHANNES SÖLL

Gamlitz, south of the Styrian rolling hills on the border with Slovenia, is home to the Söll family. Since 1806, they have run their eponymous winery on the outskirts of the quaint wine-producing town.

In 1997, Hannes Söll and his wife Maria took over the idyllic estate. Just one year later, the winemaker switched to what he calls "gentle viticulture".

"Organic farming was not enough for me. I want to keep interventions in the vineyard to a minimum; for example, I don't use any fertilizer. The result is that the vines grow more slowly and are more resistant to disease. This has an effect on the whole ecosystem. Grass, herbs, and insects all thrive harmoniously in the vineyards as a result. Instead of 25 tractor passes, I have a maximum of four to six, which not only saves a lot of fuel but also protects the soil. The soil is the heart of the vine. If the soil is healthy, the wine is healthy. Each vine is different like a young child and needs the appropriate attention and loving care. That is why we work the vines, leaves, and shoots by hand. Our harvest and cellar work is based on the phases of the moon. There are economic and humanitarian benefits to not using chemicals and tractors. Some people compare our vineyards to a primeval forest, but that is exactly how we want it," says Hannes Söll, explaining his philosophy and values.

Gamlitz

STEIERMARK/STYRIA

Johannes Söll

SANFTER WEINBAU MARIA UND JOHANNES SÖLL
8462 Gamlitz
Steinbach 63 A
T: +43 (3454) 6667
familie@weingut-soell.at
www.weingut-soell.at

Winemaker/Contact:
Johannes Söll
Production: 3 % sparkling, 82 % white, 12 % red, 3 % sweet
Fairs: VieVinum

Wine classics such as Gelber Muskateller and Sauvignon Blanc are as much a part of the winery's portfolio as high-quality red wines. These gems are fermented not only in steel and wood but also in concrete eggs. Numerous awards prove Hannes Söll is on the right track, yet the 55-year-old has opened a new chapter in his life: "We have reduced our vineyards to 2.5 hectares, and our son Christian is steering our winery into the next generation. In the future, Hannes Söll will pass on his knowledge and ideology of 'gentle viticulture' to interested winemakers. He will definitely continue his vineyard tours, which are well-known far beyond the borders of Gamlitz. These tours include wine tasting and a small snack. For those interested, the Söll winery offers a special tasting package: twelve bottles, of four varieties, for 120 euros, including shipping!

93 Gelber Muskateller Reserve
Söll la Vie – Sanfter Weinbau 2013
14,5 Vol.-%, screwcap, 500-l-barrel, €€€€€ **B O**
O V

Delicately cloudy bright orange yellow, with silver reflections. On the nose freshly grated lime zest, white tropical fruit, hints of apricot confit and orange marmalade. It is powerful, dry, finely meshed, with lovely oak nuances, taut and mineral, with apricot also on the back palate. It is a quite special muscat interpretation, and anything but conventional.

93 Riesling Gamlitz Ried Steinbach
Selektion 2016
14 Vol.-%, screwcap, large wooden barrel, €€€€€ **B**
O O V

92 Welschriesling Gamlitz Ried Sernauberg
Sanfter Weinbau 2017
13 Vol.-%, screwcap, large wooden barrel, €€€€€ **B**
O O V

92 Weissburgunder NexGen 2017
14 Vol.-%, screwcap, large wooden barrel, €€€€ **B**
O O V

89 Gamlitz Ried Steinbach Machrima –
Sanfter Weinbau 2017
13,5 Vol.-%, screwcap, large wooden barrel, €€€€€
B O O V

92 Unicus Redividus Söll la Vie Süss –
Sanfter Weinbau 2020/2022
14,5 Vol.-%, screwcap, large wooden barrel, €€€€€
O O V

SÜDSTEIERMARK DAC

★★★★★

FAMILIENWEINGUT TEMENT
ORGANIC

Nestled in Zieregg, the Tement Winery overlooks the vineyards of southern Styria as well as those of neighbouring Slovenia. Manfred Tement took over his father's winery here in 1976, turning it into one of Austria's most renowned wineries and establishing the region's international reputation. He set new standards for Styrian wines, particularly for Sauvignon Blanc, which the family has cultivated since 1959 on the now iconic Zieregg and Grassnitzberg Riff sites. In 2004, the family winery began to extend its vision of wine to the Slovenian side of its most renowned site, Zieregg. Since then, Domaine Ciringa has also belonged to the family. Today, the third generation, sons Armin and Stefan as well as daughter-in-law Monika, work with both parents. The family legacy continues with each harvest, but the love of wine and the shared commitment to unconditional quality remain constant. The grapes are hand-picked at the optimum time, spontaneously fermented, and gently vinified in vineyard-specific barrels and tanks, before being aged in the cellar in small quantities and according to variety. The winery is committed to biodynamic agriculture and has been a member of the Demeter Association since 2022 and a member of the respekt BIODYN group. However, the Tement family's commitment to quality is not limited to viticulture. The family also enriches the South Styrian region with two gastronomic region. A truly memorable getaway is guaranteed here.

95 ❂ Morillon Brut Nature Blanc de Blancs Grosse Reserve Zero Dosage 2014
12 Vol.-%, cork, used barriques/bottle fermentation, €€€€€€ ⓗ ⓢ ⓥ

95 ❂ Tement Blanc de Blancs Brut Nature Grosse Reserve

99 Sauvignon Blanc * Ried Zieregg GSTK 2020
13,5 Vol.-%, glass, large wooden barrel, €€€€€€ ⓑ ⓥ

97 Sauvignon Blanc * Ried Zieregg GSTK 2019

99 Sauvignon Blanc * Ried Zieregg IZ GSTK 2018
13,5 Vol.-%, glass, wooden barrel, €€€€€€ ⓑ ⓥ

Medium golden yellow, silver glints. Candied orange zest, kumquats, yellow tropical fruit, a hint of blossom honey, nuances of lemon balm, and soft notions of herbal savouri-

FAMILIENWEINGUT TEMENT
8461 Ehrenhausen, Zieregg 13
T: +43 (3453) 4101
weingut@tement.at
www.tement.at

Winemaker: Manfred, Armin and Stefan Tement
Contact: Monika Tement, MA
Production: 97 % white, 2 % red, 1 % sweet, 85 hectares
Fairs: Austrian Tasting London, ProWein Düsseldorf, VieVinum, Summa Margreid
Distribution partners: BY, BE, DE, GR, UK, HK, IRL, IL, IT, JP, CDN, ROK, HR, LU, MV, PL, PT, RUS, SE, CH, SGP, SK, SLO, ES, TH, CZ, UA, HU, USA, UAE

STEIERMARK/STYRIA

ness. Succulent, elegant, white peach, delicate nuances of figs and nougat, prolonged persistence, complex, unique style, exhibiting excellent length. A sturdy food accompaniment offering definite development potential.

98 Sauvignon Blanc Ried Zieregg GSTK IZ® 2015

98 Sauvignon Blanc * Ried Zieregg GSTK Karmeliten Terrassen 2018

98 Sauvignon Blanc * Ried Zieregg GSTK Vinothek Reserve 2019
13,5 Vol.-%, glass, wooden barrel, €€€€€ Ⓑ Ⓥ

97 Sauvignon Blanc * Ried Zieregg GSTK Vinothek Reserve 2018

98 Sauvignon Blanc Ried Zieregg G STK Vinothek Reserve 2017

97 Sauvignon Blanc * Ried Zieregg Kår GSTK 2020
13,5 Vol.-%, glass, large wooden barrel, €€€€€ Ⓑ Ⓥ

97 Sauvignon Blanc * Ried Zieregg GSTK Dreieck 2020
Pale golden yellow, silver glints. Pleasant herbal savouriness, yellow fruit nuances, delicate hints of orange zest. Taut, tightly woven, vibrantly structured, with a touch of red cherries and delicate apple tones, seemingly ethereal, with fine lime zest on the finish. Elegant and persistent - a delicate style.

96 Sauvignon Blanc * Ried Zieregg Kapelle GSTK 2020
13 Vol.-%, glass, large wooden barrel, €€€€€ Ⓑ Ⓥ

96 Sauvignon Blanc * Ried Zieregg GSTK Weisse Wand 2020

96 Sauvignon Blanc * Ried Zieregg GSTK Steinbruch 2020

95 Sauvignon Blanc * Ried Zieregg GSTK Die Sieben Reihen 2018

95 Sauvignon Blanc * Ried Zieregg GSTK Kiesner Berg 2018

95 Sauvignon Blanc * Ried Sernau König GSTK 2020
13 Vol.-%, glass, large wooden barrel, €€€€€ Ⓑ Ⓥ

95 Sauvignon Blanc * Ried Sernau König GSTK 2019

95 Sauvignon Blanc * Ried Sernau König GSTK 2018

95 Sauvignon Blanc * Ried Grassnitzberg Riff 1STK 2020
13 Vol.-%, glass, large wooden barrel, €€€€€ Ⓑ Ⓥ

95 Sauvignon Blanc * Ried Grassnitzberg 1STK 2020

94 Sauvignon Blanc * Ried Grassnitzberg 1STK 2019

94 Sauvignon Blanc * Ried Grassnitzberg 1STK 2018

94 Sauvignon Blanc * Gamlitz Sandstein 2020
94 Sauvignon Blanc * Gamlitz Sandstein 2019
93 Sauvignon Blanc * Gamlitz Sandstein 2018

(94) Sauvignon Blanc * Ehrenhausen Korallenkalk 2021
13 Vol.-%, glass, large wooden barrel/steel tank, €€€€€ Ⓑ Ⓥ

94 Sauvignon Blanc * Ehrenhausen Korallenkalk 2020

93 Sauvignon Blanc * Ehrenhausen Korallenkalk 2019

94 Sauvignon Blanc * Kalk & Kreide 2022
13 Vol.-%, glass, steel tank/large wooden barrel, €€€€ Ⓑ Ⓗ

93 Sauvignon Blanc * Kalk & Kreide 2021
92 Sauvignon Blanc * Kalk & Kreide 2020

93 Sauvignon Blanc * Kitzeck Sausal Schiefergestein 2020

94 Sauvignon Blanc * Kitzeck Sausal Schiefergestein 2019

94 Sauvignon Blanc * Kitzeck-Sausal Schiefergestein 2018

96 Morillon * Ried Zieregg Steilriegel GSTK 2020
13 Vol.-%, glass, used barriques, €€€€€ Ⓑ Ⓥ

97 Morillon * Ried Zieregg GSTK 2019
Medium greenish yellow, silver reflections. Fine yellow tropical fruit, hints of orange zest, soft notes of blossom honey, subtle herbal spice, mineral touch. Full-bodied, white stone fruit, fresh acidity, tight-knit salty finish, lively, finely spicy style, very good length and definition, certain ageing potential.

96 Morillon * Ried Zieregg GSTK 2018

95 Morillon * Ried Sulz Kriewetz 1STK 2018
13,5 Vol.-%, glass, 500-l-barrel, €€€€€ Ⓑ Ⓥ

94 Morillon * Ried Grassnitzberg 1STK 2019
12,5 Vol.-%, glass, small wooden barrel, €€€€€ Ⓑ

SÜDSTEIERMARK DAC

94 Morillon * Ried Sulz 1STK 2020
12,5 Vol.-%, glass, small wooden barrel, €€€€€ Ⓑ Ⓥ
94 Morillon * Ried Sulz 1STK 2019
95 Morillon * Ried Sulz 1STK 2018

94 Morillon * Ried Rossberg STK 2020
13 Vol.-%, glass, used barriques, €€€€€ Ⓑ Ⓥ
93 Morillon * Ried Rossberg 2019
93 Morillon Ried Rossberg 2017

93 Morillon * Muschelkalk 2021
13 Vol.-%, glass, large wooden barrel/steel tank, €€€€ Ⓑ Ⓥ
93 Morillon * Muschelkalk 2020
93 Morillon * Muschelkalk 2019

96 Weißer Burgunder * Ried Zieregg GSTK 2018
13 Vol.-%, glass, wooden barrel, €€€€€€ Ⓑ Ⓥ

93 Weißer Burgunder * Ried Sulz 1STK 2020
12,5 Vol.-%, glass, large wooden barrel, €€€€€ Ⓑ Ⓥ
93 Weissburgunder * Ried Sulz 1 STK 2019
94 Weissburgunder * Ried Sulz 1 STK 2018

92 Weißburgunder * Ton & Mergel 2022
12,5 Vol.-%, glass, steel tank, €€€ Ⓑ Ⓗ Ⓥ
92 Weißburgunder * Ton & Mergel 2021
92 Weissburgunder * Ton & Mergel 2020

95 Gelber Muskateller * Ried Steinbach Fürst 1STK 2020
12 Vol.-%, glass, steel tank, €€€€€ Ⓑ Ⓗ Ⓥ
94 Gelber Muskateller Ried Steinbach Fürst 1STK 2019
93 Gelber Muskateller * Ried Steinbach Fürst BIO 1 STK 2018

93 Gelber Muskateller * Ried Hochkittenberg 1STK 2020
93 Gelber Muskateller * Ried Hochkittenberg 1STK 2019
93 Gelber Muskateller Ried Hochkittenberg 1 STK 2017

93 Gelber Muskateller * Sand & Schiefer 2022
11,5 Vol.-%, glass, steel tank, €€€ Ⓑ Ⓗ Ⓥ
91 Gelber Muskateller * Sand & Schiefer 2021
92 Gelber Muskateller * Sand & Schiefer 2020

92 Gelber Muskateller Gamlitz Ried Labitschberg »Peter Kraus« 2021
92 Gelber Muskateller Ried Labitschberg Gamlitz Peter Kraus 2018

Ried Kittenberg

94 Gewürztraminer * Ried Wielitschberg 1STK 2020
13,5 Vol.-%, glass, 500-l-barrel, €€€€€ Ⓑ Ⓥ
93 Gewürztraminer * Ried Wielitschberg 1STK 2019
93 Gewürztraminer * Ried Wielitschberg 1 STK 2018

94 Welschriesling Weinstock Alte Reben 2020
12,5 Vol.-%, glass, small wooden barrel, €€€€€€ Ⓑ Ⓥ
93 Welschriesling * Ried Zieregg Weinstock Alte Reben 2019
93 Welschriesling * Ried Zieregg Weinstock Alte Reben 2018

92 Welschriesling * Ried Ottenberg Veitlhansl STK 2020
12 Vol.-%, glass, 500-l-barrel, €€€€€ Ⓑ Ⓥ
92 Welschriesling * Ried Ottenberg Veitlhansl 2019
93 Welschriesling * Ried Ottenberg Veitlhansl 2018

92 Welschriesling * Opok 2022
11,5 Vol.-%, screwcap, steel tank, €€€ Ⓑ Ⓗ Ⓥ
92 Welschriesling * Opok 2021
91 Welschriesling * 2020

92 * Tement Blanc 2021 SB/WR/WB
92 * Tement Blanc 2020 SB/WB/WR
92 * Tement Blanc 2019 SB/WR/WB

* Südsteiermark DAC

WEINGUT WOHLMUTH

★★★★

Since 1803, the Wohlmuth family has been producing wine in the southern Styrian town of Kitzeck im Sausal, the highest wine-growing village in Austria. Over the years, little has changed in their work - just as in the old days, the solid slate rocks on the surface of the vineyards have to be pounded with hammers, and every single vine has to be painstakingly worked into the barren soil. The quality of the wines is the result of meticulous manual work, from pruning to selective hand harvesting. Respect for natural resources is reflected in the renunciation of herbicides and insecticides. There is no irrigation, and the vines on the steepest slopes are still scythed. The vineyards are located between 400 and 600 metres above sea level and, with slopes of up to 90 per cent, are among the steepest in Europe. Up to 1,200 work hours are put into each hectare of these extreme vineyards yearly. A distinctive slate minerality is found in all the estate's wines, demonstrating how deeply rooted the vines are in the soil that dominates the Kitzeck-Sausal appellation.

For generations, the Wohlmuth family has owned some of Austria's earliest single vineyard sites, such as the Edelschuh vineyard, which was first documented in 1322. These historically significant single vineyards are maintained and preserved at great expense and occasionally painstakingly replanted. They produce wines of provenance characterised by a tension between warmth (Illyrian climate, ripe grapes) and coolness (alpine influence, slate soils, high altitude).

93 ❂ Chardonnay Brut Nature NV

98 Sauvignon Blanc * Ried Edelschuh GSTK 2021
13 Vol.-%, cork, wooden barrel/large wooden barrel, €€€€€ Ⓥ

96 Sauvignon Blanc * Ried Edelschuh GSTK 2020
Pale golden yellow, silver glints. Delicate notes of slate, meadow herbs and white tropical fruit, tenderly underpinned with pineapple and grapefruit zest. Firm, tightly woven, subtle stone fruit nuances, vibrant, elegant, and well-balanced. A silky Vieilles Vignes style with assured ageing potential, very alluring.

97 Sauvignon Blanc * Ried Edelschuh GSTK 2019

96 Sauvignon Blanc * Ried Hochsteinriegl GSTK 2021
13 Vol.-%, cork, large wooden barrel/wooden barrel, €€€€ Ⓥ

95 Sauvignon Blanc * Ried Hochsteinriegl GSTK 2020

96 Sauvignon Blanc * Ried Hochsteinriegl GSTK 2019

95 Sauvignon Blanc * Ried Sausaler Schlössl 2021

95 Sauvignon Blanc * Ried Sausaler Schlössl 2020

95 Sauvignon Blanc * Ried Sausaler Schlössl 2019

(95) Sauvignon Blanc * Ried Steinriegl 1STK 2022
13 Vol.-%, cork, used barriques, €€€€

95 Sauvignon Blanc * Ried Steinriegl 1STK 2021

94 Sauvignon Blanc * Ried Steinriegl 1STK 2020

94 Sauvignon Blanc * Ried Urlkogl STK 2021
13 Vol.-%, cork, €€€€€

94 Sauvignon Blanc * Kitzeck-Sausal 2022
12,5 Vol.-%, screwcap, used barriques, €€€€ Ⓥ

94 Sauvignon Blanc * Kitzeck-Sausal 2021

93 Sauvignon Blanc * Kitzeck-Sausal 2020

93 Sauvignon Blanc * Schiefer 2022
12,5 Vol.-%, screwcap, steel tank, €€€ Ⓥ

92 Sauvignon Blanc * Schiefer 2021

93 Sauvignon Blanc * Schiefer 2020

93 Sauvignon Blanc * 2022
12,5 Vol.-%, screwcap, steel tank, €€€ Ⓥ

93 Sauvignon Blanc * 2021

92 Sauvignon Blanc * 2020

SÜDSTEIERMARK DAC

WEINGUT WOHLMUTH
8441 Kitzeck im Sausal
Fresing 24
T: +43 (3456) 2303
wein@wohlmuth.at
www.wohlmuth.at

Winemaker/Contact:
Gerhard Wohlmuth
Production: 2 % sparkling, 90 % white, 7 % red, 1 % sweet, 57 hectares
Certified: Sustainable Austria
Fairs: ProWein Düsseldorf, VieVinum
Distribution partners: BE, RC, DK, DE, FIN, UK, IT, CDN, NL, PL, PT, RUS, SE, TC, CZ, USA

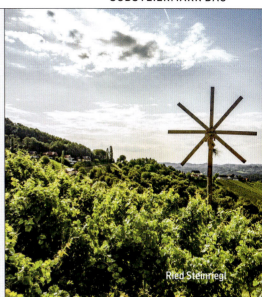

Ried Steinriegl

92   Sauvignon Blanc * Ried Urlkogl Meinhardt Hube STK 2021
13 Vol.-%, cork, large wooden barrel, €€€€

93   Sauvignon Blanc * Ried Urlkogl Meinhardt Hube 2020

92   Sauvignon Blanc * Gamlitz Meinhardt Hube 2020

97   Riesling * Ried Edelschuh GSTK 2021
13 Vol.-%, cork, used barriques, €€€€€   V

94   Riesling * Ried Edelschuh GSTK 2020
Medium yellow gold, silver reflections. Fine floral honey, ripe vine peach, yellow fruit, a touch of pineapple, soft minerality. Elegant, juicy, white fruit, fine acidity, a touch of salted caramel on the finish, balanced style, long lasting, endowed with ageing potential.

97   Riesling * Ried Edelschuh GSTK 2019

(95) Riesling * Ried Dr. Wunsch STK 2022
12,5 Vol.-%, cork, large wooden barrel, €€€€€

94   Riesling * Ried Dr. Wunsch 2021

95   Riesling * Ried Dr. Wunsch 2020

95   Riesling * Ried Steinriegl Strohbart STK 2021
12,5 Vol.-%, cork, large wooden barrel, €€€€€

94   Riesling * Ried Steinriegl Strohbart 2019

93   Riesling * Kitzeck-Sausal 2020
93   Riesling * Kitzeck-Sausal 2019

95   * Ried Edelschuh 2018 CH/SB/RR

91   * Steirischer Panther 2022 SB/CH/GM/PG/RR
12,5 Vol.-%, screwcap, steel tank, €€   V

92   * Steirischer Panther 2021 SB/CH/GM/PG/RR

91   * Steirischer Panther 2020 SB/CH/GM/PG/RR

95   Morillon * Ried Sausaler Schlössl 2020
13 Vol.-%, cork, 500-l-barrel, €€€€

94   Morillon * Ried Sausaler Schlössl 2019

94   Chardonnay * Ried Sausaler Schlössl 2018

94   Morillon * Ried Gola 1STK 2021
13 Vol.-%, cork, used barriques, €€€€   V

93   Morillon * Ried Gola 2020

93   Chardonnay * Ried Gola 2019

92   Chardonnay * Schiefer 2021

93   Chardonnay * Schiefer 2020

93   Chardonnay * Schiefer 2019

(94) Gelber Muskateller * Ried Steinriegl 1STK 2022
12,5 Vol.-%, cork, used barriques, €€€€   V

93   Gelber Muskateller * Ried Steinriegl 1STK 2021

93   Gelber Muskateller * Ried Steinriegl 1STK 2020

* Südsteiermark DAC

STEIERMARK/STYRIA

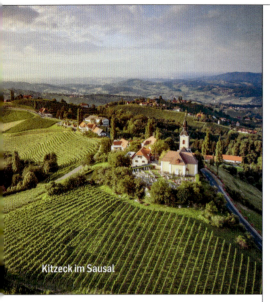
Kitzeck im Sausal

92　Gelber Muskateller * Kitzeck-Sausal 2022
12 Vol.-%, screwcap, large wooden barrel/steel tank, €€€ Ⓥ
92　Gelber Muskateller * Kitzeck-Sausal 2021
92　Gelber Muskateller * Kitzeck-Sausal 2020

92　Gelber Muskateller * Schiefer 2022
12 Vol.-%, screwcap, steel tank, €€€ Ⓥ
92　Gelber Muskateller * Schiefer 2021
92　Gelber Muskateller * Schiefer 2020

90　Gelber Muskateller * 2022
12 Vol.-%, screwcap, steel tank, €€€ Ⓥ
91　Gelber Muskateller * 2021
91　Gelber Muskateller * 2020

94　Grauburgunder * Ried Gola 1STK 2021
12,5 Vol.-%, cork, large wooden barrel, €€€€ Ⓥ
94　Grauburgunder * Ried Gola 1STK 2020
94　Grauburgunder * Ried Gola 1STK 2019

93　Grauburgunder * Kitzeck-Sausal 2022
13 Vol.-%, screwcap, large wooden barrel, €€€ Ⓥ
92　Grauburgunder * Kitzeck-Sausal 2021
92　Grauburgunder * Kitzeck-Sausal 2020

93　Weißburgunder * Ried Gola 2020
93　Weißburgunder * Ried Gola 2019
93　Pinot Blanc * Ried Gola 2018

92　Weißburgunder * 2021
91　Weißburgunder * 2020
91　Weißburgunder * 2019

93　Gewürztraminer * 2021
13,5 Vol.-%, screwcap, steel tank, €€€ Ⓥ
93　Gewürztraminer * 2020
93　Gewürztraminer * 2019

91　Welschriesling * 2022
11,5 Vol.-%, screwcap, steel tank, €€ Ⓥ
91　Welschriesling * 2021
91　Welschriesling * 2020

92　Blaufränkisch Ried Rabenkropf 2018
13,5 Vol.-%, €€€€€
94　Blaufränkisch Ried Rabenkropf 2017
94　Blaufränkisch Rabenkropf 2015

90　Blaufränkisch Red Nek 2021
13 Vol.-%, screwcap, used barriques, €€ Ⓥ
91　Blaufränkisch Red Nek 2020
90　Blaufränkisch Red Nek 2019

90　Blaufränkisch Neckenmarkt 2021
13 Vol.-%, €€

92　Pinot Noir Phyllit 2019
13 Vol.-%, cork, €€€€€
93　Pinot Noir Phyllit 2018
92　Pinot Noir Phyllitt 2017

92　Rotburger Phyllit 2018

92　Aristos 2017 CS/BF

90　Zweigelt Steiermark 2019
91　Zweigelt 2018

94　Riesling Spätlese Dr. Wu 2019

WEINGUT WRUSS

Weingut Wruss is idyllically situated on a small mountain plateau on the Kranachberg, where the third generation of the Wruss family is now devoted to viticulture. The seven hectares of vineyards are located exclusively on the chalky sandy soils of the Kranachberg. Its favourable microclimate and unique terroir give the wines their characteristic minerality. The family lovingly cultivates the steep slopes all year round, and the grapes are harvested by hand in autumn. Elegant and delicate wines are produced in the cellar, reflecting their unique Kranachberg origins. The range includes typical Styrian varieties; Sauvignon Blanc, Gelber Muskateller, Weißburgunder, Welschriesling, and Grauburgunder. " Being down to earth, visionary, and working sustainably in harmony with nature are the best prerequisites for producing authentic and elegant wines of the highest quality," says winemaker Johannes Wruss.

93 Sauvignon Blanc * Ried Kranachberg 2020
13 Vol.-%, screwcap, oak barrel, €€€€

93 Sauvignon Blanc * Ried Kranachberg 2019
Pale yellow gold, silver reflections. Ripe yellow tropical fruit with hints of guava and mango, a touch of blossom honey and candied tangerine zest. Complex, white fruit, elegant, light caramel, well-integrated acidity, chalky nuances, lemony touch, lime on the finish; already well developed.

93 Sauvignon Blanc Ried Kranachberg 2017

93 Sauvignon Blanc * Gamlitz 2021
13,5 Vol.-%, screwcap, steel tank, €€€€

92 Sauvignon Blanc * Gamlitz 2021
90 Sauvignon Blanc * Gamlitz 2018

91 Sauvignon Blanc * 2022
13 Vol.-%, screwcap, steel tank, €€€

90 Sauvignon Blanc * 2021
90 Sauvignon Blanc * 2019

92 Gelber Muskateller * 2022
12 Vol.-%, screwcap, steel tank, €€€

90 Gelber Muskateller * 2021

92 Grauburgunder * Ried Kranachberg 2020
13,5 Vol.-%, screwcap, large wooden barrel, €€€€€

92 Grauburgunder * Ried Kranachberg 2018

90 Weißburgunder * 2022
12 Vol.-%, screwcap, steel tank, €€

89 Weißburgunder * Gamlitz 2020

WEINGUT WRUSS
8462 Gamlitz
Kranach 74
T: +43 (664) 2029078
post@weingut-wruss.at
www.weingut-wruss.at

Winemaker/Contact:
Johannes Wruss
Production: 46,667 bottles
90 % white, 10 % rosé, 7 hectares
Certified: Sustainable Austria
Fairs: VieVinum, DAC-Presentations
Distribution partners: DE

Katharina and Johannes Wruss

* Südsteiermark DAC

EWALD ZWEYTICK WEIN
8461 Ratsch an der Weinstraße
Ratsch an der Weinstraße 102
T: +43 (664) 2109189
office@ewaldzweytick.at
www.ewaldzweytick.at

Winemaker/Contact:
Ewald Zweytick
Production: 95 % white, 5 % rosé,
18 hectares
Fairs: VieVinum
Distribution partners: BE, DE, CH

EWALD ZWEYTICK WEIN

Ewald Zweytick is a winemaker from Ratsch in southern Styria who cultivates a total of eleven hectares of vineyards, which are divided between the sites Ried Stermetzberg, Sulz, Ried Höllriegl at the Alter Pfarrweingarten in Gamlitz and the Witscheiner Herrenberg. His main varieties are Sauvignon Blanc, Gelber Muskateller (Muscat à Petits Grains) and Weißburgunder. Furthermore, he grows Welschriesling, Chardonnay and Pinot Gris. Since 2021, he also has a Zweigelt Rosé in his repertoire. He is very passionate about his specific site wines "Don't Cry" (Sauvignon Blanc), "November Rain" (Morillon) and "Tosca" (Pinot Gris). Since 2008, he has also been dealing with intracellular fermentation - the result is his "Heaven's Door". Ewald Zweytick's work is as straightforward as his personality particularly when it comes to his favourite wine: "Everyone who knows me knows that my heart beats for Sauvignon Blanc in general. Even though these wines are generally drunk young, it is my objective to produce long-lived, full-bodied wines.".

96 Sauvignon Blanc * Ried Stermetzberg Heaven's Door 2020
13,5 Vol.-%, cork, barrique, €€€€€€

98 Sauvignon Blanc * Ried Stermetzberg Heaven's Door 2019
Bright medium greenish yellow, silver glints. Scented hints of lychee with mint and lemon balm, white currant, as well as red berry notes, as well as floral-ethereal undertones. Taut, tightly woven, white tropical fruit, seemingly light, saline, persistent, lovely freshness, excellent length. Elegant style, already accessible, assured potential for development.

95 Sauvignon Blanc * Heaven's Door interzellulär 2018

95 Sauvignon Blanc * Ried Stermetzberg Don't Cry 2020
14 Vol.-%, cork, barrique, €€€€€€

95 Sauvignon Blanc * Ried Stermetzberg Don't Cry 2019

94 Sauvignon Blanc * Don't Cry 2018

SÜDSTEIERMARK DAC

94 Sauvignon Blanc * Gamlitz Ried Höllriegl
am Alten Pfarrweingarten 2021
13,5 Vol.-%, screwcap, large wooden barrel, €€€€€
94 Sauvignon Blanc * Gamlitz Ried Höllriegl
am Alten Pfarrweingarten 2020
93 Sauvignon Blanc * Gamlitz Ried Höllriegl
am Alten Pfarrweingarten 2019

94 Sauvignon Blanc * Ried Sulz 2021
14,5 Vol.-%, cork, oak barrel, €€€€€€

93 Sauvignon Blanc * Ehrenhausen 2021
13,5 Vol.-%, screwcap, steel tank, €€€€€
93 Sauvignon Blanc * Ehrenhausen 2020
92 Sauvignon Blanc * Ehrenhausen 2019

92 Sauvignon Blanc * 2022
13 Vol.-%, screwcap, steel tank, €€€
92 Sauvignon Blanc * 2021
92 Sauvignon Blanc * 2018

94 Sauvignon Blanc Ried Witscheiner
Herrenberg M Provocateur 2017
13,5 Vol.-%, cork, 500-l-barrel, €€€€€€
94 Sauvignon Blanc Ried Witscheiner
Herrenberg 2016

95 Chardonnay * Ried Stermetzberg
November Rain 2020
13 Vol.-%, cork, barrique, €€€€€€
94 Chardonnay * Ried Stermetzberg
November Rain 2019
Bright golden yellow, silver reflections. An exotic bouquet with notes of fine nougat, a touch of fresh guava, hints of yellow tropical fruit, soft notes of lychee and blossom honey. Juicy, powerful, fresh quince, subtle wood spice, mineral and persistent, with very good length, subtle caramel on the finish.
95 Chardonnay * November Rain 2018

92 Chardonnay * Ehrenhausen 2021
13 Vol.-%, screwcap, large wooden barrel, €€€€€
93 Chardonnay * Ehrenhausen 2020
92 Chardonnay * Ehrenhausen 2019

94 Grauburgunder * Ried Stermetzberg
Tosca 2020
13 Vol.-%, cork, barrique, €€€€€€
94 Grauburgunder * Ried Stermetzberg
Tosca 2019
93 Grauburgunder * Tosca 2018

93 Gelber Muskateller * Gamlitz Ried Höllriegl
am Alten Pfarrweingarten 2021
13 Vol.-%, screwcap, large wooden barrel, €€€€€
92 Gelber Muskateller * Gamlitz Ried Höllriegl
am Alten Pfarrweingarten 2020
92 Gelber Muskateller * Gamlitz Ried Höllriegl
am Alten Pfarrweingarten 2019

93 Gelber Muskateller * Ried Witscheiner
Herrenberg 2019
93 Gelber Muskateller * Ried Witscheiner
Herrenberg 2018

91 Gelber Muskateller * 2022
12 Vol.-%, screwcap, steel tank, €€€
90 Gelber Muskateller * 2021
89 Gelber Muskateller * 2020

93 Weißburgunder * Ried Sulz Witscheiner
Herrenberg Stermetzberg K3 2020
13 Vol.-%, screwcap, used barriques, €€€€€
92 Weißburgunder * Ried Sulz, Witscheiner
Herrenberg, Stermetzberg 2019

91 Weißburgunder * 2022
12,5 Vol.-%, screwcap, steel tank, €€€
92 Weißburgunder * 2021

91 Welschriesling * 2022
11 Vol.-%, screwcap, steel tank, €€
89 Welschriesling * 2021
90 Welschriesling * 2020

91 Zweigelt Rose in Spanish Harlem 2020

95 Gelber Muskateller Beerenauslese 2019

94 Sauvignon Blanc Beerenauslese 2019

* Südsteiermark DAC

The Traminerweg in Klöch, a popular destination near Bad Radkersburg

STEIERMARK
VULKANLAND STEIERMARK
DAC

Straden in the south of the wine-growing region

VOLCANIC CLIFFS, INIMITABLE WINES

Numerous little wine islands on the slopes of extinct volcanoes give the landscape of Vulkanland Steiermark a unique flair. 1,657 vineyard hectares are cultivated and the main centres are Klöch, St. Anna am Aigen and Straden.

One grape variety here has a special flair: the highly aromatic Traminer. The main point-of-sale are small, local wine taverns called Buschenschank. The many fortresses and castles perched high on basalt clifftops bear evidence that this was a heavily disputed borderland for centuries. Today, borders are open and Riegersburg, Schloss Kapfenstein and other castles offer an attractive ambience for an array of cultural and culinary events.

This wine-growing region offers an ample selection, because here there is a range of wines found in few other wine regions: Welschriesling, Morillon (Chardonnay), Weissburgunder (Pinot Blanc), Grauburgunder (Pinot Gris), Gelber Muskateller (Muscat Blanc à petits grains), the Traminer family, Sauvignon Blanc and even Riesling on the white side, complemented by interesting red wines, especially Zweigelt, but also St Laurent and Blauburgunder (Pinot Noir). All of these varieties express the unique geological conditions of the area through an inimitable spicy, mineral note.

Four wine routes lead through a charming landscape of rolling hills. A regional wine shop in St. Anna am Aigen provides an overview of the entire wine-growing area. Luxurious spas located along the volcanic fault line are popular vacation destinations. The number of ambitious young vintners

© Robert Herbst

STEIERMARK/STYRIA **VULKANLAND STEIERMARK DAC**

is growing. Most wines are sold in the numerous winery taverns of the region. The Ortsweine (local or village wines) in the new Protected Designation of Origin (DAC) come from Eastern Styria, Riegersburg, Kapfenstein, St Anna, Straden, Tieschen, Klöch, and St Peter. A special feature of the new DAC regulations is the Traminer, which, in contrast to the other grape varieties, is permitted to have residual sugar, and may be bottled as an Ortswein in Klöch also semi-dry or as a Prädikatswein (Spätlese, Auslese, Eiswein et. al.) The climate reflects the convergence of the hot, dry, Pannonian climate with humid Mediterranean influences. The vines grow in the warm earth of volcanic rock, basalt, sand, loam and weathered rock.

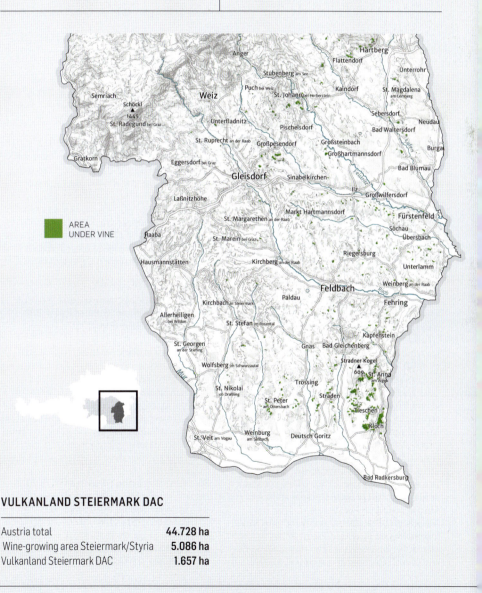

AREA UNDER VINE

VULKANLAND STEIERMARK DAC

Austria total	44.728 ha
Wine-growing area Steiermark/Styria	5.086 ha
Vulkanland Steiermark DAC	1.657 ha

SELECTED WINERIES

★★★★★
Weingut Neumeister, Straden

★★★★
Weingut Frauwallner Straden, Straden

★★★★
Josef Scharl – Charakterweine, St. Anna am Aigen

★★★
Weingut Winkler-Hermaden, Kapfenstein

WEINGUT FRAUWALLNER STRADEN

At Weingut Frauwallner, the winemaker and the wine excel together: 100% of the grapes come from the volcanic region of Styria, the vineyards are tended by hand, and each individual grape variety is vinified in its own unique way. Only wines of provenance are produced here, and Walter Frauwallner's experience and consistency result in a potpourri of individual characters that have both a clear signature and a high value of regional affiliation. "Lots of wine in the glass, the terroir clearly recognisable and always a pleasure to drink" is how the father of two sums up his philosophy, which he impressively puts into practice in three separate lines.

"Vulkanland Steiermark DAC" is the name of the wines vinified classically in steel tanks - easy to drink, but at the same time elegant and multifaceted. New in the range are the "Stradener Ortsweine" - expressive wines between regional and Riedenwein (site wines). Then there are the wines from the chalky 1STK Stradener Rosenberg, the Steintal and the basalt-influenced Altes Steinkreuz, as well as the wines from the very heart of the winery: Buch, the great STK site. These wines are profound. If you want to experience the volcanic character of Styria in a glass, these regional ambassadors are the perfect choice.

In particular, Pinot Blanc and Pinot Gris, Morillon, Sauvignon Blanc and Traminer have consolidated this family-run winery's national and international reputation. For example, 100 Falstaff points in the WeinGuide 2021/2022 for the Trockenbeerenauslese Gelber Muskateller Ried Stradener Rosenberg 2017 confirm this trend. Since 2018 the winery has been a member of "Steirische Terroir und Klassikweingüter - STK". Manual work, careful tending of the vines, quantity reduction and selective harvesting, are obligatory. Patience and time determine the development of the wines. The winery's Karbach farm shop is the perfect place to taste the wines.

97 Sauvignon Blanc * Privat 2019
13 Vol.-%, cork,screwcap, wooden barrel, €€€€€

95 Sauvignon Blanc * Straden Privat 2018

95 Sauvignon Blanc Privat 2017

(96) Sauvignon Blanc * Ried Buch GSTK 2021
13,5 Vol.-%, cork,screwcap, large wooden barrel/small wooden barrel, €€€€€

95 Sauvignon Blanc * Ried Buch GSTK 2020
Light golden yellow, silver reflections. Delicately floral, herbal spice, hints of nougat and dark berries, soft hints of candied grapefruit zest, with some mocha underpinnings. Spicy, complex, finesse-rich structure, salty-lemon, dark nougat toffee on the finish, very good length, individualistic style.

95 Sauvignon Blanc * Ried Buch GSTK 2019

94 Sauvignon Blanc * Ried Stradener Rosenberg 1STK 2021
13 Vol.-%, screwcap, steel tank, €€€€

93 Sauvignon Blanc * Ried Stradener Rosenberg 1 STK 2019

VULKANLAND STEIERMARK DAC

WEINGUT FRAUWALLNER STRADEN
8345 Straden
Karbach 7
T: +43 (3473) 7137
weingut@frauwallner.com
www.frauwallner.com

Winemaker/Contact:
Walter Frauwallner
Production: 90 % white, 4 % rosé, 4 % red, 2 % sweet, 30 hectares
Certified: Sustainable Austria
Fairs: Austrian Tasting London, ÖGW Zürich, ProWein Düsseldorf, VieVinum, DAC-Presentations
Distribution partners: DE, NL, PL, CH, USA

Walter and Petra Frauwallner

94   Sauvignon Blanc * Ried Stradner Rosenberg 1 STK 2018

94   Sauvignon Blanc * Ried Steintal 2018
93   Sauvignon Blanc Ried Steintal 2017

(93) Sauvignon Blanc * Straden 2022
13 Vol.-%, screwcap, steel tank/large wooden barrel, €€€€
93   Sauvignon Blanc * Straden 2021
92   Sauvignon Blanc * Straden 2020

91   Sauvignon Blanc * 2022
12,5 Vol.-%, screwcap, steel tank, €€€
92   Sauvignon Blanc * 2021
91   Sauvignon Blanc * 2020

(95) Morillon * Ried Buch GSTK 2021
13,5 Vol.-%, cork,screwcap, large wooden barrel/small wooden barrel, €€€€€
95   Morillon * Ried Buch GSTK 2020
Light golden yellow, silver reflections. Delicate nougat, fine caramel, ripe yellow tropical fruit, nuances of tangerine zest. Juicy, elegant, fine nuances of white fruit, a touch of vine peach, fine spice from the basalt, saline finish, fresh and persistent, certain ageing potential.
94   Morillon * Ried Buch GSTK 2019

(92) Morillon * Straden 2022
13,5 Vol.-%, screwcap, steel tank/large wooden barrel, €€€€
93   Morillon * Straden 2021

92   Morillon * Straden 2020

91   Morillon * 2022
13 Vol.-%, screwcap, steel tank, €€€
92   Morillon * 2021
91   Morillon * 2020

(94) Traminer * Ried Stradener Rosenberg 1STK 2022
14 Vol.-%, screwcap, steel tank/large wooden barrel, €€€€
94   Traminer * Ried Stradener Rosenberg 2021
94   Traminer * Ried Stradener Rosenberg 2020

(94) Weißburgunder * Ried Buch GSTK 2021
13,5 Vol.-%, cork,screwcap, large wooden barrel/small wooden barrel, €€€€€
94   Weißburgunder * Ried Buch GSTK 2020
93   Weißburgunder * Ried Buch GSTK 2019

93   Weißburgunder * Straden 2021
92   Weißburgunder * Straden 2018

91   Weißburgunder * 2022
12,5 Vol.-%, screwcap, steel tank, €€
92   Weißburgunder * 2021
90   Weißburgunder * 2020

94   Grauburgunder * Ried Stradener Rosenberg 1STK 2021
13,5 Vol.-%, screwcap, large wooden barrel, €€€€€

STEIERMARK/STYRIA

93 Grauburgunder * Ried Stradener Rosenberg 1STK 2020	89 Welschriesling * 2020
94 Grauburgunder * Ried Stradener Rosenberg 1STK 2019	90 Welschriesling * 2019
	100 Gelber Muskateller Essenz 2017
(92) Grauer Burgunder * Straden 2022	98 Sauvignon Blanc Ried Stradener Rosenberg TBA Essenz 2017
13,5 Vol.-%, screwcap, large wooden barrel, €€€€	5 Vol.-%, screwcap, steel tank, €€€€€
92 Grauburgunder * Straden 2021	96 Sauvignon Blanc TBA 2017
92 Grauburgunder * Straden 2020	
	96 Traminer Ried Stradener Rosenberg TBA 2017
91 Gelber Muskateller * 2021	97 Morillon TBA Ried Buch 2017
92 Gelber Muskateller * 2020	
91 Gelber Muskateller * 2019	96 Weissburgunder TBA Ried Buch 2017
90 Welschriesling * 2022	95 Sämling Ried Buch TBA 2018
11,5 Vol.-%, screwcap, steel tank, €€	

★★★★★

WEINGUT NEUMEISTER

ORGANIC

Christoph Neumeister is the third generation to run Weingut Neumeister in Straden. His approach to viticulture and winemaking and his quest for wine quality are fine-tuned.

At a time when very often the loudest or shrillest wines are catapulted into the limelight, he consciously pursues a long-term, holistic and painstaking approach in order to vinify elegant wines characterised by inner calm and complexity yet are still animating and satisfyingly profound.

Situated in the volcanic region of Styria in south-eastern Austria, Straden is characterised by an Illyrian-Pannonian climate, with warm days and cool nights, and ample rainfall - an average of 900 millimetres a year - to ensure a long growing season and late harvest. In this challenging climatic environment, 31 hectares are cultivated, distributed among countless small vineyards on steep slopes. The geology of these vineyards is characterised by limestone-rich sedimentary soils from two distinct origins: sandstone and shell limestone, formed from a tidal flat sea, and Sarmatian gravel, which was deposited here in the Tertiary Period originating from the Alps. Many of these vineyards have reached an age of 40 years and more and are partly still single-pole training systems, which means laborious manual work. In addition, all vineyards have been farmed organically since 2013. The result of careful manual harvesting, extended maceration periods, gentle and slow ageing in the cellar, spontaneous fermentation, long yeast contact times and late bottling are well-structured and elegant wines with a high degree of complexity and distinct origins.

The winery's premium vineyards are "Saziani" and "Moarfeitl" (GSTK) and "Klausen" and "Steintal" (1STK aka). The family runs the restaurant "Saziani Stub'n" and the boutique hotel "Schlafgut Saziani" in the immediate vicinity of the winery. Christoph Neumeister was awarded the "Falstaff Winemaker of the Year" title in June 2019 at the Hofburg in Vienna.

98 Sauvignon Blanc * Alte Reben 2020
13,5 Vol.-%, cork, large wooden barrel, €€€€€€

97 Sauvignon Blanc * Alte Reben 2019
Medium yellow-green, silver glints. Delicate cassis aroma, soft notions of yellow tropical fruit, nuances of peach and mango, a hint of meadow herbs, and dark minerality, superseded by background notes of peppermint and lemon balm. Complex and succulent, nuances of white fruit, silky, elegant texture, and finely structured marked by resonating lime nuances. Excellent length and enormous ageing potential.

98 Sauvignon Blanc * Alte Reben 2018

VULKANLAND STEIERMARK DAC

97 Sauvignon Blanc * Ried Moarfeitl GSTK 2021
13 Vol.-%, cork, large wooden barrel, €€€€€€ Ⓑ Ⓥ
95 Sauvignon Blanc * Ried Moarfeitl GSTK 2020
97 Sauvignon Blanc * Ried Moarfeitl GSTK 2019

95 Sauvignon Blanc * Ried Klausen 1STK 2021
13 Vol.-%, cork, large wooden barrel, €€€€ Ⓑ Ⓥ
94 Sauvignon Blanc * Ried Klausen 1STK 2020
94 Sauvignon Blanc * Ried Klausen 1STK 2019

(93) Sauvignon Blanc * Straden 2022
12,5 Vol.-%, screwcap, large wooden barrel/steel tank, €€€€ Ⓑ Ⓥ
93 Sauvignon Blanc * Straden 2021
94 Sauvignon Blanc * Straden 2020

97 Morillon * Ried Moarfeitl GSTK 2021
13,5 Vol.-%, cork, wooden barrel, €€€€€ Ⓑ Ⓥ
95 Morillon * Ried Moarfeitl GSTK 2020
Light yellow-green, silver reflections. Fresh yellow tropical fruit, a touch of mango, fine apple touch, underlaid with a touch of nougat, some pineapple. Full-bodied, nuances of white stone fruit, fine acidity, juicy, a hint of kumquats, taut, fine lemony notes on the finish, good length, already very drinkable, a finesse-rich food wine.
96 Morillon * Ried Moarfeitl GSTK 2019

93 Morillon * Straden 2021
93 Morillon * Straden 2020
92 Morillon * Straden 2019

95 Grauburgunder * Ried Saziani GSTK 2021
13,5 Vol.-%, cork, large wooden barrel, €€€€€ Ⓑ Ⓥ
94 Grauburgunder * Ried Saziani GSTK 2020
Light yellow-green, silver reflections. Fine yellow pear fruit, tobacco, subtle herbal spice, a hint of mango, nuances of orange zest, multi-faceted bouquet. Taut, white stone fruit, a touch of caramel, fine acidity, mineral, harmonious, seems light on its feet, a fine table wine.
95 Grauburgunder * Ried Saziani GSTK 2019

(93) Grauburgunder * Straden 2022
13 Vol.-%, screwcap, large wooden barrel/steel tank, €€€€ Ⓑ Ⓥ
93 Grauburgunder * Straden 2021
93 Grauburgunder * Straden 2020

95 Traminer * Ried Steintal 1STK 2021
13 Vol.-%, cork, large wooden barrel, €€€€€ Ⓑ Ⓥ
94 Roter Traminer * Ried Steintal 1STK 2020
94 Roter Traminer * Ried Steintal 1STK 2019

94 Weißburgunder * Ried Klausen 1STK 2021
13 Vol.-%, cork, large wooden barrel, €€€€€ Ⓑ Ⓥ

WEINGUT NEUMEISTER
8345 Straden
Kronnersdorf 147
T: +43 (3473) 8308
weingut@neumeister.cc
www.neumeister.cc

Winemaker/Contact:
Christoph Neumeister
Production: 92 % white, 7 % red, 1 % sweet, 31+4 hectares
Fairs: ProWein Düsseldorf, VieVinum, MondoVino
Distribution partners: BE, DE, UK, IT, NL, NO, PL, RUS, SE, CH, SK, CZ, USA

93 Weißburgunder * Ried Klausen 1STK 2020
93 Weißburgunder * Ried Klausen 1STK 2019

(93) Weißburgunder * Straden 2022
12,5 Vol.-%, screwcap, steel tank/large wooden barrel, €€€ Ⓑ Ⓥ
92 Weißburgunder * 2021
92 Weißburgunder * 2020

(92) Gelber Muskateller * Straden 2022
12 Vol.-%, screwcap, steel tank, €€€ Ⓑ Ⓥ
92 Gelber Muskateller * 2021
92 Gelber Muskateller * 2020

91 Welschriesling * 2021
91 Welschriesling * 2020
92 Welschriesling * 2019

92 Gemischter Satz Sarmat 2022
12 Vol.-%, screwcap, large wooden barrel/steel tank, €€€ Ⓑ Ⓥ
91 Gemischter Satz 2021
91 Gemischter Satz 2020

92 Cuvée de Merin 2019 ZW/ME
92 Cuvée de Merin 2018 ZW/ME

90 Pinot Noir 2019
91 Pinot Noir 2018

* Vulkanland Steiermark DAC

★★★★

JOSEF SCHARL – CHARAKTERWEINE

It takes a special kind of stubbornness to succeed: to do what you think is right, without pretence, but with great freedom. Josef Scharl refers to this as having character and not conforming, not adapting too much and yet not being too demanding. Generous is perhaps the word that best describes him. His wines are a reflection of his character and his way of doing things, an expression of his art.

Josef Scharl has always known what he wanted to do: live for his region, for his family, for sparkling wine and for Pinot Noir. Of course, he also likes all the other varieties in his cellar, but Pinot is his benchmark. "If you want to make wine," says Josef Scharl, "you have to listen, feel, see and find your inner self - and then do it with all the passion you can muster. The way he does this is deeply connected to the region. He's been to France, watched the idols at work, drunk their wines and then returned home to his wines. The best way to understand Josef Scharl is to meet him on-site. With grand gestures, he describes the view over St. Anna, a truly unique piece of land. A unique microclimate: humidity, cool nights, and barren volcanic soil. You taste it and you love it. There are favourite vineyards and favourite wines. "Wines are complex entities; that's what they have in common with us humans. They combine different, sometimes even contradictory characteristics, and the conformist fights against the desire for freedom and light against darkness. Diversity is important; it shapes character and therefore uniqueness," he concludes. "Because life is constantly evolving.

And what about the symbolic cap? There is a place far away from St. Anna am Aigen, somewhere abroad in the Basque country. In the coastal town of Saint-Jean-de-Luz, in a small street called Rue Loquin, the "Béret Basque" was born. For Josef Scharl, this was the birthplace of his passion for caps. He now has an innumerable collection of them.

They have become Josef's trademark in all colours and patterns. No wonder they also adorn the bottles. He's unmistakable from afar!

92 ❂ Souvignier Gris Sekt Austria Reserve brut Steiermark g.U. 2019

92 ❂ Souvignier Gris Sekt g.U. brut Reserve 2018

92 ❂ Souvignier Gris Sekt g.U. brut Reserve 2017

94 Chardonnay * Ried Schemming G-Eruption 2020
13 Vol.-%, DIAM, large wooden barrel, €€€€€

94 Chardonnay * Ried Schemming G-Eruption 2019
Medium greenish yellow, silver reflections. Delicate blossom honey, a bit of caramel, mango and quince jelly, underpinned with roasted aromas, multi-faceted bouquet. Good complexity, juicy, well-integrated acidity, tight-knit, salty, passion fruit on the finish, mineral-citrus echo, good ageing potential.

94 Chardonnay * Ried Schemming G-Eruption 2018

93 Chardonnay * Ried Annaberg 1-Eruption 2020
13 Vol.-%, DIAM, large wooden barrel, €€€€€

93 Chardonnay * Ried Annaberg Alte Reben 1-Eruption 2018

92 Chardonnay Ried Annaberg Alte Reben 2017

91 Chardonnay * St. Anna am Aigen 2021
12,5 Vol.-%, screwcap, large wooden barrel, €€€€

92 Chardonnay * St. Anna am Aigen 2020

91 Chardonnay * 2020
91 Chardonnay * 2019
91 Chardonnay * Klassik 2018

94 Sauvignon Blanc * Ried Schemming G-Eruption Auron 2020
13 Vol.-%, DIAM, large wooden barrel, €€€€€

VULKANLAND STEIERMARK DAC

JOSEF SCHARL – CHARAKTERWEINE
8354 Sankt Anna am Aigen
Plesch 1
T: +43 (3158) 2314
josef@weinhof-scharl.at
www.weinhof-scharl.at

Winemaker/Contact:
Josef Scharl jr.
Production: 80 % white, 19 % red, 1 % sweet, 20+5 hectares
Certified: Sustainable Austria
Fairs: VieVinum
Distribution partners: DE

Josef Scharl and Sophie Kirchner

95 Sauvignon Blanc * Ried Schemming G-Eruption Auron 2019
Bright golden yellow, silver reflections. Delicate herbal notes, ripe apple fruit, papaya echo, a bit of wood tobacco spice, candied tangerine zest, inviting fruity bouquet. Good complexity, fresh and lively acidity, fine spice, white tropical fruit, powerful finish, good persistency, mineral aftertaste, definite ageing potential.

93 Sauvignon Blanc * Ried Schemming Auron 2018

93 Sauvignon Blanc * Ried Annaberg Mond Reserve 2017

94 Sauvignon Blanc Ried Annaberg Mond 2015

92 Sauvignon Blanc * St. Anna am Aigen 2020
92 Sauvignon Blanc * St. Anna am Aigen 2019

93 Weißburgunder * Ried Annaberg 1-Eruption 2019
13 Vol.-%, DIAM, large wooden barrel, €€€€€

94 Chardonnay * Ried Annaberg 1-Eruption Alte Reben 2019
92 Weißburgunder * Ried Annaberg 1-Eruption Alte Reben 2018

91 Weißburgunder * 2020
90 Weißburgunder * 2019

90 Weißburgunder * St. Anna am Aigen 2020

92 Gelber Muskateller * Ried Annaberg 2021
12 Vol.-%, screwcap, steel tank, €€€
90 Gelber Muskateller * Ried Annaberg 2020
93 Gelber Muskateller * Ried Annaberg 2019

93 Gewürztraminer 2019
92 Gewürztraminer Ried Annaberg 2018

92 Eruption Rot 2019 ZW/BW/ME
13 Vol.-%, DIAM, small wooden barrel, €€€€
91 Eruption Rot 2018 ZW/BW
92 Eruption Rot 2017 ZW/BW

93 Welschriesling Eiswein Early Bird 2020
8 Vol.-%, DIAM, small wooden barrel, €€€€€€

* Vulkanland Steiermark DAC

STEIERMARK/STYRIA

★★★
WEINGUT WINKLER-HERMADEN
ORGANIC

The Winkler-Hermaden winery is located in south-eastern Styria, in the heart of the Styrian volcanic region, just a few kilometres from the Slovenian and Hungarian borders. The winery has been a family business since 1918. Regionality, sustainability and hospitality are the focus of the winery, hotel and restaurant .

Of the 37 hectares of organic vineyards (Ried Kirchleiten, Ried Schlosskogel, Ried Rosenleiten, Ried Winzerkogel), about 25 hectares are located around the Kapfensteiner Kogel and 12 hectares in Klöch and some 15 kilometres to the south (Ried Ölberg, Ried Hochwarth, Ried Grafenstückl). The winemaking is focused on terroir-accentuated, multilayered and mineral wines with a long ripening period. The practice: Selective hand harvesting, gentle processing of the grapes and as little intervention as possible in the subsequent ageing of the wines. The aim is to express the typical character of the soils and varieties in the wines.

The estate has been organically farmed since 2009, and the first certified organic harvest was pressed in 2012. Since 2022, the winery has been committed to organic regenerative agriculture. This involves redressing nutrient imbalances and building up humus and soil life. The vineyards are permanently covered with vegetation, natural pest control is encouraged, and the soil is fertilised with organic compost. The wood from which the small oak barrels are made comes from the family's forest on the Kapfensteiner Kogel.

The castle and the old wine cellars have a long history dating back to the 11th century. Another cellar, the Lange Keller, was renovated between 1996 and 1998. Red wine is now stored in small oak barrels in the 60 metre long, 350 year old vaulted cellar.

90 ❂ Pinot brut - blanc de noir 2017
12,5 Vol.-%, cork, bottle fermentation, €€€€ Ⓑ Ⓥ

92 ❂ Pinot Brut Sekt g.U. Reserve 2017 SL/PN
91 ❂ Pinot Brut Sekt g.U. Reserve 2015 SL/PN

90 ❂ Muscaris Pet Nat 2021
90 ❂ Pet Nat 2020

(93) Sauvignon Blanc * Kapfenstein
Ried Kirchleiten GSTK 2020
13,5 Vol.-%, glass, large wooden barrel, €€€€€ Ⓑ Ⓥ

93 Sauvignon Blanc * Kapfenstein
Ried Kirchleiten GSTK 2019
Medium yellow-green, silver reflections. Delicately floral, hints of acacia and lime blossom, dark savouriness, notes of apple peel, fine nougat tone. Complex, fine notes of yellow fruit, some mango, fine oak nuances, salty touch on the finish, lemon on the back palate.

93 Sauvignon Blanc *
Ried Kapfensteiner Kirchleiten GSTK 2018

93 Sauvignon Blanc * Klöch
Ried Hochwarth 2019

93 Sauvignon Blanc * Ried Klöcher Hochwarth 2018

90 Sauvignon Blanc * 2020
12,5 Vol.-%, screwcap, steel tank, €€€ Ⓑ Ⓥ

90 Sauvignon Blanc * 2019

90 Sauvignon Blanc * Kapfenstein 2020
92 Sauvignon Blanc * Kapfenstein 2019

93 Grauburgunder * Kapfenstein
Ried Schlosskogel 1STK 2020
13 Vol.-%, glass, barrique, €€€€€ Ⓑ Ⓥ

94 Grauburgunder * Ried Kapfensteiner Schlosskogel 1STK 2019

94 Grauburgunder * Ried Kapfensteiner Schlosskogel 1STK 2018

93 Traminer * Kapfenstein
Ried Kirchleiten GSTK 2020
13 Vol.-%, glass, barrique, €€€€€ Ⓑ Ⓥ

93 Roter Traminer * Kapfenstein
Ried Kirchleiten GSTK 2019
Medium yellow-green, silver reflections. Floral touch, a hint of marshmallow paste, delicate tropical fruit, inviting bouquet. Elegant, delicate notes of nut, dusty-dry style, mineral, salty echo, shows rather medium length at the moment, a touch of rancio on the finish.

© SOPHIE KIRCHNER

VULKANLAND STEIERMARK DAC

WEINGUT WINKLER-HERMADEN
8353 Kapfenstein
Kapfenstein 106
T: +43 (3157) 2322
weingut@winkler-hermaden.at
www.winkler-hermaden.at

Winemaker: Thomas Winkler-Hermaden
Contact: Georg and Christof Winkler-Hermaden
Production: 200,000 bottles 54 % white, 45 % red, 1 % sweet, 37 hectares
Certified: Sustainable Austria 🌿
Fairs: VieVinum
Distribution partners: DE, NL, CH, USA

Grauburgunder

93 Traminer * Ried Kirchleiten GSTK Kapfenstein 2018

92 Gewürztraminer * Klöch 2020
92 Gelber Traminer * Klöch 2019

92 Gewürztraminer Ried Klöcher Oelberg 2017

90 Gewürztraminer Orange 2018
13,5 Vol.-%, glass, steel tank/500-l-barrel, €€€€€ Ⓑ Ⓥ

92 Morillon * Kapfenstein Ried Rosenleiten 1STK 2020
13 Vol.-%, glass, 500-l-barrel, €€€€ Ⓑ Ⓥ
93 Morillon * Kapfenstein Ried Rosenleiten 1STK 2019
93 Morillon * Ried Kapfensteiner Rosenleiten 1STK 2018

91 Morillon * Kapfenstein 2020
92 Morillon * Kapfenstein 2019
92 Morillon * Kapfenstein 2018

91 Riesling * Klöch 2019

89 Muscaris 2020
90 Muscaris 2019

93 Hermada 2017 CS/ME/PN

93 Blauer Zweigelt Olivin Reserve 2017
13,5 Vol.-%, glass, barrique, €€€€€ Ⓑ Ⓥ

(90) Blauer Zweigelt Olivin 2020
14 Vol.-%, glass, small wooden barrel, €€€€€ Ⓑ Ⓥ
92 Blauer Zweigelt Olivin 2019
93 Zweigelt Olivin 2018

88 Pinot Noir Reserve 2018

95 Gewürztraminer Klöch TBA 2018

94 Welschriesling TBA 2018

93 Riesling Grafenschatz aus eingetrockneten Trauben 2021 Ⓑ Ⓥ

The Hochgrail in West Styria's Schilcherland

STEIERMARK/STYRIA

WEST-STEIERMARK

DAC

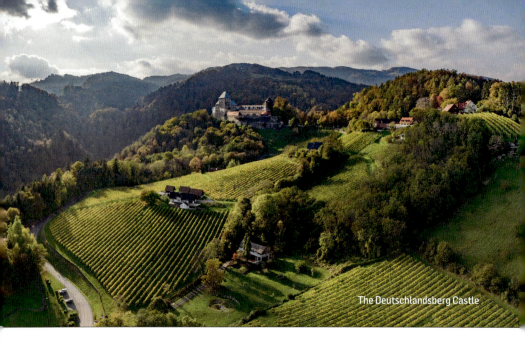

The Deutschlandsberg Castle

HOME OF SCHILCHER

Only around 640 hectares are planted with vines in Western Styria, but vintner families produce an astounding array of products: racy, tart Schilcher, powerful, tannic red wines and elegant, charming sparkling wines. All of these wines are made from a single, rare grape variety – Blauer Wildbacher. Since the 2018 vintage, Western Styria has joined the big DAC Protected Designation of Origin family in Austria.

Styria's smallest wine-growing area, Western Styria, is also where the ancient Illyrians, Celts, and Romans cultivated vines. The vineyards cover a long, narrow band climbing up to 600 metres a.s.l. (1,790 ft.) along the foothills of the Koralpe, the Reinischkogel and southward to the Slovenian border. This aspect provides protection from raw winds and rapid warming during the day. The road from Ligist in the north over St. Stefan ob Stainz and on to Deutschlandsberg and Eibischwald crosses deep valleys and travels along steep vineyard slopes dotted with quaint, tiny cellar huts. Side jaunts to the pretty wine villages Greisdorf, Gundersdorf, Wildbach and Wies offer surprising perspectives – not only panoramic views, but wine insights.

The geology of this region is unusual, comprising crystalline consolidated rocks consisting of hard, platy gneisses. Equally unique is the climate, which is described as Illyrian, a meeting of warm, humid Mediterranean influences and warm air masses from southeast Europe. The interplay of these conditions is just one explanation for the inimitable wine styles that are produced here. Western Styria is the classic "Schilcherland", a highly specialized wine-growing area with an incredible success story. The great share of its vineyards are planted with Blauer Wildbacher, an ancient variety from which pink to onion skin-coloured rosé wines are made. This was originally a rustic farm wine with aggressive acidity, but it has metamorphosed

© WSNA

STEIERMARK/STYRIA **WESTSTEIERMARK DAC**

through continuous quality improvements in the hands of ambitious vintners to become a highly sought-after beverage. New styles made from this autochthonous variety range from crisp, fruity aperitif wines to refined sweet wines and elegant sparkling wines. The red wine versions should also not be underestimated; their highly individual style enriches the terroir wine sector in Austria. Schilcher also plays a significant role in the success of wine tourism and is only permitted to carry the DAC label in Western Styria. The premiere for the Gebietswein (regional wine) will be on the 1st of December after the harvest; Ortsweine (village wines) are allowed to come from Ligist, Eibischwal, Stainz or Deutschlandsberg. Alongside Schilcher almost all of the other Styrian grape varieties are cultivated, each worthy of discovery.

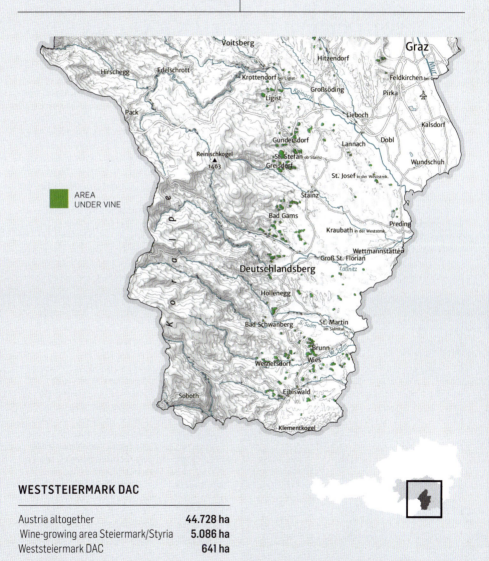

WESTSTEIERMARK DAC

Austria altogether	44.728 ha
Wine-growing area Steiermark/Styria	5.086 ha
Weststeiermark DAC	641 ha

STEIERMARK

SELECTED WINERIES

★★★
Weingut Lex Langmann, Sankt Stefan ob Stainz

★★
Weingut Reiterer, Wies

★★★

WEINGUT LEX LANGMANN

A picturesque undulating landscape in the heart of western Styria, as far as the eye can see - where Stefan and Daniela Langmann are based. This is the perfect holiday location for some, but for the Langmanns, this is where they create fresh wines full of finesse.

The star grape variety is the Blauer Wildbacher, from which the rare varietal speciality Schilcher is produced. But also Sauvignon Blanc, Gelber Muskateller, and many other varieties find an ideal environment in this region. The winemaking couple takes great care to express the unmistakable taste of the wine's origin, the terroir - with remarkable success, as the wines are in demand worldwide. The dedication and attentiveness with which they care for their vineyards also contribute to this success. The unique area is enhanced by a glorious habitat of colourful flora and fauna, abundant wild herbs, and rare bird species.

The winery is also renowned for its sparkling wines. Whether refreshing Schilchersekt, trendy Pet Nat, elegant Blanc de Blancs, or Brut Rosé: Stefan and Daniela Langmann's collection most definitely creates an explosion of sparkling delights.

Anyone who has the opportunity to visit the winery should combine this with a visit to the adjoining Buschenschank (tavern), where one can try the wines and taste the homemade delicacies and, of course, admire the breathtaking landscape adorned with grapevines.

Stefan and Verena Langmann

WEINGUT LEX LANGMANN
8511 Sankt Stefan ob Stainz
Langegg an der Schilcherstraße 23
T: +43 (3463) 6100
office@weingut-langmann.at
www.weingut-langmann.at

Winemaker/Contact:
Stefan Langmann
Production: 35 hectares
Certified: Sustainable Austria
Fairs: Austrian Tasting London, ProWein Düsseldorf, Tag des Steirischen Weines im Museumsquartier, VieVinum, DAC-Presentations
Distribution partners: DE, UK, JP, NO, CH, USA

WESTSTEIERMARK DAC

93 ❂ Sekt Austria Große Reserve Extra Brut Steiermark g.U. Stainz 2018 WB/CH
12,5 Vol.-%, cork, bottle fermentation, €€€€€ ⓥ

93 ❂ Sekt Austria Große Reserve extra brut 2017 CH/SB
12 Vol.-%, cork, bottle fermentation, €€€€€

92 ❂ Blanc de Blancs brut Sekt g.U. Reserve 2015

92 ❂ Muskateller Sekt Brut 2015

90 ❂ Schilcher Sekt Austria Reserve Rosé brut Steiermark g.U.
12,5 Vol.-%, cork, bottle fermentation, €€€€€ ⓥ

92 ❂ Brut Rosé Sekt Austria Reserve Steiermark g.U. 2020

91 ❂ Schilcher Sekt g.U. Reserve Steiermark Rosé brut 2015

91 ❂ Schilcher Sekt Austria brut
12 Vol.-%, cork, bottle fermentation, steel tank, €€€

92 ❂ Schilcher brut Sekt NV

91 ❂ Blauer Wildbacher brut nature Pet Nat 2019

90 ❂ Schilcher Frizzante 2015
90 ❂ Schilcher brut Frizzante NV

93 Sauvignon Blanc * Ried Greisdorf Himmelreich 2020
14 Vol.-%, cork, barrique, €€€€€ ⓥ

93 Sauvignon Blanc * Ried Greisdorf Himmelreich 2019
Pale golden yellow, silver reflections. Fine oak savouriness, delicate hints of nougat, nuances of ripe cassis, underpinned with yellow tropical fruit, multi-faceted bouquet. Powerful, juicy, a hint of coconut and caramel, fresh acidity, salty and lasting, a sturdy food companion with further certain ageing potential.

(92) Sauvignon Blanc * Ried Greisdorf 2021
13,5 Vol.-%, cork, large wooden barrel, €€€€ ⓥ

92 Sauvignon Blanc * Ried Greisdorf 2020
93 Sauvignon Blanc * Ried Greisdorf 2019

91 Sauvignon Blanc * Stainz 2021
13,5 Vol.-%, screwcap, steel tank, €€€ ⓥ

91 Sauvignon Blanc * Stainz 2019
91 Sauvignon Blanc * Stainzer 2018

91 Weißburgunder * Ried Greisdorf 2021
12,5 Vol.-%, cork, small wooden barrel, €€€€ ⓥ

91 Weißburgunder * Ried Greisdorf 2020
Light yellow gold, silver reflections. Fine ripe pear fruit, a

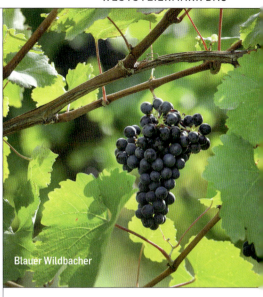

Blauer Wildbacher

touch of light nougat, soft notes of figs, some peach. Juicy, elegant, white stone fruit, fine acidity, mineral aftertaste, lemony touch on the finish, a versatile food wine.

90 Riesling * Ried Hochgrail 2021
13 Vol.-%, cork, wooden barrel, €€€€ ⓥ

89 Riesling * Ried Hochgrail 2020

90 Gelber Muskateller * Ried Greisdorf 2018

93 Schilcher * Ried Hochgrail Sonnenhang 2021
13,5 Vol.-%, cork, used barriques, €€€€€ ⓥ

92 Schilcher * Ried Hochgrail 2022
13 Vol.-%, screwcap, steel tank, €€€ ⓥ

92 Schilcher * Ried Hochgrail 2019
91 Schilcher * Ried Hochgrail 2018

92 Schilcher * Ried Hochgrail Reserve 2020
93 Schilcher * Ried Hochgrail Reserve 2019

92 Schilcher * Ried Edla 2021
12,5 Vol.-%, cork, large wooden barrel, €€€€€ ⓥ

91 Schilcher * Ried Langegg 2022

90 Schilcher * Stainz 2022
12 Vol.-%, screwcap, steel tank, €€ ⓥ

90 Schilcher * Stainz 2022

90 Schilcher * Klassik 2022

93 Gewürztraminer Beerenauslese 2017

* Weststeiermark DAC

WEINGUT REITERER

Pleasure - elegance - joie de vivre: These are the cornerstones of Christian Reiterer's sparkling wine world. He recognized early on that the Blauer Wildbacher grape, with its intense fruit and refreshing acidity, is perfect for producing sparkling wines, and was the first to press Schilcher Frizzante and Schilcher sparkling wine three decades ago. "I've always been fascinated by the Blauer Wildbacher grape and its possibilities," says Christian Reiterer, an enthusiastic rider who also sees the future for the region in this tradition: "We have unique ageing potential here with these wines, resulting from the interaction of a variety, that is exclusively from this region, with our soils and our special climate influenced by the nearby Koralpe!"

Steep sites provide the perfect amount of sunlight and the cool winds from the Koralpe ensure a particularly intense aroma development in the grapes. This benefits the Schilcher, which is pressed here classically and as a single-vineyard wine from the Lamberg and Engelweingarten monopoles, as well as the fragrant, easy-drinking white wines from Welschriesling, Morillon and Sauvignon Blanc.

93 ❂ Schilcher Sekt g. U. Reserve Engelweingarten Alte Reben Brut

91 ❂ Schilcher Rosé Extra Brut Österreichischer Sekt g. U. Steiermark Klassik NV

92 ❂ Schilcher Sekt Rosé Extra Dry
11,5 Vol.-%, cork, steel tank, €€€

91 ❂ Schilcher Sekt Extra Dry
Deep, salmon pink, copper reflections, lively mousse. Red red cherries, hints of redcurrant and strawberry confit, with background hints of lime zest. Medium bodied, red berries, racy acidity but harmoniously balanced with the fruit. Lively and lasting, ideal for enjoying on the summer terrace.

90 ❂ Rosé Schilcher Frizzante
11 Vol.-%, screwcap, bottle fermentation, steel tank, €€

90 ❂ Rosé Schilcher Frizzante

92 Sauvignon Blanc * Ried Lamberg 2021
13 Vol.-%, screwcap, large wooden barrel, €€€€

92 Sauvignon Blanc * Ried Lamberg 2018

89 Morillon * Klassik 2018

(92) Schilcher * Ried Lamberg 2022
12,5 Vol.-%, screwcap, steel tank, €€€

91 Schilcher * Ried Lamberg 2021

90 Schilcher * Ried Lamberg 2020

(91) Schilcher * Ried Engelweingarten Alte Reben 2022
12,5 Vol.-%, screwcap, steel tank, €€€

92 Schilcher * Ried Engelweingarten Alte Reben 2021

91 Schilcher * Ried Engelweingarten Alte Reben 2020

(90) Schilcher * Klassik 2022
11,5 Vol.-%, screwcap, steel tank, €€

WEINGUT REITERER
8551 Wies
Lamberg 11
T: +43 (3465) 3950
info@weingut-reiterer.com
www.weingut-reiterer.com

Winemaker/Contact:
Christian Reiterer
Production: 30 % sparkling, 10 % white, 60 % rosé, 77 hectares
Certified: Sustainable Austria
Fairs: ProWein Düsseldorf, VieVinum
Distribution partners: DE, FIN, UK, JP, LV, CH, SK

WESTSTEIERMARK DAC

SPACE FOR YOUR
WINE NOTES

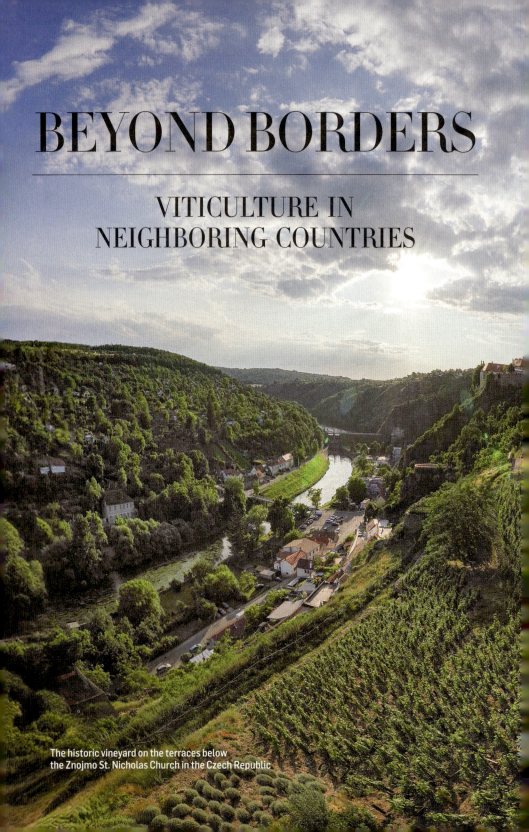

BEYOND BORDERS

VITICULTURE IN NEIGHBORING COUNTRIES

The historic vineyard on the terraces below
the Znojmo St. Nicholas Church in the Czech Republic

St.-Anna-Church, Vidošiči near Metlika, Slovenia

A VISIT TO NEIGHBOURING WINEGROWERS

Austria has a long tradition of ties with the wine-growing regions of neighbouring countries, dating back to the days of the imperial and royal monarchy. Today we are reviving these ties, which were severed by the Iron Curtain in the post-war period, by showcasing worthy wineries from Czech Republic, Hungary, Slovenia, Slovakia, and Liechtenstein.

There have been many requests for the Falstaff Wine Guide to feature wineries producing excellent wines across the borders. Until last year, it was a matter of space rather than desire that prevented this idea from being taken up. When the idea of creating a wine guide for Italy, as well as Germany and Switzerland, was realised, the South Tyrol section, which was previously part of the Austria guide, was naturally included. And so the opportunity arose to offer interested and interesting wineries from the other neighbouring countries the chance to participate. Last year's inaugural edition received very positive feedback from our readers, and this year a number of new wineries have submitted their wines for evaluation. Of course, we can only offer recommendations and not a comprehensive presentation of a large wine-producing nation like Hungary or the diverse range of wines offered by winemakers from Slovenia and Slovakia. The selection of wineries is limited, but we hope that this exciting chapter will grow over the next few years and we will be able to introduce you to a much larger number of wineries from our neighbouring countries.

CZECH REPUBLIC

Our northern neighbour has a winemaking tradition stretching back more than a thousand years. Today, Bohemia's wine-growing regions lie on the banks of the River Labe (Germany's Elbe) and its tributaries the Vltava and Berounka, with the main area of cultivation between Melnik (Mělník) and Litoměřice, and sporadically near Most in the flatter North Bohemian Basin. The wine-growing areas in Moravia are far more important, where around 96 per cent of Czech wine production is concentrated on some 17,000 hectares of vineyards. There are four sub-regions: Znojmo, Mikulov, Velké Pavlovice and Moravian Slovakia. Since the late 2000s, a new appellation-based system has been introduced in parallel with the origin, composition and quality attributes. Twelve different VOCs (wines of original certification) are currently in use. The most important white varieties are Pinot Gris, Riesling and Chardonnay, while Pinot Noir, Blaufränkisch and Zweigelt dominate the red varieties.

HUNGARY

Hungary was once a world wine power, but the country's winemakers fell on hard times. It is only since 1989 that the industry has been slowly recovering and, thanks to a great deal of private investment, is gradually returning to its former glory. There is certainly no shortage of quality potential in this truly blessed wine country with its 22 wine regions. Hungary is endowed with the best conditions for viticulture in many places, with vineyards spread across the country: from the north, with its partly volcanic soils and the influence of Lake Neusiedl, to the vast Lake Balaton and the Mediterranean south, with its many sand, loess and clay soils. Hungary boasts a large number of indigenous grape varieties, notably Furmint and Hárslevelü, from which the legendary Tokaj is made. Interesting dry and semi-dry white wines are also increasingly being produced. International white and red varieties are also increasing rapidly.orten nehmen ebenfalls stark zu.

LIECHTENSTEIN

Wine has been grown in Liechtenstein for more than 2,000 years. The Romans brought the first vines to the country. Since then, the mild climate, influenced by the warming foehn winds - a unique Alpine phenomenon - and the centuries of experience of local winegrowers have produced excellent wines. From Chardonnay to Pinot Noir and Riesling, there are four professional winemakers who produce the noble wines of the Principality. The Court Winery of the Prince of Liechtenstein in Vaduz is located in the Herawingert vineyard. With four hectares of vines - out of a total of 14 hectares in the Principality - Herawingert is one of the best vineyards in the Rhine Valley.

SLOVAKIA

Slovakia's six wine regions lie on the western border with the Czech Republic and the southern border with Hungary. They are, from west to east, Malokarpatská (Little Carpathians), Juznoslovenská east of Bratislava, above that Nitrianská near Neutra, Stredoslovenská in the southern centre, Vychodoslovenská in the east near Košice and Tokajská in the south-east. Slovakia has about 600 wineries cultivating about 10,000 hectares. Most of the wine is consumed domestically.

SLOVENIA

Selected wines from the three wine regions of Podravje (sub-regions of Štajerska Slovenija and Prekmurje), Posavje (sub-regions of Bela Krajina, Bizeljsko-Brežice and Dolenjska) and Primorska (sub-regions of Goriška Brda, Kras, Slovenska Istra and Vipavska Dolina) are among the best quality wines in the world. Each region has its own selection of grape varieties, due to differences in location, climate and wine-making techniques. Slovenian vineyards are located in the centre of the European wine-growing belt. The Slovenian wine regions share this with areas such as Burgundy in France. The combination of different climatic influences and soils enables Slovenia to produce a particularly wide variety of wines. Fifty-two different grape varieties thrive here.

VITICULTURE IN NEIGHBORING COUNTRIES

SELECTED WINERIES

Domaine Vicomte de Noüe-Marinič, Kojsko
Magula family winery, Suchá nad Parnou
Marof Winery, Mačkovci
Edi Simčič, Dobrovo

Hidden Treasures – a Moric project, Großhöflein
Radgonske gorice d.o.o., Gornja Radgona
Svetlik, Dobravlje
Verus, Ormož

Vino Gaube, Zgornja Kungota

★★
Hofkellerei Domäne Vaduz - Stiftung Fürst Liechtenstein, Vaduz

★
Atelier Kramar, Dobrovo

ATELIER KRAMAR
ORGANIC

Katja and Matjaž Kramar, a German-Slovenian couple, first studied art at the Academy of Fine Arts in Venice before devoting their attention to cultivating and producing natural wines more than 20 years ago. Their small, organically certified winery is located on the Alpe Adria Trail in Goriška Brda, Slovenia, and covers about five hectares of vineyards. They offer farm-gate sales and tastings on request, and a wine tavern is currently under construction.

93 Rebula Primario 2021
13 Vol.-%, DIAM, steel tank, €€€€
Bright, cloudy golden yellow, brass reflections. Delicate notes of blossom honey, some kumquat, in the background

Dobrovo Castle

ATELIER KRAMAR
5212 Dobrovo
Barbana 12
T: +386 (41) 317844
www.atelier-kramar.si

Winemaker/Contact:
Matjaž Kramar
Production: 13,333 bottles
25 % sparkling, 50 % white, 25 % red, 5 hectares
Fairs: Vinitaly
Distribution partners: DE, UK, IT, SLO

SLOVENIA

some apricot confit, orange touch. Juicy, taut, white peach, finely-meshed, mineral texture, fine tannin, salty finish. Textured and with depth, good food wine.

92 Zeleni Sauvignon Bohem 2020 FRL/MA2
12,5 Vol.-%, cork, steel tank, €€€€

91 Zeleni Sauvignon Bohem 2019 FRL/MA2
13 Vol.-%, cork, 500-l-barrel, €€€€

91 Merlot Garanza 2017
13,5 Vol.-%, cork, 500-l-barrel, €€€€

92 Merlot Garanza 2015
14 Vol.-%, cork, 500-l-barrel, €€€€

★★★★

DOMAINE VICOMTE DE NOÜE-MARINIČ

The de Noüe family has a long winemaking tradition in Burgundy, France, where Charles Louis de Noüe, owner of Domaine de Vicomte de Noüe-Marinič and also the grandson of Christian Jacques de Clay de Nell, is a member of the family that owns the legendary Domaine Leflaive. His passion for the most authentic and prestigious terroirs for growing wine - with a preference for white wine - led him to Brda in Slovenia, where he and his Slovenian partner, Alis Marinič, have revived some abandoned vineyards, using mass selection to recover a rich genetic heritage that contributes to the complexity of the wines. The two partners manage their vineyards without using chemicals. Instead, they naturally cultivate the soil and allow aromatic herbs to grow in the vineyard to retain moisture and protect the roots. They follow Maria Thun's lunar calendar and Steiner's philosophy. The philosophy of making wine in the vineyard is shared by her advisor, Anthony Colas, who manages the most prestigious vineyards in Burgundy. Together they choose the right moment to harvest healthy grapes. Every other procedure that follows is with minimal intervention to preserve the wine's minerality and freshness. The idea is to obtain a structured wine from the terroir, a wine capable of creating a vibration, an emotion. Today, the estate proudly stands beside these three brands: Domaine Vicomte de Noüe-Marinič, Erigone, and Marinič.

95 Chardonnay Groblja Vedrignano II Cru 2020
13,5 Vol.-%, cork

94 Chardonnay Groblja 2019
Light yellow green, silver reflections. Hints of yellow stone fruit with a touch of light nougat, delicate pineapple and mango; an inviting bouquet with subtle meadow herbs in the background. Juicy, elegant, yellow apple and a touch of new wood. Fresh acidity, a salty finish with an aftertaste of lime. Balanced and sturdy wine, yet with finesse and very good length. A fine food companion.

94 Chardonnay Sotto la Chiesa Bigliana II Cru 2020
13,5 Vol.-%, cork

93 Chardonnay Vicomte de Noüe Marinic Sotto la chiesa 2019
Light yellow green, silver reflections. White apple fruit in the underlay with fine wood spice, yellow tropical fruit, some mineral notes and white flowers in the background. Juicy, elegant, yellow peach, a touch of caramel, mineral. Endowed with good length, a balanced food companion with good ageing potential.

DOMAINE VICOMTE DE NOÜE-MARINIČ
5211 Kojsko
Vedrijan 17
T: +39 (340) 5838 551
cldenoue@gmail.com
domaine-nouemarinic.com

Winemaker: Anthony Colas
Contact: Charles Louis de Noüe, Alis Marinič

SLOVENIA

94 Chardonnay Tejca Verdrignano II Cru 2020 14 Vol.-%, cork	92 Chardonnay Érigone 2019
93 Chardonnay Tejca 2019	92 Ribolla Gialla Érigone Gaugnaz I Cru 2020 12,5 Vol.-%, cork
93 Chardonnay Attico San Pietro III Cru 2020 14 Vol.-%, DIAM	91 Ribolla Gialla Érigone 2019
92 Chardonnay Érigone Ossech V Cru 2020 13,5 Vol.-%, cork	91 Malvasia Érigone Zala Locca III Cru 2020 14 Vol.-%, cork
	91 Malvazia Zala Érigone 2019

VINO GAUBE

Some things will always remain a mystery, especially making wine, where the endless stories of the winemakers, together with the unpredictability of nature, continue to add new chapters to the history of wine.

The history of viticulture in the Gaube family estate dates back several generations. After a prolonged interruption, production was fortunately resumed in 1992, and the family began bottling their wines. Since then, there have been many changes, but the affinity with the vines and the wine has remained constant. It is a challenge for the family to create a common bond between nature and the creation of the perfect wine. The winery is located in the amphitheatre of the Svečinske gorice vineyards in Špičnik, just below the well-known road forming a heart shape among the vineyards. The location, soil, and favourable climatic conditions of almost nine hectares of vineyards allow the Gaubes to produce a wide range of different styles of wine to suit every taste. There is a choice of fresh and mostly dry wines, as well as sparkling wines made according to the classic method. The range also includes more full-bodied, mature wines from the 'Kaspar' and 'Emanuel' lines, as well as Pinot Noir.

94 Chardonnay Kaspar 2020
13,5 Vol.-%, DIAM, steel tank, €€€
Light yellow green, silver reflections. Yellow apple fruit, a background of candied orange zest, floral, fine honey nouagt touch, inviting bouquet. Taut, elegant, finely structured, mineral and fresh, white stone fruit, lemony nuances. Lingers long; a versatile food wine.

93 Sauvignon 2022
12,5 Vol.-%, screwcap, steel tank, €€
Bright yellow green, silver reflections. Delicate cassis and fresh gooseberries, a hint of bell peppers, pleasant herbal savouriness. Full-bodied, white apple, lively acidity, delicate fruit, lemony and salty in the finish, good length, squeaky clean style, has good ageing potential.

93 Sivi Pinot 2022
13 Vol.-%, screwcap, steel tank, €€

92 Zeleni Silvanec 2022
12,5 Vol.-%, screwcap, steel tank, €€

91 Rizling Laški 2022
12,5 Vol.-%, screwcap, steel tank, €€

90 Rosé 2022
12,5 Vol.-%, screwcap, steel tank, €€

VINO GAUBE
2201 Zgornja Kungota
Špičnik 17
T: +386 (41) 747151
vinarstvo.gaube@siol.net
www.vino-gaube.si

Winemaker/Contact:
Alojzij Gaube
Production: 40,000 bottles
8 % sparkling, 81 % white, 10 % rosé, 1 % red, 8.6 hectares
Fairs: Vino Ljubljana
Distribution partners: SLO, CZ

HIDDEN TREASURES
A MORIC PROJECT

The mastermind behind Hidden Treasures is the well-known Austrian winemaker Roland Velich, who has caused a sensation internationally with his Blaufränkisch red wines. For years, he cultivated the best terroirs in Burgenland in order to coax the finest nuances of this complex variety from old Blaufränkisch vines.

Hidden Treasure is a continuation of the ideas that led Velich to develop Moric, an attempt to capture a region as purely and directly as possible: traditional old methods and full confidence in the given substance, an ancient wine culture that has been successful for centuries and is a world leader.

The soils and climate of the Pannonian Plain - a lowland plain stretching from the last hills of the Eastern Alps along the Carpathian arc - the grape varieties that have proven suitable and valuable over long periods of time, and of course the people, combine to the greatest effect.

Roland Velich has decided to follow this path together with young innovative winemakers, winemakers who are ready to embark on this journey in a similar way. Starting this journey now is important to him: "It's time to make this great wine culture accessible again to the inclined public in an original and authentic form."

For the treasures from Hungary, he is currently cooperating with Gergö Filep from Tokaj, Kis Tamás from Nagy-Somlói and Villa Tolnay on Lake Balaton.

Here it is the traditional Pannonian variety Furmint, in its various manifestations, that is shone in the right light.

94   Hidden Treasures Nr.1 Tokaj
       feat. Gergö Filep 2021
12,5 Vol.-%

93   Hidden Treasures Nr.1 Tokaj
       feat. Gergö Filep 2020

93   Hidden Treasures Nr.2 Somlo
       feat. Kis Tamás 2021 FU/WR
13 Vol.-%

93   Hidden Treasures Nr.2 Somlo
       feat. Kis Tamás 2020 FU/WR

Light yellow-green, silver reflections. Delicate herbal savouriness, hints of ripe pears and figs, nuances of yellow stone fruit, candied orange zest. Juicy, mineral, white apple, taut texture. A salty, lemony touch in the aftertaste. Light-footed, full of finesse and a good companion to food.

93   Hidden Treasures Nr.3 Balaton
       feat. Villa Tolnay 2021 FU/RR
12,5 Vol.-%, cork

92   Hidden Treasures Nr.3 Balaton
       feat. Villa Tolnay 2020 RR/FU

Light greenish yellow, silver reflections. On the nose floral honey, fresh yellow apple, hints of peach and tangerine, mineral nuances. A complex palate, tightly-meshed, lemony touch, fine meadow herb savouriness. Salty and long lasting with a lively style.

93   Hidden Treasures Nr.3 Balaton
       feat. Villa Tolnay 2019 RR/FU

HIDDEN TREASURES –
A MORIC PROJECT
7051 Großhöflein
Kirchengasse 3
T: +43 (664) 4003231
www.moric.at

Contact: Roland Velich

LIECHTENSTEIN

Sommelière Princess Marie and Winery Manager Stefan Tscheppe

HOFKELLEREI DOMÄNE VADUZ - STIFTUNG FÜRST LIECHTENSTEIN
9490 Vaduz
Feldstrasse 4
T: +423 (3) 2321018
office@hofkellerei.li
www.hofkellerei.li

Winemaker: Sebastian Gunsch, Natalie Wallner
Contact: Stefan Tscheppe
Production: 4 hectares
Fairs: ProWein Düsseldorf, Vinexpo

HOFKELLEREI DOMÄNE VADUZ STIFTUNG FÜRST LIECHTENSTEIN

In 1712, Prince Johann Adam I of Liechtenstein acquired the earldom of Vaduz, whereby the Herawingert and today's Hofkellerei became the property of the Principality. The Herawingert is the oldest and most important vineyard in the Principality of Liechtenstein. With its four hectares of contiguous vineyards, it is considered the jewel of the country's viticulture and one of the best sites in the Rhine Valley. Stéphane Derenoncourt's Pinot Noirs and Chardonnays thrive here thanks to the southwest exposure, the mild foehn climate, and the slate and limestone soils. The result is wines that mature in a uniquely elegant and fresh style. The wines can be tasted directly at the Hofkellerei or at the family restaurant Torkel am Rebberg.

94 Chardonnay Ried Herawingert Appellation Vaduz Contrôlée 2021
13 Vol.-%, cork, tonneaux barrel, €€€€

93 Chardonnay Herawingert Appellation Vaduz Contrôlée 2020

91 Vaduzer Chardonnay Herawingert AOC 2016

89 Blanc de Noir 2022
13 Vol.-%, screwcap, steel tank, €€€€

92 Pinot Noir Ried Herawingert 2020
13 Vol.-%, cork, tonneaux barrel, €€€€

94 Pinot Noir Grosse Reserve Herawingert Appellation Vaduz Contrôlée 2019
Strong garnet, purple reflections, broader ochre brightening on the rim. Savoury notes underlying fine berry fruit, a hint of cherries, sweet, spicy nuances, a mineral touch, and some floral appeal. Juicy, red berry, silky texture, elegant acidity and a salty-mineral finish. Delicate style that lingers long with a hint of lemon in the aftertaste. A multi-layered food companion with good ageing potential.

91 Pinot Noir AOC Clos Domaine 2020
13 Vol.-%, screwcap, large wooden barrel, €€€€

92 Pinot Noir Clos Domaine 2019

92 Vaduzer Pinot Noir Bocker AOC 2015

© Hofkellerei des Fürsten von Liechtenstein

MAGULA FAMILY WINERY
ORGANIC

The Magula family is passionate about making natural wines exclusively from their organically grown grapes of specific Slovak varieties. Vinárstvo Magula's viticultural journey began in 2007 when they replanted an old vineyard that had been reverted to the family. Since 2016 the vineyards have been cultivated biodynamically. The estate is located in a unique place: on the grounds of an old monastery, in the leafy shade of ancient chestnut trees. The Magula family has a strong commitment to the environment and always strives to live in harmony with nature. They grow chestnuts and various fruits and keep bees and farm animals to bring life and balance to their property.

In the wine cellar, they strive to be merely supervisors with minimal intervention. The wines are allowed to mature at their own pace and in their own way, reflecting the characteristics of the grape variety, the vintage, and the terroir. In this way, harmony and elegance are conveyed to the bottle. Magula wines, especially the reds, are intense yet subtle and elegant, capturing the crisp and charming character of the northern terroirs.

93 Oranžový vlk 2021 GV/WR/TR
12 Vol.-%, cork, 500-l-barrel/amphore/stoneware/used barriques, €€€€

92 Oranžový vlk 2020 GV/WR/TR
Clouded orange yellow. Mineral, hints of grapefruit and hibiscus, fresh orange zest, backed by yellow peach and lime; an inviting bouquet. Light on its feet, white apple, fine tannin, lemony-salty, a touch of apricot. Lingers long with a freshening style.

93 Sen 2020 CS/BF
12 Vol.-%, cork, used barriques, €€€€€

90 Frankovka 2017
93 Frankovka 2015
13 Vol.-%, cork, used barriques, €€€€€

92 Rosenberg Frankovka 2018
13 Vol.-%, cork, used barriques/500-l-barrel/barrique, €€€€

93 Rosenberg Frankovka unplugged 2017
Deep garnet colour, purple reflections, ochre brightening on the rim. Delicate balsamic underlay, black cherry fruit, hints of plum, subtle tobacco nuances, backed by candied orange zest. On the palate medium-bodied, red cherry, fine ripe tannins, a mineral-salty finish. Lingers long with a red berry finish; a balanced food companion.

92 Baccara 2019
12 Vol.-%, cork, 500-l-barrel/used barriques, €€€€

92 Červený vlk 2019

91 Pinot Noir Teufelstal 2021
12 Vol.-%, cork, barrique/used barriques/stoneware, €€€€

90 Pinot Noir Teufelstal 2020

89 Modrý Portugal 2018

MAGULA FAMILY WINERY
91901 Suchá nad Parnou
Ružová dolina 908
T: +421 (905) 645 520
vino@vinomagula.sk
www.vinomagula.sk

Winemaker/Contact:
Vladimír Magula
Production: 26,667 bottles
3 % sparkling, 20 % white, 6 % rosé, 74 % red, 8.5 hectares
Fairs: VieVinum, RAW – The Artisan Wine Fair Berlin, Karakterre
Distribution partners: DK, DE, EST, FR, UK, IT, JP, CDN, ROK, LT, NL, NO, PL, SK, ES, CZ, HU, USA

MAROF WINERY

★★★★

Although Marof is a newly built winery, the methods, and procedures remain as simple as possible and are based on century-old traditions. The team's approach to winemaking is a combination of the wealth of nature and human knowledge. The natural rhythms of vine and wine are respected. With minimal intervention, they strive to express the terroir's natural characteristics, elegance, and balance.

The best vineyard sites produce healthy and perfectly ripened grapes according to organic principles. The grapes are harvested and selected by hand. The cellar master's interventions are minimal, with great respect for what has been achieved in the vineyard: spontaneous fermentation, masterfully thought-out maceration on the lees, and only the best wooden vats. The quest for perfection in everything Marof does - in the vineyard and in the cellar - is the story of this winery.

93 Sauvignon Blanc Bodonci SVL Lega 2020
13,5 Vol.-%, DIAM, large wooden barrel, €€€€€€

94 Sauvignon Bodonci SVL Lega 2017
Medium greenish yellow, silver reflections. On the nose yellow tropical fruit, a touch of herbal savouriness, white currants, some guava, floral nuances, a multifaceted bouquet. Deep, juicy and intense palate, subtle hints of coconut and gooseberries, elegant and long lasting with fine fruit on the finish. A salty aftertaste and a complex food companion. Good ageing potential.

93 Sauvignon Breg SVL Vas 2018

92 Sauvignon Blanc Goričko 2020
13,5 Vol.-%, DIAM, large wooden barrel, €€€€

93 Chardonnay Kramarovci 2020
13,5 Vol.-%, DIAM, large wooden barrel, €€€€€

92 Chardonnay Kramarovci SVL Lega 2018

92 Goričko Blanc 2020 WR/CH/SB
13,5 Vol.-%, DIAM, 500-l-barrel/large wooden barrel, €€€€

92 Breg Cuvée white SVL Vas 2018 WR/CH/SE/SB

94 Mačkovci Modra frankinja SVL Lega 2019
13,5 Vol.-%, DIAM, large wooden barrel, €€€€€

93 Mačkovci Modra Frankinja SVL Lega 2018
Deep ruby colour, opaque core, purple reflections and a delicate brightening on the rim. On the nose forest berry fruit, nuances of blackberries and liquorice, tobacco notes and a subtle touch of fine oak. A substantial palate with dark cherry and spicy well-integrated tannins. A mineral and fresh structure, black cherries on the finish. Good length, will benefit from bottle ageing.

92 Mačkovci Merlot Anna 2016

MAROF WINERY
Si-9202 Mačkovci
Mačkovci 35
T: +386 (3) 467143
uros.valcl@marof.eu
www.marof.eu

Winemaker: Uroš Valcl
Contact: Uroš Valcl
Production: 93,333 bottles
40 % white, 60 % red, 22 hectares
Distribution partners:
BE, DE, FIN, UK, IRL, IT, JP, ROK, SE, CH, HU, PT

SLOVENIA

RADGONSKE GORICE D.O.O.

Like the ripples of the River Mur flowing through Gornja Radgona, small secrets and immense knowledge have been passing through Radgonske Gorice for 170 years: How to take care of the vine so that it blooms in all its splendour.

How to take the time to care for the grapes. How to fall in love with wine, its elegance and intoxication.

How to give it a sparkle that never fades. Radgonske Gorice is the oldest and now the most prominent sparkling wine producer in Slovenia. The first Slovenian sparkling wine, known as Zlata Radgonska Penina, was produced here. Together with Srebrna Radgonska Penina, Janževec, Black Label Traminer and other sparkling and still wines in their range, they accompany us in various important and groundbreaking or simply everyday moments and create unforgettable memories.

94 • Untouched by Light 2018
12 Vol.-%, DIAM, bottle fermentation, €€€€€€

93 • Zlata Radgonska Penina Millésime Brut Nature 2008
Deep yellow gold with silver reflections and a fine delicate mousse. On the nose there is a multi-faceted bouquet of ripe yellow tropical fruit, nuances of peach, a hint of gooseberries, and notes of blossom honey. It is full-bodied, with a fresh acidity and yellow apple and delicate biscuit flavours. With vivid acidity, mineral and its gastronomic style, and although already mature, it has further aging potential.

93 • Zlata Radgonska Penina Ciconia Brut 2018
12,5 Vol.-%, DIAM, bottle fermentation, €€€€

92 • Zlata Radgonska Penina Selection Sans Dosage 2020
12 Vol.-%, DIAM, bottle fermentation, €€€

92 • Pet-Nat Renina 2019
11,5 Vol.-%, DIAM, bottle fermentation, €€€€ Ⓑ

91 • Zlata Radgonska Penina Selection Brut 2020
12 Vol.-%, DIAM, bottle fermentation, €€€€

92 • Zlata Radgonska Penina Selection Brut 2018
Light greenish yellow with silver reflections and a lively mousse. There are aromas of fine tropical fruit like mango and papaya, a hint of blossom honey, tangerine zest and light nougat. It is medium-bodied with well-integrated fruit sweetness, a lively acidity, and is harmonious and invigorating. A versatile sparkling wine it can be used as an aperitif and also as a good accompaniment to food.

91 • Zlata Radgonska Penina Brut 2017

92 • Zlata Radgonska Penina Extra Dry 2017

92 • Zlata Radgonska Penina Rosé Extra Dry 2020
12 Vol.-%, DIAM, Méthode Traditionelle, bottle fermentation, €€€€

91 • Zlata Radgonska Penina Rosé Extra Dry 2018

RADGONSKE GORICE D.O.O.
9250 Gornja Radgona
Jurkovičeva ulica 5
T: +386 (2) 5648510
info@radgonske-gorice.si
radgonske-gorice.si

Winemaker: Klavdija Topolovec Špur
Contact: Andreja Novak
Production: 4,666,667 bottles
500 hectares

EDI SIMČIČ

★★★★

Goriška Brda is where the northern Mediterranean literally merges with the southern Alps, a place where the soil is rich in salts and minerals. The region is known for its Mediterranean extravagance but also for its full-bodied and crisp white wines, exceptional wines with the potential to age for several years. Winemaker Alexs Simčič relies on autochthonous varieties: "We have faith in Rebula (Ribolla Gialla) and its potential. Rebula is our pride and joy, our identity".

But Edi Simčič has always been devoted to reds as well: "We demand maturity and longevity from them." The vineyards and climate of the Goriška Brda region can provide all this, and according to the winery's philosophy, not much more is needed. Despite the high standards, the wine is given its freedom and potential to develop. It is brought from the cellar to the table: unadorned and pure. "The wine is served as it has developed in spirit and taste: cheerful, lively, sometimes serious, but always a little liberating. True excellence is never deliberate.

EDI SIMČIČ
5212 Dobrovo
Vipolže 39 a
T: +386 (30) 602 564
info@edisimcic.si
www.edisimcic.si

Kontakt: Alexs Simčič

94 Fojana Chardonnay SVL Srednji Kos Vineyard 2020
14 Vol.-%, cork, barrique, €€€€€

93 Fojana Chardonnay SVL Lega 2019
Bright golden yellow, silver reflections. Fine wood savouriness, light caramel, ripe yellow apple fruit, delicate pear and subtle herbal touch. On the palate juicy, elegant, round and harmonious; a powerful wine with fine fruit. Long lasting. Ready to enjoy but it has certain ageing potential.

93 Kozana Chardonnay SVL Polje Vineyard 2020
14 Vol.-%, cork, barrique, €€€€€

93 Malvazija 2021
13,5 Vol.-%, cork, barrique, €€€€€

92 Malvazija SVL Okoliš 2020

93 Kozana Sauvignon SVL Kurinsce Vineyard 2020
14 Vol.-%, cork, barrique, €€€€€

93 Kozana Sauvignon SVL Lega 2019

92 Rebula 2021
13 Vol.-%, cork, barrique, €€€€€

92 Fojana Rebula SVL Lega 2020

96 Kozana Merlot SVL Lega 2016
Deep garnet, opaque core, purple reflections, ochre brightening on the rim. A touch of fine oak spiciness, nuances of cardamom and vanilla, ripe cherries, some blackberries and nougat, a hint of tobacco. Complex, substantial, ripe plum fruit. Supporting and well-developed tannin, fine minerality. Harmonious and already accessible. Shows great length and has certain ageing potential.

94 Kolos 2018 ME/CS/CF
14,6 Vol.-%, cork, barrique, €€€€€€

94 Kolos SVL Okoliš 2017 ME/CS/CF

SLOVENIA

SVETLIK
5263 Dobravlje
Kamnje 42b
T: +386 (5) 3725100
svetlik-wine.com

Edvard and Ivi Svetlik

★★★

SVETLIK

On the steep, sunny slope of the Čaven, above the village of Kamnje, the Svetliks have planted a vineyard of the Rebula (Ribolla Gialla) grape variety. Here, in the midst of the vineyards, Ivi and Edvard Svetlik are writing a new chapter in the story of their lives. The small village of Kamnje is located in the Vipava Valley, a picturesque Slovenian wine-growing region just over an hour's drive from Venice. The sub-Mediterranean climate of the Vipava Valley is conducive to wine growing. The charming vineyard draws strength from its extremely sunny position as one of the highest vineyards in the Vipava Valley. The aromatic richness of Rebula (Ribolla), an autochthonous grape variety that thrives both in the Vipava Valley and in Brda (Collio), proves that the location of the Rebula-Svetlik vineyard is ideal. The couple produces only 6,000 bottles from 8,000 vines. The grape harvest is a festive day when the Svetliks and their friends hand-pick the grapes they have tended all summer and into late autumn. The grapes turn an attractive amber colour and are aged for two years in large oak barrels before being bottled unfiltered.

A speciality is the Rebula Maximilian I, aged in barrels made from 354 old oak trees from King Louis XIV's forest and bottled in honour of Emperor Maximilian I. As early as 1503, the Habsburg monarchy had Rebula from the Vipava Valley delivered directly to the imperial court. Rebula Svetlik is not only amber in colour but also rich in aromas, minerals and complexity. It should be served at a temperature of 15 degrees Celsius in a generous red wine glass to reveal all its complexity of flavour and aroma.

(93) Rebula Selekcija 2017
13,5 Vol.-%, cork, oak barrel, €€ Ⓑ ❶

Medium orange gold, brass reflections. Herbaceous nuances, some yellow fruit, a touch of tobacco, a hint of white nougat, candied tangerine zest. Complex, subtle apricot, fine tannin, taut texture, salty and mineral, and also some nougat in the finish, spicy aftertaste, good food wine.

SLOVENIA

Božidar Grabovac, Danilo Šnajder and Rajko Žličar

VERUS
2270 Ormož
Hardek 34A
T: +386 (2) 741 54 40
info@verusvino.com
www.verusvino.com

★★★

VERUS

Verus was founded by three winemaking friends, Rajko Žličar, Danilo Šnajder, and Božidar Grabovac. They combined their families' vineyards, knowledge and labour. In the spring of 2007, the trio established a wine cellar in a former bakery. They share a commitment to family traditions, as their parents and grandparents were strongly connected to viticulture and wine.
Verus means genuine, trustworthy, factual, honest, and sincere. They have always been committed to this approach, and it is reflected in their wines. With this knowledge and meticulous work in the vineyard and cellar, they produce wines that truly express the characteristics of the variety, the vintage, and the region.

93 Sauvignon Blanc Verus 2021
13 Vol.-%, screwcap, steel tank, €€€ V
Light yellow-green, silver reflections. Attractive white tropical fruit, soft notes of guava and passion fruit, a touch of cape gooseberry, with lime undertones. Juicy, elegant, white peach, silky texture, good freshness, harmonious style, a multi-faceted food wine with ageing potential.

92 Furmint Verus - Šipon 2021
13 Vol.-%, screwcap, steel tank/partial barrique, €€€ V

91 Verus Furmint – Šipon 2020

92 Chardonnay Verus 2022
13,5 Vol.-%, screwcap, steel tank, €€€ V

92 Pinot Gris Verus - Sivi Pinot 2022
14 Vol.-%, screwcap, steel tank, €€€ V

91 Riesling Verus - Renski Rizling 2021
12,5 Vol.-%, screwcap, steel tank, €€€ V

93 Pinot Noir Verus - Modri Pinot 2017
14 Vol.-%, screwcap, used barriques, €€€€ V
Medium garnet, ochre reflections, broad brightening on the rim. Delicate notes of candied violets, red wild berries, a hint of prunes, inviting bouquet. Substantial, fine fruit expression, sour cherries, vivid, supporting tannins, salty minerality, remains lasting, a balanced food wine.

© Sean Fitzpatrick

SPACE FOR YOUR
WINE NOTES

VINEYARD ESTATES A–Z

AUSTRIA

A

Achs Paul Weingut
Gols — 298

Aigner Weingut
Krems — 112

Allacher Vinum Pannonia / Vinum Pannonia Allacher
Gols — 300

Altenburger Markus Weingut
Jois — 270

Alzinger Weingut
Dürnstein — 168

Amsee Weingut
Gols — 301

Artner Weingut
Höflein — 64

Atzberg Weingut
Spitz an der Donau — 170

B

Bauer Anton Weingut
Feuersbrunn — 206

Bauer Familie Bioweingut
Großriedenthal — 208

Bründlmayer Josef & Philipp Weingut
Grunddorf — 113

Bründlmayer Weingut
Langenlois — 80

Buchegger Weingut
Droß — 115

C

Chan Roland Domäne
Wösendorf in der Wachau — 171

Cobenzl Weingut
Wien — 44

D

Deim Gerhard Weingut
Schönberg am Kamp — 83

Dockner Familie Winzerhof
Höbenbach — 116

Dockner Tom Weingut
Theyern — 156

Doktor Wunderer Weingut
Straning — 232

Domäne Wachau
Dürnstein — 172

Donabaum Christoph
Spitz — 176

Donabaum Johann Weingut
Spitz an der Donau — 177

Dürnberg Weingut
Falkenstein — 233

E

Ecker – Eckhof Weingut
Kirchberg am Wagram — 209

Edelbauer Christoph
Langenlois — 84

Ehmoser Josef Weingut
Tiefenthal — 211

VINEYARD ESTATES A–Z

Ehn Weinhof
Engelmannsbrunn   213

Ernst Bernhard Weingut
Deutschkreutz   284

Ernsthofer Weingut
Wösendorf   178

F

Felsner Weingut
Grunddorf   119

Firmenich Weingut
Ehrenhausen   332

Forstreiter Meinhard Weingut
Krems-Hollenburg   120

Frauwallner Weingut
Straden   380

Fritsch Karl Weinberghof
Oberstockstall   214

Fritz Josef Weingut
Zaußenberg   215

Fürst von Liechtenstein – Hofkellerei
see Liechtenstein, Fürst von – Hofkellerei

G

Gager Weingut
Deutschkreutz   285

Gesellmann Weingut
Deutschkreutz   286

Glatzer Walter Weingut
Göttlesbrunn   66

Gobelsburg Schloss Weingut
Gobelsburg   86

Göttweig Stift Weingut
see Stift Göttweig Weingut

Graf Hardegg
see Hardegg Graf

Grassl Philipp Weingut
Göttlesbrunn   67

Gritsch FJ – Mauritiushof
Spitz an der Donau   179

Groiß Bioweingut
Kleinwiesendorf   218

Gross Weingut
Ehrenhausen   334

Gruber Röschitz Weingut
Röschitz   235

H

Hagn Weingut
Mailberg   237

Hajszan Neumann Weingut
Wien   46

Hardegg Graf
Seefeld-Kadolz   238

Harm David Bioweingut
Krustetten   121

Hartl Toni Weingut
Reisenberg   272

Hartl Weingut
Oberwaltersdorf   149

Heiderer-Mayer Weingut
Großweikersdorf   219

Heinrich Gernot und Heike Weingut
Gols   302

Hirsch Weingut
Kammern   88

Hirtl Weingut
Poysdorf   240

Hirtzberger Franz Weingut
Spitz an der Donau   181

Hirtzberger Mathias Weinhofmeisterei
Wösendorf in der Wachau   183

Hoegl Weingut
Spitz an der Donau   185

Holzapfel Weingut
Weißenkirchen   186

Huber Markus Weingut
Reichersdorf   158

Hutter Silberbichlerhof Weingut
Mautern an der Donau   188

INDEX

I

Iby Bio Rotweingut
Horitschon — 288

J

Jalits Weingut
Badersdorf — 262

Jamek Weingut
Joching — 189

Johanneshof Reinisch Weingut
Tattendorf — 147

Jordan Weingut
Pulkau — 241

Jurtschitsch Weingut
Langenlois — 90

K

Kilger Domaines
Gamlitz — 336

Klein Jacqueline Weingut
Andau — 303

Knoll Weingut
Dürnstein — 190

Kodolitsch Weingut
Leibnitz — 337

Kögl Weingut
Ratsch an der Weinstraße — 339

Kolkmann Weingut
Fels am Wagram — 220

Kollwentz Weingut
Großhöflein — 273

Kracher Weinlaubenhof
Illmitz — 305

Krutzler Weingut
Deutsch Schützen — 263

L

Lackner-Tinnacher Weingut
Gamlitz — 340

Landhaus Mayer
see Mayer Landhaus

Langmann Weingut
Sankt Stefan ob Stainz — 392

Laurenz V.
Wien/Zöbing — 92

Leindl Weingut
Zöbing — 93

Lenz Moser Weinkellerei
see Moser Lenz Weinkellerei

Leth Weingut
Fels am Wagram — 222

Liechtenstein, Fürst von – Hofkellerei
Wilfersdorf — 242

Loimer Fred Weingut
Langenlois — 94

M

Mad Weingut
Oggau — 275

Maitz Wolfgang Weingut
Ehrenhausen an der Weinstraße — 344

Malat Weingut
Palt — 122

Mantlerhof Weingut
Brunn im Felde/ Gedersdorf — 124

Markowitsch Gerhard Weingut
Göttlesbrunn — 69

Masser Weingut
Leutschach — 345

Mayer am Pfarrplatz Weingut
Wien — 49

Mayer Landhaus
Wien — 48

Moric Weingut
Großhöflein — 277

VINEYARD ESTATES A–Z

Moser Lenz Weinkellerei	
Rohrendorf	126
Müller Leo u. Stefan Weingut	
Krustetten	128
Münzenrieder Johannes Weingut	
Apetlon	307
Münzenrieder PMC Weingut	
Apetlon	308
Muster.gamlitz Weingut	
Gamlitz	342

N

Nastl Weingut	
Langenlois	95
Nestor	
Halbturn	310
Netzl Franz und Christine Weingut	
Göttlesbrunn	70
Neumayer Ludwig Weingut	
Inzersdorf ob der Traisen	160
Neumeister Weingut	
Straden	382
Nigl Weingut	
Senftenberg	130
Nittnaus Gebrüder Weingut	
Gols	311
Nolz Wein	
Hilpersdorf	162

O

Ott Bernhard Weingut	
Feuersbrunn	224
Ott Thomas Weingut	
Reichersdorf	163

P

Paschinger Familie Urbanihof	
see Urbanihof Familie Paschinger	
Payr Robert Bioweingut	
Höflein	72

Pesau Weingut	
Falkenstein	244
Pfaffl R. & A. Weingut	
Stetten	245
Pichler F. X. Weingut	
Dürnstein	193
Pichler Rudi Weingut	
Wösendorf	195
Pimpel Gerhard Weingut	
Göttlesbrunn	74
Pöckl Weingut	
Mönchhof	312
Polz Weingut	
Strass in der Steiermark	347
Prager Weingut	
Weißenkirchen/Wachau	196
Prieler Weingut	
Schützen am Gebirge	278
Proidl Familie Weingut	
Senftenberg	131

R

Rabl Rudolf Weingut	
Langenlois	97
Reeh Hannes Weingut	
Andau	314
Regele Weingut	
Ehrenhausen an der Weinstraße	349
Reinisch Johanneshof Weingut	
see Johanneshof Reinisch Weingut	
Reiterer Weingut	
Wies	394
Rotes Haus Weingut	
Wien	50

INDEX

S

Sabathi Erwin Weingut
Leutschach an der Weinstraße — 351

Sabathi Hannes Weingut
Gamlitz — 353

Salomon Undhof Weingut
Stein an der Donau — 133

Salzl – Seewinkelhof Weingut
Illmitz — 315

Sattlerhof Weingut
Gamlitz — 356

Sax Rudolf und Michael Winzerhof
Langenlois — 99

Scharl Josef - Charakterweine
Sankt Anna am Aigen — 384

Scheiblhofer Erich Weingut
Andau — 316

Schloss Gobelsburg Weingut
see Gobelsburg Schloss Weingut

Schlumberger Wein- und Sektkellerei
Wien — 51

Schmelz Weingut
Joching — 198

Schmid Josef Weingut
Stratzing — 135

Schmid Weingut
Langenlois — 100

Schwarz Wein
Andau — 319

Schwarz Bio-Weingut
Schrattenberg — 248

Schweiger Peter Weingut
Zöbing — 101

Seher Wolfgang Weingut
Platt — 249

Silberberg Landesweingut
Leibnitz — 358

Silberbichlerhof Weingut Hutter
see Hutter Silberbichlerhof Weingut

Skoff Original Weingut – Walter Skoff
Gamlitz — 359

Skoff Peter Weingut – Domäne Kranachberg
Gamlitz — 362

Skoff Walter Original Weingut
see Skoff Original Weingut – Walter Skoff

Söll Maria und Johannes
Gamlitz — 365

Stadlmann Weingut
Traiskirchen — 146

Stadt Krems Weingut
Krems — 136

Steininger Weingut
Langenlois — 102

Stift Göttweig Weingut
Furth bei Göttweig — 138

Strauss Gamlitz Weingut
Gamlitz — 364

Sutter Weingut
Hohenwarth — 250

T

Tegernseerhof Weingut
Dürnstein — 200

Tement Familienweingut
Ehrenhausen — 367

Tesch Josef Weingut
Neckenmarkt — 289

Topf Weingut
Straß im Straßertale — 104

Tschida – Angerhof Weingut
Illmitz — 320

U

Urbanihof Familie Paschinger
Fels am Wagram — 225

V

Velich Weingut
Apetlon — 322

VINEYARD ESTATES A–Z

W

Wachau Domäne
see Domäne Wachau

Waldschütz Anton und Elfriede Weinhof
Sachsendorf — 226

Wandraschek Weinmanufaktur
Krems — 139

Weinhofmeisterei Hirtzberger Mathias
see Hirtzberger Mathias Weinhofmeisterei

Weixelbaum Weingut
Straß im Straßertale — 105

Wellanschitz Weingut
Neckenmarkt — 291

Wieninger Weingut
Wien — 53

Winkler-Hermaden Weingut
Kapfenstein — 386

Winzerhof Familie Dockner
see Dockner Familie Winzerhof

Wohlmuth Weingut
Kitzeck im Sausal — 370

Wruss Weingut
Gamlitz — 373

Z

Zens Weingut
Mailberg — 251

Zull Weingut
Schrattenthal — 252

Zweytick Ewald Wein
Ratsch an der Weinstraße — 374

NEIGHBORING COUNTRIES

LIECHTENSTEIN

Liechtenstein, Fürst von – Hofkellerei Domäne Vaduz
Vaduz — 404

SLOVAKIA

Magula, Vinárstvo
Suchá nad Parnou — 405

SLOVENIA

Atelier Kramar
Dobrovo — 400

Marof
Mačkovci — 406

Radgonske gorice
Gornja Radgona — 407

SLOVENIA

Simčič, Edi
Dobrovo — 408

Svetlik
Dobravlje — 409

Verus
Ormož — 410

Vicomte de Noüe-Marinič Domaine
Kojsko — 401

Vino Gaube
Zgornja Kungota — 402

HUNGARY

Hidden Treasures – a Moric project
Tokaj/Balaton/Nagy-Somlói — 403

falstaff

Falstaff Publications Ltd.
Schottenring 2-6
A-1010 Vienna, Austria